PHILOSOPHICAL
TRENDS IN THE
CONTEMPORARY
WORLD

Philosophical Trends in the Contemporary World

By MICHELE FEDERICO SCIACCA

Introduction by A. ROBERT CAPONIGRI

Translated by ATTILIO SALERNO

UNIVERSITY OF NOTRE DAME PRESS

Original title

LA FILOSOFIA, OGGI

Published by Marzorati Editore, Milan, Italy
1958

INTRODUCTION

Here, reader, George Santayana wrote in the preface to *Scepticism and Animal Faith*, is still another system of philosophy, for which some justification must be given. And here, the reader might reflect upon taking up the present work, is yet another history of philosophy; and surely nothing would seem to demand justification more. Those who went on to read Santayana's work, however, soon came to realize the depth of his modesty; he had produced, not merely another system of philosophy, but the last, great *personal* statement of an entire culture, the classical humanism of the West. So, we are confident, it will prove with the present work of Michele Federico Sciacca. The book will prove its own best justification; for the reader will find here, not merely another history of philosophy, but a superb achievement in which erudition and philosophical insight combine to bring to life the drama—and not the theater—of contemporary thought.

Sciacca's work has already achieved a vast reputation, principally in the Latin countries. Its translation into English not only extends the area of its influence, but brings into philosophy a much needed countervailing force in the English-speaking world. The dominance of positivism and of the analytic school has constricted the classical and humanistic view of the value and function of the history of philosophy. This constriction has had, in turn, a deleterious effect on the conception of philosophy entertained and practiced among us. Philosophy has lost much of its humanity; it has tended to become a quasi-technical discipline, stabilized in a glacial neutrality toward human concerns. Moreover, it has tended more and more to take as its model and concern science in the restricted sense of that term prevalent today, which dissociates it from its classical relationship to wisdom. Sciacca's work should do much to correct this serious imbalance; and it can do so in the only truly effective manner—by restoring its proper place to the history of philosophy in the range of the philosophical disciplines.

In Western culture, it has been discovered that a unique relationship prevails between philosophy and its own history. This relationship has been expressed as the identity of philosophy with its own history. But it is doubtful that this expression, while so lapidary, really does justice to that relationship. A more functional or pragmatic account of the bond might prove more satisfactory. The experience of Western culture has tended to prove that it is not possible to philosophize effectively save within the matrix of the history of philosophy; at the same time, the effort has been focused upon raising the history of philosophy to the status of an authentic act of philosophical reflection. The result can hardly be called an identification of the two enterprises, in the sense which Croce implied. What ensues is rather a constant dynamic movement between the two, productive of great advantages for each. Contact with its own history imparts to philosophy a concreteness, a vitality, a humaneness, and ultimately a humility which mark it and set it apart from every other discipline. By the nature of the historical process which, being spiritual, grows upon its own expression, the history of philosophy becomes more and more the content of philosophy; it thus works upon an experience refined by reflection and not on the raw experience of the epistemologist or the psychologist. As philosophy becomes oriented to its own history, it inevitably raises the historiographic act to the philosophical level; and historical understanding becomes the most authentic form of philosophical experience.

The great merit of Sciacca's work, as well as the source of its power, is its fidelity to that insight into the relationship of philosophy and its own history. His work is a historiographic transaction and an act of philosophy, seamlessly fused. Its particular matter is recent and contemporary European philosophy. Toward this matter it has no reportorial intentions, or, at most, a very minimal one. Its concern is to understand this matter philosophically—and in the process to complete the philosophic act upon the richness of this content. The result can in no way be called an *account* of contemporary philosophy, though such an account, and a very accurate one, could be derived from Sciacca's pages. Neither is Sciacca's work an interpretation, for his is entirely free of "perspectivism," entirely true to the notion of the transcendentality of philosophical thought. It is an attempt to grasp, in terms of philosophy, the philosophical meaning of that matter.

Because Sciacca's effort is of such nature, his present work can scarcely bear an irenic tone. On the part of critics the chief allegation against his

Introduction

Philosophical Trends in the Contemporary World has been its "tendentiousness." Nothing could be more fallacious than that allegation; it reveals a lack of understanding of the kind of unity proper to philosophy. The unity of philosophy is a unity of dynamic tension, not of "reconciliation" or "amalgamation." What is generally termed "tendentiousness" by those who entertain an irenic notion of the unity of philosophy is rather conscious dialectical method. In Sciacca's pages, every position is permitted to work itself out in terms of its own inner logic and in vital historical relation to all other contending positions. But this process is not a free "natural" process; it is controlled by the philosophical reflection of the author, who assumes historical and philosophical responsibility for the kind of significant unity which emerges.

In a word, this is a mature work, a work for the culturally mature mind. What the reader will derive from it is not the elementary satisfaction of his curiosity, but the fulfillment of the demands of critical intelligence seeking to determine the meaning and value of contemporary philosophical thought and expression. The reading of this work will be a maturing experience for the student and a most illuminating one for the *cognoscenti*. And for both—in the context of the culture of the English-speaking world and the place of philosophy in that culture—it is little short of mandatory.

A. Robert Caponigri
University of Notre Dame

TRANSLATOR'S FOREWORD

The present English version of this renowned work of Michele Federico Sciacca is, with some minor changes, based on the two-volume, third Italian edition bearing the title, *La filosofia, oggi/Philosophy, Today/* (Marzorati, Milan, 1958). The changes that have been made—to have the sections dealing with Anglo-American thought enlarged—are largely due to the author himself at the recommendation of Professor Anton C. Pegis. Accordingly, in order to contain the total of this work, the number of pages in the first Italian volume, which treats European existentialism, has been decreased without impairing the unity of the text. This same work, moreover, in its third Spanish edition (*La Filosofía, Hoy*, Miracle, Barcelona, 1961), contains all the revisions and bibliographies provided by the author up to the year 1961. With respect to the bibliographies, this English version supplies only the titles of original works (besides those appearing in the footnotes) and these are directly quoted in the text. Thus the criterion adopted by the translator was to reintegrate the title in its original language wherever no English translation was extant.

The bibliographical research, magnitude of the work, complexity of the Italian sentence, and arduousness of the subject matter treated in the text made this translation a rather difficult undertaking. And, as it is best known to those who at one time or another have had this same experience, to translate is not "to transcribe." On the contrary, it is (at least to an extent) a work of composition and (always) one of intellectual self-discipline. This translator trusts that he was able to render, in understandable English, the author's thought in its integrity as well as in its basic flow and prose-flavor. All shortcomings (and there are not a few)—for which he alone assumes full responsibility—are to be imputed to him, for certainly they are not due to lack of care but only to his own limitations.

Professor Sciacca offers, in his original two celebrated volumes, a vast and perhaps complete panorama of the present-day world's philosophy. All the trends in contemporary thought (even the minor ones) are clearly defined and analyzed. And, indeed, one of the advantages for the reader of this work is that he becomes acquainted—perhaps for the first time—with so many Italian, French, German, and other philosophers who until now were hardly known to the English-speaking world.

A metaphysician with the insight of a historian, Sciacca expresses or implies "his own view" throughout the presentation of contemporary philosophical currents. Furthermore, his awareness and firm belief that the loss of the principle of being perpetrated by modern philosophy is responsible for the present uneasiness afflicting mankind, lead him to adopt a polemical spirit against all movements which have departed from the metaphysical tenets that he wishes to see re-established. The author's criticism of American philosophy is no exception to this basic criterion, even when his analyses and inferences extend to the realm of politics and ethics. The reader may agree or disagree with Professor Sciacca's treatment of American thought; to some of us it may appear not only too astringent but even somewhat unfair. Be that as it may, the intentions of this author are constructive rather than destructive, for he clearly wishes to uphold, and possibly preserve, the philosophical and religious patrimony characterizing our Western civilization.

The translator is particularly indebted to Professors Anton C. Pegis and Gaetano Vincitorio for their generous help and advice. He also expresses his gratitude to his colleagues, Professors John J. Reynold, Philip Perfetti, and Richard H. Berquist, for proofreading parts of this translation.

A. M. SALERNO
St. John's University
New York
October 1964

CONTENTS

Contents

Contents

Contents

Contents

I

THE ORIGINS

OF

CONTEMPORARY

PHILOSOPHY

---

1. Irrationalistic and
   Anti-Intellectualistic Trends
   in German Romanticism

The supremacy of the "practical" over the "theoretical," of the will over the intellect, and of "life" over "reason" is characteristic of four fifths of contemporary philosophy. It is a whole movement, both philosophical and cultural, which for more than a century has shaken every rationalistic and systematic construction from its foundation by calling into doubt all principles of knowledge, whether scientific or philosophical, thereby denying the very base of all objective understanding. Engaged in a ceaseless war against the metaphysical or theologizing "dogmatism" of the intellect, vast and manifold currents of thought have vindicated all that is irrational, primitive, and immediate in the human subject. And these are opposed to Descartes' rationalism resting on his clear and distinct ideas, as well as to Kant's rationalism resting on his *a priori* forms of the spirit; they also reject the idea of the Absolute of transcendental idealism in all its forms, as well as the idea of Nature in positivism. Such modern currents have overvalued the importance of *praxis* to the extent of dissolving it into that of "theory" or knowledge, reduced to a "tool" of action, and now, like action, changeable and contingent. The activism and the pragmatism of modern and contemporary thought has substituted a series of "philosophies of life" for the "philosophies of reason." Accordingly, it has been said time and again that there is a "crisis" in philosophy as it has been traditionally understood, and for this reason a crisis also in metaphysics. It is not possible to understand the most recent European thought—whether it be continuation, development, or reaction—or to understand the manifold aspects of the contemporary way of life without first pointing out in passing the rise and flourishing of these so-called philosophies of life.

Their common source is Romanticism, a vast and extremely rich cultural movement—by reason of its very richness really undefinable, unless one is merely content to emphasize one or another of its many aspects to the detriment of the others. In fact Romanticism has been at times a vindication of sentiment, impulse, instinct and will against reason, law and order; at times, too, historicism and antihistoricism, individualism and sociality, one an emphasis on the past and one on the future. Even when detected in the act of bursting into antithetic forms, Romanticism still presents a unitary center and, precisely, a conception of life experienced and "lived through" as inexhaustible power and energy, as activity in motion unfolding itself in infinite and diverse forms without ever being exhausted in any one of them and even without any aim except that of being supremely itself in the "impossible" attempt to capture the "ideal" in the "real." Freedom as "freedom of nature" is a characteristic of Romanticists; and, before them, it was a characteristic of Rousseau. The new and fundamental concept of Romanticism is the concept of "life" whose meaning is not only psychological or practical but also metaphysical. How is life to be conceived? This is the point where the numerous forms of Romanticism diverge; there are as many conceptions of life as there are romanticist positions.

German Romanticism flourished between the end of the eighteenth and the first decades of the nineteenth century. Its essential characteristics are *historicism* and *the creative activity of the spirit*. To this we can add its religious exigency, attachment to *tradition* (particularly to the Catholic Middle Ages, through which a spiritual unity or a unanimous humanity was achieved at the same time as the birth of national entities), and exaltation of all that is obscure and indefinite in man and history, as opposed to geometrical rationalism with its clear and distinct ideas. Philosophy, history and art are examined in their intrinsic relations, in contrast (though not complete) to the Enlightenment, which had placed history beyond rational intelligibility and art in the limbo of a confused and indistinct sensation.

A romanticism of an *aesthetic* sort places the human ideal in a life viewed as a work of art, a life that is molded according to forms of pure and serene beauty. Truth does not abide in appearances and the phenomenon, but in the inner and mysterious force lying below and vivifying the phenomenon itself. In nature this force acts unconsciously; but in man, who is aware of his development, it is consciousness and freedom. This freedom is interior harmony and so it is indifferent to the external forms of being in the world; in art, which exhausts the content of spiritual life, it fully realizes itself, so that it is also morality; but it is not a dull, impersonal, and conformist morality like that of the "Philistine." For Goethe and Schiller, Beauty and Good coincide; the ethical ideal finds full expression in the "beautiful soul," in which sense and reason, instinct and freedom, and individuality and universality do not exclude one another, as they would for Kant, but harmonize and make up that complete and rich unity constituting the human person.

Besides that of Goethe and Schiller there is, however, the aesthetic romanticism of FRIEDRICH von SCHLEGEL (1772-1829) and of NOVALIS (1772-1801), which consists in absolute freedom or, rather, in whim and in a life understood as "fancy" and "dream." According to Schlegel, the poet uses matter as an instrument for releasing the free play of his fancy, which creates and destroys at whim. Contrary to the classic poet, who loses himself in the object, the romantic poet does not take his world seriously because he creates it and annihilates it in order to create out of it another one that is closer to perfection. This approximation goes on to infinity because perfection can never be fully realized. What is the use, then, of keeping imperfect creations? *Irony* is ready to destroy what fantasy creates. When incandescent sentiments have crystallized in the expression and when ideals have become smaller in the real, reflection detects all that is lacking in the created work and all its limitations as compared to the ideal of Beauty. Like a thin-lipped ghost, the enigmatic face of *Irony* hints at a piercing smile; the work goes to ruin but the tireless artist mingles and blends the elements anew in the melting pot of his imagination; and thus, endlessly, he "amuses himself," and weeps.

Even the morality of the *Genius* is a creative will, and so morality is "aristocracy," not a utilitarian or Philistine ("bourgeois") "democratism," which is conformity to the rules of common life. The *Genius* is beyond every law, free from the tie of norms, alone and absolutely himself—in short, *unique.* He investigates nature's beauties and rejoices, yet his joy is not about things but about the inner beauty and freedom of nature. He is not in love with things but with their hidden sense; he loves things as symbols of that spiritual power operating in himself and in the world. To live is "to live in dream," to come into contact with that which is

3

impalpable and mysterious in nature and which eludes the vulgar and obtuse senses. For Novalis, poetry and philosophy are identified: to poetize or philosophize is to dream. The world is dream and the dream *is:* the poet works this miracle. Poetry is *magic* and the *magician* is the poet who transcribes and expresses the external reality in a pure world of dreams.

As the poetical world of Romanticism is not only "Apollonian" but "Dionysian" as well, so the philosophical world is not solely a "doctrine of science," a "philosophy of nature," and a "system of reason." Discordant opinions like that of FRIEDRICH JACOBI (1743-1818) are not lacking; for him the real is revealed not in the transparency of thought, but rather in *sentiment*, which is an immediate apprehension of the good and a source of *faith* whose origin and end is God. The subject-object unity is realized only in immediate knowledge and not in that knowledge which is always mediated. God is not the object of knowledge but of the indemonstrable certitude of faith.

Prescinding from these discordant opinions, however, the transcendental idealism culminating in Hegel carries within its architectonic and accomplished "system of reason" the elements of its own dissolution. The concepts of "transcendentality" and of "critique" advanced by the "enlightened" Kant—the defender of metaphysics against the confusions of the many who had made havoc of it—already give, on one hand, rise to the "crisis" (and not to the "critique" because Kant's agnostic conclusions are the result of his acrisy and dogmatism) of metaphysics and, on the other, restrict the validity of the intellect to the construction of mathematics and science, and philosophy to a methodology of science itself. Kant is, in fact, the starting point not only for transcendental idealism, but also for positivism, since both theories are less antithetic than is commonly believed or than it may appear on the surface. (If the Idea or the Act of thinking is made, in an immanent way, equal to the "fact," idealism itself is a form of positivism.) But in Kant there still is a kind of nostalgia for metaphysics together with a conflict, at times close to anguish, between the exigencies of scientific reason and those deeper and irrepressible demands of the spirit. Neither the *Critique of Practical Reason* nor the *Critique of Judgment* settles the conflict, which is impossible to compose on the basis of transcendentality, that is, on the basis of an activity that can "function" only in the phenomenal world or world of external experience.

Hegel's logical idealism undoubtedly represents the greatest effort at systematizing the problems stemming from Kantian criticism and from the first critical and orginal elaborations of it. The real and the rational coincide (absolute Thought is identical with absolute Being); but the spirit is not immobility: it is a continuous becoming and "dialecticity."

Everything is explained and justified by dialectic, the eternal fomenter of conflicts and discord and, at the same time, a universal and infallible justifier and pacifier. The faintest breeze, like the weakest of human actions, is recorded and eternalized in the perennial historicity of the Spirit, and becomes part of the life of the Absolute. Hegelian panlogism is absolute optimism.

Yet, if we look into it more closely, the system of reason reveals itself to us as gravely flawed by irrational motives. Even in Hegel, who criticizes the romantic concepts of the "immediate" and of "beauty," there is still a strong romantic *pathos*.

Beneath the systematic structure, and in spite of the omnipresent and omnipotent Reason, lies the eternal *inquietude* of the Idea which is the essence of Hegelianism. If Hegel wishes to remain consistent with his essential "dialecticism," he is compelled to admit that the Spirit never rests, even when it attains in the stage of Philosophy the absoluteness and transparency of the concept. *Dialectically* the synthesis can only be posited to infinity, as a thesis requiring an antithesis and a new synthesis which, in turn, relates to another and so on and so forth. Instead of a permanent accord, the conclusion always is an open conflict—not harmony but opposition of terms. Dialectical in its essence, the Idea is never satisfied. Yet, if there is no absolute and permanent synthesis (and if Hegel admits it, he denies "dialecticism" as the essence of thought and of reality), every thesis always requires an antithesis, and spirit is never appeased in the synthesis but is always divided in the moment of the thesis-antithesis opposition. Thus, all previous antitheses, from the poorest moment to the highest degree of the spirit, are open again and all problems remain problems. Being and thought, finite and infinite, man and history, man and God do not harmonize; they remain terms in conflict. In the becoming of history, man no longer finds himself enlightened by the light of the Idea, but alone, in all his limitations, in conflict with everything. The sense of his existence and of his destiny is lost in invincible antinomy and meaningless historicity; his incomprehensible individuality emerges and affirms itself, in all its experienced uncertainty, against the abstractness of the absolute Spirit. The magic circle of dialectic is broken and immanence yields to the transcendency of the world and of God with respect to man. The problem of the destiny of the individual arises again, and the rights of what is not repeatable, of what is unintelligible and of the "irrational" are installed against absolute rationalism. Philosophy ceases to be the lucid and compact system of reason, and it becomes involved in the immediacy of the human drama, which is much richer than pure rationality. Once more man finds himself as a limited existence in the presence of an infinite that transcends him, as well as in the presence of the world and of God.

5

Hegel is the philosopher of universal Reason and the one who identifies the real with the rational; yet, his system of reason, wherein all problems can be solved, carries the elements that will change it into a system of an ever open, inconclusive, and peremptory uncertainty. The fact is that physical reality, which has been forced into the closed circle of dialectic, continues to claim its rights (whence the positivist reaction), and human nature also goes on proposing again its problem—the problem that man is to himself and man in his concrete individuality, upon which the critics of the panlogical dialectic immediately focused their attention. Thus, the divisions within Hegelianism and the anti-Hegelian debates came into being, without the awareness that, precisely within the philosophy that was being fought, one could find the ferment and the nutriment for those needs which were being set against it.

2. THE VOLUNTARISM
OF A. SCHOPENHAUER

Although the irrationalistic voluntarism of ARTHUR SCHOPEN-HAUER (1788-1860)—a thinker still influential in contemporary philosophy—stands against the Hegelian identity of real and rational, it nevertheless lies within the intellectual scope of romanticist idealism. The world for Schopenhauer (*The World as Will and Idea*, trans. R. B. Haldane *et al.*, New York, 1961) has a cortex and a marrow. The cortex is what we know of it: the *phenomenon*, our *representation;* but the subject is not only a representing activity, it is also will, and will is the root, the first principle of the world. In all phenomena of nature, from the life of stars to that of vegetables, from the instinct of animals to the conscious will of man, the same *blind* and *irrational* Will manifests itself aimlessly; it wills because it wills, and does so in order to increase dissatisfaction and sorrow. The Will is "one and everything"; things are manifold in the cognitive act, but identical in their essence. The Will has no object; it is irrationality. It is never satisfied, and like the Hegelian idea it does nothing but generate itself for eternity; for this reason it is an "unhappy will." The world, which is the product of the Will, can only be a realm of misery and sorrow. To will, in fact, implies want, and want is pain. *Life is pain;* and if pain ceases because we grow tired of willing, *life is weariness.* Pleasure is merely negative: satisfaction of a need, cessation of a pain. Why then do we continue to live while knowing that life is sorrow, and that our sorrow has no purpose? Because it is not *we* who will, but the universal Will of life wills *in us*, and it invents a thousand illusions (love, glory, honors, and the like) in order to fill the emptiness of our lives. Also egoism and trust in human progress are deceptions plotted by the Will. Besides being an evil, to live is a crime, and to continue to live is guilt: the world does not deserve to exist. It is a duty to suppress in us the Will to live. The ways and steps (art, justice and compassion) by which man frees himself from the will, and with it from pain, culminate in the *mystic exaltation* (ἄσχησις): negation of the will in the *Non-Will*, of the self in Nothingness. The world as representation is the "Veil of Maia," and the death of the will to live is the "access to Nirvana." The world is nothing and such it is for the saints, who through this persuasion attain beatitude and peace. "In your nothingness I hope to find my everything." This pessimistic conclusion, however, which is a consequence of metaphysical irrational-ism in antithesis with Hegel's optimistic dialectic (the universal irrational Will contraposes the Hegelian universal Reason), can also be the con-clusion of this same dialectic. Eternally open to the opposition of thesis and antithesis, the dialectic polarizes in a state of inquietude, in an eternal process, exactly in that inexhausted will to live in which Schopenhauer identifies the source of sorrow. Eternal inquietude is eternal unhappiness; it is not only Schopenhauer's "suffering will," but also Hegel's "unhappy consciousness." Thus is explained Schopenhauer's opposite manner of judging history. In history there is no progress; in all its degrees the will always is the same, and history shows only the insatiable passion of the will to live (which always performs the same tragedy or comedy), even though the actors, or rather the supernumeraries, change. History no longer is the rational Idea, as in Hegel, but only the play of fortuitous circumstances which never pass beyond the sphere of appearance and the limits of an essential insignificance.

Schopenhauer's irrationalism is not an isolated phenomenon. The so-called Hegelian left gives Hegelianism a development not in harmony with the "system"; the humanistic and religious argumentations—anti-thetic among themselves, but in agreement on criticizing the Hegelian panlogism in the name of the human "concrete" and in that of the individual—become strong and peremptory; new scientific hypotheses, among them Darwin's evolutionism, do not fail to influence philosophy, and positivism is already shaped in some of its aspects. In order to clarify and explain some aspects of contemporary thought, we focus our atten-tion on Feuerbach, Marx, Kierkegaard, Dostoyevsky, and Nietzsche. On account of his importance in more recent philosophy, Kierkegaard will be treated later; the others we will mention immediately, without failing to point out Unamuno's lively and meaningful theses.

3. Aspects of Atheistic Humanism

a. The Question Regarding the "Material": L. Feuerbach and K. Marx

The "humanistic" exigency, rising from within Hegelianism and from the criticism directed against it, presents itself as a vindication of the existential and of the concrete, of the finite and of the individual which Hegel had submerged in the dialectic of the Idea. Thus, Hegelian idealism gives rise to characteristic forms of humanism (from which some currents in contemporary existentialism receive their origin and inspiration), which is either religious-theological or materialistic-atheistic, like that of Feuerbach and Marx.

Although accepting the dialectical method, the so-called Hegelian left brings about Hegel's downfall; facts are not a manifestation of the Idea, but the one and only true reality of which the Idea is a simple image, and the content of nature is richer than the Idea. Man is real, not as a purely thinking subject, but as an individual, an organism, and a *body;* man is a "conscious body," says LUDWIG FEUERBACH (1804-1872), an antiacademic thinker, the first serious and profound critic of Hegelianism, who, mistakenly, has been reduced (following in the steps of Engels' interpretation) to a sort of foot-bridge between Hegel and Marx. Feuerbach is much more than this, and some of his theses are still alive and effective today. Man, "the conscious body," is a personified need, a group of needs which he must satisfy for his happiness. In order to reach this goal the *ego* must have a *you* as its object of love; man is the ego and the you in their reciprocity (*Vorläufige Thesen, etc.*, Leipzig, 1841; *Grundsätze der Philosophie der Zukunft*, Zurich und Winterthur, 1843.)

Every man acquires a consciousness of his own humanity through the social relation, and he is the more himself the more he actualizes this consciousness. This is Feuerbach's "social" answer to the great problem concerning the "breach" between philosophy and religion, between human and divine, which Hegel had had the illusion of healing. Instead, the crisis of the European religious consciousness deepened just after Hegel, presenting itself as a final "breach" between Christianity and the new European bourgeoisie. For Feuerbach Christianity is dead, and with it the "religion of God," to make way for the birth of the "religion of man." For him religion is a purely human product (*The Essence of Christianity*, 1841.) Unable to satisfy all his needs, namely, free himself from need, man either postulates or posits an illusory Being, the fruit of his fancy, representing the picture of himself as he would like to be, that is, without needs and free from the need of needing ("man creates God after his own image"). Theology is anthropology: man ascribes the values which he would like to carry out to a being whom he calls God. Thus is born *religious alienation*, that is, the abandoning of the fulfillment of values to God, and the imposition upon Him of a task we ought to discharge ourselves. If for the love of God we substitute and realize that of mankind, the alienation ceases, and, with it, both religious consciousness and the idea of God are extinguished. In other words, if the religious fact depends on a particular human situation and lasts until such a situation has evolved to the point of cessation, man ceases to think of a transcendent God when that situation no longer exists or changes.

Feuerbach brings to maturity what is, perhaps, the only essential problem in the modern world: transforming the question of God into a question of man and transcribing theology in terms of anthropology, the discourse concerning eternity into the language of time, the happiness of the heavens into that of the earth. No longer the Son of God, man is the son of Man. According to Feuerbach (and not according to him alone) atheistic or absolute humanism arises from the "death" of Christianity as a new religion for man, who is the source of divine power, the only true and real bearer of what is sacred. Thus we see the beginning of the desperate, tremendous battle to be fought in favor of man—the "heir of the heavens"—as Ibsen has Brand say in the drama of that title. And like Brand, Feuerbach is the victim of his own impossible undertaking; in the last phase of his thought his original idealism and his subsequent absolute and social humanism (which in him finds, at times, profound and "Christian accents"—"it is the love for the other man that tells you who you are") are mortified by a heavy materialism (*The Essence of Christianity*, trans. M. Evans, New York, 1855; *The Essence of Religion*, trans. A. Loos, New York, 1873; *Theogonie nach den Quellen des Classischen, etc.*, Leipzig, 1857). Man, the creator of God, is identified with nature; the sovereign of the future universe, which is supposed to be all his and all human, is subjected to the most rigid determinism. Feuerbach starts by dethroning God and divinizing man; he ends by divinizing matter of which man is a part: "Man is what he eats." This "atheist" who all his life meditated almost exclusively on God, religion, Christianity and the soul has sown powerful seeds. With him begins the liquidation of philosophy, "which becomes a human affair only by ceasing to be philosophy." Marx is already present in Feuerbach.

KARL MARX (1818-1883) finds Feuerbach's theses still faulty because of their intellectualistic residue. For Hegel, history is identified with the dialectical development of the Idea, of which it is a necessary result, and on account of which every accomplished fact is sacred and must be justified, not chastised with death. For Marx, the founder of *scientific*

9

socialism or *dialectical materialism*,[1] it is not a question of understanding the historic process, but rather a question of transforming it. "Up to this time philosophers interpreted the world, now it is a question of changing it," Marx writes in his notes on Feuerbach (*Thesen Über Feuerbach, Frankfurt*, 1845), one of his most important philosophical works. Dialectic does not stop at the conservation of *praxis;* it leads necessarily to its overthrow. Hegel's Idea is abstract. Marx drops it into the human concrete world, transforms it from a conservative principle into a perennially revolutionary element of history; and with this he continues the dissolution of the Hegelian "conservatism" initiated by Feuerbach. Philosophy is action, not the theory of the Idea; it is precisely a man's affair and hence a "nonphilosophy," if philosophy means speculative and contemplative activity. In Hegel, philosophy—which before the human drama takes a contemplative (philosophical) attitude—has achieved its apogee and with it its death. In short, it is not a detached and contemplative thought, but thought engaged in history and the world. Such engagement is not due to our initiative; we *are* engaged and hence philosophy, as a detachment from the world, is a refuge in abstract thought, a condemnable evasion in fact condemned by concrete life and history. Marx's new attitude is not contemplation but *praxis*. The Marxist does not act without thinking, nor does he think without acting. Pure knowledge ascertains; action, instead, transforms the present state in order to build the future. It is a question of going down to the bottom of history, to the shapeless and anonymous *masses*, those who have, at all times, constituted the substance of history itself.

In short, Marx is shifting the Hegelian dialectic from the spiritual level to that of material needs, so that history and politics are explained in function of the class struggle (*Economic Philosophical Manuscript of 1844*, trans. M. Milligan, Moscow, 1959). He inserts into Feuerbach's "realistic" conception and into the immediate datum the Hegelian dialectic of "man-nature, man-work." Thus, in the preface to the second edition of the *Das Kapital* (1857-1894), trans. Eden and Cedar Paul, New York, 1929), he himself states precisely his difference with respect to Hegel: "My dialectical method does not differ from Hegel's only in its foundation, but is absolutely the opposite. For Hegel, the movement of thought which he calls 'idea' is the demiurge of reality, which is the phenomenal form of the idea. For me, instead, the movement of thought is only the reflection of the movement in reality as it has been conveyed

[1] It is already present in Marx's materialistic conception of history, which was developed by Engels and elaborated by Lenin and Stalin. It is the "official" philosophy of communism. "Historical materialism," a doctrine which is also based on Marx and Engels, teaches that the mode of production affecting our material life (economic structure) conditions the entire (political, social and spiritual) process of humanity.

to and transposed in the human brain. . . . In Hegel, dialectic walks on its head; it suffices to put it back on its feet." Back on its feet, Marx's dialectic lies on the same level as that of those feet; after all, between feet and head there is no longer any difference, since man, as far as Marx is concerned, is only a reality made up of natural objective forces acting upon things in order to transform them ("naturalism of man" and "humanism of nature"). For Marx, in fact, the dialectic of existence does not develop on a theoretical-ideal level, but on a practical and economic one, that is, on the level *of material human needs*. Moreover, the *economic* and the "material" are the sole structure in the historic and dialectical process, for the others (moral, religious, and others) are only "superstructures" and epiphenomena. "Matter" and "consciousness" are two different aspects of the same material activity; since they are not equated, they wind up opposing each other. Consequently, the "proletariat"—an expression of the propulsive force of history—gives philosophy "its material vigor" while finding in it "its spiritual weapons" (*Zur Kritik der Hegelschen Rechtsphilosophie*, n.p., 1844). Now, communism, Marx says again, wants to be the "consciousness of the proletariat," the awareness of its proletarian condition that will be destroyed with the annihilation of capitalism.

On the other hand, the end of capitalistic society is fated on account of the very dialectical movement of history. Every historic epoch or economic structure, in fact, carries and nourishes within itself the elements of its own dissolution: elements, that is, that provoke its overthrow. The slave economy begot feudalism, by which it was killed; feudalism begot the bourgeoisie, by which it was overthrown. The bourgeoisie has begotten the proletariat that will dig its grave through the class struggle, which is not a creation of Marxism but a fact observed by it. In fact, it is the capitalist system that by itself produces its own negation, the proletariat. Marx writes: "Communism is for us not a state that must be created, an ideal destined to direct reality. We call communism the effective movement that will suppress the present situation."

But at this point one can ask: What kind of antithesis is nourished from within by the future "homogeneous society" or a classless society without privileges? None, replies Marx: perfect society, without antitheses, is attained by a homogeneous society. The religious alienation which arises from the economic one ceases, too. In fact, the alienation of one's own labor aimed at satisfying the needs of another cannot take place in the homogeneous society; but each has and consumes a *quantum* of products in proportion to the *quantum* of his productive labor; therefore, the alienation in a transcendent Being ceases automatically, and the idea of

God infallibly disappears from the mind and heart of man.[2] Once man is able to satisfy all his "material" wants, superstructures are not produced. For Marx, it is to be noticed, man (and every other being) has no essence or nature of his own, which remains immutable at the same time that it develops according to historic situations; man, instead, is totally the result of the historic situations themselves, and of the social structures which correspond to them. There are neither essences nor natures (Darwin's influence is apparent): man is a purely historic product, he changes, is made, is transformable and hence there are no fixed structures, whether psychological or ontological.

According to Marxism, then, man as an entity does not exist; but men exist as they are made by a historic situation (an established economic-social structure) and they evolve with the latter's evolution. Let it be so. But the contradiction is evident: on one hand, the concept of history implies by itself process and evolution; on the other, if at a certain point man (society) does not evolve, *is not made,* but *is* and remains substantially the same, then it follows that the evolution or dialectical becoming is itself temporary and historic, whereas being is definitive. In this way, the concept of substance comes up again. But, how can there be an essence or nature of man at the end of the evolution if there is none at its beginning? Moreover, *either* evolution stops with the advent of homogeneous society and of "Marxist man" and the dialectical process comes to an end leaving us outside of history (in which case Marxism admits a nonhistoric moment in history, that is, an eternity in time, which is nonsense), *or* Marxist society has within itself an evolution of its own (in which case it must evolve into other economic structures). But in such a case it is necessary to admit that Marxist society will not be perfect, that is, it will not satisfy—in a Marxist way—all men's needs. In short, *either* evolution stops and then the dialectical process loses its essentiality, *or* it continues indefinitely and then a new structure will have to arise from the Marxist society, that is, such a society will always require two or more social classes (and it will not be homogeneous) so that it too will have class distinctions. But, being based on classes, it will have its superstructures, among them the religious one and, with it, the alienation in God. But then religion and ethics are not superstructures pertinent to this or that social-economic structure depending on class divisions; they are, instead, dimensions pertinent to man *qua* man, as they are autonomous and essential to him. Marx is Hegelian in his own way;

[2] Once man has been entirely resolved into sociality, every idea of religion vanishes: atheism becomes a certainty. In fact, writes Marx, "Atheism no longer has any meaning, for it is a negation of God and posits, through this negation, the existence of man." Socialism has no need to deny God and religion; it is the negation of negation and hence the mere affirmation of man, that is, of human society in the form of communism.

therefore, for both Marx and Hegel every thesis generates its antithesis. Although abstract in themselves, thesis and antithesis both become concrete in their dialectical relationship. Consequently, the capitalism-proletariat antinomy attains its concreteness through the overcoming of both terms, that is, through the synthesis represented by the future homogeneous society which will destroy both of them. This is all very well. But if this society cannot become or evolve precisely because it is homogeneous, it will be without its antithesis, that is to say, outside of the immanent dialecticity in every historical moment. But then, *either* the principle is not true that every thesis is concrete in its dialectical relationship with the thesis-produced antithesis (namely, the thesis is concrete in the dialecticity moving and destroying it while preserving it in the synthesis, and the whole Hegelian-Marxist system remains irreparably compromised), *or* the principle of the dialectical method is true, and then the homogeneous society (provided that such a society is realizable) would constitute a thesis without antithesis which, in terms of correct Hegelianism, is *abstract, nonreal, nonhistorical,* and *antihistorical.*

The influence of Marx and of Marxism (through the rethinking of them by the theorists of the Russian-type communism or by Leninism-Stalinism) is enormous in the contemporary world. This is so, less on account of the strength of its ideology (which is philosophically and critically very weak and, indeed, even naively dogmatic) than on account of the very close ties it has with political practice and with the so-called social question (in which the "proletariat" gains consciousness of itself) into which Marx ultimately resolves not only philosophy but any form of human activity. In communism, in fact, the Party is everything—"It is the truth," said one of its theorists—and the Party theoretically is the people. This is not the place to evaluate Marxism with respect to the problems of social justice, the concept of labor, and so forth, in which it raises some points that deserve a most careful consideration, and, in which its contributions, excepting its ideology, must not be denied. Here we are interested in presenting to the reader some of the Marxist affirmations and their consequences:

(1) Marxism relegates thought to an instrument of *praxis* on which it absolutely depends. Marxist *praxis* is radical. Technology, science and industry are the highest forms of human activity in that they help man strengthen his work, aimed at transforming and dominating nature, in such a way that his ever-increasing production will give him higher standards of material living and well-being. Only that activity is worthwhile which produces material goods. Men, too, are instruments of production, and their worth is equal to their production; men are instruments whose goal is the socialist society.

(2) Consequently, Marxism is the negation of philosophy as such, as it

is of any other form of spiritual activity whose end is not social and economic and aimed at transforming the nonsocialistic societies. Thinking is the same as doing, namely, labor; truth (and every truth) is the product of *praxis* and changes as the latter changes. Every economic structure has its corresponding superstructures.

(3) Understood in its most radical sense, the principle of historical evolution leads Marxism to deny the concepts of being, substance, essence, as well as the concept of law, whether moral or scientific. Even its historicism is radical. All beings are transformed and there are no immutable species or essences, that is, man's essence or nature (and therefore that of any other being) is not ontological but historical or historically formed, and, hence, historically transformable. Metaphysics —any metaphysics—no longer has any meaning, for the very concepts of truth and being have no meaning.

(4) There is no soul or spirit in man; nor are there fixed psychological laws, nor, strictly speaking, even scientific laws; what is true is what is produced by *praxis* in a determinate historic situation or in a moment of evolution.

(5) There is no God and no revealed religion. Religion belongs to an inferior stage in the succession of stages found in the course of human evolution. In religion man does not possess, as yet, full consciousness of himself, so that he attributes to God what belongs to himself and what will really be his in a further and more advanced phase of his evolution. Consequently, as a temporary and transitory stage in historical evolution, religion is destined to disappear when all men (and not only the more fully evolved ones) have fully acquired the awareness of themselves, that is, when there is a society and a humanity in the full maturity of its evolution. Therefore, the Being that men now worship as God is the same ideal humanity of the future, which men at the moment project outside of themselves and which they also hypostatize as a Supreme Being. Tomorrow, on the other hand, they will see that ideal realized in themselves and in their work. As long as mankind worships a God and alienates itself in Him, it has not completely realized its historic evolution, and society retains a residue of infantilism or ignorance.

It is obvious that not a single principle belonging to the Greco-Roman-Christian West subsists any longer. As we shall see, this conclusion is reached not only by Marxism, but also by many other philosophical systems which—inasmuch as they are "Western doctrines"—pretend to be against communism.

b. The Question Regarding the "Superman": F. Nietzsche

FRIEDRICH WILHELM NIETZSCHE (1840-1900) is not only the poet of the "morality of force" but also the mystic of a humanism that should be attained beyond the human, as is attested by his famous works, *Thus Spake Zarathustra, Beyond Good and Evil, The Will to Power,* and so on (*The Complete Works of F. W. N.,* ed. O. Levy, New York, 1896-1930). From this point of view, Nietzsche expresses in a conscious and mature way the torment of the Romanticists (of Novalis, of Schelling, and others) and he takes up again themes belonging to Protestant mysticism (Böhme) while, at the same time, he goes more deeply into Schopenhauer's thesis of the will to live. He also represents one of the highest points in the struggle against rationalism under whatever label, from the times of the Greeks to the age of Descartes, Kant and Hegel. With merciless coherence he teaches that an absolute humanism which involves the death of God is to be gained at the price of the death of what is human in man. If man wants to be heaven's heir, he must deny himself. With respect to absolute humanism, Nietzsche represents the tragic moment of a hopeless struggle. To Hegel's rationality viewed in the system rather than in its irrational aspects, Nietzsche opposes the will of the "individual" upon the "herd," as Kierkegaard had likewise contraposed to it his "desperation." To Hegel's Idea, Nietzsche opposes Life, no longer understood in its biological and scientific meaning (as some positivists had done), but understood as an infinitely creative "expansivity" bursting into an infinity of antithetical centers of activity. No formula can enclose or exhaust the becoming of Life: it expands *ad infinitum*, beyond any meaning or direction, into the unforeseeable.

"Once again for us the world has become infinite." In Nietzsche, life celebrates its Dionysiac orgies; at one moment life elevates itself through an enthusiastic hymn and at another it is extinguished in a lugubrious song of death.

Nietzsche's humanism is centered upon two points: the *eternal return*, borrowed from Greek philosophy prior to the "corruptive" rationalism of Socrates, and the *Superman*. The world unfolds through cycles that repeat themselves; once a cycle is closed, another begins as the repetition of a previous one. There is nothing new under the sun; what is today was yesterday, and will be tomorrow. Becoming goes back to the starting point as in a circle; becoming then is a fatal and rigid repetition of itself without any progress. Becoming is illusory; only the useless return is real. Like Kierkegaard, Nietzsche does away with Hegel's (or Hegelian-inspired) historicism. Our will as men is but the iron repetition of the "will" of nature. "Everything passes and simultaneously returns. Whatever is has already existed an infinite number of times and will come back countless times again. Everything has returned: Sirius and the spider, and the thoughts you are entertaining at this moment, and even your thought that everything is going to come back." The *instant* is synthesis and simultaneous presence of time and eternity: hence the importance of the problem of time in Nietzsche's philosophy. Bound with becoming and immersed into time, existence is one of the infinite insignificant moments in the total insignificance of universal life. Man is able to understand his life when the circle, totally unfolded, closes upon itself again. But the fulfillment of a circle is death: life is understood only through death, that is, when life has ceased, the exigency of solving its enigma has also ended with it.

The principle of the "eternal return" includes the concept of *amor fati*, which is the acceptance of one's destiny, a *loyalty* to the earth and the self: a desperate wisdom on the part of him who knows how to accept the incomprehensible and the insignificant.

The apparent becoming, representing in reality a monotonous and useless return, is already in itself a negation of life. Man does not live; he dies in the circle; in fact, in Hegel's dialectic, he lives a fictitious life. It seems that the bedrock of being is nothingness. However, the negation is dialectically turned upside down in the affirmation of existence. Breaking the circle and destroying appearance, desecrating all norms and customs, getting away from common morality, from deadly rationality, and from acquiescent and conforming wisdom—all this amounts to trying the adventure of existence, and satisfying the flame that is burning in us and that is never still or appeased. The *will to power*, of which the superman is the depository, is precisely the violent, cruel and barbarous revolt on the part of instinctive life and unconscious passion against the frigidity and insignificance of rationality. This "will" characterizes the apex of rebellion by the instinct against the shirt of Nessus woven by the millenary loom of reason. "I must bend the bow of my living and acting as far as possible so that I may achieve the highest possibilities, because what is once is always; what I am doing now is my very eternal being; what I shall be for eternity will be decided in time." It is necessary to go beyond common life, to jump over and beyond man and place oneself on the summit of the superman, in order that human nature may express itself. As Zarathustra says, "Man is something that may be surpassed." The superman is he who, through a unique affirmation of will to power, places himself beyond superficial humanity, and finds himself in the abysses of an absurd and desecrating irrationality. When reason has been defeated and the veil of Maia torn up with it, then and only then man is revealed to himself, and this takes place not in Nirvana but in a hopeless struggle and clash. No longer a slave of rational appearance, man becomes the lord of the universe and master of himself beyond himself. Life acquires meaning, and the joy of living is lavishly given to the unhappy prisoner of reason only when impulses break through and life's irrational will to power takes its full course. Man must be his own god for "God is dead"; he can be his own god only by decreeing God's death and with it, his own. However, is it not an absurdity to go beyond the human?

Precisely true; for the meaning of existence lies in the *absurd*, in the negation of reason; but the negation of reason is not the negation of reflection, which precisely by the destruction of reason leads to the conditions of a new, exceptional, and no longer human, existence. Only by placing himself outside of finiteness and beyond the bonds of rationality does man find himself again as a deep and absolute ego, as an essential existence, no longer a man but a superman.

In this nonhuman humanism, life can be only struggle and eternal war. Every being feeds his own life with the death of other beings; in all its degrees living nature is struggle for existence. In this struggle only the strongest wins, having the right to win only because he is the strongest. There is no moral law to be obeyed: law is given by the victory of one of the belligerent parties. The free expansion of life must supersede the "ethics of slaves"; *"everything is permitted, if God is dead."* In comparison with the new ethics of the will to power, common morality appears to Nietzsche as the refinement of an instinct. Every moral law is in fact nothing but an instinctive manifestation cloaked by philosophy: ethics is "the Circe of philosophers." The will to power or force (not in the brutal or physical sense) disenchants us from Circe by divesting her of her rational cloak and restoring instinct in its primitive, fresh and genuine irresistibility, that is, it substitutes for the instinct of the herd the vital and exalting instinct of risk and danger. History is a perennial conflict between the will to power on the part of the strong and the tenacious resistance on the part of codified common morality to which the weak cling. Superman is the conqueror of God and of nothingness, at the price, however, of surpassing and denying man as well.

The will to power has neither laws nor programs. Superman obeys only a hopeful fatalism (like the Greeks prior to Socrates or the Italians of the Renaissance). The cult of "Fortune," which does not judge but accepts the world, belongs to superior men, who are masters, lords, and warriors. Their supremacy characterizes the triumph of aristocratic morality, whereas the triumph of slaves and oppressed people installs the morality of the weak, the ethics of the Gospel: that of compassion, piety, and forgiveness.

History is a stage on which alternate masters and slaves, the weak and the strong, proprietorial epochs and servile epochs: compare early Greco-Roman antiquity and the Italian Renaissance, on the one hand, and the later Greek civilization, Christian Rome and modern democracy, on the other. Thus history is not the solution of the problem of existence, but the positing of the problem itself. For Hegel, history is the development of the rational idea; for Nietzsche, irrationality and a deployment of contrasting forces. And consequently, for Nietzsche's romanticist super-individualism, there is no history of epochs and cycles, but only history of heroes—superindividuals in whom the will to power is affirmed. In this lie Nietzsche's antidemocratic polemic and his superindividualistic ethics, which is also anti-individualistic in the sense that he introduces a hierarchy of individuals which culminates in the ideal of the superman, against the leveling of human beings brought about by a utilitarian and ordinary life depending on common ethics. History is made by barbarous nations in whom reason has not suffocated primitive spontaneity; it is made by heroes capable of casting off the leaden capes of civilization, and also capable of upsetting the existing order and placing themselves beyond good and evil, that is, beyond the judgment of current ethics. Even the hero's surrender and charity are manifestations of his power.

Even from the little stated here, Nietzsche reveals the spirit of a pre-Socratic philosopher. He was one of the keenest and most original interpreters of pre-Socratic philosophy. The full and vital sense of nature once possessed by thinkers such as Anaximander, Heraclitus, and Empedocles returns in Nietzsche. The pre-Socratics held the cosmos as the manifestation of a powerful and inexhaustible force unfolding itself in infinite forms of life. For them, nature is a wondrous efflorescence of a simple, divine and eternal principle to which everything returns in order to reappear, at intervals, under the sun—like a mysterious vitality presenting itself veiled in the diverse forms of existence and then hidden again when these forms fade away. Nietzsche felt the full suggestive power of this dynamic conception of life, which is at the same time naturalistic and fatalistic and hence tragic; he felt it in his own spirit and renovated it by means of the most characteristic aspects of German Romanticism. Nietzsche can be called a contemporary pre-Socratic, if we attach to this word something more than a chronological meaning.

The superman's power is only fidelity to his destiny. After all, superman is a vanquished person who finds the sense of his myth in defeat and death. He has in himself denied humanity. In order to find himself again, he had to kill himself as a man. Life fatally needs its own destruction in order to rise again. Thus, the myth of life reaches its completion through the myth of death, and the philosopher of the irrational, who had broken with desperate violence all the bonds of reason and put into motion the dreadful forces of the chaos, yields to an abstract conception of life. Nietzsche's superman still is a romanticist hero who has been cast into the unattainable ideal of a life which denies our lives as men. Irony falls upon his childish and unrestrained barbarity, as always happens with the distant reality of an unrealizable dream. Nietzsche's superman is an errant and adventurous knight seeking the absurd. The absurd is Nietzsche's last word, as nothingness is the last word of Schopenhauer's irrationalism. Nietzsche's superman is desperation presenting itself as a value; man knows that everything is useless, that it is impossible to break the fatal circle of the eternal return and, nonetheless, he dares the impossible and tries the absurd; and in so doing he makes existence worthwhile. "He was hopeless, and he *wanted the truth.*"

This stubborn denier of God, this mystic of atheism, is one who thirsts for God. Beneath his negation there is an authentic and desperate effort to communicate with the Absolute through an inexorable process of detachment from empirical appearances, an effort sustained to the point of annihilating man before God. Nietzsche seeks a truth that is absolutely veracious, a courage that really is courage, a moral nobility that is heroism, but he meets with lies, cowardice, and mean selfishness everywhere. In his hands, everything becomes nothing: the allegedly hidden treasure disappears as soon as the safe is open; he opens all the safe-boxes and always and always ashes. But then dialectic drives him back from detachment to possession, from the Absolute in itself to the absolute created by man himself, an absolute which is against man, beyond the human; the will to give is changed into the will to power, beyond religion, ethics, philosophy and science. Superhumanism, be it Nietzsche's or Feuerbach's, in its ultimate result is a negation of man and his essence, so that it is actualized outside and beyond its nonessential being, in its nonbeing; this is the proof that atheistic humanism as such is the negation of man who through it becomes either an impossible god or a beast.

Nietzsche perhaps is to be rejected *in toto,* but his lesson must be remembered and kept always: it is a lesson of desperate and absurd, yet authentic, sincerity.

4. ASPECTS OF THEISTIC HUMANISM
   THE QUESTION REGARDING THE CRISIS:
   F. DOSTOYEVSKY

A vast and at times profound influence on present-day philosophy has been exerted by the famous Russian writer FYODOR DOSTOYEVSKY (1821-1881), who is perhaps the greatest soul in the modern world. Although we do not intend to include scholars and novelists in this present analysis, an exception is made for Dostoyevsky. Not a philosopher in the proper sense of the word, he has given much to philosophy, not only because he experienced its problems but also because he influenced European thought for the last fifty years. Not men reduced to symbols of abstract ideas but ideas so embodied with flesh and blood as to become creatures terribly alive, the characters of his novels always lie between evil and good, sin and imminent act of salvation, desperation and faith, their fall in nothingness, and their "leap" to God. Each of them represents a moment, a beat in the infinite rhythm of the tragic, inward struggle man fights between his aspiration to the highest spiritual levels and evil pushing him back into the deepest abysses. What is there to oppose man's escape from the attraction of the whirlpool when he tries to reach out and elevate himself? For Kierkegaard, the opposition comes from the systematic philosophy of a miraculous reason that solves and accommodates everything; but for Dostoyevsky, the opposition stems from society with its established order, with its traditions and habits, institutions and hierarchies, with the inviolability of the rules expressed by a common ethics that inexorably condemns and casts out of life those who are not able to adjust to it. What abyss of humanity, of good and evil, is there in the scum of society, in the dwellers of haunts who, humiliated and hurt, have sickly souls? Does the right to condemn really pertain to an established society entrenched in its laws and its "virtuous" egoism, hostile to and distant from the tempest of a soul stained with crime and yet capable of enduring it in the depths of his conscience for a lifetime? Does society have, in the name of keeping "order" and in defense of "normality," the right to forbid all movement to the individual and to coerce him to live and think as the social condition wants him to live and think?

Society holds up for emulation the normal man who respects order and who has become bureaucratic even in his spiritual life. This is a man who has renounced living in his own right in order to live as others will; it is a man in the "situation," who renounces all possibilities of existence in order to cling to one only, the one in which he finds himself without merit, demerit, or even responsibility. We are born "preformed" and "premeditated." In the eyes of the "normal" man, the others, the "individuals" are the rebels, the immoral, the abnormal, the insane who wish to be themselves. They are few: normality or abnormality, so-called wisdom or so-called madness, is only a question of majority. For Dostoyevsky, however, it is not a question of denying order, as if this were almost a pure, historically contingent result, but a question of establishing an interior order against the exterior one which is inadequate to re-educate and improve. He arrives at this result through the paradoxical exasperation of the forces of evil and disorder. In this lies the ambiguous situation of his characters, who are always on the edge of either perdition or salvation, sometimes elevated to moments of evangelic transparency and at others lowered into the darkness of hell. They are souls endowed with inexhaustible resources, capable of drawing gigantic strength from their own depth as they attain salvation from the abyss of evil through suffering, grief, and expiation. Dostoyevsky identifies the school of good and redemption with the teaching of sorrow and suffering that demands indulgence, understanding, and compassion. He was profoundly convinced that in the most ignorant and oppressive environment, among the outlaws, "even down there in the cave, beneath the clothing of a convict and of an assassin, it is possible to find the heart of a man." They are the outcasts and the scum of society, the ones who are out of the established order, who wish to be reinstated after they have paid the penalty of so many injustices perpetrated in the name of this order and this morality; they wish to be reinstated, as men who have become better men, in the name of a superior and interior order, so that they may raise the others (the "normal" and the "just") to that morality and order that is not an anonymous and impersonal habit but the fruit of a strong and personal initiative filtered through sorrow.

Such is the ideal incarnated in Dostoyevsky's characters from the man of "first impulses" in *Notes from Underground* (in *The Short Novels of Dostoevsky*, introd. T. Mann, New York, 1951)—whence he cries toward the men on the "surface" that he is "a heap of miserable good sense," and whence these characters emerge, through expiation, with a great desire to be good—to the immortal protagonist of *Crime and Punishment*, trans. C. Garnett (New York, 1937), who personifies the ambivalences and antinomies of the mysterious depth of the human soul always torn by antitheses and contradictions. Raskolnikoff, besides, is the personification of the struggle against common morality that is singled out and acknowledged as legally responsible for so many crimes and wrongdoings. The triumph of good over evil, however, is not attained through the hallucinating dialectic of Raskolnikoff (the "superman"), but through the silent suffering of Sonia, the woman who lost herself in order to help others, the "sweet and beloved mother" of convicts. It is she who makes Raskolnikoff reveal himself to himself, the assassin to the assassin, and through this revelation she shows him the way to expiation and salvation. And in fact, through expiation, he is saved by Sonia, "the voluntary martyr of pure love." Dostoyevsky's nihilism is illusory, while the affirmation of the human person and of God is real and authentic; it is the restoration of ethics and religion, the vocation of every man, in which the forces of evil are overcome. Dostoyevsky's redemption is dialectical: a reversal of contraries, a profound and mysterious "crisis" and not a gradual process—a leap from sin to salvation. This is why, after all, contemporary philosophy has found in Dostoyevsky one of its masters.

On this point, however, it is necessary to state that the many currents of contemporary humanisms and existentialisms which directly or indirectly go back to, or call for, support on Dostoyevsky find themselves condemned and held in contempt by him.

Dostoyevsky's so-called voluntarism is neither pragmatic nor irrational. He does not deny the validity of reason, nor does he look upon it as being incapable of knowing truth. He is only keeping its range and extent within bounds. Man is not reason alone and truth is known with the whole man, in the concreteness of spiritual life. He is not against reason, but against its hegemony, against a reason that is disembodied and divorced from the will and humanity of man. Present-day misologists try in vain to find an ally in Dostoyevsky.

Nor is he the ally of nihilists and absurdists. True, for Dostoyevsky the being of man possesses a radical ambivalence; good and evil coexist as two opposite tendencies in perennial conflict in every creature (moral Manicheanism). This is the consequence of Adam's sin: man's heart is a battlefield for the struggle between God and devil. But good triumphs always even though amidst tears and blood. To object that good rarely appears in his novels is evidence of a lack of spiritual finesse. In its truly Christian meaning, good does not take delight in its "being prominent," but simply "in being," without external show; it is humble, hidden, and reserved, the opposite of evil that is clamorous and ostentatious. Good is not manifested through grand gestures but in small actions rich in great feelings. Good belongs to the simple and the humble, to good, ignored, unnoticed, seemingly insignificant creatures, who endure everything and ask nothing, always ready to stand aside. They are creatures who *accept* and in accepting they choose: Dostoyevsky stands for freedom as understood by Christianity, freedom as a painful and radical choice between good and evil, and as a liberation through good and truth, viz., St. Augustine's "two freedoms" called *libertas minor* and *libertas major*. The positivity of man, of freedom, and of the will are fully recognized by him.

It follows that the positivity of suffering, sorrow, and anguish is neither a sterile commotion, nor a pure negativity, nor an inexplicable and insignificant absurdity. The heroes of Dostoyevsky's humanism know what they want; they have nothing in common with the "heroes" of present-day existentialist literature, who are abulic, marrowless and absurd, for to kill someone or to embrace him is for them the same thing since everything is absurd, vain and insignificant. Existentialist heroes make a mockery of Dostoyevsky's tragedy. This is evidenced by the fact that all the solutions of the radical conflict between good and evil advanced by contemporary philosophy—which is a skeptic, pragmatic, or nihilistic philosophy—are either rejected or ridiculed by Dostoyevsky. Moreover, he considers as sterile either the masochistic enjoyment of suffering, or the desperate skepticism, or even faith in something for the sake of comfort or benefit from it. For the same reasons, Dostoyevsky makes suicide fit only for inferior souls (Smerdiakow and Svidrjgaiolov); while brutalization is the fate of the less significant or brutal figures; and madness or catastrophe befall the atheist, a spirit ostensibly strong but essentially weak (Ivan Karamazov), whom he does not spare even ridicule. For superior souls, the truly human heroes of the human drama, he reserves the true solution, *expiation,* through which rehabilitation, conversion, radical transformation, and *overcoming of weariness (metanoia)* take place. "Perhaps, I shall be better off in jail"; from this point "the story of [his] slow rebirth . . . gradual regeneration, and slow passage from one life to the other begins" for Raskolnikoff, the bankrupt and repentant superman.

Dostoyevsky personifies the condemnation of atheistic humanism in all its forms: Marxian, Nietzschean, skeptic, pragmatic, existentialist, or *absurdist;* and hence he remains one of the masters of true humanism, Christian and theistic, authentically human.

5. THE HISTORICISM OF W. DILTHEY

Anti-intellectual and humanistic positions do not end with the writers mentioned so far. The antipositivistic reaction against the abstractions of naturalism and science coincides with the last decades of the nineteenth century. Schopenhauer, Kierkegaard, and Nietzsche oppose intellectualism and rationalism of the idealistic type; between the end of the last century and the beginning of ours, contingentists, intuitionists, relativists, historicists, pragmatists, *actualists,* and so on, combat positivistic intellectualism and overthrow the new myth of Nature and Science from its pedestal, in the very same way as the myth of Reason had been previously overthrown. But there is a difference: intuitionists, pragmatists, relativists, and so on, are opposed to mathematical reason, but they believe in reason as an instrument for practical action. The pessimistic vision of existence is, in their philosophy, superseded by a more confident conception in harmony with the exigencies for man's sway over nature and perennial conquest of our daily human living; in short, a conception that fits the ideal of *homo faber,* the maker of his world and of his truth.

Science and philosophy are brought down to earth and they become effective instruments through which man builds his own "house," his new one, since the celestial "structure" has already been demolished. Philosophy loses its dignity as the science of the Absolute or as a "system" of being and knowledge. No longer do we have philosophy but only philosophies. Each one is a point of view; infinite are the points of view held by man before the universe, and hence infinite is the number of philosophies. They are ordered according to the "modes" of sensing the universe and of reacting to it, that is, as intuitions of the world and as orientation-systems or hypothetical systems none of which is true in an absolute sense, but each of which may have a certain truth of its own.

Thus WILHELM DILTHEY (1833-1911), one of the masters of

German historicism, rejects philosophy as the science of absolute truths although he justifies its existence; and although he points to contradictions in all philosophies, he vindicates for each current its own inconfutable value as a partial systemization of reality. "The last word in the historic conception of the world is the relativity of every human conception; everything moves, nothing stays still."

The foundation of ethical and political sciences on a basis as solid as that of natural sciences had been the constant and ambitious (when not naive) preoccupation of positivism from Comte to Spencer. They wished to found a sort of philosophy of history or sociology that would establish laws and concordances within the congeries of human facts. Dilthey was also dominated by the same preoccupation of organizing moral and political sciences and establishing them scientifically, that is, uncovering the "types" or "classes" in which they are organized. But Dilthey rejects (as he himself writes) the associationist psychology "which wishes to explain the constitution of the spiritual world according to its own views, laws, and forces, as is usually done by physics and chemistry in the physical order."

The empiricism of associationist psychology ignores the unity of consciousness by which alone the fragments of sense experience are composed and integrated. It is here that the new psychology of Dilthey, under the influence of Kant and idealism, resolutely departs from that of positivism, so that it grasps the sense of history (no longer sociology) in that spiritual value which had been missed by positivism. There is history wherever there is capacity for values, wherever impressions or documentary fragments are experienced as an *event*, a content of life, one that has been "vitally experienced" (*Erlebnis*). The *Erlebnis* is the foundation of the new psychology which conceives man as a teleological structure. In our psychic structure there is in fact an aptitude for values directing it in a determinate way. The spirit is not moved by external objects. Finality (teleology) is given by the capacity we have to live and experience objects in view of an end. The *Erlebnis* misses nothing; every content of life depends on the historic state of mind that has generated it. There is no knowledge that is pure or disinterested. Logical processes are bound to the psychic structure and they are pigmented with a determinate state of mind: reason is not separated from passions. Man does not know with his intellect alone, but with the totality of his being; to understand (*verstehen*) is not to explain (*erklären*), which is only a rational function, but it is knowing with all the emotive strength of the mind. Comprehension or historic knowledge is movement from life to life.

The variety of individuals, however, is centered for Dilthey in psychic structures, typical complexes repeating and reproducing themselves. Individual facts are introduced, like a system of laws, into these mental types which leave their mark on art, science, custom, and so forth, and which history has the task of discovering. In their turn, reciprocal compenetrations are established between human types and the physical and social environment (Dilthey retains positivistic influences): individualizing characteristics and permanent elements coexist in every psychic fact. "It is consonant with the individuation of the real that certain fundamental forms designated by us always reappear in the play of variations. The various characteristics, parts, or functions are regularly connected with one another in such a type. These traits, whose connection makes up the type, are in such a reciprocal relation that the presence of the type in one implies its presence in the others, and it is the same with the variation." Dilthey is not against that reason which immerses itself in life and in the flux of sentiments and which differs from the conception held by Descartes and the Cartesians, for whom reason is the depository of pure principles and the inviolable sanctuary of eternal truths. Rational propositions and principles spring from the historic man; they emerge (both the principles of Aristotelian logic and Kantian categories) from vital sentiments and from the need of understanding which is consonant with certain historic epochs. Philosophy, therefore, is only a "universalizing stylization of emotions, enthusiasms and dismays experienced by man in a moment of his history." [3] According to Dilthey, every epoch has its ideals and its values that are also elaborated under the influence of ideals and values inherited from preceding epochs. Every generation has its juridical and political ideals, its aesthetic tastes, its rules regulating customs, and so on. The new generation carries within itself its own code of values that is asserted against that of the preceding generation. Philosophy is precisely the central perspective by which the formation of an epoch's culture is determined. In other words, it may be said that philosophy—unlike religion, art and sciences—seeks to penetrate the enigma of life and to embrace the totality of the real world by organizing the materials offered by historic experience. "The philosophical spirit (writes Dilthey) moves about wherever a thinker, free from the systematic form of philosophy, investigates what in the individual is obscurely stirred up as instinct, faith or authority. This spirit is present wherever researchers, with conscious method, direct their science back to its fundamental principles and promote generalizations which establish or connect together more sciences; it exists wherever vital or ideal values are placed under revision. That which may appear disordered and hostilely adverse in the interior of an age or in the heart of a man must be reconciled by thought; that which is obscure must be illuminated; that which is immediate and

[3] L. Giusso, *Spengler e la dottrina degli universi formali* (Napoli, Ricciardi, 1935), p. 24.

scattered must be coordinated and united. Thus, in the present situation of philosophy, the characteristic is that the strongest influences do not emanate from systems, but from that free philosophical thinking permeating sciences and the whole of literature. In fact, a strong ideal action proceeds from the latter when it is represented by writers such as Maeterlinck or Tolstoy. Dramas, novels and lyric poems have become the transmitters of the strongest philosophical influence." [4] A philosophy represents the vision of the world as held by a given epoch and, for this reason, it is not outside of the historic man with his passions and sentiments.

Art, too, like philosophy, is associated with its time. Homer, Dante, Shakespeare, and Goethe express the tendencies, impulses, and ideals of the epoch in which they respectively lived. Whereas philosophy and religion give rise to definitive mental structures, poetry, however, expresses only single events. Religion and philosophy, even in the diversity of their various points of view, can be brought back to certain mental types, to determinate structures which, being eternal and not arbitrary, are produced and renewed in determinate historic moments. Each structure incarnates a type of spirituality distinct and diverse from that expressed by another; and, hence, neither a hierarchy nor a dialectical deduction of the various structures is possible. Each *Weltanschauung* or vision of the world is in itself the organization of an interior world stemming from certain states of mind impossible to relate to one another. According to Dilthey, structures thus put order in the chaos of events and constitute the laws of history, the "round-trip tracks" for the development of human spirit.

Without falling into irrationalism, Dilthey has dethroned pure truths and caused them to descend from their clear sky into the world of sentiments and impulses; he has established a tight bond between philosophy and the other ideal values without dissolving (so he thought) philosophy itself, to which instead he assigns the task of conferring universality on those values. Dilthey, in brief, changed Kantian categories, which were still confined to Leibniz' rationalism, into the forms of history as well as into the laws of our inexhaustible and manifold human life; on the other hand, he has made history a quest of values, a process of "events," rather than a series of "facts" as positivism had done. Notwithstanding the perenniality and nonarbitrariness of the structures, however, it is evident that Dilthey stands for a relativistic conception of truth, truth of an epoch or historic truth. For him, in fact, there is no such thing as *the* truth, but only truths; yet to have truths in the plural, or "more" truths—unless all truths are true by reason of *the truth*—means

[4] L. Giusso, *ibid.*, p. 25. Also see, by the same author, *G. Dilthey* (Napoli, Ricciardi, 1940).

that none of them is really truth: structures, one after the other, are born, disappear, and return. We ask, "Who is man in this coming and going of forms of art, religion, and philosophy? What do history and its many epochs—each with its ideals and values—say to every individual, to me as a person, who does not see himself fully 'explained' in the *Erlebnis*, even if in the *Erlebnis* I find myself 'laid open?'" Like all historicisms of romantico-idealist origin, Dilthey's may serve to write histories of art, religion, philosophy (provided they are not counterfeited within fixed schemes), but it never says what philosophy, art, and religion really are; that is to say, it can never speak to man one of those words having an everlasting value and carrying a never-setting light on the enigma of his restless existence. Ultimately, in it, the *factum* equalizes the *verum* and this is not anti-intellectualism; it is still naturalistic historicism.

6. THE RELATIVISM OF G. SIMMEL AND THE FICTIONISM OF H. VAIHINGER

Almost contemporaneously with Dilthey, GEORG SIMMEL (1858-1918) also delivers his pick-blows on the edifice of philosophy and of the closed system to destroy them, while simultaneously supplying his own bricks to build several dwellings for the philosophies (*Einleitung in die Moral Wissenschaft*, Berlin, 1892-93; *Haupt Probleme der Philosophie*, Leipzig, 1910). Unlike transcendental idealism, Simmel admits no absolute subject, but only the existence of individual spirits. Thus, there is no vision of the world in its totality and universality, but only partial and particular visions which, however, are shaped according to the universal forms of the spirit. With their character of universality, these visions represent the great philosophical systems. Even Simmel holds that the categories through which the human spirit creates its own world are infinite. New categories can always be revealed; no category is imposed by the datum and the same datum can be considered according to diverse categories. Human spirit is a polygonal activity, with different faces, each of which has its particular aspirations and exigencies. Each of the great visions of life corresponds to a group of such needs. Philosophy, writes Simmel, is only a "reaction of souls in the presence of the totality of being, a symbolic transcription of ineffable and irrepressible human aspirations"; it is a tendency "to achieve the unity needed by the spirit in the presence of the infinite multiplicity, variety, fragmentations, and discontinuity of the world." Philosophy is the need for "a point of unity" amidst worldly disorder and contrasts. It is the expression of individualities, but not of isolated individualities. Philosophical systems, on the other hand, are not an arbitrary or personal play as they are for

Nietzsche. Unlike the sciences, philosophy does not reflect the objectivity of things, but the "types" of human spirituality in determinate circumstances. Philosophical truths, therefore, do not have to correspond to an object, but they have to signify the type of humanity living in the philosopher; and each truth expresses only itself and is irreducible to the other; it is the homogeneous systematization of the anxieties belonging to a group of spirits. This explains why even today men find their exigencies—each according to his own needs—expressed by Plato, Spinoza, Augustine, or Bruno. In short, philosophy for Simmel is a comparative psychology, and the history of philosophy is a gallery of types or human structures, each of which is expressed by the dominating personality of a great thinker. There is in the history of thought a fixed and narrow number of ideologies and cosmologies responding to the truly original and fundamental needs, and capable of giving rise to an intuition of the world (as, for example, monism, pluralism, and the like). Metaphysics is legitimate only as a symbolic interpretation of the real: not as knowledge, but as the transformation of interests and needs to be found beyond truth and falsity. Every metaphysics or vision of the universe is partial and relative; it is an interpretation of the world as it was framed by a great thinker, who used only one of the innumerable threads making up the fabric of reality. The philosopher captures a particular trait of reality, and enlarges it so much as to include the totality in it and to elevate it beyond the relative, to infinity and the absolute. Every metaphysical vision is a relative truth longing for absoluteness: truth is relative by essence. But the exigency of totality contradicts the concept of relativity. Totality presupposes, as its foundation, an absolute, which is life with its correlative values, a life that is outside of the science of concepts. "The absolute is founded on the consciousness of probability. The absolute is *life*, the ultimate reality which we are able to reach, not by dominating it conceptually, but only by *living it*. Life is one, fulfilled in itself and in every one of its moments as an immediate reality. But each *life* is a reaction to the totality of being; it is what brings into the heart of metaphysics the fragmentariness of individual contents, and what establishes a distinction between these contents and the *process of life*, which is one and perennial, beyond the tragic limitation and dispersion of individual lives." [5] Thus understood, relativism is not a diminution of knowledge, but a satisfaction, through the dynamism of life, of the philosophical passion, which is exigency of totality.

From Simmel's conception of truth as a relative and mobile world "image" derived from the inmost part of life, which is itself life capable

[5] G. Perticone, "Introduzione" to the volume of Simmel: *Nietzsche e Schopenhauer* (Turin, Paravia), p. 31.

of producing always new as well as relative truths, it is not difficult to reach the conclusion that systems and metaphysical solutions are nothing but *fictions*. This in fact was the conclusion of HANS VAIHINGER (1852-1933), under the influence of pragmatism and the empiriocriticism (or philosophy of pure experience) of Mach and Avenarius. For Vaihinger, what is not bare and pure experience is fiction. Man cannot be satisfied with the brute sensation alone; therefore, he creates for himself some fictions (freedom, immortality, God, and so on) that are useful in practical life while they give him the illusion of gratifying his deepest exigencies. Men act as if the fictions they create were truths. For Vaihinger and the *Die Philosophie des Als-Ob* (the title of his main work, 1913) the tragedy of life consists in the fact that the highly esteemed concepts *"realiter* and not as fictions, are worthless." Philosophical, scientific, and religious truths are but "myths" or useful illusions.

7. Contingentism of E. Boutroux and Intuitionism of H. Bergson

Almost contemporaneously with the German philosophical currents sketched above, a renewal of thought took place in France between the end of the last and the first decade of this century; it received a notable response in the years immediately preceding the First World War. FELIX RAVAISSON (1813-1900) and CHARLES RENOUVIER (1818-1903) are the renovators; EMIL BOUTROUX (1845-1921), HENRI BERGSON (1859-1941), and MAURICE BLONDEL (1861-1949) are the great masters of contemporary French thought prior to the war. These thinkers mark the renewal of spiritualism (but not that of the German type) against the intellectualism, naturalism, and "scientifical-ism" of positivistic philosophy. Whatever their differences, they agree on one point: *freedom* of spirit and *indeterminism* of nature are metaphysical principles of reality as well as laws of being whose determinism and mechanical necessity represent only an appearance and a superficial aspect.

Boutroux holds that no necessary and absolute bonds exist between ideas and things (only the principle of identity, A = A, is necessary and absolute). Effect is never identical with its cause since, in the concrete, every case differs from the other and has a physiognomy of its own that is irreducible to the general law. Law, therefore, explains what is repeated but misses what is new in phenomena. Scientific laws do not grasp concrete and living reality and, therefore, they hold no objective value. Nor are the various classes of natural beings (physical, biological, psychic) deducible from one another because each one is identical with itself. Every class, then, like the effect with respect to its cause, is *contingent*, that is, it could have been different than it is or it could have not been at all. Thus, natural reality always is a new creation due to the spontaneity of the universe. The schemes and symbols of science (abstract or rationalistic knowledge) are unable to grasp the creative principle of reality, the true essence of things. They neither express nor interpret reality; they only schematize and impoverish it; thus they have a value that is not cognitive but only utilitarian, that is, they serve the practical use we make of them; or, as Mach and Avenarius say, they "economize" our mental energies.[6]

Idealistic reaction against science and scientific intellectualism finds its next genial and original expression in the intuitionism of Bergson (*Time and Free Will*, trans. F. L. Pogson, New York, 1910; *Matter and Memory*, trans. N. M. Paul *et al.*, London, 1950; *Creative Evolution*, trans. A. Mitchell, New York, 1931; *Durée et Simultaneité*, Paris, 1922; *The Two Sources of Morality and Religion*, trans. R. Ashley Audra *et al.*, New York, 1949), whose thought has exercised a world-wide influence. Although a pupil of Ollé-Laprune and Boutroux, he was attracted by the evolutionism and naturalism of the time; and yet, certainly because of Boutroux's influence too, he was able to draw some unsuspected idealistic elements even from positivism. Moreover, Bergson's thought can be considered as the most vigorous reaction against "scientificalism," that is, against that French evolutionistic empiricism of the second half of the nineteenth century, in which there is a convergence of elements from Comte's and Taine's positivism, Renan's dilettantism, English empiricism (in the form renewed by Stuart Mill), post-Kantian German philosophy, and Spencer's evolutionistic and biological positivism. Bergson could and eventually did draw the motifs of his criticism of scientificalism from the nineteenth-century French thought itself, specifically, from the psychologism of Maine de Biran, the philosophy of freedom of Ravaisson, neocriticism of Renouvier, contingentism of Boutroux, and so forth.

French philosophy has always had two fundamental directions of thought: one rationalistic according to the Cartesian type, and the other, intuitionistic, according to the Pascalian type—*ésprit de géométrie* and *ésprit de finesse*. As Cartesian-type rationalism is once more found in

---

[6] Ernst Mach (1838-1916) and Richard Avenarius (1843-1896) are the theorists of "the philosophy of pure experience" or "empiriocriticism," according to which experience, "purified, freed" of the arbitrary additions of thought, is nothing but flowing of sensations. Only to save mental energies we "condense" the multiplicity of particular experiences into general schemes. The entire value of scientific laws lies here. There is not one law that is truer than another, but there is a law that is more convenient than another—more convenient in that it condenses in itself a greater number of phenomena.

scientificalism, so the exigency for inwardness of the Pascalian type is met again in the intuitionistic current. Bergson represents the revolt against the Cartesian tradition always present in French philosophy, that is, a revolt against the *raison raisonnante*, which had found its last embodiment in scientificalism. From this point of view, Bergson expresses a historic moment that is fundamental in the development of French philosophy. His speculative effort has two converging directions: one aimed at freeing biologism and evolutionism from the heaviness of their rationalistic scientificalism so that both can be immersed in the very stream of life, and the other aimed at giving not a purely biological and materialistic significance but a profoundly spiritual sense to life itself. On the one hand, Bergson avails himself of the Pascalian type of French anti-intellectualism in order to demolish scientific intellectualism and, on the other hand, he uses new biological and evolutionistic theories to bring the former into contact with concrete reality with a view to establishing, through the principles of "intuition," "duration," and "vital impetus," a metaphysical principle of reality. Therefore, it is necessary to bear in mind: (1) that Bergson's anti-intellectualism carries a very strong polemical aspect, the criticism of a particular kind of intellectualism (the scientific one), but not the criticism or negation of every form of intellective and rational knowledge; (2) that on the ground of the criticism of scientific intellectualism, it constructs a philosophy (and a metaphysics) which, while not rejecting the legitimate exigencies of positivism, vindicates, against the latter, precisely the concrete sense of life and the reality of spiritual, cognitive, moral and religious values. Positivism, as we said, is first of all a "method"; Bergson's first problem, then, is that concerning *method:* demonstrating the abstractness of the positivistic (intellectualistic) one, and pointing out a new method of philosophizing that renovates (and it succeeded) the traditionally rationalistic (Cartesian) French philosophical environment. Bergson (as, in another sense, Blondel and other French thinkers of the time) represents the insurrection of *conscience* against *raison*. His is intuitionism but not irrationalism; intuition does not exclude concrete rationality. One must distinguish between Bergson and the "Bergsonianism" of some of his followers, who are inclined toward a dilettante-like anti-intellectualism. There is, indeed, an irrationalistic intuitionism in Bergson, but this is merely a polemical aspect; or rather, this is a shield by which he protects his conception of the spirit against scientific intellectualism as well as against French abstract and centuries-old rationalism. In fact, that which is immediate in Bergson's intuition does not exclude that mediation which is rational and reflective, concrete and not abstract.

It is one thing to say what an object is, to describe and express it in symbols; it is quite another matter to penetrate its interiorness and cap-

31

ture its very essence which cannot be expressed through symbols. The former is the method of *knowing through concepts* (analysis and synthesis; induction and deduction), which pertains to philosophical and scientific intellectualism, and is symbolic, extrinsic, abstract and relative; the latter is the method of immediate *intuition*, an intrinsic, concrete and absolute knowledge. Science and philosophy are like two bridges under which runs the stream of living reality; intuition places itself amidst the waters of the river of life whose essence is grasped in the immediate experience. "Reality is a process of perennial creation without beginning nor end; and it does not have the same appearance twice, but in every instant assumes an unforeseeable and original aspect: it is an unceasing flux wherein nothing persists, a mobile and live continuity without division of parts." Knowing through intuition means *living* a thing *from within* and, hence, intuition is an absolute mode of knowing, diverse from the relative mode pertinent to *analysis*.

Intuition is a sort of intellectual sympathy whereby we are transposed into the inside of an object and are enabled to grasp its essence, which lies beyond any symbolic expression or translation of the type made by positive science. The latter, instead, confines itself to giving a photographic representation of objects. Therefore: (1) scientific theories, philosophical doctrines and religious dogmas are obscure, relative and abstract symbols (in which true, concrete and profound reality is missing), elaborated by the intellect for practical purposes; and (2) intuition alone is instead the type of concrete and absolute (viz., metaphysical) knowledge. In fact, for Bergson *metaphysics* is a special mode of knowing, "of possessing a reality absolutely, instead of knowing it relatively; of entering into it, instead of accepting some points of view on it; and of having an intuition of it instead of making the analysis of it—all this with a view to grasping such a reality outside of every expression, translation or symbolic representation." Metaphysics, then, is absolute knowledge of the *internal* existence of beings, that is, an entering into the heart of their "individual" creativeness.

Through intuition we attain the knowledge of the *ego* that remains in time, flows, and lives without arrest. The essence of the *ego*, like that of the universe, is *real duration*, a perennial flow in which the different states enter, penetrate and are united. Introspection shows us that our spiritual life is only the intimate experience of something which continues to last even through change. The individual is a *psychological* or real *duration*. Beneath the *superficial ego* which is fragmentary and divided in so many psychic acts, and beneath the solidification of the extrinsic strata of consciousness we can grasp (if we are able to penetrate that deeply) a continuity and succession of movements and states firmly organized and animated by a common life, in which all our past is enriched with the present (*consciousness is memory*), and in which we discover our *ego in depth,* that is, our permanent and yet always new unitary life.

The inexhaustible source whence all spiritual as well as material things spring in their perennial flux is the vital impetus (*élan vital*), an impulse (diverse from evolution in a mechanistic sense) that is not substance but a force producing ever new and better forms through evolution. Originally indistinct in the vital impulse, forces spread successively in different directions; some of them developed more perfectly whereas others arrested at the initial phase. The primitive vital impulse first distinguished itself in vegetative and animal life wherein instinct and intelligence are undifferentiated and almost asleep. Successively, instinct alone develops in animals, and intelligence in men. The vital impetus rises in man as far as consciousness and freedom, but at the expense of the instinct whose function is to take hold of the essence of things (intelligence knows only conceptual relations). Instinct alone could make us know things in their reality, but this is devoid of consciousness. It is necessary to unite instinct and intelligence in intuition, the only cognitive and metaphysical faculty. Thus, as we already said, Bergson's intuition does not exclude the act of reflection, but rather includes it and makes it concrete. Intuition requires an "act of violence" and a laborious effort. To achieve our goal we must first free ourselves of our intellectual habit of applying the conceptual categories to living and concrete reality. In fact, these categories are moulded on inorganic matter and, like matter, they are crystallized and incapable of understanding life in its manifold forms of organization and evolution. When this is done and we have also acknowledged the error of the mechanistic and teleological hypotheses, which stem from our use of classifying schemes, we are then able to grasp the real characteristics of life itself. In other words, we are able to see the difference of nature between *matter,* which is inertia, dispersion, powerless and solidified energy, and *life,* which is evolution, unity, energetic integration, dynamic rhythm, uninterruptedly creative potency, ascending movement, and an inextinguishable reservoir of an always new life. The mechanistic and teleological theories, instead, cannot acquire such an understanding because both of them abolish evolution: the former by denying that there is any enrichment and originality in the process from cause to effect, and the latter by inverting the causal process and conceiving the end as ultimate cause.

Bergson, at times, gives the primitive vital impetus the name of God, "the center whence infinite worlds, like sparks from an immense fire, spring out, provided that this center is not considered as a *thing,* but as a flowing continuity. God, so defined, has nothing finite—He is unceasing life, action, and freedom."

Even in his last work, *The Two Sources of Morality and Religion,* we can find again Bergson's typical theme concerning the antithesis between "static and dynamic morality" and between crystallized and creative religion, which are variations of Bergson's classical antithesis between space and time, mechanical matter and vital impetus. Obligation, for Bergson, belongs to static morality as it was imposed by society: the everyday morality of a life conforming to the rule, effortless and without initiative, or life that is carried on through "a short-cut through the fields." Against this we have the morality of the "ethical genius," who spontaneously gives himself without imposing obligations and restrictions; this is the morality of the spirit of sacrifice and charity, a dynamic morality. Static morality is marking time, whereas the dynamic marches ahead; it is an appeal that, being launched beyond the centuries and human civilizations, always finds answers and resonances in the depth of our soul. This is the morality of mystic souls who have always marked out the road for civilized societies. The two moralities, however, meet and make up that synthesis that is characteristic of a humanity placing itself on a determinate level "higher than that of an animal society, in which the obligation would be only force of instinct; yet it would be less than a meeting of gods where everything would be creative impetus. If we consider then the manifestations of moral life as being thus organized, we find them perfectly coherent in themselves and, hence, capable of being led back to determinate principles. Moral life is a rational life."

Bergson develops the theory of the two forms of religion in a parallel and analogous way (but without direct transpositions). For the sake of their preservation and development, nature has endowed inferior societies with instinct. Man, instead, has been endowed with intelligence and the power of freedom, which, on the one hand, contributes to the maintenance, unity and social development—that is, the greatness—of the species while, on the other, it constitutes a danger for the very exercise of the function to which it is destined. Hence the necessity on the part of nature to endow man with another faculty besides intelligence; Bergson calls it *fabulation*, which is destined to counterbalance the dissolving power of intelligence. *Static religion*—namely, social or gregarious religion—originates from *fabulation* or fiction.

The fictional function, or *form of imagination*, creates "*fantasmatique*" representations, that is, images of powers, of extra-natural entities, which are believed to be real powers or real persons. The totality of phantasms and personifications, which restrain intelligence and by which nature protects the species, constitutes the content of *static religion*.

Nature has given man *fabulation* as a corrective against the following three dangers of intelligence: (1) intelligence may direct man toward selfish ends and thus away from the course of social well-being; (2) it gives the sense of the precariousness of life to man who is unique among living beings in that he is conscious of falling ill and dying; (3) it makes man aware that his work is accompanied by the feeling of the unforeseeable and the risky, that is to say by the feeling that his work may be hindered by adverse forces which may neither be foreseen nor removed. Through *fabulation* nature seeks to diminish these dangers. First, by its "*fantasmatique*" representations nature imposes some restrictions on the individual who is being led by signs and voices; second, it gives him the image of a continuity of life after death, thus keeping him attached to life and active for society; third, it makes him envisage "favorable powers," which come to take the place of natural and mechanical causes. Static religion, therefore, is "a defensive reaction of nature against what in the exercise of intelligence could be depressive for the individual (inevitability of death, discouragement because of the unforeseeable) and dissolvent for society (egotistical ends).

There is, however, not only the religion due to human fabrication, as sociologists and idealists maintain, and not only the mythology of the world *of* gods, but there is also the reign *of* God, of God the Creator. When one passes from the multiplicity of gods to the conception of the one God, then one *jumps* from static religion to *dynamic religion*, from outwardness to inwardness. There is a leap because emotion is not consecutive, but original and creative. Man no longer marks a step signifying mere augmentation of life, but he re-enters the stream of creative impetus. Dynamic religion is of a *superintellectual* nature—that is, it is a "particular and privileged" mystic experience belonging to a few men, heroes and saints, who are the elected ones. The great mystics are the founders of dynamic religion. They are the great souls who, being shaken in their depth, cease to revolve around themselves. The soul "stops as if it were listening to a voice calling; then it lets itself be led straight ahead, without directly perceiving the moving force, whose indefinable presence is either felt or guessed through the symbolic vision. At that point an immensity of joy comes: God is there and the soul is in Him." The permanent union between soul and God is attained in the *mystic action*. The soul feels the presence of God—God is in it and the soul is, at the same time, *acting and acted upon*. Now life, impetus and freedom, coinciding with the divine activity, superabound. Great is the humility and not the pride of the soul; great is its power of expansion and its apostolic fervor. The mystic longs to transform humanity, to triumph over matter, to rediscover God and to love Love Itself.

God, for Bergson, is love and thus He pours Himself out in the universe; He creates the object of love, life, and man above all. Only mysticism can attain God, for it alone is interior experience; the mystic's experience is precisely the proof for the existence of God. The mystic (and integral mysticism is just that which emerges from Catholicism through the great Christian mystics) "through God, and by God, loves humanity with a divine love." Beyond natural societies, which are the product of racial egoism, the concept of a *totally human society* is born in man who learns to love, through God, his fellow-man. Mystical love is metaphysical by nature; it penetrates with its roots into the very source of being.

What, then, are positive religions and dogma for Bergson? Dogma is the symbolic transcription of the mystical experience, the "crystallization through a gradual cooling, of what mysticism, still in an incandescent state, deposits in the soul of mankind." Mysticism and dogma alternate in the becoming of history. Experience, enclosed in dogmatic formulas, is vivified by the subsequent mysticism, whose penetration beneath the inert surface renews and snatches it from oblivion by inserting it again into the creative movement of the spirit. Bergson's position leads to these affirmations: (1) true religion, or mysticism, is an individual phenomenon, or the individual's masterpiece; (2) positive religions are inertia, that is, crystallizations of the creative spirit, or instruments used by the species to preserve itself. This is the condemnation of every positive religion including Catholicism, in whose bosom, nonetheless, Bergson finds the great mystics representing the authentic expressions of religion. Moreover, it seems that for Bergson there is no objective faith, or a content of truth that, with or without mysticism, must be accepted as revealed truth. His mysticism is energy, man's spiritual force that penetrates beyond the bounds of nature, beyond itself, to the point of transcending itself in the spiritual impetus. Thus, the content of faith has no importance for mysticism, which remains indifferent toward any form of dogmatism. Catholic orthodoxy is, for Catholic mystics, no longer the essence of their faith, nor is it the *conditio sine qua non* in order to be on the way to truth and salvation since it is an accidental aspect of their religion. In this case, then, there is no longer any religion but only a vague sense of religiousness.

8. M. Blondel's Philosophy of Action

A deeply religious and Catholic soul is, instead, MAURICE BLONDEL who, in the anti-intellectualistic reaction by contemporary philosophy, holds a place that is *sui generis*, or very personal, precisely on account of the religious interest that characterizes his thought. Philosopher of *action* (*L'Action*,[7] Paris, 1936-1937, is the title of his fundamental work), he considers it the ineradicable residue of every rational synthesis whereby the mind is shaken from its passiveness and compelled to follow

[7] Published in 1893, it was reprinted in 1950. In the meantime Blondel had gone over the first edition and published (1936) a new *Action* in two volumes.

the very rhythm of life. The principle of man's spiritual life is the *will*, which is always trying to realize itself completely without ever succeeding fully. The permanent imbalance between a will trying to complete itself and action as it has been carried out, or between a "willing will" and a "willed will," always leaves the former unsatisfied and compelled to go beyond itself. A deep or willing will always aims at affirming itself in its own fullness and integrity, but it is compelled to pursue its ideal through numerous stages because of the resistances coming to it from the outside (corporeal organism, science, society, and the like). Thus, the will conquers contrary forces for its own use and attains its goal through their cooperation. The willing will, as it progressively actuates itself, finds out something of itself but never the whole of itself; after willing everything, its capacity of willing remains intact. By the disproportion existing between the two wills, will itself is stimulated to progress and to penetrate new objects through action. No action, however, and not even all the objects of universal reality, fill the gap between the two wills. God alone can fill the abyss between "willing will" and "willed will," between what man *wants* to be and what he is, and between his infinite aspiration and his actual poverty. Our thirst for fullness and totality compels us to become what we cannot be by ourselves. We carry in our own being an essential deficiency, metaphysically necessary, and an invincible aspiration toward absolute perfection, toward God who is inaccessible in the order of nature, and who offers Himself to us in a supernatural order.

In his work, *La Pensée* (Paris, 1934), Blondel posits the problem of the origin, nature, and destination of thought itself. He proceeds from the state prior to the distinction between subject and object and follows the thinking process in its effort toward "unity and integrality," according to the method of "implication and, at the same time, integration." Prior to the subject-object distinction, thought is "cosmic thought," a global unity: the world as a *solidum quid*. The world *is* and it is *thought*, but it is not an immovable, compact, self-sustaining being identical with itself; on the contrary, it tends toward unity in a manifold process that is revealed through a multiplicity of initiatives.

Thought manifests itself afterwards as "psychic thought," a unity between organisms and things. Finally we have a "thinking thought" coinciding with the rise of consciousness. The coming into being of the latter is, at first, more thinking thought than thought already thought; it is more subject than object. Yet, in order to make human thought possible, a condition is necessary, namely, seeking for and affirming a present reality. Knowledge tends to become "the other" and it seeks "to know the other *qua* other" with a view to finding, "in this higher and more impartial science, a more certain means, that of assimilating "the other"

37

to the knowing subject more completely; thus, from its first sources thought imperiously reveals its ultimate and total goal which is *to universalize.*" But all this would be impossible if "in its coming into being and in order to come into being thought did not imply the affirmation of its own transcendence." Any initiative whatever is possible in so far as man has a deep and immediate feeling of his superiority over things, the feeling of transcendence, and that of his own power and personal aims. It is the inferior animal who remains imprisoned in and enslaved to the immanent order of things to which he adapts himself. Man always feels a nostalgia, instead, for what he is not, or what he ought to be: in this lies the common motivation for art, science, ethics, and religious aspirations. In the presence of any reality given to and endured by men, the latter introduce into it their truths as these proceed from their rational nature; yet these truths "cannot be fully applied to and justified by this reality because they are outside of and beyond the natural order and experience of this world." The consciousness of the subject-object duality implies an "everlasting appeal" to a knowledge no longer belonging to the senses or consciousness. Led by its own nature, knowledge rises to rational principles and affirmations beyond every experience in order to attain necessary and universal truths without which neither sense knowledge nor psychic or moral knowledge would be possible and conceivable. Bent on itself, thought seeks to know the universe and embrace the infinite, but without success. Objects are unified but without "attaining a total coherence and a universal unity." The invincible dualism between subject and object makes it impossible to realize an absolute unity.

The thought which thinks and vivifies the principles of reason "spontaneously and necessarily feels the need of relying on a more profound thought, on a more living and concrete ideal, and on an absolute in which it is possible to have reconciled all those terms which up to now have appeared to be irreducible, incompatible, and indestructible." The subject's life is but a passage *ab interioribus ad superiora.* The impetus toward the Absolute is not exhausted within our subjective order. In fact, the imperative need for a transcendent principle, which is not merely an idea or a mental category but rather an ontological reality, stems from the dualism between subject and object.

This thought is not an abstract thought, then, but a "thought in becoming" which, in the same way as action, is grasped within its ascending development (a thought that is civilizing and capable of organizing the sense-data, and so forth). Always dissatisfied and longing for its "beatifying fullness," this thought is endowed with an "innate deficiency" which, though tormenting, pushes it to the search for a supreme object. Neither the philosopher with his doctrine nor the man in the full course of life, nor even civilization at its fullest will ever be able to arrest this becoming and suppress this inquietude, whatever the success achieved by thought. "Consecrated by every experience and imposed on us by death with a tragic brutality, this fact is not a truth of experience only, but a truth by right. . . . *L'inachèvement est, au fond, une inachèvabilité.*" Thought not incapable of completion in itself is completed in the uncreated Being. It is, however, "naturally" impossible that thought should be united to God. Although its effort is carried to the utmost, thought still finds itself confronted by mystery. "Between human thought and divine perfection there is an insuperable abyss" to be filled only through God's gratuitous help.

Thus, within the permanent duality of subjective-objective thought, which is continuously renewed at every stage of the thinking process, a place is found for the problem of being that idealism claimed to resolve by identifying being with the subject, while agnosticism and phenomenalism ignored it altogether. The problem of being finds its place within this duality, as Blondel says in his other work *L'Etre et les êtres* (Paris, 1936), inasmuch as being according to the method of implication is not only the object of thought, but "constitutes the very conditions of its own existence and intelligibility, be it relative or absolute." The problem of the individual is posited together with the problem of being. Death is the proof of the insufficiency of the individual as "thinking thought." But the consciousness of death is the beginning of survival and a proof for the immortality of the individual. Through its consciousness of death, human thought is able to conquer death; on the other hand, through its consciousness of the perfect Thought, or God, thought cannot but wish to establish a bond with Him. Thought is thus born twice: in the consciousness of death and in the certitude of the divine Logos.

We, says Blondel, apply being to what exists; but the existence of beings relates to the eternal Being. Beings "exist" more than "being": God "is" more than "existing." Existence is the external aspect of beings; their internal aspect is their "consistency." Where does this "consistency" of beings lie?

Beings have the ability to become beings, but they are not beings as yet: an acorn may, for example, become an oak, but it is not that yet, and it might never become such. Beings, then, have an initial contingency that follows them in their evolutional and constitutive process. One, then, must not seek for the "consistency" of beings in what they are as a matter *of fact* in a given moment, but in a norm transcending them. Their being fulfilled or their coming to nought depends on whether they conform to or rebel against such a norm. It is "the internal norm that constitutes the living and secret armor of beings in search of their true and complete realization."

Consistency is normative and it manifests itself in all the elements making up the individual. The body is indispensable as a substrate and a support for the development of the individual himself. Organic life is a mediator between matter and spirit, and it sets forth the conditions for the existence of the being thinking in itself.

The passage from the vital impetus to the spiritual impetus shows the rise of the individual in which the concept of the consistency of beings is determined. However, not even individuals are completely autonomous beings. As "an outpost of being," the individual is not "a reality capable of consolidating and making himself self-sustaining like a substance that is constituted in its unity, autonomy, and in its definite and definitive consistency." He must then realize and *surpass himself*. He (the individual person) is not for his own sake and, therefore, it is an error to elevate every individual (individualism) or all individuals (democratism) to absoluteness: every individual has an end and a perfection which transcend and surpass him.

Where are, then, the "norm" and the "consistency" in the individual person? In his *relationship* with the absolute Being, with God. In this longing for God the individual completes his own personality and consciousness of being incapable of attaining God. "It would already be a very noble destiny to search for God infinitely without finding Him, and yet holding a humble, courageous, and insatiable generosity in accord with Malebranche's dictum—aiming at perfection without claiming it." However, such a solution is conceivable on condition that we exclude the possibility that the free initiative of God, dictated by His infinite charity and goodness, will ever respond to the appeal of the creature. Nothing, however, prevents us from conceiving as "possible" the free initiative of God, and then the solution of "salvation" as possible. God can grant man grace, moved by His own goodness and charity. If, instead, we deliberately oppose God's action, we remain *deprived* of being. This is the fall and "perdition" belonging to our state of dispersion and egoism, which is a "sign of the disorder, confusion, hatred and punishment stemming from the very source of our thoughts and wills rebelling against their own light and intimate impetus." It is not possible to will infinitely without willing the divine Being. The solution to the problem of the "consistency" of beings is not found in beings but in their relationship with God, that is, at the boundary of all boundaries, or in a boundless end.

Blondel's philosophy represents one of the richest and liveliest voices in our century. In this renovator of traditional Catholic philosophy, the voluntarism and anti-intellectualism of contemporary philosophy find a sound outlet, at the level of a will which does not exclude thought and of a logic which is united with the concreteness of life.

9. ANGLO-AMERICAN PRAGMATISM

In its manifold forms, Anglo-American pragmatism is similarly a philosophy of action or a philosophy of the will. Pragmatism is against English Neo-Hegelianism (Green, Bradley, McTaggart) because the latter submerges the concreteness of the individual into absolute Consciousness; and though in a certain sense it is a continuation of positivism, it opposes positivism for its different sort of abstractness. Besides the so-called religious pragmatism and other forms of the "philosophy of action," as for example that of Unamuno, pragmatism itself can be divided into five currents: (1) *logical pragmatism* (Peirce, Vailati); (2) *empirio-spiritualistic* pragmatism (James); (3) *humanistic* pragmatism (Schiller); (4) *fictional* pragmatism (Vaihinger), which we have already mentioned; and (5) *instrumentalistic* pragmatism (Dewey).

Of the first of these (and of pragmatism in general) CHARLES SANDERS PEIRCE (1839-1914) may be considered the founder. His essay, "How to Make Our Ideas Clear" (in *Classic American Philosophers*, New York, 1951, pp. 70-87) is the manifesto of the new philosophy. The problem of the nature of ideas ("what is an idea?") is not posited in terms of what they "are" but in terms of what they "do." As far as Peirce is concerned, the meaning of a conception lies in its practical consequences; in order to see what general notions (mind is developed through generalizations in a physico-neurological process) may be true, it is only necessary to apply the pragmatic criterion, that is, "to consider the possible consequences that may be relevant from a practical point of view." This criterion determines the *significance* of the concept of an object. The foundation of this epistemology is *credence* which is bound to our behavior. "The meaning of every assertion we make lies in the future" and, consequently, the whole positive sense of our ideas resides in their practical consequences. When new ideas do not produce differences in the practical results of our thought, they are only various "ways of saying the same thing." Pragmatism, for Peirce, is a "method of prevision" and having clear ideas on a subject means to be able to anticipate which present or future sensations we can expect and to prepare corresponding reactions in ourselves.

The above is followed by Italian pragmatists like GIOVANNI VAILATI (1863-1909) and MARIO CALDERONI (1879-1914), who wished to remain (particularly the former of the two) logical pragmatists so as to differ from James who, at the time, was proclaiming his "irrevocable, categorical, and frank abandonment of logic." Vailati attributes great importance both to the study of the structure and development of language and to that of the nature of the functions fulfilled by it. He is convinced that precision of terms equals the elimination of illusory contrasts, as well as the illusion of those who believe that they are "saying something even when they say nothing." Therefore, in order to avoid linguistic equivocations and meaningless words the best "methodic principle" is "that which counsels the determination of the meaning of every abstract phrase or proposition through the probing of the consequences derived therefrom, and through the probing of the *applications* made by the enunciator. In this way, two phrases or propositions can be regarded as equivalent or as two modes of saying the same thing (Peirce) by the person who, at any time, adopts them as a means of reaching the same particular conclusions." As regards both Vailati and Calderoni, Peirce's formula—the meaning of an idea lies in its practical consequences—must neither be understood in a utilitarian nor in a "subjectivistic" sense. Pragmatism, says Calderoni, is "utilitarian" only "to the extent that it leads to discarding some useless questions," that is, questions that are such only in appearance. Its formula is only an invitation to introduce "experimentalism not solely for the solution but also for the choice of the questions to be treated; it is an invitation to put into words —which are the object of our disputations—their practical and experimental content in order to avoid confusion and sophism." For both Vailati and Calderoni, experience is not only a means of *proving* assertions and theories but, above all, a criterion of their *significance*, that is, a criterion of choice and elimination of the questions provoked by the assertions themselves. For MARIO M. ROSSI (1895), whose first phase of thought is inspired by pragmatism, prevision is already in itself not only a criterion of significance, but also one of truth.

The term *pragmatism* used by Peirce was taken up again by WILLIAM JAMES (1842-1910) in a lecture at the University of California in 1898. With James, a student of medicine and physiology and a professor of philosophy at Harvard after 1885, pragmatism as a movement gained world influence and importance (as a result, too, of his widely-known works: *Principles of Psychology*, 2 vols., New York, 1890; "The Will to Believe" and other essays in *Popular Philosophy*, New York, 1903; *The Varieties of Religious Experience*, New York, 1902; *Pragmatism*, New York, 1907, and so on). Unlike Peirce's pragmatism, however, this one moves along an empirio-spiritualistic line and is wanting in "systematicity" while, at the same time, abounding in strange confusions and inexactnesses. "Radical empiricism" (as James dubbed his philosophy) is quite different from the classical empiricism of the British tradition. Experience, as understood by the American philosopher, is that of the future, a proof and verification of knowledge. Choosing the means *in view* of an end is the usual characteristic of a keen procedure that differentiates it from the mechanical method wherein neither are means chosen nor ends pursued: "In pursuing future ends and choosing means for their achievement lie the countermark and criterion by which the mental presence in a phenomenon is affirmed" (*Principles of Psychology*). In this way, volitional activity prevails over rational and sensorial activity: perception and thought exist solely in view of behavior. Both science and philosophy are constructed with human ends in view, and they serve (and this is the object of thought) action, so that man may operate in the world with efficacy. Thus, as was pointed out, "research, for James, cannot be stopped at what can be noticed objectively, and it is also quite proper to believe even in the absence of empirical objects, since the person believing in an alike thesis overcomes the state of uncertitude and attains a condition of calm empirically noticeable through introspection." Thus, James makes a defense of moral and religious "beliefs" (when these beliefs belong to the class of those which cannot be proven true or false though they are "live" and "important") on the ground that they are useful and necessary for an effective action. They are accepted as true and so there is a risk of error, but the risk is inevitable because even the person refusing to believe is assuming the risk of taking a negative decision. It is necessary then to accept both responsibility and risk by assuming what "could be," by choosing and being willing to believe.

Thus, James believes that he is saving and guaranteeing religious and moral exigencies, that he is giving a spiritualistic character to his pragmatism understood as the "will to believe." He also believes that he is laying down the foundations for his pluralistic conception of the universe in which God, one of many beings, is also *finite* and existent in time among us while He "is creating history for Himself as He creates us" (*A Pluralistic Universe*, New York, 1908). How such a God can satisfy the demands of the religious consciousness and guarantee an order of truth in the human and physical world remains incomprehensible and hence an ineffective belief, that is, one devoid of all pragmatic value.

It does not seem accurate to say that the Englishman F. C. S. SCHILLER (1864-1937), who follows Peirce's method more faithfully than James, has succeeded in bringing pragmatism back within the confines of logic and epistemology; it must be said rather that he holds to a logic very close to original pragmatism; and since he holds every thought or logical procedure to be caused by needs, feelings, beliefs and passions in the human soul, his can be considered a humanistic pragmatism, wherein everything is conditioned by the exigencies of action or practical need. In short, truth—each and every truth—is relative to man. His criticism of formal logic, which he considers a mere game or pleasant pastime of the intellect (*Formal Logic*, London, 1912), and his reduction of every nonpractical principle to a verbal proposition induce him to accept the utilitarian criterion as the only valid one, and to measure with it the degree of truth in sciences, mathematics, philosophy, and so on. In this sense, Schiller considers Protagoras' ancient saying, "Man is the measure of everything," as the greatest philosophical discovery without justifying, through this principle, the use of fictions, errors, and lies which may be convenient to someone. There is, according to Schiller, a kind of selective principle wherein the individual, during the course of his life, is led to give up some initial interests and choose truer and more consistent ones. Social actions rest on this choice; of the numerous choices always being made on the basis of a utilitarian criterion, the only surviving ones are those that have a social usefulness and that better respond to the aspirations of the greatest number of people in a given historic condition. Schiller's humanistic pragmatism is a form of subjectivism leading to radical relativism.

The "instrumentalism" of the American JOHN DEWEY (1859-1952) is the form of pragmatism most influential and most discussed today. Dewey's point of departure also lies in experience, but in that primitive and integral experience which is also error and perversity, ignorance and risk. Between man and nature there is a close and indissoluble connection; man is a part of nature and feels himself rooted in nature; but he is that part of nature which is destined by nature itself to modify its structure and to realize its meaning. As a consequence, ideas, and thought in general, are the *instrument* for the organization of future experience and "reason necessarily has a constructive function" (*Philosophy and Civilization*, New York, 1931). It is the task of philosophy to place itself at the center and at the confluence of these antitheses. In this sense, the validity of an idea is established by its effectiveness as an *instrument* for the passage from a less harmonious or nonharmonious to a more harmonious experience. Facts do not impose themselves on us from without; there is in them all that is due to our activity. Not that we create facts (Dewey is far from idealism), but we organize pre-existing experiences. Thought, in short, re-creates the world, and transforms it into an instrument used by man. Furthermore, thought has its beginnings precisely in the conflicts which experience presents. To convince oneself that error, evil, disorder, irrationality, and death are realities (rather than to delude oneself that they are but appearances) and to struggle to reduce their effects and to limit their impact—this is the task of man and of human society, a task gradually (but never completely) realized through the activity of the human intelligence which is "valid within the limits of its success." Every theory, or doctrine, or mental construction is an efficacious means (provided that it *is* so) through which man transforms reality in order to guarantee for himself the use and enjoyment of the

goods he needs. Men think when they are stimulated by need and inquietude, when they experience perturbations which must be put to
rest, difficulties which must be overcome. "A life of repose," one reads
in *Reconstruction in Philosophy* (enlarged ed., Boston, 1957), "of success
without effort, would be a life empty of thought. Men are not inclined
to think when their action is dictated by authority. Soldiers have many
difficulties and restrictions but, as soldiers, they are not famous as thinkers.
Thought comes down to them from above. Wherever an external authority
dominates, their thought is suspect and harmful." The conflicts of
experience produce systems, ideas, and theories which are the instruments
for the reorganization of a given situation. Thus, their "validity" resides
in their "success," that is, in their effective and intelligent reorganization
of reality. Otherwise, theories and systems are false. On the other hand,
since ideas have only an instrumental value, there are no rigidly closed
theories or systems or absolute truths. In fact, every conception is capable
of development and change through the use we make of it. Thought, in
short, is but a norm of conduct; the concrete notion of the "good"
dominates any logical conception of the "true" as well as any metaphysical notion of "the real." Even the sciences connected with the spirit
are to be tested in contact with reality. But, while the physical world is
to be subjugated, the moral world is to be liberated; it must be left free
to realize itself through forms and structures which are always new and
in continuous development.

With Dewey, pragmatism shows one of its most dangerous aspects:
it is no longer merely a matter of subordinating thought to action but (1)
of eliminating every trace of spiritualism; (2) of limiting the function of
intelligence to its power to transform reality (and every reality whatsoever) and, therefore, of denying that there are essences or substances or
unchangeable principles; (3) and all this with the view of satisfying the
needs of man and with them the inquietudes that stimulate them, which
are efficacious and effective when they can be satisfied within the natural
and historical order. The pragmatism of Dewey does not differ a great
deal from the fundamental theses of Marx and Marxism; it can even be
said that it is the "American" form of the latter, for the consequences
from the moral, religious, and philosophical point of view are identical.
This fact explains the sympathy received by Dewey from some European
theoreticians and followers of Marxism.

But the whole of pragmatism, except for some contribution to the
problems of science, language, empirical psychology, and its merit as an
energetic recall to the sense of the concrete, is a dangerous orientation of
thought; it is erroneous and philosophically null; it is worn out by an
invincible internal contradiction, namely, every moral, religious, or

scientific truth is provisional and contingent though each one must be considered true and necessary. Thus, on the one hand, it is recognized that truth, unless it is believed to be such, loses all its pragmatical value; while, on the other hand, it is valid solely by virtue of its pragmatic value. One or the other: *either* truth has efficacy in action only in so far as it is and is believed to be truth (in which case it is recognized that it is not to be accepted as true by reason of its practical consequences but only in so far as it is and is believed to be true); *or*, it is known that a principle is not a truth and yet it is pretended that it may have practical efficacy (and in this case one makes a statement devoid of sense because a principle which is known not to be true can have no efficacy whatsoever and exercise no stimulation). Pragmatism thus comes to recognize that the pragmatic criterion has no value as a criterion of truth, and by this fact negates itself.

There converge in pragmatism Kantian elements (emasculated of their speculative significance), positivistic and empirical elements (but of a positivism and an empiricism sometimes more and sometimes less critical or ingenuous), in addition to others suggested by the theory of evolution, in its various developments, by some recent positions in the philosophy of science and by the impact of scientific discoveries, which are immediately applied, in an arbitrary and gross manner, to problems of philosophy. All of these elements are twisted to support the pragmatic dogma that the truth of a principle or of a cognitive process is established by its practical effectiveness, that is, by its success; and this amounts to assuming as criterion of truth the contingent and the empirical, the transitory and the relative, so that the classical criterion of truth is reversed and philosophy denied. As Papini writes: "Rather than a philosophy, pragmatism is a method of doing away with philosophy." It is an attempt, which at times is exaggerated, to make of every truth a kind of "democratic" candidate on a list of so many alleged truths, in the expectation that one or another of them will obtain a majority of votes and will be proclaimed true; and the result depends on the effectiveness of the presentation and the publicity. Pragmatism denies, fundamentally, all truth and resolves itself into a form of historical empiricism or, ultimately, into a form of thoroughgoing materialism. And when it calls itself religious and spiritualistic, it resolves itself into a fideism which is in no way less disastrous, in a kind of mysticism of action and of the will, which, sustained neither by a solid rational principle nor by a well-founded idea of transcendence, leads to the most radical form of immanentism and, therefore, to a mysticism of man's ability to operate effectively. All this is done in view of establishing a future society that is ever more prepared to satisfy its needs and to enjoy the good things of the world—that is to say, pragmatism meets with Marxism.

10. Miguel de Unamuno: Pragmatism of Faith at Whatever Cost

More than anyone else among Spanish writers of our century, UNAMUNO (1864-1936) has influenced not only the culture but even the social and political life of his country. An agitator of new ideas against antiquated institutions, a fragmentary, paradoxical and genial writer without a system, and also a restless and disquieting soul, Unamuno raises many problems but solves none of them.

Like Kierkegaard, he declares himself for the individual, the human person; and like Kierkegaard, whom he had studied and known before others had discovered him, he is a deeply religious soul, a declared enemy of rationalistic thought, and a friend of solitude. For him (as for many Spaniards), it was impossible to maintain a dialogue: conversing signifies talking without listening. But unlike Kierkegaard, the Spanish thinker is far from theological preoccupations. Resting upon faith, his irrationalistic voluntarism is at times plain pragmatism. Moreover, there is in Unamuno a disquieting sense of life, an ardent and sincere mysticism, and not a gloomy theologism like that of Kierkegaard. We find both of these factors living and present in contemporary culture and in philosophy, even if the influence exerted by this Spanish writer is not well known.

Unamuno endeavors to be more of a "man" than a "scholar." In fact, animated with a religious sense and seriously engaged in his problems, he is a man who rejects every thought which is not action because he is the enemy of the unfruitful "science of the intellect." The latter belongs to those who (whatever they may be, bachelors, barbers, curates, canons or dukes) "think only with their heads when instead it is necessary to think with the whole body and the whole soul." Unamuno's work is the work of a man exalting the "science of the heart," and faith at any cost, like that portrayed by the generous Don Quixote, the knight of folly (*The Life of Don Quixote*, trans. H. P. Earle, New York and London, 1927.) In his beautiful essay "La Soledad" (in *Essayos por Miguel de Unamuno*, Madrid, 1916–1918), he writes: "Every day that is going by I believe less and less in the social question, in the political, moral and religious questions, or in all the others that were invented because of lack of courage to face resolutely the only true question of interest, that is to say, the human question which is mine and yours, the question of us all." Such a question nourishes the passion in Unamuno as both a man and a writer.

Unamuno calls upon Don Quixote in order to shake off *ab imis* and to galvanize the life of his time, which was "miserable"—"entirely miserable"

—an age without interests or passion. It is necessary to wage a "crusade," in order to find Don Quixote's tomb,[8] and rescue it from the hands of the *hidalgos* of Reason, who want to know the "why" and the "first" of everything as if there were for us a "first and a why" instead of *today* and *faith*. If the *hidalgos* of Reason, who are happy to exist but who do not really exist, "really existed in time and space, they would suffer for not being in what is infinite and eternal." Don Quixote must be rescued —the poor Don Quixote—who now is the "amusement and pastime of barbers, curates, bachelors, dukes, and the idle of all sorts." But then the purest and bitterest suffering begins for the knight of folly: he will be scorned by those who are so enslaved to "perverse reason" as to ask the "why" of everything while ignoring that one does not fight for victory, but one fights to fight, "for love of the combat itself."

If one bears in mind these exigencies, Unamuno's conception of Life is clarified both in its presuppositions and in its consequences. The fundamental presupposition is the radical antinomy between reason and life: *reason is the declared and irreducible enemy of life*.[9] Reason is identity, permanence, universality, and logical explanation of everything; it dissolves the individual in the universal and denies his most profound moral and religious aspirations. Life, instead, is diversity and inequality; continuous flow; individuality; faith without explanation, beyond logic and science, which believes in the truth of ideals, in immortality, and in God. Reason affirms that all this is *absurd*. But life replies that it is true precisely in that it is absurd, and that it is true precisely because reason considers it to be a folly. The same answer is given by the "qualitative"

[8] Cf. the essay "La Crociata," published first in the magazine *España moderna* (February, 1906) and then as a preface to *Commentaris* (Madrid, 1913).

[9] "From whatever side the matter is regarded, it is always found that reason confronts our longing for personal immortality and contradicts it. And the truth is, in all strictness, that reason is the enemy of life.

"A terrible thing is intelligence. It tends to death as memory tends to stability. The living, the absolutely unstable, the absolutely individual, is, strictly, unintelligible. Logic tends to reduce everything to identities and genera, to each representation having no more than one single and self-same content in whatever place, time, or relation it may occur to us. And there is nothing that remains the same for two successive moments of its existence. My idea of God is different each time that I conceive it. Identity, which is death, is the goal of the intellect. The mind seeks what is dead, for what is living escapes it; it seeks to congeal the flowing stream in blocks of ice; it seeks to arrest it. In order to analyze a body it is necessary to extenuate or destroy it. In order to understand anything it is necessary to kill it, to lay it out rigid in the mind. Science is a cemetery of dead ideas, even though life may issue from them. Worms also feed upon corpses. My own thoughts, tumultuous and agitated in the innermost recesses of my soul, once they are torn from their roots in the heart, poured out on to this paper and there fixed in unalterable shape, are already only the corpses of thought. How, then, shall reason open its portals to the revelation of life? It is a tragic combat—it is the very essence of tragedy—this combat of life with reason." *Tragic Sense of Life*, trans. J. E. Crawford Flitch (New York, Dover Publications, 1954), pp. 89-90.

dialectic of Kierkegaard's "existential" philosophy. "Every position of accord and harmony persisting between reason and life, as well as between philosophy and religion is impossible. And the tragic history of human thought is but a struggle between reason and life, in which the former is intent upon rationalizing while the latter endeavors to accept the inevitable and mortality. Life, furthermore, is intent upon 'vitalizing' reason by compelling it to serve as a support to its vital anxieties. Such is the history of philosophy, inseparable from that of religion," *op. cit.,* chap. VI.

Unamuno states that life has an end in itself, and this end is life in its completeness, totality, and absoluteness. But a life having *its* own end also *ends* in itself; and the will to immortality is like the desperate will of a shipwrecked sailor who lacks a raft or anything else to keep him afloat, and yet goes on hoping for rescue until he is completely submerged— he hopes in himself even while he is clinging tooth and nail to the wide and very sturdy plank of faith, which however is the faith of a shipwrecked sailor sinking with it.

Unamuno says that faith is the will to believe in what there is hope for, against the denials of reason which is fearful and cowardly prudent. That is true. But it is likewise true that there is another reason, the reason of faith, if faith has to be light and not a straw blaze—a reason in faith that is also faith in reason, in the light given us by God so that we would be made to His own image. The desperate religion of action or the exasperated mysticism of the will to live—such is Unamuno's philosophy— leads to the exaltation of action for the sake of action and of war for the sake of war. It has led to the implacable furor which has turned the world upside down and threatened our Western civilization within the last twenty-five years. Faith is made not only for waging war but also for bringing peace; it is the most shining and sharpened weapon of battle, yet its edge does not strike in order to wound but in order to heal. The "activist" irrationalism of Unamuno—who has such a deeply religious soul though his Christianity is pragmatic and generic (with a strong Protestant tinge) and thus almost abstract and nebulous—even fears God and fancies Him as an entity standing halfway between theism and pantheism.

Unamuno's pragmatism, it may be noted, is peculiarly "Latin" and is at variance with its Anglo-American counterpart. Moreover, it is in a sense a topsy-turvy pragmatism. In fact, the more a truth is *practically* useless, the more it is valid; "humanistic" pragmatism is the opposite of the other pragmatism which is based on "things" and has a criterion of truth depending on worldly success or on what is socially or individually useful. To produce for the material (or economic) well-being of all is what counts for the Anglo-American and Marxist philosophies of *praxis;* to produce, instead, for the well-being of the spirit (hence a production of spiritual goods only) and for the spirit alone, and then to live as we can, for the rest does not matter—such is the pragmatism of Unamuno who, after all, is the outstanding commentator of the life of Don Quixote, the "divine madman."

Unamuno is not a writer who belongs to any (whether Catholic or Protestant) confession, but neither is he a "lay" writer because throughout his life his true and unique problem was always God and his relationship with Him. Unamuno always stands before God, even when he struggles against *his* God. He remains on the "vertical" of faith, beyond "worldliness," over and above every "historicism," every "horizontality," even if the latter is the moral one. His driving force is faith, in contrast to Ortega who, perhaps because of his German indoctrination, wishes to give Spain the sense of history, science and sociality, that is, the sense of "mondanity" and "temporality." For Unamuno the person is constructed from within, not from without, and in order to be constructed it is not sufficient "to progress" in the world. He therefore fills a place of his own in the modern crisis of the Christian conscience. Unamuno does not believe in Christianity as a revealed religion but he believes—contrary to those who in regard to faith hold Christianity to be a conventional myth of the past—in the religious dimension, as the only thing capable of satisfying man's deep exigencies, and the only thing that may prevent him from becoming spiritless and blunted in the midst of this rapidly advancing world. In this sense, even though he fought against the "Europeanization" of Spain and advocated the "Hispanicization" of Europe, he was one of the last great "Europeans." In fact, "Hispanicizing" meant for him giving back to the rest of Europe the vertical dimension of *living* faith, as well as the religious conviction and hope that would free the Continent from the mere ostentation of Christian faith, which is now a poor cumulus of social "conventions" and a miserable custom in a society living by another faith, a faith in the world and in its scientific and technical progress. Ortega is a "European" of the time of decadence; Unamuno is a "Spaniard" of the time of Europe's Christian greatness, when the Don Quixotes still were being born. Even his fanatic love for Castile is an indication of this fact. In truth, that bare and austere land was like the symbol of Unamuno laying himself *bare* before his destiny and renouncing "scientific research" in order to face *vis-à-vis* and pry into the mystery of life, which for him is the mystery of death or of existence beyond life. The problem of the immortality of the individual is, in fact, Unamuno's great question and his torment. Of the many vain attempts to solve it, he "mystically" finds one, the only one consonant with his profound "soul," in the verses of the "Cristo de Velazquez." [10]

[10] "Sin Ti, Jesús, nacemos solamente para morir; contigo nos morimos para nacer y así nos engendraste!" ("Without You, Jesus, we are born only in order to die; with You we die in order to be born, thus You created us!"), 3rd part, xxiv.

11. ITALIAN PHILOSOPHY
AT THE BEGINNING OF
THE TWENTIETH CENTURY

The historical environment, which had greatly enhanced the fortune of positivism and which positivism in turn had made fashionable, was beginning to fade in Italy between the end of the last century and the first years of the present one. The period extending to the First World War saw the steady dissolution of positivism in Italy and the affirmation first of Croce's historicism and later of Gentile's actualism. Meanwhile, pragmatism rose and declined. However, it is true that varied forms of positivism and neocriticism, as well as critical idealism and Neo-Thomism, continued to live side by side with, while opposed to, Neo-Hegelian idealism.

Italian positivism (gross positivism embraced by "scientists," which is neither scientific nor philosophical, must be distinguished from the positivism of the "philosopher") in the person of Ardigò himself already represented a criticism of experience which paved the way for idealism. Outside of their reciprocally polemical attitudes, positivism and idealism reveal themselves as opponents fighting on the common ground: *that a person cannot surpass "the fact of experience,"* even if these philosophies differ in their mode of understanding experience itself. Both currents hold to a conception of reality based on immanentism. However, as a critique of experience and hence as a nondeterministic and nonmaterialistic doctrine, positivism is not so much the philosophy of Ardigò as it is the philosophy of his best pupils, among them, GIUSEPPE TAROZZI (1866-1958). In his studies on freedom, most of which are gathered in his book, *La libertà umana e la critica del determinismo* (Bologna, 1936), Tarozzi proposes to show how determinism is nonessential to positivism: one can be an antideterministic positivist. Determinism or natural causality is a logical instrument indispensable to science but not a principle inherent in reality. Every fact is "singular"; hence one fact is never another. Reality is an infinite variety of flowing facts in becoming (here Tarozzi is influenced by Boutroux's contingentism), facts being integrated in the process and unified in our consciousness. In Tarozzi's philosophy there are clearly some elements that agree in many respects with antipositivistic currents. Thus understood, Italian positivism (after Ardigò's or that of his followers) manifests itself as a current agreeing with other currents, in the criticism of mental forms belonging to the immediately preceding period. On the other hand, a solitary Sicilian thinker COSMO GUASTELLA (1854-1922), in his *Saggio sulla teoria della conoscenza* (Palermo, 1898) and *Le ragioni del fenomenismo* (Palermo, 1921-1923, 3 vols.) follows the footsteps of Stuart Mill in building a "philosophy of absolute experience." For Guastella all reality is phenomenal and in an indissoluble association with the perceiving subject, which is also phenomenal. Objects are but "particular and concrete representations made by the subject" and reality in itself is an illusion.

It should be noted that, on the one hand, FRANCESCO DE SARLO (1854-1937), with his own spiritualistic realism, opposes both positivism and Neo-Hegelian idealism; and, on the other, that the Abruzzese FILIPPO MASCI (1844-1922) represents Italian Neo-Kantianism and strives to confer greater concreteness on the Kantian theory of knowledge by removing from Kant's *a priori* forms that abstract and exclusively logical character which had made them be conceived as mental moulds or models fabricated prior to experience. Masci, instead, conceives them as forms which make up experience itself, and as functions which are revealed and developed along with the knowing medium. It can thus be said that before idealism was born, clearly shaped and affirmed, the Italian philosophical environment, already in ferment, was oriented toward tendencies and problems differing from those found in the age preceding it. Idealism certainly enters into this whole movement with vigor and fresh energies.

12. CRITICAL IDEALISM:
P. MARTINETTI AND B. VARISCO

One of the main currents of contemporary Italian thought, critical idealism, faces the problem of the unity of content and form, matter and spirit, with clear consciousness and in a manner different from Neo-Hegelian idealism. It rejects the doubly opposite immanentism: the reduction of being into thought (idealism) and of thought into the natural fact (positivism). Hence, we have the other essential points which distinguish critical idealism from transcendental idealism: a plurality of subjects rather than a unique subject and a unifying rather than a creative function on the part of the subject.

This explains why the principal interest of PIERO MARTINETTI (1872-1943), from his *Introduzione alla Metafisica* (Turin, 1904) to his last writings remained metaphysico-religious. For Martinetti, the theory of knowledge is an "introduction to metaphysics." The starting point of philosophical research is critical: purifying experience from the presuppositions of common knowledge and particular sciences. The critique of knowledge is not "a formal test of the cognitive processes of thought made by thought itself," but a critical examination of knowledge in general, embracing the whole of reality, and aiming at the elimination of some metaphysically insufficient points in order to find a superior point of view. Reality is neither a reflection coming to the subject from an *object-in-itself*, nor a product made by the subject; reality, rather, "is consciousness itself which, being considered in its multiplicity and in the independence of the conscious elements making it up, is the world, the object; and being considered in the unity of its total synthesis it is the ego, the subject." The world of objects exists independently of the subject, even if it is an ensemble of conscious acts. The uniting of individual subjects leads us to unity, that is, to an absolute subject. Individual subjects tend to confuse and identify themselves with a more comprehensive Ego. This fusion of individualities reaches its supreme termination in the religious consciousness, which is life in the Absolute, life in God. The knowing process is a process of reducing the sensible to the intelligible through which the subject participates in the life of the spirit. It participates, but since no *a priori* form constitutes reality in an absolute sense, even the intelligible forms are the relative expression of the transcendent Unity, or God, who remains outside of any possible form of knowledge. The One can only be expressed by means of symbols, that is, through inadequate representations, whether imaginative or rational.

In the view of Martinetti, the problem of knowledge is closely connected with that of freedom (*La Libertà*, Milan, 1928). Chance, not necessity, is opposed to freedom: "Freedom not only does not exclude but implies necessity, for it rejects contingency." Freedom in a generic sense is "that state in which a being is not prevented from realizing the inclinations constituting its nature." Freedom, in the "sense of its own spontaneity, never is without consciousness: only conscious beings can be free." As spontaneity, freedom is not in contradiction with the necessity of the causal spontaneity, for every spontaneity is always a necessary concatenation. Every moment in the process of spiritual life "is overcome by the subsequent one while being subordinated to it as a necessity from which life has withdrawn. . . . The sole and true freedom is actual freedom wherein the spirit, using the elements in which life has been fixed and determined, creates in every moment a superior living unity in which its truth is more highly expressed. Freedom finds life in its own unfolding, in freeing itself, and in creating."

Freedom of spontaneity embraces the whole sphere of impulsive life, but it is not as yet moral freedom. "When, by reason of extending itself to absolute and universal aims, the intelligent will is converted into rational will, practical freedom becomes moral freedom, which consists in opposing an always equal mind in all circumstances by identifying the self with an order of immutable principles. Will then is not an absurd faculty of good and evil; it is one and the same thing with the power and dignity of a just soul; to act against the moral law amounts to falling back under the mastery of impulse and losing moral freedom." The centuries-old metaphysico-theological problem concerning the possibility of human freedom can be resolved, once God is considered as the absolute principle of all things, and only by abandoning the conception of a God-Person in favor of a God-Reason. "Only an infinite Reason can be conceived as the living unity of an infinite multiplicity of relations and elements coessential with it." This universal Unity is to be conceived as a true *omnitudo realitatis,* in which the numerous stages of thought are retained indestructibly. "The essence and principle of man's freedom are found then in his divine personality, in his absolute being in the same way they are found in the absolute Reason with which they are coessential."

Hence, there is a religious function assigned to philosophy by Martinetti and, hence, also that accent of deep religiousness of a Plotinian and Spinozian intonation that animates his works in spite of his strictly systematic form and doctrinal weightiness. However, Martinetti's religiousness has nothing in common with the confessional forms of religion, especially Catholicism, which he implacably criticizes. Martinetti thirsts for the Spinozian "Divine," which is pure rationality, and carried to its extreme induced him to accept Schopenhauer's pessimism. Here it is, in brief, the whole process of the spiritual life, according to Martinetti: "We have a process of knowledge which, beginning with experience, is continued with conceptual understanding and reaches its highest point with the spiritual intuitions of morality and religion." The latter lead us back to an absolutely transcendent Reality, and so they are formal intuitions expressible only through symbols. "Our same practical activity, in which they are produced, is still a totally formal and symbolic participation" (*Ragione e Fede,* Turin, 1944). The transcendence of God, who is identified with the totality, is merely apparent: Martinetti's is a purely "a-cosmic" pantheism.

In the same way, BERNARDINO VARISCO (1850-1933) considers reality as an ensemble of objects of experience endowed with spontaneity and initiative. Multiple subjects are joined together inasmuch as they are necessary determinations expressed by a universal Being. Every subject or monad implies the universe, but the totality of experiences present in the subconscious is only for a small part in a clear and distinct form. The moments of knowledge (perception and judgment) are but a passage from subconsciousness to the state of explicit consciousness of the sensibles and the "thinkables" which are the components of the universal Being.

The real point of Varisco's doctrine, as developed from his *The Great Problems* (trans. R. C. Lodge, London, 1914) to *Know Thyself* (trans. G. Salvadori, London, 1915), and finally to his posthumous work, *Dallo uomo a Dio* (Padua, 1939), is the problem of the plurality of subjects connected with the problem of the transcendence of God as Person-Subject. The individual subject is limited because most of its constituent parts are subconscious, and also because it is impossible to reduce the whole of reality into the individual's thought. These limits present some difficulties, and there is only one way to overcome them: "to acknowledge them as relative only for the individual, and to admit a universal Subject beyond every individual." The subject is a singular and real individuality ("one among many"); it does not mean that it may not be universal on a logical level or that it may not interfere (as a social being) with the actions of all other subjects. Subjects condition one another reciprocally in an order that is the explication of a supreme unity animating the system, that is, of a Providence supporting their initiatives. The problem of the one and the many can be viewed from both theological and epistemological points of view: the theological unity of things is also unity of thought becoming concrete in the world's real and spiritual order. The unique thought is only the unique, universal Subject, that is, God the Creator; and man is a creature. Creator and creature are related to each other as infinity is to finite, necessity to contingency. Thus this is not pantheism, but theism.

The Italian philosophers mentioned so far share this characteristic, among others: they are far from the extreme forms of historicism, irrationalism and pragmatism characterizing German, English, and North American thought, as they also are far from the distinctly intuitionist, contingentist and voluntaristic tendencies of French thought, while not ignoring these currents and even with an adherence to some of their exigencies. Italian thinkers adhere more faithfully to classical problems and classical line of philosophical thought; and this fact has caused certain forms of novelized or "adventurous" philosophy to stay away from or have less effect in Italy, at least until a few years ago.

13. NEO-HEGELIANISM: THE ACTUALISM OF G. GENTILE

The truly renovating current not only of philosophy but also of Italian culture has been the Neo-Hegelianism of Gentile and Croce. GIOVANNI GENTILE (1875-1944) is the greatest Italian philosopher of our century, a thinker on whom centered almost the whole of Italian philosophy between 1900 and 1930; his influence, at least as a basis of criticism, is still felt today. Fundamentally optimistic and evidencing a metaphysically vigorous temper, his thought is committed to the defense of philosophy as an essentially rational act, and it concedes almost nothing to the deep-seated crisis of contemporary life because it preserves an unwavering trust in man's powers and human progress in the world. He is, per-

haps, the last thinker of significance from the historicist and romanticist nineteenth century ("romanticist" in the sense of an "Apollonian"
romanticism that is confident and enthusiastic). A man rich with generous humanity, and a very effective teacher, he considers philosophizing
as an ethical and educative process and philosophy as the perennial life
of thought, which is consciousness of itself.

The essential point of Gentile's speculation is the principle that nothing can be presupposed to thought: the object is converted into the
subject. Hence follows the other principle which states that thought
cannot be considered as object, or "thought being already thought," but
as "thinking thought," *thought in act—self-concept.* Thought and being
are identified, and philosophy is not a degree of the Spirit but the whole
Spirit. The content of thought remains absorbed in the act of thinking.
Thus Gentile, whose mind is otherwise open to many suggestions, wound
up entrenching himself in the stronghold of the pure act, that is, in the
stronghold of that philosophy which to his mind is the only spiritualistic
and Christian position outside of which or against which people are
naturalistic and atheistic.

Unlike Croce, Gentile has a greater understanding and deeper respect
for religious exigencies. And this is so because he has greater respect for
philosophy. In fact, he is led into contact with the object of theology by
his own philosophical position. His sincere and warm faith in thought
and his indomitable anxiety for research bestow on his work a truly
religious sense. It is a religiousness, however, which is faith in thought,
and which Gentile endeavors to identify with God—a religiousness,
therefore, characterizing those who resolve the religious moment into
the philosophical moment.

Although actualism is inspired and motivated by both the line of
thought represented by Kant, Hegel, and Spaventa and by the philosophy
of the Renaissance, Vico, and the Risorgimento, one must not forget,
nonetheless, that it was brought to maturity through the crisis of positivism, which was still at its apogee during the time of Gentile's intellectual
formation.

Once Gentile has posited (*Sommario di pedagogia come scienza filosofica,* Florence, 1954-1955; *The Theory of Mind as Pure Act,* trans.
H. Wildon Carr, London, 1922; *Sistema di logica,* Bari, 1917) the spirit
as *unity,* he cannot accept Croce's double dialectic of distincts and opposites: spirit cannot obey two diverse laws. There can be no becoming
with the simultaneous presence of opposites; the passage from one
moment to the other remains inexplicable. Even the distinction between
practical and theoretical activity is abstract for Gentile. *To think is to
act,* that is, spirit actualizes itself; and to act is to think. The real is
thought in its dialectical development, in its eternal *making itself,* as *pure*

act. Nothing can be presupposed to thought, for anything whatever always implies thought itself and, hence, is always thought. The other from thought (that is, Plato's idea or the positivists' nature) can only be the very act of thought which has become a *fact*, its actuality which has become past and which thought finds in its presence once again. What we call object is spiritual life fragmentized into space and time. But space is conceivable only in so far as the points existing in it are unified in the spirit, which is "spatiating activity; as the instants of time are also unified in the spiritual act, which is a "temporizing activity." Even other egos, that is, the empirical subjects which we think of as existing outside of us, become *things*, as my own ego is a thing when it is thought of and contraposed to the others. The transcendental Ego is real and concrete, and the empirical multiplicity of individual egos is unified in it.

On the other hand, the subject for Gentile would be abstract if it did not objectivate itself, if as an "act" it were not translated into "fact," from "thinking" subject into object being "thought." Subject cannot grasp itself without changing into *what* has been thought, that is, into object or nature. But the subject does not forget itself in the object: it returns to itself and includes the multiple in the one. The life of the spirit is then a perennial, dialectical movement of *thesis, antithesis,* and *synthesis.*

The absolute Spirit has three forms: *art, religion,* and *philosophy.* Art is the moment of pure subjectivity and, hence, an abstract self-consciousness expressing itself through the free creation of a fantastic world, in which the infinitely creating subjectivity expatiates boundlessly.

The artistic moment can only be distinguished ideally within living unity of the life of the spirit.[11] Religion is the moment of objectivity: the object, or God, which confronts the spirit and in which the spirit nullifies itself. The man who kneels before God is a subject feeling his own nothingness in the presence of an object who is everything. Both religion and art cease to be abstract when they are conceived as "moments" of the real. Art and religion cannot in themselves become dialectical because they have no development or process (there is, in fact, no history of art

[11] Gentile dedicated one of his last works to the problem of art: *La filosofia dell'arte* (1931). "Art, in its immediate existence, cannot be known; it escapes every effort of the mind to grasp it." Art can be known only if the moment of pure subjectivity is considered in the dialectical development of the spirit, which is thought. Pure art is not actual, "but it enters into spiritual actuality, makes itself felt there, and concurs, with its presence, to the realization of the life of the spirit, such as it is, provided that it is, actually." Art, as pure subjectivity, exists in the mediate thought, not in itself. The concrete thought is, at the same time, pure subjectivity and pure objectivity. Now "this subjectivity is pure dialectic and if we want to give this pure, subjective form of every feeling, which is art, a name common to everyday speech, we ought to call it "feeling" to be understood in its rigorously gnosiological and philosophical sense rather than in its common, psychological meaning."

or of religion). On the contrary, they become dialectical and concrete when they enter the process of history, that is, when and if both unfold themselves and attain concreteness within reality or history, which is the same dialectical unfolding of the spirit whose highest moment is *philosophy*. Artistic and religious moments are preserved in Thought, that is, in philosophy, as its dialectical moments; and absolute Spirit gains its fullness.

Gentile has been amply weighed and discussed in Italy, above all, and this is not the place to elaborate widely on certain critical aspects. Besides, in treating Gentile's school, there will be an opportunity to examine extensively the internal developments of this doctrine, as well as the critical and theoretical evaluation that has been made of it.

We may sum up the main stages of criticism leveled at actualism, even by members of the school itself, as follows:

(1) In its actuality, spirit is identified with the act of logical or reflective thought. Such a thesis encounters insurmountable difficulties. If actuality as such is a something that makes itself, an eternal becoming, the spirit can never attain the fullness of its actuality. The spirit then, in its full actuality, eludes itself or, in other words, the total and absolute act eludes the act of thinking, or it *transcends it;* but if thought eludes itself in its own fullness, thinking is not immanence, but an irreducible transcendence, that is, thought is always pursuing itself without ever reaching itself. However, for Gentile what is not act cannot as yet be spirit—it is object, nonbeing. Consequently, the full actuality of thought is an abstractness never to become concreteness, that is, a nonreality which will never be reality, and thus the spirit is not and will never be in full possession of itself.

If spirit is in its actuality and this is in its perennial self-making, spirit is everything and nothing at the same time. It remains immersed in its own act, a prisoner of its own self-identification at every point and, hence, it is ineffable. Actualism is resolved into a mysticism of the "act," which cannot be defined, because, in defining itself, it denies itself in the "fact."

What is still a "problem" is for Gentile an "object," that is, something facing thought, and of which thought has no fully reflective consciousness, which will be gained only when the problem is a solution; in other words, a problem is that which stays outside of the act, not being a concept as yet. But, once a problem is solved, another arises, and so on endlessly. In fact, as Gentile often states, if there were no more problems, thought would not be thinking, and it would cease being thought in the very act wherein every problem ceased. However, if it is so, that is, if thinking is the eternal solution of an eternal problem, if there is (and there will be) always a problem (an object, that is not an act), there is (and there will be) always something transcending thought and the act of thinking, that is, a *limit* to the thought not reducible to thought in act. On one hand, if it is only the act of thinking, one cannot understand which degree of being belongs to that which is outside of the act—it should be inexistent and devoid of essence; and, on the other, if the problem is eternal, and it transcends the act in its actuality, it cannot be conceived how being can be absolutely immanent in thought and how there can be an adequacy between spiritual activity and historicity. If there is an eternal problem (and the problem as such is an object, a nonsolution, and a nonconcept), the unavoidable presence of it nullifies the absoluteness of the act, unless it is confined to the punctual moment, or timeless instant; but, in this way, one falls back on mysticism inasmuch as one feels absolute in every act of thought. For its part the act is a perennial annulment of the problem in its solution, from which the problem comes again into being through a perennial dialectical movement of act and problem; and this is not moving ahead but marking time, that is, moving by remaining always in the same point.

Moreover, if awareness is concept and everything is reduced to concept itself, that is, to the act of reflective thought, everything is philosophy or logical act: sentiment and nature, art and religion, pedagogy and law, and so forth; but then every autonomous form of activity is annulled in the logical thought (panlogism). And this is not all: if the concept is the awareness that the spirit requires of itself (self-concept), the spirit, in its thinking, always thinks of itself; the other, whatever this otherness may be, is assimilated to it, and is annulled in it (solipsism). The transcendent Ego is omnivorous of things and of empirical or individual egos, which are its temporary moments; that is to say, they are not true as egos, but in their "being verified" by the Ego, which means in their being dissolved into the Ego. Thus, actualism does not avoid the nullification of nature and of subjects in Thought, the latter being the same thinking in act or, better, the Act itself as this alone is itself, ineffably. In other words, if the reality of the object or of the other is in the act of the thinking consciousness, then the object is never found, and there is only a subject perpetually chasing its own shadow. Actualism is thus compelled to encounter the Ego, in everything—always the Ego in its continuous pounding and pounding again on its own nature, that has been multiplied and fashioned into infinite shadows. The Ego of actualism, like Narcissus, stares at its own image reflected in the water and falls in love with it. But even in this instance the Subject, ultimately, never grasps itself because it can only be conscious of itself if it is conscious of something other than itself. Thus, it does not make sense to say, as actualism pretends, that the whole of reality is resolved into the act of thinking, and it makes no sense because the consciousness of the object is really such when the latter is not reduced to an act of consciousness. Even the consciousness of the transcendence does not signify immanence, but awareness of something transcending consciousness itself; otherwise, it would no longer be consciousness of the transcendence.

(2) According to Gentile, the subject can never be conceived as pure subject; it is always forced into mediating itself in the dialectic of subjectivity-objectivity. But, as I have said elsewhere, "The subject that cannot grasp itself posits itself as a problem, and in positing itself as a problem, it has already transcended itself." [12] The subject can grasp everything except itself as pure interiority because the act always is a dialectical mediation. Everything is immanent in the act, but the act is not immanent in itself. As absolute interiority, self-consciousness is self-transcendence. I believe this query to be of great moment. The dialectical process is missing something; it misses the subject, as self-consciousness, and pure interiority in relation not to the world, but to itself, in relation, that is, of the self to itself. It follows that if self-consciousness as such "transcends" dialectic, it posits itself not as a thing already resolved, but as a "problem." Thought as a pure act, act in its act, cannot be resolved in the Thought in act, in the thinking Thought. Therefore, it does not suffice to itself and so it posits the problem of itself, of its thinking, of thinking—that is, the problem of its metaphysical intelligibility or that of its origin, its reason for being, or its ultimate meaning. With this it posits the problem of theological transcendence.

We shall see in subsequent pages how Italian philosophy took on some new orientations from these critical queries: first, in its sense of an immanentism that was no longer metaphysical like Gentile's and no longer logical but "problematical" or "pragmatic"; and second, in its sense of overcoming immanentism through transcendent and objective idealism representing, in effect, the overturn of immanence into transcendence.

(3) According to Gentile, every scientific concept is "empirical" and so all science is empirical; it "consists of observation, ascertainment, or external knowledge of what is, happens, or is produced: it is external because, in observation, the position held by the knower, that is, by the thought carrying out the observation, is such that the object being known is presupposed outside of the subject, and the latter is thus external to the former as the former is to the latter." In other words, every knowledge is empirical when it supposes that the subject has its object ahead and outside of itself, and it is also prior to the cognitive act. Therefore, as we said, the knowledge of "nature" or of the "past" as such is empirical for its being outside of the act of thought. Natural facts fall within the

[12] M. F. Sciacca, *Linee di uno spiritualismo critico* (Rome, Perrella, 1936), p. 71. Cf. also A. Carlini, *Dialettica e filosofia*, "Giornale critico della filosofia italiana" (1924), pp. 170 ff.

logic of abstract *logos,* which is the logic of every empirical and naturalistic conception. In fact, "empiricism is naturalism because in every spiritual reality it can discern only that by which this same spiritual reality comes down onto the level of nature."

These affirmations, in which the central nucleus of actualism is summed up, contain a truth that must be redeemed against Gentile's dialecticism and immanentism which, in conclusion, deny it. In fact, once immanentism and the absolute historicity of thought are granted, the act of thought, to which the dialectical mediation in the object is necessary, finds its adequation in the same object—that is, the spirit finds its adequation in nature. A historicist and immanentist conception cannot avoid the conclusion that the historical and natural world meets and satisfies all the exigencies of the spirit. From this point of view, even actualism is naturalism and empiricism; and using Gentile's terminology, knowledge in act is also "scientific" and not "philosophical." Gentile himself perceived this, for he added that spirit is an infinity of thinking and so no object already produced in history or in nature can be adequate to it. It is perennially *in fieri* and its activity extends to infinity. However, the objection presented above remains intact and valid. In fact, temporal infinity always is finite even if it lasts indefinitely in time; it is not infinite but indefinite, that is, an infinity that is increased, but, just because it grows, it is and always remains finite. Therefore, if it satisfies all the exigencies of the spirit and the infinity of thinking, this infinity remains adequate and, as such, finite and devoid of power: spirit, too, becomes nature and fact. Such a conception of thinking and knowing is precisely the one Gentile defines as naturalistic and "scientific," that is, the one pertinent to observation and ascertainment.

As can be seen, there is in Gentile a happy contradiction. On one hand, he affirms the infinity of thinking and the principle wherein thought is not given (otherwise it would be something that "has been already thought" and for this very reason it would be denied as thought) but is thinking in act. He also affirms that the concept is concept inasmuch as it is an act of thinking and an awareness that the same thought has of itself and, on the other hand, the immanentistic position forces him to equalize infinite thought to the finite thought of, that is, to its content. But precisely the impossibility of this adequation makes actualism produce its own internal contradiction between spirit as an infinite self-act and the content already actuated, which is never adequate to such an act. Consequently, thought transcends every content and cannot be equalized. But then immanentism is unsustainable if actualism wants to preserve its principle of truth; and thus the way is open toward the establishment of transcendence. If we follow this way through, it amounts to placing under a thoroughly critical revision the whole of Gentile's philosophy;

then some elements deserving to be preserved can be saved. For instance, the critique of the "scientific" or external attitude pertinent not only to the scientist, but also to the philosopher, when the latter pretends to construe philosophy with a scientific spirit, so much so that he considers the life of the spirit in the same way as he considers the life of natural things. Significant in this respect is Gentile's conception of spiritual life as a perennial presence of the spirit to itself, whereby man in each of his acts must reproduce the whole of himself, and cause the past to be relived and re-created in the present, so that the act-in-act may be wholly its entirety and so that, once relived, it may cease to be nature. Only thus in every act can man be, in the light of the spirit, a total presence of the totality of himself.

14. THE EMPIRICAL HISTORICISM OF B. CROCE

While Gentile's main interests were philosophical (or more precisely, metaphysical), those of BENEDETTO CROCE (1866-1952) were, from beginning to end, principally cultural. For this reason, if his place in contemporary Italian culture (until about 1930) was considerable for his part in its renewal, it is considerably less in the field of philosophy. Croce's mind was open to many cultural interests (art, literature, history, politics, and the like); but the true and proper philosophical problems were felt less by him. Nurtured in the climate of positivism and acquainted since his early youth with the works of Marx, he remained fundamentally a positivist. A systematizer of culture and of cultural *facts*, he constantly maintained a negative attitude toward metaphysics without giving a critical justification for his position. Croce always tried to reduce philosophy to that really poor thing called methodology of history, and to make it an "earthly" thing through the exclusion of the "most important problems." We believe, then, that Croce's activity as a scholar, critic, and historian represents his truly fruitful and lasting endeavor, whereas his activity as a philosopher may be considered rather marginal. Again, proof of this is the fact that Croce's influence is most powerful on scholars, critics and historians, rather than on philosophers. Besides, in the last quarter century, Croce himself saw the influence of his thought gradually waning until he finally outlived it. Many new interests and problems came into being while Croce remained extraneous to them. In the last two decades his authority was principally due to political reasons. However, it is beyond question that Croce's work and the cultural periodical *La Critica* (1903) represent an important event in the history of Italian philosophy during this century. Almost exclusively through Gentile's collaboration, *La Critica* contributed to the thorough renovation of philosophical studies while through Croce's contribution it led to the reforming of mental habits in the national culture and the arousing of concern for research and work in the cultural environment.

Although Croce's thought is a reaction against positivism, it is influenced by positivism itself. Marx, Hume and English empiricism influenced Croce more than Hegel did even if this seems to be a paradox, which is not. Croce had been able to ascertain that the great theorists of positivism, though agnostic in metaphysics, considered themselves as humanists and followers of Vico, and they were also historicists and theorists of art, ethics, and law. However, positivists had a "naturalistic and extrinsic" conception of history while Croce's conception is "spiritualistic and intrinsic," that is, he endeavored to do in Italy what Dilthey had done in Germany. Herein we see Croce's thought coinciding with Kant's criticism and Hegel's idealism, as well as with the immanentist interpretation of Vico. For positivism, understood as a search for a method of studying and classifying the *facts* of nature, Croce substitutes his positivism understood as a search for a method of understanding the *facts* of human activity. To be interested in other things, Croce agrees with the positivists, is to waste time groping in the dark. It is not a question of knowing the spirit in itself or man as a spirit, but rather of knowing what the activities of the human spirit are (art, ethics, law, and so on), and what distinguishes the one from the other, and finally what their reciprocal relationships are. Moreover, his idealistic-romanticist inclination, which is indeed at variance with positivism, led him to re-establish the principles of self-consciousness and unity of the spirit, and this means unity and totality of the real in a philosophy presenting itself as philosophy of immanence.

The empiricist and positivistic character of Croce's historicism is still more apparent in his last philosophical works that are collected in two volumes: *History as the Story of Liberty*, trans. S. Sprigge (New York, 1955) and *Il carattere della filosofia moderna* (Bari, 1945). In them Croce becomes rigid in his identification of the real and the knowable with history, and in his reduction of the practical judgment to the historical judgment. No action can prescind from the situation of fact, which is the only thing that counts and which ought to be judged without regard to the intention. However, Croce recognizes that historical knowledge is not "conclusive," but rather a pure theory necessarily serving practical action. As such, the latter "stems only from a personal and original inspiration having a practical character and a practical ingenuity." Yet, it still remains to determine (and this is not easy for historicism) what this personal and original inspiration is and whence and from what source the spirit is able to draw it.

I believe that what has been said so far suffices to prove that, in spite

63

of any appearance to the contrary, Croce's mental attitude ultimately coincides with the same empirical and pragmatic mentality that is characteristic of some of the currents already mentioned.

Because of the great favor his writings have enjoyed, it is only necessary to outline here the fundamental points of his so-called "Philosophy of the Spirit" (*Aesthetic as Science*, and so on, trans. D. Ainslie, New York, 1953; *Logic as the Science of the Pure Concept*, trans. D. Ainslie, London, 1917; *Philosophy of the Practical*, trans. D. Ainslie, London, 1913; *Theory and History of Historiography*, trans. D. Ainslie, London, 1921.)

For Croce, philosophy is "philosophy of the spirit" as it affirms itself in the concrete process of experience, that is, in our human world with which all Reality coincides (immanentism). The process of the spirit, which is history (historicism), develops with dialectical rhythm, which for Croce is not only a dialectic of opposites, as it is for Hegel, but also a *dialectic of distincts*. In other words, the concrete life of the spirit always manifests itself in a determinate form of activity. Its forms are not denied one in the other as in the dialectic of opposites wherein each moment is an abstract moment becoming concrete only in the synthesis. For Croce, instead, throughout its becoming the spirit maintains its forms or "degrees" which it takes as it unfolds itself. According to Croce, this fact does not endanger the spirit's unity because concrete unity within distinction "entirely excludes the thinking of the distinction as a multiplicity whose terms are one outside of the other and thus reciprocally transcendent. This is so because each term of the distinction or each form of the spirit is the condition for and is conditioned by the others, so to speak." The dialectic of the distincts may be represented by the figure of the circle: "circularity" of the forms of the spirit.

It is well known that Croce sees two fundamental forms of spiritual activity, the *theoretical* and the *practical*, each of which has two degrees. "Intuition" or knowledge of the individual and "concept" or knowledge of the universal pertain to the former, while the "useful" or volition of the individual and the "moral good" or volition of the universal belong to the latter. Thus, within unity we have the distinction of the four degrees of spiritual activity: *Art* (intuition), *Philosophy* (concept), *Economics* (the useful), and *Ethics* (the good).

Knowledge, then, is either *intuitive knowledge* of the individual (namely, of single things) through imagination or it is *logical knowledge* of the universal (namely, of the relations among things) through the intellect. In other words, it is either a producer of "images" or a producer of "concepts." The first form of knowledge is autonomous and this is *art*, which is, in fact, intuition or representation of a mental state or of a feeling (*l'arte è liricità*, art is lyricism) that has found its "expression" in an image. As such, art is distinguished from all other forms of the spirit's activity. In it the excited sentiment is converted into clear intuitions. More than imagination, art is a "creative" or "poetical phantasy." Art is not an immediate sentiment, but a contemplated one, and the source of sentiment in it is made universal by the infinity of the expression. Art is an intuition-expression and thus it is identified with language.

From the aesthetical level the spirit passes to that of *intellective knowledge*, that is, conceptual and philosophical knowledge which cannot exist without the former, whereas the former can remain without the latter. In fact, knowing through concepts is knowing the relations among things, and things are intuitions without which concepts would not be possible. Logic is a "science of pure concepts," which is a synthesis *a priori*. The concept transcends each individual representation, but is immanent in all representations. By means of the concept the spirit grasps the individual facts that have been intuited in the web of the universal and organic order; and so the concept is a "universal concrete." When this synthesis is lacking, there are no more concepts but only "conceptual fictions" or "pseudo-concepts" that can be universal without being concrete (like the "conceptual fictions" of mathematics), or there are simple schemes in which some representations lacking universality (like the empirical pseudo-concepts of natural sciences) are grouped.

For Croce, the logical synthesis *a priori* is discovered as the "identification of philosophy with history." Each concept is a comprehension of individual facts in which the reality that is history takes an interest. Philosophy then is only a *methodological moment of historiography:* a "clarification of the categories constituting the historical judgments, that is, of the concepts leading the historical interpretation."

Practical activity is distinguished from the theoretical in that the actions-volitions are its object. Due to the principle of the circularity of the spirit, practical activity presupposes the theoretical, that is, the will is not possible without knowledge. Theory and practice form a unity and these two forms constitute and close the circle of reality and of life. The theoretical act supplies the matter for the practical act while the volitive changes in accordance with the change in the perceptive act. The "situation" and the "volition" are so interdependent that when one changes, the other changes as well. There are no fixed judgments of action. In fact, man acts instant by instant in correspondence with the always changeable historical situations.

Two forms are to be distinguished in the practical activity: a form leading toward individual ends or will of the individual (*economic activity*) and another leading toward universal ends or volition of the universal (*ethical activity*). The universal practical degree cannot exist without the economic degree. The ethical form carries within itself the economic in that the action, though universal in its meaning, can only be something concrete and individually determinate. The economic level is "pre-ethical" and as such does not suffice as it satisfies us as individuals—but not as men. Thus the moral level is necessary as a volition of the universal. "The character of moral action is such as to satisfy us not as individuals but as men, that is, as individuals only because we are men, and as men only through the means of an individual satisfaction. *Morality is a concrete universalism.*"

A detailed criticism of Croce's thought (which has already been sufficiently weighed) is not necessary, because the aspects we have already pointed out mark its limits. In essence it is only a methodology of culture remaining on the margins of philosophy.

Croce wishes to be the philosopher of "action" or of that kind of thought that can be translated into action. In fact, concreteness means for him identity of the real with doing, of the spirit with its manifestations, and of man with his actions. Indeed, man *is* his actions. Hence there is an elimination of every residue of transcendence whether this is the Platonic Idea or the idea of modern idealism, Locke's substance or Kant's noumenon, the unknowable of the positivists or the God of religion, the matter of materialists or the nature of naturalists. From this point of view he is closer to Hume than to Kant, Vico, Hegel, or Gentile; and he remains in the tradition of those who deny the concepts of being and of substance, which are dissolved into historicity or in becoming. Starting from Hegel, Marx arrives at the same conclusions, which are antimetaphysical and corrosive of philosophy, that is, he arrives at a radical elimination of every dualism—precisely as Croce does.

Croce still has faith in progress and in the values which mankind is able to achieve in the course of history. The latter has for him an immanent logic justifying every fact on the ground that as a fact it has taken place (history "is only a justifier" not an "executioner"). Croce's historicism is an optimistic and trustful "anthropocentricism"; he deifies history making a myth of it, as for example the Enlightenment and positivism had made a myth of Reason and Science, respectively. We say a myth and an "idol" because what is not God becomes an idol and a fetish at the very moment it is considered as the Absolute. This is primitivism that is characteristic of the irreligiousness of any age and that is particularly rampant in the contemporary world. From this point of view, Croce and the immanentists, still linked with the nineteenth century and with modern secularism, represent the crisis and the end of a philosophy that is not yet aware of itself. These people continue to believe in the "logicity" and validity of knowledge and in that of values, but nevertheless they do not perceive that, on account of their historicism, pragmatism, and "praxism," they have already denied all values including the value of the ego; in short, they have denied man as a spiritual existence or as a "person." The more recent philosophies (existentialism, Marxism, neopositivism, and so on) represent an awareness of this crisis as well as the fall of man from the gilded pedestal that immanentism had built for him. Man believed that he could build himself by his own power, but after a century of enthusiasm he has now observed that, once he has been uprooted from being and founded on himself, he is suspended in a void and established on nothing. The awareness of the crisis is itself the crisis of every form of immanentism confident in itself, and thus is a crisis affecting the very heart of modern thought. From this point of view, Marxism has the merit of being more coherent and, let us be frank, more sincere. In fact, if God does not exist and there is no personal immortality of the soul; if the human world is an end in itself; if the end of history (of mankind as well as of every single individual) is history itself; if "man is the future of man" and the whole trial of life is completed within historical life; if the realm of man is the earth and that is all —then the "economic" or the "material" is the supreme and authentic value. And, further, the social question is the sole question each man needs to solve; spiritual values are but the "superstructures" of a "social structure" and they are as variable and temporary as the social structure itself (that is, they are a hypocritical pretense masking ferocious egoisms); and, finally, freedom itself is the freedom of a class, the bourgeoisie, at the price of the enslavement of the proletariat. Neither Croce nor the other historicists have anything to say against these conclusions. In the presence of the problems being posited by contemporary consciousness and present crisis, Croce has nothing to say; he does not even notice them, because his philosophy which is bourgeois and Marxist at the same time (and, incidentally, one could say that every liberal is a potential Marxist) is itself an expression of the crisis of philosophy, and it is forced into crisis by the awareness we have now acquired of the inconsistency of every atheistic "spiritualism" which, just because it is atheistic, is not spiritualism.

Croce was a critic of Marx and of Marxism, but his historicism and historical materialism, both educed from Hegel, stand in the same line of thought. Once the transcendence of truth and every transcendence have been denied, religious values have been negated and man's destiny has been fettered to the earth and historical becoming, and once man himself has been made only a "historical" entity—there is no escape. Absolute historicism and absolute materialism, even in their seeming antithesis, meet and embrace. The "religion of freedom" is the pseudo-religion of being free only with respect to *things*, *facts*, and earthly *works*, that is, of being enslaved to the world. Croce is responsible for this "secularism." Some current positions of Italian Marxists are only the extreme and coherent consequence of his immanentist and empirical historicism.

As in Marxism (and in other self-styled "humanistic" philosophies which, in reality, deny the deepest humanity of man), there is in Croce's historicism another characteristic, namely, his fundamental and radical "inhumanity." There is, too, his cold and implacable destruction of all values (Croce's mind seems to be a machine producing clear, polished, and well aligned concepts) as well as the annulment of the person, which, as we said, is entirely exhausted "in his actions." All this means the dissolution of the person in the externality of actions that he performs without his interiorness, that is, without an internal nucleus of truths. Croce learned these things from Marx as far back as 1895 and never forgot them. Above all he never forgot, as he himself writes, "that the course of history has the right to drag and crush individuals." Croce, as I have said elsewhere, has neither a mind nor a heart for person or spirit, and thus he remains indifferent toward primary problems and eternal truths, which are the only ones properly inherent in the person. He propounds historical truths and thus, ultimately, he is averse to truth. He is its enemy and the enemy of philosophy as well. He is essentially skeptical, with a skepticism that is inhumanly resigned or superficially playful, in the manner of an aesthete and a man "diversely" cultivated. It is a skepticism without irony because it is not dictated by a vigorous, philosophical passion, so that it debases the character instead of strengthening it. In short, a skepticism enervating thought, alienating profound research, and destroying every faith. Croce may have been helpful to Italian culture, but he has also darkened the spirit of the Italian people.

15. CRITICISM AND
CRISIS OF SCIENCE

From what we have already said, it is evident that the antipositivistic and anti-intellectualistic polemic involves the validity of knowledge in the natural and mathematical sciences. Mach and Avenarius, Bergson and Blondel, pragmatists and relativists, as well as other thinkers such as Poincaré, Duhem, Milhaud, and Le Roy, who specifically concern themselves with the problems of science, are in agreement in denying or limiting its value in knowing.

Philosophy is turning against science the very weapons already used by science against philosophy. At the time when positivism was flattering science, philosophy was considered as the realm of metaphysical reveries and the splendid dream-world of reason. Now, instead, it is philosophy which considers scientific laws as "fictions," "schemes," and "abstractions," that disfigure reality because of their inability to go beneath the surface and skin of things so as to get into the root of life where there is no mechanism or matter, but only freedom and vital energy. Philosophy scolds science for embalming life and mummifying facts. Life must be seen, instead, with all its beauties and its ugliness, in what is bright and in what is gloomy; it must be looked at in its inscrutable sphinx-like face, like a two-faced Janus. Now, there is no scheme or scientific law capable of grasping these conflicts and harmonies or these agreements and disagreements. Science encompasses reality in stereotyped and finite forms; but life, instead, breaks out into the infinite like air and light; in fact, it is essentially an aspiration toward the infinite that gains its concreteness through finite forms which are relative, mobile and always new precisely because they are finite. Philosophy is called upon to scrutinize the very rhythm of life, of which it is the child and mother at the same time; it is called upon to emerge, like an underground river, from the irrational and unfathomable abysses of existence in order to be engulfed again in its dark bowels. Science, instead, is cut off from whatever is vital and concrete in thought and nature; it is imprisoned in the realm of immobility and abstractness, of dead formulas and fossilized schemes. At best, science can boast of a practical and economic interest; it is useful and no more.

To the criticism of science made by philosophy is added what is called the "crisis of science" coming from its own internal evolution. Philosophers and scientists, throughout almost the entire nineteenth century, regarded Newton's physics as the absolutely true representation of the universe. Mechanism and objectivity of the principles and theories of physics were beyond any discussion. But toward the end of the last century and the beginning of ours, this conception came into doubt: determinism, without being rejected as a whole, was debated; "matter," which had seemed to be the simplest datum, began to reveal itself as a complex entity; in short, determinism and mechanism came down from the rank of absolute truths into that of "hypotheses," to which indeterminism has been added side by side, as another hypothesis. As we shall see, the theory of relativity and that of *quanta*, like other discoveries have disputed the results of so-called classical physics. As a result of the intimate relations between the physico-mathematical sciences and philosophy, the whole of modern thought from Descartes to Kant has been placed under critical revision. Therefore, the crisis of science is, at the same time, the crisis of modern rationalism and Kantianism, of its epistemology and its metaphysics which, in the last analysis, coincides with its gnosiology.

Almost contemporaneous with the crisis of science and mathematics there is a revival of formal logic under the form of so-called logistic, and of mathematical or symbolic logic, which has its immediate precedents in the studies made by two English mathematicians, AUGUST DE

MORGAN (1806-1878) and GEORGE BOOLE (1815-1864), and continued by ERNEST SCHRÖDER (1841-1902) and GIUSEPPE PEANO (1858-1932). On the other hand, the "phenomenological school," though proceeding from philosophical theses, meets in some points with mathematical logic; more recently, the two schools have influenced each other. We shall speak of both later on; for the moment it suffices to remark that mathematical logic has influenced philosophy both as an instrument for the analysis of concepts and demonstrations and also because it gave old philosophical problems (for example, that of the universals) a current value. We should also note here that between mathematical logic and phenomenology there are strong differences concerning their methodology and object of research. As we shall see more appropriately when the time comes, the drawing of philosophical consequences from scientific theories, or the fact of having applied to philosophy methods and conclusions valid only in the sciences has produced a new philosophical confusion, which is worse than that of the epoch of extreme positivism; and this is caused by so many scientists-philosophers—amateurs whose affirmations often make the serious student of philosophy laugh or stay indifferent.

II

SÖREN KIERKEGAARD
THE POET
OF HEROIC SOLITUDE

"I have borne my thorn in the flesh as did Paul. I could not, therefore, enter into relations with men. Hence I concluded that my task was extraordinary." These words were uttered on his deathbed by Kierkegaard to his friend E. Börsen. They characterize the strange and paradoxical nature of this writer, thinker, and theologian whose soul was restless and unhappy. He was always dissatisfied with himself and others, always taciturn and ironical; his irony being a tragic one, he used to say: "I make witticisms; people laugh at them but I cry." Although Sören Kierkegaard was rather restricted in his problems, he was tenacious and, at times, deep in his search; although an enemy of reason, he was very bold in probing the abysses of the infinite and of mystery: he is, in a word, one of the most typical and suggestive expressions of the "Nordic soul." This thinker, who at times knows how to be a great writer, and who—as Unamuno says[1]—in the first half of the last century left his mark on Denmark's and Norway's youth was, nonetheless, almost unknown until about three decades ago. Philosopher of crisis, he was discovered in Germany during the great spiritual crisis that went with and followed the First World War (1914-1918). Since then, Kierkegaard has fed all the "philosophies of crisis" which characterize our times, and his extraordinary posthumous success is now world-wide. Most of today's

[1] M. De Unamuno, "Le Esfinge sin Edipo," in *Ensayos* (Madrid, 1916-1920).

71

philosophy, in fact, cannot be understood without Kierkegaard, so that, although he lived in the last century, he has become a contemporary; he is the philosopher of the postwar period, the thinker between two wars.

Sören Kierkegaard was born in Denmark on May 5, 1813, of a father who was well into his fifties and who, already satisfied with his wealth, had retired from business at forty. But this man, seemingly blessed (with gifts of intellect, riches, and children), in his distant childhood as a poor and starving shepherd had cursed God. With his imagination excited and obsessed by the problem of sin (which for Kierkegaard is not only a philosophical problem but also a personal one), Sören saw in his father's guilt the malediction of God weighing heavily upon his whole family. As he writes in his *Diary* (*The Diary of Sören Kierkegaard*, trans. G. M. Anderson, London, 1961)—which is a suggestive evidence of his real and imaginary torments, and also, at times, the painful document of a sick mind—after a brief mundane and skeptical period, he was shaken by "the great earthquake" which suddenly compelled him to explain his whole life with a new principle. "I suspected then that my father's advanced age was not a blessing of the Lord but rather a curse, that the spiritual gifts with which my family had been endowed were bound to be destroyed by one another; then I felt that the silence of death was increasing all around me, and I saw in my father an unhappy person destined to outlive all of us and be like a sepulchral cross on the grave of all his hopes. Some sort of guilt had to lie hard on my entire family and God's punishment was to come down on it; it had to disappear and be erased like an unsuccessful endeavor, by the powerful hand of God." In Kierkegaard the terror of sin is accompanied by a relish for this terror: he fears and loves sin at the same time; he hates it and enjoys it; he feels it as being so connatural with himself, his family, and mankind as to make of sin the category that defines it. So also he grieves for his sufferings, but he loves them and magnifies them in order to compare himself to Christ of whom he considers himself the new apostle and nearly the new prophet. The problem of sin becomes for him the problem of "Kierkegaard the sinner." Here originates the great unhappiness which is endured and enjoyed at the same time by this tormented soul, who considers himself condemned to bear a "thorn in his flesh" and to live deeply grieved and disheartened under the burden of secret faults.

He tried to gain the esteem of the world by becoming engaged to Regina Olsen. But Kierkegaard could not live as others do; the thorn in his flesh had assigned him an extraordinary task. So he broke the engagement. The hallucinating consciousness of guilt and moral abyss which he would have had to reveal to Regina's view convinced him not only to give up living like others but to live instead an exceptional life. His renunciation of Regina also signified his choice of the Christian life, the *exceptional* life *par excellence*. He gave up Regina because he could not marry, and for him Christian living was more of a literary ambition than an aim really pursued. Although tormented by his sickly mind, he lived like an Epicurean with a good deal of selfishness and narcissism, which, however, did not prevent him from writing sincere and profound pages on Christian love. Religious conscience and the presence of sin are mutually related: the want of God is felt in sin itself. Sin, melancholy, weariness, despair and anguish make man inhibit himself from living as others and, therefore, he becomes an exception; they make him ill in body and spirit and consequently unhappy. But for Kierkegaard this is a happy illness and a happy unhappiness! Sorrow makes one go beyond finite existence, and it paves the way for the infinite one; it blocks up the narrow passage toward common happiness, but opens wide the door of exceptional unhappiness that opens upon the infinite. Kierkegaard carries the thorn that had been thrust into his foot at birth and which since birth has been aching; but if he should remove the thorn, he would die in that very instant: he would become happier in the sense of finiteness, but he would be lost to the sense of the infinite. "However strange this may appear in a certain sense, it is so nonetheless; with the help of the thorn that I carry in my foot, I am able to jump higher than any other person whose foot is well." He is unhappy and, therefore, he leads an extraordinary existence. Out of sin and unhappiness he has made not only the constitutive essence of the individual, but also a pedestal in order to have his own personality rise above those of others. Together with his pride he has a taste for sorrow. Kierkegaard loves solitude and he protects his own all his life. He protects it from the allurements of the world, from the desire of riches and public recognition, and from Regina's love; but he desires just what he is refusing and scorning, and since nobody gives him these things spontaneously, he grieves and, protesting, pities himself. He knows that solitude is needed in order to perform his extraordinary mission, and that in solitude he finds a surer way of communication with himself and with others. From his fortress he can lead a better fight against the faults of philosophy and the spiritual maladies of his time. Kierkegaard is the knight of solitude.

He was really unhappy; a "son of old age," he never felt young. He calls it a mad twist: ". . . a young boy who never became a youth, a young boy who, being already old, could not get younger any more." Old before he was born! "Ah! Why were nine months in my mother's womb enough to make me an old man?" Few souls have ever felt the insufficiency and limitations of the human person with such a burning anguish. All these things are at the same time felt positively as if they constitute human essence, dignity, and nobility.

The problem of the person thus understood is always seen by Kierkegaard from a religious point of view, and in its turn religion is considered in relation to the problem of sin. This explains the gloomy concept that he entertains of Christianity. His father trained him in rigid Christian principles, but especially with the vision of God crucified by men. As a child, "he had not heard what children usually listen to about Jesus the little Child, and the angels, and similar things. On the contrary, the image of the Crucifix had been presented to him so much more frequently that this was the sole image and the only impression he could have of the Savior. . . ." But Kierkegaard—a tenacious fighter all his life in the presence of and against mystery—tried to find in Christianity the secret of life, the way to salvation, not as a redemption from sorrow but as a redemption in sorrow. Christianity is a "radical treatment" which we try to defer as long as possible, yet it is a treatment which we regret not having endured before. Christianity is love, but "fear and trembling" are the "inquietude" of Christian life. "Christianity certainly is not melancholy but, on the contrary, it is cheerful news for the melancholy. It certainly is not happy news for superficial men because it begins by making life difficult." And Kierkegaard felt deeply and invincibly melancholy—melancholy, indeed he was, but not superficial. On the contrary, he was one of those two or three individuals who in every generation sacrifice themselves in order to discover, by means of their suffering, what proves beneficial to others. "In a melancholy meditation of soul, I saw myself chosen for this task; in this I recognized the meaning of my life." In him there is already the religious reformer he became in the last years of his life; and the philosopher who is seeking in God the unshakable support of the reality of the human person, and the theologian who finds in sin, besides the essence of the individual, the tragic nourishment of religion and the painful proof of the existence of God. "Who sees God, dies," says Kierkegaard. There is something disconcerting in Kiergekaard as a man and in Kierkegaard as a philosopher and theologian. With Lombardi we may agree that "to read and study Kierkegaard means rather to free oneself from Kierkegaard." [2] But there is something in Kierkegaard that attracts and charms—the charm, that is, of a living contradiction. He was a living paradox who found pleasure and sorrow in feeling he was a paradox. "Such was in effect the existence of Kierkegaard, who was a living paradox at war against his own times and the established church; for the common conscience he was an object of horror, a stubborn witness of the truth which he hopelessly tried to achieve." [3] It could be said of him that "the victory of victories, the victory *par excellence* is to lose everything!" With this conviction Kierkegaard died a young man in 1855.

[2] Lombardi, *Kierkegaard* (Florence, La Nuova Italia, 1937), p. 47.
[3] L. Lavelle, *Le moi et son destin* (Paris, Aubier, 1936), p. 83.

These autobiographical insights drawn from the *Diary* already contain the basic elements of Kierkegaard's philosophical-theological thought. His philosophy is biographical and consequently fragmentary, consisting of paradoxical and disjointed intuitions. The central problem in Kierkegaard is that of the *person* in his individuality. Whence does one seek the weapons to defend the person? Not from philosophy but from religion, not from reason but from faith. The duel between philosophy and religion or between reason and faith for the defense of the *person* represents the fundamental trait of Kierkegaard's thought. In times of crisis like our own, there is a great fondness for what is irrational, paradoxical, immediate, and subjective. Kierkegaard's thought is essentially religious inasmuch as for him religion alone can guarantee individuality and defend its existentiality. "Individual" and "Christian" are identified: to defend the individual is therefore to defend Christianity. Kierkegaard believed he was entrusted with a highly Christian mission. He thought of himself as the restorer of faith, of the true Christianity of the Cross of Christ which forever bears witness that truth wins solely by being defeated. His exceptional life, different from the others, was truly the proof that he was a Christian. As a man he would lose, but this proves irrefutably that he triumphed as a Christian. He who wins in life is defeated because earthly success or victory is the negation of Christianity. Had Kierkegaard married Regina Olsen, he would have satisfied the desire to live like others, but he would have sacrificed his Christian mission on the altar of marriage. An accommodating and political Christianity is the negation of Christianity; Christianity and the Christian alike must not be concerned with earthly things: to win the world one has to die to the world.

The world *is* because God makes it *be:* "If God could forget it, it would collapse in the instant." In religion is hidden the secret of life, the solution of our unique problem, the problem of ourselves as persons. Nothing in fact is more terrible or great, says Kierkegaard, than to exist as an individual, and live under one's self-control alone in the whole world. "Alone" because inward subjectivity is identified with the supreme truth. Outside of us there is the appearance of us; inside of us, in our existence, there is the root of being. The so-called object is illusory, and he who is looking for the object is the victim of a mirage. "The only true objectivity is that of our own subjectivity." [4]

Is it really true that philosophy cannot give us any help in the solution of this unavoidable problem? No help: it only remains then to put philosophy up at auction without hope, however, of finding a buyer. But is it really true that Kierkegaard decrees the bankruptcy *of* philosophy and not that of *one* philosophy? Of *one* philosophy, and precisely the Hegelian philosophy then in vogue. He fights against Hegel and often

[4] L. Lavelle, *ibid.,* p. 86.

despises him; but, at least in one point, he is more Hegelian than Hegel himself. He believes that the dialectical "system" of Hegel constitutes the quintessence and ultimate conclusion of Western thought from Thales on. "The Hegelian process of rumination with three stomachs" was for Kierkegaard the process of philosophy *sic et simpliciter*. Idealism from Fichte to Hegel had found an ego that was immortal but without the fullness of life and, for this reason, it was like Aurora's husband who being immortal without eternal youth wound up becoming a grasshopper. Kierkegaard identifies speculative philosophy with the idealistic ego that becomes a grasshopper. Hegel has taken into account the impersonal rationality, and he has made man a mere genus in which the individual is drowned. On the contrary, the individual has more value than the genus; he has more worth in religion, not in philosophy. The Hegelian propositions that hurt Kierkegaard most were: that being is thought; that the individual is an unfinished determination of the spirit; that all reality, in the last analysis, is a manifestation of the idea in its eternity and transparency; that evil as such is to be denied.

Kierkegaard's *Concluding Unscientific Postscript* (trans. D. F. Swenson, Princeton, 1941) is the work that best reflects his aversion for the speculative and academic philosophy of the "professors," of "objective thought," which is indifferent toward the thinking subject and its existence. Instead, the philosophy of the "subjective thinker" centers on the concept of interiority around the principle that truth belongs to the individual and the individual alone. Speculative philosophy levels off the existence of individuals and makes them just aligned paragraphs within the "system." The "speculative" thinker is seeking for the objective truth and loses himself. He understands everything except himself. He who, instead, lives *in* and *on* his own inwardness and carries the passion of his personality in the heart of his thought is not allowed to speculate: he has the privilege of "existing." He does not imprison becoming in a frame, nor does he shut reality within a circle, but he vindicates precisely the process of becoming and himself as a living individual, against all the schemes and illusions of reason. The individual dies in the "system" and for this reason the system cannot supply an ethics. Speculative philosophy adorns the cadaver of the person with the embellishments of formulae and syllogisms in the sepulcher of logic.

What is really important for Kierkegaard is not to find the objective truth, but the truth that is our own and subjective, belonging exclusively to the individual. In a stirring page of his *Diary* he notes: "What is important is to understand what I am destined for, and what God really wants me to do; what is important is to find a truth that is *a truth for me*, and to find an idea for which I can live or die." What is the value of finding an objective truth and acquiring some knowledge of the philosophers' wisdom if the systems "did not have a deeper meaning for myself and for my life"? What is important is not to know truth, but to know that truth is accepted by me as a principle of life: "My soul longs for this as the deserts of Africa thirst for water." My thought must rest on something that is the deepest root of my existence, on something that is firmly rooted with the divine. "This is what I need and want." The immediate and most urgent task of philosophy is "to translate findings of science into spiritual life" so as to get hold of them personally. But speculative, or Hegelian, philosophy will never understand that essential knowledge is related to existence. Only ethico-religious knowledge is really essential because it harmonizes subjectivity and inward experience with truth. Not reason but *faith:* he who affirms God objectively does not believe. "The Absurd," incomprehensibility, and "objective insecurity" are necessary; the passion of faith is precisely expressed in the absurd. The system mortifies this passion and kills ethics too. Moral life is "decision" that finds its source and fullness in subjectivity. A great ethical personality can act on the external world, but it cannot allow itself to be distracted by the world, and it rejoices in its inwardness. Even here what is important is "passion," which marks the highest point of existence: the individual finds his way to infinity in the infiniteness of his imagination. We have lost indeed the logical truth and harmony of the system, but this is a happy loss inasmuch as we have found *our* truth, the truth that is inwardness itself. We have found ourselves, that is, in the dialectical contradiction that exalts passion to the point of "desperation" and "faith," and the latter as far as God. Existence postulates God and God is its only support. Then religion also is resolved in subjectivity. But is not religion the eternal truth? Precisely. Eternal truth and individual existence are placed together. This is paradox and "scandal" to speculative reason. But it is precisely the paradox and the scandal which save faith and with faith save existence, truth, and God.

Thus Kierkegaard could never be a "systematic thinker," and so he was instead a "jester," who derided every system "as a renewed attempt at having the globe blown up by a syllogism"; and he laughed at philosophers who build up a huge castle only to withdraw and live afterwards in a barn. He could not endure the speculative philosopher, the "professor," and angrily recognized the fact that his thought would be inherited by the speculative philosopher, "the figure for whom I have always entertained such a deep dislike; by him, who has so far received the best inheritance, and will go on receiving it. And even if it happens that the professor reads this passage, he will not be restrained by it, nor will he be shaken in his conscience by it; this passage too will be imparted *ex cathedra*."

For Kierkegaard, therefore, the opposition between speculative philosophy and religion is radical and invincible: Hegelian philosophy or *the* philosophy does away with the person, ethics, and faith. These truths must escape from the prison of philosophy and find their salvation in the garden of religion. The individual is made for God—this is Christianity, and it is on that point that the battle must be fought. The individual is able to receive a true communion only in his inward solitude because there alone he is in accord with God. There is no mediation, as Hegel purports, between the individual and the absolute. God and the individual face each other in the mystery of solitary intimacy; the philosophical idea or the law is unfit for the understanding of this great colloquy which is not decipherable by reason. The individual does not have the proof but the *vocation* of God. This is an appeal that only faith can understand. This is a personal word sent to us by God who is calling us by name. God is not an idea or an object that can be proved or contemplated. Every man discovers Him in the very act in which he discovers himself as an individual.

To prove God by reason is to lose God; to gain God is to be beyond reason. "The greatest provocation to scandal is to require of man that he admit as possible for God what for human reason is beyond all the bounds of possibility." Rationalistic and speculative philosophers defend the autonomy of ethics and of reason because they want to have a man who is *emancipated* from God in order to provide him with truths *emancipated* from God. In short, knowledge denies faith. God has warned man: "If you eat of the tree of knowledge you shall die." *The just man subsists on faith*, the Prophet writes; ignorance is the principle of faith; knowledge is the principle of reason. However, it is faith and not speculative philosophy that takes us to the tree of life. "Existential" philosophy leads us to the tree of life and this philosophy is the "senseless struggle on the part of faith for what is impossible for reason. Speculative philosophy remains on the surface since it lives on a plane with two dimensions, whereas existential thought knows a third dimension, viz., faith unknown to speculative philosophy." [5]

Man does not live on *intelligere*. Understanding, Kierkegaard agrees with Luther, is the terrible beast *qua non occisa homo non potest vivere*.

All this is indeed *scandalous* for speculative philosophy. Kierkegaard, however, opposes his "intrepid dialectic" to the dialectic having a rumination with three stomachs; to evident proofs he opposes infinite despair; to what reason considers impossible, he opposes both the reality of miracles and of "everything is possible to God" (*est enim Deus omnipotens ex nihilo creans omnia*). "Everything existing finds its source in God: all the eternal truths, and all the laws of morality prostrate themselves before His will. Good is good because God wills it. Truth is truth because He

[5] L. Chestov, *Kierkegaard et la philosophie existentielle* (Paris, Vrin), pp. 158, 167.

wills it. It is because of divine will that man submitted to temptation and lost his freedom. And freedom will be returned to man by the same divine will; it has already restored freedom to man: such is the meaning of the biblical revelation." [6]

Again, this is scandalous and absurd for reason. But existential philosophy is precisely the struggle of faith against reason, the senseless struggle for the possible or, rather, for the impossible. All that does not proceed from faith is sin. Only that faith which knows nothing, which wants to know nothing, is the source of the truths created by God. Knowledge is useless when it has to find the promised land; the promised land exists only for the man who knows not, but believes: *certum est quia impossibile.* For the sinful and proud *credo ut intelligam* of speculative philosophy Kierkegaard substitutes the words of the prophet: *iustus ex fide vivit.* Reason and ethics demand resignation in the presence of speculative truths that are evident and unavoidable; the Absurd and Faith bless the audacious instead. The God who can do anything lives far away from philosophy; He is the God of the Prophets, before whom man finds his own personality once again, and before whom he lives his own passions, the anguish of sin, and the sanctifying despair of the impossible. Inasmuch as there are absolute contrasts and qualitative differences between transcendence and immanence, divinity and humanity, eternity and temporality, the relationship between God and man can only be an inexplicable paradox. Only the paradoxical and "intrepid dialectic" places us before the "leap" by which existence surpasses the abyss separating it from God: not synthesis, process and rationality, but faith, grace and decision. Kierkegaard places man immediately before God; he places him as a sinner because sin is the category of his individuality. For this reason man cannot acquire truth except as a "gift" of God, through the grace of miracle and faith. Faith, not virtue, is the opposite of sin. And it is precisely here that the radical reversal occurs: freedom is revealed before God, in the state of sin, and a ray of grace penetrates and dispels the darkness of agony. The positive implies the negative. As Luther says, "One reaches paradise through the gates of hell." Existence is paradox— the abyss of sin is filled with faith in redemption.

At this point we may properly say that Kierkegaard's position is clarified with respect to his conception of the "aesthetical" and of the "ethical" points of view. In his work *Om Degrebet Ironi* (in *Samlede Vaerker,* Copenhagen, 1962) as well as in the *Diary of the Seducer* (in *Either/Or,* trans. D. F. Swenson *et al.,* London, 1944) and in the *Don Juan* (also found in the collection just mentioned), and so on, Kierkegaard constantly criticizes the "aesthetical" point of view when it is understood only as "enjoyment." The aesthete is not the vulgar Epicurean but the

[6] L. Chestov, *op. cit.,* pp. 376-377.

refined and subtle hedonist of the *Diary of the Seducer*—he who obeys the will, who knows how to enjoy life while he keeps himself above existence. The aesthete has the skill to change himself and his environment; he does not look at the future but turns to the past, to his vague remembrance in which the shape of things vanishes leaving only a trace. Kierkegaard's prototype of the aesthete can be found in some romanticists.

The aesthete's life, which on the surface appears as pleasure, is really despair. The aesthete lives in the *instant*, and the instant flees without return. "The splendid hope of youth is hurried in vain. We hurry on behalf of something that does not exist, and youth itself exists least of all! In vain the power of man progresses steadily on earth; that toward which we move is only imagination and fancy. . . . O beauty of the woods! When I was willing to contemplate you, you were faded! Run, O transient river! You are the only one to know what you want since you want only to run and lose yourself in the sea, which is never filled."

Boredom is the offspring of pleasure, "a dark knight who always escorts the lover of joy and pushes him to an ever renewed quest." [7] He who lives aesthetically is desperate. He is accompanied not only by boredom but also by melancholy, which is the "hysteria of the spirit." This is so because the intense and dissipated life of the aesthete—always longing for novelty, and always engaged in renewed efforts—tries in vain to conceal the emptiness of existence. In order to overcome despair it remains only to act desperately. But in the aesthete's life is hidden a deep guilt, the guilt of "not willing deeply and intimately." Opposed, however, to the despair of the aesthete is the despair of the "existentialist philosopher," who "despairs, despairs with all his heart, with all his soul, and all his strength." His despair is a serious act, a pledge, and a meditation; it is the act that gathers in itself the anxiety of the infinite. It is not a "passage" as the Hegelian dialectic would pretend, but a "choice," an act of will that engages the whole being, and through which alone the true meaning of life is known.

Despair is a kind of state of grace, and *irony* aids it. Irony is negativity and as such it detaches man from the world in which the aesthete is immersed. "Existing," therefore, is not possible without feeling irony, a fundamental dimension of the human person. Irony, in this way, makes man free from the aesthetical point of view and sets him on the way toward the ethical need. Irony is not truth, but an explosive that blows up bridges and scatters things. Irony creates an abyss between life on the "periphery" and "surface" of the earth, and life beyond the world, in the depth. Irony does not constitute a passage, but it nourishes the courage to "choose," and choose in despair.

[7] Lombardi, *Kierkegaard, op. cit.,* p. 97.

The act of choice depends on me. It leaves me suspended at the moment that I am about to accomplish it, and it is in this instant of suspension that I gain awareness of my deep ego, and of my *freedom*. In fact, in the instant preceding the choice I am the arbiter of my destiny, I am what I am, I am the cause of what I want to be. Before I choose, I am pure possibility, but a possibility that cannot remain in the limbo of abstraction. My existence is "directed toward a future that is nothingness (but a nothingness that is up to me to determine), toward a non-being that must be converted into being." [8] Ethics precisely implies choosing and deciding; and the choice can take place only between contrasts, namely, in the contrast between good and evil. It is here that the person finds himself to be guilty; the ego chooses only by repenting. Repentance mortifies the subject and arrests the ethical action. At the boundary of ethics, *religion* appears, or better yet, ethics almost resolves itself into religion. To Kierkegaard ethics and religion do not match but collide, as he cruelly affirms in his *Fear and Trembling* (trans. R. Payne, London, 1939). Kierkegaard goes back to the biblical narration of Isaac's sacrifice. In the decisive moment of his entire life, Abraham fulfilled the religious commandment but he had to "suspend" the ethics obstructing the road to God. If ethics had been the supreme law for Abraham he would have lost God, and with God, himself. Ethics, therefore, not only is devoid of autonomy but in the decisive moment of life, in the fatal instant—"to be or not to be"—is in contrast with religion. The ethical point is the last obstacle presented by speculative philosophy in order to exclude God from man and man from God; it is the extreme attempt by reason against faith in order to establish a truth emancipated from God. In the moment of raising his knife against Isaac, Abraham *had faith* in the restitution of Isaac to him. Abraham is acquitted before the tribunal of faith, but not before the tribunal of reason and ethics. Reason and ethics are *scandalized* by Abraham's defensive argument. For them it is *impossible* that the son be returned, but for God everything is possible: God is not impotent as are ethics and reason. Abraham had *faith* in the omnipotence of God, and *believed* that Isaac would be returned to him, and therefore he *suspended* ethics and reason. Faith triumphed! The man of faith then stands above the moral law which applies to all and has an end that is immanent in the law itself.

Kierkegaard does not always maintain this extreme position, however, and in the *Postscript* he tends to reconcile the conflict between *morality* and *religion*. There is a morality consisting of a "purity of heart" which is entirely inward and which is not absorbed, as Hegel pretended, by "ethicity," nor is it resolved into the "*ethos*" of the community and of the state. This morality moves toward religion without contrasting it.

[8] L. Lavelle, *op. cit.*, p. 83.

It does not interfere with faith, which hopes by dint of the absurd; nor does it disperse the individual in the crowd, but leaves him with his subjectivity and individuality before God. In spite of this, what always justifies Abraham is his terror and his anguish. Faith, as Kierkegaard understands it, leaves human action without any positive possibility.

At this point in the discussion we possess all the elements of the "intrepid dialectic," of Kierkegaard's thought, which centers on two fundamental themes: the person and the intimacy of truth. The defense of the person is to be sought in faith and not in reason, in religion and not in speculative philosophy. These two motives are pushed to the extent of paradox; religious faith is carried to the point of being identified with the desperate belief in the absurd. In order to realize why Kierkegaard held such a dark and irrational conception of Christianity, however, it is necessary to go back to his conception of the person, with which the all-important problem of sin is tightly bound. In Kierkegaard's view, sin is the category that guarantees the essence of individuality; the awareness of sin specifies and constitutes the individual. It "posits the individual as individual." Sin is the *existential* category *par excellence*. It regards me and only me, and affects no one else outside of me. Who can substitute me in sin? The individuality, on the other hand, is proper to Christianity. Religion deals with "individuals" not with a "public." Before God there is the single person alone: "Before God you are confronted essentially only with yourself." Therefore, if sin constitutes individuality and the essence of Christianity is individuality, then religion and sin are found tightly joined together.

Kierkegaard devotes to the problem of sin one of his keenest and most appealing works, *The Concept of Dread* (trans. W. Lowrie, Princeton, 1946). Is an explanation of sin possible? No, sin is an act of will, a *qualitative leap*, a leap from the state of "innocence" into that of sinfulness. Sin does not presuppose anything before itself: *it is posited*. Adam lost his innocence by sinning and so every man loses his with sin. However, Adam's sin has this particular aspect—Kierkegaard wants to avoid Pelagianism—that it is the "first" sin, the sin by which sinfulness entered the world. Adam's state prior to sin is the state of *innocence*. Innocence is, therefore, a state of *anxiety* and *anguish*,[9] which is expectation and inquietude, horror and tremor, dread before the *nothingness* that confronts us and that awakens in us the feeling of something terrible; at the same time, we are fascinated by the mysteriousness of this something which we must face. The soul is dream-like during the state of innocence: "Man is a soul in immediate union with its own nature." Innocence entails peace and rest, but at the same time it implies something that is neither discord nor struggle. *Nothingness* produces anguish. "The deep

[9] Kierkegaard uses only the term *Angst*.

mystery of innocence consists in its being anguish at the same time. The soul in its dream projects its own reality; and this reality is *nothing*. But this nothingness constantly sees innocence outside of itself." Anguish does not cause the loss of innocence, because the awareness of good and evil is still lacking. "He is innocent who becomes guilty on account of anguish because he is no longer master of himself; his person has been seized upon by anguish, an extraneous power which inspires him not with love but anxiety. He is guilty, nevertheless, because he has subjected himself to anguish which he loves while fearing it." Innocence is ignorance which still lacks spirit. Yet it is not animal brutality. On the other hand, it is ignorance which, being characterized by spirit, becomes precisely anguish. "There is in it no awareness of what good and evil are, and so on, but, rather the whole body of knowledge is thrust into anguish or in the monstrous nothingness of ignorance." From innocence to sin there is no passage but a "leap," a *qualitative leap*, the leap, that is, from the state of innocence or ignorance into that of knowledge or sin. It is a change of state that has taken place, and so sin cannot be explained by applying the canons of speculative philosophy or Hegel's *quantitative* dialectic. Reason is *scandalized* but, notwithstanding its scandal, it is powerless to explain sin; the "leap" holds logic at bay; quantitative dialectic yields to the qualitative dialectic of the "leap."

There is no place for sin in the philosophy of Hegel where evil is always a dialectical moment related to good. But, as Pascal states, sin is one of those things which takes us by the throat, and which, together with individuality, was misunderstood by Hegelianism. When God orders, "You shall not eat from the tree of knowledge of good and evil," Adam does not understand these words. Yet the prohibition causes Adam anguish because it awakens in him the possibility of *freedom:* the anguish of nothingness has been almost specified in the anguishing possibility of *being able.* Adam is unaware as yet of what he can do; the potentiality of power is given to him as a superior form of ignorance, as a higher expression of anguish. After the prohibition, comes the judgment: "You shall certainly die." Adam does not understand the meaning of the word "dying"; it must have aroused in him a terrorizing idea. Adam's soul is confused: "Innocence is thus driven to an extreme point where it begins to vanish. Innocence finds itself in anguish and in contact with prohibition and punishment. Though not guilty, innocence experiences the anguish of being already lost." We cannot go any further. The fall comes next. Neither psychology nor speculative philosophy can explain it, for the fall is a qualitative leap. Sin enters man and the pretense "of giving a logical explanation to the entrance of sin into the world is a silly thing that can be imagined only by people who are used to the ridiculous preoccupation of offering an explanation." What is certain is that the fall is due to knowledge—*knowledge loses man*. The anguish of nothingness, that of prohibition, and that of divine judgment are not yet sin. But they place innocence in the potentiality of committing sin, in the state of freedom in which the spirit passes from dream to waking. Anguish can be compared with the dizziness of freedom, which intervenes when spirit wishes to affect the synthesis of soul and body. "By probing the depths of its own potentiality," freedom "grasps the finite in order to lean on it. Freedom succumbs to the dizziness." When it rises again, it sees itself guilty. The mysterious leap, inexplicable to reason, is put between these two instants. For Kierkegaard, nevertheless, anguish is one of man's highest distinctions; a man who does not himself experience anguish is not a man.

As far as Kierkegaard is concerned, *man is a synthesis of the temporal and the eternal* besides being a synthesis of body and soul. Time is commonly defined as an infinite succession, that is, as present, past, and future. In time itself this distinction is not exact because it is not possible to find a fixed point, a present in this infinite succession. All the moments are in motion and, therefore, no moment is present; in time, then, there is no present, no past, and no future. The eternal, instead, is the present understood as the suppression of succession. But is it not said that sensible life lies in the instant? This is true. "The instant, then, is understood as the abstraction of the eternal, which, given as present, makes a parody of it. The present is the eternal or, better, the eternal is the present, and the present is fullness. . . . The instant designates the present without past or future; in this lies the imperfection of sensible life. The eternal also designates the present without past or future, and in this lies the perfection of the eternal." In the *instant*, nonetheless, time and eternity come together. The instant, not conceived as a simple determination of time, is an atom of eternity; it is the first attempt to arrest time. In Kierkegaard's view there is then a real contact between eternity and time. And it could not be otherwise since for him, as we know, the individual alone exists. The single person exists against the traditional logic of "genera," not of "individuals," and against the Hegelian logic that has drowned the individual into Reason. Eternity and time meet in the unrepeated individuality of the existent. What is the relationship between them? Naturally this relationship cannot be established through the dialectic of synthesis because it is a relationship of contrariety and opposition; the dialectic that unites eternity and time can only be a paradoxical synthesis, that is to say, the paradox of existence as synthesis. In fact, existence is paradox, the meeting point of infinite and finite, eternal and temporal, opposing and uniting each other. In so far as it is finite and individuality, existence is immersed in time, but in so far as it is the presence of eternity, it relates to God, to the Absolute. Relationship with itself and relationship with God coincide in existence. Existence is immediate presence and determinate individuality, but it is a presence that cannot be conceived except as an invocation of the eternal. It is the paradox of the universality of the individual, of the absoluteness of the singular. Existence etymologically means *"being outside of"* (*exsistere*), transcending oneself, and projecting oneself into space and time. Existence is distance between the instants of time and the points of space, between thought and being, and it grasps the two opposites. Existence is sin and liberation from sin, sin and redemption; it is the enclosing of man in the infinity of being. From the moment spirit is posited (for which man is the synthesis of body and soul) the instant is produced, synthesizing the temporal and the eternal. "The instant is this mixture in which time and eternity are in contact, thus producing the concept of *temporality* in which time constantly interrupts eternity, and in which eternity always enters into time. The division of time into present, past, and future only then makes sense." Temporality evidently becomes guilt in the instant in which sin is posited; and this in the sense that "when sin is posited, temporality becomes synonymous with guilt because man sins as he lives only in the instant, the abstraction of the eternal." Not that temporality as such is guilt or it would amount to saying that sin is outside of us. There is guilt when man lives in time and disregards the eternal, that is, when he breaks off the synthesis of eternity and temporality and immerses himself in the temporal series wherein he acquires the sense of the finite (the infinite series pertaining to time has nothing to do with the eternal) and loses that of the infinite. We can conquer time and achieve our pure individuality by enclosing history within parentheses.

But even in the instant there is no absence of anguish, which resides in the relationship that is established in me between finite and infinite, time and eternity. Anguish places itself in time and the instant, and I cannot separate it from my nature as a finite being compared with an infinite that surpasses me. The spirit is always tempted in the state of anguish; the imminence of sin fascinates it. It fears and loves anguish. But is not sin the strongest affirmation of the person? Is it not sin that leads to God? Is it not the sinner who finds himself before God? This is inexplicable; this is still scandal to reason. "Certainly! Believing properly means losing the intellect in order to gain God." The responsibility of single individuals as well as God are lost in the "unity" of Hegel's idealistic principle; all is leveled and settled in the *unique Reality*. For Hegel, *rational* is the unique Reality, and *irrational* is the individual. Philosophy will never understand the personality of God, which is creative of other free personalities. The paradoxical character of religion in the presence of philosophy starts from here; a paradox which in fact guarantees individuality and existentiality. Religion is the scandal of reason. The "absolute scandal" is Christ, who is truly Man and truly God. Sin and anguish are a scandal too. Faith is "miracle" and "who sees God makes himself unable to understand."

Anguish is won only by faith. Anguish is an "adventure" that every man has to understand if he does not wish to lose himself. It holds an absolute educative value only by virtue of faith. "In fact, it wears away all the things of the finite world, and lays bare all its illusions." Anguish is the possibility of freedom, and we must be educated by it, in order to be free according to the infinity pertaining to it. "When all the findings of possibility are honestly utilized, the latter reveals all finite things, but idealizes them in the form of the infinite, and oppresses with anguish the individual until it triumphs in the emancipation of faith."

All we have said explains the rebellion of Sören Kierkegaard during the last years of his life (*Training in Christianity*, trans. W. Lowrie, London, 1941; *For Self-Examination* and *Judge for Yourself*, trans. W. Lowrie, London, 1941) against official, mundane, and bourgeois Christianity. Even here the polemic with Hegel is present. For Hegel, Christ is God made man, who has unified the human and the divine; for Kierkegaard, man stands "before God," outside of the world. The Christian-bourgeois world that was sanctioned by the philosophy of Hegel must disappear. That world is the death of Christianity, and has emanated from an order of intelligence that is devoid of passion, and incapable of "really sinning." The times are not wicked, writes Kierkegaard, but are mean for lack of true and great passions. "Man's thoughts are evanescent like fog and men themselves are as fickle as grisettes. The impulses of their hearts are too poor to be called sinful." To this bourgeois world Kierkegaard opposes the existential individual, who believes desperately, who bases everything on faith, who exists only inwardly and not in the world. There is no mediation, but absolute incompatibility between the existential individual and the bourgeois Christian, just as is the case between Christianity and the world, Christianity and the State. The Hegelian proposition that the morality of the State and its religious spirituality sustain each other, becomes for Kierkegaard nonsense from the point of view of religion; and the State-Church Christianity is a compromise according to which Christianity is served with "a live human fear, mediocrity, and temporal interest." A State wishing to stunt the growth of any true poetry would only need one thousand stipends to achieve its aim. Similarly, true Christianity is lost in the worldliness of the State: "If we are Christian, *eo ipso* Christianity does not exist." It does not exist because worldly Christianity has killed it; and it has fraudulently exchanged the independence and intimacy of faith for worldliness and slavery to the State and for comforts and riches.

Kierkegaard writes with pungent irony: "Did the Apostle Paul hold a job? No, Paul had no employment. Did he then earn money in some way? No, he earned no money in any way. But was he married at least? No, he was not married. But then Paul is not a good man! No, Paul is not a good man." Thus, according to Kierkegaard, historic Christianity and bourgeois Christians have suppressed Christ.

These are the principal motives of the ethico-religious experience of Kierkegaard—motives that have been greatly echoed by contemporary European philosophy and in recent years by North and South American thought. It is really true that Kierkegaard is one of those authors people cannot read without receiving a deep impression, but it is also true that he is one of those thinkers with whom a complete spiritual intimacy cannot be established. He is not a systematic philosopher; actually he does not have a philosophy and, properly speaking, he cannot be called a philosopher according to the "canonical" meaning of the word. His meditation obeys the rules of his internal needs or, I would say, his subjective impulses. In other words, one could say of Kierkegaard's thought that it is so personal, so intimate, and filled with such "emotional moods" that it confronts us with a variety of problems (and this is the reason for Kierkegaard's fascination) whose solution cannot be our own because they are not objective problems. Kierkegaard is a writer who stimulates meditation and occasionally opens the reader's mind to abysmal problems; but this type of writer does not help the reader to solve problems. It is as if he says to his reader, "You must leave the soul to itself so that the despair of solitude may elevate the soul to the dizziness of the infinite." Kierkegaard is a theologian, not a philosopher, a theologian with few dogmas. He is one of those souls endowed with an uncommon religious sensibility, for whom religion identified with life is only inquietude and torment. Such religious souls, almost oppressed by their exigencies, are intolerant and incapable of any rigorous systemization; and so they give full sway to the spontaneity of their feelings, which never attain the clarity of the concept nor the limpidity of the intuition. In Kierkegaard we find at times the persuasive force of the concept united to the charm of his fanciful and poetical expression, but still lacking is the cogent reasoning of logic and the serenity of the artistic intuition.

Kierkegaard is not, therefore, a thinker who can be criticized. His thought is an ethico-religious experience, a personal and fragmentary one that escapes criticism. Asystematic (at times by design), his efficacy lies in his keen and deep intuition and it ends in this. Endowed with a strong, spiritual richness, he did not succeed in disciplining the restlessness of his spirit. The best teaching we can draw from his philosophy is, in fact, to understand thought as an interior meditation, a continuous and exasperating dialogue of the soul with itself. Dialectic, then, or if you will, "dialectical theology," without overlooking the fact that theology for him must serve the problem of personality. The key to which Kierkegaard attuned all his thought is precisely the problem of man, of man as a concrete individual justified by religion. Contrary to speculative philosophy, which explains and accommodates everything, Kierkegaard discovers in man a "problematic" existence, and a person that is a problem to itself; yet, within the problematic nature of the person he finds out the way to divine transcendence. Moreover, while truth is "public" for Hegelian philosophy, truth for Kierkegaard is interior and subjective. Truth exists only for him who possesses it, namely, the one who produces it with his own effort and passion. There is no philosophy or system except for the one who *suffers* in order to produce them.

Certainly these motives make the philosophical experience of Kierkegaard fascinating and appealing. But in the end these motives are not new. They are found in Christianity in their authentic form. Kierkegaard has pushed them to the limit of paradox. His restless mind was a prism deforming the problems of existence, sin, faith, and morality—in short, the content of Christianity. Kierkegaard can be considered a tormented soul seeking the medicine of his personal troubles and the conclusion of his philosophico-theological adventures in the Christian religion. After all, he did not notice—he who attributed to himself the extraordinary mission of saving Christianity—that he was killing it. The paradoxical standing "before God," the irrational and "scandalous" content of faith, these are the negation of philosophy and also of Christian revelation.[10] "With the abandonment of the Christian State, of the Christian church and of Christian theology, in short, of all the historico-worldly 'positivity' of Christianity," Kierkegaard reduces Christianity "to the pure paradox of a desperately resolute will to faith." An empty Christianity in the world is an inhuman Christianity, precisely a *denier* of that individuality that Kierkegaard wished to defend at any cost. In truth, he defended it so much as to deny it; the "individuality" of Kierkegaard is an abstraction like the "unity" of Hegel. Interiority, existentiality, effort, uncertainty of the person, despair, and so on, are concepts that feed the Christian experience; but they are deeply altered by Kierkegaard, who can be characterized as an "ingenious Lutheran Pascal" when he is not a "baroque Pascal." The dialectic that is present in Luther's theology[11]

---

[10] K. Löwith, "La conclusione della filosofia classica con Hegel e la sua dissoluzione in Marx e Kierkegaard," *Giornale Critico della Filosofia Italiana,* IV-V (1935), 353.
[11] J. Wahl, *Etudes Kierkegaardiennes* (Paris, Aubier), p. 166.

influenced Kierkegaard to the extent that he made sin the supreme category of the person and despair the joy of the soul. Evidently Kierkegaard with his "dark humor" never asked himself whether it was anguish and despair that draw us nearer God or, rather, the flash of Augustine's "interior light"; he did not ask whether we arrive at God through the violence of internal contrasts or, rather, through a profound calmness of spirit. There is in Kierkegaard a "romanticism of the absolute," [12] that ends in a pure state of mind, in a monotonous psychologism no matter how richly modulated.

Kierkegaard, to repeat, is really a philosopher of crisis and in this lies his present fortune: a philosopher of crisis not in the sense that he may give a new principle to solve it, but only in the sense that he is the expression of it and indeed, its victim. If Kierkegaard is so popular today, it means that a good part of contemporary thought is thought of crisis still far from solution. It is sickly thought that considers health its own malady, and its life, death. L. Chestov on the cover of his book on Kierkegaard adds a subtitle: *vox clamantis in deserto*. This is true, but only in the sense that the voice of Kierkegaard produces the desert; often it can hear only itself.

[12] L. Lavelle, *op. cit.*, p. 90.

III

HISTORICISM, RELATIVISM, VITALISM AND PSYCHOANALYSIS

---

1. CURRENTS OF GERMAN HISTORICISM: E. SPRANGER, W. WINDELBAND, H. RICKERT, M. WEBER, AND E. TROELTSCH

With the exception of Croce in Italy, it seems that the problems of historiography and historic methodology (and indeed historicism in all its numerous forms) chose as their home Germany where, until some years ago, the great historiographical tradition of the nineteenth century was still alive. We already noticed how Dilthey, principally, and then Simmel tried to theorize and systematize the problem of historiography along the main lines traced first by Hegel and then deepened by Hegelianism. German literature is rich with works written by philosophers and historians on these questions, even though the tradition is at present continued with scant originality and with little speculative value. We can say that German methodology of history has now fallen into a spiritless and academic formulary, when it is not simply a superficial or extravagant amateurism.

As we said, although he admits only historic truths, Dilthey recognizes in history super-subjective values constituting its unity. From Dilthey's "visions of the world" to their hypostatization as ideal moments, the step was short. EDWARD SPRANGER (1882) yielded to this temptation so that life has been divided and catalogued by him (*Lebensformen,* Halle, 1922) as the theoretical man, economic man, aesthetic man, the man who leads and commands, social man, and the philosopher. Throughout the process of history, these teleological structures make up the objective world of the spirit, differing from the world produced by whim and daily contingency, beyond which man can create values surpassing his individual existence. Contrary to Cartesian and enlightened rationalism wherein history is the reign of opinion and accident and wherein universal values are discovered and conquered within the pure world of reason, Spranger saw objective truth in the becoming of history. One must distinguish between the world of contingency and the world of history, and between the mass of impulses and whims abounding in every civilization (pseudo-ideals which are deified by man) and the true ideals "which are the realization of norms, of aims, and of a legislation of values" that transcend individual consciousness. In short, the world of subjective irrationality differs from the world of history just as experimental psychology which studies the powers of the soul differs from the new "structural" psychology, which Spranger, like Dilthey, strives to establish as the science of the concordance and uniformity of historical events.

In Spranger's view the structures or types, which are considered as moments or categories of the objective spirit or of the universal, are not enclosed each in itself, incommunicable to one another like Leibniz' monads: the "aesthetical man," for example, does not exclude the economic and religious category. The objective spirit manifests itself as totality. Similarly, the structures are not the monopoly of one race, nation or civilization. As there are no closed frontiers among individuals, so there are no rolling shutters between peoples and centuries. There is no "aesthetical man" or "religious man" of the Middle Ages, but there is man with all his spiritual structures. In the so-called aesthetical man or religious man there is no absence of, but only the subordination of all other types to, the predominating one. Man builds his universe according to the prevailing type: for the aesthetic man the world is a sea of beauty; for the theoretical man, it is a system of laws; and for the mystic, an emanation of Love and Light. Each spiritual structure is then confronted with its own metaphysics and its own ethics. Every personality expresses one of these structures in a high degree: expressing it signifies being oneself without whim or caprice; it means founding an objective order of the spirit.

It may be noted that, for Spranger, the personality is not identified with an eccentric individualism disdaining norms and rules; personality, for him, is one affirming itself as creative of an objective world of values that is reconciled with society and the laws of historic becoming.[1] In addition to the current flowing from Dilthey, German thought on historicism and historiography has also another one headed by the theorists of the "philosophy of values," namely by WILHELM WINDELBAND (1845-1915) and HEINRICH RICKERT (1862-1936), who are the greatest representatives of Neo-Kantianism within the so-called school of Baden. According to Windelband, a renowned historian of philosophy, we can consider reality from a twofold point of view: either we observe phenomena in their relations, confine ourselves to describing and classifying them, and elicit "judgments of reality"; or we judge the *value* of facts (their beauty, utility, and goodness) in relation to ends and ideal norms of the spirit, and elicit "judgments of value." This latter type of judgment belongs to philosophy, whereas the former belongs to the natural sciences whose value then is purely classificatory and descriptive. In this way, remarks Rickert (whose main work is *System der Philosophie*, Tübingen, 1921), the sciences miss whatever is particular and individual in every moment of concrete reality. Concreteness instead is attained through the historical method by which reality is not thinned, as it were, but rather fully grasped in its peculiar, nonrepetitive, and unmistakable nature; it is grasped as a progressive realization of spiritual values and as freedom because the individual, always new in each of his moments, is placed outside of the mechanism of natural laws. Windelband, and particularly Rickert, emphasize the importance of universal and necessary norms characterizing the historic judgment: norms which they place beyond becoming, in an order of values never realized nor realizable by the individual consciousness, though satisfied by the universal consciousness.

In spite of the solicitation coming from the new exigencies of German thought, Rickert persisted until the end without yielding to the allurements of the vitalists, who on many occasions scorned him for not being able to bring his rationalism up to date. This accusation is partly unfounded inasmuch as this author has also raised some problems still considered vital in present-day thought. In fact, he felt the whole importance of the problem of existence in respect to value. Do values that do not belong to the existential order represent some sense of being? This ontological problem faced Rickert as peremptorily as it faced N. Hartmann and Husserl. In his last work (*Grundprobleme der Philosophie*, Tübingen, 1934), which is a synthesis of all his thought, the problem that is properly his is very much alive: the good, the true, and the beautiful are eternal and beyond us since we are immersed in the relativity of history; this is the problem of existence and value. Our duty is to raise

---

[1] Spranger is known better as an author of important works on philosophy of civilization, psychology and pedagogy than as a theorist.

ourselves up to the sublime level of duties in all the expressions of our activity. Man is called upon to make his life a reality representing value. Inasmuch as life is flowing and becoming, it is necessary for us to organize and fashion it. Man must widen and deepen the study of theoretical laws which Kant has revealed to modern thought. As Rickert sees it then, thought is the capacity to unify the world of values and that of experience, that is, eternity and history, which becomes finite and contradictory through becoming. In the midst of so much vitalism and irrationalism, Rickert advocated the harmony of existence and value, though this was the moment, as we shall see, when existentialism stressed the contradictions of existence and proclaimed the failure of reason. Thus, he singled out the very problem which has engaged contemporary speculation so deeply. There is an obvious difference between this current and the other based on Dilthey's psychologism, which, hinging on the concept of the *Erlebnis*, produces ambiguous analogies with biological life on the one hand, and, on the other, leads to a conception of history as a catalogue or an exhibition of types or static and rigid structures liable to cause the most arbitrary reconstructions. However, if Dilthey's thought compromises the spiritual values by immersing them in the becoming of life, Windelband's and Rickert's thought incurs the risk of losing contact with the concreteness of history by placing essences in a transcendent order. For one thing, the individual and life are saved, and yet the universal and the norm become endangered; and for another, value is guaranteed, and yet it is carried to the extreme of being cast outside the existential so that it can no longer be a valid category through which history is understood and construed. Synthesis is cut off into two stumps and the fracture may cause unilateral, paradoxical, and abstract interpretations of history.

Harmonizing these two tendencies and finding a meeting point is the very problem in German historicism from Simmel to Spranger, Troeltsch, and MAX WEBER (1865-1920). The latter links himself to Comte's and Spencer's positivism as well as to Marx. Causality (determinism) explains the relations between men and social structures. Weber, however, does not deny a certain difference betwen physical and psychic phenomena which, unlike the others, are not determined by necessity since they are conscious and free. In his sociology, economics holds a favored but not an exclusive position as it does in Marx; in fact, in social and human relations there is also an intervention of factors which are due to culture, temperament, race, and so on. The structure of a social group varies, but at every moment of its evolution it presents itself as a whole that embodies the attitudes of single members. Weber's analyses, which are sometimes suggestive, remain purely phenomenological and descriptive, and, as such, external and insufficient. In reality, his explanation of religious and cultural phenomena shows that he has remained loyal to Marx's principle, wherein religions (and the forms of culture) are distinguished according as they emerge from this or that social class. Christianity, for example, began "as a doctrine emanating from apprentices-workers-pedlars. It was, and still is, primarily a religion specifically urban and bourgeois."

Concerning the problems of the spirit, we find a greater sensibility in ERNEST TROELTSCH (1865-1923), a Protestant theologian who is more important as a historian than as a philosopher. In his work *Der Historismus and Seine Probleme* (Tübingen, 1922), he outlines a complete summary of the questions regarding historiography. In it he also tries to solve the problem just mentioned through Hegel's dialectical conception of reality, but this attempt was not carried out because of his death. Troeltsch, however, points out (and this is by now a commonplace) that in Hegel the content or what is particular is understood in a Spinozian way and thus sacrificed to the monistic tendency or to the idea of the absolute. If dialectic is viewed, instead, as the dynamism of historical process in which individuality and value are opposed and yet united by their own opposition, then it helps in explaining history as a continuous alternation of contrasts which, through their involutions, while perennially composed in the creative syntheses of human consciousness, produce superior personalities, classes, religions, and so on. Historical dynamism lies, in fact, in the interpenetration of individuality and universality. History has the task of searching for the unitary tendencies within diversity, of finding out the relations and developments, and of mediating oppositions.

In Troeltsch, who was first a professor of theology at Heidelberg and later a historian of religions, the ethical exigency is very much alive as is evidenced in his last work, *Der Historismus u. Seine Überwindung* (Berlin, 1924). In this book, he inverts the Hegelian reduction of morality (values of the individual consciousness) into ethicity (values of the historical collective consciousness), and finds in the moral evaluations of individual consciousness the element which vivifies the ethical institutions of history. Thus, Troeltsch is tempted to surpass historicism.

Troeltsch's preoccupations are not unfounded, if we bear in mind that, even when it is not skeptical, historicism is always a doctrine that cannot avoid relativism, finiteness, and temporaneity of values; and this is so whatever the manner of considering it, even if that be "recognition of reality as a dynamic spiritual process in whose course universal values are realized as individualized forms never repeating themselves." [2] In Germany, in fact, it has ended by exhausting itself through naturalistic and abstract forms of typology or certain baroque forms of irrationalism.

[2] G. De Ruggiero, *Filosofi del Novecento* (Bari, Laterza), p. 262.

FRIEDRICH MEINECKE (1862-1954), who taught in Berlin and in Freiburg, is by far more interesting as a historian than as a theorist of the historical method. He considers historicism (Die Entstehung des Historismus, Munich, 1936) more a "historical relativism" than a philosophy of history. For him, in fact, historicism is the tendency to evaluate individuality, the infinite human variety, the *individuum ineffabile* as Goethe says, the acknowledgment of the autonomy of the spirit in its innumerable expressions. Historicism, for that reason, according to Meinecke, does not deny eternal truths and absolute values, but recognizes them as existing in the individual, in the infinite variety of modes in which they manifest themselves. Thus understood it is not a new theory, but an outcome of the current of thought that had immediately preceded it, that is, enlightenment, which is commonly considered antihistorical. That is why England, mother of enlightenment, is also the genetrix of historicism.

If, on the one hand, one cannot make history while drawing on the eternal, on the other hand we cannot have philosophy while leaning on the temporal. Consequently, historicism, as historical relativism (and if it is not this, then it is philosophy of history) can never be philosophy and all the less can philosophy be reduced to it. Historicism is indeed methodological, and it almost makes no sense to speak of philosophical historicism, of philosophy as methodology of history.

Even in his most recent writings, despite the experience of the 1914-1918 war lost by Germany, Meinecke holds on to his principle that ethics should be subordinated to the welfare of the State, inasmuch as what is at stake is not the freedom of the individual but the power of the State. Beyond that, on a different plane, there are the absolute values of morals and law. The dualism of ethics and power "polarizes" in the opposites of "realm of spirit" and "realm of sin." It pertains to the essence of the supreme good of the State to be guilty of the violation of ethics and law. The State must sin. This, Meinecke recognizes, is the most terrible aspect of the history of mankind. "The very human community that includes and guarantees all the others and that should, therefore, guide them with the purity of its essence, far from being possible of moralization, cannot even enjoy a theoretical purity." Power, however, is not bad in itself; it is, rather, indifferent to good and evil: it becomes bad in the hands of those who abuse it. "In lieu of confident faith in the identity of spirit and nature, there is, in Meinecke, the disconsolate acknowledgment of the incurable, perennial conflict between the two principles. History is not, by any means, all justified; it is, rather, a combination of moral life and instinctive violence, a Manichean struggle. The evil that has been perpetrated throughout history, the deception, the slaughtering, remain evil, and no superior synthesis can change its nature. And, what is worse, things are not improving. History is without hope" (C. Antoni, *Dallo storicismo alla sociologia*, Florence, Sansoni, 1940, pp. 108-109).

The theories of JOHAN HUIZINGA (1872-1945), a Dutchman who taught in Göttingen and Leiden, take a completely different course from those of German historicism. Huizinga—a historian with the temperament of an artist, well known in Italy, where his most important works have been translated (*The Waning of the Middle Ages*, trans. F. Hopman, London, 1924; *Erasmus*, trans. F. Hopman, New York, 1924; *In the Shadow of Tomorrow*, trans. J. H. Huizinga, London, 1936)—is against formulas, definitions and any adaptation of history to categories, forms, concepts (Romanticism, Renaissance, and so forth), which he considers as many labels with which historiography bottles up its wine. That is why, in history, he does not look for lines of development nor for philosophical or religious ideas to direct or govern it. With extremely fine touches and suggestive style Huizinga describes moods, aspirations, anxieties, and dreams of a given epoch or of a great historical personality. His is not a history of ideas nor of economical and speculative interests, but simply history of feelings. He grasps the irrational; he sheds light on the realm of affections and fantasy. To write about history means "to give oneself account" of the past according to the antithesis of virtue and sin, of wisdom and folly, of violence and right, and so on; and each one gives himself account of it according to his own vision of the world. We are, indeed, far from the preoccupation (when it is not, as we know, artifice) of German historiography to find and list historical structures or forms, and we are approaching a historicism which is the interpreter of the needs, nowadays so felt, of the instinctive and the arational, the unusual and the unobtainable—needs which are found, after all, at the more or less "structural" basis of any form of historicism.

2. O. Spengler and the Formal Universes

Of the vitalistic and relativistic forms of historicism we are going to mention only the most clamorous and fortunate one, namely, the theory of "formal universes" of OSWALD SPENGLER (1880-1936). He is the author of the apocalyptic *The Decline of the West* (trans. C. F. Atkinson, New York, 1926-1928), which had such a notable success in the Germany that was exhausted by the First World War and prostrated by her defeat. Only to the bad taste of the contemporary "mind" could Spengler's work appear as an original production. In reality the *Decline* is only a skilled and baroque travesty of the arsenal of German historiography. Endless paradoxes, ostentatious derangement of some accredited schemes, disconcerting affirmations and, above all, amateurism and inferiority of the intellectual climate in which we have been living for about thirty years, have built the fortune of Spengler's book as well as his fame. After all, as both an ingenious compiler of motives and an able artificer of expedients, Spengler merely imitates the style of those who novelize history or make of it a "detective" story in a Chamberlain-Keyserling-like manner. With Spengler we go back to one of the many eruptions of contemporary vitalism, and I would say of biologism; we return to the motives of Schopenhauer and Nietzsche, but far from the best in Schopenhauer, however, and nearer, instead, to the worst in Nietzsche or in Simmel. Historical becoming in Spengler is a natural and blind becoming, through which everything comes into being aimlessly, everything changes and dies merely for the pleasure of changing and dying. Historicism shows one of its faces through Spengler, and, perhaps, concludes rather badly one of its cycles.

Spengler moves from this presupposition: *cultures* (the "cycles of culture" imply, according to him, a period of about one thousand years) or *formal universes* emerge from a vital process. From Nietzsche he draws the conception of becoming as a useless development, beginning always anew and repeating itself aimlessly. It is naive to ask whether some doctrines are true or false; they are only fated. It is also inevitable that one conception be superseded by another; it is fatal that every vision of the world, inasmuch as it is a "cosmic image," imprint itself on all manifestations of the spirit (art, philosophical and social doctrine, finance and politics, fashion and custom, and so on). The aspects of a whole civilization are the incarnation of the same symbol, of the same cosmic image, of the same formal universe, a realization of the same destiny. History is not the unfolding and realization of values, but an aimless manifestation of predestined symbols.

Spengler even has a cult for vitalism: "A call to the earth, to its impulses, and passions, an abandonment of every theodicy mortifying the instincts, a revived cult of virile fortune and of the divinity of blood and sex." These are the values which Spengler, by going farther than Nietzsche, wishes to re-establish against the abuses perpetrated by the "sages." Pre-eminence does not belong to the wise man, priest and moralist who wish to improve the world, but to the worldly man, the soldier, the conqueror, the aristocrat, the noble fatalist who, in disbelieving the panaceas of betterment and progress, does his best to gain the triumph of instinctive feelings, of vital values like those of blood and honor, which are trampled on by reason. The Spenglerian man is a knight who is called upon to impose the dominion of life upon the tyranny of reason, the man who is emancipated from every myth of providential finality and of freedom and progress; a man who is the expression of a blind, cosmic force, the incarnation of living nature. As he writes—with a pessimism such that the reader does not understand whether Spengler is resigned to it or pleased with it—"From optimists we have become skeptics; we are not fond of what ought to happen, but of what happens; to be masters of what will happen is more important to us than to become slaves of ideals. The logic of natural science, the concatenation of causes and effects appears to us more superficial than ever; only the logic of the organic, destiny, and instinct, whose omnipotence we perceive in the vicissitudes of things, demonstrates to us the thoroughness of becoming. What matters is to supply man with a new vision whence another necessarily springs. Life has no purpose whatsoever."

Spengler proposes to give a historical justification of the myth of the eternal return so that he applies the mechanism of natural life to the becoming of history. Just as the seasons of sowing and harvest succeed each other in nature, so within the human world one can see the succession of historical epochs of aristocratic and democratic values, aimlessly and without any idea or plan, "like species of butterflies and orchids." Cultures, peoples, civilizations, languages and ideas blossom and become old like oaks and pines. "There are many diverse plastic arts, painting, mathematics, physics, with a limited duration, each of which is closed in itself, as every species of vegetable has its own flowers and fruits, its type, from growth to decline. These paintings, and the like, as they are living beings of a high order increase in an amazing carelessness of ends, like the flowers in the fields. Like plants and animals, they belong to the living nature of Goethe and not to the dead nature of Newton."

What then are intelligence and reason for Spengler? The supremacy belongs to blood, race, spirit of domination, love and revenge. Intelligence is only a late and derivative function and reason is the crystallizing of vital elements. Cultures are the work of these vital elements and not the work of reason or intelligence, and hence they are "living organisms" having, like all organisms, their evolutionary phases. "A culture is born when a great soul is awakened and detached from the primitive psychological state of the eternal human infancy. It is born on the soil of a landscape one can delimit with exactness and with which the culture remains bound like a plant. A culture dies when the soul has realized the sum total of its possibilities in terms of peoples, languages, religious doctrines, arts, states, sciences, and then returns to its original state. Its living essence is an intimate and passionate struggle for the conquest of the idea over the external forces of chaos and over the internal instinct in which these forces took shelter with their rancor." A culture declines when it is not agitated by the impulses of religious and warlike epochs, when it no longer feels the force of blood and honor. Such is our contemporary epoch, an epoch of "world cities," *boulevards*, exhibition halls, meetings, and a tentacular bureaucracy: a hedonistic and utilitarian epoch and an inorganic, bloodless, spineless civilization.

We shall not follow Spengler in his skillful but often sophistical and capricious comparisons of forms or "formal universes," where one is independent from the other and each is dominated by a destiny representing the sole law through which the chaos of historical facts is bound and ordained. Let us only say that, according to him, whatever has been, is, and will be, it is the representation of psychological structures or formal universes. From this standpoint everything has been "historicized," from the principles of logic called universal and necessary to the Kantian *a priori*, and mathematics as well. There is no "number in itself," but there exist "many universes of numbers": an Indian type, an Arabic type, and a Western type of mathematical thought. And hence mathematics, like art, has "its styles and its periods of style." Analogously, physics is an art; atomism and mechanism are only predominant myths, like all laws of physics, and some of them predominate in one epoch, and others in another; they are expressions of the cosmic image or formal universe in which the various aspects of a civilization are stylized. "Thus the polarized rays of light, the traveling ions, the gaseous corpuscles that the kinetic theory on gases says escape and hurl, and the fields of magnetic force are only Faustian visions and Faustian symbols," that is, they belong to Faustian civilization. This type of Faustian physics is matched by a style of architecture and of music, namely, the Gothic cathedral longing for the conquest of space and the *fuga a più voci*. The same may be said about political or social forms, and so on. The whole historical becoming is worn out by the most radical and absolute relativism: a doom of catastrophe and death is inexorably hanging over every cycle of civilization. The type of formal universe in which modern Western civilization finds expression is the "Faustian man," who strives for the infinite while relying on himself. The hero of the Western world is Venüsberg's Tannhaüser, and Dante's Ulysses, and Goethe's Faust, who are the heirs of the master's pride and of the Vikings. Even the Faustian master's civilization, of conquerors and warriors, the civilization of the pathos of distances, is bound to decline. It already shows the signs of its decadence in the predominance of the world city over country life, in the prevalence of what is standardized and mass-produced over the spontaneity of instinct and of the immediate. Western civilization has passed from the primitive incandescent phase to that of crystallization. The decline of the West initiates the end of mechanical civilization. In fact, for the colored men (and among them Spengler includes the Russians)—they who will destroy Western civilization—the Faustian technique does not respond to an intimate need, but is only a weapon to fight against the civilization that produced it. The technique of the machine will end together with the Faustian man and some day will be destroyed and forgotten. Railroads, steamships, powerhouses and blast furnaces will be, in a not too distant future, rubbish and skeletons like fossils in archaeological cities.

It is evident that Spengler believed Germany's defeat in 1918 would be the signal for the beginning of the end of the Western civilization which he had identified with Faustian civilization. In the collapse of warlike Germany, which begot Faust, and in the victory of liberal and democratic middle-class nations he envisaged the whole West swept away. Spengler, however, was shortly to be disproved: once again the Faustian myth (which is not only German, but belongs to a good part of Western and non-Western civilization) unleashed a new war. We second Spengler's wish, and this is our earnest prayer, that the Faustian man may die in the blood he has shed and in the disorder he has caused. Only in this way will true and authentic civilization, which is not Faustian but Christian, not only Germanic but above all Roman and Neo-Latin, be able to survive. This will be the victory of the spirit and not the prevailing of the biological impulse, which takes man back to the level of flora and fauna.

However, it is time now that we leave historicism with Spengler and his shining paradoxes and move on to other positions of thought, more or less bound with the irrationalistic and vitalistic persuasions.[3]

3. THE NEO-KANTIANISM OF THE MARBURG SCHOOL: E. CASSIRER AND B. BAUCH

The Marburg and the Baden schools which have already been mentioned and to which B. Bauch belongs, though with some independence of thought, also represent the most notable positions in recent German Neo-Kantianism. Though diverse, the two schools have some fundamental theses in common, such as the rejection of metaphysics and the psychological method (that has been replaced by the "transcendental method"), and the negation of every intellectual intuition, as well as a radical gnosiological idealism (knowing is not apprehension of the object, but

[3] The theory of the "cycles of culture" and of history was taken up again, with more preparation than Spengler and against his determinism, but also with a dose of superficiality and charlatanism, by the Englishman Arnold I. Toynbee (1889), who in his ample work *A Study of History* (ten of the planned thirteen volumes of this work have been hitherto published) tries to determine the general laws that govern the development and the decline of civilizations. We consider it superfluous to warn that the "history of cycles" substitutes the idea of progress, which was a typical feature of the philosophy of history of the past century.

its creation), which eliminates "the thing in itself." The Neo-Kantianism of the school of Baden, as we saw, focuses its attention on culture in its historical development and, to this extent, it represents a current of German historicism; it prefers the *Critique of Practical Reason*, maintains that axiological laws are the foundation of objective being, and reveals a sensibility concerning religious and moral values which, at times, is really profound. The Neo-Kantianism of the Marburg school, instead, is decisively oriented toward logico-mathematical sciences; its preference is for the *Critique of Pure Reason;* it recognizes in transcendental deduction the vital and crucial point of Kantian criticism and brings everything back to the immanent logical laws of pure reason; the latter is a progressive development of judgments and through its activity the object is produced. There is nothing irrational in reality, and this is a texture of logical relations; there are no intellectual intuitions, but only concepts and logical combinations of concepts. Categories are conditions *a priori* of knowledge and they constitute the objectivity of judgments. These are objective and true when they are constructed in accord with the same categories, but are false when they contradict them. Evidently the Neo-Kantianism of the Marburg school shows little understanding of religion, which is reduced to ethics and this in turn is understood as a sort of logic of duty with an emphasis on its social character.

The most important representative of this school, besides H. Cohen (1842-1918) and P. Natorp (1845-1924), is ERNST CASSIRER (1874-1945), who attenuates its rigid and abstract logicalism while building a phenomenology of knowledge which is a philosophy of culture. However, he holds to some of the tenets propounded by this school, namely, methodological transcendental principle, regulative use of the idea, and close relationship between philosophy and positive science.

Cassirer is known and appreciated for some fundamental works on the history of philosophy (*Individuum und Kosmos in der Philosophie der Renaissance*, Berlin, 1927; *The Philosophy of the Enlightenment*, trans. F.C.A. Koelln *et al.*, Princeton, 1951; he is known also because of vast works with a prevalently theoretical interest (*The Problem of Knowledge*, trans. W. Woglom *et al.*, New Haven, 1950); and finally, because of works exclusively theoretical, such as *Substance and Function* (trans. W. Curtis Swabey *et al.*, New York, 1953); the three volumes of *The Philosophy of Symbolical Forms* (trans. R. Manheim, New Haven, 1953-1957), and *An Essay on Man*, New York, 1953, and others. In accordance with the tenets of his school, Cassirer holds history of philosophy and philosophy as well as science and history of science to be closely connected with each other; actually, some scientific achievements often have a philosophical value equal or even superior to those attained by philosophy proper, although the latter elevates to consciousness the logical means which science itself creates. Science depends on historical conditions and resolves in its process the philosophical categories which are its foundation.

Thus, science is relative but not purely subjective, even if its presuppositions have to undergo the course of history; and this is so because the becoming of thought makes possible new and ascending processes of scientific developments, within which it is ever possible to gain a new concept of the subject and of objective reality, both of which go through the same vicissitudes affecting the process of scientific experience. According to Cassirer, the "Copernican revolution" worked by Kant compels us to conceive the spirit as a synthetic act, and the act as a creative activity by which objective representation or organized experience is a work of our making. Therefore, language, art, science, philosophy, and so on, are not imitations of reality (realism), but our creations. The forms of judgments are the "living elements of the content of thought, which permeate the multiplicity of its particular formations and which manifest their activity in the creation and formulation of ever new categories." Thus, the "critical philosophy" of Cassirer extends beyond the theory of science in order to embrace the world of spirit or of culture, whose categories it investigates and defines: those pertinent to "psycho-spiritual reality" differ from the categories pertinent to the mathematical science of nature. Each category sets forth its own phenomenological field and constitutes a principle through which any form of culture is tested. *The Philosophy of Symbolical Forms* (*op. cit.*) supplies in fact a phenomenology of the spirit in the Hegelian sense (and also in Husserl's), wherein logic and metaphysics as well as spirit and its manifestations are in a Hegelian way identified with each other. Against realistic gnosiology (existence of a reality in itself to which the subject conforms), Cassirer, on the Kantian basis, develops his doctrine of *concept-function*, according to which function creates the object: "The fundamental form of judgment" is "the sole condition on which objectivity may be posited." Kant's Copernican revolution (priority of the function with respect to the object) is extended to the whole of spiritual activity and is new in every manifestation made by the latter. The "critique of reason" is changed into a critique or philosophy of culture, whose "being" is grasped historically in the "action." The different products of culture (language, science, myth, art, and religion) are "manifold endeavors, all aiming at the sole end of transforming the passive world of mere impressions, in which the spirit initially seems to be imprisoned, into a world of purely spiritual expression."

Cassirer calls the structural forms of culture *symbolical*, in the sense that every being is "conceivable and accessible only through and by means of the significant concept." The significance of the universal forms of expression of the spirit is discovered in the forms themselves since there is no criterion outside of them. Thus, myth, art, language, and so forth, are symbols in the sense that each of these forms "creates and produces, from within, its own world of significant reality." They are "organs" of reality which, as such, does not exist; only the forms produced by being have existence and they are definite ways of giving significance to reality itself. "Man does not live in a physical universe, but in a symbolical one. Language, myth, art, and religion are part of this universe. They are like numerous threads forming a symbolical fabric, which is the intricate fabric of human experience." On the whole, culture "can be described as the process of man's progressive self-liberation. Language, art, religion, and science are various phases of this process. In each one of them man discovers and demonstrates a new power, the power to build his own world, an ideal world." Man's unity is not ontological, but functional; it is the transcendental ideal of humanity.

As Cassirer draws nearer the Neo-Kantianism of the Baden school resting on historicism, so F. BRUNO BAUCH (1877-1942), though belonging to the latter, comes closer to the Neo-Kantianism of the Marburg school; in fact, he shares its radical transcendentalism, which consists in making the transcendental subject the center of all conditions affecting the object. Unlike other Neo-Kantians, he finds the true sense of Criticism in the third of the three Critiques, the *Critique of Judgment.* In his *Grundzüge der Ethik* (Stuttgart, 1935), his main theoretical work, "truth," "value," and "reality" tend to be identified with each other: truth is equal to reality and this is identical with value. Ultimately, there are only "transcendental relations" ("idealistic objectivism") which develop dialectically, that is to say, the laws presiding at the formation of the object are in perennial becoming. And even on this point Bauch joins Cassirer.

The Neo-Kantianism of Marburg that, in the last analysis, substitutes the logical functions for being, eliminates whatever is still metaphysical in Kant and follows the lines of Hegelian idealism, which fatally leads to the dissolution of being and, with it, to the negation of every value whenever it acquires a critical consciousness of itself. If the first Neo-Kantianism of Baden still seeks, because of its lack of critical awareness, to salvage the objectivity and eternity of values, and if the original Marburg Neo-Kantianism confines itself to the reduction of Kantian categories to laws of logico-mathematical thought—then the last Neo-Kantianism of Cassirer and Bauch, in response to the pressure of new currents in European thought, cannot avoid the consequence of identifying being with its function, which is attainable through its becoming and historical development; in this way, no longer is it possible to justify the validity of religious, moral, aesthetical, and cognitive values since they are reduced to mere categories or historical forms of culture. The negation of being implies the dissolution of every truth and reality. Upon acquiring a fully critical consciousness about their presuppositions, historicism and immanentism cannot but arrive at the same consequences (namely, that values and the history which expresses them are insignificant) arrived at by the so-called philosophers of nothingness and of the absurd, which characterize both the crisis and the criticism of historicism and immanentism. Let us further note that every time philosophy takes upon itself the method and object of science, thus becoming a methodology of scientific knowledge or of history, its approximation to Marxism is inevitable, as we have seen and shall have further occasion to observe later on. From this standpoint, historical materialism represents the coherence and clarity of historicism and immanentism that characterize modern thought from Kant onwards; from Kant, whose *Critique of Pure Reason*, as evidenced by the Neo-Kantianism of Marburg, is a methodology of physico-mathematical science, and, as such, a theory of knowledge denying the possibility of a metaphysical knowledge precisely because it resolves philosophy into science.

4. The Development of Neo-Kantianism in Italy: M. Maresca, A. Baratono, A. Renda

Italian Neo-Kantianism developed along lines differing from those of the Marburg school. As we have said, the structure of reality of which knowledge is a sort of framework (as Masci had conceived it in the order of Kantian thought) characterizes the extreme of idealism; and the main limit consists exactly in the initial affirmation of the identification of reality and actual thought. This limit was extended by MARIANO MARESCA (1884-1948), a pupil of Masci and a professor at Pavia University for much of his life. Although idealism eliminates the difficulty which confronts realism, viz., that the process of reality is indifferent toward our knowing and is outside of the spirit, nevertheless, it raises a more serious one because of its inability to explain the action of the will on spiritual development when the process of reality is identified with the process of knowing. Thus, Maresca sees the distinction between knowledge and will as fundamental; he substitutes the formula of the identity of thought and being with that of the unity of knowing and doing, in the sense that one has to distinguish between doing-knowing and doing-willing. Knowing is a form of reality but not absolute reality. He says, "When the process of reality reaches its climax into self-consciousness, it gives rise to the course of spiritual becoming, in which intelligence and will appear as aspects of a single procedure, wherein intelligence unifies a content produced by the creative will through its unconstrained activity." As one can see, Maresca's effort, more decisively than Masci's, aims at surpassing the schematic formalism of Kant and the static concept of the categories as immutable principles in their ideal nature. According to Maresca, therefore, no form of the spirit can present itself in a definitive nature and with a final orientation. All forms are creations of the spirit itself and through them spiritual life manifests the infinite capacity of its development, which cannot be constrained by any of its finite expressions (*Moralità e Conoscenza*, Rome, 1940).

Realistic and metaphysical exigencies eventually led the thought of ADELCHI BARATONO (1875-1947), a professor at Genoa University, to assume a wholly personal meaning.

In his *Critica e Pedagogia dei Valori* (Palermo, 1919), Baratono affirms, against Gentile's and Croce's monism, the necessity of a dualistic conception of the world, which is indispensable if one is to even think of any *value* whatsoever. Consequently, it is essential to have the dualism of subject-object, of thought-reality, and of what is and what ought to be. Dualism, however, posits the exigency of unification, which cannot be satisfied in that the transcendentality of thought is unable to equalize the Unity transcending thought itself. Transcendent unity can only be an act of faith and never a philosophical demonstration. Baratono noticed the insufficiency of this metaphysical agnosticism and later on sought to find the metaphysical solution of his problem in the aesthetical judgment. His *Il mondo Sensible* (Messina, 1934) remains the most complete formulation of this new attempt.

Thought does not grasp the sensible as sensible but rather as intelligible; in fact, the values drawn from the sensible transcend it. It can be said then, that thought does not grasp the value of the sensible *qua* sensible. On the other hand, is it possible to grasp the values of the sensibles as sensibles? This problem is not gnosiological but metaphysical. Gnosiology studies how the subject unifies experience into practical and theoretical categories; here, instead, experience must be considered as the foundation of the existent (being) not yet transcended in any theoretical value (what ought to be or the conceivable). Thus, in the sensible, one can find the basis for the existence of values in themselves. Gnosiology is subjectivistic (it has as its constitutive element the activity of the subject in the production of knowledge) and, therefore, it does not succeed in solving the problem of reality, which, as a metaphysical problem, can be solved through an idea capable of unifying value and existence, subject and object. Now, for Baratono, this idea that establishes a new metaphysics is the *aesthetical value*. It is "only within the criticism of the aesthetical value, that is, of a value immanent in the sensation as such that one can seek the existential proof concerning the spirituality of contents, *before* they become contents of logical and ethical ideas transcending them: the proof being that value exists and is realized in a real unity of form and content." Aesthetical and metaphysical problems coincide. In fact, as the value is realized in the sensibles, so the idea is manifested in the intuitive form. Thus, through the criticism of the beautiful, concludes Baratono, "it is evident that the sensible world besides having a theoretical content and being a practical means to ends transcending it, is thinkable in itself as a form of existence." The antinomy of the sensibles is solved.

The ethico-religious aspects of Kant's criticism are developed by ANTONIO RENDA (1875-1959), formerly a professor at the University of Palermo. In his work *Il Criticismo* (Palermo, 1927), Renda is resolutely "averse to any interpretation which attributes a final goal to the solution of the gnosiological problem, particularly when the solution is held as a basis for scientific knowledge." Against it Renda emphasizes the instrumental value, "wherein the *Critique of Pure Reason* appears to be directed toward ends which surpass the foundation of knowledge in order to arrive at a rational justification of the ethico-religious interests of the human spirit." For Renda, the problems of God, immortality of the soul and freedom find in Kant a decisive efficacy, not only on the religious and moral level but also on the gnosiological one.

From this interpretation of Kant, he derives his speculative position delineated in his work *Valori spirituali e realtà* (Messina, 1931). In it he maintains that the highest spiritual value is religious activity, which restricts the claims of all other forms of spiritual activity. The contrasts between ideal and real, will and law, freedom and determinism reoccur in gnosiology and ethics. Religion, instead, acquires the Absolute, for only in religion is the positivity of the finite denied, and a transcendent ideal world posited, no longer in opposition to a finite world but in an inner correspondence with being and with what ought to be.

Thus, through Renda, Italian criticism finds in religion that metaphysical unity of form and content, which had been the exigency posited by Masci. On the other hand, Maresca had avoided this unity by confining his thought to a position of mere criticism of experience, while other thinkers had sought it within the transcendence of values and, finally, Baratono, within the immanence of value in the sensation.

5. SIGMUND FREUD
AND PSYCHOANALYSIS

The roots of psychoanalysis are deep in biologism (Darwin's and Spencer's evolutionary materialism). Psychoanalysis is not a philosophical doctrine,

Sigmund Freud and Psychoanalysis

even if it has been elevated to a metaphysical conception of life by those who, besides being ignorant of philosophy, lack sensibility for the problems of spiritual life; moreover, as a pseudo-philosophy, psychoanalysis had and still has a large following, particularly with the masses in nations that are culturally immature. In fact, since the end of the First World War, psychoanalysis has met with a clamorous success principally in Anglo-American countries, to the point that one wishes that, for the good of humanity, the psychoanalyst would find a method for curing minds of the malady of their own doctrine, that is, "of the psychoanalysis complex" or "complex of complex." Their success, furthermore, furnishes proof of the moral decadence of our times, and is a sign of our bewilderment and of the weakening of our religious consciousness and taste for "good" philosophy. A fondness for what is fashionable and snobbish played its part in this success, wherein we also see the need of finding comfort by expelling faults and weaknesses from our conscience, thus securing an adventurous "evasion" into the realm of irresponsibility or into psychological abnormality. Within the scope of this work, psychoanalysis interests us not so much as a doctrine marginal to philosophy, but rather as a disedifying, though significant, indication of contemporary taste. Moreover, it represents one of the components (along with some currents of pragmatism, Marxism, neopositivism, existentialism, and so on) that characterize a conception of man, which must be emphasized without attenuations in order to understand clearly its presuppositions and consequences. A critical judgment regarding psychoanalysis (or any other doctrine) means both acceptance of whatever we have received as an asset from it, and rejection of whatever in it is found to be erroneous, grossly dogmatic, simple-minded, and naive.

The founder of psychoanalysis is SIGMUND FREUD (1856-1939), a physician, a university professor, and an author of several well-known volumes translated into many languages.

For Freud, "Zone of life" signifies a phase of psychological life which is not identified at all with conscious life. For him psychological processes are not necessarily conscious and knowledge of the self is not essential to psychological activity (as idealism claims when, for example, it postulates the identity between psychological fact and fact of consciousness). Freud maintains, on the contrary, that psychological activity is fundamentally unconscious and, therefore, its state of consciousness represents a transitory aspect rather than an essential and prominent character. "Consciousness is not the essence of psychic life; it is only a quality, an unstable quality which is absent more often than not" (*Psychoanalysis*, in The Standard Edition of the *Complete Psychological Works*, ed. J. Strachey, London, 1949, Vol. I.)

Psychological activity proceeds from the *subconscious*, a sort of center of tendencies, impulses, instinctive and elementary inclinations that moves man's thought and actions and causes man's feelings, behavior, sympathies and antipathies. We do not notice the influence of the sub-conscious upon our behavior both because of the pressure of our social and family environment and because we instinctively feel repugnance toward recalling to our consciousness unpleasant memories from our infancy. The subconscious, therefore, is derivation from the instinctive sphere of our psyche, but it must not be confused with it. It is an out-come of the "repression," of *réfoulement;* and all of us, some more, some less, are *réfoulés* (in this sense, that when "sublimation" is not successful, civil society creates neurotics). Having recalled attention to the subcon-scious is Freud's undeniable merit because with it he rectifies the idealistic abstractness which reduces the human psyche to the zone of conscious-ness alone. But he is responsible for having reduced the whole psychic activity to the sole play of unconscious forces of which conscious activity is only a negligible quality. Nevertheless, the subconscious and its im-portance in man's life are not the discovery of psychoanalysis. Without going too far back in history (Plotinus, for example), it suffices to remember that Leibniz and, above all, Rosmini in his *Psicologia,* rectify the abstractness of idealism just in this sense, but they do not deny con-sciousness and freedom. And, furthermore, the "psyche" is one matter while the "spiritual" is another.

Besides the subconscious, the other two phases or zones ("psychic systems" or "psychic instances"), within which psychological life progres-sively unfolds, are the *preconscious* and the *conscious,* each of which is governed by its own laws. The normal process of psychological develop-ment proceeds from the unconscious to the conscious; the process of involution in pathological degeneration follows the opposite direction. Consciousness, not being identified with psychological life, constitutes the latter's luminous zone, which is surrounded by the faint light of the preconscious and by the darkness of the unconscious. The passage from one psychic system to another encounters resistances which either hinder or stop it.

Psychic sanity exists when resistance is overcome and the process goes on normally; and psychic malady, when resistance impedes and arrests the process. For Freud, the *normal state* of the *ego* (the conscious process) consists in discovering "the means most favorable and least risky in order to satisfy our needs" in harmony with the external world and moral duties. In this normal and balanced state, the ego is in full control of itself, and so it neither thinks nor posits the problem of its origin from the unconscious. However, if order and balance are broken, and if a need imposes itself powerfully and is frustrated as a result of the restraints imposed by environment and morality, the ego then comes out of its normal state; and ignoring the origin and nature of its need, it remains in a state of unbalance and disorder. Thus the state of neurosis rises, which persists until the ego acquires an awareness of the unconscious generating it, and until the resistance has been removed; only then is normalcy regained. Hence, psychoanalysts use this method as a cure: the psyche is put into motion once again, that is to say, the unconscious motivations provoking the neurosis are made conscious. As Freud says, neurosis is "the consequence of a state of ignorance or lack of knowledge of the psychic processes of which one should be conscious." In the psychoanalytic method, then, the passage from unconsciousness to consciousness has a cathartic function and, as such, a useful one, inasmuch as it eliminates a disorder or abnormality by going back to the source (the repression) of an instinct or of an impression which, though it lies outside of consciousness, still acts upon the ego. It is ultimately a restoration of the personality, which frees itself of impediments and pathological complexes. This method conforms to a principle that is both philosophically and scientifically valid, viz., the study of the psychic malady in its formative process, in its origin and not in its last stage. Indeed, the unconscious systems cannot be described in terms of consciousness since they lack the space-time representation and present no difference between material and spiritual reality; nor are there doubts or contrasts but only *presences*. In short, consciousness understands better the preconscious than the unconscious systems.

Thus, Freud himself (*The Ego and the Id, op. cit.*, Vol. XIX) determines the relationship between the unconscious and consciousness: "An individual is for us an unknown and unconscious psychic *id (Es)*, to which the ego is superficially added" and this ego is "the part of the *id* that is modified by the direct influence of the external world through the conscious perceptions. . . . The ego strives to make the *id* respect the influence of the external world as well as its own intentions; it seeks to establish the principle of reality against that of pleasure which dominates within the *id* without impediment. . . . The *ego* represents what can be called reason and reflexive attitude, in opposition to the *id* which contains the passions."

The doctrine of the unconscious led Freud from the psychiatric standpoint to an innovation which, though well known to philosophical psychology, is nevertheless worthy of note: psychic maladies are not always due to a somatic alteration or injury. There are some psychic maladies showing no organic injury; they have a psychic origin and must be cured by means pertaining to the psychic order. Yet, it is anything but easy to reconstruct the involuted process of the psyche throughout its slow deformations. Is there a principle to which all alterations can be brought back as to their common origin? Yes; for Freud the unconscious zone is filled with an energy he calls *libido* or *principle of pleasure*. It is not easy to define what the psychoanalysts mean by this term; it is not yet the sexual instinct in its twofold forms of coupling and auto-eroticism (*narcissism*), but an undifferentiated state not translatable into terms of consciousness, an energy in which all the tendencies, which are commonly summed up in the word *eros*, converge. Sexual love is the main point, but not the only one since there is a variety of loves (of one's self, of parents, and of children), which are expressions of the same totality of tendencies, leading in some cases to sexual union and, in others, to the avoidance and impediment of it. The *libido*, in short, is "desire for pleasure," whereas lustfulness true and proper is its fundamental form. This desire for pleasure or satisfaction of needs is implacable in human nature: it burns like fire and erupts like lava. Like Schopenhauer's will to live, this desire is always thirsty for new gratifications, no matter how many of them it may get. Freud reduces the whole man (body and spirit) to this principle: man is placed on a purely animal level. When he encounters obstacles, he withdraws and inhibits himself while losing himself in the caverns of the unconscious, wherein he determines alterations, substitutions, and *sublimations*. Psychical forces spring from the abyss of the unconscious and they return to it when their course is hindered.

Psychoanalysts explain psychical maladies and neuroses on the basis of this principle of *libido* alone. These maladies, as we know, are caused by arrests or regressions of the psychical activity in its progress from unconscious to conscious; and the arrests, in their turn, are expressions of the conflict between *libido* and the impediments hindering its free gratification. According to the psychoanalytic method, curing a neurotic signifies, therefore, singling out the form of *libido* that caused the neurosis. The physician is assigned the task of interpreting the symbols into which the *libido* itself is translated. In view of this, the neurotic is invited to tell frankly what he is thinking, all his ideas, and "dreams" wherein the best clue is found; and this is done regardless of all restraints imposed by conscience. On this point (we do not question the possible advantages from a medical standpoint) psychoanalysis has fallen into gross and often grotesque exaggerations. Every dream, even the most naive, has been interpreted in the scarcely decent language of eroticism. For psychoanalysts, even children who dream of fairies, golden stairs, shining castles, angels and paradise manifest the deep, beastly nature of man; sexual instincts are hidden in the dream of the most beautiful and purest things, and in it the burning thirst of *libido* is fermenting in a highly diversified and often repugnant range. It is certainly known that Freud wrote a whole book on Leonardo da Vinci in order to show nothing less than that the art and life of that genius are explained by interpreting with indecent language a dream Leonardo himself recounted of his boyhood: a kite trying to open Leonardo's mouth with its tail.

With the theory of the *libido* psychoanalysis upsets a fundamental principle of moral life: that morality is the discipline of instincts and feelings according to rational norms; it consists in the elevation of man's being to what it ought to be. For Freud, instead, it is evil to repress the instincts because, once they are forced back into the underground of consciousness they erode the ground sustaining the equilibrium of psychical life. Thus, in order to avoid corruptions and alterations, it is necessary to give free vent to nature as it is, that is, to the principle of pleasure. Happiness consists precisely in the satisfaction of pleasure. If instincts must be sacrificed in order to be virtuous, virtue is achieved only by sacrificing happiness to it.

There is some truth in it: repression or restraining of instincts, impulses and natural tendencies alters the balance of the psyche, without elevating the spirit to the truly moral moment. Restraining sexual desires, for example, and trying to repress and overcome them is not surpassing them; this is, rather, confusing the conscience and becoming inhibited sensualists. Chastity does not consist solely in abstention through restraint (and maybe the desire is strong, upsetting inside, and really causes confusion and immorality), but it finds its true sense when it is an interior norm.

Freud, however, besides his unilateral reduction of the whole man to the principle of the *libido,* is wrong in not taking into account the fact that discipline is really something different from restraint, as it is from impediment: it consists in following a norm or rule, freely; it is not restraining or repressing, but directing. Once he had deprived man of his moral sense, he could not see that the moral restraint, with its spiritual and self-disciplinatory value, does not restrain but liberates.

For Freud and his followers (and in truth not only for them) there is only the *libido:* civilization, society, progress and history are determined through the restraint of instincts and, consequently, they are responsible for human unhappiness and for the perversions and corruptions in the psyche.

From this point of view, Freudianism is a revolt of the individual against society and civilization, which are impediments, that make him an inhibited being when they, like leaden capes, choke the fire of the primitive *libido* without extinguishing it. The individual, for Freud, is in a state of war with society because, as he writes, the latter requires "a good behavior without caring for the tendencies that are placed deep inside the individual"; and so society accustoms many a man to accept obedience and submission even when their nature is against. The repression exercised by civilized life generates, in this way, the most dangerous deformations in character. Furthermore, no one should think the majority of men is civilized just because it conforms to society; it is only hypocrisy. In order that the individual may live "according to psychological truth," there is only one remedy, "that he live according to his instincts against civilization and society." There is in Freud, from the above point of view, an "Adamism" or "primitivism" that is upside down when, for instance, it is compared with Rousseau's. This appeal to "return to nature" is not new in the history of thought; it responds to the ever resurgent nostalgia for a spontaneous and plain life, like the primitive one, outside all heavy social structures—a life that is free from historical traditions and cultural crystallizations, bursting violently and spontaneously like a flower from the swollen bud at the first rays of the sun in the spring. It is a motive that is very dear not only to Rousseau and other thinkers, but to many romantic writers (recall the romantic "freedom of nature"). But while for Rousseau this "return to nature" signifies reverting to man's primitive goodness and free development of his personality and, for romanticism, the affirmation of the spontaneous and genuine creativeness of spirit—for Freud, a medical psychiatrist, it signifies instead a return to the pure animality of man whose humanity is denied by the principle on which the entire Freudian theory rests. In a certain sense, some (I say "certain") pages of Nietszche—like a wind blowing into a fire—act upon Freud, but always by fawning on the baseness of the material level of life; hence, if the whole man stands on this level, it is hard to understand why Freud and the psychoanalysts insist on calling this life a "human" life. Indeed, within this Freudian instinctive animal one cannot recognize the man of flesh, bones, and spirit that everyone of us is—that man whom, fortunately, everyone of us sometimes encounters in himself as a comfort to his own dignity.

Manifestation of the *libido* and *deus ex machina* of Freud's entire doctrine is the "Oedipus-complex." [4] There is in the child "from the time of nursing, a tendency toward incest ("suckling" is a manifestation of it) and an aversion toward the father in whom the child sees a rival. The maternal breast is the starting point for the *libido*, which, through its development leads the child to see in its father an obstacle to be eliminated. Therefore, as Freud says, the first object on which man's sexual desire centers (on his mother or sister) reveals an incestuous nature— an inclination repressed only through severe prohibitions. Human civilization emerges from prohibition of incest. In the neurotic we can see the savage, the man of nature being agitated by contrasting desires and

[4] Freud interprets in his own way (thus showing to ignore or to misunderstand the real deep meaning of the Greek conception of the "tragic") the legend of Oedipus, who kills his father and marries his mother, and therefore he sees in the tragical episodes of the unhappy king what he calls the innate tendencies of man toward incest and hostility to father.

lacerated by ambivalencies. Being caught in the pincers of the Oedipus-complex, this savage is an incestuous animal who falls in love with his mother and murders his father. Against the brutal and ferocious chief of the horde, who takes the women for himself and kills the sons, a *clan* of brothers is made up, an association of sons killing their fathers. In order to preserve the established *clan*, the parricidal brothers adopt exogamy and worship the animal *totem*. The father, who has been hated and killed, becomes an ideal, and out of admiration for him comes the cult for the totemic animal in whose semblance this father is in fact being worshiped. Thus, for Freud, "human civilization slowly emerges from the turbid mud of the Oedipus-complex. Nasty beasts, with their ferocious stupor and disorderly lusts, are piled up in our past; and with their howlings and their horrible gestures, they would show up again behind the shirt-front and behind the puffy décolletés of refined societies, had not the *libido* been checked through a stratification of laws diverting it from its primitive aims." [5]

However, it is precisely this curbed and confined *libido* that arouses the ideals in the *ego* and, with them, human civilization. Some kind of "desexualization" and "sublimation" of the ego's instincts takes place, and so the Ego-Ideal (*Ich-Ideal*) or *Super-Ego* is born. The sexual libido, being directed toward the object, is transformed into narcissist libido, which turns to other ends. Typical in this sense is the poet. He is, for Freud, a narcissist: he does not direct his *libido* toward objects, but he turns it upon himself. The ego's contradictory tendencies and impulses lead to neurotic "perversion," but also to "sublimation." The sexual instinct, in fact, has precisely this capacity of transforming and diverting inhibited sensuality in its normal exercise by giving rise to the "superior" states, such as poetical inspiration and mystical love. Consequently, fondness for the good, beauty, and so on, is a transformed and sublimated sensuality. Likewise, man experiences the feeling of religious humility, by measuring the distance between ego and super-ego; and the feeling of guiltiness, by measuring the distance between exigencies in the moral conscience and manifestations of the ego. It has been wittily observed by A. Stocker in his *Psychologie du sens moral* (Genève, 1949, p. 160) that Freudian sublimation *"rappelle un peu l'hommage que le vice rend à la vertu de La Rochefoucauld,"* homage *"rendu par une psychologie vétérinaire à des superstructures morales. . . ."*

From what we have been saying about Freudian theories, herewith

[5] L. Giusso, *Tre profili, Dostoievski, Freud, Ortega y Gasset* (Napoli, Guida), p. 103. Like the primitive, to whom it is close, the child, according to Freud, is "purely instinctive"; and, like the primitive, it possesses the two main instincts of aggressiveness and sensuality (in the sense of search for pleasure). Consequently, its first love is all but tender: it is instinctive, aggressive, bossy, jealous; all of these manifestations find their explanation in the Oedipus complex.

considered only philosophically, a central point emerges, viz., the principle of human life is *biological,* that is, a complex, irrational, impulsive, blind, despotic force, which is qualified as *libido* in the widest sense of the word. Man is reduced to his instincts and his "impulses" (*Triebe*). Human activity is not the progressive and harmonious manifestation of the Idea or of the universal Spirit (Hegel); it is not a dialectical process changing antitheses and contrasts into harmonies, wherein goodness and truth are always positive, but it is an antithesis of elementary impulses, a recurrence of original ferocities within an alternation of inversions, deviations, and sublimations. The "all virtuous" man, the honest citizen and good father, the active carrier of an eternal reason and messenger of the Spirit, who does not know anguishes and contradictions or, knowing them, always victoriously overcomes them, and who praises himself in his own consciousness, is not the real man, but a mythical character first created in the century of enlightenment and then dressed up anew by the romanticist and idealistic fantasy. The real man is contrast, not harmony; blind instinct, not reason; greed for lust, not wisdom and virtue; one in eternal struggle with himself between his beastly primitive ego and society's conventional ego. Freud's man is two men in one: the "apparent" man, who is produced by reason and society through the coercion of his instincts, and the "deep," original man manifesting himself through dream, Oedipus-complex, neurosis and narcissism. He is a man who, dismissing the conventional protocols of conscience and breaking the artificial seals of society, bursts in like a beast and, being reformed by discipline, yearns to return to what he was, a pure instinct of ferociousness, and a freshly free eruption of *libido.* Dream, paranoia, and neurosis are only furious sallies of instinct breaking through the thick net of social norms—savage irruptions beyond the gates of conventional consciousness. These violent evasions produce a double effect: either the sublimation of the repressed *libido,* when the individual succeeds in turning it to other ends; or the neurosis and unbalance, when the individual yields to repression.

However, how does one explain sublimation? Mystery! Is it either a mystery or a contradiction from the standpoint of Freudian "pansensualism"? It is mystery, if civilization, history, and whatever is lofty in man represent nothing but transformed *libido;* or it is contradiction if, besides *libido,* Freud admits an autonomous reason directing and restraining it. Freud himself, however, excludes the latter hypothesis so that the mysterious sublimation of the unconscious is no longer explained in any plausible way. A world of spiritual values coming out of the dregs of lasciviousness, incests and family assassinations is an astonishing thing indeed. To pretend that primitive savages transform their cries of violence and their ferocious and beastly acts into the harmonies of the

Divine Comedy or into the charity of St. Francis of Assisi just by means of sublimation of the *libido,* and to maintain that *libido* itself is the sole basis of history—all this amounts to using fanciful alchemy and pretending to extract gold from what is only mud. "Sublimation," as Scheler properly remarked, ought to take place through the pressure exercised on the *libido* by society, moral laws, and so on. But it is precisely from sublimation that goodness, ideals of morality, and the like, ought to emerge as effects. This is where the contradiction lies: on the one hand, morality should be prior to and outside of *libido,* on which it would exert its influence; on the other, morality should spring from the very depth of *libido. Libido* is truly a mythological essence! [6]

In order to fight and overcome the abstractnesses of rationalism or modern idealism—which fancies processes on a straight line, as it also fancies infinite and flawless perfectibilities and idylls which, though dialectical, still are idylls of a faultless life free from evils—Freud (and not Freud alone) makes matter take the place of the spirit, and instinct and folly the place of reason. However, the reduction of anthropology to biology and the loss of the spirit and reason by no means signify that rationalism is overcome and that concreteness and fullness of man are reintegrated; it rather means the loss of man in order to find a biped who, being dumbfounded, cannot understand how his bestiality could ever create imposing structures of civilization and centuries full of history. Vindication of a spontaneous life and victory over mortifying and arid virtue are not obtained, as Freud believes, through a revolt of animal life against spirit and through the oppression of reason on the part of instinct, but through the elevation of life—of all life—to the height of the spirit itself. From this height, the beast that is likewise in man can be really dominated, and the deficiencies of the Freudian conception of life—one of the darkest and most pessimistic theories—can be made evident.

Freud's is one of the most inhuman of doctrines. It was justly written that his theory is "the most profound analysis of the least human elements in human nature that history records." There is no animality of man without spirit, nor one that is disjoined and separated from the spirit. It is true that man is man and not an angel and, that as man, he is body and instinct, too; but, to consider him simply as a purely animal instinct it amounts to holding him only as a beast. The Freudian man, in this sense, is *inhuman.* To say that the spirit is transformed or sublimated instinct is *naïveté* and also a slander which destroys man's humanity. In Freud's biologism there is room neither for the ethical sense nor for moral conscience, to which a low origin is assigned. In it there is room only for animal-vegetative life. Freud's man belongs to zoology, because what-

[6] M. Scheler, *Wesen und Formen d. Sympathie,* p. 239.

ever is human in him is an artificial product that is imposed by society. Freud stands for the violent negation of spirit and freedom; his generalizations of *libido* are inexplicable, gross and baseless; his drawing the spiritual values from instinctive, psychical functions, and his determinism are arbitrary. Those few fragments of truth—which we did not fail to emphasize—must be salvaged (in that they are scientific data and because truth must be accepted wherever it may be found) from the accumulation of philosophical errors in which they are submerged.

Psychoanalysis, a "psychology without a soul," as it has been well defined by Stocker, is not the only anthropology to make of man only a slightly more-evolved animal, but nonetheless an animal, all body without spirit, whose so-called soul is only a reflection of the aspirations and needs of the body. Let us recall Feuerbach's definition: "Man is a conscious body." And let us also remember that for the same Feuerbach and Marx, morality and religion have come into being only as superstructures of the economic or "material" edifice. Both for Marx and Freud man is a desire to satisfy material needs; both maintain that sentiment and values, the so-called spiritual things, are born from the free play of these needs and are only superstructures and epiphenomena; both identify freedom with liberation from material needs. For Freud, this goal is attained in a society in which man's primitive instincts are to be free and unimpeded; for Marx, this is attainable through a homogeneous society. From the standpoint of the conception of man, every Freudian can become a Marxist and a communist (indeed, he is one already whether he is aware of it or not) without feeling deprived of anything essential to him as a man, and without feeling offended in his humanity and in his superior aspirations. In fact, Freudianism, like Marxism, is the negation of the human in man. Yet, how many are there (particularly in the northern and English-speaking countries) who, while accepting Freudianism (and I am not just referring to professional psychologists and psychiatrists), regard Marxism and communism with horror, so that they declare themselves sincere defenders of freedom and of human values! What values are there in a man without a soul? These people do not seem to be aware of having accepted an anthropological conception that is inhuman and contrary to every religious principle and freedom.

6. ORTEGA Y GASSET
AND THE "RAZÓN VITAL"

Within the vast current of so-called *Lebensphilosophie*, of which we have spoken more than once, we shall insert the *perspectivismo* or *raciovitalismo* of the Spanish essayist JOSÉ ORTEGA Y GASSET (1883-1955). Ortega was a professor of philosophy at Madrid and author of numerous essays gathered under the title *El Espectador* (*in Obras Completas,* Madrid, 1946-1947); of the *Meditations on Don Quixote* (trans. E. Rugg *et al.,* New York, 1961); of the *The Modern Theme,* his most significant philosophical writing (trans. J. Cleugh, London, 1931); of the *The Revolt of the Masses* (trans. anonymous, London, 1961); and of the *Invertebrate Spain* (trans. M. Adams, New York, 1937), in which he also proves himself to be a writer of great merit.

In spite of Ortega's claims to absolute originality, his thought is German-inspired (Fichte and Nietzsche on one side, Dilthey and Simmel on the other); it also shows traces of Bergsonian and pragmatist influences. After taking his doctorate at Madrid, Ortega studied at the University of Berlin where Simmel occupied an academic chair; he also studied at Leipzig and Marburg where he heard Cohen. Simmel's influence is direct, while that of Dilthey is indirect. Ortega's "perspectivism" is Simmel's "relativism" thought through again, but more in accordance with historicism because of Dilthey's influence, I believe. Even if we grant that Ortega did not know Dilthey's work until several years after the publication of *The Modern Theme* (*op. cit.*), the indirect derivation from Dilthey is undeniable because of the latter's vast influence on German thought at the very time when Ortega was in Germany. Ortega's *razón vital* is a "rethinking" of Dilthey's *historische Vernunft.* Thus, Ortega's "rational vitalism" stands between the relativism of Simmel and the historicism of Dilthey. However, it bears Ortega's personal mark even if it is not highly original in thought. In fact, to advance an idea (in this case, the "idea of life") means demonstrating it philosophically and not merely reconsidering it through the use of a new and personal style. It seems to me that Ortega clearly perceives some problems in contemporary thought without, however, resolving them philosophically. This requires the possession of a fine sensibility for philosophy (especially if philosophy is seen under the cultural and historical aspect—the least philosophical one); but it does not yet mean possessing a mind truly capable of producing philosophy.

Ortega's perspectivism presents itself as a criticism of idealism and realism, a criticism that, according to its author, solves the problems in both. Things, inasmuch as I know them, are not independent from me; and idealism is right in sustaining that things are in relationship with the subject; but there is no subject (ego) without things, and thus realism is correct in positing its question. Therefore, I am necessary to things and things are necessary to me or, as Ortega says, with an expression defining the focal point of his thought: *yo soy yo y mi circunstancia* (*Meditations on Don Quixote, op. cit.*). This is the prime reality, the *realidad radical* (that is, the one in which everything else "takes its root"), the one represented by the ego with its circumstance, by which I am I and the things which surround me (*circunstancia*) are things related to my ego. This radical reality is *life,* not a thing that is but a thing that *is made.* Life is activity or action in the world; it is not a being, but a doing. My life must be made by myself and I am responsible for it. Infinite possibilities are open before me; yet, to live is to choose and to carry things through; and that is what freedom consists of. "To be free signifies to be lacking a constitutive identity, not being ascribed to a determinate being, being able to be other than what one used to be, and being unable to install oneself once and for all in any determinate being." Ortega denies decisively that reality (life) has a substance. In short, the "being" (*ser*) of human life is its "becoming" (*hacerse*); and its reality is *history;* man is what he makes himself; he creates his form. Life is spontaneous, a free expansion of energy; it is not a forced and necessitated movement, but a free play, an unforeseeable appetite. This is vitalism, indeed, but not the positivistic and naturalistic or biological vitalism dominated by utilitarianism and adaptation and determined by the principle of self-preservation and self-defense. Ortega, too, is Nietzsche's son to a large extent: like Nietzsche, he exalts the vital tone, the unforeseeable, the risky, the barbaric. As an effective writer, he affixes his signature on the proscription-lists of all the absolutes, of reason and theology as well, and of science and progress. For Ortega, rational man is the same abstraction as mechanical man; the "organic man" is the only real and concrete one. It is necessary to make culture concrete and to reconsecrate life—culture must be dominated by life and not *vice versa.*

History, which is shaped according to the ages of human life or *generations,* develops through two phases: *ascending life* and *descending life.* The former coincides with the epochs of rejuvenation, with a fondness for warlike and sporting attitudes, and with understanding for barbarians and primitives. Passion for fighting, fondness for the aristocratic and the chivalrous, and a liking for the risky predominate in it. In the descending life, instead, the tribune prevails over the leader, middle-class comforts over the martial spirit, and mean utilitarianism in business and trade over the adventurous life of a soldier and of a knight errant. This is what marked the civilization of the second half of the nineteenth century, a civilization consisting in banks and markets, one that waged a war against all wars—and one that preferred a contract to honor and a speculator to a soldier and a sportsman. Ascending life, on the other hand, "is that which feels that its spiritual action springs from a torrent of energy, that which does not perceive its own limitations, and that which moves with a fullness of energy. This is a vital climate in which envy, small grudges, and petty resentments are not usually found. On the contrary, in other men (namely, in those who are in the descending process) one can perceive a constant impression of constitutive feebleness, of insufficiency, and of want of trust in oneself." The ascending man would rather gamble with the dangerous forces of life, because risk is the first article in his statute and death is nothing but an incident in his sporting career; and so Ortega extols sportive and warlike epochs. This explains the great importance he attributes to games and sports ("life is a matter of flutes") as well as to aristocratic *élites;* this also explains his criticism of democracy, his revaluation of the mediaeval castle and mediaeval honor, and his sympathies for the epochs of generous barbarism. It is precisely the bellicose civilizations—more worthy than those which center on the city square and on the market—that prepare the so-called superior epochs of culture. It is in the generous heart of the barbarian and savage, as in the clubs of young sportsmen, that aristocratic values of risk and struggle abide. To live means to be confident in oneself, not to hesitate on dangers but face them, and play the game of life while being prepared to lose it. "Sporting activity seems to us to be the creative and fundamental activity, the loftiest, most serious, and most important part of life; work, instead, takes the second place as something derived from it—a by-product. Indeed, properly speaking, life abides only in the first activity; the rest is relatively mechanical and a mere functionalism."

Neither great asceticism nor obedience to common life norms must be asked of an ascending man. Moreover, there is no exceptional man or "great politician" (like, for instance, Mirabeau, on whom Ortega wrote the essay *Mirabeau; o, el político,* Madrid, 1927) without a good dose of amorality. "The political man needs a substratum of organic conditions, which appear monstrous once they are isolated. Such soundness of instincts and such rich generosity are present in all the biographies of great makers of history, and they permit one to distinguish truth from falsity, Sulla from Caesar." Mirabeau, a great politician, was in need of debts and orgies, a man of bull-like virility. A stormy activity is characteristic of the politician; he has to destroy in order to create, that is, in order to create the State whose origin is "sportive." For Ortega, even art is a game. He is against the morbid and emotional art of romanticists, as he is against the art which is engaged in the conquest of the absolute by idealistic philosophers. Art is "contemplation, not impulse; that is, it presupposes a distance between the seer and what is seen. Beauty, the supreme distinction, requires that distances be kept. It is an error to believe that the worth of a work is measured by its capacity to fascinate and penetrate the subjects by violence."

Granting that man makes himself essentially through his *circunstancia* so as to be a historical entity, each man is a *point of view* that is unique; and since there is no reality in itself, the point of view and reality make up a whole. Reality is an "infinite number of perspectives," as many as there are men; in itself and "independently of the point of view from which it is observed," reality lacks "a physiognomy of its own." In this radical perspectivism there is no truth that is not historical and historical alone; even God is only a point of view. And in this lies, according to Ortega, his (and, unfortunately, not only his but also that of many others before and after his time!) "radical reform of philosophy," which had been "abstract and 'super-temporal' " and which this Spanish writer believes to have made "concrete and historical" while, in reality, he only annihilated it into history and culture. However, with one of the many contradictions consonant with him (and with which he seems to be pleased), Ortega affirms that man needs a supreme truth and that this is given to him by philosophy.

Ortega, undoubtedly, points to a just exigency, which he calls *el tema de nuestro tiempo,* consisting in solving the antinomy between "pure reason" and "vital impulse" in order to salvage both of them. Reason without life is empty, but life without reason is blind. According to Ortega we must proceed from a "living reason" which results from the "combination" of "pure reason with life" (Rational-vitalism). Very well. But, besides the fact that this "theme confronting our time" had already been presented by so many and given some significant philosophical answers long before Ortega presented his own in 1923, the problem still remains unsolved even through Ortega's historical perspectivism. At the outset, in fact, Ortega denies one of the two terms, that is to say, reason, since the latter is absorbed by *life;* and life itself is nullified since it is fragmentized in an infinite number of points of view. It makes no sense to continue to speak of a reason that must illuminate life or of a life that is blind without reason, when the latter has been emptied of the truth with the capital "T." The logico-mathematical abstract rationalism (which is the "scientific" not the "metaphysical" moment of philosophy) extinguishes life into reason; Ortega and so many others with him for over a century "toy" playfully at killing reason in life; and they inevitably kill the human essence in man's life, if reason must be understood as "concrete" reason, as "spirit," which is more than reason, but is not without reason. It is very difficult to be convinced that Ortega does not deny reason and truth, in the last analysis, when one can read that "after twenty-five centuries of mental training aimed at getting truth *sub specie aeterni,* we must start all over and develop an intellectual technique wherein we can understand it *sub specie instantis.*" In this case, then, Pascal's aphorism that thought is a "very ridiculous hero" is to be taken literally, though with a meaning not intended by Pascal. In fact, what else can be said about thought if after twenty-five centuries of such a laborious and, in this case, such a useless mental training we must start thinking all over again. We may even assume then that after another quarter century (time moves so fast nowadays), we shall be compelled to start anew once more in order to develop a technique capable of uncovering truth *sub specie absurdi*, since such is the inevitable consequence flowing from a reality that is discovered *sub specie instantis*.

Ortega views all philosophical problems *sub specie instantis;* and this explains why he states one thing in one of his writings and then writes the opposite in another. He cannot even be accused of being in contradiction, because contradiction occurs only in an order of ideas developed with rigorous coherence. On the other hand, Ortega is a brilliant writer, vibrant and intelligent, not a philosopher—an intuitive, not a systematic thinker. In almost every page of his writings one can find an idea which, though perhaps said by others, is lived through in an original way by him. Ortega is nonsystematic; he gets hold of an idea and makes it his own; that will do, and he does not go any further; he is a great writer of philosophical questions without the temper of a philosopher. He is one of the very well-read authors, but one who exerts no influence on the course of philosophical ideas. In fact, his production, so well known within the Spanish-speaking world, has had little effectiveness in the field of philosophy, and in Spain itself has been confined to a narrow group of scholars. On the contrary, as a writer and a renovator of culture, he has had a great influence. Deservedly so, because as a writer he is of the first order and as a stimulator of intellectual life he has done so much (through the *Revista de Occidente* and his library), even if unilaterally since he remained attached to German philosophical culture.

Ortega provokes problems, gives starting points and suggestions. Let us not ask more of him, and he should not pretend to give more. He is an essayist, not a systematist; the *metafísica de la razón vital* does not exist in his books, nor could it be found there. As conceived by Ortega, the *razón vital* with its infinite points of view, which are all "equally true and authentic" like Pirandello's *Six Characters in Search of an Author,* in search of a philosopher that is, who can make them true and authentic within Truth—the great maker. There can be no perspectivism without an absolute point of view, as there can be no philosophy of culture nor philosophy of history without philosophy, that is to say, without metaphysics, which Ortega condemned to death. He tells us, after so many others have done the same, that the fullness of life must be carried on to a maximum, and that living is *vivir más.* Granted! But, live for what? Life? Living for its own sake so that we may love *sub specie instantis,* without any norm, and without an absolute end? It is impossible to understand that reason can enlighten life and prevent blindness. The truth is that for Ortega, as we know, knowledge comes from life so that the relationship is reversed. It is life guiding reason, and not reason (truth), life, and life ends up filling itself with itself, that is, with its own blindness. It is one thing to say that the process of human knowing is historical, and another that truth itself is historical. These two things are not distinguished by Ortega. There is indeed a "historicity" about truth, in that truth "is discovered" in, and manifested through, history; but there is no "historicism" about it in the sense that truth is the sole product of history. The first one is concrete truth remaining immortal in its essence and independent of time through which, however, it reveals itself; the other is neither concrete nor abstract in that it no longer exists; it has disappeared in time, in one of the infinite perspectives.

Like Unamuno, with his views Ortega wanted to give a new impetus to life in Spain, and a new structure to this "invertebrate" country. Although he acknowledges that democracy possesses a vital tone, he is nonetheless against democratic morality which rests on equalization and universal suffrage, just as he is against the decrepit Spanish aristocracy. "To give Spain vertebrae and a new structure signifies to arouse in it some energies coming from industry, commerce, intellectuality, and political or military capacity. Spain suffers on account of the absence of her best people. Her trouble is that professional *élites,* having an awareness of their rights and duties and knowing how to bow to superior ideals of sacrifice and responsibility (which once animated the knights of the *Reconquista*), are no longer made there. Spain lacks active and exemplary individualities, able to organize by taking those knights as a model. Spain is the reign of anonymity, of a confused multitude, of disarticulation, and of particularism. The country lacks scientists and technicians, great ladies and strong political personalities, after whose style crowds are shaped and advanced." We do not share at all this negative judgment concerning Spain, even regarding what the country is today. Spain is not a "confused multitude," nor is she lacking great individualities. On the contrary, Spain is the land of "great individualities" who, unfortunately, remain aloof. It is a good thing that they are "great individualities" but it would be better if they were less individualistic (and as for "individualism," Ortega himself is an eloquent example). As regards the word "invertebrate," would Ortega like to correct this situation by substituting Spain's strong bones, which have the marrow of perennial truths coming from Reason and Revelation, with the feeble elements drawn from an infinity of subjective points of view? Spain would soon cease being *España y su circunstancia* and the great mine holding in custody those truths that allow us to "grasp reality *sub specie aeterni*"; it would also lose time and history in the "instant." It is precisely these centuries-old vertebrae still remaining in Spain (and not Simmel's relativism or Dilthey's historicism) that permit Ortega to posit the problem of the relation between *élites* and masses in a way that deserves consideration. Against democracy he advocates the organization of aristocracy and science in order to save civilization from the pressure coming from the masses, which have been exalted by universal suffrage and other conces-sions. The advent of the masses and their direct action would be a calam-ity to the West. It is necessary and urgent, therefore, to have the sense of hierarchy and command restored; and this sense alone is capable of forming the masses and giving them orderly progress. We concede that; but, what is there left to save in the West if everything is historical and unrepeated, as Ortega claims? Why should it be saved if everything must be discovered *sub specie instantis?* There are only perspectives, those of today and those of tomorrow. Destroying all these perspectives and with them the West itself (where the sense of truth and eternity has been lost), is a question to be considered by history. The latter will be able to account for many things, including the perspectivism with which Ortega has imprudently identified the "radical reform of philosophy."

7. Minor Forms of Irrationalism in Germany: L. Klages and Neo-Romanticism

We would have to go on for a good while if we were to give an ac-count of all the minor, small, and very small writers and all the more or less secondary currents that are characterized by vitalism, relativism, and irrationalism. But this would not be worthwhile. The motives are always the same and they are repeated with an exasperating monotony, a real mortification for these iconoclasts of what is uniform, orderly and ra-tional. Yet, we cannot remain silent about some writers who have gained notoriety in the scholarly world or with the large reading public to a greater or lesser degree. Thus, to the already long list we shall add the name of another German, LUDWIG KLAGES (1872-1956), who also follows Nietzsche and Simmel. There is in Klages a great desire to go back to nature, the ancient mother, in order to hear the genuine and familiar language of things, now become deaf and silent. He couples his nostalgia for the comfortable atmosphere of fauna and flora with a curse upon intelligence, the will, and all the forces that snatched man away from his Mother, only to cast him into a life that is a desert. Like Leo-pardi's shepherd, Klages envies animals, plants and inanimate things for their blessed unconsciousness and infallibility of instinct as well as for their sureness and full possession of existence—the eternal problem to man. Thus, in the usual and customary way he reacts against rationalistic schematism and scientificalism in order to exalt the creative spontaneity of life, that is rich and fecund.

In his *Der Geist als Widersacher der Seele* (Munich, 1954) Klages says that the person is divided by the opposition between *soul* and *spirit.* The soul is a cosmic participation, while the spirit is a reflection on life that kills life. The soul listens to the beat of universal life and seizes it in its unceasing *rhythm*, which is the essence of every form of life; the spirit, instead, unlike the soul, does not live this rhythm but only judges it, introducing into it a *beat* that breaks the perennial flow of phenomena. As a vital process of this rhythm, life is then grasped not by the spirit but by the soul; life is present in the frenzied dance of the primitives, but lacking in the beat of the spirit which suspends life and ends by killing the rhythm. To capture life in its original rhythm means to suspend the spirit, go upstream once again, and place oneself in extra-spiritual nature. The soul alone has the capacity to live the cosmic life in its intricacy of resonant rhythms without beats and arrests—a magic passage of forms from body to body and a flowing becoming.

The person, says Klages, is an indivisible vital unity in which "the soul is the sense of the corporeal phenomenon, and the body the phenomenon of the soul." The person's tendency is to be projected outwardly and have the soul really transferred into nature. But danger lies in this "being projected": if the spirit predominates, the soul becomes a mould of phenomena and a scientific activity. The flow of images is crystallized in the concept of things and so the genuine sense of reality is lost— spirit kills life. Thus Klages presents again what we already know, the conflict between spontaneous forms of life and reflexive forms of the spirit, between the categories of the spiritual objectivity (art, morality, and science) and the vital tension of experience. But what is a life devoid of any spiritual form whatever? Isn't the spirit itself richness and life too? Why, then, we ask Klages, do we not place perfection in the life of beasts and vegetables, which are entirely soul in the bio-vitalistic sense of this term?

As a glorifier of Instinct, Passion, and Nature against Intellect, Reason, Duty, God, and so forth, irrationalistic vitalism is led to these extreme and absurd conclusions by its illogical logic. A proof of this is supplied by so-called German Neo-Romanticism. The latter, in fact, has fallen into hylozoism and astrology, thus signifying a return to pre-Socratic forms of philosophy, namely, to a World-Soul, of which things and men are ephemeral incarnations or sparkles that shine for an instant in the heaven of the Whole, only to be absorbed again in the infinite fire (even in this respect, it follows Nietzsche faithfully). On earth man is a pilgrim waiting to go back into the bosom of Nature; he is a desperate knight fighting against Reason, which through its abstractions prevents him from living life; man is nostalgic, longing for the restoration of his divine essence and for the overcoming of all the errors that keep him away from his vital source. Such is the line of reasoning followed by LEOPOLD ZIEGLER (1881)—one of the new romanticists. According to him the individual ego is able to attain the power of the super-ego or

God by means of a dialectic that transcends any logic precisely because it is contradictory. The same thing is said by the well-known popular writer HERMANN KEYSERLING (1880-1946, whose name is linked to Ziegler's), who embraced magic and occultism with his conception of the genius as a vehicle of God on earth. The Neo-Romanticists also exalt the heroic vision of life, that is grasped in its tragic and religious sense, and they detest bourgeois life for being calculating and utilitarian. As Ziegler says, it is necessary to make a God out of man. All agree in opposing Catholicism, which according to them has extinguished Christian mysticism by pouring into the evangelical wine pailfuls of icy water drawn from Greek and Roman rationalism. All hold themselves to be teachers of life and of wisdom as well as prophets of new eras and great years ahead; all claim to be messianic and apocalyptic, whereas in reality they all possess a good dose of amateurism and, at times, charlatanry.

8. Minor Currents of Irrationalism and Relativism in France: L. Rougier, J. de Gaultier, H. de Montherlant

In general, the exaggerations just mentioned have been avoided in France, except for some philosophical writers (though not of the first order); among these a special place is held by LOUIS ROUGIER, a student of history of philosophy and author of the *Les paralogimes des rationalisme* (Paris, 1920), a book having a following and enjoying some success. Rougier brings out of the arsenal of skepticism and empiricism (the only two currents he respects) all the old and new weapons capable of fighting against rationalism and metaphysics. Except for skeptics and empiricists, he considers all the other philosophers from Plato to Hegel as rationalists. According to Rougier, in fact, all systems have in common an order of eternal and necessary truths *a priori*, that are enclosed either in a transcendent God or in the vast depth of a universal Spirit accessible to us through our reason. "Platonism" has up to now acted as a master and dominated our mentality. Thus, fighting against rationalism amounts to hitting the target and mercilessly destroying Platonism itself and, with Platonism, the very tenacious belief in a reason that is one and undivided in each man. For this reason, Rougier, more by sophistry than dialectical strength, does his best to demolish the centuries-old work of philosophy, to unmask the misunderstanding of reason, and to mortify the ontological mentality. Realism, which is a natural metaphysics of the human spirit, is for him the "tendency to barter the concept of a real object for one that is equivalent and adequate to this object and also to exclude from this object that which is not included in the definition of its concept." He goes on to say that being is "the most fantastic abstraction of all," and after so many destructions and catastrophes he leans toward a form of empiricism that is very close to a new positivism. Thus, this superficial iconoclast of every rationalism and metaphysics gladly places himself in the arms of a worn-out form of rationalism and metaphysics. These thinkers who oppose metaphysics because of its systematic character make themselves coherent systematizers and intransigent dogmatists of relativism, historicism, and irrationalism. They oppose the metaphysics of Platonic idealism and that of Hegelian idealism, while they themselves expound a pseudo-metaphysics of their own that stands between skepticism and empiricism; and according to it, values are degraded into fact while moral and logical principles are dissolved into contingency in the name of a "philosophy of life," which is the death of philosophy, and the philosophy of death as well.

In correspondence with a thoroughly romantic irrationalism, the French writer, JULES DE GAULTIER (1858-1942), sets forth his theory of life hinging upon the distinction between *Messianic sensibility* and *spectacular sensibility* in his essay, "Le monde comme volonté de représentation" (in *Revue de Philosophie*, Vol. LXXVI, 1913), which is a paraphrase of Schopenhauer's famous work. According to messianic sensibility, the world is imperfect, though constantly proceeding toward a better state— a day will come in which harmony and perfection will reign on earth. According to spectacular sensibility, instead, the world is not progressing from imperfection to perfection or from evil to good; it is already all possible perfection in every moment. Thus, evil and pain are necessary elements of the picture, as shadows are to light, so that this may stand out. From the standpoint of spectacular sensibility, the world is a great spectacle, a drama being made in every moment by men with their joy and their suffering, with their hatred and their love. However, he who considers the world as a spectacle outside of human passions sees only the succession of actors on the stage of life and applauds everyone who plays his part well. Everything is joy for this calm spectator. Even the purpose of life, for Gaultier, consists only in its manifesting itself, in its being a spectacle to itself. At the root of all things lies an irrational force that, out of mere whim, makes some men actors, and others mere spectators; the former are excited by passions while the latter remain free. The world, therefore, is the "will to representation, a systematic and colossal hallucination, whose object is to stage a spectacle for a spectator." The world, in fact, is the spectacle that the Absolute creates to itself in every act of its life. We are actors unaware of this drama, and we must accept our part and recite it with resignation. Life is a vital illusion, which some men, as actors, accept willingly even with all its sufferings, while others contemplate it calmly as spectators. According to Gaultier's "spectacular idealism," the world is then a pure phenomenon, a spectacle staged by an irrational force that predestines actors and spectators out of mere whim. In it lies the consequence wherein things exist only in consciousness, and wherein subject and object are real only in their reciprocal relationship. Thus knowledge is always relative. Another paradoxical consequence is that, if there is no knowledge outside of this relationship, each man knows himself differently from what he is—not as he is as an object, but as he appears in relation to the subject. Gaultier calls his philosophy *Le Bovarysme* (Paris, 1902) because he thinks that a perfect application of this theory can be found in the famous novel by Flaubert.

The same tragic and pessimistic vision (indeed one that has only a purely aesthetical meaning like Gaultier's) is in HENRI DE MONTHERLANT, the poet of sports and the exalter of rounded and strong muscles and of the rhythmical flesh of female and male athletes. He sees in sports (as already Ortega and many other lovers of vitalism for its own sake) an exaltation of life and an inebriation of pure action—action for the sake of action, for the pure pleasure of acting and moving, an all-free action without reason, and a meaningless one with respect to all ends, viz., "Search, even knowing that the problem is insoluble; work smilingly for the sake of the ideal for which the work is done; win aimlessly and without usefulness; serve and be thoroughly convinced that work has no sense; recognize, understand and endure all that, always keeping the painful and useless conviction of being right. Furthermore, it is necessary for me to gain a firm point whence I can take off toward the skies by overcoming myself. But how and with what means? Through the soul, as madness dictates, I throw myself in the arms of absurdity—O soul!" All Montherlant's theatrical characters are also "in search of an author." Their drama consists in their being always at a loss because of incomprehension and the invincible solitude ensuing from it: "Live your life as if you believed in it," but without really believing in it; otherwise, it would become a serious thing and the fresh and thoughtless joy of its sublime inconclusiveness would be wasted.

9. RELATIVISM AND IRRATIONALISM IN ITALY: A. ALIOTTA, A. TILGHER, G. RENSI

Notwithstanding the world-wide fame of both Bergson and pragmatism and regardless of the vigor of historicism and relativism, Italy has kept her distance from all the excesses of vitalism and irrationalism, at least in the field of philosophy. This is due to the sound Latin equilibrium and to the vigorous spiritualistic and metaphysical traditions of Italian thought, as well as to the strong influence exerted by Gentile's actualism, which is essentially logical and metaphysical. Relativism and irrationalism had their conspicuous representatives, however, even in Italy.

The most important exponent of Italian relativism is ANTONIO ALIOTTA (1881), a professor at the University of Naples, a clear writer and an effective critic. A declared enemy and opponent of all forms of intellectualism and of all dialectical games, he has always avoided the unilateral and extreme positions of positivism and idealism, of rationalism and irrationalism. When the various intuitionist currents were conducting their campaign against science and reason, he took part in the dispute with his important work *The Idealistic Reaction against Science* (trans. A. McCaskill, London, 1914) in order to vindicate the rights of scientific and intellectual knowledge; when new forms of realism denied the function of the subject in the knowing process, he intervened in defense of subjectivity—the irrepressible element in the act of knowing. When Italian Neo-Hegelianism reduced the object to a moment of the spirit's creative activity, he stressed the fact that the objective element in knowledge cannot be eliminated.

After studies on experimental psychology and aesthetical problems under Schelling's influence (notable is his criticism of Croce's *Aesthetics*), Aliotta, a pupil of Del Sarlo, elaborated his original position during the crisis of the First World War, when he was influenced by Anglo-American pragmatism and by Bergson. His book *Guerra eterna e il dramma dell'esistenza* (in *Opere Complete*, Rome, 1950-1954) already contains the whole of his thought.

The fact as attained in experience constitutes the real in all its living concreteness and to transcend it is absolutely impossible for us; this fact is the whole reality. "What we perceive is not the manifestation of something that is more real, for it itself constitutes reality, about which we cannot doubt without, at the same time, doubting the existence of the world revealed to us through those phenomena." The "concrete act of experience" contains in itself the subjective-objective aspects as necessary moments that are distinct though united in a living synthesis. Unity "is given us in the very act of consciousness in which subject and object are never separated since they live only in their concrete relationship with each other." Neither term can be derived from the other and, therefore, both naturalism and idealism are wrong. In the concrete fact of experience there is a subjective form *a priori* (consciousness, ego, spirit) which is neither the substance of traditional spiritualism, nor the universal Spirit of absolute idealism; and there is in it also a content *a posteriori*. Reality is concrete synthesis, *subject-object relationship*.

However, the experience we live in the concreteness of individual consciousness does not exhaust the whole of reality: it must be integrated and completed. In fact, the process of philosophical and scientific knowledge which begins with perception and culminates in the concept aims at the integration of experience. The numerous philosophical and scientific theories are, in this sense, only different points of view, which permit wider and more concrete harmonies of particular experiences. The concept does not exist as a simple entity outside of thought's concrete synthesis or beyond any relationship with the subject.

Aliotta maintains that subjects exist *ab aeterno*, "like the eternal pulsating of the rhythm of experience which attains its concrete life only in them." It is possible for the human spirit to descend from its proud eminence to ever more rudimental forms of experience (*esperienza indistinta*, indistinct experience), yet this limitation cannot be exceeded. "A plurality of subjects of experience more or less rich in content in their psychical life is the result to which our analysis leads us; endowed with spontaneity, they are active centers having a tendency to preserve and develop themselves; they are souls not enclosed in themselves within their intimate subjectivity, which has no outside windows; on the contrary, they live the life of the universe, which they perceive in themselves through the various degrees of consciousness." Experience also has an objective aspect. As Aliotta says: "There is no knowledge of the self that is not at the same time knowledge of the world other than the self; there is no experience that is not experience of an object." The world is not something standing outside of the activity performed by the subject; it is, instead, that very experience which takes place in all its innumerable centers of life and which, through its unabated motion, ascends toward superior forms of reality. "Things exist only in their perennial relationship with my consciousness, which, in its turn, does not exist except for its perennial 'rapport' with things. Subjects never had an origin nor will they ever have an end: we are *ab aeterno* and we shall live eternally. The death of the soul is an eternal rebirth, and in its inexhaustible power lies the future of the world. Nor do souls draw their origin from an absolute and most perfect Being, because, once a theistic or pantheistic hypothesis is conceded, neither freedom, nor human responsibility, nor evil in the world and not even the plurality of subjects, can be explained any longer." The reality of evil, above all (it should be remembered that Aliotta wrote this while the war was raging furiously), and his preoccupation lest he deny freedom have up to now restrained Aliotta from offering a theistic solution, which he had accepted in a previous phase of his thought. The source of evil lies "in the disorderly conflict of desires," as the souls' source of every spiritual elevation lies "in their being progressively coordinated." Every man must go on by himself in his own way without divine help and without pre-established plan. There is incertitude in life; but "only because there is some risk in it do we feel its tragic grandeur." Conflict exists in every form of society, and it is useless to hope for a harmonious definitive solution; yet it is worthwhile living, precisely because the work of the world is not and never will be perfect and complete. The drama of existence, of which we are actors and spectators, is struggle and cooperation through struggle. "We must try and try again; this norm applies not only to scientific invention but also to whatever progress we attain in life. War is the grand trial testing our ideals, just as experimentation tests the truth of physical hypotheses."

Aliotta takes up these theories again in *Relativismo ed Idealismo* (in *op. cit.*), his most mature work. A relativism that is not skepticism because "the relative itself is reality so that it leaves nothing outside of itself": a relativism that is not uniformity of individual perspectives, but gradation and progress of degrees of reality and of truth in which no point of view can be ever considered absolute. In his later work *L'esperimento nelle scienze, nella filosofia e nella religione* (in *op. cit.*), Aliotta applied this relativism to the sciences, philosophy, and religion. In it he says: "Experiment is an active modification of reality both when it starts and when it ends; it does not reproduce an order of things and facts in themselves, as gross realism feigns them before the naive imagination of people, but always produces something new." In this way, to test the truth of a theory means to see which agreements the theory is able to realize. This experimental proof must be applied to logic, metaphysics, and religion. History does not proceed along a straight line; on the contrary, history has a meaning precisely because it maintains an alternative between real progress and real decadence. "Life makes sense provided alternatives of good and evil imply an absolute risk; provided our action is able to produce an effective increase or an effective decrease of reality, and provided the salvation of the world be not certain but dependent at least in part on the effort of our will."

The concept of life as "risk" and "sacrifice" has become central in Aliotta's most recent writings (see for example, *Il sacrificio come significato del mondo*, in *op. cit.*). Faith is active thought; it "always implies some risk because it is not an intellectual evidence imposing itself with necessity, but rather a free act of choice involving the possibility of different alternatives." Indeed Aliotta tries to give a concrete content to this faith that seems to be theistic. "Our action would be useless and vain, if what we have been laboriously building throughout the centuries could be sunk in the infinite nothingness at any moment. A religious postulate is at the root of our action then: faith is a superior Consciousness from which emanates the imperative of unity guaranteeing its realization. It is possible to deny in the abstract the existence of God, and many did this with words. But when men act, it is another thing; in fact, even in their simplest movement, inasmuch as they postulate the success of it, they concretely express their faith in a continued existence as regards both the objective order and the invisible God securing it." However, this is religious pragmatism—a purely psychological position absolutely insufficient for the foundation of the theological problem.

ADRIANO TILGHER (1887-1941) was a prolific writer on many subjects and, at times, a sarcastic and sharp polemicist, as well as a critic and a journalist. He developed his thought outside of any school (indeed, he was an implacable critic of schools and academies), and yet all schools influenced him to a degree. Gradually he arrived at a form of pluralism and relativism that is very close to irrationalism. Upon reading him, one gets the impression that he is not a resigned irrationalist, but rather one who is hoping and struggling in order to find an ideal capable of giving some significance to human life. Tilgher is a relativist and, at times, a skeptic and a pessimist, perhaps only because of his inability to find a solution for the crisis afflicting the world today; yet, he did look for such a solution. We begin with his political work *La crisi mondiale* (Bologna, 1921) in order to understand the position just mentioned.

The First World War was for him one of the signs of a crisis of an epoch, rather than the crisis itself. Both the war and the ensuing peace denied the ideals of law, justice, and freedom in the name of which the best among men had fought and sacrificed. Both the French revolution of 1789 and historicism supported the revolutionary bourgeoisie, which became conservative and an ally of democracy. Neither of these forces, now in decline, is able to solve the crisis of our epoch. Moulded by Greco-Roman antiquity, by Christianity and by Germanism, European civilization is bound to decline according to Tilgher whether victory belongs to Spartacus or slaves (Russia, Germany, Japan), or to the masters (Britain, America, France). Our old civilization is crushed by the idolatry of the state sacrificing the individual and by capitalism mortifying every human ideality. The world is thrown into a wild race for the possession of things, as it is driven by an unrestrainable stimulus of needs that make it lose the sense of renouncing comforts and of giving up the domain over riches; with this the world has lost the noblest ideals and, with them, the ideal of eternal salvation.

Tilgher's ethical pluralism springs from the foregoing situation of fact: and this pluralism, as outlined in *Filosofia delle morali* (Rome, 1937), is antimetaphysical and antirationalistic. In this book he makes his own the thesis belonging to romanticist idealism, that which exalts the individual and the will of the single person, whose acts bring about the "types" of life wherein there is not *the* morality, but moralities, according to the various types realized. Thus, for Tilgher, there are so many styles of life, each incommensurable and irreducible to the other, as there are attitudes that man can take in the presence of the problem of life itself. The four most important forms of ethics are: (1) *Heroism*, a supreme synthesis on the level of "desire"; in it the will is able to overcome all natural and immediate desires that make it depend on the other and to aim, instead, at the realization of an ideal, in whose name the individual no longer acts as a mere individual but as a member of society; (2) *Asceticism*, a suppression of every desire dictated by the conviction that perfect happiness is impossible at the level of desire and will: happiness resides, instead, in the total liberation from what is outside of us; (3) *Holiness*, an inversion of heroism whereby the other is no longer reduced to the self, but the self is posited in the other: there is no longer any desire—but *love*—which becomes sanctity when realized as perfect and as a total love for all living things and for God; (4) *Wisdom*, or the ethics of intelligent action, in which knowledge is considered for its own sake.

These along with an infinite number of other types of life which may be manifested in the future, and which are irreducible to one another, coexist in a chaotic manner at a given historical moment. Man is a chaos of psychical powers, some of which are realized into styles of life; these are, therefore, creations of the individual. Heroism, asceticism, wisdom and holiness do not exist as values in themselves, but as creations due to the ethical genius of heroes, ascetics, saints and sages. Thus, there is no fixed and absolute criterion whereby moral actions and the value of life can be evaluated; but rather, every action must be referred to a creative act as well as to a style that has been already realized.

Idealistic and positivistic themes, which show some influence of relativism, phenomenalism, and materialism can be found in the nonsystematic philosophy of GIUSEPPE RENSI (1871-1941). After some uncertainties, he made his thought clear in his *I lineamenti di filosofia scettica* (Bologna, 1919).

According to Rensi, no system can say anything definitive concerning the ultimate principles of human knowledge, because no system can offer such a logical demonstration of them as to impose itself as absolute and indubitable truth. All hypotheses can be true and, therefore, no one is true; the truth of *one* condemns the truth of the *other*, and *my* reason is the negation of the reason of the *other*. A skeptic is one who recognizes the relativity of all points of view, and not one who does not admit anything as true. He is a skeptic who "becomes and is such precisely because in a given moment either a certain idea flashes into his mind as a truth, though later he perceives the impossibility of affirming it as true, or opposite ideas strike him as true all at the same time; in this way, the dogmatism of an instant and of a period is itself no more than a moment of the total skepticism. Skepticism essentially is a state of mind that can change in all directions; and yet the mind is not primarily concerned with discerning what is false, but, rather, the *possible* truth in all opposite theses." The skeptic does not remain indifferent in the presence of a multiplicity of opinions. On the contrary, he is on the side of all "beliefs" and of all "faiths," provided that they are really considered "faiths" and "beliefs," and not things presumptuously presented and passed off as "pronouncements of reason in itself," of "fantastic" pure reason. In its inability to solve problems, philosophy stands "beyond truth and falsity." As "demonstration" is impossible for art, which makes one "feel" things, so philosophy is lyrical without being amateurism.

Thus Rensi's conclusion comes close to identifying reality with absurdity: "Whatever is real is irrational and whatever is rational is not real"— that is, a fantastic construction devised by pure reason against a reality that is essentially constituted by irrationality, which governs and leads the former into a state of eternal becoming. So man is left only with despair or unconcern: "Be calm, it does not pay to busy yourself with change, since everything is, more or less, the same." In this way, we come to the last phase of Rensi's thought, his materialistic and pessimistic skepticism, of which (among other works) his two books *Interiora rerum* (Milan, 1924) and *Materialismo critico* (Milan, 1927) are evidence. Evil and error constitute the means of history; we change in order to run away from an always evil and irrational present and seek instead the rational and the good which are always projected into an unreal future: reality of the irrational and unreality of the rational. "Since every present is absurd and evil, and since reality, which is an absolute present, is always irrational, time exists for the sole purpose of enabling us to make up *later* our constant getting away from the *now;* in other words, we use time to pass on to another moment in order to free ourselves from the evil that is present in every *now*." Therefore, time "is the category of the irrational and of evil, a necessary concomitant and a condition for their existence. If, on the other hand, we were within the *good*, we no longer would have any time and we would be still." Rationality is nothingness while irrationality is being; therefore, reality "equals the absurd."

How can we free ourselves from this tormenting movement from evil to evil? By going back to unconscious nature where we do not have to evaluate, approve or judge, or think of what there ought to be; there, in our unawareness we are satisfied with what simply *is*. Reason must be silenced and we have to stop at the data of experience. Skepticism thus leads to materialistic phenomenalism regardless of the fact that it had posited itself as pessimism. Sensations themselves make up the world, which is nothing beyond the whole of sensations. Even the ego is a group of sensations; besides what we taste, touch, and so forth, there is no other reality that is distinct from the sensations due to our senses of touch, smell, and the like. From pessimistic, integral materialism one goes straight to atheism, which Rensi considers to be "the highest and purest of all religions." Believing that God exists is unimportant as far as "salvation" is concerned. Rensi says: "God, I do not see you and I deny you, but I feel you in myself; and I act" as if "you did exist, and I save myself just the same precisely because of this negation of mine." The cycle of Rensi's thought ends in nullity.

From the outline given in the first chapter as well as in this one, it appears evident that the main stream of present-day philosophy lies in activism and vitalism. This philosophy expresses itself in manifold forms, though its general characteristic is its anti-intellectualism and criticism of reason. It also presents itself, prevalently, as an immanent historicism that often and willingly is antimetaphysical. However, in the last twenty years or so, new exigencies and new speculative motives have made their way, even if anti-intellectualism and the revolt against reason and metaphysics have remained strong. Thus, a new urgent need for a more peaceful and harmonious world—less at the mercy of the torrent of impulses and instincts—has been felt at least by thinkers; such a need is, on one hand, the result of the deep spiritual agitation and the vast social movements taking place after the First World War and, on the other, the result of the 1918-1939 period of world instability, leading to a new, terrifying, armed conflict which has involved all forms of civilization. Many people are now convinced that the collapse of the traditional values of reason and religion, the dominance gained by the instinctive forces of man, and the prevalence of a technical, utilitarian and hedonistic society are among the principal causes of this upheaval in which, for the last thirty years, we have all been involved and bewildered, and which today leaves us with a tremendous fear for the future. Hence we see a rebirth of the religious exigency which, in some cultural spheres, is truly deeply felt (unfortunately, the vast majority of people is only led by the outward forms of cult, masking a radical disbelief as well as abysses of amorality and immorality), and with it a need to ask the Christian-Catholic faith to explain the why of life and give comfort to the soul. Almost all the philosophical movements within the last twenty years posit the religious problem, and even when they profess atheism, theirs is often an atheism thirsting for the divine.

The reconsecration of religious values has advanced at the same pace as the reintegration of rational values and of the function of reason—a reason, however, that, though indispensable to knowledge and action, is in its concreteness "incarnated" in life, not detached from it. Even the attitude toward mathematical and natural sciences has changed: the antiscientific polemic has been superseded by a more thorough study of scientific principles and methods, and by a closer cooperation between scientists and philosophers. Often, however, what was accomplished and continues to be accomplished is more a philosophizing scientificalism or a scientific philosophism than a philosophy of science.

Indeed, the vitalistic and irrationalistic experience has not been in vain; on the contrary, it has left profound marks. Among other things, it has imposed the problem of taking into account whatever is non-rational (but not, for that reason, any the less true) within man and society; thus, by turning to the solution of the problem of the *person* and that of existence in its spiritual and physical integrality, the most recent European thought has endeavored to surpass the two unilateral and opposite views held by both abstract rationalism and no less abstract vitalism. The problem of the person has led even the most recent philosophy to continue its dispute against deterministic and mechanistic positivism and, above all, against absolute idealism in its new historicist forms.

Some important segments of most recent German, French, and Italian philosophy are oriented in this direction: each segment, with its own physiognomy and cultural tradition, is engaged in a dispute with diverse and opposite currents such as, for example, dialectical and historicist materialism and neopositivism.

IV

PHENOMENOLOGY

---

1. NEW EXIGENCIES AND NEW ORIENTATIONS

In preceding chapters we have, on the one hand, presented and discussed irrationalistic, anti-intellectualistic, and vitalistic positions opposing the hegemonic claims and schematisms of ratiocinating reason and, on the other, the attempts at satisfying such exigencies within the activity expressed by thought itself, whose forms are no longer considered in conformity with the rigid manner advocated by the Kantian categories but, rather, in accordance with a new manner that makes them more elastic, more plastic, and more suitable for the natural and historical becoming. Both the Cartesian type and the Kantian-Hegelian type of rationalism, as well as positivistic intellectualism, have been rejected or placed under a thorough critical revision by the foregoing orientations. As soon as the categories are reduced into vital experience, they become plastic forms of a life that is grasped in its concreteness, as impetus and freedom, and as unforeseeable and indeterminate development. However, relativism, historicism, and vitalism in all their forms are unable to solve the problem of the relationship between "life" and "reason," or "existence" and "value"—that is, the problem of a reason not opposing life but, rather, making it "intelligible"; the problem of a life expressing the concreteness of reason; and the problem of an existence revealing spiritual values and being itself an "existence of value." Thus, in the last thirty years or so, speculative positions have undergone a remarkable (and at times radical) evolution: new currents and new orientations have arisen, and they have inherited exigencies and problems pertinent to the immediately preceding thought. In this way, and because of the persistent influence of its two masters—Schopenhauer and Nietzsche—irrationalism has nourished some streams of thought which refuse to call themselves (or to be called) irrationalistic. In its widest and most comprehensive sense as *praxis*, pragmatism, for instance, has assumed new forms through the criticism of science and developments of mathematical logic, as well as through the elaboration of Marxism; in this way, it has acquired an ever more determined and intransigent tendency to make knowledge dependent on action and thought on *praxis*. Moreover, the "philosophies of life" are often inclined to give the word "life" the integral meaning of incarnate spiritual activity. Anti-intellectualism and historicism characterize these and other streams of thought even in the process of evolution, which not infrequently brings them into contact with new orientations.

The experience of two world wars did not pass sowing destruction at a distance. Combat on land, in the skies, and on the seas was not carried out by abstract categories and fleshless ideas, but rather by men of flesh and blood. These men of flesh and blood turn to philosophy for an answer, which has to suit real people, not the exigencies of pure reason or those of an abstract and notional philosophy. Hence arises the first and most impelling exigency: philosophy is called to give a satisfactory response to the demands of existential and actual reality and to engage in the solution of the problems of concrete life. Truths of *reason* are reduced to (and identified with) truths of experience or of *fact*, not fact as physical event, but as a *happening* in the spiritual sphere (*Erlebnis*), in whose concreteness, singularity and contingency logical structures are adapted. This does not mean that reason is to be excluded and denied; it simply loses its rank as a supreme tribunal dictating final sentences. Reason becomes historical and problematic just like concrete existence.

The primary problem is no longer that of knowing, but neither is it that of life as understood by the vitalists. It is the problem of *being*, the ontological problem. The exigency of the "essential" or "existential" being surpasses the logical one; it is not thought that includes being, but being thought. The gnosiological question which dominated modern philosophy from Descartes to Hegel now takes the second place: being takes its revenge against knowing. However, how are we to understand this *ontological question* dominating a vast sector of philosophy at present? The most recent philosophies are not in agreement precisely on this point: some directions of thought bind themselves once more with the exigencies arising from traditional ontology; in this way, some currents elaborate forms of transcendent spiritualism characterized by a fundamentally

Christian inspiration, while others give rise to forms of ontological idealism or immanent ontologism, which cannot avoid pantheism; still others hold that Kantianism and idealism, as well as post-Kantian and post-idealistic philosophies, have eliminated transcendence in its theological meaning once and for all; and they maintain that being must be reconquered within *existence*, in the *Dasein*, beyond which there is no conceivable or existing being, and so they deny every serious possibility of building an ontology as science of being in itself, for they consider it to be a residue of a surpassed realism. The problem of *existence* is, at the same time, the problem of *being*; existence exhausts being, or, rather, it "posits" being. The philosopher, therefore, must not investigate the crystalline spheres of pure being, but must probe into the abysses of existence, the depth of concrete life, its joys and sorrows, its contradictions and truths. The singularity of existence is thus vindicated against abstract absoluteness (be it ontological, dialectical, or logical), which denies the existentiality of being. The philosophers of this school hold that irrationalistic and vitalistic theses, though inspired to a different plane and carried to conclusions at times in contradiction to each other, still retain their own truth.

Yet, the problems of concrete existence and those of the person posit the problem of transcendence, precisely because their discourse converges on the existent, which is contingency and limitation; that is, they posit again, according to other directions of thought, the theological problem. Thus, the range of philosophical problems widens more and more. In fact, what is the sense of existence? What is the sense of person? What is being? What is the relationship between existence and being and between man and God? What is the function and the range of reason for the solution of these and many other problems? The entire philosophical program is thus placed under discussion with a complexity and intricacy of problems that render difficult any attempt to clarify and systematize it critically. There is, however, a central problem—that concerning existence, its meaning, its value, and its end. There are two fundamental answers: existence is justified by itself, in its self-immanence, and in its historicity and temporality; existence has its authentic meaning, its complete intelligibility, and its ultimate end in the theological transcendence or God. Each answer implies in its scope two diverse results. The first, in its temporality and finiteness, existence is positiveness or, rather, it is the fullness of itself; finite and temporal existence is negativity, that is, an unknown entity without solution, emerging from nothing and temporarily inscribed on the blackboard of time and then erased by the sponge of death—everything is absurd or inexplicable like an enigma to be either accepted as a destiny or rejected with a futile act of rebellion, which changes nothing and clarifies or explains nothing. The second, existence has its meaning and end in God, but beyond reason and within an act of faith which is singular—the mystery of being is clarified within the theological mystery or religious life, to which every rational foundation is denied; existence finds its initial and final intelligibility in being or in God; and the theological problem is, at the same time, a religious and a philosophical problem, a problem of reason and of faith because pure fideism which is negative with respect to rational truths is also negative, in the last analysis, even with respect to the truths of faith. Faith cannot be saved without reason and, on the other hand, reason alone, without faith, cannot by itself discover the "radical" and ultimate intelligibility of itself and of existence in its concreteness and integrality. The great debate between *immanent or atheistic humanism* and *theistic or transcendent humanism* is thus reopened and the dispute goes on in terms that are new and rich in their original presentation of problems.

In such a philosophical climate, one can easily understand the importance of the theses offered by Kierkegaard and Unamuno, Feuerbach and Marx, Dostoyevsky and Nietzsche and also the importance of those offered by Augustine, Pascal, Malebranche, Rosmini, Blondel, and other authors already mentioned. Even disavowed Platonism, a favored target for the philosophers of *praxis*, is being reconsecrated by some strong currents of contemporary thought and, along with Plato, almost all great classical thinkers belonging to Western civilization.

2. THE PHENOMENOLOGY OF E. HUSSERL

One of the most fortunate currents of thought, the one which first influenced German philosophy during the decades preceding and following the First World War and which later on and still today influences even the philosophy of other countries, is so-called *phenomenology*. Its founder and master was EDMUND HUSSERL (1859-1938), a University of Göttingen professor who also taught at Freiburg until 1929.

It is not easy to give a definition of phenomenology: one runs the risk of grasping one aspect of it while missing many others. In one of the moments of Husserl's philosophy, phenomenology is a "descriptive psychology"; in another it is a method that can be summed up in the expression "to go to things." If to these two we add the other fundamental moment which makes phenomenology the study of *essences* or *forms* as "pure being in consciousness," we have the Neo-Kantian or "idealistic" point of arrival in Husserl's thought.

A pupil of Brentano and of the psychologist C. Stumpf, Husserl was influenced by the Neo-Kantianism of Marburg; a student of mathematics (his first book was *Philosophie der Arithmetik*, in *Gesammelte Werke*,

The Hague, 1950-1962), he learned from his master the art of psychological description, but immediately singled out the limitations of Brentano's psychologism: failure to distinguish in the individual consciousness what is mutable and ephemeral from what is manifested, through it, as permanent and universal. Husserl makes this distinction and in his *Logische Untersuchungen* (Halle, 1900-1921)—his first fundamental work—he points out the difference between the psychical order of connections between the elements of representation, which is relative, and the logical order of syntheses between the objective contents of knowing, which is absolute.[1] Through this important distinction, Husserl endeavors to satisfy a fundamental exigency which is also prompted by his mathematical studies, viz., to build a philosophy as a strictly rational science, an exact science. His ideal is pure rationality, scientific purity, and the perfecting of a method designed to discover universal essences that are of the same nature as Platonic ideas. His rationality does not ignore concrete reality, which indeed Husserl seeks to understand and grasp as it presents itself in the immediacy of our intuition. Yet, as we shall see, Husserl's rationalism[2] leads some of his pupils (Scheler and even Heidegger, for example) to an antirationalistic reaction which alters the course of phenomenology. However, many pupils, including M. Geiger, 1880-1937; A. Pfander, 1870-1941; A. Reinach, 1883-1916, and others, remained more or less loyal to the master's thought. The organ of phenomenology, and its minute and implacable applications, has been the *Jahrbuch für Philosophie und phänomenologische Forschung*, which was founded in 1912 and edited by Husserl himself.[3]

The starting point in phenomenological analysis is the *given world*, that is, the totality of conscious being (*für mich Seiende*); its method, the *"description of the phenomenon*, that is, what is given immediately." Thus, the word *phenomenon* does not signify that there may be an unknown reality underlying what is appearing; it is the datum, the *immediate*, that which is "present in person" within consciousness. Any object (for example, the sheet of paper on which I am writing), inas-

[1] Husserl demonstrates, against psychologism, that the laws of logic, the ideal and the *a priori* ones, are of a different order than those of psychology: the object of the former is something objective, not thought or judgment, but the content of judgment itself, its meaning. Husserl criticizes also the nominalism of the empiricists (Locke, Hume, and so forth): a) logic is not a normative science (namely, it does not set up norms of beings), and its object is, instead, being itself, the data; b) what the subject represents to itself has no importance and, therefore, the universal is not a subjective, generalized representation, but an object-idea, an ideal content.
[2] "Rationalism" for Husserl means affirmation of the value of reason, conception of philosophy as a rigorous science and research of the foundations of science itself in order to shed light on its ultimate presuppositions.
[3] The "Husserl-Archives" of Louvain contain a great number of unpublished manuscripts.

much as it is an object of immediate revelation to my consciousness, is a datum not reducible to the process by which the perception corresponding to it is formed, nor is it reducible to the network of relations with other objects. Now, phenomenology's task is precisely to grasp the immediate presence prior to any mediation or synthesis as well as to obtain an intuitive comprehension of ideas, forms, or essences (*eidos* = form, whence the term "eidetic content" is given to the ensemble of forms or essences), because, in fact, every sensible object possesses its own form. Phenomenology is thus distinguished from psychology in that the former is an *eidetic science*, that is, the science of essences, and the latter is a science of facts; and furthermore, facts are particular and contingent, while essences are universal and necessary. Although the individual is accidental, inasmuch as it is a reality it contains an essence, an *eidos*, which must be grasped directly. Consequently, two sciences exist. One concerns the facts of sensible experience while the other is about essences, an eidetic science, whose object is intuition or contemplation of *eidos*.

Although proceeding from Kant, Husserl draws away from him. Phenomenology does not reduce essences to functions and, hence, to mediating forms, but rather considers them as being outside of the mediating and functional process. Husserl abandons the theory of knowledge as the starting point, which must define *a priori* the possibilities and limits of our knowing powers. The essences or forms that we acquire by a primary intuition (*eidetic intuition*)—and of which we have an immediate vision (*Wesensschau*) that is immediately evident—are the objects of Husserl's studies. His forms are thus closer to mathematical axioms and Platonic ideas than to Kantian categories. As he explicitly states in his *Ideen Zu Einer Reinen Phänomenologie und Phänomenologischen Philosophie* (Halle, 1922),[4] the laws that make up the context of things do not come from observation through the dialectical process of analysis and synthesis, but are presupposed by it and render it possible. In brief, an eidetic reality is intuitively present in consciousness according to Husserl; it is a question, then, of exposing its structure, before turning to other problems. The aspects of life possess a meaning before we ask whether or not a world exists in correspondence with the forms which we intuit. We accept life even before positing its problems; and life within the eidetic intuition presents itself in the eternity of its ideal structures. Every form of expression coming from culture and life has its essences which intuition reveals as a world of extra-temporal, universal, and pure objects. To intuit these essences amounts to grasping the mean-

---

[4] In this work the idealistic conclusions that are emphasized in later works (*Formale und Transzendentale Logik*, 1929, and others), are already evident. Recently (1952) Vols. II and III of *Ideen* have been published.

ing of things, which is precisely their absolute and extra-temporal essence. To discover the essentiality of objects is to unveil the significance of the world. For Husserl, the universal and necessary essence, which differs from the individuality and contingency of things, is not abstract, but concrete and autonomous; in their particularity objects are abstract, as they are inconsistent, when removed from the foundation on which they depend. This is Platonism, indeed, but with this fundamental difference: ideas or essences for Plato are reality itself, outside the mind and things; but for Husserl, they are forms immanent in things and in human thought. The exigencies of phenomenology are thus satisfied: immediate intuition of the universal object or essence, which is necessary and absolute and, at the same time, concrete; and the intuition of the essence guarantees the construction of an exact science, universal and valid for all phases of reality. Phenomenology, as Husserl says, is not an acquisition of new notions that must be added to the ones we already have, but a change of perspective, "a direction of our vision, which diverting itself from experienced realities turns to consider this very character of being experimented."

Essence is contained in the datum. Thus, in order to grasp it, it is necessary to prescind from the other elements, which are unconcerned with phenomenological research, whose object is the *eidos*. To this purpose Husserl applies the so-called *phenomenological reduction*, the ἐποχή or suspension, consisting in excluding or "placing in parentheses" all that in the content of consciousness is referred to the psychological subject and individual existence. In other words, in order to grasp the pure essence we must get rid of whatever may concern our empirical subjectivity, and suspend or place in parentheses all the questions about the existence of the world, of God, and so on. The task of the phenomenologist is only that of "describing" the eidetic world immanent in consciousness, and of fixing the *regional ontologies* or *eidetic spheres*, each complete and self-justified in itself. Phenomenological reduction[5] thus leads to the exclusion of every habit, of every point of fact, of whatever impedes grasping the essence, which is the solid foundation of any science. To reduce phenomenologically means to restore its liberty to consciousness and to give it the awareness that reality has not only a scientific, dialectical or psychological meaning, but also an ontological one representing the basis for all such meanings. The catharsis achieved by phe-

[5] As it is known, Husserl gives different degrees: a) the *historical reduction* which abstracts from all philosophical doctrines; b) the *eidetic reduction*, which exercises the ἐποχή on the individual existence of the object, abstracting from all sciences of nature and of the spirit; c) the *transcendental reduction*, of which we shall speak later. Thus phenomenology fulfills its own purpose of considering pure essence, abstracting from any other element.

nomenological reduction reveals the world as a structure of ontological meanings, or intuited essences. Thus, to inquire into the world of culture, to understand a certain aspect of spiritual life, validly to establish a certain science—amounts to discovering the ontology of every form of knowing, which means discovering the essential components of each and every aspect of reality.

The idealistic thrust, by now evident in phenomenology, leads Husserl toward a new reduction. No regional ontology, nor indeed all of them, gives the totality of knowledge that justifies itself and is self-sustaining. A further reduction is necessary, the *transcendental reduction,* which places in parentheses not only *existence* and individuality (habits, psychological subjectivity, things, and the like), but also all that is not a correlate of pure consciousness, in order to discover the condition making it possible for all essences to actuate themselves. Such a condition is consciousness understood as *pure thought* or *transcendental consciousness.* This represents the phenomenological residue, or what can neither be "reduced," nor "suspended." With the transcendental reduction of the datum or object there remains only what is *given to the subject,* to consciousness. This is the idealistic conclusion of Husserl's phenomenology: the object can exist only in conjunction with transcendental consciousness or pure thought—which is grasped in correlation with an object that, in its turn, is a correlate of thought, that which is given to consciousness. Transcendental consciousness is such because of the presence of an object, and the object is what is present or given to consciousness: correlativity is necessary to both.

Transcendental reduction is clarified by the doctrine of *intentionality,* which Husserl borrows from his teacher, Brentano. Intentionality is both the manner with which something is related to consciousness, and the property of every living experience to be consciousness of an object. A judgment is a judgment about something, a desire is a desire for something; and when we know, we always refer to something that is "intentioned" in our act of consciousness, that is, to an object present to us, correlated and irrepressible. In other words, consciousess is "intentional," that is, it directs itself to an object representing not a purely interior state of consciousness, but something present with it and "reduced" to having the meaning consciousness gives it. In "intentional experiences" (*intentionale Erlebnisse*) or what is vitally experienced, existence of an object is identified with the being intentionally given to a subject. The subject is essentially bound up with the object and the object is essentially given to the subject: reality is a stream of lived experiences, an ensemble of pure acts of consciousness, of phenomena which are intentions and experiences of the subject. In intentionality, the content of consciousness presents two aspects: subject (*noesi*) or sense of perception *qua* perception, and object (*noema*) or sense of the perception of the object (the ensemble of the different data representable to pure intuition); both are complementary and correlative terms. The doctrine of intentionality avoids, according to Husserl, the extreme positions of idealism and realism; it excludes the existence of an object in itself, independent of the subject, as well as the existence of an underlying substance beyond all relations. Being is the being of our living experience. Pure consciousness, which is not a real subject in act, represents the *cogito;* its acts are intentional relations; the object is only a datum with respect to the logical subject.

Thus, we arrive at a conclusion that seems to us to be already implied in his *Logische Untersuchungen, op. cit.:* consciousness is the irreducible, absolute, and unconditioned *primum:* the world of universal essences is wholly comprised in it. Thus, phenomenological reduction seems to conclude with the fullness of being rather than with abstraction: placing the world in parentheses (*ausschalten*) is to discover the universal essences immanent in consciousness, which is the absolute. And, in the bosom of the absolute, contingent and individual existence, which had been put aside during the process of abstraction, regains its significance following the phenomenological reduction. In fact, to reduce phenomenologically does not mean to deny the things placed in parentheses; once the reduction has been effected, they are found again in consciousness itself, which constitutes every meaning, every being, and to which nothing remains unrelated. Consequently, phenomenology—a research regarding the foundations of consciousness—is "first philosophy," having in itself its own justification. Phenomenology, Husserl says, does not exclude metaphysics in general; it rejects only that metaphysics which deals with the absurdity of "things in themselves."

Phenomenology is the ascertainment of what is given to consciousness, or what is vitally experienced; it is a simultaneous presence of consciousness and datum whereby we arrive at what is purely experienced by us. Ascertaining what is given to consciousness means ascertaining the exact significance of the relationship between consciousness and its object. No other systematization is possible for phenomenology but the *description* of numerous regional ontologies or spheres of religious, aesthetical, moral and other values, each with its autonomous, enclosed and definite structure. In "showing" the datum and "clarifying it," phenomenological philosophy (eidetic science is like mathematical sciences) considers only those relations which are essential. Thus, this philosophy is purely descriptive. Its method, in fact, consists in describing essences. As was pointed out, "not only is it impossible to give any justification or any explanation, but it is even impossible to ask for one, outside of the manner with which consciousness sanctions the existence and validity of the object solely because consciousness meets the latter: the *how* is the only *why*, the only *what for* that is valid on phenomenological grounds." [6] Not even transcendental consciousness, which is supposed to unify the multiplicity of data, dares go beyond description. The *coherence*-criterion is fit for defining normality and for abstracting from anomalies; validity is given by the consciousness-datum relationship itself, that is, relationship is valid as such, only because consciousness meets with the datum. Phenomenology concludes with a form of idealism, which perhaps is nothing more than a form of critical empiricism or positivism. Notwithstanding such an arsenal of "reductions" and of analyses on the part of phenomenology, the fact is that it ends by producing an idealism speculatively inferior to the one produced with much greater metaphysical awareness in other countries during the same period (for example, Gentile's actualism in Italy). This fact is evidenced by some recent developments proceeding from phenomenology, as well as by the slight interest shown by Husserl in the true problems of the spirit.

The problem of the ego—foundation of the human personality—together with the problem of the simultaneous presence of other egos within the sphere of the ego, is posited by Husserl in his *Cartesian Meditations*, trans. D. Cairn (The Hague, 1960). In other words: if the other egos belong to the sphere of the ego, their existence is denied; if, on the other hand, they do not belong to it, as Husserl affirms, because their inclusion implies contradiction, how can diversity of subjects be understood?

The ego, for Husserl, is perceived immediately as a concrete ego with all its content of tendencies and experiences; it is perceived immediately as a monad. Confronting my ego are the other egos. How do they come to me? Not as simple representations, but as *others*. The egos are not part of the sphere pertaining to me, but are a world outside of me and transcending me. In fact, "if that which pertains to the very being of the *other* were accessible to me in a direct way, it would be reduced to a moment of my being in myself and, in conclusion, I-myself and it-itself would only become one thing." The other egos or monads are given to me; they exist by themselves, as I exist by myself; they are separated from me, and "no real bond" unites their experiences to mine.

As one can see, in the presence of the irreducibility of the ego, phenomenology makes its supreme effort. In order to restore the integrity of this sphere, Husserl admits a *transcendent Nous* as the subject of the world of things and of men—a form in which my ego is realized as object. Husserl thus endeavors to establish a kind of world of spirits. But this problem cannot be clarified and solved by remaining loyal to the phe-

[6] L. Stefanini, *Il dramma filosofico della Germania* (Padua, Cedam, 1948), p. 41.

nomenological method: the problem of the person is for phenomenology another limitation that led Husserl's best students to seek its solution outside of their master's doctrine.

Husserl's *transcendent Nous* is not transcendent, after all. It has only an appearance of transcendence like the Subject or absolute Spirit in transcendental idealism. Transcendental reduction and the doctrine of intentionality, which is its foundation, surpass, after all, the limits and aims of phenomenology and represent, we may say, a philosophical demand that arises within a method—a method, that is, that responds to certain exigencies and to a scientific-mathematical mentality pretending to be suitable for philosophical problems which, instead, cannot be reduced to the problems of the natural or mathematical sciences. In other words, at a certain point Husserl realized that his phenomenological analysis was a methodology of science; and that if he wished it to have a speculative meaning, his inquiry should begin with the world or the complex and already established datum and go from there to the discovery of the primordial datum. This explains why Husserl abandoned eidetic for transcendental reduction, and essences for consciousness to which the same essences are attributed; this also explains his further step leading him to the *transcendent Nous*, which is really nothing but a sort of universal Logos in which the first and ultimate cause of the world of things and of men should be found. But, what is this universal Logos? It is an absolute ideal present to reason; a logical essence, devoid of existence (which remains enclosed "in parentheses"); that is, Absolute idealistically is the immanent act of human thought and, as such, it is deprived of transcendence.[7] In addition, in his view, what are the sphere of religious values and the conception of God? They are as follows: every *Kulturkreis* contains a conception of God; in the different types of culture there is an authentic nucleus, which is at first identical in all; it is necessary to discover this nucleus by means of intentional analysis and then to study its constitution. Thus the conception of God is reduced to the study of the numerous conceptions that have historically been formed (the same thing can be said of religion), and God Himself is only a datum present to consciousness, that is, the immanent act of human thought. All ends in a description of the essences attributed to cultural phenomena.

At this point, the reader may be surprised by our conclusion that the philosophical nucleus (the metaphysical attempts) of Husserl's phenomenology is scarcely original and, as an attempt made by an idealistic philosophy, is speculatively inferior to other constructions much more consistent and is really marking a development and furtherance of transcendental idealism. Our judgment, which might seem to be severe, is

[7] A. Brunner, *La personne incarnée* (1947), pp. 116 ff.

substantiated, on the one hand, by the weak influence exerted by Husserl on the great philosophers of his own time (it is more or less absent in Bergson, Blondel, Gentile, and others) and, hence, on philosophy true and proper; on the other hand, by the fact that Scheler, his best student, though practicing phenomenology, went his own way. Moreover, the followers of phenomenology did not follow Husserl in his idealistic conclusions (that is, in what is more philosophical in him—"too much" for a scientific mind and "too little" for a really speculative spirit), and so they accepted and elaborated those aspects of his philosophy which can suit mathematical logic and be applied to certain theories pertaining to neopositivism.[8] This again proves that phenomenology serves interests that are more scientific than philosophical or, in other words, it applies to a scientific and, as such, nonphilosophical conception of philosophy.

After this, we are ready to recognize that "it is Husserl's merit to have considered universal knowledge not as an act which man can perform when he chooses, like a reasoning, but rather as a natural and spontaneous act like the vision of colors. The universal is not known because one wishes to know it, but because one possesses a special eye to see it. Besides, not every knowledge is knowledge of the universal: eidetic intention is distinguished from the knowledge of the pure fact."[9] It is true that knowledge of the primary truth is an act of intellectual intuition, but it is not a purely logical and essential relation; it has a spiritual and metaphysical range which Husserl does not grasp. We do not deny the merit of his method and all that is positive in it. We likewise realize that there is something of great moment in his vindication of the objectivity of knowledge as regards the distinction between subjective act of knowing and object or essence given and intuitively grasped by a faculty proper to the intellect; but we are unable to see the widely acclaimed philosophical greatness in Husserl who, unlike other contemporary think-

[8] For example one should see the North American periodical *Philosophy and Phenomenological Research*, edited by Marvin Farber (we shall speak later about the phenomenological movement in the United States of America). Among French phenomenologists we shall mention A. Koyré. As far as the method is concerned, so-called psychology of form (*Gestaltpsychologie*)—which originated in Germany and, like other currents of thought, developed in the United States where its main representatives, Wolfgang Köhler (1887) and Karl Koffka (1886-1941) had moved—has points of contact with phenomenology (although it is an independent movement). Even this psychological trend presents itself, like phenomenology, as a new prospect, a new point of view: a return to observed facts, a pure phenomenological description. The new psychology abandons the old one (that going back to the English empiricists and Condillac) which explains the genesis of complex phenomena by means of addition of simple elements combining themselves through association. According to the new psychology, at the beginning there are no elementary sensations, fruit of abstraction, but structures, forms, which, though remaining always the same, pass from the stage of inferior forms to that of superior forms: one form cannot be reduced to another (isomorphism).

[9] S. Vanni Rovighi, *La Filosofia di E. Husserl* (Milan, 1939), p. 165.

ers, does not know how to draw from the objectivity as described above (which, for that matter was rediscovered in Italy independently of phenomenology and through more positive methods and with a greater philosophical sensibility) all its metaphysical consequences. Either Husserl stops at description, which is not yet philosophical, or he ventures on a metaphysical conclusion which is idealistic and, as such, negative in the matter of the objectivity understood as a distinction between the act of knowing and the object given to the act itself.

Philosophy as pure description is reduced to a sort of "geography" of essences, which confines itself to the *how* of the world while ignoring its *why*. Hence Husserl's influence in some respects, as we shall see, has had a deleterious effect on recent philosophy.

3. M. SCHELER AND THE EMOTIONAL INTUITION OF VALUES

The Neo-Kantians of the Marburg school identify spirit and reason which unifies all sensorial contents and builds the sciences of nature in a Kantian way. Husserl, instead, restores the "intellect," or the function of grasping the essences intuitively, to the spirit. MAX SCHELER (1874-1928), Husserl's most genial pupil, explores other aspects of the human spirit and, precisely, the vast field of emotionality. He was also Eucken's pupil and taught at the Universities of Jena and Munich and after 1919 at that of Cologne. A brilliant thinker, an effective and prolific writer, he was interested in the problems of spiritual life and, above all, in ethical, religious, and social ones. His influence was and still is felt in vast spheres of contemporary culture and philosophy; his philosophical ingeniousness is, in our opinion, superior to Husserl's, and his range of view richer, more lively, and of greater present-day value. Scheler is one of the "philosophers of life" but, being Eucken's student, he is philosopher of that conception of life which places the spirit first; he chooses as his master Augustine, the philosopher of interiority and love. Not wrongfully, Troeltsch called him "the Catholic Nietzsche"; and, in fact, Scheler felt Nietzsche's influence, besides Dilthey's and Bergson's. It is evident that his temperament, interests, and development make him a phenomenologist *sui generis*. He strongly modified Husserl's phenomenology and transposed it to another plane. Husserl possesses the sense of "things," of the "world," and of "logical relations"; Scheler, instead, possesses the sense of "man," of the "human," and of "personal bonds." Husserl's philosophy rests on "description" and "logic"; Scheler's, on "life" and "love." Scheler's value-doctrine represents, within phenomenology, an insurrection on the part of human sentiment, a vindication of concrete existence, of the person—of what belongs to the person and what the person expresses—as well as a vindication of the absolute Person, which creates all other persons. In his first writings, Scheler is strongly influenced by Eucken; one of them, his *Die Transzendentale and die Psychologische Methode* (Leipzig, 1922), is remarkable and an effective criticism of transcendentalism and psychologism. His fundamental work, *Der Forma-lismus in der Ethik und die Materiale der Werte*, was published in Hus-serl's *Jahrbuch*, 1913-1916 (*Gesammelte Werke*, Bern, 1913-1916, 2 vols.); two collections were then published among other writings: *Vom Um-sturz der Werte* (in *op. cit.*, Vol. III) and *Vom Ewigen im Menschen* (in *op. cit.*, Vol. V); also the second edition of an important work (published in 1913) with this new title, *The Nature of Sympathy*, trans. P. Heath (London, 1954). These writings which represent the lasting part of his activity made Scheler one of the greatest thinkers of our century. After-wards, on account of a deep crisis due, perhaps, to his changeable and restless temperament (but not only on this account, as we shall see), he ceased to be not only the philosopher of the person, but also a theist and a Christian. Such a radical change of position is already present in *Die Wissensformen und die Gesellschaft* (in *op. cit.*) and, in a clearer way, in his last work *Die Stellung des Menschen im Kosmos* (Munich, 1947).

Philosopher of the spiritual life, Scheler considers the *inductive know-ing* of the positive sciences as the first degree of knowledge having, as its object, reality (things), and, as its foundation, the instinct of domina-tion or possession. To abstract from the real existence of things is to go beyond this instinctive behavior, and to lead toward the *a priori* and the *essences*. This is the second degree of knowledge or the *knowing of the essential structure* of that which is, of the "what" of things—the ideal and significant unities which are given independently of the subject thinking them. For Scheler, then, the *a priori* is the essence and not the transcendental form in the Kantian sense; nor does the *a priori* represent the "formal," because there is a "material *a priori*" of the contents that are independent of experience. The Kantian *a priori* is radically modified, for it is not a transcendentality whose forms are functions of the intellect —valid only to receive a sensible content and to construct experience— but it is an objective datum, an essence given to the thinking subject and not one that depends on the latter's "position." Thus, Scheler rejects Kan-tian and idealistic conceptualism, as well as positivistic and empiricist nominalism. This allows him to avoid the identification of the problem of the *a priori* with that of knowing; that is, he can thus thoroughly exam-ine the "gnosiological question" dominating modern empiricism and rationalism, as well as Kant's criticism and its developments or ramifica-tions (transcendental idealism, positivism, and so forth). The primary problem is not that of the "how can something be given?" (the problem of knowing), which if it is primary, resolves and dissolves metaphysics into epistemology and identifies the domain of knowledge with that of experience being built by the subject (Hegel, in fact, resolves metaphysics into logic or science of the concept, which is then the science of the historical world); the primary problem is instead, "what is it that is given?" (the problem of metaphysics), which is the problem of the *essence that is given,* and in which the theory of knowledge exists only as an aspect of metaphysics without pretending any longer that the subject in its transcendental activity is able to prescribe laws for nature and be a law to itself insofar as it is practical reason. In short, the *a priori* is an objective datum and not an activity of the subject. Hence, another consequence follows: understood as a form of transcendental activity, the *a priori* can only be rational as far as Kant is concerned; on the other hand, for Scheler, who sees it as an objective datum, the whole spiritual life (and not only the rational one) has a content *a priori,* that is, it expresses essences or values. Even sentiments have contents *a priori.* Thus, besides a rational *apriorism* there is an *emotional apriorism* (*emotionaler apriorismus*). In this way, Scheler not only integrates Husserl's phenomenology by developing a new "eidetic sphere," but he also transposes phenomenology itself, to which he gives a spiritual richness, an "existential" and human significance and, above all, a metaphysical interest and range which is lacking in its founder. This is the aspect of Scheler's philosophy in which Augustine's and Pascal's influence is decisive and fecund. Modern rationalism, from Descartes to Kant, had considered the domain of sentiments as a dark and indistinct zone (significant exceptions include Pascal in France and Vico in Italy); Hegelian's panlogism had made it a dialectical moment absorbed and surpassed by the logical moment. With his "logic of the heart" getting its truths *a priori,* Pascal vindicates "an eternal and absolute legitimacy pertinent to our sentiments," says Scheler; "and it is as absolute as that of pure logic, but in no way reducible to the legitimacy characteristic of intellectual activity." This is therefore autonomy, and irreducibility of the sphere of sentiments. All this, on the one hand, makes Scheler one of the philosophers of life—without being a vitalist in the sense of biological vitalism, but rather coming closer to Bergson's "vital impetus"—and, on the other, it places him in contrast with the formalism of Kantian ethics, which digs an abyss between sentiment and reason so that man is placed in a state of war with himself, a state of incurable conflict between what he does *willingly* and what he must do out of *duty.* Emotional *apriorism* is an effective criticism of rationalistic *apriorism.* It is a re-evaluation of sentiment and of emotional life, not so much in themselves (that is, subjectively or psychologically), but in that they express objective values—universal, eternal and essential data. One can certainly speak about irrationality (or arationality) of values; yet, Scheler's irrationalism (as well as his vitalism) is unlike that of other thinkers already considered, for it admits objective, eternal and absolute values like Plato's ideas or Husserl's essences; nor is his concept of "life" biological. His irrationality of values is, on the one hand, a consequence from emotional *apriorism* (sentiment, too, and not only reason, has an objective content) and, on the other, a guaranty for the values, absoluteness and objectivity.

The third degree of knowledge is *metaphysical knowledge*, whose object is represented by the ultimate problems confronting the sciences, that is, those problems which the sciences themselves cannot, nor are expected to, resolve. Even at this point Scheler's Augustinianism is apparent, and it makes him conceive metaphysics in such a way as to clarify some misunderstanding produced by modern rationalism and perpetuated until today through Kant and transcendental idealism. The objects of metaphysics are man and God: What is life? What is man? What is the Absolute or God? With these questions Scheler distinguishes the theological idea from the anthropological and the cosmological idea. Metaphysics is essentially anthropology, and without theology there is no anthropology in a metaphysical sense. Anthropology, therefore, is theistic: the problem of man implies the problem of God. Metaphysics is *meta-anthropeia*, that is, not an investigation of the first principles of nature (φυσις) but of human life in its integrity. The discovery and the analysis of every objective content pertinent to human life (namely, to the "person") in its integrity give rise from within to the theological problem, the problem of supreme Value, which is the creator of all values. This is then a metaphysics of internal experience and, as such, a *meta-anthropeia*, the only metaphysics that is genuinely "Christian" and the only one that is valid after the critical development of modern philosophy. It also opposes the latter in its dogmatic conclusions denying metaphysics as "intelligibility" of spiritual life, which all forms of immanentism have "naturalized." We do not endorse Scheler's metaphysics (which, *inter alia*, phenomenologically poses itself as a problem of the "what" but not as a problem of the "why" of man, of life, and so on), but we simply state that it is to his credit to have considered metaphysics as *meta-anthropeia*, that is, to have restored its human and spiritual sense. During the nineteenth century and prior to Scheler, only Rosmini (with a different speculative consistency and different positive conclusions) had clarified, against Kant and modern thought, this concept of metaphysics as an inquiry into the ontological and objective elements constituting the whole human person in order to attain a complete solution of the problem of life in its entirety.

Scheler views *values*—the intentional objects of feeling—as the *a priori* of the emotional. His *ethical objectivism* (there is a world of *values* or *essences* pertinent to the moral life) enables him to oppose both axiological nominalism and ethical formalism. Values (Werte) are the immediate content of the objective (*unmittelbarer Zielinhalt*) and there is an *emotional intuition* of them; they are objective, eternal, universal, absolute and immutable, and we can grasp them through a pure intuition. However, differing from Husserl, who, as we know, considers essences as correlative to a theoretical act so that he introduces a certain mediation, Scheler maintains that the value is obtained by an immediate apprehension, through an intentional act of feeling, which he calls *pure sentiment*. The "emotional intuition" is precisely an intuition of values, which, therefore, are *emotional phenomena* entirely belonging to the affective (and not to the theoretical) sphere of love or hatred, of attraction or repulsion. In other words, for Scheler value need not refer to anything else in order to be fulfilled. Value is not completed or enlightened by anything; it is complete in itself and has in itself the light to illuminate whatever is related to it. The intuition of values has no presuppositions because it presupposes nothing. In short, emotional intuition is, for Scheler, given by itself, without need for a mental structure calling it forth.

As we know, the emotional *apriorism* of values allows Scheler to admit not only *formal* or rational essences, but also those that are untranslatable into any rational meaning. Scheler calls these nonformal essences *material*, in the sense that they oppose the formalism or *apriorism* of Kant, whose error, as we have said, consists in having identified the *a priori* with the formal. In Scheler's emotional *apriorism* there is nothing that is empiristic or positivistic. Objects are not values but phenomena in which values are present, and so essences are not inferred *a posteriori* from the multiplicity of things expressing values. Similarly, for Plato, ideas are not inferred from sensible objects though the latter partake of pure forms. Scheler's essences or values, like Plato's ideas, are prior to things and their experience. Values, then, are not linked to facts: facts change and disappear but the values expressed through them are eternal and immutable; things pass, but values remain identical with themselves even in the mutability of events regarding life and history. They are not relative; what is relative is instead our knowledge of those values which can neither be identified with man's human activity (subjectivism) nor be reduced to the historical process (relativism). There are variations in the sentiment (*Ethos*) and in the judgment of values (*Ethik*), variations in practical morality and customs, but values remain intact; human behavior changes in their respect, so that they may be felt or conceived more or less adequately, but values remain absolute and immutable. Nor must we confuse our sentiments, through which we grasp values, with the instincts of biological life: they are *pure* sentiments. Vitalism confuses pure and impure forms of sentimental life. Nor does the irrationality of values signify a negation of reason, but rather an independence of sentiment from reason itself and an autonomy of those values pertinent to the emotional sphere.

Thus this "Catholic Nietzsche" is also against Luther and Lutheranism. The rigorism of Protestant ethics condemns affective life including the act of love which is rich in achievements, and it considers everything, except faith, useless for our salvation. Kant's ethics is rooted in the Lutheran doctrine of sin, and it relegates sentiments and affections to the domain of moral disorder. Lutheranism, therefore, divides body and spirit; it places life against life and, by making sin the category of human existence, it denies freedom and widens the conflict between faith and reason. Kierkegaard is a typical expression of this "inhumanism" and Protestant supertheologism. For Scheler, instead, emotional sphere has its own *a priori*, namely, the values, the intentional objects of feeling. While Husserl restores to thought its necessary and eternal object (the essences), Scheler, by means of his theory of emotional *apriorism* acknowledges the full validity of the world of pure sentiment, whose values are the intentional objects; among them moral and religious values are the highest ones. Ethics and religion are fused in a new form of nonrational *apriorism*. As Scheler writes, "Sentiment, predilection, love and hate have their own *aprioristic* content, that is as much independent from inductive experience as the pure laws of thought." Values are, therefore, *a priori* but *irrational;* reason is "blind" as regards the emotional *a priori*.

If reason is blind, the will is "unproductive" with respect to value. The latter is not produced but only expressed by the will, which is guided by it. The will has its ends, that is, it has an aspiration toward values; yet, it is not the value that depends on the ends of the will, but the will on the value. Kant's legislating and autonomous will is thus superseded by a will depending on value, which is a given object independent of the will.

Scheler distinguishes between *good* and *value:* the good is an expression and incarnation of a value (for example, beautiful things are expressions of Beauty). In fact, no beautiful thing would ever exist unless we had the Beautiful itself existing as a value before them; and this Beautiful could never entirely be realized or exhausted either by one or all possible beautiful things. The same can be said about good, just and holy things, as well as about moral institutions, and so forth. Although value expresses itself through things embodying it, value is distinct from these things and it transcends them like Plato's ideas, in whose respect things expressing them are but imitations and reflections. If good, just and holy actions could within themselves exhaust all values pertinent to the Good, Just and Holy, or if these existed only because of the existence of the things embodying them, they would no longer be absolute and eternal values, but rather relative and transitory; they would change as those goods expressing them, since they would be subject to becoming, imperfection and corruption. Good is not a value but only an intrinsic note characterizing a datum, an object, or an action. Scheler says that it is typical of Christian ethics to try to transcend all transitory and contingent goods in order to achieve the eternal Value. All creatures are goods, each according to its grade and order, so that all of them must be loved as goods; yet, through them it is necessary to feel and love the eternal and absolute values transcending all possible incarnations. Goods, then, have worth as "carriers" of values and, as such, must not be denied. Scheler's *materiality* of values is in contrast with Kant's identification of values with pure form, and in antithesis to the Protestant devaluation of so-called works. He also rejects the ethics of Pharisaism, which exhausts value in the external work.

Values are also distinguished from *duty* (*Sollen*). Scheler makes a distinction between what "ought to be" ideally, and what "ought to be done" normatively. Value lays the foundation for the ideal duty, which, in turn, establishes the normative duty. Ethics is therefore established by value and not by an imperative must. Duty is intermediary between value and action expressing it. For example, every work of art is a good; it is, then, the "duty" of the artist to realize his work, that is, to give the Beautiful, inasmuch as this is a value, a determinate expression. To do the good means to feel a duty toward the realization of a positive value (that of the beautiful, according to our example) and also to reject the corresponding negative value (that of the ugly). Duty, therefore, does not establish value, but rather depends on it. In fact, for Scheler values are divided into *positive* and *negative:* the existence of a positive value is a positive value—its nonexistence, a negative value; the existence of a negative value is a negative value—its nonexistence, a positive value. The same value cannot be positive and negative at the same time. We see, furthermore, that emotional *apriorism* leads Scheler to diminish the value of *dianoetic* virtues in favor of *charitable* virtues characteristic of Christianity. Pagan wisdom is inferior to emotional ethics, whose supremacy has been preserved by the Roman Catholic Church and by Christian philosophy from Augustine to the great Christian mystics.

Given the immediateness and absoluteness of values, it should follow that each value is unrelated; there are *the* values, not a *unitary* world of values. The same problem, troubling Plato in the last years of his life, confronts Scheler: how can the multiplicity of ideas, each of which is absolute and an entity in itself and by itself, be reconciled with the unity of the ideal World? Plato attempted the hierarchical subordination of all the ideas to the idea of Being or to the idea of the Good. However, if reason is blind with respect to values, how can a comparison of them be established? In Scheler's thought, the hierarchy of values is not established by reason, but by a *preferential sentiment* intrinsic in every value. Values are thus elevated to a superior intentionality, which in moral life is expressed as preference or repugnance. Superior values are more lasting, less "divisible," and less relative; they establish the others, and furnish a more profound satisfaction.

The doctrine of the hierarchy of values is described by Scheler with a finesse of analysis in some stimulating and enduring pages. The lowest rank in the hierarchy is held by sensible values (pleasurable and unpleasurable, useful and harmful, and so forth) and is followed by the rank of vital values (the noble and base, health and illness, youth and old age). The third grade is occupied by spiritual values (the beautiful and ugly, the just and unjust, and so forth). This hierarchy reaches its highest point in the religious values of the "sacred and profane." This grouping does not contain the moral values, which reside in the realization of other superior or inferior values. Every rank is distinct from the other and irreducible to the other, but all are part of a unitary, emotional organism. Such a unity appears evident in the determination of values. For Scheler, a good is the realization of a preferred value. How can all the ranks in the hierarchy of values be realized? Must we surrender all inferior values, sacrifice our sensible emotionality and the vital values in order to turn our attention only to the spiritual values because we ultimately aim at the summit of the sacred, whose object is the Absolute? Or is man unable to elevate himself to such a height so that it is useless and inhuman to ask of him the sacrifice of the sensible life by which he is irresistibly attracted? This alternative does not impose itself. Upon realizing a positive value, one must aim at the realization of another in the superior order. For example, an action embodying the value of the useful is good; but in order to be so, it is necessary to realize it in a way so as not to hinder the realization of values of the superior orders, that is, such an action must be performed only with a view to realizing spiritual and religious values. Yielding, on the other hand, to the desire of attaining a commodity is *evil* if this turns out to be harmful to or an impediment for the realization of superior values. This is one of the most valid contributions brought about by Scheler through his doctrine of values. Even the action expressing the lowest values can enter the spiritual sphere and become an element enriching our own spirituality. The concreteness of Scheler's doctrine here reaches its full expression against Kantian formalism and ethical rationalism, as well as against biological vitalism. It is not wrong to want what is pleasant or useful, but it is evil to will pleasure or utility for their own sake, as if the hierarchy of values which man is able to realize would go no further than the steps of pleasure and utility. Rigorists and formalists are wrong, therefore, when they condemn vitalistic values or those concerning sensible emotionality and engage man in a struggle with himself, which paralyzes action and freezes the will. Those who consider vital values as the only ones, expressing the sense of existence while not recognizing what belongs to a superior spirituality, are likewise in error. Neither the abstract and cold form of reason nor blind and violent impulse constitutes the integral and harmonious rhythm of life if one is detached from the other, and is against the other. They are only two pauses which break the unity of existence into two tonalities without agreement or harmony. Values in the sensible and in the spiritual spheres must all be reconsecrated in that they are all included, each in its rank, in the emotional organism of man: fullness of life, therefore, and integrity of the person which expresses the richness of intuitive values, and all the grades of the hierarchy as a constant realization of humanity and an uninterrupted expression of religious life. In fact, if acting well is to will the value of a rank so that it may contribute to the realization of the other belonging to the superior grade, every good act of ours always has at its root a religious aspiration inasmuch as the top of the scale is occupied by religious values. Scheler maintains that we can live the fullness of life in all its forms, and live it religiously even when we express sensible values, without having to make renunciations or becoming brutalized in our vital instincts. If I wish, I can therefore express God and recognize Him even in the simplest and humblest act of daily life, provided that, upon embodying it with the corresponding value, I express it in such a way as to take a step on the road leading to the Absolute. To will what is good signifies to live forever, and in every instant, willing God even when one wants something else; living by combining all the voices of our conscience into a single voice with infinite tonalities which, while vibrating on different chords, are all blended together into the harmonizing note of the aspiration for God. We can make life in its entirety a perennial homage to God, a reply, through all things, to the call which the theistic aspiration repeats to us at every moment in a thousand different manners and through a thousand very opposing ways.

Values are grouped not only hierarchically but also according to their *carriers* which are person and things; so they are divided into *values of person (Personwerte)* and *values of things (Sachwerte)*. Values of things pertain to "objects of value" or the "goods"; values of person are the ones of the person itself and of virtue, and they are superior to values of things. Moral values are personal *par excellence*, but (this is the way we interpret Scheler's doctrine) even values of things concerning the objects of value or goods are in a certain sense personal, in that they interest and engage the person's activity, while not remaining extraneous to morality in general, even if they are values of things and not properly moral.

Scheler wrote very well-known pages about the "person"; he is, per-

haps, the most profound and acute philosopher on "personality" in contemporary thought. All men have a soul and are "egos," but not all of
them are properly persons, in that the person implies reflection, maturity,
and capacity of choice. The person is not identified with the soul (it is
not "psychic"); it is neither a substance nor an object; it is the "concrete
unity of acts in their being" (*konkrete Seinseinheit von Akten*), and
though not identical with its acts, the person consists only in the execution of its acts. The person is essentially *spiritual* (the "ideation" or
faculty of separating the essence from existence is the human *spirit's*
basic characteristic) and wholly *individual;* every man as a person is a
unique being and a unique value (a "person in general" makes no sense).
The person is *autonomous* in the (personal) conception of good and
evil and in willing good or evil; in being united to a body, the person is
such only if it succeeds in dominating the body; nor is the person a
"part" of the world but, rather, its "correlate"; a world corresponds to
every person and a person corresponds to every world. Scheler elaborates
his ethics and his very important theory on love around this conception
of the person.

One of the highest moments in emotional life is *sympathy*, a community of identity of sentiments between two or more persons wherein each
person preserves its own personality. Sympathy is indifferent toward
moral value, which surpasses it and can transform it into a value. As soon
as sympathy loses its character of passivity, it ceases to reside in an ensemble of reactions that we are compelled to endure; it is converted into
love, the sentiment in which the emotional intentionality culminates and
in which all values reach their highest point. Emotional life, according to
Scheler, is manifested through the sentiments of love and hate, which reveal the values. To love is neither to know nor to judge, that is, we do
not love an object because it is worth more than another. Love in itself
is not social and can be directed either toward oneself or to others; it is
erroneous to identify it with altruism. Scheler discerningly remarks
(against selfish and atheistic altruism of the nineteenth century) that love
is neither "love of mankind," which is an abstraction, nor the inclination
toward "improving" or "helping" others. All these forms of altruism are
based on hatred toward superior values and, ultimately, toward God;
humanitarian ideals based on equality are the negation of love. The act of
love is completely free and does not depend on preference; it is a creative
act in that it realizes the object it loves. Love transfers a value to the
level of existence and, as it elevates itself, becomes justified through its
own motion. Evil persons who would one day look for an excuse could
find only one, that no one loved them. "What characterizes love is not
tendency toward an end or desire to realize an end represented by a
superior value. It is, instead, love itself, which in the course of its move-

ment always creates its superior value in the object, as if this value spontaneously emanated from the subject being loved, without the least intervention on the part of the one who loves." The sum of the values of the person being loved is never proportionate to the love that we have for it; there is always a *more* "without a basis," and this is the concrete person who is loved. It is the person as such who is a value and the object of our love. He who loves aims at elevating the person loved and, in elevating the other person, he elevates himself. Hate, on the other hand, is a destroyer of superior values and, hence, makes us unable to evaluate and prefer them.

Love is always directed toward a person, never to a thing. Love never stops at the things we love; it surpasses them in order to reunite them within the person, the root in which things reveal their value. In this sense, Scheler says, love is *acosmic*. Love, therefore, shines very clearly within the bonds between the *I* and *You*. Loving someone means ascribing to the other person a *You* that is like my own *I* and yet, in comparing this *You* with my own *I* there can only be a *You*. The ego can exist only through the affirmation of the personal character of the object loved. Love loves the beloved object totally; it loves its social being, its most humble feelings, its most common gestures, but, in loving them, it transforms them; it makes them be visible expressions of an incomparable spiritual reality. Love is both knowledge and joy of the essence. Even when it is the beginning of our greatest suffering, love delivers us from our subjective prison by compelling us to affirm beyond our own essence that of another being with which our life is associated and on which it depends. Knowledge is representation, while love is discovery of a value. Knowledge stops at the appearance of an object; love, instead, leads us back to a secret and invisible essence which can never die. Beings are prized for what they conceal, and love permits us to discover their recesses; love is the revelation of two beings, of each to the other and of each to itself. As the loved person is deeply penetrated by love, it opens itself to us with the increasing joy of abandonment. Intelligible knowledge asks for assent as it endeavors to overcome resistances and overcome the defenses against it; love, instead, is not willing to abolish, within a confused and indistinct unity, the irreducibility and independence of the person, but maintains all differences and the duality in order that the union between persons be effected by an act expressing their very personal and authentic will. Love never gives a perfect knowledge of the other. Love always allows to itself a sacred, mysterious, and inaccessible corner which it refrains from entering. Love strengthens, not destroys, decency. Though universal in principle, love can only be individual in its application. The subject is not universal, as in pantheism; it is not mankind, as in Kantian ethics wherein humanity is identified with rationality; but it is, as in Christian ethics, our fellow creature, a man of flesh and blood. It is not a limited but an infinite love, not restricted within the range of the person being loved, since it enables men to love other men according to a way of loving belonging to each of them.

Love's summit is love for God and for all other men in God (*amare mundum in Deo*). God is love and, hence, He must be the supreme object of love. He is the principle of love and the creator of persons; He is the object of love and becomes the reality of persons—a reality more intimate as it is more secret and inviolable. God is the supreme center of love. Love establishes the person, prolongs our action and intelligence, and reaches very far, to infinity, to God, beyond space and time. Love, as has been said,[10] does not contradict intelligence, but cooperates with it: intelligence makes the individual partake of the being that has been realized and love, of the being being realized.

Scheler's love tends to reach the source of every value, the supreme love or God. Love is, therefore, *theistic*—theistic because it is always duality and transcendence of persons, and because it is light, not the obscure necessity of the sensible impulse, that traps us in the undifferentiated unity of life. "Love is not a unified duality, but a *dualized* unity." It is theistic because it is directed to God. In their materialistic and positivistic origin, altruism, humanitarianism and cosmopolitanism are falsifications of love; they are founded on fear of seeing one's own person derogated, and on the need of forgetting in others one's own poverty. Scheler's criticism against so-called *homo naturalis* has more value today than in the past: such a man is without unity or greatness; he is always an animal, in the past, present and future. To confine man's humanity to that of *homo naturalis*, as Comte's positivistic sociology and Marx's dialectical materialism do (and also idealism and historicism, as well as any other doctrine of immanentism), and to make it an object of worship ("Great Being"), means holding great contempt for man (and in fact immanentism concludes its parabolic course with the annihilation of the person effected by atheistic existentialism). On the contrary, man's true meaning is something else: it is that deriving from his being a "seeker of God" (*Gottsucher*), a living image of God himself. From the man who prays, the person emerges and establishes itself. This is the apex of love, the Christian love which the Protestant and pietist Kant considered eudaemonism and egoism as if Christian love toward God were imposed by fear of punishment and hope for compensation. Such is Kant's lack of understanding, because the Christian love for God is the opposite of eudaemonism and egoism. The Christian martyr could say to his executioner: "Pull out, if you will, the other eye of mine but leave me my heart so that I may still love you." And he can say so because of his love

[10] L. Lavelle, *Le moi et son destin* (Paris, Aubier, 1936), pp. 49-50.

for his fellow man, which is love for God. As Saint Teresa is able to say with spiritual joy: "And even if I did not hope as I hope, I would still love as I love." Only when we ourselves become love through the imitation of God, the infinite distance between Him and us is brought closer without gangways. Love is the filling up not the joining of two abysses— the abyss of my spirit that cries out and invokes the abyss of God.

The divine is the most primitive datum of human consciousness and so religious experience is original and underived. Like any other value, the divine is revealed to us; God's *revelation*, through which the person is placed in contact with Him, is the reward of our faith: we know God through God. We would not know God as a person if he Himself did not give Himself to us and did not allow us to penetrate Him. We understand every good and every value not by moving from the things of the world to God but, only, from the top of the ladder, from God Himself. God is not to be loved for his heaven and his earth, but heaven and earth are to be loved because they come from God. Heaven and earth would be too small for themselves: my soul would not find room in them. God is the absolute reality, the Irresistible, the Holy, the Infinite; He is a Person, the Person of persons. The accusation of anthropomorphism is foolish; God is not conceived in man's image, but man in the image of God (*theomorphism*).

Revelation, like the religious value it reveals, is not rational. The content of religion, then, cannot be resolved into that of metaphysics and vice versa. The object of the one (*Ens a se*) is identical with that of the other, but what one understands of the divine is mute to the other: "Religious experience can discover attributes of God which metaphysics would never find and, reciprocally, metaphysics can find attributes that religion would never find along its way." For example, a personal God and creation remain inaccessible to metaphysics; to it the question of salvation is secondary, as the knowledge of reality is secondary to religion. Metaphysics cannot found religion though it is equally indispensable to religion; without metaphysics, religious truths would be lacking contact with rational truths and with behavioristic forms. Metaphysics means feeling the eternal in the temporal, perceiving the participation of the world in the transcendent Logos. A philosophy and a culture, which are devoid of metaphysical sensibility, cannot be religious: the antimetaphysical attitude, as such, is irreligious and atheistic. Fideism ("the God of believers") and rationalism ("the God of philosophers") are two unilateral positions—the former is wrong in depriving religion of its ontological foundation, and the latter in failing to acknowledge the categories pertinent to believers, particularly with respect to this category: the object that is proper to the religious act is "the salvation of man through participation in the life of God." The emotional intuition of love through which religion is founded makes man spontaneously religious, that is, able to see the world *"in lumine Dei,"* and love it in God, as we said. The presence of God as Absolute and Omnipotence awakens in man the creaturely feeling; man acknowledges that he is nothing in the presence of God who is Everything. On the presence of God in us, on revelation understood as an immediate intuition arising from the very act of God, Scheler founds his demonstration of the very existence of God: every knowledge of God is knowledge through God; man has this knowledge of God (the religious act); therefore, God exists.

The opposite of love is hate which feeds resentment, binds to things as it makes us, contrary to love, unable to realize the conquest of what is eternal and spiritual in us.

As we have seen, Scheler is against any generalized conception regarding the person. Person is a "substantial form," the "essence of the ego," or individual essence (Kant's "general consciousness" is nonsense). Person is able to determine all its acts and give unity to diverse intentional contents. However, it does not consist in what it has already experienced (acts and thoughts) because inasmuch as it is a person, it is itself the concrete *experience* of any possible *experience*.

The person is transcendent with respect to its acts. Because it is wholly one in each of its acts, it is not absorbed by any of them. The person is not the creator but the "carrier" of values, some of which are realized by the person alone, and others by the person in community with other persons. Originally the person is an individual reality and a reality constituting part of a community; hence, it is open to interindividual, national, and social values. There are values that, as just said, are expressed by the person in community with other persons. The person is also *plural* or *collective person (Gesammtperson)*. The pure collective persons (to be distinguished from those which are impure and incomplete because founded on bonds of blood, contingent interests, and so on) are *Church* and *Nation*. These two types of social unity belong to the unity of autonomous and isolated persons within an autonomous plural person. Nation is the emotional intuition of spiritual and cultural acts; Church, the intuition of the value of the Sacred. Scheler's concept of collective person is meaningful. Rather than an abstract institution detached from those persons composing it, a collective person is the very person carrying a value that is realized in community with many persons. Church and Nation are pure, plural persons, each expressing values consonant with itself. Values are absolute and yet they are historical, viz., "historicity," not historicism. Values are eternal, immutable, and absolute; hence, they existed prior to their possible determinations of which they are independent; on the other hand, however, they are manifested and discovered historically. As the person does not exist without its acts and sentiments, of which it is the unity without being reducible to them, so values, though eternal, cannot but manifest themselves historically. Every historical epoch is characterized by certain values expressed in forms of culture, philosophy, religion, and so on. History does not sweep away values through the flow of contingent forms; on the contrary, its process is possible only because of the essentiality and immutability of values themselves. Thus, values are historical inasmuch as they manifest themselves in events; yet, they exist antecedently to becoming and do not change with the change of things. Historicity does not lessen their absoluteness and eternity which make history possible, contrary to historicism which denies history itself precisely because it assigns to values a purely historical essentiality.

History is a continuous discovery of new values. However, history does not create them, it only *arouses* them. Exceptional men—heroes and apostles—at a certain moment reveal new values never before discovered or only obscurely foreseen. They are the geniuses of an epoch, the creators of new forms of life, of new organizations, and new institutions. Decadent epochs, on the other hand, continue to live in the past without vivifying it again, and only repeating its external forms. Those are epochs of splendor which discover new values and create new spiritual and social harmonies. Epochs of perversion are periods in which useful and vital values prevail over religious, spiritual and cultural values.

Scheler, nonetheless, in the last years of his life suddenly changed his mind and resigned his university chair, meditating on the dark night of chaos without love and without God. In a moment of discouragement and pessimism (which come easily to an emotional and restless spirit), Scheler believed that the superior grades of life are weaker than the inferior ones which in their primordial nature and with their power are blind and irrational forces within the organic world. Nietzsche prevails over Saint Augustine. The philosopher of theistic personalism is changed into a dark theorist contemplating a cosmos that unfolds itself in a Manichean way, and according to Böhme's notion, through the irreducible dualism of good and evil—two opposite forces unceasingly struggling in man. God is a Being realized through this conflict: His completion is attained through man, who is the real future of God. This is a mystical pantheism (which we shall find in the same form, in other thinkers) barely sketched and, in which, without explanation, everything is made dependent on blind forces of life.

Scheler, however, still remains the philosopher of the person and, as such, has influenced contemporary thought. A phenomenologist in his own way, he marks the transition between phenomenology and existentialism. In the fatherland of transcendentalism, Scheler represents the most energetic and effective protest against transcendentalism itself; he is one of the strongest and liveliest voices on behalf of the person's being of the transcendence and personality of the divine. In the father-land of vitalism or, at any rate, where vitalism reached its most primitive and paradoxical forms, he energetically defended the distinction between biological and spiritual life, between vital values and spiritual and reli-gious values to which he gave pre-eminence. In the fatherland that denies the true spirit of Christianity and its ethics (Nietzsche), he placed the value of the Sacred on the summit of the hierarchy of values. And in the fatherland of Hegel (who nullifies man in the Idea and the Idea in the historicist dialectic) and of Marx (who destroys man in the "eco-nomic"), Scheler represents the most effective return to man and the humane, a distinct characteristic of our epoch which otherwise is so inhuman.

The change in his thought, however, is not exclusively dependent on his temperament; the true Scheler already contains the elements which justify Scheler in his last period. In spite of his efforts he remains as a phenomenologist, a philosopher of essence rather than a philosopher of the concrete being; he leaves the spheres of the will, being, and knowing divided and impenetrable. He sees the prolific power of love without seeing the light of truth; he firmly believes in the indispensability of revelation, but he makes it an immediate intuition stemming from the very act of God; he distinguishes the religious from the metaphysical order, but he entrusts the former to emotional intuition alone and not to a metaphysics which, consistent with the truth of the Christian mes-sage, gives religion its rational foundation. He vindicates the person, but he sees it as a passive and almost obscure and insignificant support with respect to values: he declares that he is a theist, but he conceives God as something correlated to the world, as a person corresponding to the totality of the world itself, the quasi-"Carrier" of all values. In spite of everything, Scheler introduces non-Christian elements into Christianity. Pantheism (even under the form of ontologism) is already present in some affirmations made by Scheler, the theist.

4. N. Hartmann and Philosophy as Aporetics

NICOLAI HARTMANN (1882-1950), a professor, first at the Uni-versity of Berlin and, after the war, at Göttingen, is also a follower of the Marburg school and of phenomenology which he later abandoned. Hartmann had the merit of maintaining, especially with respect to Ger-man existentialism, that the ontological problem is not to be confused with that of the meaning of being.

The question of ontology is that of being as "substratum," of its qualifications which themselves are being. The problem of the *Dasein* ("to be here," "existence") cannot remain indifferent toward the question of the *Sosein* ("to be so," "essence"). The fundamental trait of Hartmann's philosophy (which essentially is an ontology) is that the problem of being has priority over that of knowing. However, what this philosophy misses is exactly being, as we are about to see. Moreover, Hartmann gives evidence of being influenced by Aristotle and Scholasticism (he interprets the latter in his own way and for his own use and consumption); as well as by Kant, Hegel, and Scheler, although he departs from them in many points because he is concerned with giving his thought an original and personal presentation which seeks to be a realism at all costs. The *Grundzüge einer Metaphysik der Erkenntnis* (Berlin, 1921), his first notable work, was followed by his *Ethics* in 1926 (trans. Stanton Coit, London, 1932), and then, by his four massive volumes on ontology: *Zur Grundlegung der Ontologie* (Berlin, 1935); *Möglichkeit und Wirklichkeit* (Meisenheim am Glan, 1949); *Der Aufbau der Realen Welt* (Berlin, 1940); and *Philosophie der Natur* (Berlin, 1950). Hartmann gave particular attention to idealism in the two volumes, *Die Philosophie des Deutschen Idealismus* (Berlin, 1960), the second of which is entirely dedicated to Hegel. Although heavy and academic like so many other German thinkers, he is a lucid and clear writer; precise and analytic, he has the merit of sparing the reader artificial abstrusities which abound in so many allegedly profound pages written by Heidegger and other existentialists.

In the name of ontology and of the implementation of the problem of being, Hartmann opposes Kant and post-Kantian idealism, Husserl and Heidegger; likewise, in the name of the autonomy of philosophy he criticizes the *extra muros* eruptions perpetrated by the sciences. However, due to his manner of positing the problem of being, he strongly criticizes traditional metaphysics and concludes with a form of "systematic" aporetics and problematicism, which greatly reduce his contributions toward a critical foundation of metaphysics and to a solution of its problems. Yet, the importance of his researches is noteworthy both as a critique of gnosiology in modern philosophy and of some positions held by present-day thought, and also on account of Hartmann's particular analyses which clarify some important problems.

Hartmann seems determined to recognize the essential character of metaphysics. He maintains that a metaphysical basis is present even in the sciences of nature: metaphysics is an element of life itself and, hence, is irrepressible. True. Yet, for Hartmann, its problems are insoluble; metaphysics signifies the irrational and there is no knowledge of the irrational; metaphysics is theologically, philosophically, and scientifically an unexplainable wonder. After this, it is no wonder that he scorns traditional metaphysics for having attempted the solution of the insoluble, that is, for having produced metaphysics! According to him, every possible metaphysics consists in acknowledging all metaphysical problems to be insoluble, and this amounts to saying that all metaphysics is impossible. The result, in truth, is neither very outstanding nor original. Hartmann adds (and he believes that in this sense he made a remarkable contribution) that, though metaphysical problems remain insoluble, their explanation can be constantly advanced through more adequate methods. Now, if the limited nature of every metaphysical solution means that truth is inexhaustible and that human knowledge is never absolutely perfect and completed, this affirmation is shared by all the great metaphysicians of classic-Christian thought. But what Hartmann means is this: (1) "adequate methods" are valid only to establish ontology (which, for him, is nothing more than phenomenology) and not metaphysics, which always remains "irrational"; (2) truth is "historical"—not in the sense (compatible with human truth which still remains truth) that it enriches itself historically so that a truth once discovered endures and becomes integrated with other truths, but in that other sense, that it is changeable, and at a certain point ceases to be truth. This amounts to saying that truth was never true. How philosophy can be a most rigorous "science," as Hartmann claims, is not understandable at all. This last remark is part of the critique that can be made against the entire thought of Hartmann, viz., he understands philosophical problems clearly; he posits them as they must be posited; he criticizes accurately the mistaken formulations and solutions offered of them; yet, he carries on his research in such a way as to arrive at results that are opposite to those which were properly intended. Thus, what happened to Hartmann is that he vindicated the indispensability of metaphysics and then denied it by identifying it with the irrational; he introduced himself as a philosopher of ontology or being, and then remained on the edge of ontology and of the inquiry on being.

Hartmann, moreover, blames traditional metaphysics for building closed systems through a method resting on the deductions from *a priori* principles. Interest no longer lies in the solution proposed by these systems but in the problems they arouse. According to him, an opposite method must be adopted: ontology (the study of being as being) engaged in grasping that unity among phenomena which makes of them an orderly whole (a "cosmos") is indeed *philosophia prima* as *ratio essendi;* but it is *philosophia ultima* as *ratio cognoscendi* inasmuch as the ultimate step in philosophy is to grasp being *qua* being or the unity of the real. Yet, in Hartmann, philosophy never takes this step, so that the *ratio cognoscendi* not only fails to make contact with the *ratio essendi,* but opposes it. This clarifies: (1) the difference which Hartmann makes between metaphysics and ontology, (2) his concept of "problem," and (3) the concept of "asystematicity."

(1) Metaphysics is not a philosophical science, but that ensemble of problems to which no answer can be given; ontology, instead, is the ultimate of what we are able to know about being. As we have said, in Hartmann's view we cannot know the unity of the real, that is, we cannot solve the very problem of ontology as *philosophia ultima:* hence, we are left only with the knowledge of phenomena. And this means that we are able to know everything about being, except being *qua* being. But, in this way, ontology is gone for good; nor could it be otherwise, once metaphysics, distinct from and opposed to ontology, is the irrational.

(2) The *problem* is any object whether unknown (the problems of metaphysical) or knowable. The known and the unknown are mingled in every problem. In fact, if a problem is distinguished from another, it means that something is known in it; but, if its solution is attempted, it means that not everything is known in it. The task of philosophy is to posit problems.

Understood as an ensemble of essential problems, metaphysics reveals insurmountable *aporias,* insoluble contradictions, which are inherent in the very nature of reality. Systematic philosophy has always endeavored to grasp the unity of the real but, in this way, it has distorted the aporetic nature of reality and supplied only apparent solutions. Open research, instead, discloses the contradictions in reality and, without attempting the impossible systematic unification, it confines itself to describing them so that reality does not have to lose any of its aspects. The "constant" in all metaphysical problems "is their insuppressible irrational element; the same condition of distance and inaccessibility of the object to the subject prevails everywhere." Hartmann remarks, however, that this is not a question of an "irrationality in itself," but, always of an "irrationality for us." Here lies the main difficulty confronting systematic philosophy: "It consists in a sort of limitation, the same one in every direction, of what is possible 'for us.' What makes this difficulty is not only the mere presence of the irrational 'for us,' but also the impossibility of rendering a direct account of it to ourselves. It is not a question of dominating the irrational, of overcoming it by knowing it, which is beyond human possibility. Neither is it enough to restrict ourselves to making a contact with it or pointing out the existence of the problem. It is precisely in the middle of these two attitudes that for us lies the task of making a rigorously aporetic treatment designed to draw the unknown near to us on the basis of its relationship with the known. If it were an 'unknown in itself,' every effort would be worthless from the outset. If it were such, it could never be shown clearly, nor could it be even sketched. As something simply 'unknown to us,' we can only perceive it at the boundaries of knowability. Moreover, in the presence of such boundaries we find problems everywhere." Forcing the manifold datum into an artificial unity means departing, more and more, from the natural unity of the world. Instead, if we simply surrender, without prejudice, to multiplicity and follow the problems in their divergent lines, we are more certain to arrive at their unity. "For the time being it is not possible to achieve this result in the unity of a closed discipline. Metaphysics as the inclusive system of a science has become in this sense impossible. However, the guarantee for the hidden unity of its object is found here. To claim to achieve the unity of this discipline at the present stage of inquiry is a utopian pretense that does not correspond to the situation of the problem."

(3) Criticism of systematic philosophy is obviously one of the characteristics in Hartmann's thought. He pursues his inquiry free of presuppositions and prejudices. He does not deny *a priori* that the outcome of a research may not be a system, but he denies the systematic position of those who have the system precede the research in such a way that they aim at the former from the start. "The task of those who wish to proceed critically in metaphysical problems requires . . . the renunciation of any hasty satisfaction of *Weltanschauung*, and of any frenzy for obtaining results at all costs; it requires the complete rejection of any kind of pre-conceived systematic construction, as well as the strong rejection of all 'metaphysical exigencies'. . . ." Metaphysical inquiry demands a long breath and a calm, aporetic procedure embracing the entire horizon of metaphysical problems, the freeing of oneself from every predilection toward cherished forms of visions of the world, and a philosophical *ethos* based on endurance and intellectual self-discipline. The incompetent man sinks unrestrainedly into solutions already abandoned and swept away by history; he has not learned anything from the great failures suffered by human thought, and every apparent "destruction of the traditional forms cannot help him" (*Systematische Philosophie*, Stuttgart und Berlin, 1942). Hartmann, the enemy of "philosophical system," is one of the most systematic (in the best sense) thinkers of our century. We must avoid every preconceived *apriorism* as well as any confusion resulting from the many "fields of inquiry." For example, the ontological problem of being is something different from the problem of knowledge, though idealism confuses the two.

As we know, Kant distinguishes between the object of knowledge and the thing in itself and confines knowledge to the phenomenon; Hartmann remarks that "to know something" and "something appears" to a subject are equivalent expressions; what is manifested in the phenomenon is its being and, hence, together with the phenomenon we group a thing in itself manifested by the phenomenon. In short, the phenomenon lets its metaphenomenal content "appear": all phenomena are phenomena of an *in se* (*Ansichseinsphänomene*). Gnosiology is thus changed into ontology. The error of Kantian, Neo-Kantian, idealistic, and positivistic gnosiologism lies in failing to distinguish between being in itself (*das Seiende*) and being-object (of a consciousness), which is knowledge. For this reason, gnosiologism cannot come out of the sphere of consciousness in order to grasp being *qua* being (ontology). These objections are also applicable to Husserl's phenomenology, which confines itself to grasping and describing the phenomena of things while missing the things themselves: by definition, it stops at the surface of problems and does not go beyond pure appearances. Phenomenological intentionality deals with "intentional" objects and not with objects subsisting in themselves. Hartmann, like Husserl, moves from the "datum," but he denies that this is a datum confronting a "naive consciousness"; he maintains, instead, that this is a datum facing a "philosophical consciousness," which is reflection and judgment and which must be distinguished even from "scientific" consciousness. To be sure, the philosopher cannot ignore the findings of science and, when he philosophizes about nature, he has to accept them; yet, scientific results are one thing, and the philosophy of the scientist is another. The scientist must not pretend to be omniscient and must not "forget that there are problems, lying beyond the bounds of science, of which he is no judge." Nature, in fact, presents problems which go beyond the competence of the scientist and the limits of particular sciences. A scientific discovery, which may be valid for the explanation of one aspect of corporeal reality, must not be generalized and used as a formula capable of accounting for the totality of reality. In such a case, one aspect of reality is arbitrarily identified with totality of reality, so that, by going beyond the limits of science, nonscientific and nonphilosophical affirmations are made about the totality of reality. These remarks of Hartmann are very exact (although not new) and possess a current value as a result of the confusion between science and philosophy—a characteristic that is found in vast sections of present-day thought.

Let us now return to ontology and to what is closely connected with it, namely, the theory of knowledge. The ontological problem of being as being is primary and essential. Thought, of its essence, cannot be but thought of "something"; therefore, it posits, as thought, the problem of being. Knowledge is *apprehension* (Erfassung) of "something," which is what is, that is, being. The "what is" is the being in itself (*Ansichsein*) and not "for us." The being in itself when it is known (and known only to the extent of its "facing" of a subject, since in itself it does remain immutably being), is the being-object: knowledge is *objection* (*Objektion*). In this sense, it is a "transcendent" act, that is, one not completed in consciousness, but which surpasses consciousness and leads it to the being which exists independently, in itself. Idealism and phenome-nology consider knowledge as something referring to objects-contents immanent in it. Hartmann, instead, considers knowledge as something referring to being-objects that transcend it: "that which is the object of knowledge has a trans-objective being; it is in itself." *Transcendent-emotional acts* undoubtedly reveal the existence of being in itself: they all are phenomena having in common something that "is opposed" to the subject. The object of transcendent cognitive acts is identical with the object of transcendent emotional acts; the former reveal to us the "mode of being" (*Sosein*) of being and the existence (*Dasein*) of being itself; the transcendence of cognitive acts is confirmed by that of the emotional acts, which is founded on the real concatenation of life.

We are not going to follow Hartmann in his ample and systematic researches on being that make up the four volumes of *Ontology*: not because they are not important (some of his analyses are clarifying and exemplary for their rigor of method and penetration), but because a detailed exposition of them exceeds the limits of our work. We confine our study to providing a brief outline centered on the theory of cate-gories.

Hartmann distinguishes *four spheres of being:* two primary (real and ideal being) and two secondary spheres (that of knowledge and that of logic). The sphere of real being is bound to that of knowledge and the sphere of the ideal being (values, mathematical being) to that of the logical. The alogical and what is contradictory in reality escape the laws of logic. The *grades of being* are matter, life, consciousness, and intellect; in correspondence with them we find within the order of knowledge, perception, intuition, knowledge, and learning (while logical being is con-structed as concept, judgment, and reasoning).

The grades of being are defined through categories, distinguished as "modal" and "fundamental." The method of inquiry as regards the cate-gories is descriptive and phenomenological (description of what is given). Modal categories are divided into absolute modes (reality-unreality) and relational modes (possibility, impossibility, and necessity). Among the fundamental categories we find the "law of force" (inferior grade) and the "law of freedom" (superior grade). The categories of nature are distinguished in "dimensional" (space and time), "cosmological" ("becom-ing" is fundamental), and "organological" or pertaining to the living world.[11]

---

[11] Regarding the categories of space (category of the corporeal world) and of time (category of the real, corporeal and spiritual being) Hartmann denies the existence of the ideal being (the only one outside of time) as well as that of the eternal real Being (God) considered as one of the prejudices of traditional meta-physics. He also goes on to deny the being of the immortality of the soul which, along with the real eternal Being, is due to extraphilosophical motives, namely, the

One grade of being is "spiritual being," to be distinguished from "psychic being," which is the grade of knowledge also possessed by animals. The category of the spirit is the most irrational and unfathomable in its structure. Hartmann distinguishes three forms: "personal spirit" (real, individual, temporal, nonspatial though bound to space, free, indefinable, and only describable, with the fundamental characteristic of personality); "objective spirit" (which is the spirit's life as regards human groups and "travels" from person to person—law, custom, language, beliefs, and so on—as historical spirit); and the "objectivated spirit," composed of the objective spirit and of the objectivation of the personal spirit.

Prior to ontology, Hartmann formulated his ethics in which Scheler's influence is very strong (phenomenological method, axiological absolutism, and the conception of values as irrational essences). Scheler, however, is stripped of personalism (Hartmann's ethics is an *impersonalistic* phenomenology of values) and of theism (Hartmann also rejected the theory of the collective person), for Hartmann maintains that man, as a moral being, has an absolute autonomy, and beyond man there is no teleological principle, no God, who in transcending man would annihilate him as person.

The task of morality is the recognition and the appreciation of all values of life. The ethics of pleasure (hedonism), of happiness (eudaemonism), and of the useful (utilitarianism) are all insufficient, and are criticized and rejected by Hartmann as erroneous and inadequate. In opposition to Kant, Hartmann maintains that law cannot be reduced to a subjective principle: the moral *a priori* is not a pure form, but an objective reality, a world of ideal objects, and of "values." We cannot know values in themselves. "The ideal and the real are equally irrational; the spheres of being-in-itself are equally indefinable"; we can only describe values according to their content and significance for us. A consciousness that appreciates values is necessary, but they are unknown, objective "essences." In the intuition of values the subject "is purely receptive and passive and is determined by its object, the value which exists in itself; the subject determines nothing on its part. Value is as little affected by intuition as an object of knowledge is affected by the fact of its being known." There is no real relationship between subject and values, but only a form of "relationality" by which the essence of values is not affected. In short, for Hartmann, values contain something which cannot be reduced to a law and which does not enter into relation—something that is "substantial" and "material." A creative energy proceeds from them. "In contact with values, being loses its balance, is set in motion,

------

desire to prolong life beyond time. He also criticizes and rejects the concept of substance as eternal and immutable (in the Platonic sense), this also due to a prejudice of classical metaphysics.

and is inclined to reach beyond itself." In order that values should penetrate into reality, we need a being "able to heed their call and ready to move into action." However, values are and continue to be what they ought to be, whether they are realized or not. Consequently, values have no irresistible force making them act in reality by themselves; they tend toward a determination, but they themselves determine nothing. "They provoke certain determinations of the will, but have no power to realize them."

We have an immediate emotional intuition of values. As there is an *a priori* of thought and judgment ("intellective *a priori*"), so there is an *a priori* of feeling ("emotional *a priori*"), the *a priori* of values, which is immediate, intuitive, and sentimental—one that penetrates into our consciousness and conception of life, conferring the character of value on everything happening within our horizon. The apprehension of a value awakens in us an intuition which is prior to experience. In fact, moral consciousness is precisely the first and direct intuition of values, the voice or appeal from a superior, ideal world. Morality must proceed from the knowledge of the *a priori* ethic, from the datum; hence, above all, ethics is a phenomenology of values. These appear to us as entities (forms) of a realm possessing structures, laws, and orders proper to them. The sphere of values is connected with the other ideal spheres of mathematical and logical entities, whose internal constitution and extension we do not know. Of all the numerous orders of being, the best known to us is the order of ethical values.

Hartmann is confronted with the same problem as Scheler: Does a hierarchy of values exist within the limits in which their world is known to us? Are values reducible to unity? Hartmann sees no purpose in a supreme unity; morality needs only a systematic connection of supreme values. We may classify them according to three basic characteristics: "specific content" (every value has its own quality differing from that of any other), "force," and "height." The height of values is in inverse ratio to their force (for example, charity is a value higher than respect toward another person; and, yet, we feel the latter value with greater force than we feel the former). Goods are distinguished from values. Ethics deals with goods only to the extent that they affect our inclination toward values. Hartmann classifies goods according to some principal types such as existence, situation, power, and happiness. He distinguishes moral values into "fundamental" values (nobility, purity, pride, and goodness, which is the first value) and "special" values which correspond to so-called virtues (justice, wisdom, and the like). Charity is axiologically the highest value. Consciousness prefers some values more than others. The value of personality resides in the personal synthesis of values. In opposition to Kant, Hartmann defends the value of personality: "Act according to your universal moral conscience but also according to your individual conscience." Love strengthens personality and is the synthesis of two ethical complexes. The value of love is not in its requital, but in loving. Love is knowledge of the ideal person. Hartmann distinguishes between "duty" and value; duty is the inclination toward something, while value is the object of this inclination. There is this connection between them, however: the duty emanating from value is directed toward man as a mediating factor in the real world.

As we have said, Hartmann maintains that values exist independent of their realization which depends on the free activity of the subject. Only the conscious subject is aroused by the ideal power of values and, on the other hand, the subject becomes a moral being, a "person" in the true sense of the word, insofar as it acts under the influence of value. As an empirical subject it is an "ego" opposing the "nonego"; as a person it is an "ego" with respect to a "you." The subject realizes values in a certain way, but it could realize them differently, or could realize them not at all; hence, the subject is *free*. Without freedom there would be no possibility for moral life. Without freedom there is a possibility for virtues but, in such an event, these phenomena would not be properly moral. On the other hand, freedom as "power to do otherwise" does not mean absolute indetermination; it means that freedom excludes causal determination, consonant with natural reality, but not every other form of determination. To be sure, there is a necessity with respect to what ought to be, and with respect to law, which is independent of ontological and causal necessity. Causality is not the antithesis of freedom. "A free will as final action is possible in a world causally determined in its totality." Freedom does not consist in "indifference," but in a personal determination which surpasses ethical and causal determination, that is, freedom is freedom even with respect to values. But then, Hartmann declares, there is no decisive argument on behalf of freedom. Because of his preconceived atheism, he concludes with a series of irrational and insoluble antinomies between ethics and religion.

With respect to Hartmann's *Ethics,* it has been rightly remarked: "Here we are in the presence of an alternative from which we cannot escape. If an 'ethics' is possible, a 'metaphysics' must also be possible. And if the latter is not possible, then 'ethics' is only a surreptitious and illegitimate commentary." [12]

This objection can be extended to Hartmann's whole philosophy, for the denial of the possibility of metaphysics renders even his ontology a "surreptitious commentary." Hartmann's discourse is indeed a peculiar one: the fundamental problem of ontology is that of being (*Sein*), but being is unknowable and irrational; therefore, ontology must confine it-

[12] P. Martinetti, *Ragione e fede* (Turin, Einaudi, 1942), p. 227.

self to the problem of *entia (Seiendes)*. The conclusion to be drawn from such an agnostic premise should have really been this: "If metaphysics is not possible, neither is ontology," nor ethics, nor a theory of knowledge unless the latter is skeptical or problematical. But this does not occur to Hartmann, who tranquilly constructs his ontology and his ethics, knotting his thought into a bundle of contradictions and compromises which are all conditioned by his antimetaphysical prejudices and preconceptions. He affirms, in fact, that being is the unknown; yet he adds that a part of it becomes known in the *entia*, in the "particularizations," where there is "something well-known." What is it? And how can that which ontology knows be said to be true? (Hartmann says that philosophy *is* science). And what is being with respect to the *entia* or particularizations? Hartmann replies that being is "identity" within the multiplicity of *entia*. But, further, how is he able to say that it is "identity," if being is unknowable and indefinable in itself? It can be identical like diversity or even absurdity, since it is unintelligible and irrational. Hartmann says that the act of knowledge, inasmuch as it apprehends objects in themselves, is a transcendent act. But, how can existence of the object in itself be demonstrated? As an ontologist, Hartmann does not demonstrate it; he presupposes it. "Presupposition of objects in themselves is the fundamental presupposition." [13] Then, if the object in itself is a presupposition, the transcendence of the act of knowing is affirmed solely on the basis of this presupposition! Thus, this philosopher—who all his life blamed metaphysical systems precisely because they deduce everything from a principle *a priori*—builds his own system on a presupposition and rambles in a vicious circle through thousands of pages. He also wanders into a blind alley: ontology, that is, *philosophia prima* as *ratio essendi* should also be *philosophia ultima* as *ratio cognoscendi;* but, unfortunately, ontology always remains as a philosophy "next to the last," in that it never reaches the knowledge of the "first," namely, being—that is, it never becomes adequate as *ratio essendi;* thus the two orders are always opposed to each other with no hope of being reconciled. There is only one thing to be done, to describe and analyze phenomena, that is, to construct more phenomenology. Ontology, then, is still to be built, perhaps by utilizing Hartmann's particular analyses (some of which are really profound and masterly) by discarding his prejudices against a philosophy that is nothing but a problem (always a problem) and by rejecting his prejudices against ancient metaphysics and metaphysics in general. Otherwise, nothing can be achieved as regards ontology because of lack of method, lack of metaphysical sensibility, and because of a deplorable confusion between ontology itself and phenomenology. Hartmann, who

---

[13] See, on this, the keen study of L. Lugarini, "Essere e conoscere in N. Hartmann," *Acme*, Parts I and II (1949), 117 ff.

is well-intentioned toward ontology, is Husserl's victim—that is, a victim of this thinker who, by reducing the idea to phenomenon, namely, to the immediateness of the intentional apprehension, deprives spirit of the truth whereby it knows and unifies. Moreover, it is no longer possible to have, if we follow Hartmann, a philosophy of being, not even one concerning its determinations because there is no philosophy of *entia* without a philosophy of being. There can be only a description of phenomena. Thus, Hartmann is unable to say anything about being, nor does he succeed in establishing freedom; rather, on account of his anti-theological preconcepts, he destroys Scheler's personalism while, at the same time, he moves away from that "return to the human" (there is no concrete "human" without a theological basis), which is Scheler's merit. Even the "scientific" nature of philosophy which Hartmann vindicates, and which in itself is commendable, is ultimately denied by his historicism of truth and his conception of philosophy as a problem, a problem forever incapable of solution.

V

EXISTENTIALISM

---

1. Historical Position and Fundamental Concepts

It is not precise, by any means, to hold that existentialism is the pure and simple progeny of phenomenology. To be sure, Heidegger was influenced by Husserl's phenomenology. However, Heidegger's theses, even when inspired by Husserl's motivations, signify something else. It is undeniable that Scheler, who underlines the nonobjectivating character of the person on which he focuses almost his entire axiology, marks the transition from phenomenology to existentialism; yet, Scheler's philosophy is still philosophy of the essence and not philosophy of existence. On the other hand, existentialism, though tied up with Husserl's phenomenology (particularly for its method) and with themes derived from Scheler's personalism, draws its most profound inspirations from other areas of the history of philosophy. It represents not only an interpretation of certain exigencies that are a characteristic of our age—which has been dubbed the epoch of "crisis" and of which existentialism is the most conscious, exasperated and, perhaps, conclusive moment—but also represents a critical "revision" of modern thought. Existentialism, in fact, denounces the latter's myths, its lack of criticism, and its lack of consequentiality in the conclusions drawn from given premises. Yet, existentialism itself which, after all, is the offspring of modern thought, dogmatizes the "myth of crisis" and identifies the very essence of existence and of philosophy with this "crisis."

Existentialism is a complex movement, not easy to define on account of its very character as a "philosophy of the vitally experienced"; even its terminology is vague and imprecise. Hence the disparity in the ways of evaluating existentialism and all the erroneous or unilateral interpretations made about it. In order to guide our reader, and in order to achieve a critical exposition of existentialist philosophy, we shall begin by tracing more exactly its antecedents, its polemic reactions to other philosophies, and the "environment" that produced it. In this way we shall be able to see how an initial "state of mind" or a "psychological situation" could become the most widespread and the most discussed philosophy of the last twenty-five years.

By oversimplification and with a *boutade* of easy effect, we could say that contemporary existentialism came into the world on that foggy day or that dark night when a young German professor, Martin Heidegger, bored and depressed, came upon the almost forgotten books of a gloomy Danish theologian, Kierkegaard, who had been a pessimist and a humorist —a pessimist because he was a humorist, and a humorist because he was a pessimist. He read them, purified them of the "myths" of Adam and Eve, of the devil and of God, of sin and grace; and, having thus secularized them, he thought them over very thoroughly, and then wrote and published (1927) the first volume of his own work in which "being" loses itself into "time," becomes existential, and discovers that it exists for nought or for death. However, it is obviously superficial to consider existentialism as Kierkegaard's (or Nietzsche's) drama which, being "emptied of its religious content and its irreproducible and very personal accent," has now been taken up again, "typified, and almost standardized by certain contemporary German professors who, on the canvas of a drama of existence, have woven *the* drama of existence."[1] Existentialism is much more than that, and it was not born because Kierkegaard was discovered and studied; Kierkegaard was discovered and studied because he responded to spiritual needs and philosophical exigencies antecedent to his discovery. The Kierkegaard-Renaissance, which characterized a good portion of German philosophy in the period following the First World War, was due to the favorable climate it found in Germany (a climate produced by both military defeat and, philosophically, by the critical revision under which modern thought had been laboring since the immediate developments of Hegelianism) and not vice-versa. Existentialism (and this is one of its prejudices) considered "the crisis of an epoch" as the "crisis of existence" or of man in general, and the crisis of a philosophical position as that of philosophy as such. Existentialism, not the solution but an expression of the crisis, embodies the uneasiness, bewilderment, anxieties and aspirations affecting contemporary European consciousness. This is so even when we prescind from its historical or *de*

[1] G. De Ruggiero, *Esistenzialismo* (Bari, Laterza, 1942), pp. 6-7.

facto derivation from Kierkegaard, who certainly was not the only one to influence Heidegger, a man immersed in phenomenology as well as indirectly influenced by the "philosophies of life." Yet, there is another consideration: existentialism, almost simultaneously with its German expression was developing in France independently of Kierkegaard, and in Russia through the rethinking of the conception of existence expressed in Dostoyevsky's literary work. Unamuno in Spain had anticipated it for about a decade (at least in some theses) and in Italy, during the same period, the critical revision of Gentile's actualism, aimed at regaining concrete existence, had begun. All these exigencies coming to maturity almost simultaneously led to the Kierkegaard-Renaissance, and led to the discovery of the Danish thinker as their remote and "current" master, who, being called into the dance was whirled now to the left, now to the right; rejected in some points, accepted in others; and in still others "interpreted" or transformed.

Depending on the various thinkers and their respective countries, the doctrinal precedents of existentialism may be found in Kierkegaard as well as in Dostoyevsky, in Schopenhauer as in Nietzsche, in Dilthey as in pragmatism, in the romanticists of the early nineteenth century and in Rilke, Pascal, and Bergson, or in Husserl, and so on. None of the foregoing thinkers is indeed to be associated simply with existentialism (some of them, if they could be asked, would reject all existentialist theses, even if they would go along with existentialism in opposing some idealistic and rationalistic currents), and many of them are not easily recognizable through the "interpretations" made of them by the philosophers of existence. However, there is no doubt that existentialism borrows for example the phenomenological method from Husserl (though not his doctrinal theses; Husserl, a philosopher of the essence, "brackets" existence "in parentheses") and finds in Husserl's incommunicable and autonomous eidetic spheres a good start for the dissolution of being, which Hartmann on his part had relegated (since 1921) to the sphere of the unknowable or sphere of the irrational. Moreover, there is no doubt that in post-Hegelian historicism in general (and in Dilthey in particular), existentialism finds (and makes use of) the "temporalization" of Hegel's dialectic and its fragmentization into so many historical spheres, each of which expresses one of the numberless meanings of existence.

However, existentialism without Lutheranism would still remain unexplained in its essentiality; and so, in our opinion, one can never insist too much on this point; Kierkegaard, in fact, is a Protestant theologian; Unamuno is influenced by Protestantism; Protestant theology received a new, vigorous, and fertile rethinking through existentialism (one has only to think of Barth). Furthermore, sin, which Lutheranism considers an act of pride perpetrated by reason, has corrupted human nature, and made it an "individualized" entity. Between God and man there is a radical opposition. Man, a slave to sin, can do nothing to save himself; whatever he does is bound to be sinful. There is then a "fracture" or a "breach" between the divine and the human, grace and freedom, faith and reason (the "meretrix of Satan"). Protestant theology is "theology of crisis" or the theology of this irreparable "breach" between God and man. Theological existentialism accepts this Lutheran thesis and exasperates it; the nontheological type "laicizes" Luther and makes this "breach" the essence of the human as such. The nothingness of man before God (Luther)— detheologized—constitutes the "being for the nought" of Heidegger. One could remark that French existentialism is not Lutheran; we reply at once that it could not be fully understood without Jansenism, which is still a breach between the human and the divine, freedom and grace, as well as an annulment of man in sin, from which only God's free action can redeem him.

Furthermore, there are still some who say that existentialism is indeed a "philosophy of crisis," but not in the sense that it is caused by an epoch of crisis like ours; they rather say that existentialism is what it is because philosophy itself, and hence existence as such, is crisis, that is to say, a "fracture," a "breach." To say this amounts to accepting the Lutheran thesis dogmatically though inadvertently, whether such a thesis is maintained in all its theological meaning or accepted after it has been detheologized. Moreover, to say this amounts to offering a cheap apology for existentialism; one naively accepts its presupposition that existence is a "breach" and, therefore, true philosophy can only be a philosophy of crisis. On the contrary, existentialism is a philosophy of crisis precisely in the sense that it is a crisis of philosophy, that is, loss of the principle of being and, hence, inability to give a real meaning to existence which, suspended in mid-air, can only be understood as a "fracture" and a "nothingness." Existentialism found its favorable environment and, as we might say, the soil prepared for its germination, in the "jolts" of the First and Second World Wars. On the basis of this situation of fact, it raised the (historical) "fractures" of a tormented generation to fractures affecting human existence as such and, therefore, making them no longer historical but structurally and ontologically inherent in man. The "crisis" thus understood as a metaphysical principle is simply a myth; and existentialism is in this sense the philosophy of the myth of crisis, of a "broken" and lacerated existence—beyond the power of any tailor to mend it and sew it up again. Existentialism marks the highest point first in the disruption and then in the loss of being; existentialism dogmatically sanctions the breach between "life" and "thought." "Existentialist experience," emptied of being, is the nothingness of life, of thought, and of existence—the gratuitous and the absurd.

On the one hand, an implacable criticism carried on for almost a century had worn thin reliance on reason, its principles and powers, just as it had gradually destroyed the concepts of being, substance, idea and essence—all of which had been historized and rendered relative; on the other hand, in Germany (and not only there) an atmosphere of distrust and weariness, humiliation and depression had been created as a result of the defeat of 1918 (the principle of the national, authoritarian State and the myth of a Greater Germany as the incarnation of God and as the guide of the world, had been undermined). War did not appear to be the means for the re-establishment of new and higher equilibriums (in accordance with the Hegelian thesis), but was itself viewed as an expression of the lack of balance and as a begetter of other imbalances; it bewildered man's spirit even more and exasperated the problem concerning the place and significance of the individual in the general scheme of life and existence. The vitalistic enthusiasms of the "philosophies of life" were quenched in the anguish of a philosophy of life understood as nothingness and death. History, as understood by idealistic historicism (revelation of the Idea and realization of God Himself in the world) appeared to be an artificial and nonauthentic myth concealing what history really is: a theater of absurd struggles, an eruption of blind forces, and an immense field for the inexplicable action of evil. What can historicism say to man in the presence of the phenomenon of war which places him in contact with death and sorrow, and on the edge of that unstable point where martyrdom and heroism share boundaries with cruelty and barbarism? What ideals can it locate beyond chaos and destruction; what experience not tinctured in blood; what feelings not poisoned by rancor and hatred? What answers does Kantian and Hegelian rationalism give to the peremptory and unavoidable questions of existence? Is historicism able to explain the destiny of a single man? These are the questions from which contemporary existentialism draws its beginning; and its answers, according to its sponsors, have enabled man to gain awareness of the "crisis"—not of a historical crisis, but of a crisis involving his human condition, whose categories are anguish, contradiction, failure, nought and absurdity. Existence does not grasp its being in being, but in the nought of being, which is its negation. Reason is always loss and shipwreck; religion is only a subjective and irrational faith, a faith in the absurd and the scandal to reason.

Existentialism is led by its concept of existence to intensify the polemic against both Kantian and Hegelian rationalism. In so far as it is individuality and personality, existence rises as a protest (already so considered by Kierkegaard) against universal reason that is held to be valid for all but to deny what is peculiar or individual in each person. Whether in the presence of a geometrical reason, or a Kantian humanity identified with rationality, or a Hegelian dialectic of the Spirit, the individual with his anxieties and his hopes, with his sense of life and death, with his profound problem of salvation or perdition remains annihilated and absorbed, neutralized and unheard; his appeals receive no messages, and his requests no answers. However, it would be one-sided and erroneous to polarize the relations of idealism and existentialism on sterile polemics and absolute opposition; as we shall see in particular, they are much deeper. In the first place, not all idealism is Hegelian, and even in Kierkegaard himself it is not a question of an antidialectical polemic, but of the contraposition of two types of dialectic. Consequently, the irrationalism consonant with existentialism must be understood as a reaction against the logical system which wishes to embrace and explain everything and as a feeling of insufferance against the same system for its failure to recognize the irreducible nature of the individual; and, finally, it represents a reaction against the nonauthenticity of rationalistic reason, which does not express the authenticity of concrete existence.

There is in existentialism a so-called theistic stream which unifies indissolubly the problems of the person and of God, and which defines existence as an essential vocation or religious transcendence: to establish the "person" philosophically is to grasp its "religious invocation." Exactly in the concrete individuality of the individual person—as Kierkegaard and, after all, even Nietzsche and Unamuno teach—there occurs the meeting of the infinite and the finite, of eternity and time, of transcendence and immanence, even if all this is paradoxical and absurd so far as reason is concerned. To penetrate deeply into concrete existence is, in fact, to understand it for the living contradiction that it is. This act of penetration enables us to feel existence in its situation, in relation to itself and in relationship to transcendence: we feel existence as the intersection of incarnation and of participation.

Existentialism, in this sense, focuses on the living experience of the "presence" of God in the ego and on the position of the individual before God. To seek God is to decide about oneself, and to seek oneself is to reach for God. The two terms of the search are mutually "engaged": the truth of man is attained in going back to God, as the truth of God is authentically revealed in the human existential state. The problem of God and man is not an abstract problem, but an experience of life lived through. To establish the person philosophically means, then, to grasp the person in its "situation" and in its "participation"; it means to investigate the person in whatever condition it happens to be: in *freedom* as freedom forms and reveals the person, in *dignity* as dignity places the person beyond transient and contingent particularity.

Another characteristic of existentialism in general is its polemic against the anonymous life of the individual, one among many, and against the customary and conventional life, in which the individual loses the sense of responsibility and of destiny, as well as the call to genuine existence. It is necessary to be oneself, and only oneself, and conquer one's own authenticity together with the consciousness of a "finitude" that is suspended, like a leaf over an abyss, between finite and infinite, time and eternity. To be oneself is to live intimately and desperately the terms of an antinomy, an existence that is broken and fragmentized in its perennial "uncertitude" and continuous "break." This is not a philosophy of rational harmony and rational unity, but a philosophy of "fracture," of existential reality which is a singularity that cannot be repeated, and a choice that implies a decision without recourse. In this sense existence is "freedom," suspension between problem and certitude, research and truth; existence is act, problem, and a drama that cannot be translated into the transparency and light of an idea, nor exalted by a vital impetus. Existence is fracture and is always suspended between two worlds, immanence and transcendence, with no possibility for a definitive synthesis, and without hope for a refuge in a super-existence. Existence is the "center," the meeting point of all antitheses, and its problem is the very problem of being.[2] The person demands the metaphysical solution.

It appears evident, from what we have been saying so far, that existentialism is not to be defined generically as a philosophy of existence (in this sense, nearly all philosophers are existentialists), but as a philosophy which defines existence in a certain way—that is, which gives such an "existentialist" connotation to existence as to make it the existence of existentialism. This peculiar manner of defining it, so difficult to state with precision, stems from a subjective experience, which has been lived through and is called "existential"; that is, every existentialist defines existence in his own way, in conformity with his personal existential experience. This starting point implies a presupposition: existence cannot be defined; it cannot be *objectified*. In fact, there is before me no objective *quiddity* extraneous to me as I to it. What confronts me is my own existence, it is *myself* existing; the philosophy of existence means philosophy of my lived experience. However, to say so, to say that experience cannot be objectified and is indefinable, amounts to rendering impossible even a "philosophy" of existence. The existentialist, in a strict sense, should confine himself to saying: "This is my lived experience." He should not even describe it, for in so doing he not only objectifies it but also deprives it of its immediateness. Moreover, for existentialism every existent (man) *has* no existence, but *is* existence. If man possessed existence, this would belong to an essence and would be definable; instead, there is no essence defining human existence, but the latter is defined by itself; every existent *is* his existence. This is equivalent to saying that it is

[2] L. Pareyson, *Studi sull'esistenzialismo* (Florence, Sansoni, 1950), pp. 25 ff.

existence which defines the essence and not vice versa; each man is not an essence having existence, but an existence giving himself his own essence. Man *exists,* not *is;* he is what he "creates himself" by existing—his existence coincides wholly with temporality. The principle of classical metaphysics is *overturned:* it is not existence that is defined from essence but essence from existence; and essence is defined in the sense that it is the historical realization of existence itself, and so the former coincides with the transitory moments affecting the latter's becoming. Thus essence is lost and denied; existence is truly indefinable, in the sense that it is incomprehensible and absurd; it is pure contingency, punctuality of accidents, pure temporality (and not temporality proper). Hence, the identification of existence and freedom: man *is* his freedom. We shall see how even such a concept of freedom is absurd.

Singular and nonobjectifiable, the existent inserts himself into the world, however; he finds himself in a determinate "situation." In truth, he does not "find himself" but rather *is* his own situation, the one "actually" defining his existence. Man is bound to the world and to other men—a bond that, like the situation, is the *being* pertinent to human existence; he is bound to the world and *engaged* in life. In it he is the whole of himself, in his absolute historicity, which he must not "evade"; he must instead accept this "destiny" of being defined by his situations, of *being* his situations (the destiny of nought and death). Consequently, such an existence which cannot be objectivated and whose essence (or essences) is constituted by its situations and its being realized cannot be known "intellectually"; in fact, to know by the intellect is to objectify: neither reason nor intellect can grasp existence in its authenticity. Existence, which is a lived experience, is had in the act of living its finiteness and temporaneity or, in its *anguish* of feeling itself as finite, "thrown into the world" and destined to death. That being said, he is not entirely wrong who defined existentialism as the *nausée de l'impuissance* (Gurvitch), the doctrine that deprives men of all his richness; but he is also right who sees in it (Pareyson) an original way of representing "to philosophical meditation the richness of spiritual life" together with a "strong manifestation of contemporary personalism," even if the inevitable conclusion on the part of existentialism is both the negation of the person as a value and the negation of all values embodied in, and expressed by, the person itself.

2. Existentialism as "Crisis" and as "Critique" of Modern Thought Resting on Immanentism and Historicism

French and German existentialism is also a fashion, snobbery, and pose; but it is not only this; it indeed is much more. It is the most mature conclusion of modern thought with respect to those aspects which characterize it as immanentism. Moreover, existentialism is the merciless and explicit consciousness of the intrinsic uncertainty in which the Cartesian "Archimedean revolution" and the Kantian "Copernican revolution" with their positivistic and idealistic developments have placed the principles of being and, with it, the principles of knowledge and action. In this sense existentialism, on the one hand, represents the consciousness of the "fracture" caused by modern immanentism (and hence the latter's "crisis") and, on the other, the awareness that nothing can be done once that fracture has taken place, so that being is lost and, with it, man and all the values, human and divine. Therefore, existentialism is a "critique" of modern immanentism. Furthermore, existentialism is, in my opinion, the most extreme (and conclusive, perhaps) point of what on other occasions I have called the "self-dissolution" of modern thought, which began with the fundamental criticism of Hegelianism by Kierkegaard, Feuerbach, and Marx. In other words, with its secularization of the sacred, with its separation of all forms of human activity from theology, with its vindication of the absolute autonomy of both reason (held to be self-sustaining and capable of creating truth by itself) and will (which is a law unto itself), and with its historicity (relativity) of all truth and of all spiritual values (human and divine) and even of God himself—the philosophy of immanence believed (and here lies the essential lack of criticism in a system that is dogmatically critical) that it was able to establish man and his dignity better, and to guarantee critically and solidly all human value (above all, freedom and the power of knowing) and the man of value. Existentialism believed in its own capacity to establish a true humanism in which man would be beginning and end to himself inasmuch as in history he would find his full development, his authentic significance and happiness. Thus, the myth of the Man-God has generated, from time to time, the myths of God-History, God-Science, God-State, God-Progress, God-Humanity, God-Freedom, and so forth; and, in spite of existentialism and other critical currents, this illusion generated by the philosophy of immanence still survives and produces new myths and holds that, after making everything temporal and denying everything (being and substance, truth and God), it can better save, establish and explain all that pertains to man and to humanity because everything has become clearer and more intelligible. Existentialism, on the other hand, is a thorough examination of these incoherent and optimistic conclusions; it accepts the critical moment of immanentism together with the latter's gnosiological and metaphysical presuppositions; but existentialism is more coherent and less dogmatic in the conclusions, for without illusion it concludes that if being and truth (metaphysically and epistemologically) are temporal and historical, then neither values nor truth exist. Man is his own existence, which is its own situation brought about by pure temporality; the final outcome—the only significant one and the only one giving a suitable meaning to existence—is nothingness and death. From this point of view, these pessimistic conclusions represent a critical awareness which existentialism has gained with repect to the mythical and optimistic conclusions expressed by immanentism; and they also signify the conquest of the authenticity of human existence (and of its value) which, ultimately, "has produced" modern immanentism itself, of which existentialism is the dissolution, viz., the "skeptical" moment overcoming and destroying the "dogmatic" one.

However, existentialism, as we have said, is not only a "critique," but also a "crisis" of immanentism, in the sense that it assumes the "immanentist-historicist" conception of life as a conception of life itself (and hence of philosophy) understood as "fracture"; and as crisis, existentialism itself is dogmatic and uncritical. As a matter of fact, on the one hand, it assumes a historical contingency (the situation in Germany and Europe after 1918) as category of human existence, and out of a number of mental states it makes as many metaphysical principles; and, on the other hand, it dogmatically accepts the theses of immanentism and historicism, and concludes that existence (life) as such is "crisis," "fracture" and "breach" without even submitting the immanentist presuppositions to a critical re-vision. In other words, its merit lies in having "unmasked" immanentism and in having made evident the fact that from "those premises" the only sincere, authentic and not "naive" conclusion is the nothingness of being, of existence, of man, and of religious and human values. In this manner, existentialism reveals the lack of criticism (and also the hypocrisy) in-herent in the optimistic conclusions and dithyrambs in honor of reason, dialectic, history, and so on. Existentialism is wrong moreover in ac-cepting "those premises" dogmatically, conceiving its own "critique" of immanentism as a "crisis" of existence and in affirming that existence as such is "crisis" or fracture and laceration, and hence can only be defined through anguish, failure, death, and the like, and not through reason, concept, eternal Idea, and so on. In this way, the pessimism of existential-ism is its ingenuousness and, in many instances, even its insincerity and inauthenticity. At this point, its "nonessentialism" becomes the "essen-tiality" of existence; its "irrationalism," the "rationality" of the irra-tional; its "lack of system" becomes the "systematic" principle of the "nonsystematic"; and "immediate" and lived experience, the constant element of "mediation." Existentialism is, then, a form of historical and transcendental idealism, the very one that does away with the illusion of "transcendentality" as an objective form of knowledge (Kant) and as a metaphysical principle (Hegel). In fact, transcendentality—which ex-istentialism considers a "possibility" or a mere and indeterminate con-dition of which concrete existence is a "situational" and temporary realization—dissolves existence and being into nothingness and makes every-thing impossible, inexplicable and absurd.

3. EXISTENTIALISM AND MARXISM

After interpreting existentialism as the solvent of modern thought (es-pecially its dominant current represented by Criticism, Idealism, and His-toricism), we must also consider it in its relationship with Marxism, the other leading component (notwithstanding its philosophical poverty) of contemporary thought. Both of these dominant currents stem from Hegel and both assume the role of an internal criticism of Hegelianism. It seems to us that in order to clarify the problems of very recent philos-ophy and in order to evaluate the consistency of its conclusions, it is best to give a more precise determination of the relations between exis-tentialism-idealism and existentialism-Marxism, which are speculative posi-tions based on immanentism. Moreover, this helps to shed some light on other philosophical currents (which we shall meet later on) whose op-position to existentialism, Marxism, and historicist idealism stems from a critical awareness of the problems of philosophy; such awareness leads them to elaborate metaphysical constructions, through which philosophy is restored to the level of its evolutional process and back into the classi-cal lines of Western thought.

Historically, Kierkegaard and Marx spring from Hegel and both em-body the "protest" of the existent against "speculative philosophy." The existential, anti-Hegelian thesis is, therefore, common to these two re-bellious Hegelians: to the Danish theologian and to the theorist of his-torical materialism. In this sense, one can speak of an existentialism issu-ing from Kierkegaard, and another from Marx. Kierkegaard represents, however, the protest of the "individual" who finds his authenticity in the existential categories of anguish and sin and in the invocation to God (existence-theological transcendence: the *other-from-the-ego* is the abso-lute Other or God). Marx, on the other hand, represents the protest of the individual who conquers his humanity in the categories (also existential) of work, production, the brotherhood of man and in the realization of the socialistic State (existence-sociality-integral immanence: the *other-of-man* is the other man, namely, "man is the supreme being of man"). Kierkegaard reduces the Hegelian Idea down to the individual and out of it makes a nonhistorical, nonrepeatable, and isolated "individuality"; Marx, on the other hand, "drops" it into history, makes it concrete in the unstable structure of the "economic," and out of it he makes "eco-nomicity," that is, a dialectical law of social evolution, which is the history of humanity progressing toward the realization of a homogeneous society. Thus, while Kierkegaard and Marx follow different and irreconcilable ways, this irreconcilability should not make one lose sight of the identity of the initial anti-Hegelian thesis in their common Hegelian origin, even though subsequently each pursues an independent path. It appears to us, consequently, that the relations between existentialism and Marxism, despite all apparent contrasts and differences, are undeniable, though equivocal, from the very beginning.[3] Not all existentialism is Kierkegaard's or of a Kierkegaardian derivation; moreover, the so-called theistic current in it is not the main current, which is still represented by Heidegger-Jaspers. The question of its relations to Marxism, then, must not be confined to the binomial Kierkegaard-Marx, but it must be extended to that of its relations with immanent or atheistic existentialism. In this case, it seems to us that the initial agreement is strengthened and, at least on one essential problem, it is complete, even though existentialists and Marxists in the end draw opposite conclusions.

As a matter of fact, Marxists are against existentialists, even against those seeking to reconcile existentialism and Marxism. They opposed, for example, the Hungarian W. Szilasi, a pupil of Heidegger, who leans toward an existentialist Marxism or a Marxist existentialism, from which (at least in some writings) even the French philosophers Sartre and Merleau-Ponty (to say just a few significant names) are not too far removed. Yet, the Marxist attitude toward them leaves no doubt. The rejection is clear and the polemic, harsh; the very harshness of this polemic, however, makes one suspect that it is a sort of family quarrel. Against the charge of lack of sociability leveled against existentialism, Sartre has maintained in vain that a writer, like every man, must *s'engager* to the service of man. It has been said in reply that "*il est engagé malgré lui au service de la réaction*"; Sartre has vainly built an atheistic existentialism of man "*dans le monde*"; the argument in retort was that existentialism tends "*bon gré mal gré à la foi religieuse*," inasmuch as "*le désespoir et l'angoisse des existentialistes, leur conception métaphysique d'une liberté humaine qui ne repose absolument sur rien sont évidemment un magnifique terreau pour tous les mysticismes.*" [4] Nor did German existentialism fare better. The Hungarian Lukács, a very renowned theorist of orthodox Marxism (at least until some years ago), rejected existentialism and viewed it as the lowest stage of the perversion of dying bourgeois thought,[5] the fetishism of the ego, closed within its egoism, fallen into desperation and nothingness. Existentialism is constitutionally antisocial, able neither to

---

[3] Cf. the cited study of Löwith in Chap. II and the important essay of C. Fabro, "Kierkegaard e Marx," *Atti del Congresso Internazionale di Filosofia*, Milan, 1947, Vol. I, pp. 3-16 and now in the volume *Da Kierkegaard a Marx* (Florence, Vallecchi, 1952).

[4] I kept in mind certain numbers of the French communist periodical *La Pensée* and of Sartre's periodical *Temps Modernes* (1946-1947).

[5] G. Lukács, *Existentialisme ou marxisme?* (Paris, 1948).

come out of its immediateness of lived experience nor to understand social and economic relations. Through ignorance of the way to sociality in which man defines himself and progresses, existentialism represents the zenith of alienation of bourgeois thought from community, the rigid enclosure in brackets of the economic categories, which (in every epoch) are the connective links of society. And here lies its condemnation: "nothingness is a myth, the myth of capitalistic society condemned to death by history." Therefore, between existentialism and Marxism there is a radical antithesis—the same one running between capitalist-bourgeois society and socialist-Marxist society. This antithesis has been considered valid by the scholar, Battaglia, who is by no means a Marxist. He considers existentialism to be lacking a social and moral principle, incapable of understanding "human sociality," and incapable of establishing freedom in a positive and concrete sense. Although rejecting Lukács' Marxist premises, Battaglia accepts the negative judgment on existentialism and its antithetic nature toward Marxism.[6]

The question does not seem to us to be that simple, and the antithesis itself does not appear to be really irreducible. To begin with, all that existentialism which Marxists consider as the ultimate bourgeois perversion stems, as does Marx, from transcendental idealism, that is, from a thought which is itself bourgeois. This fact proves the close and indissoluble relationship between capitalist-bourgeois thought and Marxist thought, to the point that one appears as the dialectical antithesis of the other. This common origin is not only historical but theoretical, in the sense that both represent more thorough analyses of dialectical historicism, which in Hegel finds one of its highest expressions. Marx and Marxists wish to make the Hegelian dialectic concrete and so they "materialize" it; contemporary existentialists also want it to be concrete, so they "existentialize" it. There is this difference: by identifying it with the dialectic of the "economic" (the only authentic structure in the historical evolution), Marxists "socialize" it; and by submerging it in the existent-individuality, contemporary existentialists "personify" it. We have already mentioned the results achieved by the two theories, results which we are not going to discuss for the time being in order to focus our attention on their common source—dialectical historicism, which pertains not to Hegel's alone, but (dialectical or not), to numerous currents in post-Hegelian thought. The salient point in the connection between existentialism and Marxism is that they both deny essence in the existents, for essence is situational and historical: every existent is his situations, and he creates his own essence; moreover, being is not an ontological

---

[6] F. Battaglia, "Esistenzialismo e marxismo," in the volume *Esistenzialismo*, Florence, "Citta' di vita" (1950), pp. 94 ff., and especially the comprehensive volume *Il problema morale nell'esistenzialismo* (Bologna, Zuffi, 1949).

entity but a historical formation. On this point, the identity between these two currents is perfect and irrefutable. In fact, can economico-social facts be predicted according to Marx? No; they are decided according to circumstances prevailing in concrete human relations, and in the conflict of forces. Here they assume their own structure, and every man is his own economico-social situation. He is as he is made by the structure of the society to which he belongs, and not merely passively in so far as he, in turn, influences the structure. This amounts to saying that he "creates," as it were, his own situation so that he *is* this situation. Once such an identity in principle (which destroys being) is conceded, it does not matter if the existent then "creates himself" or if he "situates himself" according to Heidegger's dialectic or according to that of Marx. It does not matter whether or not in his sterile solitude the existent undergoes the adventure of anguish and nought or the class-struggle and paradise brought about by a homogeneous society in community with all other men. In both cases man and the "human" person, spirit, and value (all values) are annihilated because *being* as the law and principle of reality is annihilated in the premises of dialectical historicism. Lukács (or any other Marxist) is as justified as the censured Heidegger or any other existentialist, and vice versa. "Materializing" the Idea is metaphysically identical with "existentializing" Being.

This is true, but existentialism, as the solvent of modern immanentism, represents a position that is more mature and more critical than Marxism. In turn, Marxism represents a more coherent position than that immanentism which, in its naive and uncritical optimism, had deceived itself (and still does so in good or bad faith) in the belief that it was able to salvage the objectivity of knowledge, morality, spiritual values, and even religious values. Marx understood that if being is historical and neither essences nor substances exist, and if in its historical process dialectic realizes the Idea, this Idea no longer exists. There is only the contingency of history; and history is, in fact, situations and happenings; everything is relative, and there is no absolute principle. Being is time and resolves itself entirely into temporal becoming. Marx understood well that if the destiny of man is wholly and solely historical and is realized in history, the end of man is man himself. Therefore, his goal is the creation of a better society—not as a means, but as an end—as man's fulfillment, the realization of the totality of his aspirations and his complete and exhaustive happiness. The economic appeared to him to be the only genuine structure within an immanentist and historicist conception of being, without the hypocrisies of "ideals" and of spiritual values. In this instance, too, he was right, and he shows how Marxism is consistent with immanentism and represents its more advanced and critical moment.

Yet, Marx and the Marxists stop short and do not arrive at the root.

Existentialism, on the other hand, does not stop short, and by carrying out the dissolution of the philosophy of immanence and historicism, it sweeps even Marxism away. The latter, in fact, does not mark the culmination in the involution of Western thought, as existentialism does, for existentialism advances to the point of defining being from nonbeing, existence from its being for nothingness or for death. Marxism still occupies a position of naive optimism: it believes (and this is its illusion and its "myth") in a perfect society in which man (though historically limited in his essence and reduced to his situations) realizes the maximum of his possibilities and becomes god to himself. Marxism still retains—transformed and transferred to the economico-social plane—the incoherence of naive humanism, of the thought which Marxism classifies as bourgeois. Existentialism, on the other hand, is implacable: if the existent *is* his situations, if he *is* temporality, everything comes to nothing or nonbeing. The social thesis of Marxism—undermined by the temporality of being, of every being—becomes nothing or a naive "myth," a myth "destined to death by history." Only the "existential" position remains, and it has its destiny marked out by "its being-in-the-world," which is "being-for-death." Existentialism and Marxism, common offspring of Kantian-idealistic-post-idealistic metaphysics, are philosophies of the finite (the former with a critical awareness that is wanting in the latter), of a man and a world deprived of the light of being. They are *inhuman* philosophies. Thus the antisocial and individual man of Heidegger is worth no less (and perhaps more) than the social man of Marx. From this depth, and against existentialists and Marxists alike, but with the critical awareness of the positive theses in both, philosophy begins the new work for the purpose of re-establishing itself in the light of being and within the concreteness of life. Once the supreme alienation from being has been perpetrated, the "existential" categories as well as the "social and economic" categories become worthless. To be or not to be "engaged" either with oneself or with the concrete world of human relations, to be or not to be alienated from the community, all alike leads nowhere. It is at this point that man severs himself from his human mission, and nothing can save him any longer, neither existential anguish nor social tension. Once he loses his human mission, he has no other historical mission to fulfill. Clearly then, distances between philosophical doctrines are to be measured with the sharp yardstick represented by metaphysics, and not with the flat instrument represented by what is "social or antisocial," or by what is "in favor of" or "against" economic sciences.

We believe that we have furnished sufficient data for understanding existentialism and for evaluating it as part of the complex picture offered by contemporary philosophy. Indeed, one must distinguish between the existentialism of the philosophers from that of the cafes, films, sidewalks, newspapers, *"poseurs"* and from its purely academic form expressed by certain provincial professors. These distinctions are necessary because we are dealing with a philosophical movement that has been so widespread and popularized as to interest (perhaps from motive of mere curiosity) people far removed from philosophy. Its very popularity has caused misunderstanding and given rise to superficial judgments of exaggerated praise or hasty reprobation. While bearing in mind the traits common to the whole movement, one must not confuse its major exponents, each of whom has his own personality, his own particular intellectual formation, and so forth. Such are the indispensable distinctions in a philosophy that defines itself as lived experience, as the existential experience of this or that philosopher. German existentialism differs from its French counterpart and, within the German, Heidegger's existentialism is not Jasper's; Marcel's existential philosophy is not Sartre's, even though it is possible, respectively, to establish certain lines of approach between Sartre and Barth. Even Kierkegaard's influence, which is more or less present in all, varies between the phenomenologist Heidegger and the psychologist Jaspers, and so on. One must also bear in mind that whereas existentialism was influential in Germany in 1930, its diffusion and affirmation in France and other countries took place a decade later, though in its French beginnings antedate its German counterpart. We shall first explain German existentialism of the "finite" and of the "mundane" as expounded by its two masters, Heidegger and Jaspers. Subsequently, we shall treat the theological variety offered by Russian philosophers and the Swiss Barth, and lastly the French variety in its two currents—theistic and atheistic. The conclusion will consist in some critical consideration intended to integrate the evaluation we have partially anticipated.

4. M. Heidegger's "Oudenology" or "Philosophy of Nothingness"

MARTIN HEIDEGGER (1889), after a period as a Jesuit novice, studied with Rickert at Freiburg. He met Husserl, felt his influence, and became his associate in managing the *Jahrbuch*. In 1928, after leaving Marburg, he succeeded to Husserl's chair at Freiburg. In 1945, he lost it for political reasons but has recently been reinstated. After minor works, including his *Die Kategorien und Bedeutungslehre des Duns Scotus* (Tübingen, 1916), he published the first volume of *Being and Time* (trans. J. Macquarrie *et al.*, London and New York, 1962) in Husserl's *Jahrbuch*. This is his main work and remains incomplete. In addition to secondary essays these works followed: *Kant and the Problem of Metaphysics*, trans. J. S. Churchill (Bloomington, 1962); *What is Metaphysics*, trans. R. F. C. Hull *et al.* (in *Existence and Being*, Chicago, 1949); and

Hölderlin and the Essence of Poetry, trans. D. Scott (Chicago, 1949) contained in the volume *Existence and Being, Platons Lehre Von Der Wahrheit* (1942), which was reprinted with the appendix *Über Den Humanismus* (Bern, 1954), and on *The Essence of Truth*, trans. R. F. C. Hull *et al.* (in *op. cit.*, Chicago, 1949). From these titles it is evident that Heidegger presents himself as an ontologist and a metaphysician. In the course of our exposition and in the critical evaluation which the reader will find at the end of this chapter, we shall see how his philosophy can be neither ontology nor metaphysics since both were denied at the outset when the problem of being was just posited. Heidegger promises to talk to us about Being and, instead, always speaks about the Nought because his Being is Nought. Further, more than by Husserl, he is inspired by some themes in Kierkegaard's existential philosophy. His youthful studies on Duns Scotus also had their effect. Traditional ontology, Aristotle, and Plato—whom he often quotes and interprets in his own way—serve more as critical motivation than as sources of inspiration for Heidegger's thought. Historicism and (above all Dilthey) has influenced him in a particular way: he accepts temporality as an essential category of being (metaphysical historicism), and historicism itself as a critical motivation leading to its negation. Using the phenomenological method, Heidegger carries the dissolution of being to the limit; he extends temporality to Husserl's nontemporal categories. Heidegger cannot be fully understood unless he is referred not only to Kierkegaard but also to German mysticism, to German Romanticism in all its most morbid and destructive aspects, to Schopenhauer's irrationalistic voluntarism, to the whole Protestant atmosphere of Germany, to its gloomy and turbid pantheism, which always saw, in destruction and death, the dark sense of life—a life that oscillates, according as its sense is, theological or mundane, between "sin" and "fate," which, like that weighing on Wagner's heroes or Nietzsche's Superman, is always a destiny of death, a desire and almost a passion for dissolution into nothingness. Heidegger's existentialism is nourished by the centuries-old experiences of religion, philosophy, literature and art of his people, and it is the expression of these experiences—an expression implacably "built" to the last consequences, one that has been spun out with concepts and logical discourse, with the impassibility of a person who is convinced that the only truth about which we must be persuaded is that "nothing is at the beginning and nothing is at the end." For the Greeks: "Chaos was at the beginning." For Christianity: "At the beginning there was the *Logos* and the *Logos* was with God." For Heidegger: "Nothing is at the beginning" and the Logos is at its service; and this is a coherent conclusion from immanentist historicism. Since the day when man sold his existence to history (as Doctor Faust sold his soul to the devil), nought penetrated that existence and delivered it to its essential destiny, death. Heidegger neither cries over it nor laughs at it, as the romanticists and skeptics of all times do, because he knows it is useless: one has to accept destiny and remain loyal to it. The authenticity of man is his consciousness of "being-for-death."

The central problem of Heidegger's so-called ontology is the problem concerning the *sense of being*. As in classical metaphysics and traditional ontology, the object of Heidegger's inquiry is not the being of the singular (man), but "Being in its totality as being *qua* being." However, being is not an "object" of investigation, something that is before me: I, who am positing the problem of being, *am*. Therefore, I partake of being, which makes me be; and I am a phenomenon of being. I am not *the* being, but *a* determinate, finite being, a *being-here*, a *being-in* (*Da-sein*). My question concerning being is a question concerning me, as I am. It is here that Heidegger introduces the sophism (on which all his philosophy is founded) which destroys being, ontology and metaphysics and causes his initial point of investigation—the absolute Being "in its totality and inasmuch as it is such"—to amount to a simple gesture, an assumption of illustrious ancestors that is immediately repudiated. The participation of the ego in being merely means this: being is only a moment of abstraction from the concrete *Dasein*, the *being-in*, the *being-here*. Nor is it a question of Heidegger's being motivated, as some existentialists believe, by his desire to satisfy the exigencies of "personalism" or of a "personalistic ontology" because at the very moment that being is "personalized" in the *Da-sein*, it is annulled as being, and with it, ontology as such, without the possibility of building another one, personalistic or otherwise. In fact, Heidegger has built an ontology *sui generis*, in which his discourse is not about Being but about Nothingness. From this point of view, this ontology represents a "logical" and rigorous elaboration of a sophism, which Heidegger's followers, interpreters and critics have made famous. Being (*Sein*) reaches its nadir in the *Dasein*. The starting point of this inquiry is not being, but *Dasein*, within whose limits being has been constructed and immured. The being of *Dasein* is existence (*Existenz*); consequently, the essence of Dasein is not defined by what it contains: the *essence of Dasein lies in its existence*, and existence explains it. The only possible ontology, therefore, is the existential analysis of the *being-in* (*Dasein*), that is, the analysis of every single possibility which being realizes in the single moments of our existence. This, and only this, is the "word" (*logos*) spoken by being about itself; and the numerous moments characterizing existence are all insignificant, individually and collectively, for they cannot be related to a unitary meaning giving them value and significance. The phenomenological method is the only possible method for this ontology, which, in the last analysis, is only a phenomenology, a description of the various modes of the *Dasein*, in which being is caught and outside of which it has no existence. Philosophy is the *hermeneutics* of the *Dasein,* the effort to say the "truth" (αλήθευα), and "reveal" the being of the *being-in,* its expressing itself in "phenomena"— in what is shown by itself (*das Sich-an-ihm-Selbst-Zeigende*). *Sein und Zeit,* Heidegger's most important book, stops at the analysis of the *Dasein;* its second part has not yet appeared for the reason that, given the first volume, the second could not be written. Heidegger's discourse on ontology was ended . . . before it had begun, because it begins by denying being and continues with the analysis of the moments of the *Dasein.*

Being is and reveals itself in the modes of the *being-in,* whose essence lies in its existence. Yet, philosophy, according to Heidegger, is not always conscious of this fact. For this reason, he distinguishes between a philosophy he calls *existensive (existenziell)* and a philosophy called *existential (existenziale).* The former regards the existents from without and they are assumed as entities to be classified and arranged into concepts and categories: this philosophy judges and reasons about existence while remaining outside of it. Thus, it misses the sense of being in that it is unable to grasp it in its essential existentiality. The problem regarding the mutual relationship between subject and object arises from such a spurious mode of considering existence; and with it, numerous systems (rationalism and empiricism, idealism and realism) also find their place in the philosophy called *existenziell.*

Existential knowledge needs no concept to understand being. The concept is a mode of the being of the *Dasein* and reason is its "phenomenon"; reason is understood through existence and not existence through reason. There are no true judgments *on* being. The so-called truth of judgment is only a "phenomenon of truth." Being is in its concrete revealing itself to itself, which is existing; here lies truth.

As we have said, existing is essential to *Dasein;* and more than that, the latter characterizes itself precisely because it exists, and is this thing-here. Being could not manifest itself if it did not enter into the world. Man (the *Dasein*),[7] as an existent, is *existence* itself, and so his foundation is his "being-in-the-world" (*in-der-Welt-sein*). The *Dasein* manifests itself as "being-in-a-*situation*," this situation (I was born in *this* city, in *that* year, *of these* parents, and so on), which makes the existent be what it is; the essential situation of all situations, that is, the situation that constitutes the existent, is being-in-the-world. In other words, the *Dasein* can only be *in the* (*in-der*) world, rooted in it, so that its essentiality is its "being-in-the-world." It is not only in the world, but it is essentially constituted by its being-in-the-world. If this is so, its essence is not "being" but the "*in the* world," that is, the essence *is* its situation (*this*

[7] Heidegger uses the word *Dasein* to indicate the human person.

one), and being is dissolved or annihilated in the fundamental situation of *"being-in-the-world."* It is useless for Heidegger to ask himself the why of our situation (Why are we in the world?) and the why of every situation (Why was I born in this place and not elsewhere?), since situations (and the fundamental situation) do not depend on me and since to be in a situation is essential to my being. I *find myself* in the world, I have "fallen" into it, I am "abandoned," and "thrown" there. I have no alternative but to accept the situation of being-in, and all the situations implied by that situation: I have to "assume" myself.

Being in the world makes transcendence essential to the *Dasein:* in more than one way, but above all as transcendence of being in relation to itself. In fact, the self-manifestation of being constitutes its limitation; every manifestation that being makes of itself is, then, a transcending of itself before itself. Nor can being remain in itself, because without its *being-here* it would be nothing: it would not be revealed to itself and would not exist. Being makes itself manifest by determining itself, and this manifestation is a continuous transcendence of itself. The *Dasein* is the manifestability of the *Sein*. The *Dasein*, the *being-in*, realizes a possibility of the *Sein*, which can only be a determinate existing in the world. The *Dasein*, in its turn, comports a twofold transcendence with respect to brute existents (those having no consciousness about their existing): (a) "thrown" in the world, the world transcends it; (b) but since the existent, as we shall see, is the "builder of the world," that which gives it a being (a meaning), it transcends and surpasses the world. Transcendence is essential to the *Dasein*.

The manifestation of being in the world is the *fall (Ver-fallen)*, which implies no degradation. Being falls into a particular existence and so it sacrifices infinite possibilities in order to realize one. Yet, only by limiting itself can it be manifested. It is not an inevitable or extraneous force which brings about its fall, but rather its own nature: the fact that it cannot *be* without existence, without making itself manifest to itself. Being is open to all possibilities: in "falling" it limits itself, and in limiting itself, it exists. Therefore, existing is accepting oneself in finitude, in dejection, in being "thrown" into the world, in this situation; in a word, it means assuming oneself. However, the existent, or *Dasein*, is possibility and thus it makes itself; the destiny of being is to make itself existent and the destiny of the existent is to make itself. The existent is "free to be able to be"; with respect to all that is given, the existent is a "distant" being, a "project." Man is his freedom. The *da* (here) of *Da-sein* is the sense that it acquires of itself by itself. It is not knowledge, but the existentiality which is at its basis: it is *feeling of finding-oneself-here*, the fact of being "thrown" into the world, of existing; it is to be able to be, to be a "project" (*Entwurf*), a possibility (the project is the structure of what Heidegger calls *interpretation*); it is discoursiveness (*Rede*), which is the articulation of intelligence (the foundation of language, listening, silence). It is obvious that Heidegger's being is a pure possibility: it is the Kantian-idealistic transcendentality which, inexplicably, manifests and reveals itself to itself by making itself existent. In other words, it gains its self-consciousness through its being present in the existents. *Dasein*, then, is a "mode of being" as mode of being is understood by immanentism, viz., being is its own modes, outside of which there is nothing. Essence, then, is a mode of existence. No wonder that Heidegger identifies Being with Nothingness; or, rather, that he moves from the Nought (that is, from pure possibility or pure transcendentality), and that thence all existents, like momentary epiphanies, emerge, composed, in their turn, of nothingness. Being, then, by making itself existent is also revealed to itself as Nothingness; and, likewise, the existents by "accepting," "assuming," and "projecting" themselves become the nothingness of being and the nothingness of their own existence, which is the existing of being as nothingness, even after being has revealed and manifested itself.

Things (the world) cannot be said to be really existing: they do not exist; they serve; they are "instruments," tools, and as such they are *something for*, that is, their essence is not being, but *to be for*, as any tool is in relation to others, and so on. So, the essence of a utensil (*Zuhandene*), of that which we "handle" for some use, is its very condition of being for something else. Each thing is a link in a chain, so that it is not for itself but for its relating to others. "Relating or referring" constitutes the essence of things, which are "signs," "indications," and "referments." What is called "world" is only the totality of these referments. On the other hand, things are "tools" in that they serve someone using them for a purpose, that is, they serve a "will for a purpose" (*Worum-Willen*). Things are, then, tools of the *Dasein*, which actuates their usefulness by using them. Even the purpose for which they are used, that is, the movement from potential usefulness to actual usefulness (*this one*), is assigned to them by the *Dasein*. The *Dasein*, too, benefits from it: in fact, in using *this* thing for *this* purpose, it realizes one of its determinations or situations. So, things are only a determination depending on the one using them; their existence, then, depends on the mode (and in the mode) of existing by the *Dasein*. The world is related to or connected with the *Dasein*, the existent and the conscious ego, and with that determination in which being acquires consciousness of itself, that is, makes itself the existent which is aware of existing. Consciousness is the revelation of being in existence and of existence in being. The world, which in itself is nothing, is correlated with the infinite possibilities of intrinsic realization, intrinsic to being "fallen" into existence.

In correspondence with our state of being busy in the world, there is the feeling of being preoccupied (*Besorgen*), if it is a question of things; and the feeling of solicitude (*Fürsorge*), if existents are involved. Preoccupation and solicitude (Heidegger, like Scheler, views emotion as more meaningful than reason) are feelings that are inseparable from the consciousness of our limitations, from our finding ourselves always in a situation. We are attracted by things, each of which becomes for us a source of preoccupation. Man is always preoccupied about something and preoccupation is the connective element in his existence. Man—a being "thrown" into the world and fallen among affairs—does not recognize himself in things, and precisely for this reason he loses himself and becomes preoccupied with things which constitute the motives of his anxieties and his hopes. Man is not worried about himself but about things in which he loses himself while losing his "authenticity." Worldly "cares" are channeled toward a goal to be achieved, toward an object attracting us. It is a mode of the *Dasein,* but a spurious or nongenuine mode of existence, and "existensive" and not an "existential" mode. The *Dasein* itself becomes a tool and a referment as it feels the burden of worldliness. For Heidegger, as for Kierkegaard, to gain the world amounts to becoming lost in it.

The preoccupation with things is coupled with a solicitude for other existents: being-in-the-world as regards the *Dasein* is not only being in the midst of things but also being amongst other men with whom it forms a society and among whom it lives and operates. *Being-in* as regards the *Dasein* is an *existence-with* (*Mit-dasein*). Solicitude compels the *Dasein* to concern itself about others, and to help them. From the situation of "being-in-common" (*Mitsein*), *sympathy* is born.

Led by our preoccupation for things and by our solicitude for others, we are no longer ourselves. Living in the midst of things degrades us to forms of *nonauthentic* life. This is the fall of the *Dasein* into *temporality* (*Zeitlichkeit*), into empirical time, which is succession of past, present and future. It is as if the present were crushed by the past and future, that is, by what was done and by the weight of our expectations. The state of the ego within temporality is that of "being outside" of itself, not itself anymore: harassed by the present, conditioned by the past, worried by the future. Within existensive life the past prevails over the present and over the future; it traps us with its traditions and its customs, with the burden of what others did. Man becomes anonymous. He takes refuge in the *one* or *it* (*das Man*), a neuter impersonal form, and conforms to the "one does" and "one says." The *it* or *one* is a mode of being, the *nonauthentic being* of the *Dasein*. It is a "banal existence," a degradation of authentic existence. It is every-day existence, in which conversation descends to idle talk, to the "commonplace." Social life has this in-evitable, depressing, and degrading aspect. We live according to the "time-clock" (where time differs from "primary time" of being): the time after the fall in which, at every moment of the chronological suc-cession, man finds himself preoccupied and solicited by the cares of things and the concern for others, as he is intent upon providing and foreseeing, while remaining ignorant of himself, a thing among things, and anonymous in the midst of a mass of anonymity.[8]

For Heidegger man is not in time, he *is* time; it is necessary for every moment of the *Dasein* to ever surpass itself in another successive moment. Temporality is, then, immanent transcendence; and history is being in-finitely transcending itself, being in its infinite self-determination, and *Dasein* transcending itself in successive moments. Being, then, is an in-finite self-"existentialization" and an infinite self-transcendence. This go-ing beyond itself on the part of the *Dasein* is essential to the finiteness of existence through the three "ecstasies" (*Extasen*) of temporality: past, present, and future; temporality in itself is essentially "ecstatic," an orig-inal "being outside." History (*Geschichte*) is the organization of time —time filled with the past, with facts which have already occurred. History does not tell the authentic being of man; it does not reveal to man the sense of his being himself time, a sense that lies in the future rather than in the past.

Heidegger, who excludes any dimension beyond time (Kierkegaard's "qualitative leap" from temporality to eternity) and, therefore, the religious or theological solution of the problem of existence, draws the extreme consequences from this metaphysical historicism. The historical process of Hegel's Idea unfolds itself in a circular movement so that everything draws its meaning from the Idea itself. For Heidegger there is only temporality, essential to existence and to being itself, which is and is revealed by existentializing itself. There are no categories, for him, as there are for Dilthey, *Grundformen*, in which the multiplicity of facts gains meaning; nor, as for Scheler, values which are revealed by history, while transcending history itself. Categories are only "existential modes."

But, why does man expend himself in his concern for things and in the preoccupation of a banal and nonauthentic life? In order to escape

[8] It is significant what Heidegger says regarding banal existence, our petty, shabby and impersonal every day life, which is so much a part of our mechanized, stand-ardized, extremely bureaucratic society, which is engaged, body and soul, in utili-tarian interests, uniform, and rubber-stamped, devoid of any spirit of innovation. Our unsatisfied, greedy society, says Heidegger, disperses the interior sense of our existence and makes us too solicitous of and preoccupied with that which interests our external life; it makes us ignorant and forgetful of the inner meaning of our personality. We shall see later the positive and negative aspects of these antihistoric and antisocial instances.

himself, replies Heidegger, in order to "evade" the consciousness of his true being, the *nothingness* assailing, surrounding and constituting him.[9] Man is afraid to know the whole truth concerning himself, and so he tries to forget himself by "going out" in things and in daily life. To withdraw from the *one, people, everyone (das Man)* is to make a *choice*, the choice of being able to be himself, his authentic self. *Consciousness (Gewissen)* is the re-entrance into itself of the *Dasein*, when it ceases to listen to the indefinite *Man*. The "common man" seeks an escape from the world by freeing himself from any preoccupation concerning this or that thing. He reduces all objects to one level so that he has no preference among them, no concern with any of them. Solicitude ends, boredom enters. Things do not attract; the wholeness of being is present, but in an abyss of indifference in which beings and events are found confused, without value, without attractiveness. Weariness frees man from the world; it makes him change from preoccupation with everything to indifference toward everything.

The profound man, by contrast, conquers his own being in *Anguish (Angst)*, in which he regains his authenticity. Just as solicitude is the emotional correspondent of the fall, so anguish is the feeling of *redemption*. Anguish rescues man from the world. As solicitude is the loss of the authentic sense of our existence in things and anonymity—an enslavement to referment and to the preoccupations and expectations from temporality—so anguish is the recovery of existence, of original freedom, and of the original sense of time. To escape from the agony which reveals our nothingness, we fall into worldliness: to rescue ourselves from the dispersion of ourselves, we re-enter into consciousness of ourselves. Anguish is beyond the antinomy of joy and sorrow for it is their common source. Man volatilizes things through anguish; he grasps the infinite sense of his possibilities and the essence of his existence. Anguish immobilizes the word and gives an incomparable sense of totality. In its presence the universe withdraws before it, revealing itself as unstable and suspended. Anguish reveals the nothingness essential to being and to us.

In anguish, the things of the world suddenly lose their importance: man no longer worries about them. All the questions that once perplexed him (Why this thing instead of another? Why must I pursue this end instead of another? Why is there something instead of nothing?) interest him no longer.

In all the things of the world being is present, but man, immersed in things, forgets or is afraid to ask them what being is. Now that in anguish

---

[9] It is natural, here, to recall Pascal's concepts of "misery of man" and of *divertissement;* this recalling, however, should not cause equivocations. What Pascal says makes sense (man is conscious of his "misery" because of his "greatness"; his rescue from *divertissement* is the conquest of his true nature, the calling of God), but what Heidegger says, as we shall see, does not.

things have become faint and "slip away," and "sink into the depths," [10] man questions being, desires to grasp its meaning, which is that of his existence. But to question being is to jeopardize our existence. What is being? Being is nothing. Anguish reveals me to myself and reveals my nothingness as the authenticity of my existence. Anguish has rescued me from the banality of worldly life and made me find myself; it has revealed me my destiny, the destiny of all, of being and of existence: the Nothingness. It remains only to accept it and through such an acceptance to be free. This dizziness of the void, this sinking of being in nothingness, is liberating and authenticating anguish.

Let us not misunderstand: anguish does not annihilate what exists; what exists is the same as before—the stars are still stars, the trees, trees. But, in anguish, what exists, interests no more. Existing things stay the same but for me they sink into insignificance. I, too, continue to exist and entertain relations with others but, in this respect, I am insignificant to myself. Each thing is as before, but all "slip away," and say good-by to us as they pass by. The existent accepts his fate, receives it with "open arms." He, then, is not "thrown" any more, because he accepts and "repeats" his destiny, he takes the responsibility for it upon himself; he lives in the awareness of being nothing and in the acceptance of his nothingness. He accepts his "debt," his fate. His lot is to be an accumulation of "debts" of which death is the last installment due.

Anguish reveals the primary freedom of being (the referment to something else ceases) and the primary sense of temporality. For Heidegger, as we know, temporality is essential to being—being is *time*. But primary time differs from time made worldly by banal life, which is the succession of past, present, and future: three moments, each of which is "outside" of the others. Primary time, instead, is interpenetration of past, present and future, gravitation toward the future: the *Dasein* anticipates in the present its further possibilities and so, somehow, it makes the "future" the "past."

Yet, if existence gravitates toward the future, it means that the present is insufficient. Time is infinite in the sense that it has no end, though in itself it is finiteness. The future, which is present in every present, an *after* accompanying every *now*, indicates that the present is incomplete and inconsistent; it reveals the essence of existence and of time, which consists in not being sufficient to itself, in being transcendence and finiteness. When the future is prolonged in an infinite series of states, it gives rise to worldly time, to the time of "history" (the infinity of time is "history" as an unending series of events, one referring to the other, as

[10] Anguish differs from that fear which is fear of something that threatens us; in anguish nothing definite is threatening us: what anguishes us is the absolute indefiniteness in which everything collapses.

effect of the fall). Anguish recalls existence from its dispersion in things, and restores it to primary time which is not history but *historicity* (*Geschichtlichkeit*). This sending back, proper to history, is the nonvalue of history: history, as becoming, is a succession of events. What counts is not history but historicity, not temporality but primary time, not solicitude but anguish, by which the sense of historicity is restored. Upon pulling us out of the flux of history, anguish delivers us from dispersion and we are restored to ourselves. Inasmuch as it is temporality and because it has been expended by "care," our existence moves from one thing to another: it is concentrated in the present, laden with the past as well as with the future, that is anticipated by its present interests (it is a "situation" moving toward a "project"); on the other hand, as primary time our existence concentrates on the future by projecting itself forward and discovering its own inconsistency, its being for nothingness and death. Even the past gravitates toward the future: death ratifies birth, the initial condemnation to the situation. Man defines his destiny within primary time. The voice of his conscience tells him to accept it; the man who listens to it makes destiny his own will. Confronted with destiny, the will can only accept or endure it. Each one of us is placed on a "potential" horizon, in an inescapable destiny. Life is the development of a Necessity, an ἀνάγκη. Man is faced with a choice already made and to which he is already committed. My destiny is already there; it is the realization of what already is. All moments are enclosed in time, in an iron chain—"the future of what already is." To launch into the future is to go ahead, but always the realization of what already is. Freedom to do this thing rather than another is abstract freedom. The only true freedom is the acceptance of our destiny. What destiny? *Either* that of living lost in time, within which the future always sets us outside of ourselves, the past causes us to fall back into what has already been done, and the present worries us; *or* that of going beyond temporality by means of anguish, through which we again discover true freedom—the freedom represented by death and the sense of being which is nothingness. The thread of destiny is already cut, and it is not I who cuts it. (The existent, in his every situation, from birth to death, is authentic only in his consciousness of death, which reveals his essential nothingness to him.

Death signifies the end as well as the goal of the *Dasein*. It is not a rupture, something invading life from without; it is the component of life itself. Existence does not precipitate into nothingness as if an indifferent, blind, omnipotent force destroyed it; death does not come from the outside to annihilate the being of existence, but it coincides with the being of existence. "Being in the world" is "being for death." *Dasein* equals being for the end (*Sein zum Ende*) which equals being for the nought

(*Sein zum Nichts*) which equals being for death (*Sein zum Tode*). There is no opposition between Being and Nought: once being *is* its existence, and existence is time, the lot of being is tied up with the bounds of existence, which is its situation. The nonbeing penetrates being, which is made up, bounded, and annihilated by it in the sense that nonbeing causes being to *be nothing*. In this way, being is unable to give existence any reality, any meaning or value because, as it is understood here, it has no reality, no meaning, and no value itself. From the Being-Nought, to the nothingness of existence: from Nought to Nought. Being and the existent, we and things and the infinite possibilities, realized or not, are so many moments of nothingness, which in turn are buried and sunk in their initial and final nothingness. A catastrophe without protests, rebellions, or useless desperations once anguish has revealed that the being's being is Nought and the authentic life is life for death: that is, awareness that "*I*" will die rather than "*people die.*" It is not a question of "any death," but of *my* death. Death is the most personal possibility of being. The *resolution* (*Erschlossenheit*) consists in accepting the destiny of one's own existence in silence and anguish, as loyalty to oneself and freedom for death. Accepted destiny is a decision, the decision of carrying out one's own duty in the world. The *authentic ego* (*das eigentliche Selbstsein*) is found in the authentic historicity, in the anguish disclosing the essential nothingness of the self, of everything, of being, and of being in the world.

However, how is it possible to talk about Nothingness? Isn't it nonsense? *Being-Nought* undoubtedly is nonsense, a logical contradiction; but logic, says Heidegger, cannot give us the "fundamental experience of Nothingness." The "Nought making up being" is revealed to us by the feeling of anguish, as well as by that of weariness. Being-Nought is not a condition "mirrored" by the intellect, but a truth (a fundamental truth) that is felt and suffered, an understanding that everything is "destined" to be lost, a reaching for the primary root of existence. For Hegel, the concreteness of being and nonbeing is becoming and the supreme synthesis is philosophy or the absoluteness and transparency of the Idea to itself; for Heidegger, on the other hand, the being of being is Nothingness, and anguish is the emotional transparency of existence to itself— that is, the transparency of nothingness which constitutes existence itself. The being of Nothingness and the nothingness of Being: Nothingness does not confront Being, but it is Being itself. "In the state of anguish, nothingness exhibits itself to us simultaneously with the totality of being." Nought is not a logical category but an ontological category. *Dasein* comes from the Nought (from the being of the Nought or the nought of Being), and its being in the world is a race toward nothingness, its nothingness (death). It cannot be said that *ex nihilo nihil fit,* but the *ex nihilo omne ens, qua ens, fit.* From Nothingness to Nothingness: man is the "sentinel of Nothingness."

In the beginning there is no chaos, no being, no Logos—Nothing is in the beginning and Nothing is in the end. Hegel posits Being and Nonbeing in a dialectical relationship, and, through dialectical becoming, he concludes with the absolute Idea. Heidegger does not reject Hegel; he only continues and furthers him with merciless coherence. If Being and Nonbeing are in dialectical relationship and if the essence of reality and of thought is dialectic, there is no Absolute to be revealed to itself, but only Nothingness at the beginning and at the end. The so-called existential metaphysics is this and only this, as it springs from the "critique" of transcendental idealism, that is, from transcendentality taken as a metaphysical principle.

To sum up: we gain true freedom, "freedom for death," when, in the state of anguish, the nothingness of being is revealed to us. Genuine existence is conquest of the true sense of being, which is the sense of nothingness. Our destiny is entirely clarified: being in the world is being for death, which is not the negation of existence but that which constitutes it. "As a being which degrades itself in the mediocrity of daily life, the being for death is a constant flight in the presence of death." Instead, outside of worldliness, the fear of death and, with it, that sense of rebellion we experience in its presence, are dispelled: to exist in anguish, before ourselves, is to be "loyal to death." Anguish, then, gives true freedom, the freedom for death. The alternative, whether we are to resume our destiny or not, is posited before our being free for death. If I take back my destiny, it becomes mine but is different from what it was before; it becomes mine as a fundamental freedom. No one can force me to take it back: I can only be forced into enduring it as a burden. "Here lies the foundation for a possible ethics. This acceptance of destiny is, for Heidegger, a decision consonant with man. Thus, within genuine time in which man expects nothing but his already chosen destiny, he chooses himself in a certain way. Returning to himself and *repeating himself,* man is his own foundation and finds in himself a new tranquillity, wherein he marvels at nothing." [11] Such freedom is the wisdom of accepting our destiny. Death, the most existential thing, is what pertains to me most; and to accept it amounts to remaining loyal to my authenticity. Who can take my place in my death? Only upon accepting it, each *his own,* we restore ourselves to the original being, reveal the self to the self, and reach the abyss of Being, that is, the abyss of Nothingness in which lies the whole of being and the whole of existence: being's Being is Nothingness and nothingness' being is Being.

[11] C. Mazzantini, *Il tempo* (Como, Cavalleri, 1942), p. 75.

Heidegger's latest writings contain, according to some interpreters, the cues, cautiously stated or hardly hinted at, of a new orientation toward the positivity of Being. In our opinion the so-called last Heidegger is still the first Heidegger, the one found in *Sein und Zeit* and in the other minor works. It is true that Heidegger in his *Letter on Humanism* rejects the atheistic interpretation of his thought; yet, all that can be read in it is still a confirmation of his absolute, dogmatic, and preconceived atheism. To say that "through the existential determination of man nothing has been decided concerning the 'existence of God' or his 'nonbeing' " and that, consequently, theological Transcendence is a "possibility" toward which existence is still "open," amounts to saying nothing, because, as long as Being is Nothingness, such a possibility can only signify the identification of God with the Nought; it amounts to repeating the old position maintained by the "first Heidegger," wherein Being is Nothingness. As long as Heidegger does not abandon this position (that is, his "metaphysics"), though he speaks about something divine revealed to men by poetry (*Hölderlin and the Essence of Poetry, op. cit.*), and about truth as a "revelation" (*Unverborgenheit*) of being to the existent or as an "overture" (*Offenheit*) of the existent toward being, he still repeats the same and identical things with equivocal words, which, perhaps, signify that he himself is aware of the insurmountable difficulties of his philosophy. When Heidegger now states that man is the "custodian" of Being, he changes nothing, if being is still Nought; man is always the absurd "sentinel of Nothingness." The "last" Heidegger leaves the impression of a man thinking in a vacuum: he proceeds by hints and suggestions using a language that is a play on words—a language that says something and says nothing as if it were an obscure prophecy, a revelation in which "openings" are "closures" and in which "disclosure" is also a "concealment," and so on. The "first" Heidegger wished to conceive and write the "Philosophy of the Nought"; the more recent Heidegger, fallen into an artificial search for the "word" (to the point of making it lose all meaning instead of restoring it to the true and genuine one), and in self-commentary, seems to be writing a "mystique of nothingness" entirely "of this earth."

5. KARL JASPERS' EXISTENTIALISM OF THE "LEAP INTO EMPTINESS"

KARL JASPERS, together with Heidegger, represents German existentialism. He was born in 1883 at Oldenburg. A graduate in medicine, he was known first as a student of psychology before becoming known as a philosopher. From 1921 to 1937 he taught at Heidelberg. Even while pursuing studies in jurisprudence and attending courses in philosophy, he was unsatisfied with official knowledge. In his autobiographical essay "Über Meine Philosophie," in *Rechenschaft und Ausblick* (Munich, 1951) he himself states: "I was seeking a vision of reality." This quest, still representing his fundamental exigency, was rendered more urgent by the First World War. For him, too, that war did not pass in vain: "Lo! in 1914, with the First World War came the great collapse of our European being." From that time forward every single life was determined by historical events. All problems reached a new depth. What shook everything so violently during the war also revealed what had been partially veiled before: the foundations and conditions of every existence. That paradisiac life of the prewar era, ingenuous as it was even in its sublime spirituality, could never return. Philosophy in its depth became more important than ever." Besides his works on psychology, Jaspers wrote *Philosophie* (Berlin, 1956, 3 vols.), which still remains his fundamental work. His lesser works are: *Man in the Modern Age,* trans. Eden and Cedar Paul (Garden City, 1957); two essays on Nietzsche and one on Descartes; and other writings gathered in the volume *Reason and Existenz,* trans. W. Earle (New York, 1955). More recently he published his ponderous volume *Truth and Symbol,* trans. J. T. Wilde *et al.* (New York, 1959), which had been announced years before; *The Perennial Scope of Philosophy,* trans. R. Manheim (New York, 1955); as well as other writings which do not add much to his thought.

Jaspers lacks Heidegger's phenomenological formation: he goes back to the existential experience of Kierkegaard to whom, of all existentialists, he is most loyal. Yet, Kant's influence, together with Nietzsche's and M. Weber's, is no less decisive; nor should we forget the influence exerted on him by some representatives of classical or Neoplatonic pantheism such as Plotinus, Bruno, Spinoza, and Schelling. Of all the existentialists, Jaspers is the most systematic within the limits permitted by existentialism which identifies philosophy with existential and hence non-objectifiable experience. A clear writer, he does not have Heidegger's mania for neologisms, nor does he adopt that obscurity which often indicates emptiness rather than depth of thought. Like Kierkegaard, Jaspers argues against the "system" that explains and deduces everything and arrives at a definitive completeness wherein each detail finds its place and meaning in the totality of the real. He vindicates his concept of *Transcendence* against the "system" (not against the "systematic," representing order of concepts and method): thought "transcends" itself continuously because Being always escapes it; thus, the system is impossible, and totality unreachable. Thought, whose task is to clarify existence, reveals that there is a continuous "clarification" about existence; but the definitive and ultimate "clarification" is always missed by thought: the latter's supreme clarity is its "shipwreck" before the supreme clarification. Existence cannot be repeated and so it cannot be arranged in any system; it breaks into infinite perspectives. Totality denies rather than explains it. Objective and systematized truth knows everything except existence, which is "choice" and "faith"—to conclude existence is to deny it. The system tends to conclude existence in a "round-off" process. The Hegelian dialectic is "passage," "conciliation," and "pacification" suppressing antitheses: existence, instead, is involvement of positivity and negativity, and paradox, as Kierkegaard said. As we shall see, at any rate, Jaspers' dialectic is the same Hegelian dialectic carried to its extreme consistency in an opposite direction: not from antinomy to synthesis, but from partial syntheses to the supreme and unsurmountable antinomy. Jaspers destroys the "dialectical truth" of Hegelian dialectic. It can also be said that, unlike Heidegger, Jaspers shares with Hegel a lively historical sensibility.

Jaspers (whose idealism is more evident than Heidegger's) borrows the principle of transcendentality from Kant, "the philosopher *par excellence"*: object is for the subject; the objective is determined by our "consciousness" of which it is an "appearance." Furthermore, Ideas of pure Reason (world, soul, God) are assumed by Jaspers as the three "in-globing" or "circumscribing" (*Umgreifende*), as the three possible "horizons" capable of encircling all others. Kant, as we know, concludes that metaphysics as a science is impossible and that the value of those three Ideas consists only in their regulation of reason; Jaspers arrives at the same conclusions namely, "failure" on the part of the *Umgreifende-World* and *Umgreifende-Consciousness* in the presence of Being, which escapes both and determines the shipwreck of metaphysics. The unseizable Transcendence is still there; all steps made in order to get close to it, all strategic maneuvers by our dialectic of approach are in vain—Transcendence withdraws at the very moment when distances seem to be brought closer. The only thing we can do is to "jump," but Jaspers' "leap" is more paradoxical than Kierkegaard's. We leap into Transcendence without reaching it; we do not know whether we remain suspended in air or fall back to earth. However this may be, it is a fact that we are wrecked before Transcendence, and we sink into ourselves. *Das Scheitern ist das Letzte:* "Failure is the last end."

Jaspers speaks about being in three ways: *being-in* (*Dasein*),[12] existence (*Existenz*), and Transcendence (*Transzendenz*). *Being-in* is that which exists, its mere presence circumscribed in time and space, the things. *Existence*, instead, is presence, which is invocation, that is, a transcending of the *situation*, and at the same time, ego and "being as for itself." *Transcendence* is the horizon of all horizons, the infinite embracing everything, the "circumscribing-Whole" (*Umgreifende*), or Being in itself (*Ansich-*

---

[12] For Jaspers *Dasein* are the "things" while for Heidegger it is the existent (the ego, man), which Jaspers indicates, instead, with the word *Existenz*.

seiende). Philosophy is the clarification of existence with respect to Transcendence. "Philosophy is the journey that leads us to ourselves," that is, that takes us into a state of *anguish* in which consciousness, seeing the world as it withdraws, senses the void beneath itself. The ego is ever engaged in time, in certain circumstances and in certain situations, some of which are definitive and insurmountable ("situations-limit"—*Grenzsituationen*—like sex, the epoch in which the ego is living, and so forth).

I do not choose my place in the world; I, instead, am this very place; I only exist by integrating myself in an irreducible and historical situation. Therefore, if I know all possibilities but take part in none, the world will not be visible to me. Existence is realized through an act that shatters the real, through an act that causes all the contradictions to shine forth in the world. I am never going to grasp Being in its totality whatever starting point I may accept: both the horizon of the world and that of existence cannot go beyond their frontiers; even metaphysics fails in the presence of Being, but it is through this failure that *Existence* is revealed. Thus, philosophy is *transcending*.

Jaspers' philosophy is summed up in three questions: "What can we know in the sciences? How can we effect the deepest communication? How does truth become accessible to us? The goals of this research are man and Transcendence, that is, existence and Transcendence. "Man is the place in which, and through which, all that can be for us becomes real. To neglect the human Being would amount to submersing ourselves in nothingness. What man is represents for man the capital question. Man, however, is not a self-sufficient being shut in himself." Man's question is, then, indissolubly connected with that of Being. Therefore, the question "What is man?" is tied up with the question "What is Transcendence?" We can only use human terms when we speak about transcendence. For Jaspers, who is far from Kierkegaard's theocentrism, the problem of transcendence is only a human problem—the immanence of a transcendence not superable by immanence. For us, God is "only in the manner in which He appears to us in the world, in the manner in which He talks to us, and in the manner given through man's language in the world. He is for us only in the form in which He assumes an 'aspect,' an aspect which always hides Him in the measures and thoughts of men." Consequently, philosophy, even for Jaspers, is research of the absolute Being, who circumscribes everything while being circumscribed by nothing. Thus, philosophy by essence is metaphysics. Yet, Jaspers immediately informs us that being cannot be objectivated, that it is an unknown entity, so that it is unknowable: "No being objectively known is being itself."

Such are the motivations and exigencies in Jaspers' thought, the fundamental aspects of which we shall explain and clarify. To philosophize is the need to clarify ourselves to ourselves: therefore, to philosophize is to posit a question, not so much about the meaning of the world, as about that of our existence. The man who undertakes to philosophize calls himself into question, commits his own person completely, and he must therefore accept the risks which the quest involves. To philosophize is an act of courage; it is the adventure which existence undertakes in order to clarify itself to itself.

Every position we take with respect to being is a point of view, a "horizon," a limit. Thought shifts from one limit to another, from a narrow to a wider horizon, while looking for a horizon capable of including the whole of being. Thought, thus, is led to transcend itself though not possessing the horizon of Transcendence by which, instead, it is always encircled. Yet, can existence renounce the clarification of itself? Such renunciation is the pure "situation," the *being-in*, the loss of existence in daily life, in which it disguises itself. To recover existence is the attempt to get close to being; but, the more the existent progresses the more totality gets away from him—he always remains included and imprisoned in a point of view, while perceiving that the infinite draws away from him as he gets closer to it. He does not conquer the infinite, he only loses himself in it; either he loses himself by imprisonment within the brute situation, or he is shipwrecked in the presence of Transcendence.

Man's deep aspiration to understand being in its totality is always unsatisfied though remaining unquenchably alive. True philosophy is not philosophy offering solutions (dogmatic philosophies), but one positing problems while remaining itself eternally a problem. Existence is clarified to itself as a problem; thus, if philosophy wants to clarify existence, it can only be an existential philosophy. Philosophy is an "invitation" to the search for truth. He is not a philosopher who possesses truth, but he who looks for it and experiences all its inexhaustible uncertitude. Truth invites us because we do not possess it; philosophy, then, is an invitation to Transcendence. Every point of view approaches Transcendence without being able to embrace it, since it always remains beyond us.

In this way philosophy expresses man's drama, which is his tendency toward an infinite that is always beyond his grasp, and that, because it eludes him, both tests and invites him. Thought and existence are fragmentation, a "fracture." Even if man realized all his possibilities of research and discovery, the point of view he might achieve would always be a partial vision of the whole. Dogmatic conclusions are only a presumption on the part of philosophers and scientists who deceive themselves into thinking that they can include the whole of being in one formula.

It seems that for Jaspers the horizon of the *World* is identified with that of the *Whole:* the totality of the World is the totality of the absolute

Being. *Science* is the typical orientation in the World (and, by way of interpreting Jaspers, let us add that "scientific" describes every philosophy assuming the World in its totality as the horizon coinciding with that of Being), but its results give an "image" of the World which, as an image, is not the World at all. Provided that Being is identified with the World as a whole, science leaves me "outside of Being," its knowing is "the not-knowing what Being may be." "Scientific knowledge of things is not knowledge of Being," both because the image of the world is not the world and because scientific research misses *me*, who investigates, and also misses my life for which science is unable to provide a foundation. In short, science is "always merely particular, unable to embrace the whole of being and be a total knowledge of things; and so it does not offer goals to life, nor an answer for those essential questions which agitate man. It has nothing to enlighten the significance of man or to tell him whether or not it pays to turn to it. To exchange the convictions by which I live for a knowledge that I can demonstrate, disturbs the entire human attitude." Why, then, should there be a science if within the limits of its unquestionable and universally valid knowledge it can help so little that it abandons us without a reply when we face those eternal substantial questions? There is a science because the will to know the unknowable is an irresistible impulse and also because science today exerts an extraordinary influence. However, in spite of this, the orientation of the world supplied by science strikes against the limits of the circumscribing Being, which is not the image of the world that science itself gives. Inasmuch as existence is a movement toward the *Umgreifende*, it demands another type of thought in which man can discover the being he is. Sciences must then be distinguished from philosophy, which is not a science, and of which sciences are means. "Philosophy, in fact, though bound to the sciences and never without them, remains something absolutely different: it is thought in which I sense Being itself through my internal acting wherein I become myself; again, philosophy is a thought that makes me feel an impetus toward Transcendence; philosophy reminds me of this impetus and in a sublime moment it is even capable of producing it as a thinking act affecting the whole of man." We shall evaluate Jaspers' criticism of science at the end of this chapter; however, even now we can remark that it is a criticism against both positivism, for which mechanistic thought and "objective" knowledge are absolute, and against idealism, which, like positivism, misunderstands existence. In fact, idealism changes existence into an object and makes of being a thing which is demonstrated and "comprised" in the image of the world constructed by idealism itself. In this objectivity of the world, however, there is no room for my individual ego.

Once it has been proven that a hold on Being is not possible through the orientation of the World, existence is pushed back upon itself to move from the being that it is to the encounter with Being. For Jaspers, as we have already hinted, there are three modes in which we may have an intuition of our being:

(1) The mode of *Reality* or nature is that I know myself "as matter, living organism, soul, consciousness." But it is evident that this mode of knowing my being does not coincide with Being, with the encircling horizon. To know myself is to objectivize myself, reflect myself as in a mirror, that is, to make myself the object to myself. What is objective in me is a *thing* I investigate, so that which I investigate remains outside, "hidden" behind the ego objectivated by the knowing act. Once again, objective knowledge does not pave but bars the way of access to Being, in that "every object is a determinate being standing before me in the scission of subject and object, but is never the whole Being." On the other hand, I am myself to the extent that I do not become object and, therefore, I am unable to say what I am. Thought, says Jaspers (whose dialectic aims not at making evident the positivity but rather the negativity of a principle), is "the enlightenment of existence" (*Existenzerhellung*), but is never able to grasp existential reality. In fact, to clarify existence is to objectivate it; and objectivating it is to let it escape us. The existent, rooted in being, is never totally objectivated, but always remains enclosed in the circumscribing horizon.[13] Thus, within the mode of "reality" or objective mode of knowing my own being, Being escapes; it "exhales its soul," as Jaspers says in one of those poetical imageries of which he is fond. Consequently, the knowledge of the being I am as reality does not reveal Being. This is a second "fiasco" after that concerning the orientation in the world.

(2) The mode of *Consciousness in general* is to be distinguished from the individual or empirical consciousness (personal mode of knowing and evaluating things), which cannot be circumscribing at all. As regards consciousness in general (in the Kantian sense), which is the fundamental mode of our being, things become "object of experience and thought." It is the "space of the sciences," the place of universally valid knowledge. However, precisely because reality becomes "object of experience and thought" it is reality no longer, but only a "form" wherein we know it. This time, the wall of objectivation between existence and Being interposes itself, and a third "fiasco" must be added to the other two.

(3) The mode of the *Spirit* includes the preceding surpassing, and authenticating them; it overcomes the atemporality and abstractness of Consciousness in general in order to realize the comprehension of all

[13] The fact that existence is not objectivable does not mean that it is subjectivity. It is beyond any reflection on itself and, therefore, it is beyond subjectivity and objectivity.

things in the concrete becoming of history; and it overcomes Reality because "its becoming takes place within reflective thought and not within immediate bio-psychic occurrences." But not even the Spirit gives us the circumscribing-Whole: existence (*my ego*) remains outside once again. The "very vast and complete vision of the Spirit is just a *vision*, a spectacle before me wherein I lose and never find myself again. And another 'fiasco.' " All paths lead to the same conclusion: "If I want to grasp Being as Being, *I am shipwrecked.*"

These three modes whereby we know our being and attempt to grasp Being foreshadow—as we shall see clearly later on—three historical philosophical positions: the positivistic, the Kantian, and the Hegelian one. Their "fiasco" in the presence of Being is Jaspers' criticism against these philosophies, which were like three "illusions" in their attempts to grasp the Absolute.

One mode still remains, *Existence*, which is posited as clarification of itself and its voluntary acceptance; it cannot be objectivated beyond the distinction of subject-object (which is the screen separating existence and being); and it cannot be either measurable or experimentable. Existence is free *ab origine* and in its absolutely historical reality, which is confirmed in time. Existence, which is *historicity*—within time without being in time—is union of brute existent and existence, of necessity and freedom; it is the union of time and eternity and so a historicity manifesting itself in the *instant*, because it is the identity of temporality and nontemporality and, as such, it is unthinkable; yet, as unthinkable, it is not irrational since the irrational is purely negative whereas historicity is wholly positive. Existence always is in *situation* and it cannot modify the *situations-limit* (*Grenzsituationen*) of which being always in situation is one of them (death, sorrow, and so on are the others); and they are "like a wall against which we fatally collide." Existence is *freedom*, existential freedom which cannot be objectivated (and, thus, one that is beyond the question of determinism—indeterminism); and as *not-objectivable*, it cannot be either demonstrated or rejected. One is aware of it only through the *existential choice*, that is, through the decision to become oneself—a decision in which *guilt* is intrinsic for the simple reason that existence is free (the choice that I *must* make represents the rejection of other possibilities). Such is this paradoxical Existence, which is this thing and its opposite at the same time (without the possibility of explaining itself by reflecting on itself, since this is the way of not explaining itself any longer); and Jaspers places this existence before Being which has been missed by all other approaches. Such Existence can only be clarified in the presence of Transcendence, the supreme horizon, beyond all horizons. Historical becoming is this antinomic tension of existence, which always reveals itself in its paradoxicalness—freedom bound to necessity, eternity united to time, being to nonbeing, communication linked to solitude. This is the tragic face of existence, its authenticity and its life: if oppositions artificially disappear, existence fades away into nothingness; if antinomies are fictitiously pacified, as in a "mirror" in which the total and objective image of the world is reflected, existence reverts to the nonauthentic.

Truly primary freedom (*Ursprung*) is discovered in the presence of Transcendence, and existence finds itself as possibility of being and as free space. In order for existence to be discovered as freedom, it is necessary to transcend the external situation, the ego dispersed in the world and placed in a given situation of objective space and in a given amount of objective time. It is necessary to choose one's own present and nonobjectifiable being. It is necessary to accept one's own individual situation and to develop one's intimate possibilities. In short, it is necessary for me to discover myself as *Existenz*. But to discover my existence and, with it, my freedom, means to enlighten my primary situation and discover that it is not up to me to decide my own existence. I am only taking what has already been decided. I am left with the sole possibility of accepting my existence as a *destiny*. Jaspers' freedom coincides with Nietzsche's *amor fati*.

Bound up with the problem of the modes of being of my being is that of *Communication:* I am myself in relation to others. "It is only through the bond uniting men that knowledge gains its meaning."

What does Communication signify for me? Am I a stimulus or an impediment to communication?" The following fundamental, philosophical question arises here: "How is communication possible? Which of its modes can be realized? How do they stand in relation to one another? In what sense are solitude and the power of isolating oneself bridges of communication?" Jaspers recognizes all the positivity that communication holds as a power "clarifying" existence: "The individual man can never become a man by himself alone. Being-oneself is real only in communication with another Being-oneself. Absolutely alone, I remain in the darkness of a world all shut off; together with the Other, I can manifest myself in a movement of reciprocal opening. One's own freedom is possible only if the Other is free. A Being-oneself, that is isolated and isolating, either remains mere possibility or vanishes into nothingness."

Thus, communication is essential to the existent. For each of the three modes of being of my being (Reality, Consciousness in general, and Spirit), there is a corresponding type of communication.

In the mode of Reality men communicate only externally, as they cooperate with an objective society. They communicate and understand each other in all that is convenient and useful to them. In the mode of Consciousness in general they find themselves united by the universal and common form of knowing things: they communicate in the unity of the abstract and the generic. In the mode of the Spirit individuals reveal themselves in a whole and communicate on the basis of the organic character of the real. However, all three forms of communication are insufficient. Each mode sets a communication and gives a truth, but none of them singly, nor all of them together, can give the truth and reveal existence before Being. There is a truth which is called *utility*, another which is named *scientific truth*, and still another which I call *spiritual-unity*, but each one of these is relative and does not grasp the absolute truth. Therefore, if truth always escapes, no point of view must be assumed as dogmatic and held as absolutely true. Without dogmatisms, says Jaspers, there would be better understanding among men.

It seems there is for Jaspers a form of truly authentic communication, the *existential communication*, a process of revelation and realization of the ego as "self," in which existence struggles to be itself. In this "loving struggle" every existent is at the disposal of the other. To reveal oneself to others is to expand one's own being, to come out of isolation, to establish a reciprocal understanding, and to advance through a scientific collaboration. "We do not philosophize by moving from solitude, but from communication." It is not a question of establishing a supremacy and a victory; in such a case we use others, making them instruments of our realization. In the communication as a "loving struggle," the others are each himself, making up the multiplicity of the unique ones, the plurality of persons, each being "exceptional" and himself; yet, the common efforts are unified in the search for the Being-One, in the tension toward Transcendence, which unifies individual persons and draws them, singly, as close as possible to the highest revelation of the sense of Being, that is, a transcendent, spiritual, and personal unicity (*Einzigallgemeine*). But, even this authentic form of communication is bound to suffer a "fiasco," as it is swept away by its destiny of being a "shipwreck" which constitutes the essence of existence. In the presence of Being, the individual remains the existent, who, in his "isolation," still perseveres in his endless quest.

Jaspers' doctrine of communication is better clarified in the distinction between intellect and reason. Truth is more than a simple possession on the part of the *intellect*. "Scientific exactness which imposes itself is not the whole truth. This exactness, in its universal validity, does not entirely bind us as real men, but only as intellectual natures." The intellect, whose measure is exactness, sees the rest as sentiment, subjectivity, and instinct. "With this bipartition, the bright world of the intellect still remains besides the irrational in which there is a convergence of everything that is either despised or extolled to the skies, according to circumstances. Every bipartition paralyzes motion and makes man slip here and there between the dogmatisms of an intellect overflowing its bounds and the inebriation of vitalism, the accidentality of the fleeing instant, and life. The soul becomes mean in the variety of experiences lived disparately. . . . Truth is infinitely more than scientific exactness." We are led to this "more" through communication, which discovers Being, the circumscribing-Whole, and Transcendence. Such a passage beyond objectivity and toward Transcendence, in which we really exist, cannot be given to us either by our intellect or by the sciences; philosophy alone can give it to us. "What we call Reason is a movement in which we disclose ourselves unlimitedly and in which we would like to express everything existing; through it, we almost attract to us what is most extraneous and farthest from us; within it we seek a relationship that is valid for all things; and we are indebted to it for not breaking our communication with anything. This word (Reason) is to be radically distinguished from the intellect since it invests with itself the condition of truth as truth may come to light from the modes of the circumscribing-Whole." Getting close to truth does not mean confinement to one mode alone, but a consideration of the forms in which the infinite Being manifests itself. Precisely, here resides the attitude of reason or philosophy, as it differs from intellect, which shuts itself in the objective, which is but one of the modes of Being.

"Reason does not reject the intellect's truth but passes through it in order to move freely beyond all restricted horizons, thus revealing that truth resists all attempts to be enclosed within a system. Reason is always open to all modes, to all forms of experience affecting Being, even to forms that are instinctive, passional, and irrational. Reason also listens to the voice of religious faith, but does not allow itself to be shut up in any one of these modes. Reason does not exclude anything *a priori*, with intolerance; it accepts contrasts as well as harmonies. It has no mania for system because it is sensitive to the lesions which tear existence." Reason "like a magnetic force, conquers every scission," so achieves a unity far superior to that of scientific knowledge. It "inserts itself there where unity is destroyed, in order to salvage a truth from this very lesion and in order to prevent a metaphysical collapse—the crash of Being itself. Reason, the origin of order, pursues everything that destroys order. Reason remains as the patient, unceasing and infinite force facing the extraneous, irruptive, and destructive element which proceeds outside of logic and is antithetic to "intellectualistic" logic. Although reason does not reduce Transcendence to itself, it still makes Transcendence present in existence through transparent allusions which announce Being. Consequently, Reason (*Vernunft*) and Existence (*Existenz*) are unified: "Existence achieves clearness only through reason and reason possesses content only through existence."

Yet, this highest degree of clarification realized by existence through reason is positive in the sense that, by clarifying existence, reason reveals its inability to get a firm hold on Transcendence. When Jaspers writes that reason "puts" being "into light," he simply means that reason gives existence the maximum of light or awareness concerning the inaccessibility of Being; that is, reason clarifies existence and causes it to be itself, in the sense that it definitely convinces existence of its failure before Transcendence in whose presence it is shipwrecked. Only the "leap" into Transcendence remains, but a leap without arrival, and so a real shipwreck, not *in* but *before* Being. Such is the existential clarification. Reason has priority over all other forms of communication, because, by coming closer to Being than the other forms can, it reveals existence to itself better than the others, but only in the sense that, better than the others, it reveals existence as shipwrecked before Transcendence.

Furthermore, first in *Reason and Existenz, op. cit.* (and later in *Truth and Symbol, op. cit.*) Jaspers speaks of his peculiar "logic," which proceeds outside of logic and is antithetic to "intellectualistic" logic, in that it holds paradox, contradiction, and the vicious circle as its principles. Jaspers' logic is, then, "rational nonlogic," since for him one is "rational in the true sense of the word," only if reason "is based on the irrational." The only possible logic for him is (and must be) a logic that characterizes the "failure" of logic, and, likewise, the only existential philosophy is that which ends with the "failure" of philosophy. Only in this way are logic and reason existential and capable of clarifying existence, because existential clarification is shipwreck before Being.

Hence, this is the paradoxical conclusion: I and others reciprocally communicate more by what we do not know than by what we do know, that is, communication is better if we do *not know* what Being is, if we are *never* to reach it, and if we remain outside of Unity. Existential communication, which is the cessation of every illusion concerning knowledge, consists in the common awareness about our not-knowing. We all feel united before Transcendence, but like fellows in shipwreck. Hence, solidarity and even solitude: existence communicates in solitude, inasmuch as in the presence of Being it experiences its solitude. We discover the deep sense of existence when we find ourselves before Being; yet, "to be before Being" is to be shipwrecked and to be without any of the modes of being, including reason. As long as I think, I never find myself before Being, but only in the presence of a mode through which the Whole manifests itself. In order that I may grasp the Whole, it is necessary for me to come out of my thought. Therefore, in order that existence may find itself in its own presence and before Transcendence, it is necessary that I cease thinking. In the "shipwreck of my thought" I realize myself and discover my destiny. When I have lost all possibilities of reaching the Absolute through a mode of being of my being, only then do I have the sole possibility of grasping the Whole. "A thought which truly grasps transcendence—on the basis of the impossibility for any communication to become perfect and on the basis of the failure of every form of truth in the world—is a thought which demonstrates God."

Such a motif is Kierkegaardian, ultimately. In fact, even for Kierkegaard God is not object of knowledge but of faith: transcendence is the scandal of reason. Yet, in Kierkegaard there is religious faith and a recourse to grace that is lacking in Jaspers, whose conclusion is Neoplatonic in its inspiration. Existence, in the presence of transcendence, is discovered as pure possibility and also as absolute freedom; that is, existence takes notice of itself in that moment in which it can be everything and nothing. In this possibility existence is truly itself, completely realizing its historicity, and accepting its destiny. Only in the presence of our destiny we acquire a sense of greater understanding toward others and toward their truth. Transcendence reveals the profound sense of our humanity. Thus, we do not exist in Being but *for* Being, in our decision to be for it, and in our feeling that we are in its presence. In the *instant* in which I suspend myself on the edge of Transcendence, I exist no longer because I exist in the presence of Being; I am and am not; I lose myself and find myself again; I am shipwrecked and realize myself in the final shipwreck. In this situation-limit "the instantaneousness of the invisible Whole can shine; in the world, on the other hand, such unity disappears and remains incommunicable because communication would lead it to our horizon, wherein it would be falsified and misunderstood. Its possibility lies in its instantaneousness, in its unrepeated historicity. It is in time and, yet, it is outside of any time." The point of arrival for thought and communication as for Plotinus is *silence*.

Existence is engaged in the presence of Transcendence and so is philosophy, which cannot pretend to do what religion (founded on revelation) alone can do. Religion gives guaranties to man, to whom it shows the path to faith. Philosophy can do nothing of the kind. Nonetheless, since "philosophizing encircles Transcendence," it is essentially related to religion.

"In order to remain true, religion needs philosophy; and in order to remain meaningful, philosophy needs the substance of religion. . . . Philosophy will have to affirm religion at least as a reality from which it has drawn its own being. If religion were not the life of humanity, there would be not even philosophy." [14] For Jaspers, however, as we have seen,

[14] Jaspers has dealt again with the problem of religion in "Von der biblischen Religion," in *Die Wandlung*, Vol. I, No. 1 (Heidelberg, 1945-1946), pp. 406-415. It looks, however, as if he is saying nothing substantially new: he recognizes the impossibility to replace religion which determines, "in a decisive way," the bulk of human events—which, in their turn, are illustrated and clarified by philosophy. He tends, Neoplatonically, toward a "philosophical religion."

no "rational" answer can be given to the question of the nature of Being. Indirectly an answer is given through the clarification of existence. The bounds of existence lead us to admit that the existence of an "outside" is as certain as that of an "inside." "The feeling about the laceration of Being in every aspect, as well as the radical manifestation given by contradiction, shows us that everything we succeed in knowing does not receive its consistency from itself." The manifest sign of Transcendence lies in the sense of limitation. Thought is unable to furnish proofs of the existence of God because the categories of the intellect are for the knowledge of things; yet, it is precisely the contradictions and lacerations of our lives, and precisely the shipwreck of our thought and existence, which constitute the direct proof (neither "intellective" nor "rational") of Transcendence. It is not a demonstration of God's existence, but a *meeting* with the Being of existence, which is shipwrecked before Him. The "outside," then, always remains unknown, whereas the "inside-being" is the *ciphered* structure of things. "Inasmuch as the limit and the root are to be made tangible in every Being, it is almost necessary to trace everywhere the shining thread which holds it united to Transcendence." In other words, the modes whereby Transcendence manifests itself are its *symbols,* a ciphered scripture, whose mysterious meaning we must discover. Every existent is a *cipher* of Transcendence. Existence, therefore, both unveils and hides Transcendence. Every horizon is such that, when it is broken, it reveals transcendence.

Reality is to be considered not only for what it indicates, but also for what it hides; and each thing, each existence, within its bounds and imperfections, is a cipher and speaks the mysterious language of Being. To clarify and to understand it in its existential depth, and not in its empiricalness, is to comprehend the secret message of Transcendence. All the modes of reality are unique, infinite messages of Being. Each thing is a cipher, a cryptic word, which, if well understood, gives testimony to Transcendence. To philosophize means to know how to decipher this message; in this sense philosophy is *metaphysics*. Metaphysics is not objective knowledge—Transcendence is enveloped in a myth within metaphysical objectivity. Therefore, metaphysics can only use symbols.

Thought does not comprehend the profound meaning of these ciphers: silence is its last word. Thought itself is a cipher that needs to be read. Metaphysics is left with only three ways: (1) the way of *formal transcendence,* by means of which we transcend the categories of the intellect and our own existence; (2) the way of the existential relations of Transcendence, in which is included that of the two laws, "law of day" and "law of night." Existence presents itself to me as order, loyalty and reason, and I follow the "law of day." It requires that I realize something constructive and productive in the world. Yet, existence breaks before me, it makes order fall apart, it renounces itself as false and vain, and I am sent down into the abyss of nothingness. The "law of night" holds sway over me. "The law of day is aware that in the end there will be death; however, in its enthusiasm for life existence does not believe in death after all, and so it seems to be certain about its immortality. . . . The passion of night, on the other hand, in its thrill for death feels a communion of love with it as in the presence of one who is an enemy and a friend at the same time." The law of day feels the law of night, but it withdraws and goes on acting; at any rate, the passion of night surprises us with its frightful sense of death. The day commits us to positive construction through historical becoming, whereas night warns us that everything is vain, and everything shall be destroyed; (3) the way of the *reading of ciphers*, in which it is impossible to distinguish the symbol from what is symbolized: Transcendence is in the cipher but it remains impenetrable. Existence is the place for the reading of ciphers, which are the light of Transcendence, an obscure and shining light "announcing" but not revealing. This is again a shipwreck. However, in this indissoluble implication of positive and negative, man discovers himself in the presence of Transcendence. The cipher, which is man, is the presence, not the proof, of Being. Everything is a cipher: history, language, art, life, and so forth. The highest cipher is metaphysics, which, like all ciphers, does not demonstrate but witnesses. Thus, the decisive cipher of Transcendence is the failure of metaphysics, the shipwreck of Existence. Here is its supreme clarification—failure. "At the end there is a shipwreck." In such a shipwreck all ciphers resound: existence is shipwrecked in silence, accepting its destiny without protest. It is the revelation of non-knowledge on the part of thought. This is "ignorance," which nonetheless is knowledge of the human drama and a definitive clarification of existence that is enlightened by Transcendence at the very moment when the "illusion of philosophy" is dissolved. Thus, Transcendence is not known, it is felt and lived; "one leaps" not into it but before it. Man truly becomes himself before Transcendence, in the presence of such "immense amplitude which seems to be set as a pure void." But, with the shipwreck of thought and the failure of metaphysics, existence discloses its true possibility. Once again, opposites involve each other. Final shipwreck is final triumph. In fact, "transient being becomes historical substance only through Transcendence." To philosophize is *to learn how to die*, yet this means that "through it, I emphasize the significance of the present by means of an active energy having Transcendence as its measure." Only man is open to possibility, freedom, transcendence, and shipwreck; and more than that, all that exists, including Being, is for man so that he may reveal his destiny to himself, meet the nothingness of his being, and accept his fate as authenticity and fulfillment of his existence. The individual is an "exception" and he tests his exceptionality only by "sinking into Transcendence." [15]

6. THEOLOGICAL EXISTENTIALISM:
I. ESCHATOLOGISM AND NIHILISM OF RUSSIAN "RELIGIOUS PHILOSOPHERS"

a. Introductory Remarks and Immediate Antecedents

It seems to us proper to subdivide so-called religious or Christian existentialism into "theological" and "theistic," not only because of its different confessional character (the first is Orthodox and Protestant while the other is Catholic), but also for purely philosophical reasons. In fact, theological existentialism is founded on the Christian religion, and it is like a commentary on or an interpretation of the "Word of God" or Revelation; on the other hand, the other form which we call theistic does not qualify itself as Christian, nor does it take Revelation as its starting point, though in reality it is inspired by Christianity. Furthermore, the former is anti-humanistic or *pan*-humanistic and is more concerned with God and his interior drama of self-revelation than with man; the latter rests on humanism and regards faith as a conquest and a guarantee of man's human authenticity and of the positive sense of existence. Obviously, such a distinction does not exclude either the points of contact between the two currents (for instance, their common aversion toward reason and "objective" knowledge), or the differences of "accent" and "tone" in each individual exponent within the two movements of thought. Almost all these writers go back to or invoke Kierkegaard at a later stage, after their own thought has been well developed, and each approaches him with a particular intellectual formation. The group of Russian "philosophers" ("philosophers" in an oriental way, for whom metaphysics is not distinct from religion, since it is, ultimately, a problem of "wisdom" and "salvation") is more immediately inspired by Dostoyevsky and Soloviev; on the other hand, the other group of theorists associated with the "theology of crisis" is inspired by Luther and Calvin; finally, G. Marcel is inspired by the Pascalian tradition and modern idealism. In this respect, let us observe that all these writers share in common a bond

---

[15] Existentialism has been widely studied and discussed in Italy. That of Heidegger and Jaspers has been re-expounded by Nicola Abbagnano (1901), a professor at the University of Turin, who has tried to confer to it a positive character in his volume *La struttura dell'esistenza* (1938). Later (*Filosofia, Religione, Scienza*, 1947) Abbagnano reduces existence to "possibility," but he deems it necessary to have a criterion of distinction between the illusory possibilities and the others. Such a criterion is given by the "possibility of possibilities," that is, by the transcendental possibility.

with idealism (a bond expressed with or without a polemic spirit) and some points of contact with Nietzsche. Even some Catholic writers and theologians have attempted to engraft upon existentialist themes the stock of traditional metaphysics (Thomistic or Augustinian), which they have preserved. On the other hand, in the Russian-Slavic and Swiss-German strains of existentialism, the thing of great interest is the act of faith in which they emphasize (sometimes to a paradoxical and exasperated degree) its originality and irrationality, which invest even the moment of philosophy. The latter, in fact, is not well distinguished from religion and as an "existential" thought it opposes the objectivity of abstract and deductive knowledge, as well as ontology for its being concerned only with being in itself, in a way that the necessary link between being and existent is neglected. Faith, understood as an intimate, lived experience (be it an act of man in collaboration with the action of God or an exclusive work of Grace), leads the so-called existential theology to the establishment of an irreducible opposition between Faith, Religion and Church, Christianism and Christianity, thus concluding (as Kierkegaard had done) that one cannot be a Christian unless he is outside of the Church (any church whatsoever) and that faith and religion deny each other reciprocally.

All these themes cause existentialism to be characterized as an anti-humanistic supertheologism opposed to and in antithesis with absolute humanism. For the latter, everything is time and historicity (negation of the eternal, of God); for the former, on the other hand, all must be judged from the highest point, from the viewpoint of eternity, in which history, time, and even man—insignificant and negative in themselves—acquire the sense given to them by God: it is the act of faith that founds authentic existence by setting up a communication between God and man. The two antithetic positions, as we shall see, deny both the human and the divine.

The "nihilist" tendency in Russian thought, which we are going to consider first, is already characteristic of the major writers of the nineteenth century. In opposition to Western thought, Russian-Orthodox thought always looked upon the various forms of "humanism," "culture," and theological and philosophical "rationalism" as the negation of existential experience, the negation of human freedom and sin, and as the usurpation of the divine, the death of God, the loss of the *meta*-historical and the weakening of faith; and it considered the Catholic Church as a political, juridical, and bureaucratic institution. Russian thought, in this sense, is openly in favor of "nonculture" and "nonphilosophy," in that culture and philosophy, as expressions of humanism, are the negation of religious faith. Hence its so-called nihilism, which is consonant with a supermysticism, the carrier of an apocalyptic, eschatological, and prophetic tendency through which everything representing the work of reason or having a human and temporal character is considered worthless.

Besides Dostoyevsky, whom we have already considered, the spiritual father of the Russian "religious philosophers" is VLADIMIR SOLOVIEV (1853-1900), the national philosopher of Czarist Russia. Ivanov, Chestov, Berdyaev, and Bulgakov depend on him to a greater or lesser extent. The critique of Western "rationalism" from Scotus Erigena to Edward von Hartmann, was the theme of Soloviev's first notable work *Krizis zapadnoi filosofii* (St. Petersburg, 1874), which is rooted in Russian orthodoxy and "slavophilism." In it, Russia's universal and mystic mission is clearly set forth: to revivify decayed Western Christianity and remotivate Roman Catholicism (ill with sclerosis and sterilized by the rationalism stemming from Greek philosophy) by means of the Orthodox religion, so as to resolve the crisis in Western thought, which has lost the sense of reality and the purity of "metaphysics" because of its severance from concreteness.

Western philosophy, according to Soloviev, rose from the exigency of making reason independent from authority (religion). "The new philosophy has the task of unifying the logical perfection of the *Western form* with the *fullness of content of the religious conceptions of the East.* . . . The achievement of this *universal synthesis* of science, philosophy and religion . . . must be the highest goal and the ultimate result of intellectual development. In this way, the perfect internal *unity* of the *intellectual world* will be achieved." In short, Soloviev rebukes Western rationalism for its abstractness (loss of any contact with the existent, personification of concepts, and artificial, doctrinal antinomies) and autonomy from religious faith. Such is Soloviev's critical motivation. On the positive side, however, he identifies metaphysics with religion, religion with Christianity and Christianity with Russian orthodoxy. The latter has the mission of carrying out a general "integration," that is, a "universal synthesis" of science and religion, an elaboration of the metaphysical revelation of the real, a reincarnation of man, a unification of theory and practice and of thought and life, a preparation for the advent of the "concrete total oneness" of the spirit, leading to a "reign of spirits embraced by the universality of the absolute spirit." The West has separated man from God because it has built a philosophy severed from life; thus, it has either ignored or betrayed truly metaphysical thought, which is not "rational knowledge" but "religious (Christian) and existential revelation."

Soloviev's attitude toward the West unlike that held by almost all orthodox theologians is not wholly negative: he prophesies, as we just mentioned, a synthesis between the logical perfection of the Western form and the religious conceptions of the East. He always believed in the realization of a Christian society, in which the two inferior human elements (rational and material) would be united and willingly subdued by the divine principle, even if, after so many disappointments, he thought of man's salvation as something to be effected through an apocalyptic catastrophe in a universe dominated by the antichrist. In all his brief and troubled existence, Soloviev entertained the hope of a spiritual transformation of the world and the salvation of civilization.

He felt, after all, the influence of Western "rationalism" and, to some extent, was conquered by it. Yet, what really is lacking in him is precisely the synthesis between Western thought and Russian religion. Nor could he produce it. In fact, by identifying metaphysics and religion he already eliminates the problem of harmonizing reason and faith, because, in this case, only faith survives, while reason is either suppressed or considered as a source of error, sophisms, and abstract analyses. What prevails in him is orthodox tradition, ancient gnosis, and a mystic-religious interest (with a pantheistic background, as is evidenced by his "Sophia" theory), in which the influences of Western philosophy (of Kant, Hegel, and, above all, of Schelling) are disguised. The main aspects of his thought are: Christ's cosmic function and the deification of man, who is regarded as an intermediary entity between primitive chaos and Supreme Being. The latter creates and supernaturalizes all of his work through the incarnation of His divine Wisdom wherein humanity becomes the center of the world in which God realizes His design.

We do not deny that Soloviev has tried to harmonize theology, experience and reason. His position seems clear: the absolute Being, inaccessible by empiricistic and rationalistic means, can be reached through mysticism supplemented by experience and reason. Thus his *free Theosophy* (or complete knowledge, whose object is the Absolute) is a synthesis of theology, science and philosophy, a system of religious and logical knowledge. But it is this very synthesis which is missing in Soloviev; on the one hand, he rationalizes mysticism and, on the other, on the basis of mysticism, he sees a divine revelation in every act of knowing. His doctrine of "Sophia," influenced by the cabalistic and Neoplatonic tradition, by Böhme and Schelling, is a mystical pantheism, modeled on the Neoplatonic-Schellingian scheme of the logical deduction of the three Hypostases from the absolute Being or divine Unknowable. The absolute Being, by process of emanation, objectivates into the *Logos*, "the intelligible world which God sees, *ab aeterno*, as His Wisdom," which man should carry out into the universe, putting thus into effect the *free Theocracy*, the society in which he acquires consciousness of his "uni-total" essence. Thus the "free theosophy" (harmonious union of theology, philosophy and science) or integral knowledge, which surpasses all abstractions and logical formalisms, resolves into "free theocracy," namely, into the unitotality of universal society. Reunited to the Divine principle, by means of the mediation of Christ, humanity is the Church, body of the *Logos* (incarnate in Christ), the community of Christians which, at the end of time, shall comprise all of humanity and of nature in a universal theandric organism (M. Herman, Introduction to the *Crise de la philos. occid.*, Paris, 1947, p. 42).

Until the revolution of 1917, Soloviev's influence on Russian thought was equal to and perhaps greater than that of Dostoyevsky and Tolstoy. Moreover, according to Wenceslaus Ivanov (one of the heirs of Soloviev's thought who was later converted to Catholicism), he (the singer of the Divine Sophia) was "the true maker" of the "religious tendencies" and the "carrier of a principle for a constructive order." The revolution interrupted the ferment of such ideas so that Ivanov, Bulgakov, Chestov, and Berdyaev emigrated to Germany, France and Italy.

b. L. Chestov: Faith in the Absurd

Among the Russian "religious philosophers," LEO CHESTOV (1866-1938) is a passionate and paradoxical writer more than he is an original thinker. He has won a place for himself on account of his implacable and intransigent, antiphilosophical and antiscientific polemic in defense of religious faith, which for him is faith in the Absurd. Chestov starts with a criticism of science or of those "minds" which Dostoyevsky calls "Euclidean," and with a critique of Nietzsche's ethics (*Dobro v uchenii gr. Tolstogo i F. Nitshe*, Paris, 1907; *Dostoevskii i Nitshe* [*filosofia tragedii*], Berlin, 1922); his initial position is negative with respect to both reason and ethics. During his years of exile in France he thought that in Kierkegaard's and Pascal's thought he had found a sound basis for his own position of radical criticism of rationalistic philosophy. Thus, these works came into being: on Pascal, "Gethesemane Night" (in *Job's Balances*, trans. C. Coventry *et al.*, London, 1932); on Kierkegaard, *Kirkegard i ekzistentsial'naia filosofia* (Paris, 1939); his "Revelations of Death" (in *Job's Balances, op. cit.*) which again deals with Dostoyevsky and Tolstoy; and his series of essays (his most expressive work), *Af'iny i Jerusalim* (Paris, 1938). Chestov finds that in Pascal, Kierkegaard, Dostoyevsky, and in Nietzsche—the masters of "existential philosophy"—there are still corrupting rationalistic elements such as Pascal's apologetic exigency ("apologetics is a justification of God before reason"), Kierkegaard's and Dostoyevsky's nonradical negation of ethics, and so on. For Chestov, on the other hand, between "existential" and "speculative" philosophy there is a total opposition: "existential philosophy is so intimately united with faith that it can carry out its task only through faith, in which it acquires the dimension detaching it from speculative philosophy." Speculative philosophy as such is atheistic: "It is an abominable thing, precisely because it is an attempt against the omnipotence of God." Speculative thought "prostrates itself before so-called evidence" while existential philosophy, whose source is faith, surmounts all evidence.

All things created by God were good. Man corrupted himself through his desire to eat the fruit of the tree of knowledge. Upon becoming *sapiens,* he ceased to live in the state of "innocent ignorance," in which he was unaware of good, evil, and death. For Chestov, sin is science (philosophy) which was unknown before the fall. From that moment on, man knew his limits (the possible and impossible, beginning and end, the ought and ought not): "As long as he was without lights, he had no limits—all was possible; all was *perfect,* as written in the Bible." Since then, this *homo sapiens* has been trying to take possession of the word of God, to replace faith with reason by changing it from a "believed truth" into a "known truth." The *concupiscentia irresistibilis* leads man (this is punishment due to his desire for knowledge in spite of divine prohibition) to seek his salvation in knowledge wherein lie his slavery and death. Passion for knowledge is a "diabolical pride" and an attempt to chain God to our truth, or (what amounts to the same thing) an effort to disengage ourselves from Him with a view to subjecting everything including God to reason. Speculative philosophy is "sacrilegious" and "atheistic" even while speaking of God and, precisely in this case, it is more so because it violates God's inscrutability and destroys the mystery.

Theological and apologetic doctrines, rational demonstrations of the existence of God, or the alleged mystical intuition are so many endeavors aimed at reducing God to our human proportions and capacity, at imprisoning Him within our cogent reason, and rendering Him superfluous. "Man hates Revelation above all because it is the *awakening,* the liberation from *abstract* truths, to which the fallen Adam's descendants are so accustomed as to be unable to understand life outside of them. Philosophy . . . using great care, rejects what is incomprehensible, enigmatic, and mysterious, avoiding all those questions for which it is unable to supply ready answers."

The divine mystery is a veracious truth and the "mysteries of being are silently whispered in the ear of him who knows when it is necessary to be all ears." This is an ineffable truth that is understood only by the good listener, a truth that requires a type of communication differing from that of ideas. It is individual, secret, and *one,* as faith is *one:* "It can be seen only by the one who seeks for himself and not for others, by the one who has made a solemn vow neither to transform his visions into judgments binding on everyone nor ever to make truth tangible." Truth is faith, and faith is subjective, for it belongs to the person *hic et nunc,* as a gift of God bestowed on innocence, while denied to proud science. "The promised land does not exist for the man who *knows.* It, instead, is found where the man of faith has arrived: it becomes a promised land *because he has reached it: certum est quia impossibile.*"

Even ethics, the other offspring of the tree of knowledge of good and evil, is a necessity. Virtue cannot be distinguished from knowledge, the "you must," from the "you know." As principles of contradiction and identity are imperative, so is the command of the will. This command suspends faith and paralyzes it, depriving us of that absolute irrational trust that Abraham had upon accepting the "impossible" (for reason) word of God (for whom all is possible) promising him the restitution of Isaac. Chestov remarks that even Kierkegaard wound up yielding to the siren's call and decided for the conversion of ethics into religion. Likewise, Nietzsche ended by accepting the Greek *amor fati,* and by letting himself be bewitched by what he had even called the "Circe of philosophers." Law is nothing but the alibi for sin, and the attempt to disguise it as virtue, the product of pride, the exaltation of man and his autonomy.

To free oneself from knowledge (science, ethics), is to free oneself from sin, and it is also to return to "innocent ignorance," to the *not-knowing.* The *not-knowing* is faith; and faith is what Chestov calls "existential philosophy," which does not exact logical justifications or rational explanations. Faith is a decision for the impossible, the "infinite despair," which projects "man into a dimension of being, wherein compulsions cease, and with them, eternal truths—or rather, wherein eternal truths end, and with them, the compulsions." Faith is the dimension of existential philosophy, beyond proofs and death. Authentic existence is discovered in despair. "Do they want to save men from despair? But despair is an immense, formidable force not inferior to any ecstatic impetus." Eternal beatitude is the gift of faith, which "knowing nothing and wanting to know nothing," triumphs over death. Existential philosophy is "philosophy of tragedy"; it experiences the tragic reality of sorrow and death, which it overcomes through faith. When we convince ourselves of the uselessness of our miserable human efforts, when all our weapons of ethical science are cast aside as blunt, dull weapons because they are the products of sin—faith brings about the "crisis" precisely in this moment of despair. We abandon ourselves to the "impossible," to the "absolute will" of God, to the Absurd.

It is necessary to accept the Absurd, to rescue faith from reason's claw, and to realize—through faith, the Absurd, and Holy Scripture—that liberation which rational thought denies man. There is no room for the "necessity" of science and ethics. Just as the opposite of knowledge is faith or the *not-knowing,* so the opposite of sin is freedom; faith, in fact, is liberation from the sin of knowing good and evil, from *concupiscentia irresistibilis;* it relies upon the Absurd, upon God, the only one who saves or frees us while being indifferent to our works whether they be blasphemies or prayers. Just as, for Barth, God can condemn St. Francis while absolving Cesare Borgia, so, for Chestov, Nietzsche's *horribiles blasphemiae* are worth the *laudis jubilationes* of Pascal and *vice versa*. In this way, instead of being redeemed by faith, man is annihilated in Chestov's nihilistic and antihumanistic supertheologism; and with man, God, too—for He is identified with the Absurd.

c. N. Berdyaev's Impossible Eschatologism

NICHOLAS BERDYAEV (1874-1948), the greatest Russian thinker after Soloviev, defines himself as a "religious philosopher." He was first persecuted by the czarist regime for his criticism of the Holy Synod, and later expelled from Russia by the Bolshevist government as an enemy of communism. He twice found shelter in Germany, and later took refuge in Paris where he lived until his death. There he edited a periodical on religious studies, *Le Chemin*, around which many of his other exiled countrymen, including Chestov and Bulgakov, gathered. A restless and deeply religious spirit, he was formed through the study of German idealism and Marxism, of which he later became an implacable critic. Later still he became a follower of Dostoyevsky and of Kierkegaard, and felt the influence of Dilthey. His writings reflect the drama of his tormented spirit and a sense of inquietude inherent in the very problems which preoccupied him.

Berdyaev makes the philosophy of Dostoyevsky explicit and, in some aspects, carries onward the thought of Soloviev with whom he shares a sympathy for Böhme and German Protestant mysticism, as well as the defense of Russian orthodoxy. Among numerous and memorable writings touching on many speculative problems (religious, philosophical, social, and political) we mention the following: *The Meaning of the Creative Act*, trans. D. A. Lowrie (New York, 1955); *Freedom and the Spirit*, trans. O. Fielding Clarke (London, 1944); *The Fate of Man in the Modern World*, trans. D. A. Lowrie (New York, 1935); and his meditations on existence, *Ja i mir ob-ektov* (Paris, 1934). The last two books were considered by him as his most important philosophical works, and he himself defined his thought as "a philosophy of freedom—of the creative act, of the person, and of the spirit—and an existential philosophy." Other memorable works are: *Dostoyevsky*, trans. D. Attwater (New York, 1934); *Slavery and Freedom*, trans. R. M. French (New York, 1944); and the *Opyt eskhatologicheskoŏ metafizik* (Paris, 1947).

Existence is an ontological category; and to say existence is to say being or person: "The subject itself is being, and communicates with the mystery of being." Philosophizing starts with it, because the source of philosophy is the experience of human existence in its fullness, which is experience of being; being is not deduced from knowing, but knowing from being. The person is an unrepeated and individual "universe," and "the subject must be a person at the beginning and at the end." The person is totality and "participates in its entirety in all the creative acts of man." Only the person or individual knows, not the universal Subject or "Consciousness in general"; thus, knowledge is "personalistic" (while personalism is not to be confused with "egocentrism"). "The decisive function in knowledge belongs not to the logical process of thought, which has only an instrumental character and prevails only halfway, but to the volitive and emotional tension bound up with the whole spirit." The *spirit*, not the intellect, is fullness of knowledge and existence. Knowledge is an *intuition* representing the person's direct participation in being. Existential knowledge is not "objectivation," but rather the negation of it.

Berdyaev, like Kierkegaard, states that "truth is subjective." "The category of the general . . . is an erroneous category. The general has no ontological existence . . . ; it is, first of all, of social provenance as it results from sociological interpretations. . . . Thus, it is up to existential philosophy to overcome the general in order to arrive at authentic existence. . . ." Generalizing objectivation, whose tool is the concept (which Berdyaev opposes to intuition) is alienation of the subject, and externalization. "The subjectivity and personal character of metaphysics open the avenue to a higher knowledge." To surpass the "Euclidian mind" is to affirm the true sense of freedom and, with it, God, because God is found only in freedom. It means overcoming the "gnosiological fracture," and having the subject reintegrated in being, from which it had been "expelled" by objectivation. Modern thought from Kant onwards has the merit of understanding the need for surpassing realism and, with it, the merit of acquiring a critical consciousness regarding the centrality of the knowing subject. Both Kant and idealism are, however, wrong in identifying subjectivity with the abstract transcendental subject rather than with the concrete existential subject. For this reason, with the loss of the person the true sense of being is lost. "Knowing is not only casting some light on being; knowing is not a clarification of being, but rather a light in the heart of being, light inherent in it. Being is not immanent in knowledge, but knowledge in being. By supposing the identity of being and thought, one does not take into account the irrationality of being, which is replaced with a being already rationalized." This is not a transcendental idealism, nor a realism which is the naturalistic aspect of objectivation. Berdyaev's position is to "reject the naturalistic, *objective* conception of being and replace it with that of existence, existent and *essente*, that which has essence. Subjectivity signifies neither subjectivism nor psychologism. "The ego must overcome its solitude; but this cannot happen through objectivation, and not even through romantic subjectivity; it can be brought about only through the conquest of spirituality, in the intimate heart of the subject, by affirming oneself as a person, which remains itself even when going out of itself." Freeing oneself from objectivation is like being freed from sin: "The original fall was like a loss of freedom, like an enslavement of man to objectivity, and like an externalization."

The two levels of objectivation and of existence give rise to two modes of knowing (the objective and the existential). They also produce two forms of freedom, religion, history, and society: one is nonauthentic, the other, authentic. We must, therefore, free ourselves from the knowledge, society, history, freedom, and religion produced by objectivation, so that we may once again find being in its ontological significance, that is, being as "existence" which Berdyaev distinguishes from "life," a biological category.

Objectivation on the social level gives rise to *socialization*, to impersonal and anonymous "socialized knowledge." The person is aligned within classes, institutions and laws, wherein each *ego* is no longer in relationship with a singular *you*, but wherein the *ego* and the *you* are *things: communion* is supplanted by *communication*, which is the loss of the intimate, of the subjective, and of freedom, which we give up "in the name of peacefulness, social well-being, and organization of human life. The infinite of the spiritual world disappears, "being replaced by the juridical and the organizable, through which individuals are swept away in the anonymity of "technical" gears. History is the theater in which the conflict between the objective and the existential, the antihuman and the human is staged; and it is extremely difficult both to "humanize the behavior of history," and to "humanize the State," which is "favorite creation of history."

As abstract confessionalism, religion has no soul because it represents only an objectivation of faith. Faith, on the other hand, is without dogmas because it represents an emotional intuition of God, who is pure love and a giver of truth to life: a truth we seek in vain in science and speculative philosophy. Revealed truths are unknowable, and in presuming to know them we end in negating them. So-called religious knowledge is what human reflection adds to divine Revelation. Theology is the objectivation of the word of God, that is, religion degraded to social phenomenon, to collective knowledge, to communication: it has ceased being existential experience, communion of spirits, and participation in Being.

If we pass from the objectivation-level to the existential-level, we again find the authenticity of the spirit and, with it, philosophy, society, history, religion and freedom, which also, at this level, are authentic.

A philosophy that is existential "by vocation" cannot be but religious.

Philosophy and religion harmonize when they experience life in its fullness, and when they do not replace metaphysical or mystical intuition with scientific truths or dogmas. Philosophical knowledge also has its root in the emotional ecstasy, personal and subjective, which occurs when the philosopher delves deeply into being. Yet this ecstasy should not be egocentric, a "folly of the self" and a consequence of original sin. True knowledge, in fact, is knowledge of being, a discovery of the sense of life and of our personal destiny. Existential knowledge—which, as we have said, is not a knowledge pertinent to consciousness in general or to universal reason but rather to man as a concrete existence, as a person—is a very singular penetration which each spirit makes in the same mystery, and a spreading of one same light into a myriad rays. As fullness of knowledge, philosophy gains "creative consciousness of the sense of human existence." However, precisely at the point of contact between philosophy and religion, the rupture between them is also evident. The abolition of mystery was the pretense of atheistic humanism which became antihuman once it had lost God and, with God, the vertical sense. Existential philosophy lives on freedom and mystery, on time and eternity; and, for this reason, it is a philosophy of existence which is a single consciousness that bears in itself its *duality*, and a philosophy that lives in its own contradiction and represents a living paradox.

The person that socialized knowledge or communication nullifies affirms itself in the "communion wherein each one comes out of self in order to reach others." This communion is not actuated in any of the external forms of societies that are organized for the well-being of the masses, but in "solitude," which is not selfish isolation, but a relationship of love with the other person, who is not just "another before me," but "the other ego," my second self, a singular *you*. *You* and *I* are shut in ourselves and isolated, if God is absent; ours is a communion of three: *you*, *I*, and *God*, the *You* of every *I* and of every *you*. Only such a communion makes possible a Christian and human society (human because Christian), in which the person maintains the supremacy over society without being alienated from it. This, in our opinion, is the way we must understand what Berdyaev calls *personalist socialism*. The communion of spirits can be realized neither by the official Church which has middle-class habits—the church of those who believe through birth and tradition and of the one who lacks doubt and inquietude—nor by communism, which is both a technical organization for material well-being and a total negation of spirit and freedom (with its disregard for man's spiritual freedom, communism denies this "communion" at the very moment it tries to "impose" it). Yet, Berdyaev recognizes (1) that "the Church represents and protects, in an organized manner, the unity of the spiritual expression of all Christian generations; (2) that it guarantees one and the same meeting with Christ; and (3) that it points the way to salvation to all mankind, to all those who still find themselves in the inferior levels of the spirit." On the other hand, although he sharply criticizes communism, he acknowledges, with Dostoyevsky, the truth in it—the material or economic factor is the condition of human existence on earth. He says, with a profound sensitivity to the problem of social justice (but against Marxism): "Bread for oneself is a material worry, whereas bread for the others is a spiritual worry." In this sense communism is a lesson, a reproach to every Christian in that it represents "the evident proof of a duty not fulfilled, of a mission not carried out by Christianity." If we do not wish to see the anti-Christian idea triumph, we must practice "a Christian spiritual education," and reconquer "a Christian disposition toward faith and sacrifice"; we must realize, that is, an integral Christianity, "which is not rhetorical, incomplete, and decadent," but, rather, a "regenerated Christianity, capable of realizing its eternal truth in a concept of universal life, universal culture, and universal justice in society."

On the basis of this universal Christianity and against *historicism* or "immanent history," which is succession of facts and in which existence is at variance with objectivation, Berdyaev recovers what he calls the *Historical*, the *existential time* or eternity in which man participates. The succession of facts—which has no authentic meaning within the "horizontal" order of immanent history advocated by historicism—acquires significance within the "vertical" order of eternity, which is judgment upon time. "Order and harmony can only be conceived eschatologically." Therefore, "the true revolution of the spirit is the end of objectivation, that is, the end of the world." The advent of the spirit, its supremacy over the material world—once objectivation has come to an end—will determine "the transfiguration of this decayed world." The person's participation in God—the *You* or absolute Person which is simultaneously communion with other persons—realizes that fullness of existence which is the fullness of the spirit.

It is also the fullness of freedom because the person, the man, is *freedom*. Man is spirit in that he is capable of initiative. Even freedom is twofold, "formal" and "substantial": freedom upon truth and freedom in truth; or, as taught by St. Augustine, freedom of choosing the good [a freedom which is bound with the possibility of sinning (*libertas minor*)] and final freedom in God and in good, which is the freedom of not being able to sin any longer (*libertas maior*).

Libertas minor is the corruption of the first freedom: it affirms itself as separation and revolt, rebellion, free will, and whim; it proceeds from nothing, from a refusal of being, and posits itself autonomously. It is the *audacity to say no*, the freedom of the "superman" Raskolnikov, and of the atheist Ivan Karamazov: freedom that leads to crime and teaches that "everything is allowed if God does not exist." It severs itself from Being and relies on its own might; it is Lucifer's freedom, the one that must be converted in order to escape its own nothingness. However, if man had no freedom of choosing good and perpetrating evil, and if freedom were not freedom to deny itself and to rise against its destination of being free in the good, in which case alone freedom is authentically free—then there would be no freedom in man. The latter is free in that he can choose his own destiny and also choose either to remain faithful to it or to fail it. Freedom as such is tragedy; there is evil and there is sorrow in the world because there is freedom; but, without freedom, there would be no good either, and no man as spirit. Freedom is not, then, a right but an obligation, a burden, a responsibility, a suffering. Hence, the tendency in man to "unburden himself," to "do away with freedom," and to accept the slavery of a rationalized world that is devised and constructed technically, and a world-machine made by the "Euclidean mind."

To burden oneself with freedom means to burden oneself with sorrow, and to place oneself in the position of human dignity, which is the position of the spirit, but is very uncomfortable. Freedom is always in danger: *either* it is denied in the will which rebels against Being, *or* it is denied in self-renunciation by accepting the "idyll" of a world that is mechanically ordained and mechanically made uniform. If man overcomes these two tremendous temptations, it is possible for him to realize the ultimate freedom in Truth, in God. Man's destiny is the same as the destiny of freedom, which is a duty to fulfill, a burden to be carried, and a free acceptance of that burden of duty and of sorrow. It is our profound humanity in time and in the spirit ("freedom in time" and "freedom in the spirit" are inseparable). To be free is the engagement to be men, in view of the realization of final freedom making us free in God. This last freedom, being impetus and love, is not merely human; it reveals to us an infinite which is ever present and real. It is the freedom of Adam redeemed through Christ and in Christ.

Of all the existential philosophies treated so far, Berdyaev's is the only one that has a deep sense of the human; his is a philosophy concerned with the positivity of existence and its values—one that speaks of God, being, freedom, and so forth, without adulteration of words and invention of a terminology laden with emptiness. For this reason we have emphasized only one facet of Berdyaev's existential philosophy, without intending to conceal the other but, rather, with the aim of distinguishing between them; for we are convinced that the one we have described possesses an intrinsic positivity. In fact, with respect to religious, moral and social problems (Church, freedom and communism), Berdyaev wrote pages that are among the most meaningful of our times, not only for the sincere and experienced, human and religious *pathos* that animates them, but also for their philosophical depth. Having said this, it is necessary to add that Berdyaev's metaphysics, in fact, reflects another facet of his thought—a facet that brings him back to Oriental nihilism and renders his eschatology "impossible" and absurd. Berdyaev's metaphysical construction, indeed, evidences the following traits: a legacy from Soloviev (who identifies metaphysics with religion, and reduces metaphysics to eschatology); a reduction of rational knowledge to objectivation (as if rationality were only this) and a reduction of existential knowledge to the emotional intuition alone; and an influence stemming from semi-Manichaeism, that is consonant with Russian orthodoxy and with Dostoyevsky, as well as an influence resulting from Böhme's mysticism.

Berdyaev himself (*The Meaning of History*, trans. G. Reavey, London, 1949) rebukes the Reformation for having denied human autonomy in the presence of God's action in man; he rightly points out that Hegelian monism—which "sacrifices the personal soul to an absolute Spirit" in such a way as to become "the opposite of personalism," that is, an "anti-personalism"—stemmed from the Protestant error in that Hegel's absolute Spirit is Luther's grace reduced to the status of being in the world. Yet Hegel and Schelling (with their logical dialectic pantheism and mystical pantheism) have entered into Berdyaev's mind as well, along with Böhme and the ancient gnosis (already incorporated in Soloviev's thinking), thus corrupting the authentic Augustinian strain in his thought. Consequently, his eschatological conception—which differs greatly from St. Augustine's—ends, on the one hand, by depriving history of any value and by nullifying time to such an extent that Christian eschatology itself becomes insignificant and absurd; on the other hand, it ends by denying God Himself (who is internally characterized by a dialectic of good and evil) with whom Berdyaev links the destiny of authentic freedom and, with it, that of the person, which is freedom because it is spirit.

The struggle between God and the devil is not only in the depth of human nature (according to Dostoyevsky's thesis); the tragedy of polarity is "in the very depth of divine life." If Dostoyevsky "had gotten to the bottom of the science of God, of the Absolute" (luckily, we say, he did not do that), "he would have been compelled to recognize the polarity even in the divine nature itself, the abyss in God, something similar to Jacob Böhme's theory of the *Urgrund*"—that is, he would have, like Berdyaev, admitted an indeterminate "primary being," a nonbeing more original than divine being, and from which the cosmic drama gushes out, a drama in which God too is involved. And with that the Christian God, on whom Berdyaev always calls (when he forgets Böhme and the gnosis), is lost, and the Russian philosopher does not escape the pantheism of a God lacerated by an evil within himself, of a God whose tragedy is the same as the cosmic tragedy. Hence, it follows that: if the whole natural

and human world (the world of time and history) is tragedy and catastrophe (and with this, the positivity of "immanent history" as well as
that of the "historical," is denied); and if God Himself is (by essence)
the tragedy of good and evil, and if universal history is identified with the
eternal struggle God undergoes in order to free himself—then Berdyaev's
"tragic" God is Hegel's absolute Spirit, whose development is a process
of self-liberation and self revelation to itself; then persons or subjects are
nullified in it as tools or phenomena of this immense cosmic struggle of
which God alone is actor, a God who is troubled with the "tragedy of
polarity" which essentially constitutes Him. The difference between the
two philosophies is this: Hegel's secularizes Protestant theology (and we
must not fail to remember even his Neoplatonism) and resolves religion
—a dialectical moment of the absolute Spirit—into philosophy, which is
logic; that is, he drops the curtain at the moment when the Absolute has
wholly conquered itself in its self-transparency and beatifies itself in
contemplation of itself and, perhaps, of the remains of the Prussian State.
Berdyaev, on the other hand, is not willing to secularize theology, so that
he continues the tragedy indefinitely (even when the curtain has dropped
at the end of time), with no significance, and absurdly. In fact, if good
and evil coexist with God, the two freedoms constitute His tragic polarity.
But, then, what sense is there in the redemption of man? And what is the
sense in man's rising from *libertas minor* to *libertas maior*, to freedom of
God? Provided that man could rise to that height (though he cannot), he
still would find that in God there is the continuation of the tragic struggle
between the two freedoms, that is, that God has still to redeem Himself.
Since God's tragedy is identical with the cosmic tragedy, if God *is*
this tragedy and is unable to resolve it (as He cannot) then, man, too,
is incapable of freeing himself, because he is the essential manifestation
of, or the essential participation in, that tragedy. Therefore, *libertas maior*
is an impossible freedom.

7. THEOLOGICAL EXISTENTIALISM:
   II. THE THEOLOGY OF "THE ASSASSIN-GOD"
   AND OF "USELESS SALVATION" IN K. BARTH

Protestantism in our century has found a powerful reaction and new
accents in the so-called *theology of crisis* or *dialectical theology* of the
Swiss Calvinist KARL BARTH (1886), a Protestant pastor who became
a professor at Göttingen, Münster, Bonn, and from 1935 on at Basel, his
birthplace. His book, *The Epistle to the Romans*, trans. E. C. Hoskyns
(London, 1933), strongly stirred German Protestant circles, as it roused
arguments, harsh criticisms, discussions and polemics which even today are
not extinguished. Barth's *Epistle to the Romans* goes against the whole

tradition of biblical studies, not only in opposing historical-philological criticism, but by reason of the intransigence that characterizes some of its theses and the meaning he ascribes to "dialectic." Even the theology of crisis is related to the *Kierkegaard-Renaissance* and to existential philosophy, in fact, began as a theological existentialism with the Protestant Kierkegaard. However, whereas the Danish theologian, through the existential categories of anguish, sin and faith, aims at saving the individual man from the omnivorous Hegelian dialectic, Barth wishes to save God or Revelation from secularization as it was brought about through the subjectivism of the "religion of sentiment" (characteristic of the romanticist-idealist Protestantism of Schleiermacher and Ritschl); through conservatism and the mythologies of the Reign of Humanity; and through bourgeois pietism and humanitarianism of the liberal or socialistic environment that preceded the First World War. Barth is not an existentialist in the sense that he would make Transcendence a "position" of existence (in this respect he is poles apart), but rather in the sense that he grasps the meaning of existence at the very moment of "crisis," which is, after all, the presence of God operating in us. As he himself states in one of his autobiographical writings, his theory claims to be neither a philosophy nor a religion (if the latter signifies a study of man in his relationship with God), nor, least of all, a natural theology, but only a theology having, as its exclusive object, the Word of God, which is the mystery of God Himself in His relationship with man—a theology, therefore, having as its center, beginning and end God alone, exclusively His Word, Christ, and not man.

Barth's thought did not cease to develop with his *Epistle* of 1919 but, under the influence of his brother, Henry, and of the theologians Edward Thurneysen and Frederick Gogarten (who represented the first group in the new theology), he has modified the harshness of some theses in the second edition of the *Epistle* (1922) and in his other fundamental work, *Church Dogmatics*, trans. G. T. Thomson (New York, 1955), of which thirteen volumes have been published since 1927. Nevertheless, it seems to us that there are no substantial changes between the "first" and the "last" Barth.

There is no doubt that Barth's theology exercises a suggestiveness which is *sui generis* and, I might say, dialectical; it attracts and rejects; it commands attention but is never able to secure assent; it is a disconcerting suggestiveness.

Barth himself states that (at the beginning) he constantly kept in mind, in its positive and negative aspects, Kierkegaard's qualitative infinite difference between time and eternity, that is, as we know, the absolute detachment between God and man, between whom every relationship becomes inexplicable and constitutes a scandal to reason. From man to God there can be no dialectical passage but only a *qualitative leap*. For Kierke-gaard, the individual is alone in the presence of God, alone in a relation-ship of negativity. Man is a sinner: the category of sin is the category of his individuality; the abyss dividing him from God can only be filled by grace, by faith, which is a miracle, not an act of knowledge. God and man, qualitative opposites, meet in the absurd: in revelation, in which the infinite descends to the finite; in Christ, in whom the divine descends in the human; and in the instant in which the eternal enters time. These are the paradoxical syntheses of the "intrepid dialectic." The negative im-plies the positive, existence is simultaneously mortal malady and life (Luther's *simul justus et peccator*); it is negativity of sin which, being denied by grace, is converted into redeemed positivity.

Barth says that this is the conception of life for Dostoyevsky. Raskol-nikoff seeks *life* and finds *death;* but death is reversed into its opposite, in the negation of itself; God finds Raskolnikoff and the resurrection takes place. Such is the dialectical implication of opposites, typical of the theology of Barth, who evidently cannot refrain from "polemizing" with the "religion of conscience" of idealistic and romanticist Protestantism (liberal theology), and with "religious experience" as understood by Schleiermacher and his school. Barth's theology aims at a complete separa-tion of the divine from the human and at placing the former beyond the practical, psychological, and physical datum.

The language of reason is unable either to say or to comprehend any-thing about God. God is not "to be demonstrated" since He is "that which demonstrates." He is not to be founded, since He is the foundation of everything. Man does not know God; it is God who knows man.

For Barth, as we have mentioned, there is an "eschatological, cosmical and radical dualism": *God and man; God who is God and man who is not God,* two worlds, one confronting the other. *Man is not God* signifies that he *is* man in that he *is not* God: God's being is not-being man and man's being is not-being God. God's transcendence is absolute, radical, without any remote possibility of analogy. To think of God as God is already to deny Him since it means rooting Him in man thinking of Him —God, the *absolutely Other* from man, is not even thinkable. "God is in heaven and you are on earth"; there is no relationship, only a reciprocal negation. "A passage, a development, an ascent, a construction of this side toward the beyond are excluded in principle." Man lives in his world, the world of nature, history, space, and time. His civilization and culture fit his condition or status, which is that of sin and fall. Such is the world of the finite, of the temporal, and of the contingent wherein the funda-mental law is represented by *eros,* a fullness and impetus of life, a "libido" and vital impulse. But this *eros,* a despot of the world of sin and vanity, finds its limitation in death; beyond the line of death looms the impassable abyss of the transcendent world of God, of the *absolute Otherness*. Every attempt at crossing this line is a sacrilegious Titanism: all we can know is not-knowing. Such is the situation in a sinful world fallen in the abyss of death. Similarly, man is also radically immersed in the "perishableness of things as he is hurled at the conquest of vanity under the irresistible thrust of *eros*, which in appearance looks like a carrier of life but is, in reality, an instrument of death."

Facing the world of man, who is not God, stands the eternal world of God, who is God and is not man: the world of the absolutely other, of the Invisible, of creation and redemption, of cause and end. What man thinks of, worships and invokes as God is not God but an idol, the idol of his pride that cannot resign itself to its ignorance of God and cannot renounce the existence of someone satisfying his exigencies. Barth does not conceive the abyss separating God and man, however, as a static equilibrium between two equivalent forces, but as a dynamism of continuous creation, in which the new world always surpasses the old one by denying it. For Barth, in other words, it is not a question of a rigid opposition, but of a duality moving toward unity. The dualism of temporal and eternal vanishes into eternity in that the latter term qualitatively surpasses the other.

Once an absolute divine transcendence and an absolute human negativity are posited, nothing that comes from man has either a value before God, or a positive function in the determination of the crisis: neither philosophy nor ethics, nor religion, all of which are a sacrilegious effort and a Promethean Titanism. Evidently, Barth's polemics are directed against the philosophies of immanence and of subjectivity, and against that humanism and softening of the Christian message which pretend to attain transcendence by moving from man (from the low)—that is, they pretend to resolve transcendence into the human, and to reduce Revelation to the intellectual categories and the Christian Life to a convenient system of rules. The certainty of philosophy (and also of ethics and religion) consists in its negativity: "We know that God is what we *do not* know, and that precisely this not-knowing is the problem and origin of our knowing."

No human word can have a "likeness and correspondence" (*Aehnlichkeit und Entsprechung*) with the word of God, but can only be in "contrast and contradiction." Even good works (such as morality) are worthless, no matter how noble and excellent they may be; they are worthless before God. Like man's life and being, they "are only death and nonbeing from the viewpoint of the beyond"; they represent another attempt, on the part of our satanic presumption, at getting hold of God through thought or action, sentiment or virtue. Sin makes man absolutely incapable of thinking and willing anything having any possible value for

God. Man is a sinner, and sin is not an act of the will but is constitutive of his nature, that which makes him essentially an absolute otherness from God. In so far as they are human, our works are neither meritorious nor nonmeritorious before God. God qualifies them in one way or another, according to his impenetrable designs. Even at this point God turns man's upside down, the plus sign into the minus sign, and *vice versa*. God's verdict may be "the condemnation of a St. Francis of Assisi and forgiveness of a Cesare Borgia. He can change every human *yes* into a *no*, and every *no* into a *yes*. He is impassible, whether we are going toward heaven or toward hell." The saints "fight against God while struggling in favor of God."

Since God is what we *do not* know, the *absconditus*, we must exclude natural theology which, as a rational elaboration of the concept of God, knows what God is not, that is, the negation of God and, therefore, still another diabolical work. Mystical experience must be denied because it presumes that we can communicate with the Inaccessible—as must the Church, which is a visible society, a human and historical organization to which the divine allegedly descends.

Even religion (rites, practices, and dogmas), like the Church, is a work of sin, an attempt at establishing a bond with the absolute Transcendent: an attempt, as always, to lay hands on God. The Church is not a mediatrix between God and man; on the contrary, she makes man aware of the abyss separating him from God; she places man before his sin and his death, on the impassable border beyond which there are redemption and life. No "religious pathos" can lead us out of the unbreakable circle of our negativity. It, too, is smoke in the midst of smoke, and insignificant to God. Yet, religion, on the other hand, represents the apex of our negativity; in fact, it places us before the abyss of God and before our "negatively positive" being, wherein "the void becomes visible," as it is for the saints. Just when man tries to get near God, the latter strikes him with lightning as He did the ancient Titans. It is at this point, nonetheless, that man really recognizes his negativity; he finds himself before God, before the One he cannot be, and as a sinner and a nothingness, on the line of death which, with all his possibilities (including that of religion), he cannot change into the line of life. Man is like a person behind an electrically-charged barbwire which he cannot touch; man remains an enigma before the infinite enigma of God. As Kierkegaard (and, before him, Luther as well as Job and Paul, according to Barth) had said, religion is not man's salvation but the delicate and disquieting juncture wherein the whole problematical nature of human existence is revealed: and with it, man's malady, not his health; his torment not his peace; his disharmony, not his harmony. Religion is not a dimension having man as its base and God as its vertex, but a line breaking just at this side of the abyss separating man from God, the old from the new world; it does not end in itself, but it is the juncture at which man places himself in order to be reached by God; it is the acknowledgment of man's dependence on God, on that total Otherness never to be attained by him. In short, religion discloses man's negativity, exacerbates man's sin, and places him in the infinite distance dividing him and God. The religious man, as such, is a sinner; religion is his death before God. However, the positivity of religion lies precisely in its negativity; the negation is resolved in the affirmation of God. This is not all: "A negation maintaining itself as negation, once it has been posited, would not be true negation; it, too, must, in its turn, be denied." In other words, once all the negations have been effected, man must not consider himself as the negative before the positive (God), because then God would not be everything, in view of the fact that He would be found in a dialectical relationship with the negative (namely, man). It is, then, necessary to have the *negation of the negation* (that is, man's nonacknowledgment that he is the negative element before the positive element). Only at this point of total negation, when even the negation of the negation itself takes place, can faith intervene and deny the negation of the negation and carry out, in this way, a shift to positivity, to the advent for which there cannot be, on the part of man, any preparation, not even a negative one.

Who then is the subject of faith? If it were man in the position of waiting for the Divine Word to convert his negativity into positivity, man once again would place himself before God, who would be subordinated to him. On the contrary, it is the divine Word that, being everything, "says" and "does everything" while realizing itself through creation, so that there is an appropriation, a "requisition" (*Inanspruchnahme*) of the being that is realized by the Word itself. Faith, therefore, comes from God Himself: "Man knows God because he is known by God"; he would not seek God had God not already found him. Faith, then, is not one of our acts, but a "gift," God's grace rejecting every human participation; it is a miracle, a mystery; it is not man's faith in God, but God's act; it is "God's faithfulness" (since God does not forget His creature) toward man, not man's faithfulness toward God. "Therefore, the true subject of faith is God Himself. Faith is the *yes* granted by God to him who has accepted the *no;* it is the life given by Him to the one who has willed to die." The *no* pronounced by God against man's negativity invests it, invades it, and changes it into positivity. Faith makes man lose his nonbeing, which is his being, and it gives him being, which is God. Reformers and martyrs carry out the great social and religious upheavals: they are the "possessed" by God. Psychologically, faith "is a continuous leap into the uncertain, into the obscure, and into emptiness"; it is the audacity of being, knowing and willing in God; it is the extraordinary courage to believe "in spite of everything"; it is the supreme risk, the absolute and radical "nevertheless."

The act of faith by which God assumes man, "happens" at the moment of *crisis*—the miraculous sign of intervention that changes death into life. At this point true *existence* is established; man lives by dying; he finds salvation by losing himself. In fact, God establishes freedom through the enslavement of the flesh; and He also establishes the human personality on His pre-eminent and sovereign personality; He nullifies the negation of man within His divine positivity—which is dialectical for it affirms itself by solving every *yes* and every *no*, sin and grace. At the moment He denies the negation, God assassinates man and then commits suicide, as we shall point out at the end of this chapter; and all this is done in a Hegelian way. Thus, everything becomes useless: sin and grace, perdition and salvation, condemnation and redemption.

The crisis is in no sense a human possibility; for man it is an impossible possibility precisely because it is a divine possibility. The crisis is the situation of man being judged by God. By accepting God (once man has given up all satanic attempts at assimilating Him), man is a *nothingness*, a *darkness*, which God in turn accepts and lights up; man "allows himself to be chosen" and God chooses him for his inscrutable ends. To allow himself to be chosen by God is man's *freedom;* to choose the human negativity and change it into positivity is the grace God gives to whomever He chooses and in whatever manner He pleases. Man can do nothing about it; whatever is his is worthless, even his negativity or death before God. Redemption is our success and our failure, which is success, too. God alienates and loses us with His wrath; whereas by His grace we are drawn nearer, affirmed, and saved.

In the *instant* of crisis, the past (time) is doomed; the fleeing instant is an interruption through divine intervention, in the order of the *before* and *after*. The divine grace bursts in and strikes like lightning, and, on his way to Damascus, it converts Saul to Paul. The instant of crisis is not, however, inserted in the succession of facts, in the chain of causes and effects; it remains outside of any prevision and of any predisposition, outside of time, for it is annulment of time. The instant is *nontemporal:* "In the presence of every 'before' and 'after,' the instant is a *quid* that is new, a something else that is extraneous; it is not continued in the 'after'; it is not rooted in the 'before'; it is not placed in any logical, causal or temporal connection, because it is absolutely new everywhere. The instant is always God's being, God's doing, and God's having, for He alone is immortal." Grace is outside of anything connected with the world; but, "without this nontemporal instant, the past remains dumb, and the present deaf." The *futurum aeternum*, that which comes toward us, is fixed in the nontemporal instant of crisis, differently from the temporal future (in which our sinful world is sunken) that gradually becomes past. The radical dualism between God and man is resolved in the eternal future, the point of crisis: and so, too, the *no* of God, the Creator, is changed into a *yes* by God, the Redeemer.

Existence is established by the crisis. Barth, too, distinguishes between the "being-in" (*Dasein*) and "existence"; the former, under the toll of sin and flesh, is man in the world, subject to historical determinism; existence is the negation of the "being-in," the miracle worked by grace (but it is not a mystical union with God, nor an anticipation of final grace). God establishes our "existence" and constitutes our personality on the negation of the *Dasein*. The death of the old man, who is sin, is the negation of the union of the spirit with *this* body; the new man no longer is the one who lives in this body. Eternal existence ("I am I"), which is the work of God, is constituted through the negation of the nonbeing of the *Dasein* ("I am not I"). This is the work of faith, and it means to die and to rise again in Christ and with Christ. In God's decision dies the flesh, which is the significance of death, a temporal decision occurring to man against God and to God against man; and the spirit lives, an eternal decision that takes place in man through God, and in God through man. The decision between flesh and spirit is God's alone. It is Christ who discovers man the sinner and his indigence; and Christ forgives and saves him.

We are confronted with the mystery of predestination, a fundamental point for Barth, the Calvinist. Predestination is an inscrutable mystery. The predestined one, he who is chosen by God, will never be able to say he himself chose God. Our negativity, our *no*, is converted into positivity, into a *yes*, only through God's decision. Barth argues with Augustine and the reformers who conceived predestination as governed by the cause-effect principle. If it were so, it would be inserted in the temporal series. The instant of salvation, on the other hand, is of divine "origin," absolutely nontemporal. God is an absolute despot in the presence of man: predestination, in fact, is precisely the most perfect expression of divine freedom and divine sovereignty.

However, the possibility is twofold; predestination includes salvation and perdition. God says to Rebecca: "I have loved Jacob and hated Esau." Is there then duplicity in God? A God who saves and a God who condemns? But God is absolutely one. He is the God of Jacob and the God of Esau; and He is Jacob's God because He is Esau's God; and Esau's God because He is the God of Jacob. God's duality is dialectically resolved into unity; Esau's God is denied in the God of Jacob because God, who is Esau's God in every temple, is Jacob's God in eternity. "We can understand that we cannot *understand* God outside of the dialectical duality, in which one must be two, in order that the two may be really one." We know "that such duality in God absolutely cannot signify an equilibrium, but only an infinite overcoming, an infinite victory on the part of grace over judgment, of love over hatred, and of life over death." But, if there is no duality in God, can there be duality in a humanity divided into chosen and rejected ones, into saved and doomed souls? In order to answer this question, Barth says that it is necessary to give the mystery of predestination not a quantitative sense, but a qualitative one. Predestination is not the mystery of *this* or *that man,* but the mystery *of man.* In the temporal instant, Jacob is also Esau, and Esau is also Jacob in the eternal instant (*simul justus et peccator*).

What meaning is there in human acts, once the crisis and man's recovery through faith have taken place? Is there anything man can do? Such problems are of interest to the so-called last Barth who, allegedly, has attenuated the extreme nihilism of the "first" Barth, the Barth of the *Römerbrief.* As far as we are concerned, the last Barth remains substantially identical with the first. In fact, the abysmal distance between God and man is retained, even when he speaks about "an immanence in the world on the part of a totally transcendent God." In fact, precisely the Barth of the *Dogmatik* excludes the *analogia entis* in that the finite or created being, namely man in himself and by himself, signifies nothing. Likewise: the world, history, dogmas, Christ's earthly and historical episodes, and so on, signify nothing.

Barth emphasizes the difference between Christ and the historical and contingent Jesus. Even though we knew Christ according to flesh, what we know now is the crucified and resurrected Christ. There is nothing exceptional in Jesus, He is a man like so many others, the founder of an oriental religion. His death underlines the relativity of all human things, including those that pertain to His historical life. Similarly, the Church, from the historical and human point of view, is a society like all the others; even the Bible, the Word of God, closed in the "prison of the world" (*Welthaftigkeit*)—as are closed also the Church and the historical Jesus—is not light that illuminates darkness, but is enveloped by them. Hence the means by which God "unveils" Himself is the same that "veils" Him (hence the independence of truth from whatever dresses it up); on the other hand, the veil that hides the Word of God is the vehicle of His Revelation. There is, then, no intrinsic capacity in man that can in any way draw him near to God and establish between them an analogical relationship of some sort. There exists, indeed, an analogy, but only "by virtue of the divine act wherein God confers on man a capacity that continues to be a capacity of God." This is the *analogia fidei;* but faith is an act of God, His gift (and man has absolutely nothing to do with it); consequently, even *analogia fidei* is an entirely divine initiative, so that the capacity still does not pertain to man but to God. Thus, in the "last" Barth everything is really the same as it was in the "first." All that is insignificant in itself (things, happenings and words), and transposed, becomes significant and allusive through that capacity. Even the most trivial facts can be "occasion" in the sense that God can give them a meaningful content and use them as a "veil" through which the *Deus absconditus* is indistinctly seen. A fact is *historical* (*historisch*) when it belongs to *history* (*historie*), that is, to a succession of human events which are all insignificant—a succession dominated by the principle of causality. That fact, instead, is *historicistic* (*geschichtlich*), which God chooses out of the *historical* and uses as a veil through which His mystery transpires: whatever God takes from *history* and makes meaningful (a "sign," an "occasion," a "pretext") through *historicity* (*Geschichte*). Historicity, then, is the divine sense of history (*Historie*), all that may serve God as an "occasion" for revealing Himself. Hence, the whole of history is insignificant, except for those events God chooses as occasions or means, to which He (and only He) gives a meaning wherein He reveals himself as it were, through a veil. No physical or human being, then, in itself has any meaning; out of the whole of the world only that thing has meaning (divine and not human meaning) which God, for incomprehensible reasons, and gratuitously, chooses in order to reveal Himself. The fall of the Roman Empire and, tomorrow, that of the Catholic Church (we speak from Barth's point of view), and the death of a louse are three equally insignificant events, unless God chooses one or the other (or all three of them). The "last" Barth writes: "God can speak to us through Russian communism, a flute-concert, a shrub in blossom, or through a dead dog." That being granted, the problem of the meaning of our actions remains unchanged—namely, human acts have no meaning. And the question: "Is there anything for us to do?" should be answered in all sincerity. We can do nothing, because whatever we do has no meaning whatsoever, except for the meaning God may choose to give it, and He may use this or that, indifferently. Barth's distinction between "ethics of Grace" (*"soli Deo gloria"*) and "ethics of conscience" has no positive meaning, in that man's negativity and God's essential dialectic allow no meaning for it. Even more meaningless, as we shall see, is the expedient of the doctrine of the "as if," that is, the absurd imperative to act "as if" the justification in it were a human possibility.[16]

[16] Although Emil Brunner (1889), a professor at Zurich, accepted at first many theses of the theology of crisis, he departed from Barth (*Die Mystik und das Wort*, Tübingen, 1928) and polemized with him. During the early period he conceded a certain relation, a point of conjunction (*Anknüpfungspunkt*) between nature and the elevation of man to the supernatural order, and also a certain natural knowledge of God, even though the act of faith (and the Catholic doctrine does not state otherwise) transcends human nature and remains a pure gift of grace. (Since 1946, however, when the first volume of *Dogmatik* was published, Brunner has adhered to the integral position of Barth.)

8. A CATHOLIC POSITION WITHIN THEOLOGICAL EXISTENTIALISM: E. PRZYWARA

On account of the distinctiveness of his theological thought, the Jesuit priest ERIC PRZYWARA (1889), a professor at Munich, can well stand as the representative of that Catholic theology which knows how to take into account philosophical and theological existentialism. For this reason we thought it more effective to place him immediately after Barth and his followers. Otherwise, he would have been mentioned in another chapter.

Przywara's position appears at once precise and exact; the religious act is tension between two real and living beings—God and man, the Creator and the creature. To suppress one of the two terms is tantamount to denying the tension. Philosophical superhumanism denies God, Barth's supertheologism denies man, for different reasons, but with an identical result; both deny the religious act, so much so that Barth, we may add, dialectically transfers the tension to God Himself, thereby denying Him as God. Immanentism resolves religion into philosophy (Hegel); radical transcendentalism with its Absolute Otherness resolves philosophy into religion; both deny the tension and, with it, the religious relationship. God exists in Himself and by Himself, independently of and before the creature, prior to the human act; to deny this transcendence and absoluteness of God is to fall either into cosmic pantheism wherein God is swallowed up by the finite (the world), or to fall unto a noncosmic pantheism (theophanism) which absorbs man and the world in God. On the other hand, the transcendence of God—from whom the creature comes and toward whom he aspires (outside of and without Him nothing subsists)—does not exclude His presence in any way, nor is He an absolute and absurd extraneousness. Therefore, God, though remaining a transcendent God, can save man.

Against Barth and the theology of the exclusive *analogia fidei*, Przywara metaphysically explains the relationship between man and God through the doctrine, the *analogia entis*, without which the being of the creature would be absurd and contradictory. In the creature which becomes and evolves, essence and existence do not coincide; yet, this does not mean that one can subsist outside the other. The creature's being is, then, analogous to the Being of God. It is dissimilar because in man essence and existence never coincide fully; it is similar because the creature tends toward the fullness of being, in that it is capable of surpassing itself. The religious problem is solved through this metaphysical doctrine of the analogical relationship between man's being and the being of God: "God is in me because my essence is correlative to existence; He is outside of me because my existence is limited by my essence." Religious life, then, surpasses every limit and cannot begin with and end in man; it is a feeling of divine presence, but also one of absence, love and respect, the affirmation of man's value together with his inability to absorb (intellectually and mystically) God in himself. Yet, what is impossible for man is not impossible for God; man cannot make himself God, but God can make Himself man, not in order to deny man but in order to elevate him (*Analogia entis*, n.p., 1932; "Metaphysik, Religion, Analogie," in *Metafisica ed Esperienza religiosa*, 137-187, Rome, 1956).

Although Przywara maintains the classical line of Christian-Catholic metaphysics, he knows how to incorporate into it (not merely for the purpose of dressing it up fashionably) some existentialist exigencies, which he cogently draws from the very depth of metaphysics itself.

9. THEISTIC EXISTENTIALISM

a. G. Marcel's Philosophy of Mystery

French existentialism, with the exception of Marcel, developed more than ten years after German existentialism (which, in turn, is later than the theological variety). This French philosophy is also imported from Germany and, above all, is a "Parisian" interpretation of Heidegger's *oudenology* (Sartre), or of Husserl's phenomenology through Sartre's *meontology* (Merleau-Ponty); and everything has been finally refined through and baptized by Wahl's "subtleties" and critical judgment. The chronological difference accounts for the existentialist fever subsiding in Germany at the time when it was raging in France. In fact, Marcel's main work, published the same year as Heidegger's *Sein und Zeit*, went almost unnoticed (except for some authoritative criticism by persons such as Lavelle) and, in any event, it did not receive then the great attention it was to gain later. Existentialism in France only began its ascent[17] and its diffusion, perhaps never matched by any other philosophical doctrine, in 1940. This is also due to the fact that French existentialism is more literary than philosophical; or it is, rather than a true and real philosophy, an "experience" of philosophical ideas by novelists and playwrights. Its greatest representatives, in fact, are novelists and playwrights and,

[17] German existentialism has to do with it, but its influence is limited to a restricted group of scholars who aired their views in the periodical *Recherches philosophiques*, which, from 1931 up to the Second World War was published, under the direction of A. Koyré, in large yearly issues and had carried articles of Koyré himself, of Wahl, Marcel, Sartre, and so forth. But up to the beginning of the war France was still under the overwhelming influence of Bergson, Blondel, Brunschvicg, Hamelin and Lachelier.

with one exception, they do not belong to the academic world of the Sorbonne or of any other university.

Generally the distinction is made between two currents, the left and the right, also called "atheistic existentialism" and "theistic existentialism." The former, naturally, made more noise and enjoyed great celebrity with the public at large.

Theistic existentialism can be reduced to the name of GABRIEL MARCEL (1889) alone; and the latter's "success" cannot, by any means, compare with that of Sartre; nevertheless, his name has attracted the attention of the most serious critics. Marcel's position is, for many reasons, unique: his formulation is neither phenomenological, Kierkegaardean, nor Nietzschean; his existentialism is anterior to the German type and also, considering the initial date of the *Metaphysical Journal*, trans. B. Wall (Chicago, 1952), to that of Barth. It is more or less contemporary with Unamuno's most significant writings. His ontology is existential, though it would wish to be linked up with traditional ontology. Marcel is included in the non-Cartesian French tradition from Pascal to Bergson, even though his thought developed through the study of Schelling—the idealist with the unfinished system—and, as we have said, through that of the Neo-Hegelians Bradley and Royce (*La Métaphysique de Royce*, Paris, 1918, which was republished in 1945). His "existential" and "subjective" philosophy, from this point of view, is his liberation from idealism through a deeper study of idealism itself. Marcel's philosophy, like Kierkegaard's, is autobiographical, personal, and averse to rational analyses. It proceeds from existential experiences within which we are to look for the best Marcel, a spirit endowed with a rare finesse and an uncommon psychological penetration. Some of his pages, however, lack spontaneity: they are lukewarm as if written by a man accustomed to the theater. The religious motivation (even before 1929, the year of his conversion to Catholicism) undoubtedly dominates Marcel's thought; but, unlike theological existentialism wherein the existential moment is regarded only in the act of faith (namely, in the supernatural intervention of grace), Marcel sees the religious category as the only authentic category of existence and not as something to be added to it; consequently, the others ("faithfulness," "hope," and so on) are to be borrowed from religious experience, within which existence is revealed to itself.

This fact makes Marcel different not only from theological existentialism (including Berdyaev), but also, and even more, from the German type (including Jaspers), to which he has been compared. Such a difference, however, does not deny Marcel's points of contact and affinity with the other currents.[18]

[18] Marcel himself, a contributor to the *Recherches philosophiques*, has emphasized his points of contact with German existentialism.

Once the religious sphere has been assumed as the one revealing the authenticity of existence, philosophy can only be a philosophy of the "concrete" or of "experience" through which being is revealed; so, it is "superior existence" or "mystical empiricism" or "existential ontology": an experience that is existential participation in being and a being that reveals itself in the immediateness of existential experience. Rational mediation is left out; existence is beyond any problem; it is the "metaproblematical," a "mystery." The stages through which Marcel deepened his thought are characterized by the following works: *Being and Having*, trans. K. Farrer (Boston, 1951); *Du Refus à l'invocation* (Paris, 1940); *Homo Viator*, trans. E. Craufurd (London, 1951); and the two volumes *The Mystery of Being*, trans. G. S. Fraser (Chicago, 1950-1951), his only organic work, for the others are all collections of essays, besides the dramas prior to and after his conversion. Marcel's philosophy focuses upon two concepts: "fundamental feeling" and "mystery of being" (*sphère de l'être*), problem and objectivation (*sphère de l'avoir*). A deepening we have called it, not a systematization. Marcel's "experience" remains fragmentary, expressed through sudden flashings, through promises of returns to it and of a further deepening of it—*a diary*. Musicality accompanies it as "a luminous commentary"; the Catholic religion has become its spiritual nourishment.

Marcel's experience is still, from a negative standpoint, one of the many protests against "the oppressive sadness of contemporary world," whose roots are in a dehumanized culture ruled over by the abstract, the rational, and the technical (*Man Against Mass Society*, trans. G. S. Fraser, Chicago, 1962; *The Decline of Wisdom*, New York, 1955). This modern world, in which everything is to be so explained, so catalogued, and made so functional as to leave no room for the individual, creativity, and wonder, is corrupted by a radical rationalism (Marcel the *"moraliste"*). To this generalized culture and life deprived of personality wherein universality becomes the highest goal; to this adage, "It is good for everybody," so that *"n'importe qui"*—Marcel opposes his thought whose concern is the concrete life of intelligence, which is regarded as research and creative investigation, an intelligence being formed through a dangerous and perpetual acrobatism. Contemporary spiritual life feels the influence of factors which come from the political and social order and compress it on an inhumanly mechanical level. Man and the person do not count; what counts is a leveling society by which an intolerable mask of habits and external acts is imposed. Existential philosophy aims at tearing off such masks, and at demolishing false and deforming artifices in order to restore to the human person his sense of existence outside of "current experience."

The philosophy of Marcel, as a philosophy of concrete experience, opposes idealistic "objectivation": the "I think" is not a source but "a breechblock"; it is the *sum* which prevails over the *cogito;* therefore, not "I think" but *I am.* Only the initial and mysterious being of the "I am" assures us of being; hence, *existence* and *objective being* are two completely different dimensions of being itself. Being is not a "spectacle." I cannot place myself either "in front" of being or stand behind its shoulders in order to observe its "behavior," because I am "engaged" (*engagé*) and "enrooted" (*enraciné*) in being. Concrete philosophy is not an abstract and closed system; it is a "research" which is not to be only an "investigation" of being. It is not a question of *the* being but *of* being. It is not possible, according to Marcel, to have "a concrete philosophy without a continuously renewed tension," that is, "without the most ardent reflection exerted on lived experience." Thought cannot go outside of existence: "such a passage into existence is something radically unthinkable, something without any sense whatever. . . ." The starting point then for an ontological research can only be existence, the "I am" which is involved in the questions it posits concerning being. All our relations, our body, existence, the others, and God become falsified if "seen" objectively and driven out of the existential. To objectivate is no longer *to be* but *to have,* and it means losing *my* being, *my* body, and so on. The meaning of the Cartesian or Fichtean *cogito* lies not in its ability to absorb being within itself, but in its inability to reduce it to pure and objective transparency. The *sum* has priority over the *cogito:* "If the existential is not at the origin, it will be nowhere; there is no passage into existence which is not a trick or a deception." Primary and indubitable experience is not either logical or rational; it is existential, instead; it means "to feel fundamentally," that is, to feel "not the sensation materialistically understood as a transmission or conveyance of a message which proceeds from one subject and is captured by another," but sensation as an act of sensing like "a corporeal, fundamental feeling," as Rosmini would say. The fact of sensing is the mysterious condition in every sensation, its initial immediateness: "Sensing is not receiving but an immediate participation." Sensation is not rational; it is irreducible to thought. It is the fundamental sensing that makes sensation itself possible as a *detecting;* and it is this sensing that represents a datum we cannot objectivate, and a "situation" in which the ego sympathetically partakes of the universe. "The fact of sensing is the fact of partaking in a universe creating me." In a certain sense, sensation is a "mystical apprehension" of the real and the foundation of every experience and of thought itself. For Marcel, in fact, "questions are possible only on the basis of the *hic et nunc* or on the basis of the immediate presentation." The fundamentally immediate is *incarnation:* I cannot be without my body and yet I am unable to identify myself with it. I cannot think of *my body* because, *ipso facto,* it would become a body. Thinking of "my body" signifies placing it "in front" of me as an object and, hence, making it cease being mine. This "intimacy with myself"—without being identified with my body—places me in a relationship of "presence" (of an "incarnated ego"), that is, such that I cannot exist without "my body." The "incarnated ego" is the original indistinctness, beyond the objectivating distinction.

There is a sensation as a transmission from one object to another, and there is a sensation as a fundamental and immediate sensing; there is a body as an instrument and an object (*l'avoir*) and a body as "my body" (*l'être*) immediately given (*incarnation*). On the one hand, there is the existent as "a phenomenal unity" bound to a "body-object" and, on the other, as a "real unity," a position not to be objectivated and through which I establish a sympathetic mediation with other things. The indubitable certitude of my existence and the existence of the world rests upon the immediateness of this fundamental sensing. Is it a problem or a mystery? A mystery that is an immediate certitude of *my* existence which from the beginning possesses all the values of religous experience. The "I am incarnated" does not signify the identification of my body with my soul: it, instead, indicates the intensity of the incarnation. In fact, to feel the incarnation is neither to identify nor to distinguish; it is to *partake*. "To be incarnated is to appear as a body, as this body here, without being able either to identify oneself with it or distinguish oneself from it, because identification and distinction, as correlative acts, can be exercised only at the level of objects." When a *quid* is related to a *qui*, the original intuition of unity is broken through objectivation; or this happens when from the level of "being" one passes to the level of "having," from "participation" to reflective analysis. The same unity is established not only with our body but also with things of the world through sensation as a fundamental feeling, which partakes of their life, almost as if we "incorporated them in ourselves" and formed with them "a unique complex which cannot be decomposed." Such is the man who feels, who lives: the man of internal experience, of the sphere of being, of the indistinction between subject and object, and of a lived participation in which *qui* and *quid* realize the *accrétion vivante*.

The "ruinous dissociation between the intellectual and the vital takes place as soon as "thought" intervenes; the living unity is disintegrated. Man does not "feel" or "see"; he "is not," he "has." He does not "participate," he "conceives." He does not "love"; he "analyzes." Everything becomes an object, instrument, a spectacle; everything becomes a problem. The body is *mine* no longer; as an object of my thought, outside of the immediate intuition and of that unity which is incarnation, my body becomes a problem—a multiplicity of problems. I no longer know if it is mine; if it *is:* whether I am my body, whether it is generated by the soul, or whether it itself generates the soul. Even those things with which I used to be very familiar become problems, become distant from me; I see them outside myself. Then I say I *have* a *body;* I *have* a house; I *have* a friend; I *have* a flower, and so forth. I have so many experiences about objects, which are to be analyzed, inventoried, classified. "Science" (opposed to existential experience) is the birth of "problems." To posit a problem, in fact, is to disassociate the unity between me and my body, things and my sensing them; it is to divest myself of my body and of things, and to devitalize experience. "The very act by which we question ourselves as to whether or not the unity of terms has a foundation is the act which separates them." Once they are separate, we rely on the sphere of "having," of objectivation, of the technical, of science, of the nonincarnated, in which every man becomes "an object" for others, a function, a tool. This is the sphere of "having": *one has,* not *one is.*

If problem characterizes the sphere of "having" or of objectivation, it cannot characterize the sphere of "being" or of existential experience. Incarnation, in fact, is not a problem, in the same way as our lived and immediate participation in things is not a problem. The sphere of being is, then, that of the *metaproblematical,* that of mystery, and of the indistinction between subject and object. In this sense incarnation is *mystery* (not in the religious sense); it is, precisely, the "situation of a being which presents itself as bound to a body; it is a nonrational (metarational) certitude and a lived experience: a truth "surpassing" and "comprising" us, which we cannot deduce discursively because it is *given* to us as immediate intuition; or, in other words, it is not a "problem" to be solved (since a problem arises with the reflection "concerning the basis for the union of terms"), but a "metaproblem." It is not, however, a passive acceptance, but freedom. I convert the *having* into *being* through my free activity; an incarnated being, I reduce the situation given to me, to my being. "I build *myself* out of what is *mine.*" The "I am" is the affirmation of my insertion and participation in being: existence is the mysterious insertion of "being" in the "being-in"; it is "incarnation" (feeling of my body and union with an external world through sensation) and "invocation," namely, a relationship with Being through participation. Metaphysical intuition is not objective or reflexive knowledge, but "certainty" of the presence of being in the incarnated being, a reflection "of the second power." It is not a question of "going around" being, but a feeling of sharing it. Regarding the *I am* there is no problem of being, but an "impetus toward affirmation," and a "calm waiting." Being is experience of a presence that cannot be discovered through thought, but through the revealing spiritual data, which are proper to the existential and themselves existential and not-objective. Thus there is a twofold participation or implication: in the being of sensible world and in the Being-in-itself or God. It is this participation that makes existence question Being in which it is itself engaged; it is possible, then, "to arrive" at being by moving from its affirmation, from the immediate datum of my existence. Participation is not identity; if it were, I would not feel the need to surpass my being in order to arrive at Being. It is tension, the mystery of being and of participation: "The question as such is suppressed and converted into a request." God is a "presence" and so the request made to transcendence has its answer in the immediacy of existence, which is participation in being. The existence of the ego, things, and God is not demonstrated rationally; it is experienced within the immediacy of the sphere of being. It is attained in the zone of the "metaproblematical" or of "mystery." To accept the "ontological mystery" is to consent to being —an act of humility, a pledge, and a loyalty; it is "sacred knowledge" and enlightened participation. This, for Marcel, is metaphysical thinking.

To posit as a problem the ontological question (to inquire "about the totality of being and about myself as a totality") is a corruption and a degradation of intelligence. Such a question transcends the sphere of the problematical and of doubting. The "ontological mystery," in which the *appetit de l'être* still persists, transcends every doubt which is characteristic of a problematizing thought. "To think, or more exactly, to affirm the metaproblematical, amounts to affirming it as indubitably real, as something I cannot doubt without contradiction. We are in a zone where it is no longer possible to dissociate the idea itself from the certitude or degree of certitude penetrating it. In fact, such an idea is certitude; it *is* its own guarantee; and, in this sense, it is something else and more than an idea." The ontological question positing itself as a metaproblem contains in itself, as we have said, its own answer; it is "an appeal changing its sign": that is, it is already to have found; it is the presence of Transcendence. The metaproblematical is not to be understood as the problem-limit (the unknowable); on the contrary, it is a resolution of the terms of the problem into unity; mystery is not what is unthinkable, but what cannot be objectivated. It is grasped with a "second reflection." Such reflection is the organ of metaphysical knowledge; while it negates objective or problematizing thought by which the certitude of the metaproblematical is threatened, it also clarifies the presence of Being within the spiritual data of moral and religious experience. The second reflection is, then, a negative dialectic and an "ontology of invocation"; it is a "blinded intuition" (*intuition aveuglée*), a concentration, an unbreakable union with being, an acknowledgment of the mystery, the "positive act *par excellence*." To adhere to mystery with humility means to free oneself from a problem and its constricting and trying limits; it also means to gain the zone of "being" by surpassing that of "having"; in short, it is a realization of freedom. "To have" means to possess and be possessed; "to be," instead, means to be free and to be able to regulate oneself. He who *has* cannot dispose of, or regulate, himself; he who *is* can. To change having into being is to dispose of oneself fully.

It is obvious that in a "metaphysics" understood as the negation of objective thought, there can be no valid proofs for the existence of God. "No demonstration of the existence of God is possible; there is no logical passage permitting us to elevate ourselves to God by moving from what is not God." In fact, "when we speak of God it is not of God that we speak," because God is neither an object nor a spectacle. The "rational ways that should lead to God" are not paths, but false ways, for God is not an object, the prey of logic. His sphere is the metaproblematical, the mystery.

On the side of being one finds then the "ego," the person I am, existence which is participation in being and body, "incarnation," which is contact with the world and "invocation": to pass from "having" to "being" is to free oneself from the "refusal" and to become free through "invocation." Thus, this participation in a *you* and in God, the absolute *You*, is attainable from the side of "being," of the metaproblematical.

Being locked in ourselves is still "having," still objectivation; it is refusing the "you" as "you" and holding it as a thing. "I communicate with myself in proportion as I communicate with others"; "if others escape me, I escape myself." The "other" is an *ego* that must be penetrated (loved) and not "that one there," one among many, a thing to be utilized or taken apart like a gadget, whose functioning we wish to observe. Such is the attitude of science, that is, of those seeking to know how a thing is made and what its use is. The "other," in such a case, does not exist for me as an *ego*, because I am not "disclosing" myself to him as to a *you*. The level of the other as a "he" or "that one there," or as a represented idea, is transcended by *love*, which is the affirmation of the *you*. Love is a mystical meeting between *ego* and *you*; each adds something to the other, as each creates his own freedom by creating the other's freedom. Love is the "*you's*" defense; it prevents me from disposing of the other as an object of analytical knowledge; it prevents me from confusing him with myself or confusing myself with him. Love preserves the initiative on the part of the *ego* and of the *you*, precisely because both are in relationship with the *you*—a presence of the *ego* to the *you* in the communion. Together we free ourselves from the "having" in the relationship of invocation of the absolute *You* or God. In the mystery of love we go to Being and Being comes to us. The "others" and God are not "objects of love, but the opposite of objects: they are "other selves," a *you* and the *You*. To love is to embrace the other's cause, and "to sympathize so much with the sick that one has to become the sick one himself."

Love is an unconditioned *availability*, a liberation from "having"; to be unavailable is "to be concerned about oneself," and "to be encumbered" by oneself or about things, or even possessed by something.

The affinity of love with poverty is great. A saint is always available because he is not possessed by things; he does not carry a burden impeding him from "disclosing" himself to others. The *you* to whom I am *present* is available for me and, being present, "he is capable of being with me when I need him." The one who is unavailable is always in a state of uneasiness, inquietude, and anguish.

"Such anguish contains an *inespoir* which, in relation to a determinate object, becomes a *désespoir*. If a basis exists for all this, the metaphysical roots of pessimism are the same as those of unavailability. All this is to be related to hope."

In fact, the bond between this other spiritual rhythm and love is very close. "Hope essentially is the availability of a soul, very intimately engaged in an experience of communion for the purpose of fulfilling the act which transcends the opposition between willing and knowing; through this act of transcendence, hope affirms the living eternity of which experience offers at once a pledge and the premises." The need to participate in a higher destiny and a purer joy rises from the despair of being in a hedonistic world, in which all desires and accomplished goals are useless. At the root of hope there is always a situation inviting to despair, the situation of this functional world wherein there is nothing "allowing me to open a credit-account in favor of hope and to give it some guaranty": a situation of "absolute insolvency." A man remaining in this situation is immersed in the sphere of "having," and, once all the possibilities of existence have been exhausted, he arrives at the "refusal" of being, whose extreme conclusion is suicide. Despair is treason to and the negation of being. Nothing remains save to oppose loyalty to refusal and hope to despair. "I hope that upon snatching me from myself, death may affirm me in being." Hope is a "vow," a "prophecy," and an "act of faith."

"The bond is close between hope and affirmation of eternity, that is, of a transcendent order." Hope is not only desire, but an affirmation with all my soul and being, that what I am hoping for *will be*. Such is the "prophetic resonance that stems from true hope." Hope is the weapon of those who are disarmed; or, rather, it is the opposite of a weapon and in this its efficacy mysteriously lies. Hope is the companion not of pride but of *humility*. It is not only a protest dictated by love but an appeal, a passionate recourse to an ally that is itself love. "And that supernatural element found in the depths of hope clearly manifests its transcendent character, because nature unlighted by hope can appear to us only as the theater of a vast and inflexible bookkeeping."

"The zone of hope is the zone of prayer." Our fundamental condition is to be "threatened" by despair, in that "the structure of the world in which we live allows and, in a sense, almost counsels an absolute despair; yet it is in such a world that an invincible hope can arise." Hope "exorcizes" our despair, and opens the way to the life of Being into which life returns.

It prepares a "creative faithfulness" because to live on hope means to succeed in remaining "faithful" during the dark hours. *Faithfulness* is the spiritual rhythm summing up all the others; it is "what counts most . . . on the ontological plane." Faithfulness means perpetuating a "testimony," which is a *pledge* made with a person, an idea, or with God, with the promise of keeping it in the future; consequently, it is "a manner of transcending time." Faithfulness, like promise, makes sense only if a relationship implying inalterability is established. It is not "a theorical or verbal acknowledgment; it is an effective one with a certain ontological stability, a stability which endures and in relation to which we endure." To fail to keep the pledge is to refuse to "go out of one's way" in order to fulfill it; and it means to "shrivel up" in our own misery, and to fall back into "having," outside of the spiritual rhythms of being.

How can I "engage myself to entertain tomorrow the sentiment which I experience today? Though tomorrow I may have no will to keep the word I have given, still, if I am engaged, I will know that I am bound to keep it. One must distinguish the act of feeling and the act of recognizing obligations and admit that recognition is independent of the feeling which may accompany it. But what is the nature of this bond (implicit in the act of swearing, and the like)? And in which measure do I have the right to find myself? I have no right to contract an obligation which I ought to know I cannot fulfill. It is thoughtlessness. . . . But I perceive the existence of an absolute obligation contracted by myself as a whole or, at least, by a reality in myself, which I cannot deny without a complete disavowal and which, on the other hand, is directed to the totality of being and is accepted by that totality itself. This is faith."

Faith is an absolute pledge. Disavowal is possible but it cannot be justified through a change either in the subject or object; it can only be explained through a *fall*. In this fall I deny the whole of myself. The absolute pledge, the pledge to God, is the grip that Being has on me; through faith I reply to the ontological exigency that arises from my participation in Being. The hold of being is presence of Being namely, the presence of God in us and *engagement* on our part toward God. Confidence in God is the mysterious relationship between faith and grace. Faith is realized as pledge, loyalty, love, and trust. We cannot be pledged to ourselves because we change. However, if there is an absolute pledge, a faith in God as a foundation for all other pledges, it means that all of them are no longer based on simple and changeable psychological states.

God is the ultimate goal in the existential itinerary: the impetus toward Being stops only at the feet of Being, before the presence of God. Loyalty (which as an absolute pledge is faith), hope, and love are forms of spiritual communication, ways of existential metaphysics, the sole effective barrier against the dissolution of the problematical and the degradation into the objective. The categories of the metaphysics of the problematical are all summed up in "creative faith," which is fullness of freedom, a protection against the forces of dispersion, and an executor of the deepest aspirations of existence. Man realizes himself only by remaining faithful to the situation of being incarnated.

The best in Marcel is found here in his penetration into spiritual experiences that reveal existence as participation in Being.

b. P. Wust and His "Incertitude" of Existence and "Securitas" of Faith

A form of existentialism in some respects similar to Marcel's is that of the German PETER WUST (1884-1940), a professor at Münster in Westphalia. After his return to Catholicism, he renounced Kantian philosophy and elaborated a theistic interpretation of existentialism in *Ungewissheit und Wagnis* (Munich, 1946), a work preceded among other writings by his *Die Dialektik des Geistes* (Augsburg, 1928).

For Wust, the moment of philosophizing is always characterized by the sense of "incertitude" (*Ungewissheit*), by the fact that we are never sure; yet man aspires to certainty. Certainty and uncertainty are found dialectically combined in concrete life. More than that, great decisions are not taken with proven reason but through an act of faith in spite of rational incertitude; consequently, they imply in themselves a "risk" (*Wagnis*). The logic of life, while not denying the logic of abstract reason, surpasses it, as Pascal—to whom Wust reverts—would say. It seems, however, that Wust is impelled by existentialism to maintain that this is not a reciprocal integration of the two types of logic but, rather, a defeat of reason, whose history (the history of philosophy) would be a millenarian bankruptcy.

Thus, according to Wust, the history of the proof of the existence of God is the history of the uncertainty of all proofs; and, in the last analysis, this is, more than a question of the undeniable limits of reason, a question of the latter's impotence or, as Jaspers would say, reason's *fiasco*. Now, if it is true that reason must acknowledge its limitations in order to preserve faith, it is also true that faith cannot be saved without reason. Fideism is as destructive of faith as rationalism, which denies it, is. Indeed, the life of the spirit cannot be reduced to rational activity alone (particularly to the activity of an abstract reason) since it would be impoverished; yet one is outside of spiritual "life," and therefore of truth, when one identifies, as Wust does, the rational moment with that of incertitude or of invincible *insecuritas,* and certitude and sureness are placed "outside" of thought in the abandonment of the sphere of objectivation and of problem, as Marcel says. Even for Wust, after all, the problems of metaphysics belong to the metaproblematical. Consequently, the choice is determined by sentiment, emotional states, passions, and so on. Neither *homo faber* nor *homo philosophus* can attain and offer that certainty to which man aspires and which is given only to the *homo religiosus,* even if "ambiguity" may be found in the religious sphere as well.

Of all animals man alone is not secure and guaranteed, because he is spirit and freedom. Hence, every act of his always involves risk. To choose is to risk. And up to this point we may agree with Wust provided that risk is not a leap into darkness. But Wust's weak position (and the inanity of his attempt to give German existentialism a positive sense) lies in the alternatives of the choice: *either* an immanent conception of life (purely human), in which case incertitude is insurmountable, the *insecuritas* is invincible, and the distrust absolute, as risk is absolute, gratuitous and unjustified ("irrationalism of the decision," the *Entscheidungsirrazionalismus,* typical of Heidegger's and Jaspers' existentialism); *or* a theistic conception supported by faith in the supernatural and in Providence, in which case the risk no longer is a nonreligious and blind temerity, because it is now enlightened by faith in which man's security is found. Yes, indeed, but what is the basis by which I choose to go to the right or to the left? The existentialist who advocates an immanent conception can always say that another believing existentialist will agree with him: in conceiving existence as an invincible incertitude and as a risk; in acknowledging the "failure" of reason; and in minimizing all objective knowledge—then, on his own account, he takes his "leap" and believes in God. On what basis? None. It is an act of faith and, as such, it is subjective; it is valid for the one who attains it. Yet, there is a more serious question: how can one arrive at the theistic conception and at the idea of Providence when everything in the world is obscure and uncertain, and when reason itself does nothing but create clouds, obscurity, and problems? From such an all-problematical human reality, we can only arrive at a God who is also problematical, ambiguous and dialectical, provided that the analogy makes some sense; this is the same as Barth's God, Jaspers' Transcendence, or Sartre's Absurd. In other words, one cannot deny the certainty of human truth, pose everything as a problem, and then assert the existence of the Christian God in order to give a meaning to life and avoid the absurd. It is not from nonbeing that one arrives at Being, but rather from being (by analogy), at Being *per se.*

This fact proves that every attempt to "Catholicize" existentialism or even only to arrive at theism through existentialism is bound to fail. As existentialist philosophers, Wust and also Marcel profess a philosophy which is not in harmony with their very sincere and ardent faith. This explains why the positive (and more ingenious) parts of their writings are those that deepen and clarify religious experience and its spiritual categories. This is so because they really live their religious experience; however, their existential metaphysics (not metaphysical, after all) denies the rational values while resting the whole religious moment on pure sentiment. Such philosophical "incertitude" makes their positions a "risk" for the religion that is theirs and ours; it becomes "insecure." Now, the problem for philosophy today is not to ratify the failure of philosophy and open a new credit-account only at the bank of religion, because God does not recognize any solvency either in a bankrupt reason or in a proud reason as symbolized by absolute humanism; the problem of philosophy (and, above all, of Christian-Catholic philosophy) is to reconquer *reason's health*, a sound reason (and by *sound* is meant that reason must have flesh, sinews and heart, since skeletons never abound in health), which may, with *its* truth (a light from God), *humbly* stand before truth itself. Even this is risk but the trust stands on *firm ground*.

10. EXISTENTIALISM AS A METHOD AND A PERSPECTIVE

a. J. Wahl's Realistic Dialectic

Many French students of existentialism (a numerous group) may be called existentialists, not so much for the specific existentialist position that they personally assume but for the studies they have devoted to existentialism. It is not, indeed, within the scope of this work to consider, *ex professo*, the critical literature pertinent to the numerous currents of thought we are presenting; yet, among French students of existentialism there are some who have greatly contributed to the clarification of existentialist problems; and even if they have not built a new existentialism, they have adopted it as a method of criticism, of interpretation, and of treatment of specific problems or doctrines (whether existentialist or not) having a historical and theoretical background.

JEAN WAHL (1888), a former professor at the Sorbonne, is a leader of this French group. He is a historian and critic of existentialism, especially with respect to its proximate and remote origins. Very notable is his *Étude Kierkegaardiennes* (Paris, 1938), as well as his other works, *Du malheur de la conscience dans la philosophie de Hegel* (Paris, 1929), *La pensée de l'existence* (Paris, 1952), *Existence humaine et Transcend-*

ence (Paris, 1944), and so forth. Wahl is a keen critic though often subtle and captious; at times he is successful in his comparisons between positions that are seemingly distant not only in time but also from the theoretical point of view. His writings are more skillful than profound, and they evidence his ability to utilize the reasons of one man in order to question those of another, and then to adopt the reasons of the latter as a retort to the former, making all positions problematical in the end. This is not merely his canon of criticism, but his "philosophy" as well; his very method of criticism is accepted as philosophical doctrine—in other words, the *sic et non* doctrine. Wahl is a skeptic (but with a faith, perhaps); he probes deeply in order to demolish and to pose problems, but never to present solutions. He has a keen and fine intelligence, which employs criticism for the sake of criticism, negatively, like the skeptic who demolishes without the knowledge or the power to rebuild. Yet Wahl's skepticism has this positive aspect: it includes a strong and sincere "mystical" accent.

In his *Vers le concret* (Paris, 1932) he compares the positions of James, Whitehead, and Marcel, who, in opposition to the Hegelian criticism of the immediate, emphasize the *mine* and the *here* and the *now* in order to vindicate the very concept of immediateness. Moreover, by placing our spirit among things, they demonstrate that the relationship is not only what idealism wishes it to be, for it is a "contact," a "kinship," and a "knowledge" affecting spirits and things. They view relations not as something added to the original datum, but as part of it; or, better, relations translate a nonrational foundation. Their empiricism cannot be defined as one that explains the whole through its components. "There is an explanation of the whole by means of its parts, but there is also an inexplicability of the whole with its parts. Let us rather say that empiricism is defined through its affirmation of the nondeducibility of being and its affirmation of the datum, that is, through something immediate which is received and accepted. It is necessary for empiricism to posit the problem of the datum. In short, the problem of the three philosophers studied by Wahl is that of being, which they maintain cannot be reduced into knowledge. They deny the intelligibility of being which they see as more a feeling than an idea, something rebellious to reason rather than reason's essence.

There is immanence and transcendence in their metarational realism. Transcendence is "the idea of a beyond through which knowledge gains a meaning, and toward which it leads while receiving nourishment from it. Immanence, on the other hand, is the idea of a compact truth in which no one element is absolutely transcendent with respect to another."

This is what Wahl calls "realistic dialectic" as simultaneous presence of transcendence and immanence, of objectivity and subjectivity. The fracture shows up in the *choc* felt by thought when confronted with the irreducible reality. "Immanence and transcendence come to a reciprocal completion within the domain of descriptive knowledge, in the same way as they are completed through the description of the characteristics of space and time." Spirit "meets" the object; spirit finds itself in the "presence" of, *vis-à-vis* with the object. Spirit may recognize itself in the object but also knows that there is something there it cannot assimilate or completely exhaust. This is the fracture.

There is also a domain of profound values which is in its turn subjective-objective. "It is subjective in that it is the life of sentiment, and it is objective inasmuch as much life is real." Besides a "material density" there is also a "spiritual density." In correspondence with the exigencies there are, and there must be some realities—philosophy is an appeal to reality. The religious problem is inserted at this point: religion is "the idea of a living relationship between spirit and universe, a person to person relationship." When the religious sentiment reaches all its depth, there will be neither a content nor an intellectual message. This is the way in which such higher transcendence and higher immanence appear: on the one hand, this Being beyond being to whom prayers are addressed and, on the other, the confluence of spirits and their communion. For Wahl, they are "ideas or calls conveyed to reality, and we are unable to determine whether the reply we receive is anything but their echo."

Realism, then, oscillates between the immanence of a subject in the object and of an object in the subject; the transcendence of the object is in relation to the subject. Realism cannot be censured, for this oscillation characterizes the very life of thought. It is due to this dialectic that we may talk about going *toward concreteness*. "The concrete is never given for the philosopher; it shall be what is pursued. The concrete can be revealed to us in the absence of thought. . . . There is a necessary dialectic precisely because there is a realism. The real is the limit for dialectic; it is its origin and its end, its explanation and its destruction." This dialectic is not Hegel's, indeed; here the movement is not immanent in the idea or, if it is so, this is due to the fact that it tends toward something other than itself. This is more of an oscillation than a dialectic, but an active and tense oscillation of ideas. It attaches itself not to the idea but upon a mystical agnosticism. Only through dialectic we can advance toward reality. "Living thought is made up of innumerable cancellations. The dialogue of the soul with itself is a perpetual negation. This is what Hegel meant when he said that in the negation of reason he saw the essence of affirmation. Beyond the real we see the *no* of dialectic; and we find again the idea of the Hegelian negativity. To the *yes* of the dialectic is opposed the *no* of the real, and this is another negativity we find, and, properly speaking, this is nothingness." Thus we are led to distinguish two

257

negatives: the *no* of dialectic and the absolute *no* of negative ontology. "Every *no* has its *yes* and every *yes* its *no*. Yet, thought cannot stop at this point; there must be for it a *yes* without a *no* it cannot define, and a *no* without a *yes* that is also undefinable." We are able to escape this antinomy of dialectic and real only through a mystical vision. This is true enough. But even this is a *yes* having its unfailing *no*. Human existence and transcendence are united; the latter offers itself to the former thus creating the anguish, which is not an appeal to God and a disposition to receive His message; it is rather existence in the presence of transcendence, though the recourse to God does not eliminate the paradox. Wahl, indeed, is interested in maintaining the paradox, the antinomy, and the *yes* and *no*. What interests Wahl is this lack of an element of certitude and the constant and irrepressible tension in a problem which is ever open; through his too subtly critical interpretations, he aims at showing that both in Kierkegaard and in Jaspers, as well as in other thinkers, once the theological presuppositions are put aside, there is always a problem at the beginning and at the end; and the problem can never be solved because it is forever confronted by an antinomy ready to defeat any such attempt.

Even the *Traité de métaphysique* (Paris 1953), which is Wahl's most ambitious theoretical work, is based on the same method; it, too, moves from the *yes* to a *no* and from the *no* to a *yes*. We can call it a metaphysics that is like a "pendulum" whose supreme oscillation is the one between "nature" and God. The ineffable in nature, or on this side of reality, is in a relationship of dialectical reciprocity with the Absolute or God, the Ineffable of the beyond. Hence, there are two ecstacies: a mysticism of matter and a mysticism of the divine. Dialectical movement is like a sound arising from infinite sounds and enclosed between two silences: silence in the presence of the ineffable on this side of reality and silence before the Ineffable of the beyond. Is it the one or the other? No disjunction is involved; once again we are confronted with the one *and* the other, with a certitude and its contradictory. At this point, Wahl's curiosity becomes terribly painful and serious; the discussion is interrupted and the dialogue ends. The *tension* between *pros* and *cons*, *sic et non*, is transformed into a mute discourse between man and the absolute-*Otherness*. The dialectic of thought is lost; yet, it must be lost if it does not wish to lose but rather wishes to find the lost paradise of the immediate. In Wahl's view, rather than noontime—during which an immense, new light pours its luminous and illuminating rays into the depth of a soul in ecstatic adoration—this is the hour when the soul plunges into a very dark night, into a darkness, dense with near and distant mysteries, immense with their thousand utterances. The Absolute still is what separates and unites; the Ineffable of the beyond can only be described by antitheses and paradoxes. "The Absolute and the transcendent are the furthest limits of thought, and we are unable to say if they come from thought itself or from some other thing. A thing without name, that which Lawrence calls the obscure God."

Is it possible to return to immanence without losing transcendence? Does the philosopher have the strength to transcend transcendence itself, and then revert to immanence without having his effort at transcendence lose value? Here is Wahl's final answer: questions of this kind make up philosophy as such, in that philosophy is better able to query than to answer. It is a movement more obscurely perceived than seen; philosophy goes from reality to ecstasy through dialectic and antitheses.

"In the presence of works of art—those finished and unfinished worlds at the same time—or, more simply, in the presence of things, we experience fullness and no longer separate intrinsic from extrinsic, and infinite from finite. The unceasing dialogue arrives at its conclusion in silence." And thus Wahl ends in pure mysticism.

b. V. Jankélévitch's Dialectic of Consciousness and of Alternative

VLADIMIR JANKÉLÉVITCH (1903) analyzes the two faces of consciousness, not in order to stop at the antinomy but in order that the positive may shed light on the negative, and the spiritual life may be understood in the concreteness of the two aspects. Jankélévitch's best pages are psychological analyses, which are very fine though not always free of affectation. He is a "moralist," in the French sense of the word, and his philosophy is psychologism.

Consciousness is inquietude, pain and anguish; yet, the spirit increases through inquietude and suffering, as it gradually learns how to purify and cure itself. Such is the fundamental motivation of his *Valeur et signification de la mauvaise conscience* (Paris, 1933).

"Being conscious" is the same as "being dissatisfied"; consciousness is, in fact, always "incomplete." Dissatisfaction and discontentment precede and follow every action of ours; before we act we ask ourselves what we must do; then we feel pushed to go farther. "Bad" conscience compels me to duplicate myself and become the spectator of myself, and it also prevents me from recognizing myself both in myself and in the object. I am unable to coincide with and contain myself. Consciousness is always a dialogue—an open, endless debate between the power of knowing and of justifying and the effort to surpass knowledge itself. It always changes the internal unity arrived at in a new object, which it distinguishes from itself in order to reflect upon and judge it. Consciousness is reflection on myself and, for this very reason, it is inquietude, a never-ending process. The ego as consciousness becomes itself a problem and assumes the responsibility for what it wishes to be: it refuses to make itself a reality which it could ascertain before having created it by itself. However, precisely for this reason, the ego succeeds in giving itself a spiritual existence and not being a thing. As Lavelle writes, its clairvoyance in effect divides the ego; but it must be divided in order to cease being a thing and in order to be able to become its own creation.

Can the ego escape itself and avoid the tormenting dialogue of its consciousness dividing and tearing it asunder? Yes, indeed, through purely intellectual activity whereby it does not consider itself but its object: it glances at the immense Whole of which it is itself a part—not a *vis-à-vis* with itself but a face to face with the world. This is Spinoza's wisdom. Yet, here is consciousness waking up again and with it, pain. The ego finds itself divided, not a unity any more, but a bundle of internal dissents preventing it from agreeing and coinciding with itself. Nonetheless, it is precisely in dissent and in contradiction, as well as in the open problem and in the dilemma (rather than in contemplation), that existence is revealed to itself as a painful, infinite dialogue. Consciousness feeds its own life with the shreds of flesh it is compelled to rend from itself.

Moreover, to be conscious of ourselves is to realize our value and the value of our actions. Consciousness is moral conscience. Yet, even in this way, consciousness is duality between what we are and what we shall be. Time splits consciousness between present and future. The present becomes a longing for the future and so it is still inquietude, debate and dialogue, not unity. To wish is to hope—the future is hope. But not so for the past—it burdens us with actions that we can neither modify nor reject. Remorse, which is the presence in me of my past, reveals the tragic aspect of a life that is fixed in an unavoidable act and hence in an incurable sorrow. It is precisely in the past that the duplicity of consciousness presents itself as more impatient and intolerable. On the one hand, I see a number of actions which are not mine and, on the other, the impossibility of rejecting this past which is mine no longer. This is still a divided consciousness.

Furthermore, the past does not only present this tragic aspect; when the present is too painful, it is a relief and a sweetness to contemplate the past. Moreover, the remembrance purifies and spiritualizes all the events experienced by us; it regenerates; it has the power to convert flesh into spirit. But, in order that conversion take place, it is necessary to experience pain. It is not oblivion which delivers us from the burden of our past, but its living and bleeding presence. Suffering is the bitter medicine capable of producing the cure. A truly and deeply suffering soul is a convalescent soul. Sorrow is the sustenance and light of conscience. The anxious, painful, "bad conscience" sets the stage for a good conscience, which is wholesome and strong, rooted in the present, and looking not backward but ahead with tranquillity and trust. Virtue lives in a present that is to be the "top of the soul." We may fall back into the "bad conscience," but we can measure the depth of our falls.

The dialectic of "bad conscience" is continued in the dialectic of the "alternative" (*L'alternative*, Paris, 1938), which was elaborated through a closer inspiration coming from German existentialism.

The human act is always conditioned by the double perspective of real and possible; in the instant of realization the possible becomes real. Yet, the realization of a possible implies the sacrifice of other possibles: realization is exclusion and abdication. We cannot realize all the possibles; one has to choose: existing is deciding, not hanging on indecision and thus being paralyzed. The act then (except the gratuitous one, which is pure *charitas*), always implies attrition, or a *choc en retour*. Life, therefore, is to be taken seriously, not tragically; it must be accepted courageously. The sentence "one cannot be everything and something at the same time" governs the dialectic of spiritual alternative.

However, *tediousness* is tied up with the dialectic of alternative, conditionality of the act, and the lacking nature of our lives. "We suffer before and after the option. Before the option, we suffer from an uncertainty that goes as far as a lack of will power, and we wonder which is more important: the infinite nonexistence or the poverty of a good and strong will. And during this time we are unable to decide and unwilling to sacrifice anything. After the option there is tediousness, a pungent tediousness." Yet, why this tediousness? It is because the act, at the moment of being realized, reveals its nonbeing, its incompleteness, and the immense sacrifice of so many possibilities forced back into nothing. Tediousness is a revenge on the part of the possible and a fatal dissolvent of the value in our acts. The being of the act which, as an act, reveals its nonbeing: a deep tediousness in our existence and our internal human misery. "Bad conscience" presents itself as an alternative, that is, still as a divided and dualistic conscience, sacrifice and tediousness.

Is it not better, then, to kill time and hide from consciousness the destiny that persecutes and torments it? Is it not better for us to escape this oppressing thought by plunging into action so that we leave no time for reflection? "Amusing ourselves" is useless when the spirit is ill; it is the spirit that needs to be cured.

However, according to Jankélévitch, the cure is in the alternative as well as in the same "bad consciousness." Pessimism is founded upon an existential analysis which is unilateral. There is in the choice both a negative and a positive aspect, and around the latter we must build our personality. The act of becoming is a spiritual tension, an attentive watcher of consciousness, and a factor of movement and conquest. When this spontaneous and generous state collapses, tediousness then takes its place, and this signifies the fall of the spirit. Consciousness, which is no longer intent on the choice, refrains from transforming existence into life and time into duration. The life that is relaxed manifests the dark abyss of existence, the richness of duration and, as Jankélévitch says in accordance with Bergson, it fades away in the monotony of time. "In a certain sense, therefore, the evil of existence is the radical unhappiness, but not because life in general is bad as pessimists believe. Our solution, then, is not nothingness; on the contrary, it is existence that has been cured, beautified, and completed; instead of making it leaner, let us make it fuller; instead of having it rarefied to the point of annulling it, let it become richer and fuller." We must not deceive or kill time, which is to be "spent" and made duration, instead. We must become fruitful in the action, and life is to be enhanced not stopped; life is affirmation of will and not a tired, inert, and resigned suspension.

Thus, existentialist pessimism is corrected through Bergsonian motivations, though Jankélévitch does not go beyond the description of psychological states (his *Traité des vertu* [Paris, 1949] is also remarkable), within which he still seems to abide even in his more recent and meditated work, the *Philosophie première, Introduction à une Philosophie de "Presque"* (Paris, 1954).

11. J. P. Sartre's "Hylology"

According to J. Wahl,[19] the "École philosophique de Paris" consists of Sartre, Simone de Beauvoir, and Merleau-Ponty. There is in this declaration perhaps a bit of irony; if not, let us add some, without bitterness, because we know that things in Paris fortunately have not yet reached this point. The leader of this philosophical school is JEAN-PAUL SARTRE (1905), an existentialist endowed with a great deal of fancy and an author of very widely-read plays, novels, short stories and even books of philosophy: the fictional characters of Sartre, the writer, embody the ideas of Sartre, the philosopher, and the two types of writings clarify and complement each other. His first philosophical works relate to psychology and phenomenology (*L'imagination*, Paris, 1938; *Sketch for a Theory of the Emotions*, trans. Philip Mairet (London, 1962); *Imagination*, trans. Forrest Williams (Ann Arbor, 1962), but in his novel *Nausea*, trans. L. Alexander (Norfolk, 1959), the reader can already find the central experience of his philosophy which was expounded, after a long preparation and with the help of such a shrewd and crafty logic that it can hardly conceal its juggling ingenuousness, in the more than seven hundred pages of his *Being and Nothingness*, trans. H. E. Barness (New York, 1956), to which the mediocre pamphlet, *Existentialism*, trans. B. Frechtman (New York, 1947), must be added.

[19] J. Wahl, *Petite histoire de l'existentialisme* (Paris, 1947), p. 13.

Sartre (like other existentialists) borrows from Husserl the theory that ideas are objects of consciousness to be ascertained, described, and inventoried without capacity for the solution of contradictions in experience. Hence, a phenomenological description: he takes from Hegel the concept of opposition between being and nonbeing, but without its synthesis, and consequently the two terms in the antinomy devour their respective viscera for eternity; from Heidegger he accepts the principle that being is "mundanity," being-in-the-world; from Freud he literally takes the theory of love as a form of possession; from Kierkegaard he detaches the concept of the fall, which he secularizes in order to have it fit his plans properly; he does the same thing with French Jansenism which he detheologizes; from Feuerbach (and Marx) he draws the postulate that man is an organic matter of which consciousne is only a manifestation (a doctrine that also belongs to Freud).

This list of filiations, which could be extended (with the name of Nietzsche, for example, and someone has even mentioned Pascal, poor Pascal!), is not intended to signify, by any means, that Sartre's existentialism is like a sample book of ill-combined doctrines and that it is devoid of originality. This would be a polemical judgment and, as such, exaggerated and unjust. On the contrary, the list serves to emphasize the meaning and the importance Sartre's existentialism has for us.

Even this philosopher's existentialism presents itself as an ontology, an analysis and a sense of being. However, without hesitation and unequivocally, Sartre tells us that "Being is without reason, without cause, and without necessity," and that modern thought, therefore, has achieved a great progress—this progress: it has reduced the *existent* to its acts, to what it reveals, and to what makes it manifest, thus overcoming, once and for all, the dualisms between potency and act, phenomenon and noumenon or substance, and so on. Therefore, only phenomena exist and existence is its phenomena. The phenomenon of being is one among many; yet, there is not only the *phenomenon* of being but also the being of the phenomenon. Such a dualism is insuperable and it makes the phenomenal character of being be transcended toward the transphenomenal and the ontological; but the being of the phenomenon is such for a consciousness knowing it. Consciousness is always "consciousness of something," of an object, that is, it is knowledge, but a knowledge that itself (Sartre says against idealism) is a mode of being and, precisely, the mode of being of the knowing subject. There is, then, a being of consciousness or being *pour-soi* (thought, we could say, understood in a Hegelian way, as a perennial motion) which refers to a being *en-soi*.

How does Sartre understand the *In-itself?* This is for us the fundamental point in his thought; what is left is a consequence. The expression *en-soi* could be misleading on account of the dialectical layout Sartre gives it, that is, of an *en-soi* for a *pour-soi* and of a *pour-soi* for an *en-soi*. This is not so: the *en-soi* is not in relation to itself because it would imply a duality and, therefore, consciousness; it is not created, otherwise it would not be the *en-soi*, but from "other"; and yet, it is not *causa sui* because it would have to be intelligence; it has neither an *in* (it would have to be interiority) nor a *self* (it would have to have either an essence or the implication of an "outside" of itself); it is neither active nor passive. What then? Then it *Is, only* is. It is not "ce qu'est l'étendue chez Descartes"; nor is it accurate to say that Sartre's being "characterizes itself as having *deux formes*," the *en-soi* and the *pour-soi;* nor is it difficult to say whether the *en-soi* or the *pour-soi* comes first; and it is an error to consider Sartre now a "realist" (primacy of the *en-soi*) and then an idealist (primacy of the *pour-soi*).[20] In Sartre, the *en-soi* (or the being which is *en-soi*) is simply and gratuitously given, only given, neither to itself nor to anything else, a brute datum, one that is "massive," as this author says, and "kneaded with itself." Thus, neither idealism nor realism which, in different ways, would imply a duality of subject-object: the *en-soi* excludes every duality, even one that is immanent to itself, as well as every affirmation or negation. The *en-soi* is an *Is* which denies everything, a shapeless mixture, *matter* in the most "compact," "dense" and "thick" sense of the word. Think, if you wish, of Parmenides' being, but in the sense (contrary to Parmenides) of pure matter, an unintelligible and ineffable datum: *it is without a thing which is.* This is the being which is *en-soi,* and Sartre's ontology, which we have called *hylology* not out of a desire to be witty, gratuitously proceeds from such an *en-soi.*

This *Is* (which corresponds to Heidegger's transcendentality whence Sartre's concept of existence emerges or is "clipped off") becomes in accordance with determining causes whereby its becoming is rigid, like a motionless becoming, a necessity, an *ananke.* The *Is* is its very becoming; being which is *en-soi*, the *en-soi*, is its apparition or its phenomenal manifestation. But the being which is phenomenon of being, as it were, has become dualistic, it is no longer a solid and thick compactness, it "posits itself" before itself, thus becoming being *per-se*, consciousness, that is, a necessary phenomenon of the "massive" and compact *in-itself;* the latter, in turn, is a phenomenon of consciousness, an object, which is both a phenomenon and the being of the phenomenon. Consequently, being's necessary becoming is a necessary, immovable and dialectical relationship between being that is the *in-itself* and being that is the *By-itself* so that logically there is no *in-itself* without *by-itself*, as there is no *by-itself* without an *in-itself*. Thus, at the outset, it is postulated that the *pour-soi* is only a *by-itself* in relation to an *in-itself*, that is, it is already defined as a Nothingness ("Being and Nothingness" as the title of Sartre's book

[20] J. Wahl, *ibid.*, pp. 53-54

says); and it is also postulated that consciousness is a manifestation of the being that is *en-soi*, the pure *en-soi*, that is, matter; and another postulation is that the world is a phenomenon of the *pour-soi*, the "ballast" that fills (in the most "heavy" sense of the word) that vacuum which is consciousness, so that it may have a consistency; yet, as it is being filled, it becomes "nullified" as, likewise, the *pour-soi* is the *nullification* of the *en-soi*.

The game is over by now and the series of nullifications in which Sartre delights neither frightens nor surprises us any longer; in fact, the game can be analyzed and all the moves reconstructed in the same way that a child does with a seemingly complicated toy. A game, whose preparations and tricks are known, amuses no longer; it annoys; and Sartre annoys because he is monotonous. One drama of his pleases, if it is among his best; the second one wearies; and the third is left unread because one knows how it is going to end. Yet, what can one do! It is like parlor games still played by people, who are deadly bored with them and yet say they are amused.

Sartre's dialectic moves but does not progress; it marks time: upon raising its right leg (*the en-soi*) it nullifies the *pour-soi;* then, with the lifting of the other leg (the *pour-soi*), the *en-soi* is *nullified*—and so on, with no reason, always endlessly and gratuitously. Sartre takes as his starting point (though to say this is not exact because the starting point is the massive *Is*, which is also a point of destination) the concrete, that is, "man in the world," Heidegger's *Dasein* as being-in-the-world or worldliness which, after all, is being *per-se*, or consciousness, that as such exists in relation to the "other," to something extraneous, the object. Is there any need for saying that consciousness or the *per-se* or the man-in-the-world represents a "nothingness" as posited by Sartre? No, because we already know that. In fact, positing myself before the world, as something "other" than the world, signifies that I *am* not the world; therefore, consciousness that exists only in relation to the "other" is "nullified" by the *en-soi* because it is *not* the "other" with respect to that which it is as consciousness. Or else: consciousness (the *pour-soi*) is the condition by which there is a "known," which is "other" than itself, and is what consciousness is not; thus, knowing, which is consciousness in relation to the "other," is a negation of the *pour-soi;* it consists in being conscious of what one *is not*. The *per-se* is not determined but rather is denied by the known object. Consciousness is the *not* (it is not the other) by which objects are posited. This negation is the man-in-the-world. It must be observed that in this case negation is not a judgment (I am conscious that I am *not* the object) but rather an ontological condition, that is, it is not negation to posit nothingness because it is rooted in the depth of being (it nestles in being "like a worm" according to Sartre)—nothingness is a "nullifier" and thus consciousness which is *not* the object is the *nothingness* through which the object is posited. Thus, nothingness enters the world at the same time as man does (the *en-soi* is compact and massive): the duality of being through the *en-soi* and *pour-soi* determines the rise of consciousness (the *pour-soi*) in relation to an object, which is "other" than consciousness itself, and which is *not* consciousness; so, consciousness or *pour-soi* comes into being as a nothingness through which the object is posited; consequently, nothingness enters the world together with man, that is, with the *nothingness* of consciousness (or of man) which is not the world with which it is in relationship. Thus, man consists in this nothingness, and it does not mean that man as a whole is nothingness. He is not only consciousness (*pour-soi*); he is also *en-soi*, that is, he is his body, his ego, his habits, and the like; he is the massive and compact entity that he is besides being matter and consciousness. Then man is the nothingness of consciousness and the massiveness of his body, of his ego, and so on, a matter that belongs to man but is not man's alone; it is not the human. The human or consciousness is *nothingness*. Sartre's materialism is absolute; it is derived from Freud's *ego* and *super-ego* and coincides with that of Feuerbach and Marx (consciousness is the epiphenomenon of matter). All the personages in his dramas, novels and short stories are a *nothingness* of consciousness (of the human) ballasted with heavy and thick matter—the brutal and pure *en-soi*. They are man as man was conceived by Marx and Freud but without the lie of those "elevated ideas" consisting in the homogeneous society or in "sublimation." Moreover, consciousness is that nothingness which represents the condition through which objects (the *en-soi*) are posited; thus, consciousness is the condition through which the world becomes an object in relation to it; consciousness is the condition of the body rather than the body, the condition of consciousness. Yet, on the other hand, negation does not envelop only consciousness or the *per-se* in man, but also the world.

Even things have an *in-se* (their massiveness) and a *per-se*. Inasmuch as they are things they are what they are, an in-itself, and as a *per-se* they are the *per-se* of man in that they have no consciousness, that is, their *per-se* becomes something for man: the means (or tools) that man uses for his plans. The *per-se* in things is created by man at the moment he uses them and so things are no longer what they are, their massive *in-se*. However, things do not find their *per-se* in that which is our own, because our own *per-se* is nothingness. Man is without a meaning and so he cannot give one to things or to the world; he gives them his own human meaning, which is nothingness; so, nothingness is even the *per-se* created by man in things. What then? If the *per-se* is nothingness (consciousness or the human in man) and nothingness is the *per-se* that man gives things (the human in the world), only the *in-se* is left or, rather, the massive and primitive *Is* which is kneaded with itself and is gratuitous matter. What is our psychological reaction in the presence of a world which is a "nothingness" of meaning? *Nausea*, an emetic. Nonetheless, is man a "nothingness" of meaning and a nothingness as a *per-se?* Exactly; and, in fact, he feels sick with himself. No, even more, man *is nausea*, a permanent emetic: "*la Nausée . . . est moi-même.*" Sartre's man (his characters) *is* nausea; he is a matter that falls apart, crumbles, decomposes and then is kneaded again. Heidegger's "anguish" is legitimately Sartre's "nausea"; existence as understood by existentialism (or by Marxism and Freudianism, and so forth) finds its authenticity in nausea and not in the lie of "anguish," of "failure," of "faith" as pertains to Barth's or Chestov's God. Hegel's spirit has completed its cycle; it is no longer an *in-se* and a *per-se* as absolute Spirit (in this way it was a lie), but it is, in its absolute authenticity, as an absolute Matter or as an *Is* which is kneaded with itself. "If God does not exist, everything is allowed" and everything is conceivable, even what Jean Paul Sartre is willing and able to conceive in the cafés of Saint-Germain-des-Près. In reality, what we have just said represents the thought not only of Sartre but also of any man who has "in his heart" denied God; whatever such a man may say after that denial makes no sense. Sartre, the pure immanentist, the systematic atheist, the absolute materialist, and the Jansenist without God or grace (though no less Jansenist in his conception of existence as nothingness or as "original fall"), represents the nausea in all theories denying God and man. He accepts these theories as categories of existence and concludes with a double nausea: a nausea which man has about the world and a nausea he feels about himself.

The nothingness of the *per-se*, of man, is clearly manifested through freedom, which is not a property of the *per-se* but something identified with it: man (does not have) is freedom, which denies the *in-se*, that is, man posits himself as "a being which is not what is and is what is not." Man as freedom has then no definite essence; his essence is freedom which is absence of an essence or, if you wish, is the essence of the *per-se* that is existence, which is not defined *by* or *in* an essence. Otherwise, existence would be decided and nothing would be left to be decided on. His essence, instead, is freedom, the absence of the essence and so a pure possibility. Man is a "project," his own project; he makes himself at every instant and he is what he makes of himself—man invents himself at every instant. Choice itself does not presuppose any reason (reason would deny freedom within rational necessity); "every reason comes into the world through freedom," which is freedom of choice without any reason. Yes, indeed, but this freedom is not free not to choose; so it is determined and decided as freedom capable of choosing this or that, and this means that it *must* choose. "Hence, the absurdity of freedom": man "is condemned to be free and he is a slave of freedom"—*elle est une malédiction.* Sartre is right: freedom for the existentialist (as well as for the Marxist) truly is a curse; he does not know, in fact, what to do with such an absurd freedom. He is bound to choose and burden himself with a responsibility—and for what? For nothing; and without reason he is condemned to choose though there is nothing worth his choice: everything is the same within the insignificance of everything, within the nothingness that the *per-se* (man) is, and the *per-se* that man lends to things. What then? Then, to choose this or that is the same (for Sartre and for Barth, the Jansenist without God and the Calvinist without man, respectively), and it does not matter upon *what* or *whom* the choice falls; I obey only the necessity of choosing, as I accept the tremendous destiny of being free at the same time that I know all this serves no purpose. To choose is absurd and, yet, I must choose. It is at this point that Sartre's existentialism reaches a dramatic intensity and "interrupts" the "nausea." Freedom becomes *a nemesis,* a fate, an absurd and cruel destiny: to choose and the necessity of choice, to burden oneself with responsibility and to engage oneself—all is done for *nothing.* Tragedy lies in this being condemned to be free for *nothing;* and it is the tragedy of some Sartrean characters, the tragedy of a man who is without a reason, an essence, a God, or anything—a man "without support," "without excuses," a helpless man and a project that must be worked out, a man that must invent himself. In this lies the real anguish, a tragedy in the authentic sense of the term: that of being forced to play a meaningless part that nonetheless one must continue to play to the end—until death and for no reason —in all its insignificance and with pain, even if a crime is perpetrated, for a crime, too, is meaningless. This is the tragedy of history (of the individual and of humanity as a whole), which is the beginning and end of itself, and the tragedy of the history of historicism and of freedom as a liberation that is immanent in and to itself and hence absurd—so much rushing toward liberation for *nothing.* Hegel's subject and Marx's *homo economicus*—the *homo faber* and the *homo philosophus,* the man-in-the-world and for the death—all reveal their authenticity in Sartre's freedom. "The man who is master of himself and of the world is a free man; the man who is all and only man, is God": such is the ideal that has been held by modern man from the days of Bacon until today. Yes, such a man is free, indeed, and a master of himself and of the world; but he is a free master for no purpose; he is free to *exist for nothing.* Too bad Sartre has not developed this point to its fullest extent; above all, this could have been done by Sartre, the writer whose characters would have had a human intensity instead of a corporeal "density."

Yet, the gratuitousness of freedom seems to clash with the *situation.*

"Man is but a situation"; freedom is man and, thus, freedom cannot prescind from the situation; on the contrary, freedom, as an impossibility
of not-choosing, is itself in situation. However, it is precisely the situation
which prevents freedom from remaining pure possibility or an empty
choice of itself. Freedom is the absence of everything, and man is freedom and, therefore, man is empty: the situation fills him; like the Orestes
of *The Flies*, it prevents him from being as light as "thread" and from
living "on air." It is condemned to choose, to exercise itself without any
reason, since choice itself matters and not what is being chosen. And this
in order to fill itself with something, so that it may not "live on air."
In fact, Orestes fills himself with crime; he perpetrates the "irreparable
act" in order to "ballast" the emptiness of freedom and thus acquire
weight. Once the decision has been taken and the choice made, and once
he has put himself in a "situation," there follows the "obligation" to
execute the "plan," to *become somebody*, and to be *something*. It does not
matter what you are going to be or who you may be, because nothing is
serious and nothing has meaning; what matters is choosing something
(killing or catching butterflies, it is all the same) in order to be *somebody*
and ballast freedom, that is, existence, because man is freedom. There is
nothing serious, but what one has chosen to do must be done, whatever
it may be. "Everything is gratuitous" and existence (freedom) is the
"perfect gratuitousness." Once the choice is made "is there a way of going
back" or must one stay engaged forever?" Not at all; man is always a
project aiming at the *future* but, since all that he does he does *for nothing*,
he must start all over again and dispute over the past and present (like
Orestes, after he had "ballasted" himself with his matricide). The nemesis,
the curse to choose without having anything worthwhile from which to
choose, goes on: I am in the "necessity of choosing myself perpetually"
without having, within my acts, a unity, a welding, a continuity, a
seriousness of purpose, a fulfillment of duty, and so on. Nothing at all:
absolute gratuitousness as such is the original *In-se* that is kneaded with
itself—a *gratuitousness* that is unable to grasp the tragedy belonging to it,
so that it provokes, instead, a *nausea* with ourselves condemned to choose
ourselves (the nothingness of the *per-se*); and a *nausea* with the things to
which we give our nothingness as a meaning. What is there left? In the
presence of the nothingness of the *pour-soi* and *en-soi*, dialectically only
the pure *In-se* remains, that is, the *Is*, the heavy matter whence this absurd
man and this absurd world, this immense nothingness and universal history, emerge like nauseating and dense exhalations from a huge and
perpetually rotting matter. Human consciousness is the *décompression
de l'être*, the decomposing of the massive being; it is an excrement that
is a *nothingness* making everything a *nothingness*.

However, Sartre states that existentialism is a humanism; and this he affirms in his pamphlet, *Existentialisme est un humanisme,* which must be considered along with the third part of his *Being and Nothingness* dedicated to "*Le pour-l'autre,*" and with some of his plays as well (*No Exit,* above all). Man's relationships with others are essential to him; sex in fact, is the proof of it: essentially man is sexual and this signifies that he is a being-for-the-other. The other for the *per-se* is *look,* first of all. "Shame" is an evident example. If I am peeping into the hole of a lock and at a certain moment an extraneous eye appears—the other who is looking—I feel ashamed. The other, then, is a "look" which comes to interfere with the field of *my* objects, with the environment in which I have organized *my* things; and this bothers him and me as well. From the moment he appears he is my "opponent," the one who is trying to attract to himself my things and myself. "What I call the apparition of *a* man is the apparition of an element within the objects of my universe—an element disintegrating this universe." In the person of the other, I see the appearance of a competitor, one who wishes to use me as a means whereby his project may be realized and, thus, one who "steals from me my world" and myself. In turn, I try to include him in the execution of my project. I and the *other* tend to be each for himself and, consequently, we oppose each other in order to prevent that one of us fall as an object within the domain of the other; or, better still, we struggle so that one may dominate the other and may succeed in including the other within the execution of *his* own project, that is, to make the other be one of *his things.* The conquered one is dominated by the "judgment" of the dominator; he ceases being a *per-se;* he does not live *his* project but the other's project; he becomes the *per-se* of the other, that is, the relationship is identical with that of the *per-se* in comparison with the things of the world. As man is condemned to be free, so he is condemned to live with others; he cannot avoid the other's "look," the interference by the stranger who makes him feel "shame." And this is man's *honte,* his "original fall," this not being able to be absolutely *per-se,* his having to endure a judgment, and his being forced to disclose himself as a "guilty" one: "*c'est en face de l'autre que je suis coupable.*"

In its concrete relationship with *le pour-l'autre* the *per-se* tries to dominate it as object and freedom; this, for Sartre, appears evident in sexual love, which, typically, is a form of *possession* whose extreme behavior consists of masochism and sadism. Love is a proof of force: one wishes to possess and dominate the other *qua* other, and not only as a body or for pleasure. Sexual love is a reciprocal plundering on the part of two souls. Whatever the relationship between two men, it is a conflict. And social life as such is a conflict: "The others are the Inferno." At this point Freudianism and communism find Sartre's assent, a proper and serene assent as befitting the person who describes, at the same time, things as they are and all his *nausea.* When, after all that, Sartre writes (to refute the charge communism lays against existentialism that the latter is an antisocial, individualistic and bourgeois doctrine) that existentialism itself is a "humanism" because all men are united through the universality of their human "condition" in spite of individualities, we know what the meaning of this "feeling united" is, as we know the significance of the choice that man makes for himself and for all: man *"se choisit"* and upon "choosing himself," *il choisit tous les hommes* (indeed, he must do this; he is compelled to have a "rival," to enter into a "conflict") and so he is responsible for himself and *pour tous*. Certainly, this is his "shame." After all, Sartre need not demonstrate his implicit communism; Marxists, rather, should realize that Sartre's man is metaphysically identical with the Marxist man—they are Siamese twins born of Hegel's brain and grown into two rascals.

However, what is man looking for in all this coming and going from the *in-se* to the *per-se*, and to *"le pour-l'autre"*? He seeks what he has always sought from the sinner Adam on: to be God. Man wishes to become an *en-soi-pour-soi: "c'est cet idéal qu'on peut nommer Dieu"*; and so the "fundamental project" for human reality is that "man is a being who seeks to become God. . . . Being a man is to aim at being God or, if you prefer, man fundamentally is the desire to be God." Man's passion is inverse to that of Christ, who as God became man; man, instead, has the passion to become God. But his effort is vain, and his torment a wasted passion; "the idea of God is contradictory," an *en-soi-pour-soi* is absurd, and *man is a useless passion*.

Man, who cannot be God because God is absurd, rids himself of his sickness and guilt only when he incorporates himself in the "viscous" and pure *In-se* which is kneaded with itself, and when he ceases being *une passion inutile* and *becomes* his true possibility, viz., a purely *digesting* organic matter. Man's illusion that he can make himself God finds its concreteness in his making himself a beast; and this is so because of the inexorable dialectic that is intrinsic in such an illusion. Once the immanentism of all times and of all forms lost its mask of "elevated ideas" or foolish words, it gave us its perfectly made man: *this* biped with his "unhealthy velvety color of vomit" who "screams and bleeds when others kill him," and who, in turn, kills when he is not eating to sate himself or when he is not busy "taking his *siesta* on a bench."

12. Other Forms of Existentialism

a. A. Camus' *"Absurdism"*

It is not within the nature of our work to give even a brief account of the existentialist literature (dramas, novels, etc.) that abounds particularly in France. After all, even in the case of Marcel and Sartre we have confined our references to those literary works that were necessary for the clarification of their philosophical works. For this reason we cannot dwell much on ALBERT CAMUS (1913-1960), who, in many of his works that are highly valuable from the standpoint of literature and art, makes his characters play the part of the *absurd man*—a man who is indifferent to everybody and everything in this irrational world, one who does this or that, even "placing himself" in what is good and virtuous, not for any reason, but "out of mere whim." When all is said and done, "all actions are the same" in a "world devoid of any importance," wherein "everything is permitted." Their consciousness vainly seeks (and this is the "absurd") the clarity of reason in the presence of an irrational world. Camus' characters reason formidably in order to give a "logical" proof that man is "absurd"; but they pay no attention to the contradiction involved in this absurdism . . . that, precisely because it is "demonstrated" denies itself. For Camus the world is irrationality (and "nausea") only because God does not exist; if God existed, it would cease to be such, and everything would make sense. "The certitude in a God giving sense to life would greatly surpass in attractiveness the unpunished power to do evil." Camus is not Sartre, however; he feels the need for God and the attraction of faith. Yet, he is contradictory by definition (particularly in his last volume, *The Rebel*, trans. A. Bower [New York, 1954], which is supposed to be philosophical but, instead, is a jumble that could only be the product of inexperienced and unprepared hands), and with the same "obstinacy" with which he cannot renounce his longing for God, he denies Him by presupposition. In this way, for him, man is not absurd but he *must* be so; God *is* not and yet He *ought* to be.

b. M. Merleau-Ponty's "Corporealism"

MAURICE MERLEAU-PONTY'S atheism, on the other hand, is radical and satisfied. Born in 1908, he is a professor at the College of France and the author of many books, including *La Structure du Comportment* (Paris, 1942), the *Phénoménologie de la Philosophie* (Paris, 1953), and *Les adventures de la dialectique* (Paris, 1955).

His existentialism is without either nausea, anguish, or absurdity; it is a happy one, contented and pleased with the fact that man is a being-in-the-world without a God to deny him his autonomy. He considers as a source of consolation all that other existentialists view as a reason for despair or disgust. Merleau-Ponty is a dogmatic and candid existentialist, who proceeds from presuppositions he does not question and arrives at the conquest of a happy world—the world of Marx with all its dogmatism and the lack of criticism it implies. A phenomenologist like Husserl, Merleau-Ponty simply states that the world is "*toujours déjà là* prior to our reflection," and all our effort consists in finding again the "ingenuous contact," wherein we give it a "philosophical statute," and make of it a *compte rendu* or a "vitally experienced world." Thus, this is pure objectivism: the world is there, an "inalienable presence." What can we do with it? *We can describe it.* And, what about man? What is he? At this point Heidegger is called upon: there is no "inner man"; man is in the world and he is known in the world. Merleau-Ponty immediately and without discussion discovers man's fundamental and sole vocation: "Man is a subject *voué au monde*." That being granted, the trick is done and everything becomes a matter of consequence.

In brief, his thought is that perception is the fundamental fact of knowledge whereby man is in the world and in relationship with it; but, precisely because man and the world are indissolubly bound, it follows that the world (*le réel* that is there) is "what we perceive"; the *being* of the world is the *intersection* of my own and other's experiences—the world is what I perceive and man always knows himself more and better in the world that he perceives. Man "open" to the world is well locked in it; as Merleau-Ponty says, he is all exteriority. It is not well understood, then, what aspect of man is "incarnated" since the "sense of the self" and the sense of corporeity are the same thing. It is more simple to say, as does Feuerbach, that man is a conscious body. In fact, for Merleau-Ponty, our body "actuates" our existence in the world. Historical materialism is accepted, even if reproved because of the fact that it considers the economic factor as the sole signification of history. The world would be our world and we, in the world, if we did not have the *ambiguity* of our consciousness; in fact, on the one hand, consciousness causes it to be ours and, on the other, causes it to be in itself. The same ambiguity is manifested in relation with the others. Consciousness relates me to another, who denies my knowledge through his knowledge while, on the other hand, I am locked up in my subjectivity. The others' world is a *violent act* (this is not the only point of coincidence or affinity with Sartre).

Merleau-Ponty, as one can see, confines himself to mere description and avoids ontology; he assumes that man is being-in-the-world in the most radical sense; thus, to be exact, he does not avoid ontology but he radically identifies being with being-in-the-world, and consciousness with being "to" the world, whereby man (conscious body) and world (which is the phenomenological world) constitute a unity. Man "is in situation" but with the power of knowing and directing it. The study of the "structure of behavior," hereby identified with the structure of existence, shows that man is *débat et explication* with respect to things and to others (society). The situation in which each man is engaged is his world outlook; the numerous situations make up the "common situation." Man must recognize man; nonrecognition is violence which Merleau-Ponty admits only in the case of its subordination to recognition and when it tends to destroy itself. The task for mankind is to carry out a real community for all individuals (inter-subjectivity), one which is able to establish, at the same time, the possibility of their individuality.

Once it is granted that the object of our knowledge is the world, to which man assigns a meaning, it follows that the only conceivable transcendence is the one being immanent in the world, that is, a movement that is intrinsic in the world (a "horizontal," not a "vertical" transcendence). The whole world of man (of philosophy, science, ethics, and so on) is this world within which man enriches himself "without dying in the presence of an Absolute," for if He were, if the Absolute existed, "perfection would be already realized," and man would have "*à la lettre, rien à faire.*" Therefore, in order that *une nouvelle histoire* may be written . . . *il faut que Dieu n'existe pas.* Besides, "on account of an inevitable dialectic" the evolution of man will lead toward changing theology into anthropology. Religion is born only when man regards himself as incapable of carrying out the fullness of himself in this world (*ici-bas*); and so it (Christianity above all) is "man's fantastic effort aimed at rejoining other men in another world." Merleau-Ponty's Marxism is literal on this point. Within the negation of God, Sartre and Camus see the absurdity of consciousness and the irrationality of the world; within atheistic humanism Merleau-Ponty sees the full realization of man and of a perfect society. Thus, absolute humanism returns to its old, nineteenth-century dogmatism; in Merleau-Ponty, it does not lack some good analyses (particularly psychological analyses) which can be scarcely saved from the mediocrity of a pretentious and superficial thought.

13. A General and Essential Criticism of All Existentialism

From our exposition of existentialism which at times is an already explicitly critical presentation, one fact, I believe, becomes clear: existentialism is only a phenomenology and not an ontology nor a metaphysics as it purports to be. The term "being" is encountered in the titles of very significant works (of Heidegger, Marcel, and Sartre), but then everything is reduced to a "description" of being and, in point of fact, a description of the *Dasein*, man, and the existent—an anthropology set on a phenomenological and psychological level. Existentialism abounds with analyses of this type, some of which are really notable, even if the fineness in them often becomes affectation (also morbidity, decadence and artifice) and the acuteness, sophistry and subtlety. However, on this point, it has the merit of having given philosophical dignity to the concrete human relations (communication, the "other," and the "you") and of having emphasized (especially French existentialism) the importance of the "body," particularly in a philosophy defining itself as existential and winding up with a description of the sphere of the human and of man in the world. Even theological and theistic existentialism does not separate itself from the phenomenological and descriptive point of view; and it does this while keeping the problem of our relationship with God from becoming the theological moment wherein lies the solution of all the problems of existence. All existentialists promise to found a metaphysics and an ontology; their promises even today are still promises (and will so remain), and their utterances are only verbal because the "metaphysical objectivity" mentioned by Jaspers is not in him, nor is it in the other existentialists, nor even in Marcel, who goes so far as to talk about a "metaphysical knowing" or, as has been said, about a "methodology of the unverifiable," whose definite limit is precisely not to render metaphysics "verifiable" (or empirically clear). Metaphysics, instead, must be relegated to the "metaproblematical," as if one still using philosophical terms could speak of metaphysics, once the latter has been placed outside of and in opposition to reflected thought, and as if metaphysics and reflected thought themselves were not life and engagement but only —who knows why—extraneousness and a spectacle. Heidegger, for his part, speaks to us about the exigency of being, the preoccupation of being, and so forth, but not about being itself, that is, he talks to us about the subjective reactions on the part of the *Dasein* but not on the part of *Sein*. The truth of the matter is that for existentialism *being is not*, the existent *is*, and so, speaking of being in terms of existential philosophy amounts to speaking about the personal experience of each man; consequently, every existentialist, regardless of his promise concerning the *Sein* or *être*, actually tells us his own life and, sometimes poetically and other times with an abundant use of technical terms, writes his autobiography. Hence, their common characteristic, great and small, is this: they all emerge with an ontology of dilettanti and a use of terms (being, nothingness, essence, existence) so superficial and unconstrained as to confuse being, grades of being, manner of being, and so on and so forth; in other words, they mix up all that a philosophy, unengaged in a fight with logic, modestly tries not to confuse.

As a counterpart (which, however, does not make up for the ruin of an *ontology without being*, since such is existentialism), existential philosophy has the merit of having focused on the problem of man and of existence. It has, in this way, eliminated from philosophical speculation what is detached and spectacular in abstract rationalism, Kantianism, transcendental (German) idealism, and positivism—within all of which ideas and concepts act on their own as undisturbed inhabitants in the monarchical state of a "consciousness in general" or of an Absolute subject, in which physical and human experience enters only as a domesticated content easily managed and ready to let itself be "arranged," "surpassed," "resolved" and "dropped" into the "forms" like liquid in a bottle. It is true that soon after Hegel things started to go the other way, and the uprising of existence against speculative philosophy occurred in many places within the rationalistic territory; yet, idealism, Kantianism, and positivism succeeded in suppressing the risings, which, after all, present themselves as a rebellion on the part of the instinctive and irrational, and of life understood in a biological sense, rather than a rebellion coming from existence in its fullest sense. With existentialism the battle flares up with new weapons used on the very ground of the opponent. In fact, existentialism is connected with the idealistic tradition (and, in some instances, even with the positivistic one) and, through it, terms such as "being," "essence," "ontology," "metaphysics," and so on, that had been excommunicated for about half a century, come into circulation once again, as if a return to the Greek-scholastic tradition were about to take place; yet, it uses them in order to build an ontology and a metaphysics that are "existential," not "objective"; so, it reduces the content of these terms to their existential meaning which is understood (we should not forget this) according to the manner of existentialism. The problem of man, as the problem of the existent and of the person in his individuality, becomes a central problem, but, once everything is reduced into an impassable and unobjectifiable individuality, the existent surmounts being, and existence places itself prior to, and posits, essence. Thus, after a vigorous defense against speculative philosophies and against the "objective," the existent is now aware of its *existence;* and, indeed, it is aware that dialectic, God or Nature, will not devour it; but, unfortunately, the existent *is not.* Besides the term "being," other words such as "humanism" and "man" are affixed to the titles of their works. Their preoccupation is great indeed to give their anthropologies a truly concrete and constructive sense; yet, afterwards it is discovered that man macerates himself in his nothingness, in anguished and useless solitude (even if he is called wise and virile), and that social life is banal and humiliating or even an *inferno,* so that the final conclusion is that I and the other *are nausea.*

However, one cannot deprive existentialism of the credit for making the problem of the person one of the first order and for focusing attention on man, who is placed before himself and his responsibility as (I would say) the sole being having consciousness of his existence and of his death. This peremptory position on the part of man before philosophy and of philosophy before man caused many merely academic exercises on obsolete positions or secondary problems to retire to the sidelines. For better or worse, existentialism has reminded the philosopher that the first problem is the problem of man, of the sense of his existence (on which that of the world depends), and the problem of his destiny; and such a problem does not regard man in general but the man that each one of us is. Moreover, we must not speak about life and death as a matter that may interest "contingency" but not "reason," since reason is made for the universal alone; "on the contrary, we must speak of these things as things which are our own, for example, the death and life which are *mine*, the existence which is my existence, and the philosophy which is my philosophizing. Indeed, this reduction of all reality and all experience to the subject is an idealistic theme; yet, in opposition to idealism, the subject to which everything is reduced is the individual and concrete subject (*this man here*), so that, for the individual, the totality of experience coincides with the individual himself, that is, it coincides with his existential experience—that which is, is *my* being as a point of view or a perspective. To clarify existence is to clarify the whole meaning of being, which is this meaning. However, that "clarifying" precisely signifies "describing." Therefore, the meaning of being, which is the sense given to it by existence, coincides with existence itself. Thus, with two strokes the traditional concept of metaphysics and ontology is reversed. It is existence which gives meaning to being and not *vice versa;* existence is its making itself, or its being in situation; consequently, being, which is the meaning that existence gives it, is wholly exhausted in the acts of existence itself.

Let us make, then, two observations: (1) The criticism we leveled against existentialism as being a phenomenology or a descriptive method, and not an ontology true and proper, must be emphasized. It means that existentialist philosophy cannot do otherwise, not because its being existential renders it incapable of speaking of being, but because it reduces being to existence and existence to its acts and situations (even transcendence is a situation); it follows, then, that phenomenology or description of existential acts is itself an ontology in that the *whole* being *is here*. This, too, is an idealistic position (and, it seems to me, positivistic as well) if one bears in mind the shifting from the universal to the individual subject. (2) Consequently, those persons who object that philosophy, after all, has always been philosophy of man or of existence without so many anguishes, desperations, failures and falls do existentialism an injustice. Likewise, the existentialist on his part unduly claims a meaningless merit when he retorts to the said charge by maintaining that the whole history of philosophy has labored only to bring forth existentialism which, he believes, represents the ultimate conquest in the "clarification" of philosophy itself and of existence. This he believes to be the great achievement and final goal as if, from now on, philosophy can only be existential philosophy in the existentialist sense alone. On the contrary, from our preceding remark a diverse consequence follows: existentialism is defined not as a philosophy of existence but as a particular mode of conceiving existence; it is an ontology in that being is existentiality itself, that is, being is denied as being and affirmed instead as *nonbeing of being,* whereby the sense of being is grasped within the sense of existence, which makes it be; and since it is existing that *makes it be,* being as such *is not.* There is an identity between *I-situation-being;* hence, phenomenological and ontological are identified. For the existentialist, being exists, *exists only: I, you, he;* not in the sense that it exists *in* me or that I "consist in it." Not so indeed, but in this other sense: being *is* this existing *of mine, of yours; it is here, like this.* Being *is not.* Yes, indeed! Therefore, *I am not,* I only exist. A being existing as being and not as *my* existing is not understandable to an ontology which is an "existential" experience of "being," for it is able to understand *only* the experience of being (that is, each man is able to understand *his* existing in which there is the whole sense of being). Not only existence cannot be objectified but also that being which is *not* as being; hence, being is uncommunicable.

Existentialism is given the merit (and existentialists pride themselves on it) of having grasped the "dramatic" sense of existence, which is "tension," "paradox," "ambivalence," and so on. Almost all existentialists have some poetical moments (and some of them, the temperament of a writer), and so they undoubtedly succeed, against their illogical logic, in translating into spiritually rich pages (and also pages of throbbing suffering) the tension of an existence in suspense, and unsafe, always in desperate dialogue with itself, with things, and with the others in an attempt to grasp the sense of being and to burden itself with its destiny. Yet, this typical moment of existentialism, one of its best points, stems from the abiding and unsubdued human depth of these thinkers, from their poetical temperament, and from a more authentic experience than the one they theorize as existential philosophy, which is negative of any really dramatic or tragic sense of existence. In fact, wherever everything is nothingness and is a proceeding from nothingness to nothingness, there is no longer either drama or tragedy, nor is there any tension; there cannot be even a consciousness of nothingness, for consciousness too is the nothingness of consciousness. A consciousness of nothingness makes sense only if nothingness is not the nullifier of consciousness; and, on the other hand, I can feel to be nothing only in the presence of being and if I partake of being—a misery and a greatness of man, but, without greatness man does not know his misery—which means that man is consciousness of his misery (negativity) because he is consciousness of his greatness (positivity). If being itself is nothingness and consciousness is a nullifier, let that suffice, for there is no drama and no tragedy; and even if it is granted that there might be, it would be a ridiculous farce, for when I come to know the game, all that is over and the tension of the uncertain and insecure is wanting. The dramatic sense of existence in existentialism is nonexistential; and so all this is rhetorical.

Precisely because existence is nothingness, it can be "made" anything; and in this respect existentialism reveals one of its most negative, destructive and corruptive facets as regards the individual and society. Existence which gives itself essence and the situation of being implies the leveling off of all situations because of the insignificance of all of them. The existent (and being) is wholly *consumed* in its actions and these are chosen arbitrarily, without justification, just for "whim," since each and every one of them is a mode of the *Dasein:* each matches the other in value, that is, all are worthless and insignificant. The possibility that existence is—this empty "spider's thread"—can ballast itself with any choice whatsoever, with a stab or with a hug. Consistently with his theory, the existentialist can make himself anything; he can place himself in any situation without repenting of anything, without having to gain or lose in his human dignity because, after all, there is no essence either in man or in things. The existentialist is neither a traitor nor a hero; neither a devil nor a saint; neither good nor bad; neither a liberal nor a communist—and yet, *he can make himself be* all of these things. Today he can place himself in one situation, and tomorrow in another, indifferently. The *da* driven into being makes being blow up; and once being has been blown up, everything is likely *to be:* Heidegger a Nazi, Barth an anti-Nazi, Sartre a socialist, and so forth, and not because they were such or remain so today but because they placed themselves in a situation and accepted it on the ground that a *da*—any *da*—must, somehow, be attached to existence (and this is its curse). All was done indifferently, without anything being detracted from the merit of their action; Heidegger, in fact, could have chosen Barth's "situation" and *vice versa.* What counts is that man makes himself be a project and "places himself beyond himself"; and that he "ballasts" himself with a matricide perpetrated without any aim except that of giving himself a burden through an irreparable choice. "To be or not to be" no longer is an alternative; Hamlet has been emptied of his doubt and drama and now can well become a Punchinello. There is room for everything within the existentialist's existence, since existence no longer has a place and is like a thing "shifted" toward nothingness. Man is annihilated within his situations and all the situations sink in man's nothingness; man is an annihilating consciousness. Such are "humanism" and the human, morals and morality, as well as sociality of existentialism.

The existentialist concept of Transcendence allows identical considerations. Existentialism has its own religious soul, a "nostalgia" of God, and a preoccupation regarding Transcendence; unlike the verbose atheists and peaceable agnostics of the nineteenth century, or the parlor-skeptics of the eighteenth century, existentialism knows very well that to affirm or to deny the existence of God is not the same as choosing to take a long holiday either at the seaside or in the mountains: it knows very well that it is a radical choice in that it radically changes the meaning of the human and physical universe. Hence, existentialism denies God and yet speaks of Him continuously; it also affirms that He is absurd and yet it states that if this God existed even as an absurdity, things would be better (Chestov even admits that God exists, that He is the Absurd, and that things go very well for those who believe in Him); and it also expresses the great tension of the finite toward the escaping Infinite, which shifts us always farther and farther while revealing itself as a mirage or, almost like a joke played by Nothingness on man, who troubles himself to grasp the Infinite without being able to convince himself that, as he wears himself out in a "useless passion," he is, instead, moving toward nonbeing and finitude. The theological problem is felt poetically as torment, desperation, nostalgia, or a hope that "exorcizes" desperation. On account of its nihilism, this doctrine philosophically does not justify this "passion," which, theoretically, is verbalism without meaning or life. Hence its suggestiveness and what I would call the magic which existentialism exercises, especially on young men who are always in search of something that can torment them aimlessly. He more quickly and more effectively enchants a woman who, skeptically, indifferently, and with nostalgia, continuously speaks to her about the nonexistence of love and the insignificance of life ensuing therefrom. There can be no greater seducer nor greater corrupter than he. In point of fact, existentialism as a philosophy of finiteness or "humanism" is atheistic (its transcendence has nothing to do with God; it, rather, denies Him); theological and theistic existentialism admits the existence of God, but it posits the problem of the rapport of God-man in a manner that seriously compromises the existence of God and the problem of the relationship with man, unless it denies both (proof of this ambiguity is the fact that almost all existentialists, believers and atheists alike, go back to Kierkegaard). Consequently, the whole human drama of Transcendence, though so alive, for example, in Jaspers, ceases being a drama and becomes a pure and simple affirmation of atheism, like the following one: "To penetrate the human being means to penetrate entirely Being in time. Man is the circumscribing-Whole that we are . . . ; inasmuch as he is a possible Existence, he is in relationship with Transcendence through which, in his own freedom, he feels himself given to himself." Transcendence arises from the finite and ends within the same finite as its clarification; and this does not signify a religious solution of the problem of existence but the positing of it as awareness of its nothingness before Transcendence. Existentialism is immanentism and, in moments of sincerity, open atheism; but, unlike immanentism (which is enthusiastic because of its lack of criticism and because of its unawareness of the implications inherent in a coherent immanentism), existentialism makes the effort, as Sartre writes, "to draw all the consequences from a coherent, atheistic position." Here are the consequences: the destruction and annihilation of God, man and the world ensuing from the secularization of the sacred and the historical character of God, values, man, being, essence and substance. Existentialism, which is also a seducer and a corrupter, is a useful and violent purge against the corruption of humanisms and historicisms exalting the dignity of man, his absolute autonomy, his capacity to perform on earth what (according to religion) a fantastic God does in heaven. Existentialism has dealt a mortal blow to such a myth invented by dilettanti and professors in the eighteenth and nineteenth centuries, and inherited in our times by other dilettanti and professors: today, nobody believes in it, not even those who profess it.

The preceding critical points are to be accurately integrated with those we are about to formulate on the individual representatives of existentialism. Let us begin with Heidegger, the metaphysician who only went halfway. In fact, *Sein und Zeit* has not gone beyond its first volume published more than thirty years ago, that is, it has not gone farther than the study of the problem of existence which, according to Heidegger, is only an introduction to ontology or problem of being. However, the study of human existence, after the manner of Husserl, is but a phenomenological analysis and so, from the start, the way to construct an existential metaphysics is precluded because the latter is identified with a phenomenological description. That being granted, the phenomenological analysis of human existence is no longer an introduction or preparation to a general ontology; it is, rather, the whole ontology. Heidegger's metaphysics could never materialize simply because the research on being, as this philosopher posits it, is entirely exhausted within the analysis of human existence. This is not a metaphysics (Heidegger himself recognizes that metaphysics should have followed), but is a positing of the problem in such a way that the possibility of a metaphysics, a research on being as being, is excluded; thus, that first volume presented by Heidegger as an introduction paving the way to metaphysics is, instead, a barrier to all metaphysical possibilities. In other words, his method and his laying down of the foundation shut off rather than open the solution of the metaphysical problem: method and foundation are, then, mistaken. The fact is that, at the start, Heidegger eliminates the problem of being, for he denies being by position; and, then, there is no longer an existential metaphysics, but only the existential, which is baseless, for it is founded on its own existing; and this existing is not established by being through participation; on the contrary, it is the existing that lays the foundations of being, which is thus resolved into the being of the existent, that is, into the-being-in-the-world. Therefore, against Heidegger's very promises, ontology begins and ends with the phenomenological analysis of human existence and no room is left for writing a metaphysics. To express the matter more correctly: there never was an ontology, nor will there ever be one, because Heidegger denies being at the start; being is not; it is Nothingness. In short, Heidegger's whole being is the-being-in-the-world of the human existence (of the *Dasein*), and as being-in-the-world (finiteness, mundanity, temporality) it is the nothingness of being. Heidegger's *oudenology* is written with the first volume of *Sein und Zeit* (where *und* means *ist*); he no longer has any metaphysics or ontology to write; the only thing left is to describe the finite of an existence that is engaged in an absurd adventure, running from Nothingness to Nothingness. "For man there is no being to be known; he has only to become conscious of the being he generates by superimposing it upon the brute existent." The analysis of human existence is not a simple preparation, "but the very content of the whole metaphysics," because "the affirmation of being in general is identical with the development of man's being." [21] Heidegger's metaphysical program is ambitious, indeed; but it is based on a personal ambition that cannot be carried out.

Heidegger's Nothingness, whence everything emerges and to which everything reverts, is the Kantian-idealistic transcendentality. In his *Critique of Pure Reason*, which is concerned with the elaboration of a methodology of science, Kant makes the subject's knowing activity a "spatial" one, so that subjectivity as transcendentality becomes a kind of "space" for phenomena; Hegel, who is concerned with the problem of history, identifies the transcendental with temporality; and, at the same time that he proceeds with his transformation of Criticism to transcendental Idealism, he converts the transcendental to the transcendental Subject. In other words, transcendentality is no longer the condition *a priori* for experience, but the metaphysical principle of experience itself, and so transcendentality is identified with Time. In this way, being is converted into the "whole of becoming," and the metaphysics of being into the dialectical development of the Idea, which *is making itself* and, through its development, becomes history and temporality. From this starting point Heidegger draws his consequences. He does not question the historicity of Being, its making itself through becoming, and its perfect coinciding with the latter; Hegel has the development and fullness of the Absolute or God coincide with time and with the world (the totality) with no other "openings"; Heidegger has his *Dasein* coincide with

---

[21] A. De Waelhens, *La philosophie de M. Heidegger* (1945), pp. 313 ff.

time and the world in such a way that the "world" is not an "opening," as he says, either contradicting himself or palliating the difficulties of his philosophy, but it is rather an hermetic "seal": being is shut in the world and *is* the world. However, we were saying that Heidegger, moving from his *Dasein*, draws his consequences from Hegel's conclusions, that is, he asks himself: What is man (*Dasein*) in a metaphysical conception such as Hegel's? In this way he posits the existential quest (following in Kierkegaard's steps) within Hegelianism, and all the syntheses are blown up in the air, even the supreme one allowed by Hegel's dialectic of antinomy; and Heidegger does this not by using the theological dynamite of sin and faith used by Kierkegaard, but by tormenting the concept of transcendentality to the point that it must "reveal" its "truth," that is, its Nothingness. The Kantian transcendental is valid in the (sensible) world; Hegelian transcendentality is historicity itself—therefore, its being is being-in-the-world; but the one to be questioned on being is man, and so ontology must begin with the description of human existence (and, at this point, Husserl aids him). This is all very well, but the fact is that ontology begins and also ends because if being is the whole of becoming and it consists in its *making itself*, there is no Being outside of becoming, that is, being is all mundanity. One has only to stop at the *Dasein* and describe it in order to possess the whole being. Which being? Evidently, that which *makes itself*. In other words, if being *makes itself*, if it is the history of the world, being is the situations of the existent and consists wholly in the "*Dasein*." Then, ontological and existential questions coincide with each other: outside of the *Dasein* there is no being; the transcendental subject is abolished and, with it, all syntheses, *the* synthesis, and the Hegelian Totality. Even Transcendentality loses its logical transparency together with its "rationality" and becomes an obscure background that is irrational, indeterminate, and a kind of ἄπειρον, whence the *Dasein* emerges—like the ancient Fate characterized by an inexplicable destiny—on account of an original and absurd guilt. Upon emerging, the *Dasein* causes Transcendentality to acquire (still in the Hegelian way) consciousness; and it emerges from Transcendentality only to be "thrown" into the world where it places itself in a situation as "Dasein" and, in situating itself, it makes being be in the *da*.

At this point there is a critical question within transcendental Idealism: if being *makes itself* and is this very *making itself*, being is the situation of the existent; therefore, Being, as conceived by transcendental Idealism, is Nonbeing. Consequently, in the beginning being is Nothingness from which the existent emerges, as it were, clipped off by destiny; and this existent, representing being as "Dasein," as being-in-the-world, and, thus, as "being-for-the-death," and for Nothingness, remains reabsorbed in the obscurity of the original indeterminateness. It is the destiny of the "finite"; being is this finite and so it is also the destiny of being. Transcendental Idealism has lost its splendor; it has been deprived of its rank by utilizing its own principle, that of immanence. Heidegger makes sense from this point of view: if being is the whole of becoming, which is finite, being is Nothingness; and the world, which is finiteness, is also Nothingness. There is still another meaning in it: if being makes itself and is this making itself, there is no ontological essence—the *essence is historical,* instead; therefore, it is posited by existence, it is its determination, a situation, a *da,* chosen arbitrarily, and tomorrow it will be another *da* no less arbitrary and insignificant than the first. Spinoza "geometrized" the One of Plotinus by making it the Substance, which is a rational necessity manifesting itself with the rigorousness of passages as in a geometrical demonstration; Hegel inserted into Spinoza's Substance his dialectic, and out of this deep hollow swallowing up the world he made his transcendental Subject which is self-revealing in the same world and which step by step will swallow it up until its own fullness is conquered. Marx lowered the idea into history and buried it there, in order that it would produce the moments of dialectic which are identified with economic forces and social classes, and he pushed historicism and the mundanity of being to the point of its total resolution into the mundane and historical; Heidegger, following in Kierkegaard's steps, carries the existential exigency to a maximum and makes being coincide with being-in-the-world, that is, with the existent, of which it is a historical affirmation, and a situation. Theological pantheism thus evolves (coherently) toward the mundanization of Being, which, already in the same pantheistic position, is world—the World. As such, the latter is "finite," a finiteness emerging from an obscure indetermination, that is, from Nothingness. However, in the philosophy of the finite and of original indeterminateness, whence everything emerges and is like a void on which the apparition of the world rests, Heidegger has preserved something that is theological: the Lutheran concepts (assumed in an atheistic philosophy) of "original fall," of the veiling and unveiling of Being (that is, of Nothingness) and that of "mystery" which, as we know, after all, always reveals itself as Nothingness.

Heidegger not only reduces the metaphysics of transcendental Idealism (and immanentism as such) to a metaphysics of Nothingness (and we give him credit for this), but he adopts this metaphysics as his own and presents it to us as a clarification of existence and the conquest of its authenticity. We remark at once (though accepting his reduction of mundanized being to Nothingness) that he lets himself miss the profound truth of Idealism lying in the concepts of spirit and self-consciousness which can be elaborated with a view to founding a truly existential metaphysics if they are critically assumed (from this point of view

Heidegger's speculation is inferior to Gentile's actualism). We add that all his philosophizing (even in the manner of procedure) is dogmatic and almost prejudiced by an emotional, obscure situation he endeavors to put forth in a form that is scarcely conceptual (in spite of its technical apparatus), since he proceeds with enunciations, hints and indications which are dropped like the leaves of the ancient Sybil, who, in this case, resembles a hysterical Cassandra always foretelling disasters.

First of all, we deny that a *Dasein*, an ego, a subject, can emerge from Nothingness. From Nothing comes nothing and least of all, as Heidegger claims, an *ens*, that is ego. The *ens* can come out *ex nihilo* only through the creative act of God. In other words, a metaphysics that makes the world rise from Nothingness is a creative one by implication; if it excludes God's creative act, it also excludes the birth of the world from Nothingness and so it must follow another way out (the world exists *ab aeterno;* it springs forth from a primary principle—air, fire, or whatever it may be—that is, from an original and living matter, and so on). Ancient metaphysics was right on this point. Heidegger rejects creation (naturally he denies the existence of a creative God) and, yet, he has *omne ens* be born *ex nihilo,* thus gratuitously affirming an absurd hypothesis: the *ens* comes from Nothing, without a God creating *ex nihilo.* Now this is no longer a philosophy but an alchemy. Heidegger's hypothesis is a magic formula rather than a philosophical proposition. However, even if it be granted that from Nothing something can be born, what is begotten is a "thing," not an "ego." The ego is a *here, someone who is.* Now, *someone* cannot be born from "Nothing" in that from "nothing" (οὐϑέν) nobody (οὐϑείς) can come. The *Dasein* can emerge from the οὐϑέν not as an ego, a person, someone, this man, but only as an οὐϑείς, an anonymous nobody, a kind of shadow of Nothingness without either determinations or the possibility for acquiring any. In fact, how can one individuate that which is an emergence from Nothing, that is, a negation of being? Every determination is impossible once being is denied. What emerges from Nothingness is always a nondetermination or, if you wish, its determinations, that is, some "nothingnesses" and a "no-one"; and the *no-one,* precisely because no-one, cannot be an ego or a person. When Ulysses wants to hide from Polyphemus he does not reply to him, "I *am* Ulysses," but, simply, "No-one," thus losing his personality and becoming a "thing," something coming from nothing so that nobody knows what the thing is; and he could have said "a chair," "an apple," "a horse." That is, a "thing," an anonymous tool relating to some other tool; that is, still that world of the nonauthenticity spoken of by Heidegger. Only this can be granted (without conceding) as coming from Nothing, namely, things, the "non-ones," nonmen, nonsubjects, and nonconsciousnesses. If Heidegger had been coherent he should have said that everything is absolutely nonauthentic. His oudenology could describe some οὐδείς, the non-ones, because without being there are no thinking and conscious subjects, there is no thought: there is darkness and that is all. A metaphysics of Nothingness is a sad, intellectual exercise by a professor in a bad mood and with many presumptions. Heidegger's world, which emerges from the Night and primitive darkness, like a shadow among shadows, soon sinks into the night of Nothingness; we can understand it only as a state of mind, as a spiritual rhythm characterizing a gloomy soul, or as a subject for poetry (lines that could have been composed by a Novalis or a Rilke, for example), but not as a metaphysical thesis conceptually elaborated with the presumption of solving nothing less than the problem of the meaning of being, as well as with the claim of renovating metaphysics from the times of the Presocratics on. We are not in the least surprised that this willful denier of Transcendence, in his last works, tries to find a remedy for finitude within a mysterious transcendence toward an Earth deified in the manner of a quasi-Nietzschean or cosmogonical pantheism. Going on at this rate, Heidegger, the metaphysician of existentialism, risks becoming a speleologist.

That interpretation seems to us to be very kind, which views Heidegger as a thinker who does not arrive at "absolute idealism" only because of the opposition presented by the "brute existent" since, for him, "man is the measure of pure intelligibility." [22] Idealism, which, even in its Hegelian form implicitly reduces being to nothingness, is another thing and it contains elements of truth representing a conquest for modern thought, even if they are to be vindicated against Idealism itself. Heidegger does nothing of the sort: led by the intrinsic logic of immanentism, he reduces Being to Nothingness, but, at this point, he builds up a cabalistic metaphysics which endeavors to draw the *Dasein, ens cogitans,* and man from Nothingness. The "coherent" conclusion to be arrived at from these premises, however, is completely different: even man, the *Dasein,* is a brute existent, a thing, a no-one, a measure of pure Nothingness. Thus, contrary to De Waelhens, one must say that Heidegger, led by his own internal coherence, overthrows absolute Idealism while he reduces man to a brute existent. Instead, he calmly draws the *Dasein,* man, from Nothingness, and he describes him without explaining how the τις (used as a noun) can come out of the οὐδέν in place of the οὐδείς. Sartre, who is another Heidegger (in spite of his efforts to disavow such a filiation), is more coherent; ultimately he reduces everything to unauthenticity, including existence whose authenticity is that of "being too much" and a nauseating thing like everything else. What Heidegger calls "authentic" is also reduced to the unauthentic in another way.

As we know, Heidegger distinguishes "unauthentic" life—which is the

[22] A. De Waelhens, *ibid.,* p. 316.

banal, every-day routine of the anonymous, neutral being of the *one* (man) says, which is "gossip," "commonplace," and so on—from "authentic" life, to which anguish elevates us; and anguish does this by revealing to us the insignificance of things and by uncovering to us the destiny of the *Dasein* (which is being-for-the-death) and the nothingness pertinent to the authentic being of the existent, so that "nothingness presents itself to us together with and at the same time as the totality of being." Such a twofold level of life is unjustifiable within Heidegger's philosophy. The *Dasein*, as a cure for the world, is not in any way degraded in the unauthentic life; in fact, for one thing, it neither causes a dispersion nor a loss of being, as Heidegger says, because it never had any being to lose (it loses not even the consciousness of its own nothingness, of being-for-the-death); secondly, even a banal and anonymous life is nonetheless a situation and a project; and, in an existential philosophy one situation is worth another (as stated by Sartre, the joy-killer of Heidegger's lie concerning "authenticity"): it is only necessary for the existent to assume and accept the situation, to plan on it, and make it his destiny in order for it to become authentic. Existential experience is expressed only if a person places himself in a situation wherein he gets himself involved in the things of the world; likewise, he also expresses existential experience who places and involves himself in "anguish," wherein he dissolves cares and preoccupations as he faces the nothingness of his being-for-the-death. Heidegger wishes us to believe that if one is dispersed in the world's cares, he is distracted and so loses the consciousness of his destiny of being for nothingness and death. That is not so: he who immerses himself in the world's cares and loses himself in this preoccupation, has already identified his destiny precisely with his being-in-the-world, so that he is convinced that he is living for the end and death after which there is nothing. Such a person is already a follower of Heidegger, that is, he is an immanentist and an atheist. In fact, what else is there to give a mystical impetus to Marxism, other than its deep conviction that man's destiny is fulfilled in this world within which everything, even paradise, must be carried out? A Marxist, the busiest man on earth and the one most concerned with things and with "utensils," knows very well that his destiny is being-for-the-death, more and better than the authentic *Dasein* in anguish. Furthermore, he is more coherent: Should he rise at the height of anguish and be estranged in the name of any authenticity? The authenticity of being conscious that he is nothing? But such an authenticity is more unauthentic than the life of a man who is concerned about the world since being convinced that he is a being-in-the-world, he is concerned about that world. Both bet their whole destiny on the nothingness of being, on being-for-the-death; granting this and since the final result is the same whether it be care or anguish, it follows that it is more authentic to live in the world totally engaged. This is because, I repeat, living completely immersed in the world with an absolute pledge to the earth requires the consciousness that man is solely for death. In his own way Heidegger made use of Pascal's *divertissement:* man distracts himself with a thousand futile things in order to forget his condition. Now, however, Pascal's warning makes sense because it reminds man that his distraction or dispersion in the world diverts him from God while seriously endangering his "destiny of eternity." For Heidegger, instead, there is nothing of the kind: withdrawing from the world and seeing it, philosophically, in its insignificance through an act of grace by anguish (the secularized Lutheran concept of grace) is pure rhetoric (emotionally, it is another thing); and it is so because, once the *Dasein* has withdrawn from the world and acquired his authenticity, he discovers that this authenticity is the consciousness of his destiny of being-for-the-death, a consciousness also possessed by the one engaged in the world. Why, then, should one withdraw from the world? In the presence of nothingness or, rather, since nothingness belongs to the totality of being, all situations are identical and different at the same time: the "care" reveals what "anguish" reveals and vice versa, without the possibility of distinguishing, except rhetorically, the authentic from the unauthentic. Can one say that Heidegger lost his authenticity when he situated and projected himself into Nazism? Certainly not. As he would not lose it tomorrow if he projected himself into communism or any other situation whatsoever. That is, in any case he would be conscious of being-for-the-death, except in that case in which he would recover the sense of being, or Being. But he rejected it; and it is just this refusal that renders radically unauthentic all his conception of existence, care or anguish as it may be. An anguish that is inexplicable since Nothingness is Being and Being is Nothingness; yet (alas!), the two "understand" each other "mutually." How can anguish make things fall and sink into "insignificance" if, at the same time, it reveals my (and also its own) insignificance? It could do it (as in Pascal and all great Christian thinkers) if, by revealing to me Being and my destiny before the infinity of Being, it made me feel the finiteness of the world before the infinity of Being; that is, it could do that only through a philosophy of Transcendence, not through one of immanence. However, if anguish reveals nothingness to me, then I cannot notice the insignificance of things because I myself am insignificant; even anguish itself is insignificant, and everything is so—even insignificance itself, which in this way becomes purely rhetorical. If a destiny is to be assumed by me in the presence of the negation of Being, and before the finite to which I am condemned, or before universal historicity (of being, essence, existence, and so forth), well, such a destiny is that of taking a plunge into the world and using the "utensils" in order to produce others endlessly. In fact, Hegel brings into being not only Kierkegaard, Heidegger, and so on, but also Marx and communism, which, at least, are not "annoyed" and, as far as one can judge, are instead determined to take away from us that terrible tediousness which, as Heidegger says, "invades us when *it annoys us*." The same thing is true for "unauthentic time" and "authentic time" which, as usual, would rescue us by disclosing to us our-being-for-the-end and death. Even this future is banal and unauthentic like "clock-time," which, at least, is useful and also rejoins the end to the beginning and nothingness to nothingness, as Heidegger wishes.

Here is how: in Heidegger there is no redemption because there is nothing to redeem, but everything to be sunk into Nothingness, into the Night, whence the illusion of the world and of man arises. Things are utensils and the care makes them "appear" to me as significant; anguish, on the other hand, makes them "slip" into insignificance and Nothingness: by doing so it reveals to me my own nothingness or my being-for-the-death, that is, my insignificance as an absolute insignificance. In this nothingness besetting being and presenting itself to us together with the totality of being, how can one distinguish the authentic from the unauthentic, if, in their nothingness, both are nothing in the same way? Nothingness is the "common-place" of the care and anguish, of things and *Dasein;* everything is "common-place," banality, and "idle talk." The same is true of anguish. But, what is there, then? Then, Sartre's *nausée* is more authentic, as more authentic are his *Heideggerian* heroes without weight or all weighty on account of their compact and thick "flesh." Absolute pessimism gives rise to an absolute hedonism or utilitarianism (and vice versa), as well as to vice and crime. In fact, Heidegger, Chestov, Barth, Sartre (Hegelians, Orthodox, Manicheans, Calvinists, and so forth), all of them, are peacefully in agreement on this score.

Heidegger accepts historicism unreservedly: if temporality governs life and being (and eternity is a myth), being is the same temporality and it rejects (rightly) that adventitious substitute of eternity represented by the "forms" of Diltheyan historicism, and also the perennialness of values and forms of spirit, and so on. At the same time Heidegger devaluates "history" as a succession of facts, a series of happenings having an alleged meaning and a real insignificance, in that they do not tell anything concerning the meaning of existence (which, according to him, as we said, is revealed by "historicity," instead; yet, historicity, as a revelation of nothingness, is as insignificant as "history"). From this point of view Heidegger represents the coherence of historicism and its criticism at the same time (the awareness of the myth of historicism). From another point of view, Heidegger has what can be called a utilitarian conception of social life (of the relations with others and with the world's things): things *serve* man as utensils or instruments while other men are also utensils in his daily life; man finds that his fellowmen are, like himself, busy about things; their talk, then, is set on an anonymous and banal level, as it indeed is in a "crowd" intent upon using the goods it produces as well as upon producing other goods in a life regulated by "clock-time," and in which no one says anything but all exchange their "hear-say." Heidegger, from this standpoint, is a devaluation and a criticism (and, in this case, a contempt) of what can be called the utilitarian man engaged in things that are "material" or "economic": a criticism against a society focused on "things," such as the Marxist or any other society whose emphasis rests on "goods," which call for other "goods," a society governed by the principle of social well-being, wherein all individuals must have those "things" to occupy them.

Yet, Heidegger does more than that: he devaluates the history of historicism while revealing its insignificance; nonetheless, he *accepts* this method of conceiving history; through him historicism is led to manifest its ultimate coherence when he rejects all its palliatives regarding immortal principles or eternal values. Heidegger, in fact, reduces being to temporality while *accepting* such an absolute and integral historicism; he devaluates life in the world, both in its relation to things and in relation to others: life is seen as a banality and degradation of an existence dispersed in the utility of things and the anonymity of the masses. Yet, he *accepts* this conception of life in the world and in society. In other words, he can be considered wholly a historicist who does not believe in the myth of historicism, since he is a person who makes being temporal and finds the authenticity of historicism itself in a "historicity" revealing the nothingness of man and his being-for-the-death (this means that Heidegger is critically conscious of the insignificance of historicism and that he destroys the strongest and most alluring myth in modern thought); yet, at the same time, just by accepting historicism and because of this acceptance, another "myth" is created—that of history and man (and even of historicity) sinking into nothingness and death. Heidegger does all this without bothering to examine historicism, from which he draws this consequence. Thus, out of the same question which he "critically" injects into historicism, he dogmatically makes the constitutional "crisis" of existence and history, both of which become annihilated into insignificance. He removes the mask of positivity from historicism, thus revealing its negativity; and then with the same pall of the negativity of historicism he wraps up existence and lets it meditate on and clarify its destiny of death. The same thing can be said about man with respect to the world and others: Heidegger maintains that life in the world (as possession and utilization of things) and in society (as an anonymous crowd busied about things) is unauthentic; yet, he does not try any new way to conceive these relations (for instance, a relation of sympathy toward things and one of brotherhood toward men). Not at all; he accepts the devaluating conception: he judges it as unauthentic and negative; yet, he makes it his own, and is convinced that there cannot be a better and less unauthentic relationship between man and the world and between man and man. Even at this point he posits a critical question within the pragmatic conception of life and of society while he reveals with contempt its limitations; and then "dogmatically" uses the same question to make a chronic, perennial crisis of man's life with respect to the world and others, as if no other relationship with things and no other social structure were possible. This position of his is not too far from some Marxist theses, except that Marxism considers human activity and production as an affirmation of man's power and sway over the world, which man subdues in order to "serve" his needs; and in human activity and production, Marxism sees also the way to attain a perfect society in which man realizes his end and fulfills his destiny. Heidegger, on the other hand, sees in it the fall of man into unauthenticity (and with this he is critically conscious of the myth of praxism and of that conception of life focused on "things" alone); but he does not discern the possibility of another way of life, so that his opposition comes only in terms of his unauthentic and insignificant authenticity, which is the negation of sociality as such. His position is identical with that of an integral historicist, who has freed himself from the myth of historicism; or it is identical with that held by a *praxist* (not incorrectly Enrico Paci spoke of "pragmatism" in this respect) whose conception of the problem of the relationship between man and the world, and between man and man, is not far from the Marxist conception, though without the myth of Marxism. Therefore, Heidegger can be interpreted in two antithetic ways: on the one hand, as an antihistoricist, in the sense that he destroys the positivity of historicism (and of immanentism) and as an historicist, in the sense that he totally accepts the more coherent historicism; and, on the other hand, as an antipraxist (and anti-Marxist), in the sense that he considers *praxism* as a fall, a dispersion, and a degradation of existence, and as a praxist (and also a Marxist; cf., Szilasi), in the sense that he accepts such a conception as the only possible one. In this way Heidegger has led the immanentist conception of existence (existence as a refusal of Transcendence and a negation of being in historicity) to its sterility; unfruitful in fact is a position that, after noting its mythical character and along with it its negativity, presents itself as a position of this same absolute negativity in which no longer is there any sense in its speaking about being, meaning of being, significance of existence, of authenticity, and so forth because everything is enveloped in the original and final Nothingness.

Heidegger (and existentialism in general) represents the decline of immanentism, the critical age of a philosophy which no longer has any trust in the productivity of the principle of immanence. On account of its decadence, fatigue and senescence, it is an impossible "situation" and a useless "project" for it to be fecund; and yet this is a doctrine which still believes dogmatically in the myth of realizing the fullness and positivity of man within an immanentist-historicist experience or within an "atheistic humanism" (as for example Marxism, the last illusion of immanentism). Such a doctrine, however, as a philosophical ideology constitutes an empty and discounted dogmatism, a coin out of use, and a non-project; it is not even a "referring to something else" in the Heideggerian sense.

The full criticism that we have made of Heidegger's philosophy induces us to be briefer with the other existentialists and thus avoid repetition.

Even Jaspers' ontology, in spite of his philosophy of "ciphers," ultimately is a theory of the structure of human existence. In it there is undoubtedly a metaphysical nucleus which is entirely lacking in Heidegger's phenomenology, by which Transcendence is identified with being-in-the-world, that is, with human existence, which alone is described. For Jaspers, on the other hand, man is not the Transcendence but he is *before* Transcendence; in his "failure" man makes tests of being and then prepares himself for his "leap." [23] Yet, Jaspers' Transcendence still remains an ambiguous concept even if he calls it God. Jaspers can be considered as the existential experience of pantheism. His Transcendence is the unknowable and hidden One, an Absolute beyond all categories: an elusive one that can be translated only into symbols which are inadequate to make it understandable. The One is immanent in existence and in the world, but it is also beyond them (man's language and that of things are a cipher), and it hides itself while being present—the presence of an absence and the absence of a presence. Nor is it a person because personality —Jaspers repeats, in the company of pantheists of all times—exists only in relation to other personalities whereas the One is one, the Absolute. From this standpoint Jaspers is a Neoplatonist and closely reminds us of Plotinus and also of Spinoza; a position similar to this has been recently held in Italy by Martinetti with his mode of conceiving the One or Whole. However, Jasper's pantheism is not the religion or mysticism of reason (Spinoza, Martinetti, and others), but a *mysticism of reason's failure*, which acquires the existential experience of its unsufficiency in the presence of the Absolute; it remains powerless within a zone of silence, and in the cessation of a thought which clarifies itself; and it gains its authenticity not in its reunion with the One (Plotinian "ecstasy" or Spinozian *amor Dei intellectualis*), but precisely in the experience of the

[23] On the relations between Jaspers and Heidegger see M. Dufrene and P. Ricoeur, *K. Jaspers et la philos. de l'existence* (Paris, 1947), particularly pp. 363-372.

absence of such a reunion and in the failure of all attempts at grasping the Absolute. Jaspers' existent, indeed, is a spark from the Whole (and so it is divine); but still this Whole or Transcendence is only man's horizon which, in itself, is a "pure void" and yet the existent is always bound to face this Totality without ever reaching it. Consequently, he is not shipwrecked *in the* Transcendence (such a shipwreck would be his salvation), but he is shipwrecked *before* Transcendence and so his experience is failure and negativity; and this is the authentic possibility of the existent. In other words, the existent makes his experience "before" Transcendence but not that of Transcendence, which is always beyond; such an ultimate experience is the impossible possibility.

At this point Jaspers' Transcendence is revealed as fictitious, an improper word, in whose place we should find more appropriate the word Immanence. The failure of existence before Transcendence is not explained by Jaspers on the basis of the impossibility on the part of the finite to immerse itself *in the* Transcendence, but on the basis of the inability of the finite to "understand" Transcendence and to make it coincide with the realization of its possibility to "encircle" the "encircling Whole." In other words, it is impossible for the existent to realize the horizon of the "circumscribing-Whole" or absolute Unity although this may be his supreme possibility; therefore, this possibility, inasmuch as it is impossible, is presented to him as Transcendence, as a beyond that is always going to be a beyond; and not because it is a beyond in itself (as in classical pantheism), but because it is *his* beyond, that is, the unreachable thing, the nonrealization of the self on the part of the existent. Thus Jaspers' Transcendence is only the impossible possibility on the part of the existent, his future never to be a present, and the unreachable absolute Immanence of the self to itself. In this case the failure of the existent before Transcendence is only the failure of the absolute Immanence of the existent himself, who cannot realize himself as a circumscribing-Whole, and so is destined to never grasp himself fully and hence to be encompassed, never encompassing. The failure with which the existent is revealed to himself and becomes aware of his destiny is his impossibility of being the Absolute, God. His silence before Transcendence and the shipwreck of reason are the silence and shipwreck of the existent in the presence of his possibility and his awareness concerning his impossibility to surpass the finite (although surpassing it is his possibility); in the finite, then, the existent sinks in silence, while being enveloped by ciphers giving no consolation, that is, by ciphered messages sent to him by his impossible being beyond the finite (a being which is therefore infinite); in his possible impossibility of being the Whole, the existent sends such messages to the existent (that is, to himself) in his insurmountable situation of finitude. This situation of finitude aiming at the whole Infinite is called by Jaspers authenticity of the existent; Sartre calls it "useless passion." Then, Jaspers' pantheism is not an "incomplete atheism," as it was called, but a complete though not declared atheism; and it is so not on account of insincerity on the part of Jaspers, but because he is an atheist with a religious soul. I would call Jaspers' pantheism a critical one (because of the awareness that every pantheism is atheism and a shipwreck of the world in God and of God in the world), that cannot bear to declare itself atheistic and so it refuses to be such. It is also a critical one because it is aware of the impotency inherent in pantheism with respect to the solution of the questions pertinent to religious consciousness and of the problems laid down by the theological exigency—in short, a pantheism without the "myth" of salvation and liberation of man in the immense sea of Totality.

We said that Jaspers' Transcendence is the supreme and impossible possibility of existence, the horizon that, being unrealizable, is never that in which the subject can situate itself, but always that before which it is situated and shipwrecked. Such Transcendence is the Kantian-idealistic Transcendentality and its failure. The idealistic transcendentality is represented by a subject (the transcendent Ego of idealism) which endeavors to realize the absolute Unity, the Whole or perfect adequacy between totality of knowledge and totality of reality. Jaspers assumes the idealistic transcendentality and makes it the supreme possibility for the existent; the possibility, however, upon becoming an existential experience cannot be realized, so that now it is an impossibility. From a horizon of knowledge entirely immanent to the Ego and in which the whole reality is also immanent, it changes into a horizon of Transcendence that is always the possibility of the existent; yet, precisely because it is unrealizable, transcendent, and a "beyond" always confronting the existent, it has become the existent's failure in the presence of his impossible possibility of being the circumscribing-Whole, that is, the horizon of Transcendentality pertinent to the idealistic Ego.

"Certainly we know," writes Jaspers, "that this being of ours, as a circumscribing horizon, is in no way the *being in se;* however, the latter will be revealed to us in a truly critical manner only when we have covered the entire path indicated by Kant," that is, that direction moving from the subject or being as we are. Jaspers' words imply that Kant failed to cover the road that he himself had opened and so he could not "critically" reveal the being in itself. Jaspers travels it all the way with his analysis of "Consciousness in general" and of "Reason": the former corresponds to the "intellect" and the latter to the "reason" pertinent to the three metaphysical ideas of Kant. In fact, "Consciousness in general" is the "form" of that which is the object of our experience, that which gives universal validity to our knowledge, the "space of sciences," but not the circumscribing-Whole. Kantian transcendentality (the intellect's forms *a priori*) is the "place" or form in which we recognize the objects of experience; so, it should be also the form in which we recognize the circumscribing-horizon; but precisely because it is the form in which we should know it, it is not the circumscribing-Whole itself and it amounts to saying that transcendentality as a form of a content could receive the circumscribing-horizon. In other words, the transcendental activity of the Kantian intellect is not the horizon of the whole, but is a form missing such a horizon, which remains in the beyond, as Transcendence. After all, even Kant is of the same opinion, but it is not so with positivism and "scientificalism" whose criticism is represented by Jaspers' analysis of consciousness in general; this criticism categorically objects that "the scientific knowledge of things is not the knowledge of Being" and so science's horizon is not that of metaphysics or philosophy; on the contrary, scientific knowing is "not-knowing what Being is."

However, besides Consciousness in general, the existent is also Reason; in Kant, too, besides the intellect there is a reason, the activity carelessly trying the metaphysical flight without the obstacle of the sensible. Such a flight, as we know, is not a success and the three metaphysical ideas remain as such and are enveloped in the antinomies and paralogisms of pure reason playing the more modest role of "regulating" reason itself. Being, for Kant, remains *in itself*, since it escapes reason in all its attempts. For Jaspers, Reason inheres in the existent and becomes existential experience and inquietude launched out toward the unseizable Being. A relationship of dialectical tension is established between the existent that exists and reveals itself before Transcendence (which is not "objectivated" as it is in Consciousness in general) and Transcendence that is before the existent: if the latter disappeared, the former would, too, because the existent—of which transcendence is a supreme possibility—would be lacking. In that case the existent exists for the Transcendence or Being which it tends to grasp, and Being is transcendent because it escapes the seizure by the existent, that is, because it always remains his unrealizable possibility. This is how Jaspers, upon covering the whole way opened by Kant, but not traversed by him, clarifies (and this is also the clarification of the existent and his destiny) Being in itself in a "truly critical" way. In a "critical" way because Being is not *in se;* it is, instead, transcendent *in relationship with* and *before* me as an existent; it stands as my unrealizable possibility in whose presence I am shipwrecked. We are left then with the shipwreck of the existent (who is never shipwrecked as a shipwrecking being), or with the existent as a perennial shipwreck, and with Transcendence in the presence of which the existent is a shipwreck; in short, there is the existent as a shipwreck of the full Immanence of Being to Itself, which is Transcendence precisely because it is an unrealizable immanence (since it is not the Immanent in act). The existent forms itself "only in relationship with Transcendence," and Transcendence, we clarify, is constituted *only* in relationship with the existent. There is tension, but a fictitious one because Transcendence is not really transcendence but an Immanence which is not really immanent; it is "horizontal," not "vertical"; it is the moving of the existent toward his becoming absolute and so there is neither a religious nor a metaphysical tension—there is only man's shipwreck in the presence of his impossible (and absurd) possibility of making himself a God. "At the end there is a shipwreck." And what does this signify? What destiny does it clarify to me? This one: "in vain you try" to understand "Transcendence (to enclose it within yourself and to take its place) which always escapes you; yet, the sense of existence is here in the situation of shipwreck, in the passion for forever trying and forever being shipwrecked"; that is, it lies in my situating myself in a "useless passion." After all, Jaspers himself notices it when he writes with both a Kierkegaardian and a Nietzschean accent: "Everything is a shipwreck and so it does not pay to start all over again, since everything is meaningless." The sense of metaphysics, for Jaspers, lies in its lacking a meaning; neither the existent nor being has one. Even Jaspers' existentialism is a dissolvent of the person and of Being, before which the person itself "does not assume a positive and axiological dignity"; nor is this done by Being in the presence of the person. Jaspers' tension and implication of opposites are an illusion just as are the opposites themselves. Even Jaspers is an immanentist who protests against immanence, who recognizes its complete negativity and accepts this negativity as fundamental to existence and as its "crisis."

However, the existent is also Spirit and, as such, is no longer the "space of the sciences" (of things), but the "time" of history and becoming; it is not Consciousness in general (or Kant's intellect), but Hegel's Spirit. Jaspers' analysis of the Spirit, whose result still is a failure, represents the criticism and failure of the Hegelian absolute Spirit making and conquering itself through dialectical process. Jaspers acknowledges that the mode of the Spirit is the highest effort toward achieving the "comprehension" of the circumscribing-Whole, that is, a "totalitarian vision"; yet, this is an effort bound to fail, because it is not a "comprehension" but a "vision" of Being, in which what is lacking is the subject-object unity; and the supreme synthesis or the Whole in itself and for itself is missing because of the persisting duality. Thus, Philosophy (in the Hegelian sense of the word) is not a circumscribing-horizon: history and logic are condemned to insignificance. Once a total comprehension is the illusion or myth of transcendental idealism and once the supreme synthesis is impossible, it is evident that all other partial syntheses (the moments of religion, art, ethics, law, and so forth) lose the importance gained in the Spirit's process; the *no* of the supreme synthesis falls upon partial syntheses nullifying all of them while carrying the shipwreck-Transcendence dialectical antinomy, back to its pure state, as the ultimate result of all forms of human activity. It is not exact to say that Jaspers, almost contradicting himself ingenuously, first recognizes the positivity of the numerous modes of comprehending Being and, then, in the final position, provokes the emergence of "a conclusive contradiction capable of destroying the edifice previously built"; [24] the positivity of the numerous modes is conditioned and, I would say, suspended on the final position, that is, on the last synthesis, the attainment of Being. In fact, it could not be otherwise in an immanent philosophy; once the positivity in the last synthesis of Hegel's dialectic is denied, the entire process of the Spirit becomes insignificant. This is what Jaspers does: he denies the possibility for the comprehension of Being and dissolves immanentism as a positive conclusion, as a philosophy capable of understanding the whole Being, thus revealing the mythical nature of its very pretense. Yet, since this critique is conducted within the perspective of immanentism itself, Jaspers identifies the failure of this philosophy with the failure of existence as such, and in agreement with Heidegger and other existentialists, he creates the new "myth" that philosophy and existence are "crises," rupture, insignificance, and absurdity. At this point, religious faith did not help him as it did Kierkegaard or Chestov, so that he stops at the "existent-shipwreck" antinomy (it, too, is insignificant) in the presence of Transcendence. Like Kierkegaard, he indeed speaks of a "leap," but this "leap" is not made *in* Transcendence, nor is it an irruption of God (grace) into man, but a leap of the existent before Transcendence. However, a "leap forward" is not a jump but a dance. It is an unsuccessful leap; after leaping, the existent still is before Transcendence (and this fact proves that it is not possible "to leap" into God without God's help, but Jaspers has not thought of it), whereupon he hobbles like a lopsided, crippled fellow, or he remains suspended in the air, like a balloon launched without Sartre's ballast. What else can be done at this point? One can write, as Jaspers does, the logic of the absurd, of an absurd, hopping existence before an absurd Transcendence, and its impossible possibility—the logic, Sartre would say, of a "useless passion." Thus existentialism loses precisely that existent (the person) it had the merit of vindicating, the existent, that is, it had posited in his irreducibility and burdened with the supreme problem of the sense of his destiny as a peremptory critical demand against rationalism, idealism, and positivism. However, can it recover man if at the outset it refuses God? In its best moments, existentialism is the tragic experience (and not a

[24] L. Stefanini, "Esistenzialismo ateo e Esistenzialismo teistico," *Il dramma filosofico della Germania* (Padua, Cedam, 1948), p. 69 and *passim*.

happy experience like that of the eighteenth and nineteenth centuries) on the part of atheism, the experience of an absurd existence without God.

The philosophy of the finite experiences the negativity of finite existence whose being is its situations; theological existentialism should be the existential experience of a faith which salvages existence and restores the positivity and validity of an order resting on the true and the good. Instead, it follows the same path as the other, indeed in such a direction that even theology becomes involved in the absurd, in the irrational, and in the negative, so that to the disconnectedness of logic and destruction of being is added that of Revelation. Oriental nihilism and Protestantism play their part in this game. Thus Chestov radically denies science (knowledge) and human ethics.

Berdyaev at his best, unlike Chestov, preserves the sense of the human as well as that of the divine, which he keeps distinct but not separated; and, because of his clear, theistic position and his abandonment of immanentism, he is able to criticize the latter without later assuming the same immanentism reduced to its negativity as the negativity of existence (which happened to Heidegger and Jaspers, who reject the experience of theological Transcendence). His critical considerations on Kant hit their mark (for example, Kantian criticism of any possible metaphysics is simply the criticism of a rationalistic and naturalistic metaphysics, that is, of metaphysics as Kant himself conceived it), as do those on atheistic superhumanism, which represents the negation of man. Thus Berdyaev is able to recognize in "historicism" the loss of the "historical," as well as that of every sense of history in "immanentist history." His criticism of Marxism is also remarkable. Its positivity regarding the social question is well recovered and made part of Christian *praxis;* also noteworthy is his doctrine of freedom with its foundation inspired by authentic Augustinianism, even if Berdyaev later spoils this theory with the insertion of a gnostic-Böhmean motive, wherein the rescue of human freedom within truth becomes impossible and wherein even God is involved in the tragedy of good and evil investing and wearing Him out from within. Besides, Berdyaev's eschatologism makes God ineffectual because of the abstraction and indetermination (and moreover He is no longer a Person); and besides he nullifies history by considering it a completely negative work of evil which will be erased through divine judgment. Where then is man's positivity, that of the human, and of creation itself, which Berdyaev vindicates while contradicting himself?

It is not with Berdyaev but, rather, with Barth that theological existentialism presents itself in all its negativity; when the economy of the sin-freedom-grace relationship has been broken, and all positivity has been denied to sinful man so that it can be entirely attributed to God, Christianity remains profoundly altered.

Barth proceeds with violent suppressions: "Religion is a human activity (and, hence, it is negative) having the sinful man as its beginning and end; so it is opposed to faith, which has God as its cause and end." Man cannot be a Christian; such a possibility pertains only to God who breaks into man through faith. God alone makes us lost and redeemed; man has nothing to do with it; man is nothing both as a sinner and as a redeemed person; man is a guinea pig on whom Barth's God tries out his contradiction and realizes his internal *dialecticity*. Barth's God strangely resembles Hegel's: a God who, in making and freeing Himself, crushes men as He posits and "resolves" them according to the aims of His self-making. Man's perdition and redemption, according to Barth, signify self-perdition and self-redemption on the part of God. It is God who triumphs over the *yes* and *no* as He frees Himself from the nothingness of creation. Barth sees redemption as nullification; even creation signifies positing the nothingness, in that the creature is essentially sin (what God *is not* and so it is the negation of God); to create is to posit the nonbeing and death in which God exercises His redeeming action by reversing the *yes* into a *no*. This is all a satanic game by a satanic God. God is "radically the Other," absolutely the Other, which cannot be even thought of. But, if He is unthinkable how can I think that He is radically an Other? And if one grants that only that much can be thought of God, one should not say anything more. However, Barth says a great deal more, like those mystics who write entire libraries on the Ineffable. Barth mysteriously knows everything concerning the "radically Other," because he resolutely denies the presence of any truth in man (even this one: that there is in man no truth whatever?) to the point of always violently suppressing the problem of knowledge. Nonetheless, having eliminated this problem and denied the possibility of the smallest truth in man, Barth writes, among many things, a *Dogmatik*, which has already exceeded five thousand pages; and he still promises that he "will talk" more. The fact is that he must possess God's truth, the revealed Word in its absolute entirety. There is no greater pride than that of a philosopher who abolishes reason on the ground that it is vain and inept (for example, the skeptic; and Barth is a skeptic, for he denies man any truth); such a philosopher rejects this gift as useless only because it does not make him be a God, the Absolute, and only because he believes himself to be in possession of a suprarational truth that surpasses that poor instrument which is reason, a faculty common to all men and hence not "exceptional." Likewise, there cannot be greater Satanism than that of a theologian who refuses freedom (nullified by sin) and who refuses reason (powerless to know), as well as anything that is human in man; such a theologian acts as a superman, and when he has refused everything given to him by God, his Creator (and this is a contempt for both God's gifts and God

Himself), he places himself before the Gospel and says, "this is the Word of God," which is as he interprets it. But, what is his means of interpretation if he has refused everything? Evidently he holds himself to be "possessed" of the grace and "elected" *a priori;* and, indeed, it is God Himself who speaks through his lips. Hence, the sureness, the radicalism, and the satanic pride of him who believes himself to be an instrument of God, a saved one: "It is God speaking, not I." Such is Barth, who considers God as the ultratranscendent, beyond all analogy (except that of a faith beginning and ending in God Himself, wherein man has no other role than that of being an instrument in the divine drama). And then about God Barth knows everything, above all the fact that the Hegelian dialectic has become so incarnate in him as to make him proceed with the same logic used by the philosopher from Stuttgart.

We acknowledge in Barth's radicalism a just exigency: that of attacking all "humanisms," even those defining themselves as "Christian," to the point of making them confess their "atheism." Barth's intransigence aims at making room for God against the invasion of these humanisms which deify man, as well as at making room for a "Christ" against the sweet honey of the "Lives of Jesus" of the Arcadian type, which make the "Sermon on the Mount" and the "Night of Gethsemane" the subjects of short octosyllabic stanzas. Barth also disowns the pretension of a philosophy that objectivates God in order to reduce Him into a "concept" that the human mind is capable of "containing" in itself. So far, so good; but it is a mistake and an absurdity to proceed, as Barth does, by means of radical and violent negations. Making room for God is right, indeed, but on condition that man is given his just place; otherwise, the deicide perpetrated by atheistic humanism is simply substituted with the homicide perpetrated by dialectical theology, and all remains as before. Make room for a "Christ," yes, but without denying the value of "Jesus' life" in an absurd "Christ-Jesus" dialectic, wherein the annihilation of "Jesus" is also the annihilation of "Christ"; react against the Hegelian "objectivation" which resolves God in the world (in history), yes, but without either depriving knowledge of all its value or resolving the entire sense of history in God through a sort of "theological occasionalism," which ultimately is an inverse Hegelianism, that is, a pantheism and, therefore, atheism.

Barth's Hegelianism is unquestionable. The Hegelian dialectic of contradiction hinges on the concept of "preserving by destroying," that is, by denying; and this is, however, an assumption and an inclusion that is also an affirmation of the position within the negation of the negation; the synthesis, upon denying them, retains the two opposites and, in retaining them, denies the negation within the affirmation of the position. For Hegel such a dialectical circle is the life of the Spirit, which, because it is immanent in becoming resolves itself in the same becoming. Consequently, God is resolved in immanence. For Barth the negation of the negation (and so the affirmation of the position) does not take place in the circle through immanence, but is worked out by God during the act in which He assumes the negation (the *no*) and transforms it into a *yes*. Hegel's dialectic (the being-nonbeing-becoming triad) is literally transferred to God and it becomes the game of the *absconditus* and of the *revelatus*, as a passage from death (*no*) to life (*yes*), wherein the synthesis of human history is produced. For the immanentist Hegel, the supreme synthesis is realized within the absolute moment of Philosophy; for the ultratranscendentist Barth, it is carried out eschatologically in God's triumph; Hegel resolves theology into philosophy (the "abstract" religious dogma into the "concrete" philosophical concept); Barth resolves philosophy into theology (philosophy is the human symbol of the drama of a dialectic realizing itself in God). Contradiction is, then, an intrinsic element in divine as well as human nature.

Barth's shift of the solution from the *world* (Hegel) to the beyond changes nothing; by resolving philosophy into his theology, he reproduces a position identical with that of Hegel, who resolves theology into philosophy; the ultratranscendentalism of dialectical Theology is an absolute pantheism and an ultraimmanentism. Even Hegel could accept Barth's position and acknowledge it as his own. Hegel, in fact, could say he also resolved man into the absolute Subject (thus denying him); he could also say that he caused everything to be the work of the Subject and nothing to be done by man (by empirical subjects), who is a mere instrument of the conquest that the Absolute makes of itself; again he could say he gave history a sacred significance (the whole of history is "sacred history"), while events were made to appear as veils through which the depth of the immanent Absolute is transparent; and, finally, he could say he conceived humanity as a symbol of the great drama which the Absolute lives within the self, in order to conquer the self through a logic of contradiction that is intrinsic and essential to it. Barth in vain replies that for Hegel everything happens along the path of immanence rather than along the path of transcendence. What transcendence can be found when the nothingness of creation is *necessary* to God, when the human *no* becomes the divine *yes*, and when, in short, this nothingness represented by the world and by man is necessary to the essence of God, that is, to His intrinsic *dialecticity*? An acosmic pantheism, if you wish, but one in which the nothingness of the cosmos is the necessary condition for the divine *yes*; and this still is a radical immanence. Barth in vain defends himself by saying that God is absolute freedom revealing Himself when and as He pleases, and that He always remains the absolutely Other which man cannot attain even when God communicates with him. He reveals Himself when and how He pleases, indeed; but He *must* reveal Himself since He *needs* the *no* in order that His *yes* be possible (a necessity stemming from the tyranny of the dialectic of contradiction); God is freedom, but in the sense of the freedom of Spinoza's God, that is, a necessity (still pantheism). Moreover, if the human *no* is necessary and the *yes* of faith is God's work within the *no*, and if the whole is the same drama of God, then man's essence is identical with the divine; and so there is pantheism and a radical immanence.

The act of faith with which God assumes man "occurs" in the moment of *crisis*, the sign of the miraculous intervention which changes death into life. At this point true existence is established: by dying man lives; by losing himself he is saved; God founds freedom on the slavery of the flesh; He founds his personality, pre-eminent and sovereign, and the human person, and He denies the negation which man is, in his divine positivity—a *dialectical* positivity affirming itself by resolving the *yes* and *no* and sin and grace. If the interpretation is correct, the dialectical synthesis, which Barth denies *a parte hominis* when he exacts the negation of the negation (that is, that man is not to posit himself as a negative element before God, who is the positive one), is carried out by God, who posits Himself in the absolute pre-eminence of the *yes* before the *no* of man and resolves the nothingness of man himself (and of creation). God triumphs over it, as He "frees Himself from it"; He also realizes the dialectical synthesis and, with it, His absolute sovereignty over the two elements composing the synthesis itself. Now, if this is the case, as basically it appears to be, by the transference of the Hegelian triad of being-nonbeing-becoming to God, the "Hegelian" Barth causes the divine *yes* to assassinate the human *no* (man loses his nonbeing, which is his being, and he gains nothing, since it is God who "invades" him, annihilates his nonbeing or his being-a-man, and takes his place and possession of him); and the "instant" of the "assassination" of the nothingness of the creature (its being) is also the instant of the "suicide" of God because, by dialectically resolving the *no*, the divine *yes* denies itself within the dynamics of dialectical synthesis; the *no* is necessary to the *yes*, as the nonbeing is to being, and nothingness to God; dialectically God frees Himself of it, yet, for His realization and liberation this *no* is dialectically necessary. In this way everything becomes "useless," the *yes* and the *no*, sin and grace, condemnation and redemption, perdition and salvation; and God Himself. Grace without freedom, redemption without collaboration, God laden with a *no* which gives being to his *yes*, though it annihilates Him as God: the whole of Christianity is corrupt.

Barth's radicalism can only portray a God in contradiction and place on the same level a St. Francis and a Cesare Borgia. However, if this is so, it becomes perfectly useless and insignificant to resist communism or to protest, as Barth did, against Nazism: in fact, if it is so, God can use communism or Nazism, St. Francis' benedictions or Cesare Borgia's daggers and poisons and, indifferently, give a meaning to either communism or to the poisons, whereas no meaning is given to the Saint's stigmata (which, in this way, are to remain within their negativity and insignificance). Yet, this Hegelian Calvinist theologian was either lacking in sincerity or, perhaps, he did not have the courage to assume all the responsibility implied in his "dialectical theology," so that he did not draw such extreme but coherent consequences. He was unable to resist the temptation of the flesh, or of the noble gesture of resisting inhuman tyranny (an insignificant gesture unless Barth thinks that God chose precisely his gesture as an occasion to reveal Himself to us), to the point of deserving "recognition" even from renowned Catholic scholars; otherwise, if we wish to be even more lenient, he found, for a moment, the courage to react against his own dialectic and to disown it through action. However, in such a case he should have rectified it on the theoretical level also, rather than uselessly appealing to the Kantian and Vaihingerian "as if." Here is his expedient: our works (everything in the world) are insignificant; yet, we must act, not stay still, "as if" justification were a human possibility, that is, "as if" what we do carried a positivity within itself. Now, the "as if," that in Kant (and even in Vaihinger) makes some sense, though it solves nothing, is such obvious nonsense in Barth as to leave one stunned. In fact, besides the point that, if man is convinced about the insignificance of everything, it is very unlikely (because of the psychological situation he creates) that he will act "as if" it were not so; and aside from the fact that, even if he overcomes his skepticism, which leads to inertia, and decides to act, he can indifferently act in favor of Moscow or Rome as either a brigand or a saint; but prescinding from all that (and other things), precisely from Barth's point of view, if man behaves in accordance with the "as if," he not only refuses the negation of the negation, but all other negations, thereby satanically positing himself before God with the full burden of his sin and flesh. The thought alone that man acts "as if" what he does has some merit or positive value, and "as if" the justification were a human possibility, leads him in the very act of his action to deny God, grace, radical transcendence and faith as a gift of God, and so on. This is so even if man admits these values theoretically, since, in this case, "theoretically" is used with its worst connotation. Evidently, in such a case, life and thought are made to be at such variance as to cause man to be annihilated by hypocrisy and immorality. The "as if" represents the negation of Barth's whole theology; it is another way of reinstating the same humanism destructive of God, against which Barth has fought without balance or moderation and in the name of an exaggerated supertheologism.

The atmosphere changes when we come to Marcel's theistic existentialism. In this case, we are dealing with a philosophically questionable experience (and we shall question it); yet, from a human and Christian point of view, Marcel's experience is extremely meaningful. Marcel possesses a concrete sense regarding man, the world, and God; and he has the artist's touch. His three spiritual rhythms are almost living persons within the human drama; they come forth with a human countenance and gait; they are disarmed before the world and are yet able to conquer it, as if they were a defiance against all the disprovals, disownings and betrayals of life; they represent an energetic and vigorous affirmation of the spirit against an impersonal, weakened, hedonistic and anonymous society. Within the implication of presence and participation, of invocation and reply, God, man, and things converse: a dialogue between things and the existent, between *you* and *me*, between us and God. Solitude, perhaps, but not isolationism: Marcel's inwardness and his positing of the individual as individual gather the voices of humanity in the name and love of God. Of all the forms of existentialism Marcel's is the only one that does not refuse but, rather, fulfills the experience of a Christian existence. All this had to be acknowledged without delay; yet, this acknowledgment also implies the limitations characterizing Marcel's experience from both a philosophical standpoint and that of a Christian philosophy.

Marcel is concerned lest the "objective" kill the "existential," and lest the impersonal "problem" mortify and degrade the intimacy and personality of the "mystery" (not in a religious sense). Thus, to the metaphysics of the objective and problematical he opposes that of the existential and metaproblematical; indeed, the metaproblematical is the zone of metaphysics. However, is objectivity only rationality and the opposite of the existential? Is a metaphysics of the metaproblematical, or of what has been experienced but cannot be objectivated, still a metaphysics, or is it only a subjective experience that, as such, has value only subjectively in just the same way as all other personal experiences, among which there may be one denying Marcel's own experience? Can a metaphysics that refuses mediation be in conformity with Christian-Catholic theology (Marcel is a Catholic) as well as in harmony with a Christian-Catholic concept of life?

"Mystery," for Marcel, is that which is known immediately, that with which I find myself involved; it does not stand *before* me as a problem, as something splitting indistinctness and original totality; "mystery," instead, is the "metaproblematical," "a seizure of being," and an "apprehension"; it surpasses the endless doubting of that "problematizing" thought, which not only destroys immediateness and separates what is *in me* from what is *before me*, but also deprives me of my "seizure of being," and depresses me by casting me into one doubt after another until I am in "despair." In short, the metaproblematical is the *safety-zone* guaranteed by immediateness which, as such, is beyond the problem. We agree with Marcel on this point if all that he means is a rejection of the "problem" and a rejection of objectivating thought when the latter is understood in a rationalistic and detached way (and I would say in a mathematical-scientific way) whereby the problem of being is there, before me, and I coldly go over it, with my mind, as if the result would not interest me since I am led by an alien and indifferent attitude. If that "seizure of being" or "apprehension" (expressions that are not easily determinable because they communicate an emotion more than an idea) implies an original, *intellectual* intuition of being (to be determined with precision in order to avoid the ontologism Marcel risks with his conception of "immediateness"), that is constitutive of rational or reflexive thought, then in this too we are in full agreement. However, one cannot clearly see in Marcel how this intellectual intuition of being is understood because it is not determined, elaborated, and developed. Nor does the metaproblematical oppose the act of problematizing in an abstract and rationalistic sense, but rather it opposes the act as such because it opposes reflexive and objective thought as such; and, at this point, our dissent is open and irreducible because it rises in defense of metaphysics and of a theistic metaphysics of existence. Marcel rejects all objectivation and believes that he is making metaphysics safe by getting it out of the labyrinth of problematizing thought; but, if this is so, if there is no mediation, Marcel's "problematical" is only his subjective "seizure of being," and a purely autobiographical experience, that is enclosed in itself and secured by its immediate certainty, without any concern for being mediated and developed into a philosophy that is rationally justified. However, this is not a solution of the problem of metaphysics and, least of all, does this lay down a "methodology" through which a metaphysics could be founded, as is believed by some of Marcel's students; on the contrary, this is an attempt to solve the problem of one's own personal salvation, which, in the last analysis, is the perennial problem in French philosophy from Pascal to Blondel. Indeed, by positing a relationship between Being and the existent on the metaproblematical or mystery-level, that is, on the basis of immediateness, no questions can arise any more; but, precisely on this account, once the relationship is posited as a vitally experienced one and we stop at it to describe its spiritual rhythm, philosophy and metaphysics will never rise again. A metaphysics of what cannot be rendered objective, or one restricted to a lived experience, is a contradiction of terms; there is an interior life expressed emotionally, mystically, and so forth, but this can be anything except a philosophy or a metaphysics, which is objective thought and a problem and its solution. Existential experience either mediates itself or it remains outside of philosophical problems; the *aut-aut* in this case does not allow a third term. Marcel's metaphysics of the metaproblematical reminds us of Bergson's "metaphysics," particularly as a penetration of reality instead "of an adoption of points of view on it," or as "an intuition of reality instead of an analysis of it, so as to grasp it outside of every expression, translation, or symbolical "representation" or—as Marcel would say—outside of every objectivation. In fact, Bergson, who did not exclude the rational mediation, never built a true metaphysics because he wound up identifying it with mystical experience.

Furthermore, why should reflexive thought and the problem degrade lived experience and lose the original unity? Even reflexive thought and the problem are a personally lived experience that can be shared and suffered. Concrete philosophizing does not mean that we catalogue, as spectators, the moments of the drama of search, which is life; it means rather to live those moments by unifying and clarifying them within that superior unity offered by reflexive thought. Philosophy is precisely that lived experience expressed by reflection; and the objective is not what is unexperienced. Indeed, we do not exclude a primary immediateness (there is no need to say in what sense because at this point we are concerned with Marcel's and not with this writer's point of view) as a *starting point* for philosophizing, that is, a starting point that is not immediately a point of arrival either. Otherwise we confine ourselves to a philosophy that is "edifying" only with respect to a person "living it"; yet, a philosophy that, as such, is not really edifying without thought, which is objectivity, the only philosophically edifying thought. It seems to us that, unless we are mistaken, Marcel's position is as follows: everything becomes insoluble and wrapped up in doubt if it slips to the level of objective thought and this is true of *everything* (the problem of the relationship between body and soul, of the existent and the others, of the existent and God, and so on); everything, on the other hand, is clear, certain and infallible provided that it is within primary indistinctness, beyond thought, and within the zone of mystery or of the metaproblematical. The consequence then is that whatever is certainty and clarity is not philosophy, and whatever is philosophy is doubt and insoluble problem. This, however, is philosophical skepticism to which you add an immediate faith that is pure fideism. On the other hand, the *spontaneous* certainty of lived experience or of immediateness belongs to instinctive life and sentiment, and this must be highly regarded because, at times, it is more certain than the sophistic certainty that belongs to reason; yet, between recognizing the truth of this point and denying objectivity on the ground that it is all problem or a problematizing thing, there is a great deal of difference. If it were so, man would have a spontaneous certainty only a degree higher than that belonging to animal instinct. One is unable to understand what Being and man himself are for a Marcel who confronts us with his "refusal" and his complete devaluation of discursive knowledge. We are face to face with a pure phenomenology (that is very fine in its analysis of psychological life) unable to justify either itself or all the "mysteries" on which it is founded. To reduce everything to "mystery" is as abstract and nonexistential as to reduce everything to a "problem." Man is not only subjective feeling; indeed he is this thing, but also, intellect, reason, will and fullness of spirit. "Nous évoluons tous à tâtons entre les énigmes." That is true, but if everything remains an enigma, we stop there at an abstraction. Do we know everything through the immediate? Let us entrust ourselves to spontaneous impulse and to *intuition aveuglée*. However, how can we oppose another person like Jean Paul Sartre who, on the basis of this radical skepticism, goes through a diverse, existential experience? We cannot tell him that he is wrong or in *error* because we would have to demonstrate it, that is, we would have to objectivate, to "discourse," and to mediate the original immediateness. This means that we would have to include reason within the spiritual rhythms revealing being, and beside faith, hope, love and loyalty; reason, after all, was not given to us in order to degrade us (this could be, too, but it would be against reason itself) but in order that those feelings may be inserted within the objective order of a truth vivified by them at the same time that they, in turn, are enlightened by it. The renunciation of reflexive thought makes Marcel's being really "problematical"; one cannot say what it actually is. By exasperating the opposition running through the problematical, the objective and the existential, faith is no longer certainty (this objection also is directed at Wust), but is a pure "tension" characterizing an opposition that "chooses" and "leaps" in God because of anguish or "despair." However, it can "leap" even in the absurd of Sartre or in the Nothingness of Heidegger, in the Christian God, or in Jupiter, or in Buddha. Marcel's criticism against the objective and the problem can be assumed only as a polemical position, that is, as a corrective of the opposite, rationalistic tendency by which everything is to be transcribed (even God's mystery) in terms of rational clearness, wherein existence is made abstract and null; when it is assumed as a philosophical position, on the other hand, it becomes the negation of knowledge and even of faith if it is carried to its extreme.

The zone of the objective cannot be, in any way, identified with that of "having," with that of the spectacular, or that of external "seeing." Objectivating is an act of thought, which is interior life and zone of "being." In the *ego sum cogitans* there is the ego, as well as being, feeling, thinking, reasoning and willing—the whole man, body and soul. If the *ego sum* is assumed as a pure and immediate feeling, it becomes as much of an impoverishment of the *sum* in man as the pure *ego cogito* is. Marcel (and existentialism in general) sets the abstraction of the *ego sum* against the abstraction of the *ego cogito,* that is, they reject the level of pure thinking and replace it with that of pure and immediate existing, as if there could be an existence without thinking and a thought that did not belong to an *ego sum.* The *ego sum cogitans* eliminates the two abstractions by accepting the *sum* and the *cogito,* namely, it implies subjectivity in existing as well as objectivity in thinking, also interiorness and truth; more precisely, it implies an "objective interiorness" that is not only rationality but, above all, an intellectual intuition of being as "object" or idea founding the objectivity of reason. We cannot go beyond the immediateness of existential experience unless we take into account the initial objectivity found in the very concept of "existence." Otherwise, we remain as prisoners of concrete existence and outside of it though we think that we possess it. Marcel rejects mediation because he believes it to be extrinsic to existence and not intrinsic as it is in effect.

Thus, he is confronted with a dilemma: immediateness and mediation, ineffable and *objectifiable,* which are by him located far away from each other and are opposed to each other. The consequences are serious from both philosophical and religious points of view. Marcel finds himself agreeing with Barth that theodicy as such is sacrilegious and atheistic, also that God is pure existence without essence, and that there are no rational proofs concerning the existence of God, and so on. I am not going to remind Marcel that all these affirmations are condemned by the Church (I am not an ecclesiastical censor), but I remain perplexed by the possibility of harmonizing them with Catholic orthodoxy. It was rightly remarked that without a "mediating reflection" one cannot be a Catholic even in thought. To condemn the entire world of objectivation (which, after all, means the world as such, except the relations concerning *you* and *me*) means to have at least a leaning (against one's own intention) toward Lutheranism or Jansenism. He is not even like Pascal, who not only does not condemn reason at all, but writes an apologetics and holds as valid the proofs for the existence of God. The problem is not to oppose the two worlds of "being" and "having," or to condemn science, technology, reason, society, and so on; the problem is instead to see how the two worlds meet each other (that is, a problem of mediation), and how it is possible to attain an authentic objectivation (and not that of idealism, positivism, and the like) which is not abstraction, possession, slavery, and impoverishment of the immediate. However, this is possible only through objectivation itself, through reason, and not through the condemnation of reason. Marcel, instead, identifies the inhuman contemporary world with objectivation as such, and so he turns away from it. As soon as we come out of lived experience and mystery, the inevitable befalls us and we lose ourselves in desperation. It remains only to lock oneself up tight and stay in the little corner of the meta-problematical, whence one can send messages and invocations to the many "you's" and to Being so that we may be spared from falling into the "hell" of "philosophy" or of the "objective" (and does not all this remind us of the theses sustained by Orthodox-Lutheran theological existentialism?). Now the problem, I repeat, is another one: that of mediation that is not a solution into, but a distinction within unity— and so not a nullification but a reconquest of unity or original indistinction through mediation itself. However, Marcel's existentialism lacks the element of an objective interior truth capable of effecting the mediation without "exteriorization," that is, it lacks the philosophical moment within existential experience, so that it becomes exhausted within the mystical moment of the immediate or of the ineffable.

It seems to us that Marcel is unaware of the fact that, by exasperatingly confronting the metaproblematical and the problematical, he ascribes the whole "tension" to the problem, to the extent of making uncertain the strength and positivity in both metaproblematical and faith itself. If I must remain outside of the problematical and objective thought in order not to miss the original indistinction (immediate unity), it is clear that I do not solve the enormous problem represented by the whole world of the problematical, which I leave still as a problem besetting and incumbent on me. The terms of the tension are, then, the problem (the sphere of the problematic as a problem) and mystery (the metaproblematical), within which I am secluded. Yet, the relationship is solved in a way entirely detrimental to mystery: as regards the zone of the problematical (of reason), the mystery is the nonproblem and thus the relationship is between a nonproblem (mystery) and problem; in this relationship the whole force of tension pushing me toward mystery is given by the despair produced by the zone of the problematical, that is, by the terror of the problem (of skepticism), which is so charged with full positivity while hope and mystery are only a refuge whose sense and attractiveness are given solely by the problem. In such relationship the metaproblematical receives all its positivity (and even its weight) from the "intensity" of the problem. In other words, the exasperation of the problematical (namely, of the doubting and objective thought) gives it an "intensity" superior to that of mystery, which almost receives its intensity from the other. Then, even the intensity and strength of faith are not given positively through love for a God who is entirely for the creature, but through the intensity of a desperation that is strong and infinite, since it is granted that the objective as such is despairing and negative to the point of suicide. Metaproblematical and faith in God, also God Himself, are unimportant in this position: I love God and believe in Him intensely in order to escape desperation. At that point the best part is played by subjectivity (intensity of hope and despair, problem and mystery) and not by Being, by God. All this means believing and philosophizing within the terms of the problem of perdition or salvation. Is there in it trust in God or a desperate trust in my salvation?

In this lies the mortal error of theological and theistic existentialism: it devaluates reason and objective thought, and also denies an essence in God and man; it reduces man to negativity, rejects all mediation and devaluates history and society; in short, its thinking, up to this point, more or less is similar to that of atheistic existentialism. Then it adds: ". . . but God exists; I believe in Him because of pure faith and *in order to save myself* from skepticism and all previous denials. In this way everything makes sense; the negative becomes positive either through grace or invocation." But it is not so; it is not so at all. If everything is negative, one cannot arrive at God—not even through faith. One cannot say that everything is absurd; but, if we have faith and believe in God, everything becomes comprehensible, since, in this case, only an absurd faith can emerge from the absurd, and God Himself can only be conceived as an absurd in the same way as He is conceived by atheistic existentialism which, being more coherent, denies his existence. In order to arrive at God we must, against existentialism, reconstruct the positivity of man (by giving him an essence) and the value of existence, and also of thought, reason and objectivity. Faith will help, but only on this positive foundation. After all, existentialism and all modern thought have not been in vain! To repeat, we must restore the positivity of man and of reason, the objectivity and meaning of existence, and these values can no longer be the same as those propounded by abstract rationalism. On the contrary, they will be able to bear any criticism only if they satisfy the exigencies whence a radical criticism had arisen against them.

Using Berdyaev's expression apropos of Marxism, we may say that Sartre symbolizes the denunciation of the "lie found in great ideas" as well as the denunciation of the game played "by French professors" at the end of the nineteenth century (one should move the beginning back at least to the end of the eighteenth century and extend the discussion in such a way as to include other countries). These people thought they could produce Copernican revolutions, have the State or History play the part of God, change the world through a class-struggle, and turn man upside down in order that the ballast of his spiritual ideals would fall out of his pockets. In this way they would have man cast out of his consciousness and thrust into the unconscious; the sacred would be secularized, the spirit materialized, everything *historicized*, being dissolved; and they could shout that God is dead, and so on. Then, with every negation they would repeatedly say that man was attaining more and more his autonomy, his critical maturity, his happiness, his freedom, and his most profound truth! Sartre causes all these people, who are as rash in their denials as they are timid and hypocritical in their refusal to draw the legitimate consequences from their negations, to take notice of their absurdity in talking about morality, values (whether they are economic or moral), progress, well-ordained society (of *un monde policé*), human dignity and many other noble things, because once being is denied there is no substitute. In fact, once truth is *historicized*, it no longer exists; once God is denied, there are no longer any obligations, prescriptions, rights and duties that obtain: since there is not even the human in man but only the animal, for man then is wholly gratuitous matter, like a worm or a stump. To think that values can exist *tout de même*, after saying that *Dieu n'existe pas*, is an illusion. Existentialism, on the other hand, believes that it is *trés gênant*, Sartre continues, and that God does not exist, "because every possibility of finding values in an intelligible heaven disappears with Him," just as disappears the possibility of having a good *a priori*. Once God has disappeared, there is no place where it is written that the good should exist, that we must be honest, and so on, "because we are on a level where there are only men." "Everything is allowed if God does not exist," in the words of Dostoyevsky's character, Ivan Karamazov. And Sartre comments: "This is the starting point for existentialism. In fact, everything is permitted if God does not exist and, consequently, man is *délaissé* because he finds no possibility to cling to, either within or without himself. . . . If God does not exist, we are not faced with values or orders legitimating our behavior. Thus, neither behind us nor ahead of us have we justifications or excuses in the bright domain of values. We are alone, without excuses."

This position held by Sartre must be considered from several points of view. With respect to modern historicist-immanentist thought (negation of being and of God), it has the undeniable merit (which is, after all, common to other thinkers whether existentialists or not, though Sartre goes to its root) of arriving at the extreme consequences drawn from the blind alley represented by a man who starts from himself and returns to himself. Moreover, it has the merit of decolorizing and emptying all the myths of absolute humanism (including the Marxist one), to the extent that at present one can say that man has neither a nature nor a given essence and that God is absurd, as Sartre himself maintains. However, one can no longer be "enthusiastic" about these "discoveries," because it can no longer be said that they imply a more critical and more valid foundation for man and for spiritual values, and so forth; nor can one go looking for diversions and expedients with a view to giving existence some positive meaning, as happens with some existentialists who do replace the old lies with new lies regarding the high ideals, while using a dogmatism that is less pardonable and more naive than that used in the past and also in our own times by the deifiers of man and of worldliness. In this sense Sartre's criticism against immanentism is the most explicit, the most radical and brutal of all. Yet, precisely because it is such, it is only a negative polemic; the presuppositions and consequences of immanentism and of absolute humanism are pushed to the extreme by Sartre; however, he allows himself to miss whatever there is that is positive and recoverable in immanentism itself as if in obedience to a drive toward the total destruction of that conception of life he himself shares. Consequently, one must not be so naive as to accept Sartre as simply an immanentist who dissolves immanentism and atheistic humanism, so that with a stroke of the pen we can blot out modern thought and Sartre himself and happily return to the past. This limitation in Sartre's criticism against the "professors" who believe that, following God's denial, everything would remain the same as and better than before, becomes a more serious limitation if considered in relation to Sartre's own philosophy. This is the reason: Sartre dogmatically accepts and ratifies historicist, materialistic and atheistic immanentism; he accepts Hegel's dialectic, Husserl's phenomenological method, Kierkegaard's Protestant man who is annihilated by sin (like the man of the Jansenists), the "man-matter" of Feuerbach, Marx and Freud, and being as "mundanity" of Heidegger, and he says that all of them are right; then he says of Hegel that his dialectical antinomies are without synthesis; he says of Husserl that since there is nothing to solve contradictions, these must be left there and we can only describe them; he says to dialectical materialism that social progress and earthly paradise are myths; and he says to Heidegger that his ontology of being as being-in-the-world is an ontology of the body because supremacy pertains to the compact and massive "thing" before which we feel ourselves *n'être rien*. Consequently, Sartre's criticism proceeds from dogmatic presuppositions; or, rather, his position is a critical furtherance of atheistic immanentism dogmatically accepted, however; or, even better, his is a critical (negative) position that doubts everything pertinent to atheistic or materialistic immanentism except immanentism itself. Atheistic or materialistic immanentism says: God does not exist, so we must get Him out of those hard-headed or immature people who continue to believe in Him; without Him (and more than that, precisely because He does not exist) things are going better than ever and man can *make himself* this or that. Sartre replies to all that: Yes, indeed; God does not exist and on the part of man it is absurd and useless to try to make himself a God; and, then, everything is permitted; everything is absurdity and gratuitousness, massive and thick matter, and man *makes himself* this thing and that thing, but now and always he is nothing, because nothing is serious in life. However, what is then truly gratuitous and nonserious is exactly Sartre's position, since he "critically" takes upon himself immanentism in its consequences, making them coherent with their premises, demonstrating how secular ethics, secular freedom, secular progress, and the like are nothing but mythology, and how from those premises the consequence is an all-material man with neither spirit nor humanity. And then, after the "criticism" of those consequences, Sartre maintains the premises "dogmatically" firm, and out of what constitutes the "ruin" of a philosophy and the dissolution of a principle, he makes the "ruin" of being as such, as well as the dissolution of man and concludes: "This is man," this is existence." This amounts to saying that he assumes the crisis of immanentism as the "crisis" of existence, as if the former constituted the latter, and as if the latter were resolved into the former, so that existence, man, and philosophy as such are fracture, rupture, and nothingness. In this way, the destroyer of all myths jealously keeps alive the myth that has generated all the others. Sartre, therefore, dissolves the noncritical, positive consequences from immanentism, while (with total noncriticism) keeping immanentism alive in all its absolute negativity, so that he identifies this negativity with the world in its totality without a shadow of the remotest critical advancement. Thus, Sartre is not the end of immanentism; he is its most rigorous and coherent affirmation, but entirely gratuitous with respect to premises and consequences. One could state that he is an immanentist and an atheist precisely because this doctrine leads to negative conclusions. He is like someone who—having denied existence and things of any value to the point that he does not know what to do with his own life—is not in search of a philosophy to guide him and free him from such a state of mind, but, rather, in search of one that is apt to justify and sanction him. Heidegger was (and with good reason) his favorite philosopher, for he is the thinker whose principles, if carried to their conclusion, could lead to the same conclusions arrived at by Sartre.

Even when Sartre is a skeptic and an atheist, he can also be regarded as a moralist to be inserted in the tradition of French moralism inspired by Jansenism.

As a moralist Sartre does not believe in "good actions," for he holds that virtues are the alibi for vices, and that men preach them without practicing them. His is naturally an absurd moralism, in that he denies not only morality but also virtues and moral principles; once these are denied, moralism itself ceases, and, everything being negative, it no longer makes any sense to reproach men for failing to practice the virtues. In fact, Sartre is not complaining at all, and he neither condemns nor does he absolve—he observes and describes. However, at this point vice itself ceases to be such and leaves us almost indifferent: garbage makes an impression when it is in a parlor but not when it is in the incinerator.

Sartre's man is neither attractive nor repellent; he just remains there and we do not know what he is; he has no drama, as he is a shapeless mass that wrinkles his skin, moves a limb, curls himself up or stretches. And one cannot know what his man is, or whether or not he wishes to do what he is doing for he is not even an experience of vice and of nonvalues since he is outside of the human level; and his words are meaningless, empty like pumpkins in which one can put anything, at pleasure, as it does not make any difference whatsoever—this thing or that thing makes no difference, since everything is absurd. With Sartre, existentialism ceases to be an existential experience and it destroys itself while it reveals its nothingness of human consistency. This is Sartre's greatest limitation as a writer and as a philosopher: a writer who is not an artist, an arguer but not a philosopher, and an ἐριστιχόσ, but not a dialectician. Everything seems to be written coldly, particularly *Being and Nothingness*, a skillful but not meditated work, one that is technical but not scientific, postulated but not deduced—a work in which innumerable identifications and "nullifications" are often a mere play on words or superficial inferences, that only to mediocre or hasty or unprepared readers may seem like profound thoughts. Sartre's philosophy, like some of his characters, is as light as a straw; and it is empty, though well "ballasted," just to give itself "weight," with sophisms and plays on words, that are undoubtedly executed with the skill of a juggler and, hence, with elegance and facility —good gifts to ensure success.

Sartre is a writer who lacks in whatever he writes the sense of responsibility (there is nothing serious, as he himself says) just as responsibility is lacking in his characters; he has nullified freedom in the absurd, and so he has nullified responsibility. No one, for Sartre, is responsible for anything either toward himself, society or God; the self is nothingness (matter), society is hell, and God is the absurd. *Everything is ballast,* good only for filling that emptiness which is existence or freedom to which we are condemned. However, in all this hell of nothingness and absurdity there is still an element worth being brought to light.

The "In-for-the-other" as "hell," about which Sartre speaks, represents society as possession, greediness, a sway over and in the world; it is a society whose structure is the "economic" and the "material." Sartre is a socialist and it seems that he likes to have communists consider him (or such was his desire some time ago) one of theirs. Indeed, he is one of them since many of them are common to him, Feuerbach and Marx (Sartre's "consciousness" belongs to the body, as for Feuerbach, and I could give other examples); but he is one of them without the myth of Marxism, that is, he does not believe that the society which would possess and dominate the world represents an earthly paradise, the authenticity of humanity in man, and the fullness of his positivity. He is a

Marxist who calls Marxist society a "hell," a Marxist by necessity, I would say, because the nihilism of his philosophy and his gloomy and absurd moralism prevent him from conceiving a better humanity or entertaining a less radically negative opinion about man. Even for Sartre, as for Feuerbach and Marx, man thinks of God because he projects beyond himself the same ideal that he himself wishes to be, that is, a God. The *en-soi-pour-soi*, Sartre writes, is *l'idéal qu'on peut nommer Dieu.* Marxism, however, believes that man will be able to attain such an ideal on the day when—through social revolution, rational conquest of the world, and homogeneous society—he will be freed from the need of need. Sartre, on the other hand, has no illusions: this is the ideal, but God is absurd, and man will never realize *l'en-soi-pour-soi;* and since this is his fundamental passion, man is a *useless passion.* All this amounts to saying that the new man of Marxism is a useless passion. Indeed, in these days burning with such a passion it is highly significant to have an atheist call it useless.

Should Sartre's affirmations be confuted? It would be an undertaking as easy as it would be useless. His negations can be made to stand up with an ease far greater than that met by Sartre to align them. Sartre's interest is negative, not positive: reduction to its consequence of a philosophical position, such as that of immanentism and historicism, which deny being and God; and a reduction to its consequence of existentialism itself. In this respect, Sartre proves how useless it would be to attach any positive meaning to existentialism (and he has thereby excused us from speaking about Italian existentialism) and to existence as existentialism conceives it. Now, since existentialism defines itself not as a philosophy of existence in a generic sense, but through its particular mode of defining existence, Sartre proves that the existence of existentialism is pure negativity. Indeed, even this has its importance, although it is negative.

We come to the following conclusion: the world (and, in the first place, human thought, which is the sense of the world) stands on an accented vowel—*è* (is); suppress it and we shall have the senseless world of Heidegger or Sartre, of Chestov or Barth, the world of the περί μή ὄντος of Gorgias without even the charm of the "persuasion" played for Helen of Troy by the flute of the shepherd Paris.

VI

IDEALISM AND
ITS DEVELOPMENTS

---

1. ANGLO-AMERICAN IDEALISM

A. Neo-Hegelians at the End of the Nineteenth Century and Other Idealists

Around 1870, as already mentioned, there was in England an idealistic movement inspired by Kant and Hegel (and linked with the "Hegelian right wing" and its pantheistic theologism), that reacted against the prevailing tendencies coming from empiricism and utilitarianism. Its date of birth can be identified with *Hegel's Secret* (London, 1865) by Stirling; and the "metaphysics of the Absolute" represents the common denominator or meeting-point in the otherwise diverse perspectives of Green, Bradley, McTaggart, Royce, and so on, thinkers who are not within the chronological limits of our exposition. However, we are going to mention them briefly in order to better understand the developments among their followers, as well as the anti-idealistic reaction from the beginning of our century up to date, and also in order to realize how idealism and neorealism have their points of contact in spite of their mutual opposition.

J. H. STIRLING (1820-1909) and T. HILL GREEN (1836-1882) represent the phase of idealistic absolute monism as opposed to materialistic monism: each perception and each particular relation, everything, must be related to "total Consciousness," to the "unique Subject," and to the Whole that is in every single thing as every single thing is in it—"the

One is many and the many, one." This metaphysics of the Absolute soon arouses, as we have just said, the "pluralist" and "pragmatist" reactions, which must be taken into account by the same idealism, since the latter subsequently is compelled to characterize itself as an effort to salvage the "concrete" within its monistic metaphysics. Such an exigency is right but is impossible to satisfy within a metaphysics of the Absolute such as Hegel's. Hence a consequence I would call paradoxical: on the one hand, the Neo-Hegelians lack an intrinsic logical coherence as well as a critical and thorough analysis of their own position; on the other, in their attempt to justify the "concrete" in spite of their monistic system, they do not lack motivations and points which are the vital part of their thought, making it alive and, in some respects, giving it a present-day value. In saying this we are thinking, above all, of the Englishman F. H. BRADLEY (1846-1924), the greatest exponent of English idealism, and of the North American J. ROYCE (1855-1916).

According to Bradley (*Appearance and Reality*, New York, 1902), by reducing things to "external" relations and to a spatial explanation, science misses their concreteness which is to be found, instead, in their internal relations, none of which is absolute, however; but all are intelligible through "integral experience," wherein everything is harmoniously contained as well as identified with the very life of the Absolute. Within this position Bradley is critically assuming both Kant's transcendentalism and Hegel's panlogism. He clearly realizes that the Kantian "universe of relations" (representing transcendentality itself) cannot define the totality of the real except in the sense of the phenomenal totality and so transcendentality, thus understood, is limited to the relative which relates to the Absolute (it builds, we say, a science but not a metaphysics of the real). It is from this point, in fact, that the question of transcendental idealism comes into being, first with Fichte and then developed and systematized by Hegel. Bradley makes this position his own and yet for him the Absolute is neither posited *a priori* nor dialectically deduced; this is his departing point from Hegelian monism and also the point at which he vindicates the exigency of the concrete, bringing him closer to pragmatism and pluralism. Thus, on the one hand, in the name of idealism Bradley fights against hedonistic ethics (*Ethical Studies*, Oxford, 1927), psychological associationism (*The Principles of Logic*, London, 1883), and naturalistic metaphysics but, on the other hand, in his work *Appearance and reality* (quoted above) he breaks away from Hegelian panlogism through the criticism of the concept of relation that, being reduced to a sham, ceases being a mediator between what is "apparent" (finite) and what is "real" (infinite). For him the Absolute is not only something produced through concrete experience (and this is not so different from the Hegelian concept of "historicity" of Reason), but even

317

individual experience is so integral as to represent the life of the Absolute itself. In reality, since for Bradley contradictions are not reconciled through a logical mediation as in Hegel, he makes the fullness of experience coincide with a moment beyond reflective thought, that is, with an immediate intuition of the Absolute, wherein mediate knowledge is only a degree of approximation, Neoplatonically surpassed and nullified within the mystic or intuitive moment. The inadequate unity of knowledge is a symbolic "appearance" of the totality obscurely present in every single appearance. In other words, differences and relations presuppose a totality within which they are comprised and by which the foundation of experience is constituted. Once the contradictory as appearance is rejected, we make use of an absolute criterion: "Ultimate reality is such as not to contradict itself." The Absolute is a harmonic system of experience, but philosophy cannot grasp it because every human experience is imperfect. However, if everything is appearance, the Absolute is its own appearance.

Scholarly ELLIS McTAGGART (1866-1925), the author of two volumes on Hegelian dialectic and cosmology, thought he would solve the problem by transferring pluralism into the absolute Spirit mythologically understood as a "society of individual souls." Each of these souls is a single, conscious, and immortal individual among whom God is the most complete Ego, a sort of Jupiter in the midst of many gods making up a kind of Olympus less quarrelsome than the Homeric one. Instead, none of these gods is omnipotent and each realizes his fullness within this "association," which respects their individuality. In short, we have a "celestial" democracy made up of gods whose leader is not a despotic one. Each one of them corresponds to a mode of harmonization that is to be realized through the experience of individual human subjects, for whom dialectic is necessary since they reconstruct the Absolute within time. Such a theological pluralism is very close to that of James.

The problem of the individual's concreteness is strongly felt by Royce, who tries to rescue it from its being nullified in absolute Consciousness; he is, at the same time, convinced that the individual is realized only by being incorporated in it. In order to demonstrate the inconsistency affecting the "external" relations, Bradley had, above all, availed himself of the observation that these relations imply a necessary process to infinity; Royce, on the other hand, makes the infinite process be a positive character of the Absolute. Under the influence of pragmatism, he identifies (*The World and the Individual*, New York, 1901) the truth of an idea not with the latter's correspondence with an objective entity ("extrinsic significance") but with its "intrinsic significance," that is, with the end it proposes to carry out. The problem of reality, then, is posited as a problem of relationship between its two significances. After rejecting the "mystical" and "realistic" solutions as well as that which pertains to "critical rationalism," Royce expounds his own solution. The latter consists in bringing the idea's extrinsic significance back to its intrinsic significance, since the idea conforms only to an object to which it wishes to conform. The idea seeks its own object; it contains a purpose determined through a "decision" that eliminates other possibilities in order that one alone be "defined." Thus, reality is the complete and explicit determination of the intrinsic meaning or purpose in the idea. The determination process is a process of *individuation*, wherein reality is individual and as irreplaceable as that which fully satisfies its purpose; that is, it is a whole, or a world unitarily and individually realized as a totality of meanings. Consequently, the end of an idea is not to be considered in itself but relatively to the absolute end of which it is a moment. Every act by our will is only a fragment of the infinite Will, which in its actual present includes the whole process of time. All times are completed and preserved within the all-inclusive Consciousness or God, together with all truths and individual, finite intellects. Eternity is the inclusion of the infinite series of time within the eternal present; with its mistakes, guilts, and sorrows our life is the carrying out through us of God's eternal perfection. The infinite is a "self-representative system"; although remaining as an individual, in itself it contains, as its own parts, an infinity of individuals made after its own image and likeness.

God's world is ours also, and each single individual's. "A cathedral may appear unique and, yet, its bricks, arches, and sculptures may also be unique. In the universe, likewise, if the whole is an expression of the absolute and unique Will, each fragment of life holds its unique place within divine life." In all of Royce's writings (besides *The World and the Individual* [quoted above], the fundamental ones are *The Problem of Christianity*, New York, 1913; *The Philosophy of Loyalty*, New York, 1936; *The Hope of the Great Community*, New York, 1916), there is a contradictory position that is expressed in two formulas: "only the Absolute is" and "each individual is unique" in the Absolute. Royce's solution is illusory, however. In fact, individuals are not separated but they "belong to a total Thought which in itself contains them all . . . concretely, not in a potential or ideal manner." Each individual consciousness realizes to a maximum its own ideas, which, however, are to be fully carried out only within absolute Thought. Everything is an expression of the divine Logos living in the multiplicity of concrete experience. On the other hand, all experiences attain their perfection through their victorious struggle against finiteness; that is, they rise to the concrete unity of the Absolute.

In his works following *The World and the Individual* (already quoted), Royce takes up again Peirce's "interpretation" theory as a relationship affecting three terms: the interpreter, the thing being interpreted, and the person for whom the interpretation is made. The world is a complex of *signs* to be interpreted, and that interpretation is true which establishes a community among those three terms in the relation. The soul of Christianity, for Royce, is the idea of "religious community," and Christian love is *loyalty* to the same community, which we must love as a person. The Church is the relationship between the unique absolute individual and the single ones constituting it. For him *loyalty* also is a criterion of morality. In fact, that man is moral who stays loyal to a task or mission freely chosen and established in concert with other individuals in the community.

BORDEN P. BOWNE (1847-1910) belongs to the same age as Royce; he was a disciple of Lotze and a professor at Boston. A critic of Spencer and the chief exponent of the school of American "personalism," Bowne (whose writings—*Metaphysics*, New York, 1882; *Philosophy of Theism*, New York, 1887; *Personalism*, Boston, New York, 1908—were widely known even in Latin America) formulates his own conception of the ego both in opposition to the empiristic psychology of human faculties and through a criticism of Kantian thought. His "transcendental empiricism," as he himself called his own theory, reduces all reality to conscious experience. Every real thing is an ego or an idea pertaining to the ego, which is dynamic and identical with itself; and more than that, the ego's self-identity is produced by its own dynamism. According to transcendental empiricism, intelligence cannot be studied through categories, but the latter can be studied through the former, for intelligence itself is a fundamental phenomenon explaining everything except understanding itself. Therefore, the person, or self, which is the ultimate datum of experience, is self-consciousness, and the source of categories or norms. Even the Infinite Being or God is a person ("personalistic theism") and this is proven by the fact that the universe is intelligible—the fact that we do not understand the universe with our thought points out that it has been founded on thought.

More than with his writings, JAMES EDWIN CREIGHTON (1861-1924), exerted his strong influence with his teaching; with the editing of *The Philsophical Review* and of the *Sage School* at Cornell University as well as president of the American Philosophical Association. His objective-speculative idealism (expounded in the posthumous, *Studies in Speculative Philosophy*, New York, 1925) is opposed to "atomistic realism" within empiricist tradition, against which Creighton sustains that existence and value are inseparable, and that whatever exists is part of a system of relations and values. Subject and object are correlative terms: there are no objects without a subject (that is, without a process of interpretations in terms of ideas and universal relations), and there is no real subject without real objects. This relationship with other subjects constitutes our experience, and so the exigencies of relational life are exigencies of social life. For Creighton, as for almost all American thinkers, the nature of thought is social in the sense that our thoughts can be said to be true only after they have been checked and weighed by a more complete experience than that of the individual.

As one can see, between empiricism and pragmatism, on the one hand, and on the other, that idealism which also accepts some naturalistic elements, there are obvious likenesses. Moreover, on account of the coming into being and prevalence of other currents, Neo-Hegelianism is already weakening and is gradually moving toward radical transformations both in England and North America.

B. Developments in English Idealism: B. Bosanquet, W. R. Sorley, J. S. Mackenzie, J. B. Baillie, and R. G. Collingwood

BERNARD BOSANQUET (1848-1923), for a few years a professor at St. Andrews, is linked up with Bradley's idealism. Besides Bradley's influence he strongly felt that of Plato and Hegel as well as that of Lotze whom he translated into English. In the last years of his life he came in contact with the Italian Neo-Hegelianism of Croce and Gentile and also sustained a polite polemic with Carlini. Having a mind open to manifold interests, Bosanquet sympathizes with many intellectual movements and he is attracted by almost all speculative problems: logical and aesthetical ones (*A History of Aesthetics,* New York, 1934); moral problems (*The Principle of Individuality and Value,* London, 1912; *The Value and Destiny of the Individual,* 1913); political-social ones (*Aspects of the Social Problem* [by various authors; ed. by B. Bosanquet], London, New York, 1895; *The Philosophical Theory of the State,* London, 1920), as well as religious problems. Like the other English idealists, Bosanquet is interested in the problem of the individual in relation to the Absolute. More than Hegelian, his idealism is characterized by a Hegelian origin. As he himself writes, Plato was a revelation to him: a "dualism" in this world and in the "other," but a unity within duality, immanence together with transcendence on the part of the Absolute. For Plato, according to Bosanquet, the "other world" is not far away, but it is "here" and "now" —it lives in our experience. Plato is confirmed by Hegel, who "told us that the object of philosophy is never abstract or far away, but always something concrete and present in the truest sense of the word." [1] In short, for Bosanquet, the dualism between *this* and the *other* world must

[1] J. H. Muirhead, ed., *Contemporary British Philosophy* (New York, 1924). For some English philosophers I also refer to this work in which each thinker expresses his own thought.

not be understood as separation of the two worlds, but as a duality involving unity, and as a transcendence of the *other* with respect to *this one* although both are mutually related as well as present in one another. Aesthetical experience expresses this transcendent presence of the Absolute: "It gives us a present world, a world that is really one with that in which we live, and one which, even if it has been reproduced, is immediately the truest and most profound self-revelation of it." Universal and particular, freedom and necessity, as well as spiritual and natural are unified within art. Understood in this way, art does not differ much from religion—both experiences show reality as a concrete unity and an overcoming of abstract antitheses. Also moral experience is a synthesis though different from the religious one. Morality is the acknowledgment of what "ought to be" in relation to an individual will; in essence religion "consists in a unity of will and faith with a supreme real perfection within which finite imperfection—no matter how effective—is bound to be transcended and surpassed."

All such forms of experience converge into thought as a determinant of reality as well as into logic as a theory of thought itself. Bosanquet is against "pure thought," "pure logic," and against the "purely logical." "Thought always is an affirmation of reality posited through the process of particular spirits. Its character is closely related to that of reality. If one asked, then, what reality is, ultimately only this could be answered: that it is the Whole on which thought always seeks to affirm itself. Moreover, if one asked what thought is, ultimately only this could be answered: the central function of thought consists in affirming that its particular world belongs to the real universe. A thought having nothing to do with what is given, and building no order, is a *res nihili*." Thought is self-revelation of reality. Not an abstract "pure logic" resting on peculiar principles, but a logic giving a "clear perception of the mode wherein natures making up the universe, through their connection and cooperation, regulate and mould the assertions making up our thought." Logical adherence to a principle means its application, that is, "an appreciation of it in all its consequences as that which, if considered in an adequate way, necessarily attains some individual, living reality from its own application. The universal, which is the very life and spirit of logic, does not signify a general predicate, but the plastic unity of a comprehensive system." The opposition between system and sentiment is "foolish." In fact, "the emotional power—which absorbs or carries away, and actually pertains to great ideas, great characters, and great works of art—is measured by the depth and extent of the roots and sources which those ideas have in reality, which, in turn, is measured by their logical power—that is, the power to develop and sustain a coherence with the Whole."

In genuine logic the Whole operates as a criterion. "Implied in all the modes of experience which attract us in any manner, the Whole is now studied in its typical manifestations wherein the central essence is represented by the idea-system, or spirit of the universal concrete—in other words, in the spirit of individuality." The same thing can be said with respect to freedom (social and moral freedom) whose condition (and criterion) is given by its participation in the Whole: "Only by uniting itself to the Whole, can finite spirit become in it what it ought to be." Being free means knowing the good as well as getting accustomed to practicing it; it means "an identification of goodness with a moulded and educated character that enthusiastically aims at realizing the ideal Ego, which is the Whole."

Experience, then, as Bosanquet says, is "revelation" of the Whole, of the world of values, which, however, experience is never able to understand by itself since it is impossible to solve "all contradictions that are incompatible with the self-revelation of the universe through particular beings." For Bosanquet, on the other hand, there is no doubt that levels of life and points of view, though partial, are correlative with levels of thought, "and that there are foundations and evident conjectures in favor of the idea that ultimately the 'Whole' means more than that which is manifested of it in imperfect souls or in their consciousness." The totality of the universe is being within which reality and value coincide. When we see that a particular experience is realized in such a way as to constitute the best one within its genus (religion and art represent, for instance, the best experience of life), we say that we find "the real thing" —that is, that it concentrates in itself strength and value, and that it surpasses all the rest. It possesses what we really want, and is "that which satisfies." In the "real thing we experience the positive quality of the Absolute" and "the intrinsic connection between reality and value becomes transparent to us." To those who try to deny it, the Absolute says in its defense: "I am all there is, the whole essence and value. Nothing can be willed outside of me; and any other thing whatever can be thought only abstractly outside of me." Yet, no "real thing," no experience of ours, no matter how perfect, is ever able to become adequate to or express the Absolute, which, thus transcends, while being immanent. The Absolute is immanent in the relative, which, however, never loses its character of finiteness. Even by admitting the individual wills (by whose cooperation the social value comes into being), ultimately Bosanquet does not recognize a true individuality in finite persons, so that for him, as for Bradley, the Absolute alone is an individual.

A strong, personalistic tendency and a conception of reality representing a teleological order (freedom is realization of the supreme values of life), characterize the idealism of WILLIAM R. SORLEY (1855-1935). A professor at Cambridge University, he sought to probe the problems of ethics in all his writings from the *On the Ethics of Naturalism* (Edinburgh, London, 1885) to *Moral Value and the Idea of God* (Cambridge [Eng.], 1918); and he is still connected with McTaggart's idealism. For Sorley, values belong to our experience although it is not possible to contain them within the conceptual schemes which are used by science to describe natural phenomena. Science can even ignore them; yet, a total theory on reality has the obligation to know them. Sorley argues with those holding values and value-judgments to be subjective, in a sense in which things and the perception of them are not so. To say that value is subjective, is to admit "that value depends on the subject experiencing it, in a way in which the objective world, instead, does not depend on it." Certainly, experience, intuition, and sentiment are subjective, but that does not imply that value is such. We must distinguish between origin of the judgment, possibly founded on the subject's affective or appetitive experience, and criterion on which the judgment is based—this being something surpassing the limits of individual consciousness. I who wish, affirm, by judging, that what I wish is beautiful, good, and so on; value, therefore, is not purely subjective. Values, says Sorley with Scheler, presuppose the persons who are the "carriers" of them: "Nothing has value *per se*, except for the person or the person's state." This is valid for the superior values (Goodness, Beauty, and Truth); the others are instrumental.

In the first place, value is objective on account of the very reason for which it is generally held to be subjective, that is, because value is a characteristic of the person, in the sense that it is something the individual "considers as belonging to personal life both in itself and with respect to others. Now, for Sorley, persons belong to the objective order or order of reality, and they are carriers of values which are manifested through them. The person is something positive science may look upon indifferently, but not philosophy, which cannot ignore individuality and the conscious persons. In this sense it can be stated, therefore, that value is something objective. A good man's goodness is as much objective as the man himself."

Values are objective also in another sense. Both natural laws and values are never realized completely but only to a certain extent. Indeed, it is precisely in the nature of value not to be ever fully realized in the fact. In fact, the imperative character on the part of duty is rightly so, precisely because what ought to be is not so, as yet. However, while natural law describes factual events, moral law does not pretend to describe man's factual behavior. Thus nature's laws and moral laws, equally objective (though realized within certain limits), differ through their relationship with the actual data of experience. Lastly, values are objective in the sense that they pertain to the system of reality which philosophy has the duty to understand, in that they are a factor and an aspect of it, simultaneously.

On the basis of the objectivity of values, reality presents itself as distinct according to two levels: the domain of things governed by the mere causal process and the domain of values. Yet, such a distinction serves only as a practical convenience. On the other hand, a theory of reality must embrace both orders (causal and moral) and find the link joining them. To the question: "How is it possible to conceive a world in which causal and moral orders are equally valid?" we reply that it is necessary to have a synthesis embracing the "whole" of reality, that is, a "synopsis," a "vision" rather than a "discourse." To philosophy "the two orders must appear as correlative aspects of a sole reality, and the capacity to solve such a problem is the criterion according to which philosophical systems are compared and judged."

Which theory of reality is able to justify both experience and the realization of values? Not naturalism, indeed, but idealism. The history of philosophy is acquainted with many kinds of idealism, of which two are fundamental: idealism advocating a unity of the real (truth conceived as an order of absolute or objective thought) and pluralistic idealism (reality as a plurality of centers of consciousness)—in short, monism and pluralism. Both are confronted with insurmountable difficulties summed up in the problem of the One and the many. "However, every difficulty disappears if the unity of the universe is conceived not as an impersonal order of 'bloodless categories' but as a Supreme Mind to which finite minds and their world owe their truth, and if the Supreme Mind, God, is conceived not simply as a Creator but as the essence and source of all values, in which He wants the free subjects to share. The visible world is an image of the Eternal but a temporal image, not a photograph. It is only in time and in the form of activity, made possible by time, that finite minds are able to attain those values of which they are potentially capable; and, if freedom is a value or something exalting other values, these can only be achieved through a slow and gradual process of errors and bewilderments in a world where the journey is painful and filled with torment." Theism alone, therefore, is able to set up a conception of reality capable of justifying the domain of values as well as that of facts. Sorley's theism, however, is an ambiguous one; it is more of a pantheism than a theism, so that the difficulties posited by the problem of the One and the many remain unsolved. Finality of nature and freedom of persons to whom values are intrinsic are the two postulates in Sorley's metaphysics. In order to guarantee the individuals' freedom this philosopher states that God has self-restricted his omnipotence.

J. S. MACKENZIE (1860-1935), in his *Elements of Constructive Phi-*

325

losophy (New York, 1918), develops an idealism which, though inspired by Hegel, is not Hegelian. He was first a disciple of the Hegelian E. Caird, and later professor at Cardiff University. In the last analysis Mackenzie maintains a moderate form of *critical realism*. In fact, he writes: objects do not exist in a region completely independent of consciousness, but are "in consciousness" in the sense that the subject perceives them without their being creations of the perceiving subject. Such a form of idealism is to be accepted "if it is true that none of us recognizes the existence of extramental conditions in knowing." Borrowing it from Meinong, Mackenzie makes his the concept of "intentionality"; that is, by moving toward an object, consciousness constitutes, within itself, an objective reality which "signifies the object" rather than being the object itself. The forms of intentionality are subjective and variable, and they need not assume a definitive and fixed form. This is confirmed by the fact that the "real" world, no matter how variable, varies according to well-defined modes that are communicable from subject to subject. On this rests the foundation of our conviction that the world is an ordained system.

However, do objects of experience really constitute a systematic order? Besides the problem whether or not such an order subsists, we "as rational beings cannot refrain from seeking in the world we perceive an intelligible order which, in its turn, cannot be conceived without granting the existence of an intelligence." The problem is not whether any universe whatever is able to subsist without the spirit, but, rather, whether a universe, like the one we know, can be substantially conceived without being related to self-conscious subjects. This conception of reality, which one can call indifferently "critical realism" or "critical idealism," is "a doctrine according to which extrasubjective reality must be interpreted on the basis of the spirit rather than on that of matter."

It is not exact to speak of degrees of reality; it is better to say that what appears is the appearance of a reality. Reality must be considered "as a systematic Whole, which cannot be rightly understood simply as one or simply as manifold, but only as a multiplicity in the unity." The concept of a unique substance is untenable; it is better to speak of "orders," of reciprocal relations among things, and of a "structure" of the universe. Moreover, the space-temporal system, as confirmed by Einstein's theory of relativity, is to be conceived as a limited system. "The acknowledgment of such a limitation seems to imply, on the other hand, that the universe is only a partial aspect of a wider Whole," which we call "Cosmos" in order to distinguish it from "our universe." The definition of "Cosmos" requires some research of a higher order, and it cannot prescind from the concept of value. In fact, in its perfect form, religion coincides with the veneration of what is considered the supreme value and it implies the conviction that the universe is a Cosmos, that is, a perfectly beautiful Whole. Mackenzie links this concept to the Platonic idea of the Demiurge. The Cosmos is created in the sense that every being is a creator and contributes to making it: "Within life every man makes God to an extent." Creation, indeed, but a "creation of creators" wherein the divinity comes rather at the end of this evolutive process, as Alexander says.

It is true that all the conceptions implied in the religious vision of the universe are to be held as hypotheses rather than as dogmas, "but if these hypotheses are the only ones capable of making intelligible our universe, each one of us is entitled to support them with a remarkable degree of conviction."

Two facets of thought must be distinguished in J. B. BAILLIE (1872-1940), who was a professor at Aberdeen University until 1924, and from then to his death Vice Chancellor of the University of Leeds. In the first phase of his speculation (The *Origin and Significance of Hegel's Logic,* New York, 1901), Baillie advocates an absolute idealism with some religious coloring, one having its origin in Hegel whom he translated. The experience of the First World War turns his meditation to the problem of man and his destiny, as well as to the problems of concrete existence, without taking into account the Hegelian presupposition concerning the universal rationality of the real. This second phase is represented by his *Studies in Human Nature* (London, 1921).

For Baillie there are some problems of capital importance: How can we reconcile the claim made by knowledge to the attainment of a universal and valid truth of the World with the fact that the human mind —and therefore knowledge—is subject to temporal becoming and has a history? How can we demonstrate that the numerous kinds of experience are expressed by one principle alone? How can it be explained that scientific and philosophical interpretation appears to be necessary, when, reality, once it is interpreted, does not reveal itself to be created by the results of our interpretation, nor connected with them? An answer to these problems can only be given through a general conception of the individual considered in his development.

Philosophy rises from a reflection on the following situation: "The human individual is single and he is conscious of being such; on the other hand, his relations with the world which he calls experiences are manifold and so diverse that, in some cases, they have no apparent relationship with one another. Philosophy tries to understand such a situation in which man finds himself; it could then be called almost an attempt at obtaining a unitary or full vision of man and his world."

The World before the individual is as real as the individual himself is. In experience, one is not mingled with the other—individual and World

327

subsist and coexist together. Thus, there is no reality "outside" of and "beyond" man and his world; the two terms "outside" and "beyond" can acquire an appropriate meaning only through the relations between man and the world. "Experience could then be defined as a process through which the individual discovers reality, or as a process wherein reality reveals itself or 'realizes itself' through the individual's own experience." In short, the entire human experience is an active and reciprocal relationship between a living individual and the surrounding World. Therefore, the fundamental aspects of experience are as follows: "singularity of the individual," and a gradual and experimental character as well as a "relative imperfection" even in the highest success of man.

Baillie really possesses a concrete and active conception of human experience which must be grasped in all its forms, each of which does not determine the other. In this way, logic does not determine practical action or perception. This is not to say that the process of the world is essentially logical, but rather that the process through which the reality of the world is discovered assumes a logical form. Individuality in such a case is neither illogical nor logical, it "is more than logical"; and "no logical process can exhaustively express its experience." The full consciousness in man's personality is developed when man enters, as a welcomed guest, among communicative souls.

There is a complex variety of modes by which man enters into relationship with the other beings constituting the world. Each mode is a form of communication with the world, from sense-exercise to intellectual activity, so that the individual does not find himself separated from the world itself. "When the intellectual process is full and complete, then he finds himself in his own world, more at home than he had been at any time prior to the undertaking of such a process; and this is so probably because thought establishes durable and universal relations with the world." However, a wider sense of individuality is gained by the individual in communication with his fellow-creatures, that is, in moral life. In every form of experience there is the presence of the same general character regarding experience itself—"a conscious distinction and a concrete relationship between a concrete individual and his world, a process of conscious relationship between some form in act and some part of the world."

In the diverse forms of relationship between individual and his world, one must note that: (1) each form of experience produces a different consciousness of reality; (2) in some forms more than others, the individual gains a greater affinity as well as a superior degree of confidence; (3) his individuality is fulfilled through diverse genera of experience.

Often with a keenness and finesse of analysis and always with enviable clearness, Baillie tests the numerous forms of experience (sensible, moral, scientific experience, and so forth), none of which succeeds in exhausting, in his totality, man and his world. Truth is a risky, experimental, and gradual conquest, always incomplete and never in its fullness. Hence the problematical and tragic nature of man's life. "Experience is a continuous process of attempts, experiments, and errors. This is one of the most remarkable and, in a certain sense, most tragic characteristics in the human individual's life on earth, for he is moving within a partially realized world, always bound to encounter, at each turning point, 'the obstinate doubtfulness of the sense of eternal things.' For this reason, he seldom loses the sense of his childish wonder so particularly manifest in the primary stages of his earthly career." Some forms of experience may have more success than others and be more certain than others, but in none of them is man able to avoid the danger of error, misery, and misfortune. He is trying to capture the fullness of his individuality, but he finds himself only in one degree of experience at a time. He, therefore, is led to place "the forms of experience on a scale of values so as to show that individuality is not exhausted within any part of experience but is rather realized more in one form than in another." The individual's greatest achievement is found in religion, which represents the highest form of human experience. "The consciousness of the individual's relationship with the transcendent inspires in him a sense of more durable stability, otherwise impossible to attain if he were conscious of being only one of the many other finite beings. Therefore, while in religion the individual transcends all other finite beings—he is defying the scoriae of finite things and their unceasing mutation—he does not transcend, however, his own finiteness and his bounds, thus remaining a finite individual in comparison with what is transcendent. Religious experience, like any other, then, is a process that, from beginning to end, realizes itself in conformity with the elements—energy, thought, and action—which make up one's individuality; and, as an experience in general, it is one of the gradual discoveries of the self as well as of the transcendent."

Baillie's position is very significant within contemporary English thought, not only because it represents the evolution (and I might say the crisis) in idealism, but also because it is at variance with prevailing neorealism. Against the latter Baillie holds that concepts have to maintain their character of being mental functions with respect to objects, and that it is not possible to put on the same level the knowing mind and things being known, in that the mind always transcends its object. The mind does not copy things because it always brings something new into reality; indeed, as we know, for Baillie the mind (that is, knowing) does not aim at discovering an objective world, but at realizing itself in its free individuality.

Overwhelmed by neorealism and other currents (that we shall treat later on) idealism had a momentary revival with REINHOLD F. A. HOERNLÉ (1880-1943) and R. G. COLLINGWOOD (1889-1943). First a professor at St. Andrew's and then at Capetown and Johannesburg, Hoernlé does not go beyond a form of eclecticism (such is in essence his "synoptical philosophy") with a prevalence of ideas drawn from Bosanquet (*Idealism as a Philosophy*, New York, 1927). Its application to the question of universals deserves mention, for these are considered in a Hegelian sense, as entities making up the structure of the evolution of reality as well as of the axiological evaluation ("Concerning Universals," in *Mind*, 1927).

A professor at Magdalen College at Oxford, Collingwood is the author, among other works, of the study *Speculum Mentis* (Oxford, 1924), which remains his best even after the posthumous publication of his two volumes: *The Idea of Nature* (Oxford, 1945) and *The Idea of History* (Oxford, 1946). Of all English idealists Collingwood is the only one to be under the direct influence of Italian Neo-Hegelianism and, precisely, of Croce's historicism. He accepts the Hegelian dialectic of opposites, but unlike the German philosopher, he distinguishes five moments in spiritual activity— art, religion, natural science, history, and philosophy. The dialectical passage from one form to the other is due to the fact that each of these moments, as a definition of the Absolute, reveals in itself an incompleteness to be filled by the higher grade.

For Collingwood, art is "imagination" in the sense of Croce's concept of "fantasy"; and it is the most elementary form of spiritual activity. However, thought, which is intrinsic to art, leads the latter to surpass itself. In fact, in the artist's consciousness there is an antithesis between art and criticism. Every artist is a critic, but, as an artist, he must forget that he is one. Art, therefore, gathers in itself two contradictory elements. Moreover, it claims to have a meaning and to achieve a goal; yet, it cannot reveal its meaning; indeed, as art, it is "a meaning without a meaning." To discover the meaning in art is to surpass art itself: "Art dies with the growth of knowledge." In short, the aesthetical moment is led from within to surpass itself.

Religion, too, is imagination but, unlike art, it affirms what it imagines. Religion, then, is the dialectical overcoming of art. It, too, carries within itself its antithesis between symbol and meaning, and this antithesis leads religion to surpass itself in science, which does not personify those abstractions, but shows them as they are. However, to acknowledge science as an affirmation of abstract concepts means transcending it already. The historical moment arises from the overcoming of the scientific moment; the historical one is a synthesis of universal and individual, that is, not the position of an abstract universal detached from the particular, which also is abstract, but a universal ascertained through the particular, and a particular gaining veracity through the universal. Even history cherishes in its bosom a killing snake: the residue of abstractness represented by the "fact" which the historian finds before himself as an object he must discover. The historian does not change the world; he discovers it, for the fact exists independently of the historian thinking of it. Philosophy alone overcomes the abstractness of the fact because the philosophical moment includes the fact and the consciousness of it.

According to Collingwood every theoretical moment of the spirit has a corresponding practical moment. Thus, the aesthetical moment has an action that is considered like a game; the religious moment has a morality that is founded on the "commandments," and is formalistic and conventional; the scientific moment has a utilitarian one; the historical, an individual morality; and the philosophical moment, an absolute ethics.

We do not think Collingwood's thought is very original, but it is significant; first, because under the influence of Croce's historicism, it represents a form of idealism that differs from Bradley's and that of the other thinkers within the same current of thought; and secondly, because at any rate it still is a reaction, however weak it may be, against prevailing realism.

We must remark, however, that just as English metaphysical idealism, including Bradley's, remains speculatively much inferior to that of Gentile, so also Collingwood's "historicist" idealism is only an echo (though one not devoid of a personal character of its own) of Croce's, of which it accepts even the purely historical character regarding metaphysics (*An Essay on Metaphysics,* Oxford, 1940).

C. Developments in North American Idealism

Notwithstanding the prevalence of neorealism, critical realism and, then, logical positivism, even after Royce's death (the latter's ideas influenced even the philosophy of his opponents), idealism is still today at odds with so-called naturalism—one of the secondary currents in North American thought. The dissension-point is to be found particularly in the mode of solving the problem of the essence of reality—naturalistic monism on the one hand and idealistic dualism on the other (value is autonomous before nature). However, under the pressure of criticism by naturalists, the most recent North American idealism, though maintaining its dualism, emphasizes, let us say, the historical aspect of value and gives more weight to (historical and natural) reality in which man realizes such value. Let us note at the start that North American idealism is far from the metaphysical maturity attained by European idealism—as, for instance, this was expressed by Lachelier and Hamelin in France, and Gentile in Italy. Moreover, it often indulges in forms of empirical idealism, which stand beside and occasionally coexist with other forms of Platonic idealism. Finally there are in it so many influences and adaptations that only one of its governing principles can be called idealistic in a generic way. This principle is: The universe constitutes an intelligible system or order immediately manifesting itself through the sensible datum, which, therefore, is only an indication (a sign, a symbol) of the objective reality of essences. Such an objectivity being granted, idealists consider themselves as true realists and charge those, who are realists, with nominalism. The same notion of "probability," they rightly remark, would be meaningless in a world without an order of intelligible relations.

ALFRED H. LLOYD (1864-1927), a University of Michigan professor, elaborates a "dynamic idealism" (*Dynamic Idealism*, Chicago, 1898) along the lines of evolutionism. Thought is a dynamic activity of adaptation between consciousness (which does not exist as consciousness in itself) and environment, which is its object. However, for Lloyd the object "is the same as the subject": there is identity between them. The ego is part of that totality represented by the nonego, and so its nature is social. The universe for Lloyd is a combination of changeable relations, both as totality and as parts of that whole. Each thing is a totality as a single relational system, and it is a relational part of another system or other systems. The totality of dynamic relations constitutes the significance as well as the reality of each thing. Thus, as a world of changeable relations as well as one creating new relations, the universe is intrinsically intelligible and animate—a self-active, living and evolving organism.

Strongly realistic and naturalistic influences characterize the "idealism" of FREDERICK J. E. WOODBRIDGE (1867-1940), a professor at the University of Minnesota, and a professor and dean at Columbia University. Intent upon avoiding both materialism, wherein thought is exiled, and excessive idealism, wherein nature is reduced to thought itself, Woodbridge attempts a compromise (*The Realm of Mind*, New York, 1926; *Nature and Mind*, New York, 1937) through the analysis of the spirit understood not as a thinking activity but as the realm of being within which thought explicates itself. In other words, spirit or the "mental sphere" is a "logical structure" that precedes and conditions thought. There is, then, an intelligible world endowed with an objective order and integrating the two aspects of being—the physical and the mental—in which we live. We know such a world by means of ideas that are not copies but signs of reality; they enable us to predict and check events because, as Spinoza said, order and the connection of things are identical with the order and connection of ideas. Santayana's influence, together with that of critical realism, is evident in Woodbridge. His metaphysics is purely descriptive and close to the scientific naturalism at present prevailing in the United States of America.

Elements from Royce's absolute idealism, and from the personalistic one of Bowne, as well as the objective idealism of Creighton, along with elements from German neocriticism (Windelband and Rickert) and from Dilthey and Simmel, all converge in the "naturalistic idealism" of WILLIAM E. HOCKING (1873), a professor at Harvard and one of the most influential American thinkers. Nature, which Hocking identifies with the Absolute, has an objective significance man can know, though it exists independently from its being known by him. As a branch of knowledge inquiring into such a nucleus of mental life that constitutes the universe, philosophy can only be idealistic. To discover the meaning of Nature is to discover those values which are eternally "emerging" as we increase our knowing capacities. Values are unified within an Infinite Ego, and meanings of things are fused in a unique will. The human person is an incomplete image of the universe and, as a natural entity, it is determined by the laws of nature; yet, this person is free and thus it transcends nature itself (*Types of Philosophy*, New York, Chicago, etc., 1939). The universe is not exhausted within a particular ego, but it serves the community of persons in the same way as the body, which is indispensable for the realization of the ego, serves the individual of which it is an organ. As the body belongs to the ego rather than the ego to the body, so nature belongs to the community of persons and not vice versa. The persons constituting a community ("man's will to live always is a will to live with others"), are historically and socially realized (*The Self, Its Body, and Freedom*, London, 1928).

Three years after Royce's death GEORGE P. ADAMS (1882), a University of California professor, in his *Idealism and the Modern Age* (New Haven, 1919) took up again the idealistic theme of the existence of an objective order, considered as the sole criterion for stating and solving the problem of knowledge and that of value. Adams properly emphasizes the qualitative difference between philosophical and scientific problems, between world of spirit and world of nature, dialectical method (resting on the rational deduction) and scientific method, and between the mediateness of reflection and immediateness of experience. Philosophy, therefore, is not a rethinking of the problems of science, which is restricted to facts, but an original and irreducible research aiming at attaining the meaning or value in those facts. A spiritual experience is irreducible to a physical experience (*Man and Metaphysics*, New York, 1948): the spirit transforms and evaluates the objects as it interprets them. Things have no experience since experience belongs to man only. "In the movements of a mass of air there is neither meaning nor value. There are only movements in time and space and a play in the distribution of energy. Moving human masses, on the other hand, carry within themselves and on themselves meanings and values because here we have spirits, or centers of conscious life and experience. Here alone there is value and there is meaning."

In 1932, eleven articles by several authors (some of whom have already been considered in preceding pages) were gathered together in a volume (according to a typically American custom) entitled *Contemporary Idealism in America*, edited by Clifford L. Barrett. Absolute idealism is hardly considered in that volume where the advocates of pluralistic idealism are predominant. Hoernlé speaks of a "resurrection of idealism in the United States" and counts among idealists even Whitehead. Evidently this "resurrection" is to be understood in the sense that idealistic elements are accepted by other philosophical currents and are operative in them.

WILBUR MARSHALL URBAN (1873), a Yale University professor, deserves particular mention for his polemic against positivists, while at the same time he defends the objectivity of value. He writes that "with the exception of some few thinkers, for whom the notions of being and existence move within the circle constituted by ideas pertaining to scientific positivism, there is no one who sustains that the mode of existence of values is limited to subjectivity." Urban is a defender of what he calls *philosophia perennis*, that is, the great tradition in Western ontology, by which the existence of an intelligible world and that of an objective order of values are affirmed (*Valuation: its Nature and Laws*, New York, 1909; *The Intelligible World: Metaphysics and Value*, New York, 1929; *Beyond Realism and Idealism*, Riverside, N.Y., 1949). He holds that his philosophy is beyond realism and idealism. In fact, he can call himself a naturalist, if he is opposed to idealism, and an idealist, if he is opposed to realism. In point of fact, his philosophy wishes to be one oriented toward realism, as it avails itself of the two directions in order to avoid the two extremes. As he himself writes, "both relative and idealistic postulates are necessary to a theory of intelligible knowledge; both realism and idealism are necessary parts of a natural metaphysics concerning the human spirit, and so they are part of *philosophia perennis*." Values and reality are two polar categories and, while they cooperate, they cannot be identified with each other. Here we have not an opposition but a "tension" dissolving itself in a mystical experience. Objectivity and eternity in values are not disjointed from their temporality: value is realized in time, to which it gives meaning.

The idealism of BRAND BLANSHARD (1892) is closely related to that of Urban. He is a disciple of Royce and a professor at Yale. His main work remains *The Nature of Thought* (2 vols., New York, 1940), in which he also proclaims himself to be a continuator of the *philosophia perennis*, that is, of the "doctrine of the autonomy and objectivity of reason." The development of thought is a creation of a totality represented by the same reality within which everything is included, and determined; such a totality is understood in successive stages, along which experience is constructed as a coherent system. Ideas cannot be considered either as images only or solely as logical entities—there is a connection between psychical images and the universals, as is proven by the fact that the latter are present even in the most elementary perceptions.

Also for the neoidealists the religious problem or, if you wish, that of the divine is still a fundamental one. Even when based on immanentism, idealism always bears a "theological" character. The American one is sometimes theistic according to the tradition of Christian Platonism (a personal God), and sometimes only Platonic: God (or, rather, an impersonal Divine) is the same objective, intelligible order.

Although idealism is not a predominant current in America today, it represents, nonetheless, one of the few philosophical positions which, unlike scientific naturalism and neopositivism, preserve the sense of philosophy and that of the problems of the spirit.[2]

The thinking of WILMON H. SHELDON (1875) can be defined as a form of Christian spiritualism. He, too, is a professor at Yale and the author, among other works, of *Strife of Systems and Productive Duality* (Cambridge [Mass.], 1918), *America's Progressive Philosophy* (New Haven, 1942), *Process and Polarity* (New York, 1944), and *God and Polarity* (New Haven, 1954). On the basis of the Leibnizian notion of compossibility and the theory of statistical frequency, Sheldon formulates his proof of the existence of God: Whatever is not contradictory is real; all possibilities are initially real including that of a being containing in itself all possibilities as well as the whole of reality—such an omnipotent, indestructible, free creator and good being is God.

D. The "New Humanism"

The so-called New Humanism, represented by IRVING BABBITT (1865-1933), a Harvard professor of comparative literature, and by PAUL ELMER MORE (1864-1937), is also a form of idealism characterized by a Platonic or classical inspiration. A noted student of Plato, More was a brilliant writer, literary critic, and a professor of Greek at Washington and Princeton Universities.

The process of European culture in the last centuries is guilty of having destroyed Christian religion, as well as the foundations and prin-

---

[2] For completeness of information, besides those mentioned, other works of a certain importance are cited: J. E. Boodin, *Cosmic Evolution* (New York, 1925); R. F. A. Hoernlé, *Idealism as a Philosophical Doctrine* (London, 1924); A. S. Brightam, *A Philosophy of Ideals* (1927), and *Nature and Values* (1945); G. W. Cunningham, *The Idealistic Argument in Recent British and American Philosophy* (New York, London, 1933); B. Blanshard, *The Nature of Thought,* 2 vols. (New York, 1940).

ciples of the social and moral order. Naturalism, romanticism, relativism, and so on have done so with respect to literature and philosophy; socialism, nationalism, and imperialism, with respect to politics—they have upset human living and have led to the First World War, the most stupid war in history according to Babbitt. The same process, through which Christianity and the values resting on it were destroyed, has not been able to find a new principle replacing it, as well as one on which a new form of life could be built. Not that for Babbitt Christianity is eternal and thus impossible to be replaced but, rather, it would have been necessary to wait for its destruction until the moment when a new and solid principle capable of substituting it had been found. The unforgivable guilt on the part of the modern world is thus to have consummated the ruin of Christianity prior to the finding of a new way toward a new reconstruction.

However, it is by now impossible to go back, and so the new synthesis to be carried out is an absolute Humanism, a purely human one, in which there is no room for God, the immortal soul, or for other metaphysical and theological reveries. Irving Babbitt (a good writer but a superficial philosopher), does not notice, then, that his atheistic humanism (like any other form of it) will not stop the ruin caused by the de-Christianization he regrets; his philosophy, instead, completes such a ruin and makes it definitive because, within an atheistic conception of life, no single human value can be really saved. Humanism accepts the dualism of spirit and body, constituting the very essence of man, who is twofold—superior man and inferior man. As taught by Plato, Aristotle, Buddha, and Confucius (all masters of a purely human ethics that is independent of religion), the inferior man must be subject to the superior one, and so the body has to be checked by the spirit, and the vital impulse, by the "vital check." At any rate, what is this superior principle? And, what is this check? It cannot be demonstrated; it can only be felt, experienced, and intuited. It creates the good and truth, which through practice and habit produce in us, as Aristotle said, a second nature, a virtuous one which is our rugged conquest. Man is not born good; he becomes such through the discipline exerted by the "vital check." In this way the "humanity" of man is formed; and this is temperance, moderation, the golden mean, as Aristotle says. Such a civilization made of equilibrium and lack of excesses is set by Babbitt against that mode of *comforts*, masses, and machines, that is typical of our times. These ideas, among others, were expounded in *Literature and the American College; Lessons in Defense of Humanities* (Boston, New York, 1908); *The Masters of Modern French Criticism* (Boston, New York, 1912); and *Democracy and Leadership* (Boston, New York, 1925).

P. E. More, who is Babbitt's most brilliant disciple and collaborator, also opposes the tradition of classical culture to the modern one. With a greater philosophical preparation than Babbitt's he builds on metaphysical ground an anthropological dualism between spirit and flesh, body and soul, and with Plato he conceives a world of matter and an objective world of ideas. Such a duality of nature compels man to seek not only a material progress but also, and above all, a spiritual one. More reproaches American naturalism and pragmatism, which, for the sake of theoretical progress and science, sacrifice religious and aesthetical experience, within which man realizes himself and his true humanity; the latter is to be realized within the classical ideal as perfected by the Christian ideal (*Platonism*, Princeton, 1917; and the five volumes of *The Greek Tradition*, Princeton, 1921-1931). However, he argues also against romanticism which exalts man beyond his limits, because it yields to the "demon of the Absolute"—an incarnation of evil (*The Demon of the Absolute*, Princeton, 1928). What is needed is neither a materialistic technicalism nor a romanticist absolutism, but a love of beauty, of spiritual richness, and of a dialogue beyond dogmatism. More admits the existence of a personal God, the personal immortality of the soul, and the dogmas of Christianity.

2. ITALIAN IDEALISM AND ITS DEVELOPMENTS

A. General Considerations on Recent Italian Philosophy

As we have stated in Chapter I of this work, for about the first twenty years of this century Italian philosophy is at first characterized by Croce's empiricist historicism and, in a second phase, by Gentile's actualism. The two currents were not able to dominate, totally uncontested, even during the time of their greatest influence; and this is so because of the survival of other orientations inspired by positivism and Neo-Kantianism and, above all, because of the contemporary current of Martinetti's and Varisco's critical idealism. Following the end of the First World War, the generation that had endured it found in Croce's historicism no answer for its exigencies, and it gathered around Gentile for some time. From then on "Crocianism" inexorably began to decline; Croce's influence on philosophy, in fact, was very scanty, and only accidental political circumstances held his fame high until his recent death. Moreover, even Gentile's philosophy has suffered, particularly in the last two decades, a sharply critical revision by Gentile's own followers (besides a revision carried out by the younger generations reared in a different cultural climate); and this revision has led actualism either to its radical evolution or to its dissolution. However, actualism still remains operative in both cases.

337

An outline of Italian philosophy in the last twenty years, or thereabout, can be sketched as follows: (1) a continuous evolution of positivism to the point of losing almost all its characteristic elements, so much so that it has fallen into forms of relativism, phenomenism, or even neopositivism; (2) evolution of Neo-Kantianism to the point of a quasi-coincidence with critical idealism; (3) further development of critical idealism whose most significant outlet is critical ontologism; (4) a thinking anew of Gentile's actualism to the point of its decadence into forms of empirical idealism, "praxism," or "problematicism" representing its dissolution; (5) development of traditional Catholic thought (Thomistic Neo-Scholasticism), which has come more and more in contact with the problems of contemporary philosophy; (6) birth of a new Christian spiritualism out of an internal criticism of Gentile's actualism as well as under the influence of Christian Platonism from Augustine to Rosmini.

In this chapter, limiting ourselves to the most typical representatives, we shall only consider the developments of critical idealism and Gentilian actualism, excluding Christian spiritualism which represents an autonomous current.

We think it is once again proper to point out that none of the three currents presently in fashion in world philosophy—pragmatism (Dewey), existentialism, and neopositivism—finds a truly representative position in present-day Italian philosophy. In fact, the first of these three currents aroused the interest of certain pedagogues devoid of philosophical ideas, or of certain students of philosophy notable in the field of history of philosophy, whose position, still not well defined ("transcendentalism of praxism"), is on the edge of Marxist praxism. As an example, I allude to MARIO DAL PRA (1914), a professor at the University of Milan, according to whom the metaphysical constructions are all undermined by the unlikely possibility of grasping the universal and the totality ("theoreticism"). The intentionality of the universal is therefore to be abandoned from the theoretical point of view (antitheoreticism) and assumed instead from the practical point of view, without any ontological support, for a "gratuitous" decision (*Problematicismo e teoricismo*, 1950; *Sul concetto di criticità*, 1953, and others). The second one, as we said, though widely expounded and criticized, has not gone beyond some academic elaboration as an autonomous current. And the third current has only lately begun to exert some influence, for it receives some consideration among those people who, lacking criticism as well as philosophical sensibility, are unable to distinguish between science and philosophy, or among the highly provincial "antiprovincials" always hunting for something new and foreign. Therefore, present-day Italian live and militant philosophy is not represented by any of those three currents, nor is it represented by the Marxist one; also no current of contemporary psychology (Freudianism, for example, or any other) has attained the importance of a philosophical current. From this point of view the most recent Italian speculation, even within the scope of world-wide philosophical problems, presents its own physiognomy, its own "tone," and character. In spite of everything, Italy still today is one of the very few countries in which philosophy has preserved its metaphysical sense, and in which the supremacy of thought over *praxis* is validly protected—a country where psychology, pure phenomenology, and description of mental states are not labeled as theories of knowledge and, maybe, even metaphysics. The credit for this is due to our ancient and recent tradition; it is due to Neo-Scholasticism as well as to Gentile and Martinetti. Through them philosophy has maintained its rational and metaphysical sense while reflexive thought has preserved its rank. This has been a vaccine giving good results so far, and we hope it is going to keep all its effectiveness until we see the end in the epidemic of the overvaluation of the fact over the spirit, of the practical over the theoretical, of the scientific over the speculative, and of the naturalistic over the spiritual. This does not mean, however, that the most recent Italian philosophy is not taking into account the element of positivity and the problems posited by the new currents; it considers them (at least the part of it still loyal to the true sense of philosophy and of philosophizing), but in a way that is consonant with the philosophical moment within the spiritual activity, that is, by assuming them on the level of reflexive thought and of a thoroughly speculative search, so that the solution may always be rational and resting on the metaphysical viewpoint, which alone is authentically philosophical.

B. P. Carabellese's Critical Ontologism

PANTALEO CARABELLESE (1877-1948) was a professor at the University of Rome for about twenty years. His lifetime goal was the foundation of a critical metaphysics, at which he was to arrive by disputing with post-Kantian idealism as far as Gentile's, by moving from Varisco's critical idealism (he was Varisco's disciple), and by rethinking the problem of metaphysics in its historical context and, above all, in Descartes, Spinoza, Rosmini, and Kant.

Carabellese rejects the Kantian position wherein being is left outside the reach of our knowledge, as well as the idealistic position, through which thought is identified with being (loss of objectivity) while multiplicity is reduced to mere appearance. For him absolute idealism and realism are abstract positions to be surpassed by the philosophy of the "concrete" for which the object is neither outside of thought, nor a creation of the subject. Being is distinct from thought as *its* object, of which thought has certitude. "Every subject is certain of the object, in that they are concretely together in the same act," writes Carabellese in his *Critica del Concreto* (Rome, 1921; 2nd ed., Rome, 1940). Thought and being separately taken are two abstractions: "Thought, concretely, is thought that is; being is the being that is thinking; it was, is, and will be always being." Thus, the idealistic position must be reversed—the absolute unity belongs not to the subject but to the object. In its individuality every spirit has the universality of being as immanent, but this does not mean that its individuality is universality: "The pure object, therefore, is unique, and its essence is universality." The universal is not a production of the subject, but its objective essence. Therefore, Kant's merit does not lie, as idealism erroneously believed, in having said that the object is produced by the subject, but "in having precisely brought the ideal world into reality through the unity of experience." The universality of the object is the validity it has for all possible subjects; it is the unicity of the subjects and it constitutes their objectivity. The subject is only individuation of the unique universal; and the pure subject *per se* is "the abstract singularity of consciousness," as the object *per se* is "its abstract universality." Thus, subject and object are the abstract aspects of that unity that the concrete is. Subject is not consciousness, but the singularity of consciousness; it is not an agent (nor is it the object) since the concrete alone is an agent, that is, an individuation. Only individual beings are real, "but through the universality of their being."

The concrete, therefore, is not identified either with the universal or with the particular. Consequently, neither the absolute incommensurate unicity of the universal nor the infinite multiplicity of the singular is ever sufficient for the concrete. Consciousness can never achieve either of the two abstract terms, although each of them always is a term of consciousness. The abstract cannot be posited either as something only transcendent nor as something immanent only. That being said, the exigency of the real must be satisfied even after abandoning the position of an absolute transcendence. Absolute transcendence condemns itself at the very moment of its being posited—affirming God is placing sparkles from the divine as immanent in concrete reality. Every transcendence is compelled to concede that much to immanence. If one wishes to speak critically about transcendence, he must not take it as "the affirmation concretely made about something that is outside of this concreteness."

As we know, my concrete subjectivity is in the universal consciousness, which is the unique absolute. Consequently, to individuate the unique, universal consciousness is to comprehend within myself the single consciousnesses not as such, but solely as consciousnesses. Yet, no matter how close I get to the other, *just because it is another*, that is, a *you*, the other transcends me. "The universal consciousness, then, by allowing our reciprocal comprehension also causes our reciprocal transcendence." In this way the transcendence of the purely abstract object is, concretely, the reciprocal transcendence of the subjects among themselves. "Inversely, the transcendence of the purely abstract subjects determines the relative transcendence of the concrete object, which cannot always and only be the same and wholly enclosed by single consciousnesses. This can be considered as objective transcendence which affirms itself within the bounds of concrete consciousness." All this clarifies the relationship between religion and philosophy: "The believer begins with the need of affirming himself and ends with the denial of the self in the motionless perfection of the unique Absolute; the philosopher moving from the need of grasping the pure Universal ends with making it live only through the effort he has made to arrive at it. Religion and philosophy, then, tend to reach the boundaries of life; they try Being in its depths, and only through such probing do they solve their own being."

Carabellese worked out these concepts in a systematic manner in his work *Il problema teologico come filosofia* (Rome, 1931), his best work and one of the most significant in Italian philosophy during the second quarter of our century.

"Either philosophy is metaphysics, too, or it is not philosophy." Metaphysics, in fact, is "philosophia prima," that is, true and real philosophy *sic et simpliciter*. Carabellese's book can be held as the demonstration of this task. But, indeed, after Kant, the metaphysical problem can be posited only in terms of a thorough study of the Kantian Critique itself. That was not done by post-Kantian idealism, which denied metaphysics. In this way idealism did not fully understand Kant and the true result of his Critique, which is not the unknowable-ness of the realistic being (*the thing in itself*), but "the noumenical-ness of being in itself as pure object, that is, the reduction of the thing *in se* to Idea. In short, as a result Kant's Critique demonstrates that the being in itself is the object of consciousness." Therefore, "the thinkable-ness of the Kantian thing in itself is only this living the 'in-itself' in the concrete consciousness; its unknowable-ness, instead, is only the resolute denial that the abstract being of consciousness can be the being in itself." Thus, for its part, the critique cannot be a criticism of knowledge, that is, an evaluation of the knowing power which reason holds in its pureness, but "it must become a critique of consciousness, that is, a criticism of concrete, spiritual activity, a criticism of being in its concreteness"; and, as such, the Kantian question "How is it possible to know?" is to be superseded by: "How is concrete being possible?." The critique, inasmuch as it is a critique, is called upon to solve this problem: "Once concreteness is placed in consciousness, how is it possible (within concrete consciousness) to have the establishment of that form of consciousness, which, in its willingness to grasp being as being, is willing to grasp the Absolute and so to overcome the implicit and the relative which take place in concrete consciousness and without which concreteness itself would vanish. In short: How is metaphysics possible in the concrete?"

According to Carabellese, modern thought has failed to grasp the problem of the object. This is due to an erroneous conception of the object itself, realistically understood as an object to be known in its own existence as a something *other* than the consciousness we have of it. Instead of rectifying the realistic concept of object, modern thought has suppressed it; it is a question, instead, of not suppressing it, but of demonstrating that the character of the object is not that of being something other than the subject, but that of being the *being in itself that is present in consciousness*, the unique being constitutive of the subjects in their *alterity*. It is unicity not multiplicity. "The alterity, then, is not a characteristic of objectivity."

To have demonstrated that it is necessary to remove the concept of alterity from objectivity, does not mean that alterity itself is eliminated: as the object is positive so also the subject is positive. Alterity is multiplicity of subjects, but it must not be confused with the phenomenal multiplicity in the external world of which Kant speaks. This *other* is neither a pure object, nor a phenomenal object, and not even an empirical subject. "The 'other' which is found in the conscious ego (and so each one of us finds it) as an essential moment of consciousness (the 'other' of which the conscious subject must be aware) is the *other* ego, that is, the other from me, but one which like me is, evidently, the pure *you*." Alterity is the other subject. Post-Kantian idealism has denied the multiplicity of subjects and "has arrived at the unique absolute Subject, thus confusing the singular with the Unique."

Remarkable also is the criticism Carabellese makes of the concept of "thing in itself," which he finds to be contradictory. In fact, "when we affirm it with our minds the thing in itself can only be a concept or an idea, a 'something in us,' always a something that is in our rational consciousness and never a something that is a 'more' than it or a 'more' realistic than it." There cannot be a thing *in re* and a thing *in mente*. The being of the thing in itself is a something "more," the existential "more" that cannot be known. The realistic "more" always is beyond the consciousness which affirms it; "but in order for it to be outside our consciousness, it must be inside of it, and once inside, no longer is it what it must be." However, the abandonment of the realistic concept of thing in itself does not authorize one to deny the very concept of the thing in itself. At this point idealism was mistaken; while thinking of confuting realism, it was instead compelled by the latter to take into account only the realistic concept of thing in itself. If, on the contrary, the Kantian, idealistic concept of the noumenal Absolute is considered and if the contradictory character of the Kantian concept of thing in itself is eliminated, then the Object of consciousness in its pure objectivity is recognized as such.

However, does such objectivity satisfy the common consciousness in need of a thing that is independent of consciousness itself? For Carabellese this exigency is satisfied by alterity, that is, by the existence of the other *subject,* and not by objectivity. The inquiry into the subject and in the object has led us to admit the positivity of the unique Being in itself (Object) as well as the positivity of the other, which is manifold, relative, and reciprocal (subjects). In the positive consciousness "we find an *Object* which is *ideal* precisely because it is *object;* and, some *subjects,* which are real precisely because they constitute a conscious spirituality. These subjects realize the ideal Object while that Object substantializes the real subjects, because it is Being in itself. Being in itself, with its ideal objectivity, is the constitutive principle of the relative being with its real subjectivity; this is what we are told by concrete consciousness when it makes us notice the necessity of its individuation." Philosophy, therefore, has its own object, which idealistic historicism has denied, thus destroying philosophy itself. Its object is Being *in se* in its objective noumenal character, which is distinct from the concrete. This noumenal Object (Idea), a pure Object, is God; God, therefore, is the object of philosophy. Yet, how can the problem of God and His existence be posited today? In order to answer this question, we must first examine the traditional manner of stating this problem.

That manner rests on a realistic conception: the presupposition of the existence of a Being which we have to worship. Now, in this concept, says Carabellese, "Being *in se*—an object of worship precisely because it is a pure object—is mistaken for the existence which, instead, belongs to the subjectivity of the worshiper." In this way the worshiper's existence is nullified precisely because we affirm the existence of the being we worship. There can be neither a demonstration *a priori* nor a demonstration *a posteriori* regarding the existence of God, since existence does not pertain to God. In this respect Kant's criticism is definitive. It is necessary, then, to abandon the traditional (realistic) position and recognize the fundamental exigency whence the problem of God arises; that exigency is: "the objectivity of consciousness."

"If God is Being *in se,* and existence, instead, is 'being in relation,' to say that God as such exists, no matter how we conceive existence, we only utter a verbal contradiction, we say nothing: to affirm the existence of God is to deny God. The error concerning the existence of God rests on the prejudice that there can be alterity with respect to the absolute Being." Nor can the Absolute be the totality of the relative as claimed by Hegelian idealism. That is confusing God with the concrete, from which, instead, He is distinguished as "unicity of Being in its absolute-ness, which is not negation, nor the opposite of what relative existence is; it is, instead, the immanent principle which does not deny but mul-tiplies itself through existence."

God, therefore, does not exist: existence is subjectivity, alterity, recip-rocity. The Absolute, however, is neither alterity nor reciprocity; if it were so, it would no longer be the Absolute. From this point one can explain how Carabellese understands the ontological problem. The start-ing point in this argument is the Idea; in order that it be valid, the Idea must be absolute, or a pure objectivity of consciousness; and in order to be such, existence must be removed from it. Only in this way can the ontological argument be accepted by critical metaphysics. *Inseity* belongs only to God and God's immanence signifies nothing but this very *inseity*, which is negation of existence. Only in this way God is the Unique one rather than one of the singles. There is no God without immanence, and in order that He may be the immanent unique Being, He must be the very objectivity of consciousness: "God is the pure Object of conscious-ness."

To deny God mentally is denying the objectivity of thought through an act of thought itself; and that is contradictory. "*I think, therefore I affirm God; if you deny God, you do not think:* that is the ontological argument in its positive as well as its negative form."

Carabellese deserves credit for having remained loyal to the meta-physical essentiality in philosophy, against every easy-going fashion and all superficial "surpassings." The statement "philosophy is metaphysics" is explicit and constant in him. Likewise, his criticism against transcen-dental idealism, his original elaboration of Kant, and his thorough study of the concepts of subjectivity and objectivity rank among the most remarkable contributions not to Italian thought alone. There are not too many contemporary thinkers who, I would say, felt the sense of Being so totally and radically as Carabellese did. Outside of being, one sinks into the empirical and nothingness; man feels, thinks, wills, believes, and hopes in Being. All thinking beings, inasmuch as they are thinking, find them-selves in Being, in whose objectivity they understand each other. From this point of view critical ontologism signifies objective pureness of "ontic" [-ὄντος] thought—a thought that belongs to no one of us and yet it conditions all thinking individuals who, in thinking, *are*. To say "this is *true*" is to leave out the individuating notes making one man foreign to the other. This is experiencing one's own freedom, regaining the ego in the objective Consciousness, which is not that of each thinking person, but the environment for all thinking ones, for the innumerable dialogues through which thought manifests itself. Each single individual finds again all the thinking ones in the objective unity of this Being-thought. Upon entering into it, he gives up his accidental notes in order to acquire *what is* in this Being of Consciousness, within which every thinking individual loses his phenomenal character separating him from the others; there he finds himself to be again with all the thinking ones within the essentiality of this unifying Being of consciousness.

However, Carabellese's Being is the Idea or pure Object that is immanent in the single consciousnesses, that is, the objective form of thinking. Therefore, this is "ontologism": an intuition of Being and, more than that, its immanence in our own individual consciousness—a "critical" ontologism in that Carabellese's Being is not the transcendent God of traditional ontologism, but the theological Idea of Kant's *Critique of Pure Reason*. In other words, God is conceived as a pure Idea, so that Being exists just in the thought of individual thinking subjects. He cannot exist in Himself because existence is a characteristic of individual subjects and not of the unique Object. This is pantheism, unquestionably; and more than that, this is atheism since the existence of God is denied, and God is identified with the pure idea of being, that is, with the very form of thinking in which it is immanent. Obviously, Carabellese calls God what is not God, and he uses the concept of existence in his own way. In traditional ontologism existence as attributed to individual beings differs from existence as attributed to God. In an individual subject essence is not all and one with existence, and from the analysis of a particular being one cannot necessarily deduce its existence. In God, on the other hand, essence and existence form a oneness; consequently, as existence cannot be denied of Him without necessarily denying His essence, so God cannot be thought of as an essence without being admitted as existent. The concept of existence related to God has nothing to do with the existence of finite beings. In fact, when existence is related to God it loses all its particular character in that it is identified with God's essence. Only when the infinite concreteness, which God is, is abstractly separated can one say that existence does not agree with Him.

Carabellese's God, moreover, no longer is that of religion and theology. In fact, who could pray to and worship a pure Object that is just immanent in our consciousness? And besides: Where is the ontological argument? No argument whatsoever exists here any longer. We have just the affirmation of the "I think," and God is identified with this affirmation. It is one thing to say "I think, therefore I am affirming God" and it is another to say "I think, therefore God exists." The two formulas are antithetical: the former denies God while, contradictorily, it affirms thought, which exists precisely because God exists; the latter infers the existence of God from thought, which exists as thought precisely because God exists. St. Anselm moves *from the idea of God* and from it argues His existence; Carabellese states that *God is Idea*, Idea alone, a pure and immanent Idea and he denies His existence. What kind of ontological argument is this? And whose Idea is this? This is the Idea of single consciousnesses and so it is immanent—and thus an Idea that is adjusted to the finitude of the world, which, in turn, becomes proportionate to it. Hence, if God is all immanent, He is finite like the world in which He is immanent, and to which He is relative.[3]

It seems to us that these difficulties have not been overcome by TEODORICO MORETTI COSTANZI (1912), a University of Bologna professor; he is the best of all Carabellese's disciples, and besides Spinoza's influence he felt that of Schopenhauer as well as, lately, that of St. Anselm. A deeply religious and mystical soul (*L'asceta moderno*, 2nd ed., Rome, 1952), particularly in his last work (*L'argomento di S. Anselmo e l'ascesi di coscienza*, Todi, 1950), he made a thorough philosophical analysis of the concept of "asceticism." The latter is to be understood as a purification of what is empirical in values, so that these may be recovered within the purity of "consciousness" or within the purity of thought, in which they do not constitute a hierarchy (as is the case with abstract intellectualism which, for example, holds the sensorial to be inferior to the intellectual) but are all valid in their absoluteness through which the Being of consciousness is revealed.

3. G. GALLI'S CONCRETE IMMANENTISM

Due to its uncertainties, found particularly on the metaphysical level, Varisco's philosophy exerted varied forms of influence and it had some developments which were carried out independently of this teacher's thought even though they had been originally inspired by it. An example of this is offered by GALLO GALLI (1889) who in his writings links his thought to the fundamental concepts of Varisco's metaphysics. He shares with the latter, who was his teacher, some exigencies and problems whose solution, however, is not in consonance with his master's thought. Evidently, in Galli there is also the influence of Berkeley and Leibniz as well as that of Kant and Rosmini, whose "idea of being" he is inclined to understand in the sense of the Kantian *a priori*. A greater autonomy of thought is to be found in his more recent writings in which he develops a position polemically oriented toward three main directives: "against immediate and vulgar realism; against intellectualistic abstractiveness; and against the dynamic conception in general and the Bergsonian one in particular." The last two points were thoroughly developed by Galli, who recently has revised, through a new and more profound elaboration, all his theoretical works in such a way that greater clarity and depth have been attained (*Saggio sulla dialettica della realtà*

[3] M. F. Sciacca, *Filosofia e metafisica* (Brescia, Morcelliana, 1950), pp. 217-218 ff.

spirituale, 2nd ed., Milan, Genoa, 1950; *Prime linee di un idealismo critico,*
Turin, 1945). Galli assumes a constantly critical attitude not only toward
Gentile's actualism (he vindicates the needs of multiplicity against the
universalism of the "pure act") but also toward objectivism, against which
he uses Berkeley's subjectivism viewed through Kant. We have, then, an
absolute subjectivism, but one that is able to account for the world of
experience and justify the synthesis of particular and universal, so that
the result is a concrete conception of the absolute. Philosophy is logic
of the concrete, but, as logic, it is a demonstration and a deduction of
what it affirms from pure principles; it is not a dialectic of opposites
after the Hegelian manner, because for Galli the negative cannot be
resolved into another term. In fact, once the negative has fulfilled its
mediation, it gains by itself a positive value distinct from within the
thesis it had provoked as an internal opposition to thought itself. Spirit is
a complex system of acts of syntheses which Galli reduces to four main
forms: sensorial knowledge; rational knowledge; impulsive activity; and
volitive activity. Each of these forms is a moment of the unity-multiplicity
synthesis. "They result from an immanent and ever differently renewed
opposition (which, however, is endlessly conciliated and reconciled) between effectual act and universal idea; wherefore, one or the other
[the act or the idea] predominates although both proceed from their
conciliation within the general process of development and although they
both return, through the fundamental moods, to this kind of process for
a truer integration of the specific affirmation by which spiritual life is
expressed in them" (*Per la fondazione di un concreto e vero immanen-
tismo,* Turin, 1944). Besides the four forms of synthesis, Galli distinguishes
the sentiment which is a principle of individuation, as opposed to thought,
which is a concrete universal, as an integration of the particular acts of
individual life. The unity in the subject is dialectically constituted
through these diverse and distinct activities of the spirit. However, concrete, spiritual reality never carries out such absolute unity, so that individuality in the single forms and multiplicity of acts persists always.
Unity-multiplicity thus projects itself beyond our concrete experience
and the supreme synthesis tends to constitute itself as a reality in itself.

Galli's fundamental problem, then, is that of multiplicity (matter) and
unity (spirit). The exigency of unity is actually found even in the world
of matter, as, likewise, the exigency of multiplicity is found in the world
of spirit; and it is not refractory to unity, in that multiplicity is apt to
become an effectual affirmation of unity. Galli, "on the one hand, extends
the validity of the category to pure mind itself, because the images of
the act, inasmuch as they are images, are not valuable for themselves, but
for the merely possible, infinite reality they represent; and, on the other
hand, he makes the effectual act rise up to the region of the mind through

its own intrinsic expansion, in which it does not lose itself according to its most characteristic and immediate affirmation or affirmation *in se*, but gains its own fullness of meaning and value in relation to the total being, that is, it gains a moment that is essential to the absolute affirmation of its own being." The whole being is reduced to spiritual reality, which is a synthesis *a priori*, a multiplicity-unity dialectical relation wherein the universal does not "exclude multiplicity but, rather, finds in the latter a moment of its own affirmation: the universal, that is, is a category of relation." The effectual [the real] is contained in the universal, and this is what Galli calls *formal relation*. The infinite is never wholly in act and, thus, it must needs be recognized that "some other finite acts always exist beyond the finite in act; and so, once we have been not only able but also obliged to speak about the act of finitude in general, we can also say that by virtue of the very existence of the finite subject we can and must affirm the existence of other infinite subjects." Thus the way to transcendence is open and the contrariety of experience should find its solution therein. In fact, Galli speaks of God in whom the opposition multiplicity-universality attains its absolute conciliation: "The world of experience signifies only a mere negation with respect to the Absolute —it is intrinsic in the Absolute, and essential to it."

4. ACTUALISM AND ITS DEVELOPMENTS

Up to the present, three main orientations have originated from actualism: (1) An unconditional defense of the act in all its speculative scope, whether pertinent to its gnosiological (Kantian) meaning as a transcendental apperception, or pertinent to its metaphysical (Hegelian) meaning as a unity of the real identified (in an immanent way) with the Absolute. (2) An elaboration of those elements which rest on transcendence and which actualism was not able to resolve in the immanence of the act of thinking; this elaboration goes so far as to hold immanence as a transitory moment and so far as to change actualism itself into a form of transcendent and objective idealism decisively theistic in the Christian-Catholic sense. (This current has regained the religious impetus and metaphysical sense of Gentile's thought even against Gentile himself. Thus, men who were of different formation and age but who initially had all been actualists or close to the problems of actualism agreed in their effective effort to renew Catholic theism; and so they found themselves on the other camp siding with the Neo-Scholastics but always with their unmistakable attitude.) (3) An elaboration of Gentile's act in its purely gnosiological or empirical meaning with the exclusion of its metaphysical sense. The first of these movements is represented by V. FAZIO ALL-MAYER (1885-1958), and has no development since it is a purely academic position; the second one can be more rightly called actualism and, at present, as already mentioned, it constitutes the autonomous current of Christian spiritualism (Carlini, Guzzo, Sciacca, and so forth); the third and last one can be considered as the dissolution of Gentile's actualism which, through the criticism of whatever is metaphysical and theoretical in it, has been both mutilated of the principle of transcendental self-consciousness and pushed into positions which rest on empiricism, pragmatism, skepticism, irrationalism, and so on, as this is attested by Saitta's Neo-Enlightenment, Calogero's moralism, and Ugo Spirito's problematicism. Actualism, then, has been drawn nearer Croce's antimetaphysical and empirical historicism, so that it has suffered an evolution that is both dissolution and involution. Through these developments actualism has wound up meeting some existentialist exigencies, without, however, assuming their pessimistic and desperate tone.

Of the three mentioned orientations we are going to treat only the third one (commonly labeled, together with the first one, "Gentile's left wing"); the second orientation, improperly labeled "Gentile's right wing," will be discussed in another chapter.

In GIUSEPPE SAITTA (1881), formerly a professor of theoretical philosophy at the University of Bologna, the dominant problem is the relationship between religion and philosophy, and he understands philosophy as ethics. For him, it is not a question of a duality but of "a simultaneous presence" of the "many" in the "one," of "consciousness" and "self-consciousness": we must grasp the "presentness of self-consciousness in every shudder of our being" (*La teoria dello spirito come eticità*, Genoa, 1921), and the eternal, in the transitory. Matter, constituting externality, is "what makes self-consciousness itself real." Not the Hegelian dialectic of pure thought, then, but the dialectic of the determinate in which the absolute Idea fails to distinguish itself from its determinations; and not Gentile's dramatization "of a double ego—empirical ego and pure ego—but the dramatization of the unique ego," in which the universal is resolved "in the personality of the spirit, as absolute individuation or living being." That is what Saitta calls "spiritual synthesizing"—a unity of sensation and intellect, knowing and willing, body and soul, "becoming as freedom" which is creation of ends, and mediation between being and what ought to be, a synthesis of *happiness and duty*, that is, an absolute ethicity of the spirit. Once the transcendental Ego has been resolved into the infinite plurality of subjects, that is, in the concrete world of single individuals, Saitta is led to vindicate the value of sentiment, sensation, and the corporeal by addressing himself to the "most audacious and revolutionary subjectivism"; he identifies the latter with the "enlightened consciousness" (*La personalità umana e la nuova coscienza illuministica*, Genoa, 1938; *L'illuminismo della sofistica greca*,

Milan, 1938; *La libertà umana e l'esistenza*, Florence, 1940), and winds up with a revaluation of nominalism as well as a negation of all political and religious institutions, which for him are "a true and real congealment of the human spirit." Hence, his violent polemic against religion (especially the Catholic religion), which, according to him, is a denial of the dignity of the human person, a "philosophy of death," a "plain materialism," and so forth. Not a transcendent God (which for Saitta would lead to an "ethical nihilism" and a "morality of slaves") but a "living God" identifying Himself with the same human person, that is, a "modern God," which is, after all, a deification of man. Saitta's attempt at eliminating every metaphysical and transcendent residuum from Gentile's thought ends inevitably in atheistic materialism and nominalism.

Another endeavor to analyze actualism thoroughly and with a different philosophical finesse is represented by UGO SPIRITO (1896). A professor of theoretical philosophy at the University of Rome, he at first was an apologist of actualism itself and also an appreciated student of law and economics. In Gentile's act of thought as absolute unity, even Spirito finds a theological residuum from traditional metaphysics and, consequently, a persistence of the dualism between transcendental Ego and empirical egos, between the Act and its modes, and so on. He, therefore, identifies the act with its modes and with concrete experience, and philosophy with the particular sciences. Thus philosophy finds its true expression in history (*Scienza e filosofia*, Florence, 1933). Philosophy is not a science by itself, the science of the "mythological" concept of God —the object of ancient and abstract philosophy—but it identifies itself with the numerous concrete forms of the activity of the spirit (politics, law, and so on). Every judgment about reality is both particular and universal, and every knowledge is both scientific and philosophical: not two forms of knowing, but two necessary moments in every knowing. Thus, actualism is drawn nearer the Crocian understanding of philosophy as a "mundane" not theologizing science.

In successive order (*La vita come ricerca*, Florence, 1937; *La vita come arte*, Florence, 1941; *Il problematicismo*, Florence, 1948; *La vita come amore*, Florence, 1953), and always within actualism, Spirito has elaborated what is now his characteristic form of thought, *problematicism*— that is, inasmuch as "antinomy" constitutes the essence of thought, no solution is true; it remains only to accept problematicalness itself, and the ever open research, as well as the ever unsolved dilemma. Hegel deserves credit for having placed the essence of thought in its antinomic or dialectical process; however, he considered dialectic to be the solution. Consequently, dialectic has become a "myth," like actualism and historicism which are also "myths," as is also any position presenting itself as a solution. It is true that either a metaphysical system is arrived at or there is no philosophy, in that the "research" is not philosophy but only a desire and a need for philosophy; but it is also true that self-possession is unreachable: the only thing left for us is the research or immediateness of life as art, which is not self-possession or metaphysical system. Moreover, Spirito acknowledges the radical insufficiency in every solution based on immanentism (his criticism of modern thought from Descartes to Gentile is remarkable) and, hence, the necessity for a theological transcendence ("actual necessity"), which, however, he also holds to be "mythical."

GUIDO CALOGERO (1904), at present a professor of history of philosophy at the University of Rome, also wishes to eliminate the intellectualistic residua found in Gentile's actualism, in which he recognizes the merit of identifying reality with the act of thinking as well as with theorizing thought rather than with thought already theorized. However, if this is so, we must give up the task of constructing a theory of the act of thought, and a logic, as well as a gnosiology (*La conclusione della filosofia del conoscere*, Florence, 1938). Logos, knowledge, and dialectic are the very act of a "judging consciousness" and never a "judged fact"; therefore, a logic and a gnosiology are impossible. Rules of logic and principles of gnosiology are not referred to knowing but to *praxis:* "The logos has no laws except that of its absolute superiority with respect to every law; and, then, if those laws attributed to the logos are real laws, this means that they are not the logos' laws, but laws pertinent to *praxis.*" The ego's reality is in the consciousness of the self as *will* or *pure ethicity*. There is no theoretical philosophy but only a practical one, that is to say, an "absolute moralism" (founded on a purely moral faith) or even an "absolute pedagogism," since morality and pedagogy are the moments of a unique act—"the pedagogical exigency that first makes the *ego* set its own limit in the (moral) *you,* and then makes the *you* set its limit in the *him* (education)." Such is the thesis developed in *La scuola dell' uomo* (Florence, 1939), where Calogero gives systematic form to his thought, which he has expounded again in his volumes *Etica giuridica e Politica* (Turin, 1946), *Estetica Semantica Istorica* (Turin, 1947), *Logica Gnoseologia Ontologia* (Turin, 1948), *Logo e dialogo* (Milan 1950), wherein, as it appears, there is neither a logos nor a dialogue.

GUIDO DE RUGGIERO (1888-1948), renowned more as a historian of philosophy, at first was a more intransigent actualist than Gentile himself, and also an advocate of a more concrete, absolute immanentism. There are no categories or spiritual forms to be replaced by a series of forms, in which the "spirit's organizing activity is multiplied and distinguished in its acts."

Later, De Ruggiero came nearer Croce, from whom he accepted both the reduction of philosophy to a methodological moment in the historical inquiry and the principle of action as a "vital moment in the surpassing" of history itself. In his article "Revisioni idealistiche," in *L'educazione nazionale* (Rome, 1933), De Ruggiero abandoned his initially actualist tendency and appeared to be leading toward a form of realism or, rather, toward a more concrete form of idealism. For De Ruggiero, act of thinking and content of thought are not identified and *"the fact that* a thing is in our thought does not suffice for the explanation of *what* that thing is; and, yet, the metaphysics of knowing is founded on the exchange between the *what* and the *what is* and on the fallacy that the latter is to be by all means resolved into the former." Obviously De Ruggiero stopped at a form of moderate idealism, that is, at that idealism which is entirely absorbed by the sense of the particular, the sense of things and events, which may respond to the exigencies of a historian of the Crocian type; however, as a philosophical theory, it quietly rests on a form of empiricism hardly concealing its skepticism toward true and real philosophy.

Finally, in his last works he critically revised Croce's historicism, in which he recognized the merit of having defended civilization and culture "in the name of historicism and against irrationalistic aggressions" (*Il ritorno alla ragione*, Bari, 1946). A vain defense, in our opinion, since Crocian historicism itself is, though disciplined and cautious, a form of the crisis of reason; besides, it is unable to act as an embankment for it lacks a consistent speculative foundation. In fact, De Ruggiero himself emphasizes the limits of such a historicism, with which he says he is unsatisfied. It is necessary for the concrete man to "place himself beyond history, on that ideal vertex spoken of by Nietzsche, there where the supreme values of man's humanity were brought together; it is from that height that man may be able to judge the past, to measure the insufficiency of that which is not what it ought to be; and it is from such a vital want of balance between real and ideal that man can draw a vigorous impulse for his new endeavor and prepare himself for a new action." Now Croce denied precisely such a "metahistorical vertex on which the perennial philosophy had focused itself; and in doing so he indicated that he preferred a portable lamp throwing some light on the road of his historical research to a beacon shedding from its high position so much light as to illuminate the whole of life." However, De Ruggiero did not ask himself whether, without that "beacon," the portable lamp is capable of clearing up anything identifiable (I say) with the depth of, and not just with the surface of history, at which Croce, who was a positivist in spite of everything, had stopped. De Ruggiero would have liked a synthesis "of the one and the other," of the historical and the metahistorical, and it would have been interesting to know what he would have suggested in order to carry out such a synthesis. Again he writes:

"Historicism offers us a vision of the world we are to protect and preserve. Its logic, its ethics, its religion were instruments and appanage for an optimistic conservatism which by now is going down together with that world which is crumbling before our eyes. We aim at the vision of a world to be reconstructed and renovated beyond historicism." Therefore, even De Ruggiero was convinced that Crocian historicism has faded as a theory and that, precisely because it has a logic, an ethics, and a religion that are instruments and appanage for anything you please, it has never had either a logic, an ethics, or least of all, a religion. However, De Ruggiero did not tell us what this "vision of a world to be reconstructed and renovated" is. Is it still another form of enlightened immanentism based on historicism or materialism? Well, in that case it will be still another "portable light" illuminating nothing and no one but rather leading everyone astray.

The critical revision of Croce's historicism and Gentile's actualism is one aspect in the more vast revision confronting not only modern philosophy but the very principles of reason. Neo-Hegelianism believed it had effectively opposed the dissolution of philosophy into *praxis* by vindicating the theoretical moment, and the disintegration of reason and values by reaffirming the validity of the logos in which value is immanent. The critical revision of Crocianism, however, has given evidence of the nonphilosophy in Croce's "philosophy" together with its lack of a philosophical solution for the problems which it had failed, from the beginning, to posit philosophically since they were not posited metaphysically. Gentile's actualism, instead, possesses, as we have already said, a metaphysical essentiality which led it to be developed in two opposite directions: one that regards the foundation of metaphysics within the framework of classical idealism and, hence, within ontological truth (Augustine-Rosmini) in which the concepts of being and interiority have been recovered outside of immanentism, since it was shown that authentic interiority as such, implies transcendence; and the other that carries actualism to its extreme consequences and loses its metaphysical core as well as its rationality intrinsic in a philosophy identifying being with the act of reflective thought, to which all the moments in the life of the spirit are reduced. Consequently, on the one hand, actualism has given rise to a philosophy tending to surmount and solve the "crisis of philosophy"; and on the other, it has allowed some positions which, in destroying actualism, also show that they are the expression of the same crisis.[4]

[4] The exigency of the human historical concreteness was vindicated—at first from within actualism and then departing from it evermore—by Franco Lombardi (1906), a professor at the University of Rome: *L'esperienza dell'uomo* (1935); *Il mondo degli uomini* (1935); *La libertà del volere e l'individuo* (1941); *Dopo lo storicismo* (1951); *Nascita del mondo moderno* (1953). In contrast to Lombardi and other idealists, Santino Caramella (1902), a professor at the University of Palermo, has

5. C. Michelstaedter and G. Chiavacci

CARLO MICHELSTAEDTER (1887-1910), a man from Gorizia who died a suicide at twenty-three, stands alone in Italian philosophy. He had time to write, besides some poems, a volume entitled *La persuasione e la rettorica* published posthumously (Florence, 1922). It is a work done with ease and inspiration in a very personal and, at times, powerful style; it is a work more literary than philosophical as it expresses a thought sincerely experienced and rich in suggestion; it is one of the most authentic testimonies in contemporary philosophy.

Michelstaedter's intuition of life can be briefly formulated as follows: there is opposition between *persuasion* that is possession of life and *rhetoric,* or false persuasion, that lures men with illusory goods while pushing them into an unceasing race toward an unreachable good. "No life is ever satisfied with living in any present, since it is life in so far as it is continued, and it is continued into the future in so far as it lacks living. In fact, if it were able to possess itself entirely here and now, wanting nothing at all, so that nothing would wait for it in the future, it would not continue itself—it would cease being life." So many things attract us in the future, but in the present we wish in vain to possess them. "I shall climb the mountains; the height is calling me and I want to possess it; I ascend it and I dominate it; but I cannot possess the mountain. I am standing very high on the plains and on the sea; and I see the vast horizon belonging to the mountain; but all this is not mine, and yet it is in me when I see it; and precisely because I yearn to see more, I have never seen, for I lack sight."

The social organism determines itself more and more, and the individual, already a slave of society, is a link in this mechanism: he has the right to find in it his place to live, but he pays for it since he has to give up his autonomy. The human soul always desires new goods; attracted by the future, it evades the present and runs after a tomorrow that always is "outside of its reach"—a tomorrow on which all unseizable happiness rests. This unsatisfied thirst for living makes man never be a master of himself; never live in the present; believe that to be true which is not; and prolong his misery to infinity. It is "rhetoric" which fools him as it makes him believe he is living in the midst of pleasures; it deceives him and makes him escape from himself. "That which he wishes is in him and in willing he moves life away from himself; he does not know what he wants. His end is not his end; he does not know why he

---

arrived at a critical spiritualism, which is decidedly oriented toward theistic transcendence: *Religione, Teosofia, Filosofia* (1931); *Senso comune, teoria e practica* (1933); *Ideologia* (1942); *Metalogica* (1945).

does whatever he does; he acts as a *passive being;* in fact, he *does not possess himself* as long as his hunger for life abides in him irreducible and obscure. *Persuasion does not abide in the one who is not able to live only by himself;* but man is a son and a father, a slave and a master of that which surrounds him, of what was already and is bound to come again—a thing among things." "We are a heavy body which, once it has been pulled off the hook that keeps it hanging on the ceiling, would tend to come down, more and more down, endlessly . . . because we are the result of an original deficiency which wishes to be filled out . . . and we live in an attempt at filling it out without being able to do so, precisely because life itself would cease if we were able to fill it out once. We are not free but passive since we are compelled to look for the self in the other thing that conditions us . . . in that nonego in which the ego can never find itself. . . ."

Michelstaedter vigorously rejects the illusory self-sufficiency, to which he opposes "persuasion," that is, the real possession of reality and life, which is not desperately hoping in the future, but is living in a present that is really ours. He who is *persuaded* achieves self-possession, sufficiency, and autarchy. In fact, he has freed himself of all his bonds with a world that is not his own, thus triumphing over rhetoric. He has made time stop, he is outside of time, and he is not afraid of death since he has overcome it within himself (in fact, he has everything in the present). Moreover, such a state of autarchy is not an escape from the world, because only he who is convinced that the world is rhetoric can truly dominate it.

Michelstaedter's position is one of the most rigorous expressions of immanentism; it makes the idealistic principle of the absolute autonomy of the subject its own, and, precisely in that which is external and within a good always placed outside of the act, it finds the rhetoric-motif together with the metaphysical root of sorrow, which rhetoric, with its deceptions, tries only to hide (while in reality it makes it more exasperating)—only persuasion can overcome this sorrow through the possession of the self. However, such self-possession representing an absolute rejection of the world and a rebellion against life is ultimately reduced, in spite of everything said to the contrary, to a desperate isolation that can be a gesture of great pride, or else, perhaps, one of great humility.

Some people have been saying with reason that Michelstaedter is an "existentialist *ante litteram*";[5] and he is just that, in the sense that existentialism is the critical awareness of the intrinsic insufficiencies in transcendental idealism from which it derives. A philosopher of immanence, Michelstaedter represents in Italy the first existentialist "crisis" within the thesis of immanence; and he is Unamuno's first companion.

[5] T. Moretti Costanzi, "Un esistenzialista ante litteram: C.M.," *Studium* (1942).

The "rhetoric" of which he is speaking is the position of the idealistic Ego compelled to grasp itself in its relation to the nonego (external world), and thus compelled to escape from itself and never be able to possess itself nor to ever achieve its own fulfillment and fullness. Once Michelstaedter has unveiled the misery in the historical vicissitude of the ego, as he continues to hold fast to the immanentist thesis, he is left only with despair: existence as individuality detaches itself from the world and becomes shut in itself with an absurd present, an empty interiority, and an impossible freedom. Michelstaedter denies both an immanent Absolute (idealism) and a transcendent God;[6] he denies the constructive possibility for a speculative philosophy and thought itself;[7] he is left only with his own aching ego, that is rebellious and desperate while trying in vain to be God.[8] Is not God an eternal present or the instant that is eternal presence? And Michelstaedter the man wants to be God and live such an instant, in which a life without hope retreats as in its own "haven" and there, "in a point" makes itself flare up into a flame. Moreover, by committing suicide he made life a flame, at a point, as if he were to attain, through death, the fullness of the absolute present and deny the limit. In it lies the sense of Michelstaedter's philosophical suicide. However, in doing so he yields precisely to that limit, and bows to the empirical as he replaces the rhetoric of life with that of death or, rather, persuasion itself is in him a rhetoric since in this philosophy of absolute immanence being is nothing.

Michelstaedter is Nietzsche's spiritual brother and, outside of Italy, an almost unknown forerunner of existentialism. In the crisis of philosophy, as a crisis of being and of the validity of thought, he is the first cadaver that this crisis placed before our eyes, almost as if it were the first stone in a road paved with skulls.

Michelstaedter has nourished the thought of GAETANO CHIAVACCI (1886), a professor of theoretical philosophy at the University of Florence, who has always considered himself as a spiritual disciple of this thinker from Gorizia; in fact, he availed himself of Michelstaedter's thought even in order to revise Gentile's actualism from within. For Chiavacci, therefore, Gentile's act can be considered in its interiority, or as the principle through which the existence of every being is posited. In

[6] "I have never known the absolute, but I am acquainted with it in the same way as those who suffer from insomnia know sleep, or as those who look at darkness know light" (*La persuasione e la rettorica*, p. 63).

[7] "I think, it is true, and by thinking, I am," but *cogito* does not mean *I know*; *cogito* signifies that I try to know, that is, I lack knowledge, I do not know. "If I knew, I would be, for thought alone can exhaust being; I, instead, *non entia cogito, ergo non sum*: my existence as it is affirmed by the *cogito* is in short a nonbeing." (*Ibid.*, p. 69.)

[8] Michelstaedter arrived, forty years earlier, at the same conclusions as Spirito and Sartre.

the latter sense, Gentile's act is an "illusion" not a "reality." Hence, it is necessary to distinguish between *act* and *actuality:* "Actuality is an illusory affirmation of life in that present which is found between past and future; the act, instead, is the real affirmation of that present existing outside of time—existence belongs to the former while reality belongs to the latter"; "actuality" is rhetoric or "illusion"; the "act" is "persuasion" or "reality" (*Illusione e realtà*, Florence, 1932). To philosophize is not to know external things but ourselves, whatever is "valid to gratify our richness of life, our will, and our consciousness: in it our life may satisfy itself and find that peace many in vain seek through the usual ways." Life has no solution outside of itself; it has in itself its *persuasion* and one has to live it through in order to recognize it and persuade himself about its reality. "Philosophy is the very profound persuasion on the part of him who always knows what he is doing."

Spirituality always stands above natural transcendence; the *becoming* of things in space and time differs from the *development* of the spirit, which is only present, without either past or future. Between these two poles, unfolds the drama of human consciousness which longs to win the spatial-temporal finite multiplicity, in order to conquer the unity of itself within a present in which time has no value. In this yearning one gains consciousness about the *nothingness* of the world—a nothingness that is sufferance and, therefore, *catharsis*, because, through his consciousness regarding the nothingness of things, man paves his way toward the solution of his own problem as well as the problem of things. This problem reveals man to himself: "His being before the nothingness of other things is his sorrow, his perennial tragedy," and no solution, not even that of mysticism, is allowed by the contrast between illusion and reality. However, to acquire a consciousness about reality is to live with "disenchanted" eyes; it is looking not for illusions but for reality in the world, in which we must live with the persuasion of being able to carry out the same reality, that is, spirituality, the infinite, and God.

Chiavacci's position is clearer in the occasionally profound pages of his *Saggio sulla natura dell'uomo* (Florence, 1936). Nature has an autonomous existence and, as such, it posits a problem whose solution determines that of the spirit. "The absolute ideality and freedom of the spirit cannot be conquered unless we oppose to it, as a fact existing in time and as a fact we must overcome, an effective nature representing the problem which the spirit must solve. In fact, the spirit will solve it through the act: the act is a *process* because, in order to maintain itself real, it must reconquer unceasingly its reality by overcoming that ever resurging nature."

The spirit will take possession of itself when it recognizes the relativity of human nature. Only in this way it "detaches itself" from the world and from its natural personality, "which it feels to be no longer its own but nevertheless accepts." Suicide and asceticism are affirmations of the life one wished to deny through them. In fact, "he who arrives at a true devaluation of life, finally understands this paradoxical truth—that *it is worthwhile to prolong life if, in this way, one succeeds in devaluating it.*" The consciousness of the tragic character of life gives us an immense and solemn peace. We look at life with another eye and we feel the presence of the divine in it. In order to perceive the divine, one must refuse any support, even that of God. Here lies the essence of every religion. We grasp things in their eternal being since we have detached ourselves from them. The culmination of spiritual activity is represented by *art*, through which we are freed from the painful labor and transparency of the Absolute. Spinoza and Schopenhauer are found here again, through an idealism fashioned after Schelling's. Spiritual life, which in its development becomes more and more fulfilled within itself, is a realization of God in us, and is the conquest of the Absolute as a victory over our particular ego (illusion), and a perennial discovery of our consciousness concerning God (reality). (*La ragione poetica*, Florence, 1947).

"To detach oneself" from things is to seize them in their eternal being. This is a wisdom typical of Spinoza and Schopenhauer and, therefore, a wisdom of desperation and a useless heroism. Once the world is an illusion and once transcendence (God) is denied, interiority or the act of spirituality, spoken of by Chiavacci, is only an empty interiority trying in vain to fill itself with an immense silence and a solemn peace. Yet, such a tragic conclusion is truly suffered and intensely experienced by Chiavacci; and that makes him one of the few authentic philosophers.

6. RATIONALISM AND IDEALISM IN FRANCE

A. General Remarks

As we said already, Boutroux, Bergson, and Blondel (without overlooking the influence of J. Lachelier's idealism) can be considered as the masters of French thought up to the end of the First World War; Bergson, above all, has influenced all currents even in depth. However, even before the spreading of existentialism, the irrationalistic, subjectivistic, and vitalistic currents (from which philosophy generally kept itself aloof) did not spare French culture as is attested by novels, plays, literary criticism, and so on. In spite of all this, with the reawakening brought about by Bergson within dominant positivism and also by Blondel, French philosophy is prevalently oriented toward forms of "idealism" up to the time of the existentialist irruption. In this same denomination one can include not only the same Bergsonian intuitionism arisen from the still unconsumed ashes of positivism, but also that "rationalism" of Cartesian and enlightened origin, which is to be found even in the positivists and which characterizes other sectors of French thought. What has been called the "transformation de la philosophie française" began (as in Italy) about 1930, when Husserl's phenomenology, the new logical theories, and particularly existentialism made their influence effectively felt; Lavelle's and La Senne's *Philosophie de l'esprit* made its appearance almost contemporaneously. For the last fifteen years existentialism has been the center of all discussions and polemic in French thought; there is no philosopher who has not felt the need to take a position regarding it. Such widespread interest has led otherwise distant and opposed positions of thought to meet today on the ground of the problems laid down by existentialism. Idealism and rationalism are obviously questioned by a movement whose attention is focused on human existence and existential problems, in opposition to the "systematic spirit" and absolute and totalitarian truth.[9] Questioned on the same ground of immanentism, they were not able to defend themselves well; in fact, they either confirmed their own position dogmatically, or barrenly lamented the end of philosophy as a "science" and a system of rational truths; in some cases they even adapted themselves to the positions held by the opponents. It must also be noted that to a certain extent, existentialism tried to enter into the two great traditions of French philosophy: the "Cartesian" and the "Pascalian" traditions; the latter, in fact, is found again, as we already mentioned, in what is called Christian or theistic (and not only in it) existentialism; the former, on the other hand, has been restored even from within existentialist positions. Finally, the current that represents, let us say, the counterbalance to existentialism is the *Philosophie de l'esprit* in its best exponents; and, unlike idealism and rationalism, it has been successful because it was able to make some theses posited by existentialism its own, within an ontology resolutely oriented toward a theistic and Christian spiritualism in spite of its idealistic origin. In other words, the *Philosophie de l'esprit* (as in its own way, Christian spiritualism in Italy) knew how to place itself in a position of effective criticism against the dissolution of philosophy (and of human values as such) effected by existentialism, Marxism, and new scientificalism; it was able to do so only because it abandoned the immanentist prejudice and, with it, the presumptions of absolute humanism and atheistic historicism and rationalism, from which the dissolution of philosophy and annihilation of values originated. Therefore, within the framework of contemporary thought, the latest French exponents of positivism, idealism, and rationalism represent (as in Italy) a position, I would say, of "nostalgia" for that peaceful

[9] We indicate in passing that existentialistic motives are already to be found in Paul Valéry (1871-1945). The mind of the philosopher is creative like that of the artist.

past which was naively convinced that, once God and Christian religion had been put aside, human reason would be happily and freely autonomous; it could then construct its own world, that is, the world of history as an uncontested field reserved for the eternal thought operating through man and producing an infallible progress. The ruin of reason and the crisis of truth originated with that reason which believed itself to be always right and even more and more infallible by proclaiming itself divine and creative of truth and of all values. In fact, the more recent currents, from existentialism to neopositivism (and their kin and derivatives), are only the extreme consequence of that ruin and that crisis. Therefore, when we hint at the survivals of positivism and at the most significant rationalistic and idealistic positions, it means, in short, speaking of the last "illusions" of an atheistic immanentism which, in its naive or intentional blindness, still believes that truths and values (created by man through the historical becoming and immanent in it) are "divine" and absolutely valid without a transcendent God; they hold the latter to be a superfluous remnant from a mythical mentality which progress or historical evolution has taken upon itself to eliminate entirely.

In France, more than in Italy, positivism was slow in dying, and its theories even today find some followers, perhaps less outspoken, in the science of law, sociology, historiography, psychology, and so on. This proves how Comte's influence first and, later, that of Durkheim have been deep and traceable even in sociological doctrines that are not positivistic, such as, for example, those of Dewey (or inspired by him) or even the Marxist ones or close to Marxism. In spite of all this, it is easy to ascertain that, out of the more recent currents, only neopositivism has had, at least until now, in France (and also in Italy) a scanty influence and originality even though it was widely made known there (by Boll and Vouillemin). However, that is perhaps explained by the fact that French positivism was able to develop its positions to the utmost and to compare them critically with others, as happens in countries having a truly philosophical tradition (that is, maturity). Logical positivism and naturalism (prescinding from the small and marginal contribution they may have afforded to philosophical problems) denote a scientist-like mentality, and they arrive at such a gross nominalism and such a naive (since it is so drastic) refusal of philosophy, that they can gain followers and arouse interest only in decayed countries or in those that lack a speculative and humanistic tradition (and therefore a critical sense).

In France, however, as we have already mentioned, so-called rationalism is still recognizable as that which, together with idealism (and even other currents), has had its organ in the *Revue de Metaphysique et de Morale*. This periodical is the expression not only of the autonomy of philosophy and of scientific research but also of "free thought," which holds that any contribution not coming from itself is an improper and unjustifiable interference, as well as an intolerable intrusion; hence its "pure secularism," as well as its indifference toward religion (which is considered only as a coefficient of social life to be explained only rationalistically). We are going to limit our remarks only to A. Lalande and E. Bréhier, and to O. Hamelin and L. Brunschvicg; the last two are important exponents of French idealism that also falls within "rationalism," of which the most recent philosophy (criticism of the principles of knowledge and of sciences, existentialist problems, and so forth) represents the crisis and a criticism, as we have already said.

B. The "Assimiliation" Theory of A. Lalande and the "Humanism" of E. Bréhier

ANDRÉ LALANDE'S (1867-1956) rationalism, like Bergson's intuitionism, is in its own way a reaction to Spencer's evolutionism, while still maintaining the positivistic positions. A former professor at the Sorbonne, Lalande is particularly renowned for his famous *Vocabulaire technique et critique de la philosophie* (Paris, 1956). To the principle of "differentiation," making beings more heterogeneous, Lalande (*La dissolution opposée à l'évolution dans les sciences physique et morales*, Paris, 1899; rev. ed., *Les illusions évolutionnistes*, Paris, 1931) opposes the principle of *assimilation*, marking the progress of reason in human history. Time, therefore, does not multiply the differences, but rather it equalizes them. Matter does not evolve from the homogeneous to the heterogeneous, but it proceeds by abolishing differences and re-establishing equilibriums through a progressive assimilation that can be noticed in nature, as well as in human society, in ethics, in art, and so forth. In short, the "constituent reason" (the one that assimilates and grasps identities beneath differences) tends toward unity and homogeneousness, produces science, reduces the multiplicity of things and eliminates qualitative differences, and so on (it must be distinguished from "constituted reason," which is made of fixed principles, "Raison constituante et raison constituée," in *Rev. des Cours et Confer. à la Sorbonne* (Paris, 1925). Such is the law of the material world, being also a law of reason, the opposite of that of life, which tends toward differentiation. Consequently, reason agrees with matter but not with life; as was well pointed out to Lalande, reason is not the highest form of life itself, but its negation. Lalande excludes the possibility of attaining the state of perfect homogeneousness (fortunately, we may add), but he grants that such is the tendency in matter and reason, that is, a tendency toward the annihilation of the individual and the particular within an undifferentiated Unity, which is ineffable and indefinable like the One of Plotinus, and yet is such as to be conceived only as a Matter no longer with reason. In fact, if all quality were annihilated, the function of reason would cease, leaving only pure Quantity. Moreover, an assimilation process without a model directing its course, makes no sense. What is this model, then? Lalande does not say; and from what he does say, only this affirmation can be deduced: it is the law of matter and thought to abolish differences in order to realize the purely quantitative homogeneous; if this, however, were realized, it would be a product of the same process of matter and reason. Yet, how is it possible to be assimilated to something that is not, and is the product of a process that can be said to be of "assimilation" only contradictorily, since it itself produces the model for its assimilation?

EMILE BRÉHIER'S (1877-1952) rationalism is, I would say, more erudite philosophically. He was a professor at the Sorbonne for many years, and also a renowned and esteemed historian of philosophy. Possessing a mind open to all currents, old and new, he had what one might call a "Greek" conception of philosophy, that is, one that is so rigidly rational as well as rationalistic, as to reject the religious question as such, in that it may interest faith (thus constituting a moment that is inferior to the philosophical or rational one) but not reason and the philosopher in any way: there is no such thing as a "Christian philosophy," as there is no "Christian" mathematics or "Christian" physics; there is only one philosophy, a rational and autonomous science, to which religion can be of no help. Bréhier finds a way to sustain this thesis even in his booklet *Science et humanisme* (Paris, 1947).

According to this author (and we concur with him), science does not have within itself a discipline that forces it to be at the service of mankind; in the past it had found one within humanism; today humanism is in crisis; it is a question, then, of finding out whether humanism can be re-established. Science and humanism are two diverse values; they, then, indicate two values, each with an independent origin: one claims to establish our domain over nature, and the other wishes to free us and have us be men, not as a biological species but as moral beings. Consequently, science can neither "absorb nor replace humanism"; and it is not even able to "blend" with it.

Naturalism, democracy, and *religion* in general are for Bréhier dangerous enemies of humanism. He also counts Christianity as its "opponent," and the reason is that Christianity denies the power of man, his initiative, and his ability to save himself, so that man is put in God's hands; or else, Christianity surpasses human nature, which is thus "transformed," "deified," and placed out of its own condition—"L'homme est comme aspiré et absorbé par la transcendance." Therefore, humanism is compelled to defend its type of wisdom against "theological transcendence," as well as against "mechanical science" because both "nullify" it. True humanism is Greek wisdom and, in the case of Bréhier, the stoic wisdom.

Bréhier recalls the conflict that took place between paganism and Christianity in the first centuries; one can easily object to him that many fathers of the Church considered the pagan philosophers to be Christians before time; that St. Augustine canonizes Plato and Plotinus, as St. Thomas does later with Aristotle; and that, in general, all Christian thought was formed on the basis of Greco-Roman thought, which was kept by Christianity, though revolutionized by it without being subverted. The fact is that Bréhier does not distinguish between Catholic Christianity and Protestant Christianity. Certainly Luther was antihumanistic and Bréhier opposes the *De servo arbitrio* of the "Christian" Luther to the *De libero arbitrio* of the "humanist" Erasmus who, like Pelagius, is "dans la lignée des Stoïciens" as he makes "the initiative of man's salvation rest on man's will." There is no stoicism at all in Erasmus, but only Christianity; his opposition to Luther is that of a Christian humanist against a nonhumanist theologian. Bréhier would not say that Augustine was a Pelagian; and yet he, too, wrote a *De libero arbitrio*—he fought against Pelagius in order to defend true freedom, the one pertaining to man, who is not God. It seems to us that all Bréhier's argumentations move from a gratuitously postulated antithesis: humanism is man's autonomy; Christianity is negation of such autonomy; therefore, Christianity and humanism are antithetical and inimical. There is antithesis, indeed, if by humanism one understands emancipation from God and abolition of God himself; in that case, however, there is no humanism but a deification of man, that is, a fatal mockery on the part of humanism, which is responsible for what Bréhier calls (and we with him) the "crisis of humanism" as well as for the crisis of philosophy or of reason which he regrets in his *La transformation de la philosophie française* (Paris, 1950).

Even in this work (which has a well-defined critical and theoretical line) Bréhier vindicates the autonomous and rational character of philosophy, which distinguishes it from religion, politics, and from the existential description of mental states. Now, it seems to him (and we cannot say he is wrong) that most recent philosophy (and not only French philosophy) tends to be confused (and dissolved) with either science, politics, or religion, and so forth. Hence the transformation of French speculative thought which, until the beginning of the century, had preserved "intact" and also "amplifié ce souci d'universalité de conscience claire, d'humanité, qui reste malgré tout notre tradition véritable," which is to be defended even against the so-called naturalism of Bergson and the latter's anti-intellectualism. The epoch that followed has a truly different intellectual character from the preceding one: "The spirit is focused upon self and declines to undertake the vast explorations of the real as well as the expanding of that experience with which Bergson had identified the future of philosophy." The main traits in the new philosophy are there to point out, according to Bréhier, its profound transformation: (1) toward the end of the second decade of our century, the image of a continuous universe is, with a remarkable insistence, replaced by an image of a discontinuous universe, and that is done under extremely varied forms; (2) the confidence in the human spirit and its sufficiency (immanentism) is failing and such distrust "se traduit par un constant appel à la transcendance"; (3) hence the need for the construction of "theories of values" expressing the "necessity for seeking a guidance for conduct and a rule for evaluation outside of the reality that we are"; and, thus, there is a need for transcending the self; (4) as in the Middle Ages one of the new directions is represented by Christian Revelation ("that, by essence, is outside of every philosophical reflection")—which has become the very substance of philosophical thought—and the other direction is represented by Marxism ("so extraneous to western humanism"), which, indeed, is an objective interpretation of history, but one that has been assumed unconditionally and, therefore, not critically. These last two examples, according to Bréhier, express the need for "doctrines préalables, antérieures de droit à la réflexion philosophique," and they also show the "mediaeval" character in present-day philosophy.

Bréhier concludes that the true danger threatening historical and moral sciences is intrinsic in them rather than coming from natural sciences: "il est dans une sorte de glissement de problèmes qui les fait s'évanouir peu à peu et comme se dissiper en des genres de pensée très variés et qui n'ont rien à voir avec la philosophie, dont l'unité et par conséquent l'existence sont ainsi profondément atteintes." The only thing left, then, is to eliminate the "prephilosophies" in order to restore *the* philosophy, that is, the critical sense in the rational research. It is not a question of "giving up all hope," but one of continuing to work "sans fièvre." There is to be neither an "irrational panic" nor "angoisse et délaissement"; "the vocation of philosophy is still, as always, to inject *sang-froid* and reflection."

In short, for Bréhier philosophy is a rational and critical science that presupposes nothing to itself, neither religious dogmas, ideological dogmas (Marxism), nor anything else amounting to a "prephilosophy," that is, a philosophy (and thus a nonphilosophy) which is preconstituted and, I would say, "premeditated." Up to this point we agree with Bréhier and, what is more, he deserves credit for remaining to the very end loyal to the essential rationality of philosophy and its criticalness, against atheistic and religious dogmatisms and fideisms, as well as against exigencies and sentimentalisms. However, our agreement ceases when Bréhier identifies the rationality and autonomy of philosophy with its self-sufficiency, of which the only true and "philosophical" (and, therefore, critical) form is immanentism. We say that if philosophy must not presuppose anything to rational research, it must not even be conditioned by the "dogma" of immanence. Bréhier should have critically justified this conception of philosophy of his, rather than to have accepted it as a presupposition on the basis of which he tried contemporary philosophy. In other words: Is it true that the only form of truly philosophical rationalism is the immanentist one, having an absolute confidence in the work of human thought that is unconditionally self-sustaining since it has in itself its own principle and its own end? Unquestionably, such a self-sufficient immanentism is the heart of modern thought; but there is no less doubt, either, that the crisis of philosophy has sprung precisely from the critical thorough study of the concept of human self-sufficiency, as well as from the collapse of the trust in the absoluteness of thought coupled with the concomitant dissolution of the very principle of immanence itself. It is not possible, therefore, to propose again such a principle as if nothing had happened; it can be proposed again only as a limit-concept, that is, as a conception to be held as already discounted, and one that must be discarded precisely because of its twofold dissolution caused by most recent criticism. The latter, being a consequence of immanentism carried to the point of nullifying philosophy as such, also dissolves the same immanentist conception, of which present-day disunited and disuniting philosophy is a filiation. In so far as we are concerned (and our point of view appears evident from the critical layout of this work), the problem is to be set up according to the following terms: (1) philosophy is a rational autonomous research and it is to be constituted rationally; (2) modern thought believed that such rationality and autonomy are incompatible with transcendence and, above all, with a theistic transcendence, so that it arrived at the conclusion that rationality and autonomy in philosophizing are to rest on the principle of absolute immanence; (3) yet, precisely from this position of immanentism sprang present-day philosophy (which itself points out the crisis of philosophy) as a critical awareness of the dogmaticalness and insufficiency in immanentism itself, whereby the crisis involving the latter has also involved philosophy as such so that both have been destroyed simultaneously. We agree with Bréhier on the first point; we also accept the thesis that philosophy is a reflection and an activity of the thought and that, therefore, its reconstruction is possible only by critically reconfirming the objective validity of rational principles; yet, precisely for that reason we deeply disagree with him since we hold that the autonomy of philosophy is no longer to be vindicated on the basis of the immanentist principle since the latter caused the loss of rationality in philosophy and the loss of philosophy

365

itself as such. The critical dissolution of immanentism is permanent because of the very fact that it has, through criticism, revealed itself not as a solid foundation for the building of philosophy and its rationality, but rather as the loss of both. Consequently, a truly critical position in philosophy today implies a twofold rejection: of the currents denying its rational validity, on the one hand, and, on the other, rejection of immanentism, not only because the latter has revealed itself to be erroneous but also because a critical study of the autonomous process of thought intrinsically and rationally leads to transcendence, which is thus rationally justified. To assume immanentism as valid even now and to identify with it the sole possibility for the foundation of a rational and autonomous philosophy is to move from a position that is dogmatic for want of criticism and, I would say, for an insufficient sounding of spiritual life in its integrality; it is, moreover, moving from a position already surpassed because of its internal development which constitutes its self-dissolution. Bréhier, instead, holds all "transcendentist" elements to be so many deviations from philosophy and so many mortal threats as to place the currents having a religious (Christian) character on the same level as Marxism. Now, it seems to us that there is a misunderstanding here: we agree with Bréhier if he is protesting against those who, in denying the objective validity of philosophical knowledge, build religious metaphysics founded on Revelation-data, inasmuch as those constructions are not philosophical and, least of all, do they follow the line of classical Christian thought, be it Augustinian or Thomistic; but, if he affirms, as he actually does, that philosophy must ignore religion under any circumstance, and that theological transcendence is the fruit of imagination, so much so that even by talking of it one puts oneself outside of philosophy, then we must object; in fact, in that case Bréhier did not vindicate the rationality of thought, but has only defended a rationalism that is as abstract and dogmatic as fideism is. A rationally-founded theological transcendence and an objective rational knowledge expressing itself so critically as to justify a theistic metaphysics imply no lessening of rationality in philosophy, but rather are consonant with the most critical position, which, being the least dogmatical, is the most philosophical. For Bréhier, on the other hand, "la transcendance, telle que elle est comprise, a pour corollaire la négation d'un sens de l'histoire en tant qu'histoire humaine. . . ." And why should this be so? Is admitting (*through reasons*) the existence of God perhaps the same as denying history as human history? Elsewhere in his writings one can read that "l'invasion du transcendant dans la philosophie . . . est le signe d'une crise de civilisation qui laisse l'homme solitaire, s'interrogeant sur les valeurs." We say that it is not a question of invasion but one of critical awareness, since it is the same rational research to arrive at the existence of the "transcendant"; and that the sign of the crisis of civilization is not given by such an invasion but rather by the invasion of immanentism, which caused the dissolution of principles and values. Transcendence does not cast us "dans les ténèbres de la théologie," as Bréhier writes apropos of Lavelle, but rather it frees us from the darkness of a dogmatic rationalism as it came into shape through the *siècle des lumières.*

Bréhier sympathizes with Brunschvicg and his "intellectualism"; he agrees with him in viewing the passage "from the immanent to the transcendent" as an act of giving oneself up to fancy and to the contagion of imagination, as well as to the whim of the will." Yet, immediately after, he writes that Brunschvicg's doctrine is, "above all, a philosophy of culture." Well, precisely because it is a "philosophy of culture," it cannot be philosophy but its dissolution and, as such, it contributes to the present-day dissolution of thought lamented by both of us, Bréhier and myself. However, it is clear that in order to lift up philosophy again one cannot appeal to the same point of support which led philosophy to deny itself.

C. O. Hamelin's Idealism

OCTAVIUS HAMELIN'S destiny was a curious one; born in 1856 he died tragically in 1907 in a generous attempt to save a life. His main work, *Essai sur les éléments principaux de la representation* (Paris, 1907), was passed over in silence. Moreover, his influence as a teacher was slight, having taught first at Bordeaux and then at the Sorbonne, at the time when Boutroux and Bergson were gaining laurels. The new edition of the *Essai* (Paris, 1925), together with other works on Descartes and Aristotle, was due to the good offices of Brunschvicg and Robin, and it has had such a vast repercussion on contemporary French philosophy that its author is placed side by side with the great masters. Parodi considers Hamelin to be the initiator of the rationalistic insurrection against philosophical irrationalism. Due to its recent discovery, Hamelin's philosophy falls within the limits of our work even if, chronologically, this may not be strictly true.

The *Essai* is hard to read; at times it seems like an arid and formalistic formulary and, yet, not infrequently it contains the deepest analyses revealing a truly speculative mind trained through the study of the great classics of human thought. We are going to indicate only the essential points of Hamelin's idealism, which holds a place *per se* within the history of idealism.

Hamelin holds himself to be the continuer of the rationalistic phenomenism of Renouvier, the greatest exponent of French Kantianism and Hamelin's master.

In fact, Hamelin's theory of opposition between analytical thought and synthetical thought is borrowed from criticism. The former thought expresses itself through deduction and is the method used by exact sciences: analysis and reduction of what is compound and organic to ever more general and ever more simple laws. Yet, precisely because of that, the analytical method includes the synthetical method immanent in reality which organizes itself according to ever more complex forms. Is there a thought that is proportionate to as well as capable of formulating this procedure of the real? This is the problem confronting Hamelin; the dialectical method of opposites becomes his own, and he holds it to be a law of reality. His task, then, is to study the synthetical (not a deduction as in Kant) "progression" of the categories, the rational forms constituting reality itself.

Hamelin, unlike Hegel, makes the synthesis reconcile the opposites without denying them. The opposites are not contradictories "but only contraries, that must be held as correlative in order to characterize them adequately. We replace Hegelian contradiction with a correlation. When we isolatedly consider that which is determinate not because it is contradictory in itself but only because it is incomplete in each of its determinations, we are faced with the following consequence: the synthetic method, far from developing through successive negations, as Hegel claimed, must proceed, instead, through affirmations completing one another, reciprocally; and, in the process, the last affirmation will not be the nothingness spoken of by the negative theology, but it will be a complete and totally definite being, such as had ultimately been claimed by Aristotle, whom Hegel misquotes in this connection." Hamelin's dialectic, unlike Hegel's proceeds, then, not through negations but through affirmations, as well as through positive determinations which are always more concrete. The becoming of the real takes place within the categories-series.

We are not going to follow Hamelin through his description of the connection-process established by him between two categories—a process of self-production wherein an inferior category exacts the superior one. Yet, we cannot pass over in silence his concept of "relation" considered as the very law of thought; in its three moments of "positing," "opposing," and "modifying," it constitutes the rhythm of becoming. There are, above relation, the categories of quantity (number, time, space, and motion), whose dialectical relationship is as follows: things appear to be bound together within the order of relation; from the point of view of the number, on the other hand, they are isolated and distinct from each other. The synthesis, within which relation and number are reconciled, then tells us that "something exists which is both and indissolubly a bond and a dispersion, a gathering of discrete terms that are not separated nonetheless." This something is time, each part of which is the negation of the others and, therefore, time is a successive series that is irreversible and unique in kind. However, the characters of time are only understood through an opposition of contraries, so that in antithesis with temporal quantity there must be another quantity, namely space, "in which the parts, excluding themselves only in a certain sense, present themselves simultaneously and as reversible and multiple." Time and space which Hamelin, unlike Kant, elevates to the rank of categories, are integrated within motion.

Hamelin continues this procedure by antithesis: quantitative categories require the antithesis of qualitative categories and so on, as far as the categories of cause and finality, the first of which is in itself incomplete, and the other, alone, does not do anything. They must not be considered separately; it is a purposeful organization carried out through mechanical causality: that which acts, the agent, is a cause destined to an end. With finality and life we are now reaching the threshold of subjectivity and consciousness, the organic development of a reality which in me is subject and object. The representation, then, is not of an object to a subject that is outside of it, but it is subject and object together, the whole real.

In the analysis that Hamelin makes of representation he follows the triad-procedure. Thus, he divides representation into theoretical, practical, and affective, and each of these is further divided into three moments: the theoretical, into the moments of concept, judgment, and reasoning; the practical, into those of the technical, aesthetical, and moral activity; and the affective, into the sensitive, aesthetical, and moral sentiment. At this point, the dialectical process in the subjective spirit is concluded.

Both for transcendental idealism, and for Hamelin, thought as a total synthesis of subject and object is the Absolute. For him, however, the Absolute is not human but divine thought. He wishes to avoid idealistic pantheism for two reasons: "First of all, because substantialized thought with which it is satisfied is a thing for us, and as such it partakes of the intelligibility of matter. Secondly, pantheism does not admit but one individual. If we, then, notice the existence of a plurality of consciousnesses, pantheism is not acceptable." Then we can only accept theism as the most "probable" "hypothesis," in the expectation, says Hamelin, that *"a genial discovery* will reveal a third outlet for idealistic philosophy."

Naturally, a system that ends with a precarious and probable "hypothesis" leaves us at least perplexed, while it also exposes itself to an inconfutable criticism: that the whole system is to be revised from its foundations. In fact, this is so. Hamelin claimed to reconcile many points of view; he wished to stay on idealistic grounds and, at the same time, make room for realism; he wanted to think as a pantheist while being willing to arrive at theism; he wanted, on the one hand, to vindicate the rights of experience while, on the other, he entrenched himself within irrational-istic intransigence. We could still go on, but it is better to conclude with a comprehensive objection: Hamelin's "system" is not a system because it creaks on all sides. Aside from the system, however, some acute and most thorough analyses remain. Hamelin must also be given credit for something else: no matter how abstract his construction may be, like Gentile in Italy he has kept a metaphysical sense for idealism (and, hence, for philosophy).

D. L. Brunschvicg's Cultural Idealism

Idealism, on the other hand, loses its metaphysical character with LÉON BRUNSCHVICG (1869-1944), a disciple of Lachelier and a professor at the Sorbonne; he is also one of the most authoritative thinkers in con-temporary French thought. As Hamelin made us think of Gentile, so Brunschvicg makes us think of Croce. Although lacking systematic unity, his thought presents, as has been pointed out, a unity of development based on an idealism that cannot compromise with any form of realism; and that is evidenced in all his works: from his *Spinoza* (Paris, 1906) to *La raison et la religion* (Paris, 1939); and in his other works (*La modalité du jugement*, Paris, 1897; *Introduction à la vie de l'esprit*, Paris, 1932; *L'idéalisme contemporain*, Paris, 1905; *Nature et liberté*, Paris, 1921) including his posthumous ones *Héritage de mots, héritage d'idées* (Paris, 1945), *La philosophie de l'esprit* (Paris, 1949). Brunschvicg is not only a declared enemy of all the metaphysical entities belonging to realism, but even an enemy of whatever there is of the metaphysical in Kantianism and transcendental idealism; neither a thing in itself nor the Idea anterior to thought can have existence; nor are there categories capable of ex-pressing once and for all the nature of the spirit. Thought alone is real (not as a soul or a spiritual "substance") as an activity that is in evolution perennially. His is not the idealism of a metaphysician, but one that, as we are going to see, pertains to a historian of sciences and culture.

According to Brunschvicg, Hamelin's error is that of attempting to construct a philosophy outside of every experience; instead, experience must be placed prior to reason. It is not Nature that follows the course we wish to assign to it, but it is Nature that takes us by the hand so that we may discover worlds whose existence we were not even able to sus-pect. Brunschvicg rejects not only deductive idealism but also pragmatism, and he denies that science is a simple instrument for action. Here is how he himself defined his point of view: "Philosophy does not force us into a dangerous choice between a sensorial appearance (which is essen-tially mobile, incoherent, and, therefore, incomprehensible) and a meta-physical reality, which being outside the universe of experience and action is not less incomprehensible, precisely because we wish it to be free from change. Instead it is a positive study having the only truly concrete object, that is, the spirit that each one of us is in effect; its task is to clarify the laws to which it conforms, that is, the relations which are the condition of our intellectual progress, through which we are enabled to elevate ourselves beyond the sensible without, however, getting out of nature and humanity." As an absolute science of the universe and God, metaphysics stays beyond idealism, in that it is beyond the human spirit; skepticism, on the other hand, stays behind idealism in that it disregards the effective value that is in the same spirit. Brunschvicg's idealism aims precisely at "knowing the spirit." It is not a question of deducing or knowing the world, but one of "perpetually comparing the achievements of spiritual inventiveness with the unforeseeable relations of the empirical *choc*." In fact, it is precisely the resistance offered by experience that gives back to reason freedom, by forcing it to surpass its own artificially imposed limits, and by gaining consciousness of its power in all its extension.

The duality between experience and thought does not imply a realistic position. Brunschvicg explains that it is not a question of admitting the existence of a nature of things that have been given and that are in themselves, in the presence of the spirit. "As I see it, instructive experience is that which in its attained development the spirit receives as a *choc;* but I refuse to hypostatize it beyond that *choc*, and, therefore, I resolutely keep away from realism. Experience is not the revelation of something definitely impenetrable; it is an invitation to shake the dogmatic quietness of reason." Brunschvicg is not asking himself the reason and the nature of such a *choc;* he is not on the metaphysical level but on that of history, that is, on that of the spirit historically considered according to the course of its victories and defeats. Thought's activity is grasped in history (particularly that of the mathematical and physical sciences), in that which man produces in his perennially inventive progress. Herein lies the reason that makes Brunschvicg—the theorist of an idealism called concrete—be completed by the very learned Brunschvicg of *Les étapes de la philosophie mathématique* (Paris, 1912), *L'expérience humaine et la causalité physique* (Paris, 1922), *Le progrès de la conscience dans la philosophie occidentale* (Paris, 1927).

Brunschvicg defined his speculative position from the time of his *La modalité du jugement*: philosophy is a work of reflection; it is reflection itself. The spirit does not posit an object standing fixedly before itself, but it tries to know itself through its movement and activity. He makes his own the fundamental thesis of idealism: "Knowledge constitutes a world that is our world. Nothing is outside of it; a thing beyond knowledge would be by definition the inaccessible and indeterminable; that is, it would amount to nothing in so far as we are concerned. Philosophy, then, can only be the critique of thought, and this is all the more true in that thought is transparent to thought itself. The main object of thought is not representation but the very activity of the spirit, so that philosophy can be thus defined as an intellectual activity gaining consciousness of itself—here is what the total study of a total knowledge is; here is what philosophy is."

It is not the concept that is first but the *judgment*, which is a living relation amongst things and a fundamental act of the spirit. Necessity between ideas (a union of two notions in an indivisible act of thought) establishes the intelligible world in which ideas are, in fact, one "interior" to the other. The judgment of reality, on the other hand, sets a contact between us and nature. This second form of judgment, unlike the first one, is defined on the basis of its exteriorness as related *to another thing*. "The impossibility for the intelligence to reach the internality of its representation compels it, in order to analyze and understand it, to posit being, that is, to acknowledge that this is." The relationship between the two terms is given by the judgment of possibility founded on knowledge which, in fact, is exteriorness and interiorness, and which has as its character, compromise. "The being attained through the science of nature results from a compromise between the intelligible and real; it marks a stopping-point along a double movement of approximation that is scientific movement."

Neither idealism nor realism: "In the work of perception as a whole there is so much ground for keeping realism at bay; likewise in the total endeavor made by science there is so much of experience that idealism can be kept also at bay. Even at this point the solution is a human solution, that is, a compromise."

Apart from this ambiguous solution, Brunschvicg brings about a real contribution through his effort to give concreteness to reason beyond Kantian formalism. Also, at this point, Bergson's influence is obvious. His conception of the spirit as a free activity represents the most significant aspect in his idealism: a free activity held not as fixed in formulas or channeled into the eternally determined categories (the evolution of reason is not the necessary development of the Idea, as it was for Hegel) but as progress that is neither totally experience nor entirely pure reason ever. Hence the consequence that problems are not solved by personal theories but by the collaboration of all human efforts throughout history: "Philosophy must not invent a solution to the problem of truth; it must find out how the problem was solved in effect." His historical inquiries, particularly on mathematics and physics, led Brunschvicg to the conclusion that in philosophy the real goal is to acquire awareness of human philosophizing in its becoming. In this sense he calls his philosophy "humanism": man has to gain consciousness of his activity without going beyond the path traversed by knowledge. "To know oneself is to feel as being within one's own constituent power; it is changing oneself into a watching consciousness that speeds up the dynamism within rational progress. During his uninterrupted dialogue with the universe, man becomes the world of science. Intellectual consciousness is *unity*, but not an abstract unity. Considered in its concreteness and dynamism, reason does not impoverish interior life, which is, instead, enriched and organized by it. Consequently reason represents both the universality and concreteness of spiritual life and, in this sense, its unity. Unity is also the aim of moral consciousness and of religious consciousness."

For Brunschvicg, the history of the human spirit is all that is real and knowable. Outside and beyond it, nothing exists except reveries. Its stages are perfectly identified with the degrees of the life of the spirit, whose infancy always coincides with belief and whose adult age coincides with the stage of mathematics or that of rational man. Thus, infancy ends with the Pythagoreans, who invented mathematics; then, with Aristotle and as far as Descartes, Europe lives through a new infancy of about twenty centuries; with Descartes, who again discovers the mathematical way, adult life begins anew and, though it is threatened by romanticism, it definitely affirms itself with Einstein and the prevailing of the scientific spirit; through the latter, the progress of consciousness is guaranteed until the triumph of the spirit of freedom, which coincides with the liberation of reason from the senses, imagination, idolatry, and from whatever else hinders its development in the historical present.

The poverty and arbitrariness of this scheme are evident; and if Brunschvicg had rigorously conformed to it, he would be a belated mediocre repeater of the enlightened-positivistic idolatry of science and scientific reason, ill-representing the philosophical one. Fortunately he was a man of vast and profound culture, which allowed him to articulate the scheme and break its artificialness and rigidity. Yet, it does not save him from doctrinairism to which his philosophy leads irremediably, and as such it represents the liquidation of philosophy itself. He is convinced that science delivers man from all bondage (of nature, tradition, religion, superstition, and so on) and that in order to achieve its fullness, life must change itself into mathematical reason. Through the logic of such a thesis Brunschvicg is led to identify historically the whole man with the *homo sapiens*, and all history with science. Mechanicalness (*homo faber*) and religion (*homo religiosus* and *magicus* or a mythical power-seeker), language (*homo loquens*) and politics (*homo politicus*) are obstacles to science; yet for the purpose of bringing about that communion of spirits and that reign of freedom identified with the learned society, science, through its omnipotence and miraculousness, will convert those obstacles into instruments of truth and means of internal liberation. We ask: Can one have a more mythical conception of science? The following, neither more nor less, would be the development of "Western consciousness": to create a science that, like a monstrous idol, swallows up everything that is not reducible to it! Man needs only rational truth, that is, science, which, to be more precise, is mathematical physics. Such is the West, and such is the great conquest that humanity has made, is making, and will make for itself! Brunschvicg says that he wishes to free us of all forms of idolatry; and, who is going to free him—the liberator—from his idolatry of science?

This author assigns a conspicuous place to religion as one of the "superstitions." Since he is devoid of any religious experience whatsoever, his many writings on religion are a blunder. One can say that he had only one concern: denying religion as faith in a God who is transcendent and a creator (a childish myth and the fruit of imagination) and affirming that philosophy (that is, science) is itself the authentic religion of adult humanity.

During the meeting of the "French Philosophical Society" (March, 1928), Brunschvicg expounded his theses on the problem of God and religion, and they are contained in *Le Progrès* . . . , and others; a memorable discussion ensued with Gilson, Blondel, Le Roy, and so forth, and it was continued in the *Revue de Métaphysique et de Morale*.[10] According to Brunschvicg, as we mentioned, the spirit begins, with Descartes, to discover again its creative, unconditioned freedom. Its evident sign is that in order to understand reality thought avails itself of "mathematical Physics" in place of "metaphysical Physics," through which it had, after Aristotle, made up a web of abstractions about the supernatural. Through the other physics founded on analysis, thought has gained instead the true spirituality of the real, resting on the realism of matter and life in which there is no room for the supernatural. For Brunschvicg, the transcendence of God as "Maker of heaven and earth" is a fruit of our imagination. God is discovered in consciousness, as the root of values universally acknowledged by all consciousnesses. Such a God is the *Verbum rationis*, that must be freed from every ontological hypostasis. Naturally, between this God of the "philosophers" and Abraham's and Jacob's God no compromise is possible.

In one of his last works, *Raison et religion* (Paris, 1943) Brunschvicg again occupied himself with the problem of religion. Not only reason (whose goal is the unification of experience) but also true religion (all positive religions are excluded) tends to carry out human values—the

---

[10] All the writings were gathered, after the death of Brunschvicg, in the volume *De la vraie et de la fausse conversion suivi de la Querelle sur l'Athéisme* (Paris, 1950). Cf. M. F. Sciacca, *Il problema di Dio e della religione nella filosofia attuale*, 3rd ed. (Brescia, 1953).

spiritual unity of the living and universal love. The conflict is not between reason and religion, but between concrete, historical reason and material religion based on external cult. The conflict ceases when religion is divested of its symbols, of its dogmatic letter and narrowness, and becomes rational religion, which cannot be identified with any positive religion. We have to free ourselves from that religion which is founded on the "loyalty of birth," that is, on our past as children, and then to adhere to religion as a "loyalty of spirit." Birth-loyalty is the selfish, utilitarian, social, and anthropomorphic moment in a religion (*static* religion, says Brunschvicg together with Bergson) pertaining to the *homo faber*. Spirit-loyalty, instead, is dynamic and founded on an unselfish love amongst all creatures: it is the religion pertaining to the *homo sapiens*, through which all positive religions must become true and be surpassed.

History evidences the many difficulties encountered along its course by religious rationalism in conflict with opposite conceptions: a conflict between a *vital* ego, which is shut up within its bounds and is a feeder of anthropomorphism, and a *spiritual* ego, which is the overcoming of materialism and selfishness; a conflict between an *imaginary world* and a *veracious world*—between a *human God*, who is the ordainer of the world for our use and consumption, and a *divine God*, who is not a *faber*, but a *sapiens*.

That is all very well, but what is God, then? Nothing except a scientific reason, totally manifested as mathematical physics; or, better still, God is that degree of progress carried out by human thought up to now; tomorrow the ulterior degree will be more splendid, indeed. God is human thought (or, more than that: He is the philosophy of Leon Brunschvicg): "God is such that we cannot consider ourselves as being something distinct with respect to Him, as He cannot be something distinct with respect to us." And human thought is Science, the impersonal thought which, inasmuch as it is impersonal, is a "thing," an immense and gratuitous thing like matter—it is the Thing. Brunschvicg's sophism is the same one found in modern idealism from Fichte to Gentile: human thought has the notion or the presence of the infinite (and up to this point, if the terms are well understood, one is within truth, in that truth properly belonging to Plato and Christian Platonism); therefore, human thought is infinite and is God. But, are we not to realize that infinity does not belong to human thought, which is the thought of a finite subject, but that, instead, it belongs to an objective truth being present in it? The sophism is evident; an identification of the act of thought with the objective presence of the infinite, whereby infinity, writes Brunschvicg, is "inherent in thought inasmuch as it is thought." That is enough: God is the same human thought. True. But the "notion of the infinite," spoken of also by Descartes, is all gone and thought remains in all its invincible finitude and subjectivity. At this point God can be identified with any one activity of the subject; for Brunschvicg, He is identified with mathematical physics, with science, which establishes love among men, as a kind of universal embrace. Brunschvicg, who died in 1944, had time to experience in his own person what kind of communion of spirits is realized by the "spirit of science" and what kind of monster its god is; he had time to notice that it is the "machine" and not the spirit that always constitutes a model for science, which being devoid of any intrinsically moral or religious value, cannot give itself such a spirit. "Humanism," as Bréhier would say, can give science a spirit, but humanism itself ceases to be such when it denies the true God, who is not, least of all, to be identified with the *homo sapiens* of Brunschvicg's scientist rationalism. This author was so busy persecuting idols all his life that he had no time to notice that he himself was an idolater of science; he could have also noticed that very few scientists were not idolaters or worshipers of a well-arranged matter, of a god-clock or Euclidian-god.

However, the criticism of Brunschvicg has to be further investigated in order to recover whatever positiveness can be found in his so-called idealism. A quick comparison with Croce will be helpful to this effect.

Croce gives philosophy the task of determining the fundamental forms of spiritual activity; Brunschvicg, on the other hand, does not see any compulsory itineraries to be followed by thought; yet, if spiritual activity is attained, as he claims, through the historical progress of its forms, it is still attained through those forms no matter how mobile and varied they may be. For Croce mathematical and natural sciences give rise to pseudo-concepts; for Brunschvicg, instead, they constitute knowledge true and proper; however, this does not change the fact that both of them agree on the conclusion: that there exists no problem of the spirit in itself in that the spirit is only its historical manifestations. The difference, then, consists in determining which ones are the manifestations revealing the spirit, in which the spirit entirely resolves itself; for Croce they are art, philosophy, economics, and ethics; for Brunschvicg, mathematics and physics, principally. However, the result is the same: the spirit is in its concrete acts and philosophy is a methodology of history for Croce and a methodology of sciences for Brunschvicg. The two thinkers come to an empiricist-positivistic historicism, which can also be called idealism, but one that has been deprived of its essence, its metaphysical element. Having arrived at the conclusion that spirit is its acts (its discoveries and its facts), Croce and Brunschvicg could continue their philosophizing only by reconstructing the spirit-process as a historical process, that is, by making history. In fact, Croce and Brunschvicg stopped their theorizing in order to write history: literary, political, and civil in the case of the former, and a history of sciences in the latter's case, so that both might grasp that spiritual activity that is identified with the historical process. Once again it is proven that transcendental idealism cannot go beyond a form of empirical historicism in which philosophy is dissolved and the spirit is dead and buried, if it abandons its metaphysical structure which it has in Fichte, Schelling, Hegel, and Gentile.

In fact "knowledge of the self," both for Croce and for Brunschvicg, is equal to the knowledge of man as he made himself throughout the course of history. Thus, the knowledge of the self is attained always in the moment of exteriorness, that is, in the moment of the spirit as the spirit is making itself or as it is becoming externally manifest. For these two writers there exists no problem of the subject as such, of the single man as a problem to himself, of self-consciousness as the initial positing of itself as subjectivity-objectivity, and of the concrete man; the existing problem is not that of man (you and I), but that of human history, that is, of impersonal reason. We are not denying that, as Brunschvicg writes "knowing ourselves is indeed a leaning on our own past in the hope of reviving it"; however, we hold that a "philosophy of the spirit" cannot overlook the fact that the one that leans on the self is the single subject, the ego, which by leaning on its past, is first of all positing itself as a problem, through which a solution clarifying its own personal existence is sought. History, otherwise, is a pure anonymity, that is, the history of an impersonal reason which believes to gain its maturity through mathematical physics or whatever it may be, and, instead, it remains as an eternal unconsciousness because consciousness and thought signify personality, conquest, and affirmation of personality.

Our criticism reveals itself to be more appropriate, when one considers that for Croce and Brunschvicg there exists no problem of the person, for the simple reason that, for them, the person is nobody, as it has no value at all. In fact, for example, man (the person) *is* his works and *only* his works: I am my actions, and these are all that I am, and the whole that remains of me; that is, I am not. Brunschvicg, as a matter of fact, identifies the person with the individual, and the individual with the vital ego and corporeal egoism; the person, as such, is an obstacle to the progress of reason, an obstacle to be eliminated and surpassed. In a word, I must think and act according to reason in order to deny myself as an individual, as a man, and in order to regain a united "humanity." This is Spinozism, indeed, and also Hegelianism, but in a degraded form, in that unity is not realized at the level of Substance or Idea but at that of history, that is, at the level of what is factual and empirical. In such a strange world there is no room for me and for the other person, for the feelings and for the truth that may inhere in me so intimately; there is room, instead, only for reason, which wants to make me happy at all costs, even at the expense of my own personality, since reason is fanatically intent upon becoming mature and enlightened through mathematical physics. My fellow men and I, as Croce says, can only offer our services, because we simply are obliging and transitory carriers of a "torch" passing from hand to hand, so that history may go on, reason may free itself, and freedom may delight in being free. In fact, although they lived for a long time, until only yesterday, Croce and Brunschvicg died thoroughly convinced that this is progress, and that progress is infallible, and that it is moving always rapidly toward the better even when the worse happens.

These are irremediably dead philosophies and they are particularly ridiculed by existentialist and problematical currents, which, in turn, represent their dissolution while being their legitimate heirs; from these pseudo-idealistic philosophies (which negate authentic idealism), culture and cultural problems have drawn undeniable advantages; yet, such gains cannot make up for the ruins caused by them, in that they destroyed the spirit and spiritual (human) values, even if they think that they are validly establishing and defending them. They are philosophies of might and of what is "God-reason," that is conquered through scientific development by which Nature and society will be transformed, and wherein the exaltation of man, as the artificer of science or of history, ends with man's negation in the monstrosity of the "machine" he himself has built. Marx and Marxism also have given life to the same myth. Brunschvicg and Croce object that theirs is a philosophy or, rather, a "religion" of freedom outside of which there is nothing. Thus, they too, like idolaters, create their fine theology in spite of their being against metaphysics and against theology: Croce builds that of "historicism," representing the fullness of human history, including Christianity; Brunschvicg, the other theology based on the "spirit of science." In fact, as with respect to Croce "we cannot say that we are not Christians" since through twenty centuries of historical process on the part of thought Christianity has been completed, made truer, and de-mythologized, so with respect to Brunschvicg the New Testament is the completion of the Old, and his "religion of spirit" (identical with the Crocian "religion of freedom"), or of scientific research, is the "Third Testament" completing the New one. Yet, all these conquests and new gospels end miserably by teaching us that freedom is that of nineteenth-century liberalism, and that justice (Brunschvicg writes this) is carried out by politics, that is, by democracy and, to be more precise, by the French Masonic Radical Party. With all these pitiable things in its hand, humanity can do away with God and Christianity! So great are the Westerners, the "great Europeans" of our century, at least according to the opinion of politicians in the West, including those who call themselves Catholic Christians.

The new collection, *Philosophie de la matière*, edited by R. Bayer, was initiated with Brunschvicg's volume entitled *Philosophie de l'esprit* (1949).

Thus, a volume that is entitled "philosophy of the spirit" can be inserted (and not extrinsically) in a collection of "philosophy of matter." In its preface Bayer remarks: "Philosophy of the spirit is for Brunschvicg undoubtedly defined in opposition to the philosophy of matter, and critical idealism in antinomy with immediate realism"; but, immediately afterwards he observes acutely that when Brunschvicg writes, he draws the terms "infinitely closer": "Autrement dit, nous ne pouvons pas appuyer la spiritualité sur la transcendance, sous quelque forme qu'elle se présente à nous. Il nous restera donc à rechercher comment la philosophie de l'esprit peut être définitivement conçue en tant que philosophie de l'immanence." Thus, the philosophical opposition between philosophy of spirit and that of matter is so attenuated as to vanish, precisely because spirituality cannot (and this is only a dogmatic exclusion) "rest on transcendence." This means that within a philosophy of immanence, whatever it may be like, the concept of "spirit" no longer makes any sense, and it comes to be identified with that of "matter" if it is developed critically. We agree with Bayer because we see a confirmation of what we have long been maintaining: that every immanentism is a materialism and that it may be called "idealism," "philosophy of spirit," or anything else, only because a critical investigation is lacking in it. In the particular case of Brunschvicg, everything is reduced to "matter," that is, to "things" and the mode with which thought thinks of them; and this is so because of his resolution to reject transcendence and identify spirit with scientific progress, wherein philosophy ceases to have its autonomy, and religion is relegated to the sphere of imagination and myth (unless it be scientific philosophy itself). If the spirit is only that, then there is no longer a spirit; for more than a century immanentist idealism believed itself to be a "philosophy of spirit" and, instead, it is only a "philosophy of nature" in that the spirit-nature perfect adequacy, as exacted by immanentism, leads of necessity to the imprisonment of the spirit in things. The "spiritualizing nature" formula, within a philosophy of immanence, is identical with the other one—"naturalizing the spirit." What Bayer calls "réalisme opératoire," is a form of philosophy of matter and pragmatism equal to other so-called materialistic currents including Marxism. However, it represents a more mature and critical position in the sense that, by pushing immanentism to its ultimate and legitimate consequences, it denounces its materialistic character as well as its illegitimacy as idealism and philosophy of spirit.

Nevertheless, through this "réalisme opératoire" the dogmaticalness present in Brunschvicg's philosophy has been emphasized; and Brunschvicg remains what he is—more a man of culture than an original philosopher, excelling more as a historian of science than as a historian of philosophy true and proper. His historical works, in fact, though they undeniably present a vigorousness of construction and a marked line, manifest, at sight, a unilaterality of view and a certain insensibility regarding the very problems of the spirit (ethics, aesthetics, religion). His reconstruction of the "progress of consciousness in Western philosophy," and that of "European spirit" (*L'esprit européen*, Neuchâtel, 1947), in some respects are among the most anti-Western and anti-European reconstructions we know of; they are the negation of Western philosophy and Western spirit (a negation pursued with perseverance and richness of culture and keenness), because Brunschvicg accounts only for the scientific tradition. *Progrès* is one of the most significant books in the crises of Western culture, which is carried to the point of identifying itself and the "progress of consciousness" with those elements and results representing its antithesis and destruction, when they are considered isolatedly and unilaterally. In fact, it could not be otherwise because Brunschvicg makes *scientific thought* be supreme; he identifies consciousness with mathematical and intellectual consciousness; he reduces "love" to a symbol of pure intellection; he distorts Christianity and Christian philosophy from Augustine to the present time, and he identifies the life (and progress) of the spirit with a progressive humanization of nature (that is, with its conquest), which means (and from the viewpoint of immanence it cannot signify any other thing) progressive naturalization of the spirit as well as the spirit's enslavement by Nature itself, just when the former believes that it has conquered the latter. Immanentist or scientist historicism is not Marxist only on account of incoherence and naiveness, the incoherence and naiveness of so-called Western democracy, which also makes freedom and human fullness rest on purely technical progress and on the play of production and consumption. Therefore, while denouncing all its negativeness, we hold as negatively positive the revision of immanentism made by those immanentists who have criticized its dogmaticalness even if not its premises.

Deschaux, author of a complete and systematic exposition of Brunschvicg's thought, about which he is enthusiastic, defines this thought as an "idealism of culture." Granted: idealism of culture and historicist culturalism or, if you like, culturalist historicism. However, philosophy is much more than that and something altogether different; culturalism, like historicism, is its death. Bayer on the one hand is drawing Brunschvicg's "philosophy of spirit" closer to the "philosophy of matter" while Deschaux, on the other, defines it as an "idealism of culture"; now, in doing so, both point out the limits in their countryman's pseudo-idealism.

However, one has also to acknowledge the merit due to Brunschvicg (and to others) for his protecting and upholding the theoretical value of truth and of thought together with the critical-scientific tradition, which is an essential characteristic of European culture. In times like these it is already an achievement to have some thinkers uphold, with loyalty and intransigence, the theoretical nature of thought (of philosophizing) and the validity of the principles of knowledge; today, in fact, there is a reborn neopositivistic barbarism, and the pragmatic is so overestimated that every truth is reduced to it. A useless defense, however (and even a contradictory one), in that the "theoreticity" of thought is being denied at the very moment when one affirms truth to be the outcome of history and the spirit to be its works and its action. Likewise, the true concept of European "culture" is lost when it is unilaterally and dogmatically confined only to the critical-scientific tradition; and such is the case when "culture" excludes the religious tradition, as if it were a negative one or an obstacle to its development, that must be disposed of. The authentically European "culture" is a synthesis of both traditions; and only if and when such synthesis (unity and distinction) takes place, is there true humanism and also true rationalism; instead, through their historicism, which is destructive of philosophy and, hence, of theoreticity, Brunschvicg, Croce, and others led true humanism to crisis; in fact, on the one hand, they gave support to the "crisis of principles" and of value and, on the other, they helped praxism to be so coherent as to identify philosophy with political-social action.[11]

E. E. Le Roy's "Idealistic Exigency" and Religious Pragmatism

As we know, for Kant, the existence of God is one of the three postulates of practical reason: man cannot be the adequate cause for the accord between morality and happiness; we must, then, postulate the existence of God as an intelligent Cause embracing all nature. It is, therefore, "morally" necessary to admit the existence of God. It is not a question of a theoretical proposition that is rationally demonstrable, since it is a postulate held necessary for the practical use of reason. Morality is fulfilled through (natural) religion, that is, through the action of a spirit conceiving the idea of a moral Author of the world: metaphysical agnosticism, on the one hand (indemonstrability of God's existence), and religious pragmatism, on the other (practical postulation of God). This Kantian position was elaborated and reconstructed in many ways, and it influenced the attitude of many modern thinkers, who were led by a

---

[11] Brunschvicg had some influence on contemporary French thought even after his death in Bachelard, *La philosophie du Non* (1940); in George Bastide, *De la condition humaine* (1939), and in Ferdinand Alquié; finally in Stephan Souriau, *Instauration philosophique* (1939) and *Les différents modes d'existence* (1943).

voluntaristic, anti-intellectualistic and, in general, pragmatist orientation; in this way, even James's "will to believe" is inspired by Kant though, in other respects, these two philosophers are not close to each other.

The Frenchman EDOUARD LE ROY (1870-1954) also entertains a pragmatist conception of religion (and of dogma); a mathematician and a philosopher, he was Bergson's follower as well as his successor at the Collège de France. We are not going to deal with Le Roy as a critic of science and as a theorist of religious pragmatism linked to the modernist movement, because the writings regarding these problems are prior to the chronological limits of our work. Yet, we have to mention his volume, *Le problème de Dieu* (Paris, 1930), which gathers together previously published articles and lectures (among them the two famous writings on how one must posit the problem of God, 1907), and his *Introduction à l'étude du problème religieux* (Paris, 1944).

Le Roy moves from the "idealistic exigency," that is, every question on existence postulates thought or consciousness and it is nothing outside of it. Therefore nothing can be presupposed to thought which is "an integral action of the spirit, in that it aims at knowledge." For Le Roy, thought is a "perennial initiative," and an "exigency for an infinite impetus beyond every given necessity." This Bergsonian theme, together with the concept of "intuition" opposed to analytical thought, is present in all his works; on the one hand, "intuition," as antecedent to the distinction of subject and object, penetrates reality, grasping its change, mobility and creative flux beneath substance and conceptual frames; analytical thought, instead, breaks the indivisible frame of reality, which it immobilizes within a net of inert concepts, whose value is utilitarian and economic. The immediate is the very act of thought, which is a perpetual creation. Whereas immovable being is represented by a "thought already acted upon," creative being is "acting thought" (Gentile would say: "thought already thought of" and "thinking thought," but Le Roy lacks the dialectic of the two moments); synthesis is produced by action whereby intelligence is not excluded. "Every thought implies the affirmation of God." God is the supreme value, the "first and absolute subsistence," that which is above real, "above and not beneath, beyond and not on this side of every perceptible and conceivable reality." Even when one denies God, in the last anaysis one believes in Him, because "when one affirms Reason, Truth, and Justice as superior and sovereign realities deserving every sacrifice, and such that, morally, they dominate us, one believes in God." God is not *my* thought, but *the* Thought, and I am intrinsic in it. Thus, He "is more intrinsic in us than we are in ourselves, because He is a vivifying inspiration in us; and as an inspiration soliciting us from within so that we may overcome ourselves, God transcends us infinitely." He is both immanence and transcendence. We grasp God in ourselves as an interior and profound infinite source of all our person. "However, in grasping Him, we perceive Him as a supranaturalizing grace, that is, as an impulse which, like a call to transcendence, always and infinitely is leading us to surpass our present nature as well as every finite nature." There is only an inner experience regarding God. To affirm God is to affirm the principle of moral exigency.

In other words, being intrinsic in thought the idea of truth implies the Absolute; yet, thought always knows itself incompletely; for this reason it is unceasingly led to surpass itself in the direction of the Absolute or supreme Thought. This does not mean that we demonstrate the existence of God (indeed, Le Roy disputes the validity of all traditional proofs) in that no logical necessity can explain God Himself ("deducing God is the same as denying Him"); it only points out the fact that in his consciousness man has an explicit experience of Him.

What this idea of a truth being intrinsic in thought really means is not clear; and this is so both because for Le Roy a knowledge going beyond discourse and logical necessity is a perfect knowledge (though it does exclude the rational moment), and because, according to him, more than reason God is essentially a will being present in our own will. Thus, on the one hand, we have "faith in God" and, on the other, the affirmation of His existence as the affirmation of the "supremacy of moral reality," which is "the first root of being and the principle of existence"; therefore, under the impetus of God's presence in our will and of the inquietude ensuing from it, there cannot be a demonstration but an "elevation" to God. At this point, Le Roy's "idealistic exigency" loses its theoretical character (nothing is antecedent to thought), and it resolves into a pragmatist and purely voluntaristic exigency which, on the one hand, is fideism and, on the other, runs the risk of denying God's transcendence and eternity. Lavelle rightly remarks: "After identifying substance with change devoid of any support and after holding duration as a creative entity, is it still possible to escape from the idea of a God who is simultaneously 'becoming' with creation? It seems impossible that we find a way whereby God still maintains a character of eternity, unless His duration, rather than the essence of reality, is made a particular dimension of the universe, through which all finite beings can, indeed, be distinguished from each other and each one can make its own being through an act of its own will."

The thesis of modernism is also a voluntaristic one; it is a religious movement that in the first decade of our century tried to shake from its foundations the whole dogmatics of the Catholic Church. Both as an effort to reform the church from within and as a doctrinary content, modernism has lost almost all its importance in the last twenty-five years or thereabout; as a live movement it precedes the limits imposed on our exposition. We think, nonetheless, that it is useful to fix some of its fundamental concepts, particularly those concepts having a present-day value provided they are transferred to a different level.

The greatest representatives of modernism, whether considered for their theoretical contributions or for their contributions to the history of Christianity in its first centuries, are Laberthonniere, Le Roy, and Loisy in France, Tyrell in England, and Bonaiuti in Italy. Modernists, unlike some pragmatists, first of all admit that the content of religious experience is supernatural; yet, in agreement with the pragmatists, they affirm that it corresponds to exigencies of life, that is, to a practical and not to an epistemological need. God is not an object of knowledge, so that it is impossible to give a rational demonstration of His existence. God is living in us as He is an integral part of our being; therefore, it is through action that a contact is established between us and Him. The supernatural is not the object of reason but of faith, and it is exacted by action. Nor does it imply a contrast between religion and philosophy, because the two actions are found on two diverse levels: the former is founded on exigencies of faith and action and the latter on speculative and hypothetical affirmations. Dogma itself is not in contrast with philosophical truths, both because dogma is subject to historical evolution and because religion experiences its truths *ab intra*, while philosophy experiences them *ab extra*.

ALFRED LOISY (1857-1940) insists on the essentially social character of religion, particularly in his work *Religion et humanité* (Paris, 1926). Religious activity is a vital impetus because it aids man in his ascension from animality to spirituality and also guides him toward his ideal of a "good society." Besides being mystical, the character of religion is moral; that is, it is a sentiment of respect and reverence man entertains toward himself, his fellow men, and the universe—morality is an essential character of religion. This does not mean that morality and religion are identified; the former considers things as being *compulsory*, the latter as being *venerable*. Both, nonetheless, tend to become one thing: "Morality and religion jointly refer to the superior life of humanity, of which they represent two aspects rather than two distinct spheres. This superior life, inasmuch as it is life, is movement and action. If one deeply examines the two notions of religion and morality so that they may be brought back to their pure concept and be given their highest realization, one finds that they tend to be only one thing, the very perfection of humanity. Religion always is a spirit animating morality, and morality always is like the practice of religion. It is religion that gives a sacred character of obligation to the principles of morality; it is religion that aids in respecting them as duties; and it is through this duty-observance that religion is fulfilled."

Besides being related to pragmatism, modernism is closely related to modern idealism: the Hegel-Feuerbach-Strauss-Renan-Loisy line is uninterrupted and it indicates a historical succession. In fact, with the so-called historical method Loisy wound up denying miracles (they are not historical "facts," but "visions" by the first Christians) as well as dogmas, that is, all revelation.[12]

7. J. BENDA'S IDEALISM WITHOUT IDEAS

The writer JULIEN BENDA (1867-1956) is to be placed outside of all currents in present-day philosophy; at times an effective and keen essayist and polemist, he is the author of novels which, to tell the truth, are not novels, and of books of philosophy that are not philosophy; yet, his writings are significant as a criticism of some aspects of contemporary thought and life. As an implacable and venomous criticism against the aesthetic of contemporary French society, *Belphé-gor* (Paris, 1919) remains his best work for keenness of analysis and force of argumentation. All aspects that are characteristic of today's French cultural thought—and not French only—are made the object of his attacks and they are rebuked mercilessly. Aspects that are typical of many sectors in contemporary culture are put on the spit (life as absolute dynamism; art as passion and immediateness; the struggle against intelligence, order, rationality, and law; the exaltation of instinct, of the mobile, contingent, subjective, and so on). Benda calls it an "aesthetics for women," created and used by women; for him the highest exponent of this aesthetics is Bergson of whom he is as fond as he is a severe and, at times, unjust critic.

What does Benda oppose to this ethics of feminism and of superficial and decadent "pan-lyricism"? He opposes two worlds armed against each other: on one side, the beautiful world of women, of loves, and of earthly and erotic emotions; on the other, a kind of Platonic superheaven containing all essences, all pure forms, order and intellectual beauty—in this latter world the passions are lightly felt and they slip away, silently. From the loftiness of that intelligible order, the earthly vicissitude appears as being unworthy of being lived through. There is, then, an irreducible dualism between flesh and spirit, sense and abstraction. The object of philosophy cannot be the problems of political and social life, which are shaken and excited by passion, but the traditional, eternal problems of metaphysics, the Eternal, the Absolute, the Necessary, God, Parmenides' and Plato's world. However, Benda, who points to this heaven of salvation, cannot forget the earth, women, and love. In reading him one gets

[12] The modernistic doctrines were undoubtedly influenced by Blondel's *Action* (1893), but it is an error to number Blondel among the modernists.

the impression that his limpid and immovable, metaphysical heaven is furrowed and shaken by the quivers of the flesh.

With his effort to find a reconciliation-point in sentiment, in his *Lettres à Mélisande* (Paris, 1926) he seems to be attempting a mitigation of his metaphysical dualism between heaven and earth; on the other hand, in his *The Betrayal of the Intellectuals* (trans. R. Aldington, Boston, 1955) and in its continuation *La fin de l'éternel* (Paris, 1928), Benda sharpens his dualism once again.

Clerics, he says, "essentially act not in seeking practical ends but for the purpose of getting their rejoicing in the exercise of art and science or in that of metaphysical speculation; in short, they aim at a good that is extratemporal, and their motto is: 'Our world does not belong to this world.'" *Laymen,* on the other hand, are all those engaged in a practical action resting on personal gain and led by earthly and temporal passions. In short, clerics are the dwellers of the world of spirit and laymen those of the domain of the flesh.

Now, according to Benda (and he is not entirely wrong), since the last century or thereabout, and particularly in our days, the *clerics* have become used to tilling the laymen's land; that is, they indulge in the world of social, political, and economic passions in such a way that spiritual goods and theoretical values are neglected by them. They ended up sanctifying earthly things (Class, State, Nationality), while desecrating the traditional values of Justice, Humanity, and the like, which Benda wants to defend at all costs. The *cleric* has wound up applauding the *layman;* and this is what "the betrayal by the clerics" signifies. The sure consequence of this betrayal, wrote Benda in 1928, will be the downfall of our civilization under the rumble and weight of a very deadly war. Péguy, Barrès, Kipling, Maurras, and D'Annunzio must especially bear the responsibility among the betraying clerics; while Fichte, Hegel, Marx, Nietzsche and, more than anybody else, Bergson are brought to trial in the *La fin de l'éternel, op. cit.* Thus, Benda confirms the fathomless abyss between practical and spiritual, politics and justice, philosophy and practical activity, and between sin or the reign of Caesar—negation of God —and justice, truth, charity, eternal and extrahistoric values, and affirmation of God.

However, when, on the ruins of his polemic Benda tried to rebuild his thought (in his *Essai d'un discours cohérent sur les rapports de Dieu et du monde,* Paris, 1931), he could not give us anything better than a coacervation of Oriental and Greek theology, of positivistic evolutionism, and Schopenhauerian themes, all of which were summoned to give their support to his dualism between a God being conceived as the Infinite and the Indeterminate, and a world that is finite and determinate. There is no passage between God and the world; the world exists because it has detached itself from God, it has fallen, and it has turned against Him. The origin of the world is due to an act of bad will by the world itself. The world is an evolution from inert matter to man, from what is indistinct to what becomes distinct; and it had only one aim, that of being always more opposed to and always farther from God. Man is the culmination of this evolution process *against* God. Yet, it is precisely in man that the will to renunciation is manifested together with a will to go back and be drowned in God Himself. It is the *clerics'* duty to redeem themselves from their own betrayal, as well as to incite the laymen toward hastening their absorption in the divine Nothingness. Thus, the Platonic idealism is deprived of its Ideas and the only thing left is emptiness. In that which I believe to be his last work *La France byzantine*, Paris, 1945) Benda displays another denunciation; and this time the latter is at the expense of the existentialistic currents which substitute intelligence or thought with "availability" (a hint at Marcel), a sort of magic mysticism or a mysticism of the senses, and the like, which is a sensual exaltation at the expense of reason, idea or objective truth. Philosophical categories are by now substituted with dream, delirium, the subconscious, hallucination, novelty, the fluid, the primitive, the gratuitous, and so on. Well, not all the fault is his; yet it is not enough to play the part of the public accuser; one must also know how to build and to do this in conformity with truth and reason.

VII

REALISM AND NATURALISM
IN ENGLAND AND
THE UNITED STATES

---

1. Orientations in Anglo-North American Thought

In this chapter and in the next we shall dwell on some currents of thought (at present dominating, together with phenomenology and particularly with existentialism, in vast areas of the world) which border upon philosophy true and proper as they often lack understanding toward spiritual questions or represent a negation of philosophy itself, which they reduce to a mere problem of sciences and even of technology. Their fortune, even in the Western world, is a symptom of the crisis and a sign that the spirit of philosophy (and of culture) in the West is, by now, confined to a few oases (fruitful oases, indeed) surrounded by the desert. The "collapse of being," the "crisis of the foundations" and of principles, the decadence of the critical and "humanistic" tradition and of "culture" in a European sense have struck the millenary structure of the so-called West, and they continue to eat away its roots more than phylloxera does with vines. Although the pseudo-philosophical orientations we are about to treat possess some positive elements (one, for instance, is their calling attention to problems that must not be neglected), they are the measure (even more than some of the worse aspects in existentialism) of the confusion, superficiality, and coarseness with which some people write about and discuss philosophy; they also denote an insensibility to all the problems of the spirit, metaphysical, aesthetical, moral, and religious. A new, scientist barbarism that is greater than that expressed by positivism in the last century is unable to distinguish between spirit and nature (matter), between morality and biology, or technology and truth of reason, and so forth. It seems, at times, that millennia of classical and Christian thought all of a sudden have sunk, and that the critical sense, which is a finesse of shades and neatness of distinctions, has disappeared from European intellects in order to give place to mixtures properly belonging to primitives. England and the United States of America are the countries that, besides the communistic ones, suffer most from the attacks of the new Ostrogoths of philosophy (and of culture); although already injured by corrosive and destructive forces, the Latin West (including South America) as well as Germany are defending themselves as best they can. In the course of these last chapters we shall have the opportunity of touching again on this topic and presenting some critical remarks.

Around the beginning of our century, at the height of idealism, the neorealist movement made its appearance in England; idealism, since then, has witnessed its own gradual decline and naturalism, its rising affirmation, that paved the way to present-day logical positivism. The difference has greatly decreased between Cantabrigian philosophy, which is dominated by the influence coming from mathematics, and Oxonian philosophy, which in its humanistic and historic character is open to the problems of metaphysics and ethics; as a matter of fact, scientificalism is prevalent even at Oxford. Realism itself is in decline by now, and an occasional more recent idealistic flash (which we have already noticed) is almost extinguished; logical positivism seems to be in the process of absorbing almost all other currents. Yet, since the end of the last war there is in England a certain revival of religious and theological studies; and, without preconceptions or ill will, even Protestant writers show an interest in Catholic theology and in Thomistic philosophy; even existentialism has aroused some interest there. In addition it must be said that, more than any other in Western Europe, English society lately has been going through a radical transformation. In spite of everything, one notes a certain weariness toward naturalism, scientificalism, and logical positivism, whose outcome is skepticism. There is a chance that the few ferments together with the many inner inquietudes may concretely lead to a revival in the moral and religious values; however, at the present stage it seems to us that precisely these two countries—England and the United States—are in the greatest danger of accepting some Marxist doctrines. And this is said in spite of the fact that they are free from both a strong communist nucleus organized as a political party, and from an official Marxist culture that is doctrinally well prepared and aggressive; moreover, such an acceptance cannot be due to the social conditions prevailing in the two countries, but, rather to the dominant philosophical doctrines (having so many points in common with Marxism), which have debased or unhinged the spiritual values.

The discourse is, perhaps, more complex when it is related to the United States of America; this young nation is without a truly autonomous, philosophical tradition, if an exception is made for that Christian Platonism (engrafted upon the indigenous, religious tradition) which, imported by the European colonizers, is still enrooted and present more as a moment of immediate life than as reflective consciousness. In the curiosity and, I would say, in the wonder and impetus with which the American receives the most disparate doctrines, more with his imagination than with his reason (as children do with tales), undoubtedly there is a good dose of ingenuousness and critical immaturity, even if united to an almost youthful freshness. The lack of an autonomous, speculative tradition and of mental structures matured through a long philosophical elaboration gives American mentality both a certain malleability (which is not plasticity) and a capacity of absorption, which is not yet a force of assimilation. "Their wisdom," writes Santayana, "is rather tenuous and, principally, made up of words, so that it is neither fully certain of its grounds nor aware of its ultimate meaning; consequently, their physical and emotional development may have to endure an arrest detrimental to a normal course."

People speak quite frequently about American "pragmatism" as a philosophy truly consonant with the *forma mentis* belonging to that nation. More than a philosophy true and proper, that term signifies an ensemble of national characteristics: a distinct "realism" in the sense of conforming to the "facts" or to concrete things, coupled with a repugnance for the abstract and for aprioristic and metaphysical constructions; an explicit or implicit supremacy of the practical over the theoretical, which is considered to be valid only as an instrument of action through which the natural or social environment is to be changed or conquered; an immediate trust in common sense without the complications of reflective thought, making difficult what is easy and complicated what is simple— after all, reflective thought causes the action to be preceded by a rational process, and this slows down the action and takes away its impetus, while the risk, enthusiasm, and conquering power in it are diminished. With a view of their being more effective and more "productive" this pragmatism and this empiricism are not to be entrusted only to their disarmed and pure immediateness; we must organize and equip them with "methods" and with all other weapons or "instruments" supplied by reason, in order that a maximum of success be achieved by the action; and, measured by the "practical outcome" and by the conquests already attained, this success indicates also the progress and betterment of the human community.

However, if the action and even the sense of life are understood in this way (and in America he is "honest" "who produces" better and at a lower cost; and he is a "benefactor" who knows how to give humanity a new comfort), from where can we get methods and instruments? They cannot be obtained from metaphysics or from philosophy (as we understand it—or as we used to understand it?—in Western Europe or, I would say in "Mediterranean" Europe if I could also include Germany), which are "disinterested" since, as their object they do not have things but being, which is spirit, that is, their object is not practice but the "theory" of practice; those methods and instruments cannot even be gotten from a humanistic culture as we are accustomed to understand it. Only science and technology can supply them adequately. Hence, for a people that technically and economically has realized such a great development (one could paradoxically say that this development is the true "culture" and even the substrate of American "spirituality"), it is not difficult to arrive at the following conclusion: scientific knowledge is the prototype of all knowledge and, thus, the only valid form in that it is practically effectual and experimentally verifiable. After all, that development has, almost exclusively, occupied and preoccupied this people, to the point that it conditions and defines (with few exceptions) even the religious and moral custom. Philosophy, then, must assume the same object and the same methods as science; the several forms of spiritual activity (aesthetics, ethics, religion, and so on) must also be studied "scientifically," as empirical facts that are to be observed, checked, and accepted for what is verifiable in them. Hence, another generalization becomes possible: between nature and spirit there is no substantial or qualitative difference—spirit is one of the natural phenomena. Naturally, as a result of such a conception, in the very act with which philosophy posits its own problem, it renounces not only its autonomy but also itself as a philosophy *tout court*, since it is bound to identify its own development with the progress in mathematical and physical, biological and psychological sciences, and so forth; that is, philosophy must accept as problems and solutions of its own, such problems and solutions as science posits and gives to itself.

Even though some significant exceptions continue to be present, things may not change in the United States for some time; and this, we believe, for two reasons: (1) simultaneously with or prior to its technical and economic development, North America did not have (and still does not have) either a philosophical thought in the Western sense nor a humanism of the spirit and of spiritual values and, consequently, it has increased its body, to use Bergson's happy expression, beyond measure while remaining small in its soul; (2) it was colonized by the least European people of Europe, the British, who always conceived colonization according to the economic terms of exploitation and production, so that British colonies were given not a "culture" in the humanistic sense, but a "civilization" in the sense of technology and external progress, as the most valid and most "rational" means of economic exploitation. Christianity, as it spread along with the European conqueror, had to cope with the latter's politics and interests: faith was to be engrafted both on a mentality resting on technical progress and economic exploitation (of which the conquered people were only instruments or "things") and on an empiricist philosophy (British philosophy) that is suitable for and connatural with that mentality. The United States (and other peoples) in the first place came to know the worse aspects of Europe, and this acquaintance was brought about by the people least endowed with "European spirit." One could say that for centuries the United States went on knowing the European "nonculture" through the economist, mercantilist, and empiricist mentality of England, for which progress meant, prevalently, the exploitation of riches, the conquest of new markets, and the extreme degradation of the human dignity of the people being dominated, and so on; that is, progress has been identified with that "Marxist" element which has always been present in the history of mankind, even if while having its origin in Protestant, Calvinist, and Anglican capitalism, its importance became predominant only since the last century, approximately. Marx, perhaps, became a "Marxist" in London, in the midst of that liberal society, whose ethics was utilitarianism, whose "spirit" was the great industrial concerns, and whose god was technological progress; and all this had to be harmonized with the evangelical parables and the "Sermon on the Mount."

It seems to us, therefore, that the United States of America, a young people endowed with so many positive qualities that we Europeans perhaps no longer possess, may be exposed to the following danger (which is also our danger): that the empiricist-scientist mentality may prevail in such a determinant way as to be considered true "superiority" (and such acts of national pride are possible when a formidable economic and military might is involved). Should this occur, then a contempt would follow for anything that is not reducible to that mentality, and also an attempt to impose it on all (even if it were to be imposed with the method of democratic . . . "freedom") without there being any opportunity for assimilating (and I say "assimilating," in its truest and strongest meaning) the critical, philosophical, and "humanistic" mentality belonging to authentic Europe (or to that little portion of it still vitally surviving); in such a case, the West would be confronted with a threat from within no less grave than the threat coming from without, so that the

392

whole Occident in its way of conceiving life could find itself reduced to Marxism, even if governed by the most comfortable, political democracy. However, there is a not entirely vain hope still resting with America. Precisely on account of what we called its malleability and its lack of a centuries-old tradition, the contact with spiritual values, as these have been elaborated in the course of thirty centuries by the Mediterranean civilization, may convince this nation of the following: that technical progress is not spiritual elevation at all; that philosophy has the spirit as its object, and truth as its end; that truth guides action and it does not derive from action; that science is not philosophy and that spiritual freedom is quite different from political freedom, which can subsist even in a society that has killed the spirit in matter and man, in the midst of the most perfect, technological progress. Only if the Western world (Europe and the Americas) succeeds in reconquering this conviction, will it be able to say that the battle was won; and only in that case will its resistance to the so-called Russian-Asiatic Orient truly gain significance. Otherwise, all resistance is senseless; there is no need to oppose a barbaric invasion when the people resisting it have already perpetrated the same thing in their own way. Once this barbarization has been perpetrated and the spirit is dead, it is all the same whether a purely earthly humanity be governed by a political democracy or by one that is social or popular; this is a question of concern to the politicians only.

Through the exposition of the philosophical currents treated in this chapter and in the next, the reader can become aware of the truth of what we have been saying with extreme frankness. Somebody else before us and like us has already joined together realism, naturalism, Anglo-American logical positivism, and historical materialism under the common label of "philosophy of matter." We grant that that is a label, but it does not affect the surface only; the reader can see by himself the relationships and points of contact. Therefore, since today those philosophies are predominant in the universities of England and of America (and in those of other smaller countries), and since even Husserl's phenomenology has been weakened into a form of naturalism, it follows that a conception of life, at least akin and not repugnant to the Marxist one—as regards, I say, the philosophical thesis and not as a method or a political *praxis*—is predominant in those countries. The difference, then, and the conflict which today is so acute can only be a question of political method and of economic interests; all this is remarkable, indeed, but it still is a meager consolation to be materialists in a regime based on a political democracy rather than in one based on a popular democracy. The invasion in process against the spirit still remains a factual datum whether it is coming from the Goths of the East or the Goths of the West.

It seems to us that we gave some essential reasons why North American thought prevalently is pragmatist, naturalist, and scientist; with its emphasis on science and technology it denotes a poverty of critical spirit and even scientific spirit, in the sense that the two terms have within the European cultural tradition. When theoretical activity is dominated by the practical one (of which it is an instrument), its truth is both measured by actual success and replaced by a "technical means" capable of assuring a greater result. Under these circumstances the political and social moment acquires, of necessity, an interest and an importance that become predominant and almost unique (as in Marxism). Furthermore, the salvation of the world and the universal panacea rest on a political category, democracy, that is, on an external structure, which in itself is destitute of a moral content. Morality, like truth, is not a question either of majority, of organization, or of "plans"; it is another thing entirely and when it is wanting cannot be given by any political form whatsoever. Otherwise we have a prevailing of social ethics over personal "morality," and yet the latter is the only one that expresses principles that are truly universal and capable of realizing concretely a human communion not on the basis of a socially well-distributed egoism, so that each person satisfies his own wants, but on the basis of a scale of values, the vital ones of which (and their corresponding goods) represent the condition and the means for the establishment of the spiritual values, which are qualitatively superior. Only an intrinsic adherence to these values will permit man's betterment and elevation (even this is an interior and personal achievement though within the human community); that is, it will permit the realization of spiritual freedom (in the spirit), of which political freedom, though not a negligible aspect, becomes an insignificant one if it is by itself. Spiritual freedom, unquestionably, is the freedom of man as a spirit. Otherwise, just when we think we are resisting communism (or Marxism)—according to the current use of the terms—we fall into it, causing its victory through the same stratagem with which we hoped to defeat it. If the repugnance is confined only to a political method rather than to a conception of life, there can be no doubt concerning the outcome of this conflict.

We do not believe that all men of thought in North America have a clear awareness of what we are arguing here; on the contrary, many of them, upon reading these pages, will be surprised and baffled at so much apparent misunderstanding on our part. This results from that bit of ingenuous freshness persisting in them, through which they are, to an extent, redeemed (unlike the British). Theirs is an easy and enthusiastic optimism; an immediate feeling of human solidarity (which has been shown in so many cases); a certain shallowness in their mode of judging; horror for human miseries, sorrows, and sufferings; a repugnance toward evil which they carry to the point of believing that it can be eliminated from man and from society through technological progress and through the "school of democracy." And, in spite of all the disproofs, they persistently and with a missionary zeal want to carry such a progress and such a democracy everywhere, trusting that the lesson can be learned in a fortnight in the same way that one learns the keyboard on a typewriter or on a calculating-machine. All this (and more) has its good sides, but it is also very dangerous; it makes life tasteless and obtuse, as life becomes restricted to a sporting competition and to a kind of permanent advertising-board with revolving characters; and, by pushing things too far, man becomes a very comfortable and satisfied animal, whose consciousness is reduced to the pleasurable sensations of enjoyment or of risk. Now, Christianity (and Western thought, even of the non-Christian type, has been investigating and digging out these principles for twenty centuries) has revealed to man his misery and his greatness—a misery of sin and, therefore, evil and sorrow, but also a greatness of thought. A Christianity free from sin (and one that considers evil eradicable from man through man's action) is negated at the start; and, likewise, that Christianity is anti-Christian which does not recognize the rational and spiritual values and the possibility of man's elevating himself by incarnating them. A conception of the human person and of the person's betterment must make room for the spirit and for the problems of the destiny of each individual man, of suffering and of death, and of the freedom of the spirit. This is the only conception that can establish a true communion of spirits. Otherwise, it is not a conception of the person, but that of a biped cut out from the fauna of the earth's crust and "observed" with special attention to his individual and social behavior, as well as to the mechanism regulating and determining that behavior.

All this had to be said without a distortion of words or intentional mitigations (which often show self-interest and hypocrisy). After all, we are not here foolishly condemning either science, technological progress, or the material betterment of human society. On the contrary, it is a good thing to favor them; but let us not say that science and technological-social progress are a remedy for all evils, or that they by themselves make mankind advance and man attain his fullness as a man or as a person, which, instead, they can dishearten and oppress. At this price, the country that is technically most backward but capable of expressing the spiritual values is immeasurably preferable to any other highly advanced nation; it is in the former that man and his humanity are still living. Only when "matter" is an instrument of the spirit, and methods of organization or observation of nature are distinct from those fit for spiritual life, only then are forward steps achieved. Otherwise, as is happening under the appearances of who knows what kind of progress, we take one hundred steps toward man's animality and more than one thousand backward with respect to his spirituality.

Going back to philosophy true and proper, we can say that in the last thirty years it has undoubtedly gained in America an ever increasing interest and a hitherto unknown consideration; there are numerous publications, periodicals, philosophical organizations, and so forth, as well as curricula in the many universities. Evidently, such interest is principally directed toward a determinate philosophy, namely, the one that, produced by sociologists, concerns itself with social problems; or that of the scientists which concerns itself with scientific methodology; and finally the philosophy of the politicians, which concerns the problems of politics. We would have nothing to say against all this, if such questions were posited on a philosophical basis, since as philosophical questions they would have to rest on speculative conceptions that had already assumed a theoretical position with respect to the greatest problems of the spirit. Unfortunately, it is not so (or it is so very rarely): it is the philosophical problems that are treated (or mistreated) with the methods of science, so that only a scientific methodology is produced (which is not, as yet, even the "problem of science" as a philosophical problem); the speculative problems true and proper are, instead, neglected as making no sense, in that they are not "verifiable"; or, else, a naturalistic and materialistic metaphysics is produced. However, be that as it may, in these last years philosophy has gained importance and even prestige in the United States. The establishment of the "Carus Conference" is one of the most conspicuous proofs, even with respect to the quality of the many volumes already published, as well as for the quality of the authors who are among the most representative. Publications based on a multiple or collective collaboration have come out at an increased pace; and through them, the orientation in present-day thought is better indicated than it is through the writings of individual authors; what is more, it seems to us that, through these short syntheses of his thought or self-presentations, the American philosopher gives the best he can of himself, and in the works with a larger scope he shows, on the other hand, that the architectonic systematization is not suitable to him.[1] Even this method of collective collaboration (leaving aside the intrinsic value in the works) is of significance. In fact, science is collective, whereas philosophy, like art, is the work of individuals, it is a "monastic" activity and, like mysticism,

---

[1] Cf. *Contemporary American Philosophy Today and Tomorrow*, by H. M. Kallen (1935); *Naturalism and Human Spirit*, by Y. H. Krikorian (1944); *A Philosophy for the Future: the Research of Modern Materialism*, by R. W. Sellars, V. I. McGill, and M. Farber (1949); *American Philosophy*, Vol. I of 2 vols.: *Philosophic Thought in France and the United States; essays representing major trends in contemporary French and American philosophy*, by M. Farber (1950).

I would say, it is anchoretic; for this reason philosophy is universally human and capable of carrying out (after religion) the highest form of spiritual communion. However, this spirit of collectivism and "co-opera- tive society" is typical of the "industrial" mentality; one of its most apparent expressions is found, in fact, in the United Nations, this ple- thoric and confused institution has, it seems, the ambition of defining even a philosophy acceptable to all! To arrive at a philosophic *trust* is a bit too much, at least until we are allowed to distinguish it from petroleum or other commodities. It may be that we will have a "Charter" for phi- losophy or a Statute such as the one we have for the United Nations; and then conflicts and confusion will be greater. However, let us hope that some honest European or American may continue to survive and exert the right of veto even if this not be granted.

North American philosophy, as we mentioned, still lacks the character of a national philosophy. True, philosophy is never national; yet a people may express exigencies and a philosophical "spirit" characterizing its thought, which in itself has a universal character. Now, to date no philo- sophical system has originated in the United States; all the tendencies en- countered there were imported, and not one was expressed on American soil, even if, once there, it went through a particular and also original acclimatization. Moreover, this judgment of ours is shared by Schneider, who is the author of a scholarly history of American philosophy: "When a new idea comes to us we project it semi-consciously, against one his- torical perspective after another to discover what meanings or sig- nificances it may acquire when placed in various contexts. After a series of experiments in interpretations, we discover how and where the new idea can best be used and assimilated." [2] American philosophy, in short, is the ensemble of the reactions aroused there by philosophies born and elaborated elsewhere.

2. British Neorealism: G. Moore, B. Russell, S. Alexander, J. Laird, C. Broad, and L. Morgan

Conducted with a polemical spirit against idealism and pragmatism, the following is the program of British neorealism: adherence to concrete experience; progress of science through the perfecting of its methods, so that advancement may be attained in technology also, which in turn stimulates social (and also moral) progress; solutions of the problems of real life according to contingencies and independently of abstract apriorisms, ideological presuppositions, and religious beliefs. Most im-

[2] H. W. Schneider, *A History of American Philosophy* (New York, 1963); A. C. Benjamin also affirms that in American philosophy it is not possible to discover "the distinctive characteristics of a national philosophy" (*American Philosophy, op. cit.*).

portant are the problems of method and of science, which are identified with scientific knowledge. For idealism there is only one method of unification of reality (the unity of absolute Consciousness); for neo-realism, instead, the methods are numerous according to the various forms of experience: the pluralism of methods warrants the validity in the many plans of scientific knowledge relatively to each one of them.

On account of its radical naturalism and scientism applied even to moral and religious thought, most recent Anglo-Saxon thought presents some traits that are opposed to those of French, German, Italian, and Spanish philosophy. Even this is a form of absolute humanism, but one in which man is a being among the so many beings of nature; consequently, this is a naturalistic humanism. For the neorealists, for example, the greatest interest in knowledge is not represented by the epistemological fact but by the content of knowledge itself. Is it a materialism, then? No, they say, as we shall see, because materialism is a static doctrine; on the contrary, for them time is an integral part of the cosmical system; the primary element is not the atom, but the *event*, that is, "the spatial point taken in the instant of time." This spatio-temporal primary element is an evolutional complex, whose phases are ordained by the categories, that is, by the forms constituting the very reality of objects. Through these various forms the spatio-temporal becoming is specified in different de-grees of reality, from the lowest to the highest one, which is the organi-zation of the human spirit. Therefore, for the neorealists the subject, though the most important, is only a particular case in the universal objectivity; it is a moment within the cosmical becoming. North Ameri-can neorealists go as far as to reduce the so-called acts of knowledge to natural events; there is for them no difference between an act of knowl-edge and, let us say, raining. Physical and human facts, as well as physio-logical and spiritual ones, are placed on the same level. Perception and the photograph of a star, says Russell, can be very well substituted by each other.

On the one hand, neorealism puts consciousness (the center of reality for idealism) on the same level as other things; on the other, against the subjectivism of pragmatists and intuitionists, it holds a decisive objectivism as it overestimates science already underestimated by the idealistic cur-rents. Scientific concepts and abstract schemes held by idealism as a fiction, or pseudo-concepts through which the concreteness of reality is not attained, are given by the neorealists an honored place and considered objective entities, that is, a true essence of reality itself. Reality is not, as Bergson says, a continuous flux, but a plurality of objective essences: consciousness does not constitute the reality of objects, which are not necessarily bound up with thought; spirit itself is only one among so many groups of external relations running through real entities. Thus neorealism links itself to classical British empiricism but, unlike the latter which stops at the analysis of the subjective datum in knowledge (sensation), it accounts for the content in knowledge, for the *res,* in which not only physical facts but also spiritual acts are solved. In short, for neorealism the point is to establish the foundation of "being" independently of the "being already known."

Neorealism is: (1) *naturalistic;* in fact, man is an integral part of nature and nothing can essentially distinguish him from the other beings—even spiritual acts are corporeal or material phenomena; (2) therefore it is *materialistic*—even if its materialism differs from the classical one; (3) it is *empiricist*—every knowledge comes from sensorial experience and, consequently, the only form of knowledge is the scientific one and the only valid methods are those of the natural sciences; (4) thus, it is *scientistic*—the only true method is the scientific one, through which we must study even morality, aesthetics, and religion and, since these do not constitute an autonomous source of knowledge, they offer less interest than physics, mathematics, and biology; (5) it is *antimetaphysical*—all that is not reducible to science and to the methods of the science of nature is pseudo-problem and nonsense; (6) it is *antisystematic*—research must be confined to particular problems, since the truths in the sciences are particular and their methods various; (7) it is *rationalistic*—only rational or analytical methods are valid.

What is philosophy, then? Only this: an analysis of the scientific notions of physics, biology, and so on, and, as used to be stated also by positivism in the last century, a kind of synthesis of the particular findings by the particular sciences of nature. What about man, then? Only this: he is a natural being having essentially nothing to distinguish him qualitatively from a stone or from a cabbage. These theories are not upheld by the philosophers, however; they are upheld by the scientists who say that they are philosophers. There is no greater misfortune for philosophy than that of being entrusted into the hands of a pure mathematician (if only a mathematician and not *also* a philosopher); such a man will treat being as an unknown factor in an equation; or if philosophy falls into the hands of a biologist, he wants to see the spirit through the lens of a microscope. The positivism of the last century was worked out by philosophers and scientists; the scientists' form was so inferior that it caused the other form to be calumniated also; the present-day form is a positivism by scientists only. Consequently, all their speeches interest philosophy very little; they interest the problems of science and scientific knowledge. From this point of view some of their particular researches having a gnosiological-logical character are to be taken into consideration.

We said that these theories do not interest philosophy or that they may interest it only marginally. Yet, in the presence of such a "philosophy," all of us should ask a question. Suppose that such doctrines are going to become (and let us notice that their diffusion is enormous both in England and elsewhere) really the "philosophy" of a people that in its thought and action (that is, in its life) becomes so permeated by it as to reject any religious quest (religion is already denied by these doctrines); the question, then, would be: What elements are there to prevent such a people from becoming materialistic and atheistic in the same way as any other people governed by total Marxism? There would be none. Perhaps while maintaining a materialistic, Western democracy, it will continue to reject the form of a dictatorship and a democracy of the bolshevik or sovietic type; but it will always be materialistic as it will embrace a materialistic-rationalistic conception that does not differ essentially from that held by Marxism. In fact, the real danger lies in this: to have death at one's bedside and, at the same time, to believe that it remains outside of the house. Russell, the most renowned figure in this current, was already a communist; Russell is the most accredited philosopher in England and all politicians in the West honor him as a great European "intellect."

Initially, G. E. MOORE'S (1873-1958) neorealism is Platonizing. A former professor at Cambridge University, he opened the polemic against idealism with his famous article "The Refutation of Idealism" (New York, 1903), which was reprinted in his *Philosophical Studies* (New York, 1922); he is also the author of two works on ethics and of the *Defense of Common Sense* (New York, 1922). Moore rejects all idealistic positions including that of Berkeley's empirical idealism; he directs his attention to nineteenth-century British empiricism, whose methods he adopts; he sets the stage for the restoration of Hume's phenomenism. Moore (as does Russell) portrays himself as the defender of common sense and of common man held as a constitutionally incorrigible realist. The method he applies is called "analysis"; it consists in purifying the meaning of a philosophical proposition and that of a belief universally accepted by common sense; next, in showing the contradiction existing between these two propositions and in justifying the latter. For Moore what has been experienced is not identifiable with the subjective act of experience: in sensation and in the idea we have the consciousness of something objective, which is distinguished from our act of perceiving and thinking. "There is no reason for supposing that either every physical fact be *logically* dependent on a mental fact, nor that every physical fact be *causally* dependent on it. With this I am not affirming that there are physical facts entirely independent (logically and causally) from mental facts; I only affirm that there is no *sufficient reason* for supposing the opposite; and this amounts to saying that none of the human beings endowed with a living body on earth has ever had reason, during his life, to suppose the contrary." The objective reality of the pen with which I am writing does not, for example, depend on my perception. My being conscious does not mean that the real fact depends on that mental fact; consciousness is a "transparent means," a kind of mirror, in which the experienced object presents itself exactly as it is independently from my knowledge. There is a reciprocal independence, which, at any rate, does not exclude the relation between physical facts and those that are mental or pertinent to consciousness.

I am, says Moore, absolutely certain about some propositions: about *my* body's being born at a certain time in the past and about its continued existence; and I am also sure that from birth it has been in contact with the surface of the earth; moreover, I am sure that in every moment of its existence there are many other things in relation to which my body is at *diverse distances*, just as there are still other things with which it is in *contact*—among them, other human bodies like mine, which were born at a certain moment in the past, and so on. I also know that I have had many diverse experiences, that I have nourished some hopes, and that I have felt some feelings, and so forth. I am certain of all that, as I also am certain that "many a man had, like me, various experiences during the life of his body; and this is so because the other men must have belonged, the same as I, to a class made up of human beings, who were endowed with a body, and who were born and lived on earth for a certain time." Such experiences must have been similar to those just listed and ex-perienced by me; "it is true that, only in relation to *himself* and to *his own body*, each one of those human beings has acknowledged as true . . . a proposition that was *corresponding* to *anyone*" of those enumerated above; and that it was "corresponding only in so far as it regarded *him* and *his* body, as well as the time during which he had certitude of it, in the same exact way as the corresponding propositions (listed above) are affirmed with respect to *me*, to *my body*, and to the time during which *I* wrote them." In other words, "as I acknowledged (in the act of writing about it) that actually a human living body, which is my own body, exists," so, in relation to himself and his own time, each man, likewise, has acknowledged the truth of a proposition that, even being different, he might have formulated thus: "*Actually* there exists a human body that is *my* body." Now, if my experiences correspond to those of other in-dividuals, it follows that their existence does not depend upon this or that subject experiencing it. They have a character of universality giving them the value of conceptual entities true and proper. And for Moore the world is made up of concepts, which are the sole object of knowledge. Our consciousness, then, does not make up truth, but it receives it from the outside, since there are certain objective propositions existing in themselves, which are true.

Upon reading Moore one is often induced to think of Reid and the philosophers of the "common sense," for whom the reality of things is given and assured by immediate belief (without the mediation of "ideas"), and the objectivity of knowing by the correspondence between perception and object. However, in Moore (and, generally, in neorealism) there is more than that: due to their character of universality, experiences are reduced to conceptual entities; thus reality is made up of a structure of such entities. Neorealism is a "logical" realism; it is, ultimately, a form of conceptualism not far apart from nominalism; from Hume one goes back to Ockham. For Moore, in fact, there exists a given series of *things* that are what they are, so that they are both irreducible to thought and undeducible *a priori;* some of these data are "universal," in the sense that they surpass what is immediate and spontaneous: they are logical or conceptual entities, and relations constituting objective reality of which there is, one among many, consciousness. This realism does not stop, then, at the immediate datum of experience (at objective reality as it is given in itself), but it conceives experience as a structure of logical relations. Obviously, it cannot avoid nominalism; in fact, on the one hand, universality is not given by principles *a priori;* nor is it given through the participation in an absolute subject (neither in the sense of modern idealism nor in that of Platonic-Christian idealism); and, on the other hand, the always open multiplicity in the relations cannot constitute a deducible and total system. What is, then, the objective and axiomatic sense of these "universals," which are not an immutable system of categories, or of principles, nor the result of a logical deduction? There is no sense—with its empiricist origin, this logical realism is, ultimately, a skepticism, or a reduction of knowledge (and of reality) to a multiplicity of perspectives and methods, namely, to that multiplicity which is "peculiar" to sciences, and which has been generalized and assumed as a model or a unique type (the only one valid) of knowledge. The whole philosophy of Moore can be reduced to the following formula: only material objects exist and the experiences we make of them are logical or conceptual constructions. This formula expresses a definite mode of conceiving scientific knowledge, with which philosophical knowledge is identified. However, this is a mode of philosophizing that is somewhat strange. He who, apropos of Moore (and, above all, of Russell), has thought of Leibniz' rationalism (and besides Russell himself, this person was Couturat, who is only endowed with the *esprit de géométrie*), has rendered this philosopher a great disservice.

BERTRAND RUSSELL (1872) is a former colleague of Moore at Cambridge University. A world-famous mathematician and polygraph, he expounded his logical-mathematical theories in his *The Principles of Mathematics* (Cambridge [Eng.], 1903) and in his celebrated work in three volumes *Principia mathematica* (Cambridge [Eng.], 1957), which he wrote in collaboration with Whitehead. His scientific philosophy was expounded in many other works (*The Problems of Philosophy*, New York, 1912; *Our Knowledge of the External World*, Chicago, 1914; *Introduction to Mathematical Philosophy*, London, 1953; *The Analysis of Mind*, New York, 1921; *The Analysis of Matter*, New York, 1927; *Religion and Science*, New York, 1936, and others). Russell has written about everything: about political, social, moral, and religious problems. He writes with a fine style that is lively, free and easy, and rich in *humor*, but also with an astonishing and, at times, exasperating superficiality. The most difficult problems of the spirit as well as the highest human experiences, for which he is constitutionally unfit, are disposed of by him with such an ease as to reveal his impressive incomprehension and, at times, also his gross ignorance of them. Like all dilettanti, he is a contradictory writer lacking an established and solid, intellectual position; his mind changes according to the impressions of the moment. One cannot say that this is due to his intellectual development because this word signifies an intrinsic coherence and a seriousness of purpose completely unknown to Russell; his purpose is volubleness. As a scientist no one questions his merit; but as a writer on ethics, religion, and so forth, Russell is only a high-class newspaperman. However, philosophy is not interested in the witty remarks that are out of place and in bad taste when they concern problems representing the seriousness and dignity of thought; they reveal an intellectual crudeness beneath the surface of a learned aristocrat. Yet, these are the qualities that make an author very popular and widely read; as a writer Russell has all of them; his materialism as well as his political (always extremist) and antireligious radicalism make up for the rest, in an epoch that, like ours, is afflicted by a decadence in taste and a want of sensibility toward spiritual values. The same qualities made the fortune of some materialists and positivists (the worst of them) in the last century and of Voltaire (though Voltaire is another thing) in the eighteenth century; Russell is a smaller Voltaire to be kept at hand in one's waistcoat pocket. When he writes about mathematical logic he is a clear writer and so "scientific" as to be unable to understand that philosophy differs greatly from his mathematics; it is something so aristocratic that it cannot be understood simply by being a mathematician and an English lord. Let us not be misunderstood; we are not saying that Russell's logical-mathematical researches and points of view do not carry a remarkable scientific weight; we say, rather, that his reduction of philosophy to logic and of logic to mathematics, that is, his scientificalism and his materialism, have no philosophical weight; and we also say that Russell's perspective, as a philosophical perspective, is a coacervation and a muddle of Humian phenomenism, nineteenth-century positivism, Leibnizianism (in which Leibniz is hardly recognizable), and of a great deal of fancy; again we say that Russell's is an extravagant abstraction reducing all spiritual life to physiological and material phenomena and matter (and the ego) to symbols of mathematical logic, and philosophy as such to mathematical logic itself. All this is affirmed gratuitously only because this author holds that mathematics is the entire human knowledge and that the whole man is to be found within this knowledge. We are not going to follow Russell in his logical-mathematical researches; we shall confine ourselves to his "philosophical" conception, as it flows from those researches and also see how it is applied to the problems related to philosophy.

Like all who are atheists through indifference or insensibility, Russell creates for himself an idol he must worship. His idol is mathematics; he has the "religion of mathematics" which he considers as "one of those elements in human life deserving a place in paradise." Indeed, mathematics is the only corner of paradise existing in the whole universe, a kind of serene and comforting shelter. Pythagoras and Plato also considered mathematics a very high knowledge and God a geometer, but Pythagorean-Platonic symbolism expresses (not adequately) the metaphysical world of the Idea, which is being, and, consequently, mathematical knowledge is the interpretation and expression of an ontology transcending it. Russell, on the other hand, suppresses being and denies metaphysics and, with it, the spirit as well; his, therefore, is pure "mathematicism" and, as such, no longer a philosophy. In one of his famous *pensées* Pascal exalts the genius of geometry as it shines in Archimedes; but, beyond it, he contemplates the genius of charity shining in Christ, as he also contemplates man's greatness of thought, whose light is being. Yet, precisely on account of this, he takes up his position against pure scientificalism and he plans (*pensée* 76) to "write against those" who "approfondissent trop les sciences" as well as against Descartes' mechanism; he points out that scientist philosophy or pure scientificalism (mechanism and not philosophy as such) is not worth "one hour of labor." Exactly so: from the speculative point of view, whatever it may be, philosophizing scientificalism is not worth one hour of labor. Again it was Pascal who pointed out (and I quote him for he also was a mathematical genius) the "vanity of the sciences" relatively to the truly human problems, that is, problems of the spirit or philosophical ones, because the "knowledge of external things" can never console man about his "ignorance concerning morality."

Russell does not reason in this way, both because he does not think as a philosopher and because of his preconceived and acritical materialism. In the last analysis he is a skeptic and a pessimist (with moments of bitter sarcasm), who considers the world of men only as a messy confusion. For him morality and spiritual values in general are a question of physiology, and religion is a matter of fear and the fruit of suggestion. In the presence of this human world Russell takes refuge within the symbolism of his mathematical logic, which enables him to disregard men and things. Thus to him mathematics is a refuge, an oasis of consolation, a religion, and a mysticism. "Far away from human passions and far away even from the pitiful laws of nature, little by little the human generations have created an orderly cosmos wherein pure thought can dwell as in its own abode, and at least one of our noblest instincts can find refuge there by evading the gloomy exile of the existing world."

Undoubtedly there is here an attempt at affirming the superiority of the theoretical, which we cannot overlook nor fail to appreciate; yet, this theoretical world is reduced to pure formalism without either foundation or ontological value, so that it is demolished at the very moment it is posited or built; there is also a certain suffering on account of the desolation produced by the skeptical materialism of that "gloomy exile" which is our "existing world." Here is why: there is neither the naive optimism (even if Russell believes in progress) possessed by the many North American naturalists and materialists nor that optimism dogmatically and fatalistically built by many Marxists. From this point of view Russell's conclusions are not different (even if the starting points do not coincide) from those of some existentialists. By making all that is human and divine devoid of value, Russell is left only with a purely mathematical world, which constitutes his paradise—in the same way as some existentialists are left with only the wisdom of accepting "fate" or a pure faith in God without either any foundation or any plausible justification. In order to exorcize the "desperation" in which the world casts him, Marcel finds his refuge within "hope"; Russell, a materialist, escapes into the symbolical world of mathematical logic in order to avoid the "gloomy exile" of life.

Russell began his long and very active writing career with his research on formal logic and pure mathematics, and from there he drew his philosophy. Or rather under the influence of Peano who, as Russell writes, "represents the extreme arithmetization of mathematics," and that of Frege, who "logicized" it (the latter held as valid in the field of logic those notions previously considered valid only in the field of mathematics), Russell's researches led him to believe in the philosophical nature of mathematics itself. From this conviction he arrives at his arbitrary generalizations and his most exaggerated and unjustified extrapolations: identification of pure logic with pure mathematics, which is in turn identified with valid philosophy. Yet this is not sufficient to explain Russell's position and his discouraged and discouraging philosophical poverty. His pure logic and pure mathematics are purely formal: it does not rest on an ontology, namely, on a metaphysics of being; that is, it does not represent the *organ* for the intelligibility of the real. However, according to Russell, it must be accepted as true because it can be applied to things exactly. "We do not simply wish to have our numbers verify mathematical formulas, but we want them to be exactly applied to the objects with which we are in contact. We want to have ten fingers, two eyes, and one nose. A system in which the number one signified one hundred and the number two, one hundred one and so on, could go very well from the point of view of pure mathematics, but it could not be applied to daily life. We want that 'zero' 'number' and 'successor' have a meaning that agrees exactly with our finger, eyes, and nose."

Let us bear in mind that mathematical logic is assumed here *as if* it were true, that is, as a conventional technique useful to daily life. Logic had been emptied of every truth (of its principles, that is) and reduced to an instrument or technical formulary to be applied to things. Relativism, which, after all, is skepticism, and the practical use of the principles (assumed as true only because they respond to this use) are already postulated within pure logic with which Russell identifies philosophy.

What then are things or objects? "Be they material or real, they are what and where the mind says they are, and exist independently of it." Some general ideas are good not only for thought but also for the objects, although between things "some relations may subsist or disappear without in any way affecting the things themselves." For this reason "the nature of everything is just what it is, and it must not be confused either with its origin nor with the aspirations that can be entertained about that nature." Things are given, but they are *without being*, as Hume's phenomenalism and nineteenth-century British empiricism teach; nor do they receive being from thought (as idealism claims); nor is thought made to understand them. Within a phenomenal materialism reality is rendered useless, as it (man and his history) is cast out by the highly rational world of numbers and the technique combining them. "Pure logic and pure mathematics (which are the same thing), according to Leibnizian terminology, wish to be true within all possible worlds and not only in the complicated mess of this world in which chance has imprisoned us. The logician should maintain some distinction for himself; he must not agree to deduce his argumentations only from what he sees around himself." Again, in these same lines Russell confirms the intrinsic nontruth of logical truths and, above all, his want of confidence that they "may be verified" in this "complicated mess of the world" in which "chance" has imprisoned us. However, chance is irrational and if it has placed us in this "complicated mess" of the world, the world itself is irrational (and so are we). True. It is a world without being, an ensemble of material phenomena, some of which—excrescences of the nervous system or who knows of what gland—are called "spirit." But then? Here is what: once the numbers and mathematical logic have well assured us about our fingers and our noses, we escape this "complicated mess" by taking refuge in . . . the numbers, which after all are not true, or they are true only to the extent that they "are applied" to things and to our daily life; the latter, due to chance, unfortunately is a mess, and no "technique" whatever can in any way make it intelligible. Russell's "paradise," then, is purely conventional; and it is unable to make even a purgatory out of the "hell" of life in which we are imprisoned by chance, to which, I believe, numbers do not apply—chance is "unverifiable."

The *Principia mathematica* (written, as we said, in cooperation with Whitehead) certainly marks a relevant stage in the study of mathematical logic. The task in this rigorous research is to demonstrate that pure mathematics (including pure geometry) is a branch of logic, and that its propositions are analytical (and not synthetical *a priori*, as held by Kant). Following in Peano's and Felge's steps, as initial propositions Russell (and Whitehead) posits a few logical principles represented by formal symbols from which other propositions are deduced through a logical calculus. With this method, then, principles and mathematical theorems are gradually introduced and demonstrated. A process that is purely analytical and *a priori* (deductive), independently from things as well as from spirit. Subsequently, Russell came nearer and nearer to a form of skeptical phenomenism along the lines of the Humian-positivistic tradition: the universals, too (mathematical or not), are reduced to a simply practical instrument of science and, as we already remarked, to a technique that is useful to the perfecting of man and to progress. However, it seems to us that skepticism is not going to spare even this generic faith in an indefinite betterment of humanity.

Russell's realism, like Moore's, is pluralistic; there are no "internal relations" among things (as Bradley claims) but only external or extrinsic ones; consequently, things are what they are and their essence is independent from relations, by which nothing is added. The world, then, is *pluralistic*, an infinite whole of atoms, which are independent, and bound up together only by extrinsic relations. The "idea" does not signify only the subjective act of knowing (Berkeley) but the thing known, which does not exist in consciousness, since it is *given* independently from it and is indifferent toward it. Even knowledge is an external datum. A subject perceives a star; this perceiving subject can be replaced by a photographic plate, whose passive behavior is the same as that of the subject; the photographic plate reflects the star in the same way as the sentient ego does. Physical, physiological, and psychological facts are all on the same level. We know only the sense-data, that is, qualities (colors, sounds, and so forth) but not matter; we can suppose, but not demonstrate, the existence of an object supporting them. Independently from the subject (empirical or absolute), are sense-data objectively real? It does not seem so; I would say that, for Russell, they are phenomena, not substances independent from the subject. As the universals (at least in what has been called the second phase of Russell's thought, which, after all, is a consequence of the first) are practical instruments of science, so in the same way pluralism becomes identified with a kind of "logical atomism": the world is an ensemble of sense-data logically united, and the various modes of establishing these purely logical relations are manifold. Thus we have again the skeptical conventionalism, and the combinational technique in which knowledge and reality are dissolved without any light of truth or being.

What are for Russell the "laws of thought"? They are certain rules by which certain symbols are manipulated; from these manipulations the propositions or theorems of formal logic follow. Are these rules (the laws of thought) universally valid and inviolable? Not at all; they can easily change or be replaced by others; and then we have another variety of logic which follows from the new propositions of formal logic, which in turn derive from the new manipulation. Thus this manipulation of symbols can go on to infinity because infinite are the varieties of logic: there will be a new logic for each new group of primary propositions; in fact, symbols are only signs on paper, and their properties are determined only according to their relation with primary propositions. Yet, are these propositions at least true? No. They are not because they are always deduced from certain initial definitions through certain manipulations. In this way we arrive at the tautology of the propositions *a priori*, that is, at the *nothingness of truth*. Such is the inevitable conclusion of a purely formal logic that is emptied of every objective content of truth: a logic taken in its pure formalism without an ontology to rest on; a logic that is not an *organon* of intelligibility; a pure and inconclusive void, in which all manipulations are possible. Logic is degraded to a technique that can serve only a practical use. In fact, in so far as its meaning is concerned, it is well in agreement with our "fingers" and our "noses," even if the world remains, on its own account, a "complicated mess." This, perhaps, could satisfy Lord Russell's aristocratic "intellectuality" and it also would preserve the "distinction" that according to him must always be found in a logician.

All this may be so, perhaps, but it is not sufficient either for man or for philosophy, which has a "distinction" that must be vindicated against those who are spiritually obtuse. This philosophical "distinction" is its autonomy from mathematics (and from any other science whatever) in its method and in its object; and, with its logic (the only one valid), it is philosophy which judges the validity of mathematical formalism and of the principles of science, and not vice versa, because thought is not technique and it refuses to be degraded to a technique; and it is not so because thought has an objective content of truth, which is constitutive of human thought as such. Moreover, truth leads all the techniques without being reducible to any of them, in that it is the opposite of every technique; and thought, like truth, is constituted by an objective and "divine" element, of which philosophy (metaphysics) is the highest expression; philosophy, then, is absolutely autonomous from science as a whole, even if it is not indifferent toward science and its developments. For Russell, instead, the ideal of philosophy is a scientific one as it draws its nourishment from the sciences of nature; in fact, the task of philosophy is to check and clarify those scientific concepts through a process of logical analysis. However, not caring for philosophy at all (and he ignores it a great deal), Russell afterwards changed his mind even with respect to this concession which had been maintained by old positivism; consequently, he came to the conclusion that philosophy is useless (like morality and religion) and that only the natural sciences can tell us something probable concerning the world.

Russell applied the method of analysis even to spirit or ego which, like Hume, he conceives as "a bundle" of perceptions. The ego is a logical function to be used only for grammatical convenience. Beginning with the individual sensations, even material objects are a token of logical constructions. Consequently, there is neither matter nor spirit (a "neutral monism"): what we call matter and spirit are only *sense-data* variously grouped by different logical laws. Being only *sense-data*, things no longer call for a material substance to support them; things are a support to themselves, just as the ego, which also is identified with the "sense-data," does not call for a spiritual substance. In short, the ego is an ensemble of sense-data bound up in a certain way (sense-data are the sensations of things with which we come in contact); the ensemble of the sense-data regarding different objects (that is, the different aspects of a table, of a chair, and so on) represent the things—what we call matter.

The bonds between psychic life and physiological life are very tight, to the point that thought is determined by the brain and by the nervous tissue, that is, by the laws of nature, of which man is an insignificant part. Russell finds that the immortality of the soul is an absurdity and that religion is an evil, in that it is founded on fear (and, in fact, the saints were fearful beings terrorized by God) and, therefore, it is to be eliminated as, after all, it will be, when men have achieved their maturity (even if it may not be exactly like Russell's).

Within the order of values, each man is free to pursue the ideal in life that pleases him most. Naturally there are no moral principles (they are useless); each one has to seek his happiness with love and knowledge and by contributing to the perfecting of man and to progress. Russell founds his morality on the desires: for me to say that something is good, amounts to saying that "I like it"; and to say that it is not, is another way of expressing a different reaction of mine toward it. It is not a question of true or false objective affirmations but a matter of personal desires. Ethics has the task of promoting those positive desires causing happiness while weakening those that cause unhappiness. According to the ideal in democracy, it is necessary to bear in mind the good of society and not that of the individual. Moreover, progress will be immense and happiness overflowing the day when we free ourselves from the superstition of respecting outside nature, and even man's nature (as that "enemy of goodness and decency" which is religion, would have us do); we shall, then, be convinced that man too (like a worm or an insect) must be for the sake of society's happiness the object of a scientific study. Russell certainly must be satisfied that this is practiced on a large scale by Russian scientists (and not only Russian ones). We would like to ask whether among the values of Western civilization, which we are continuously invited to defend at all costs, there is also room for Bertrand Russell's philosophy (since, for many intellects in the West, it seems to occupy a high place). Even in his *History of Western Philosophy* (New York, 1945) which abounds with elementary blunders (stated with elegance but still blunders), Russell has demonstrated (except for a few pages), his vigorous ignorance in this subject.

Australian by birth, though trained in England, SAMUEL ALEXANDER (1859-1938) was a professor at the University of Manchester; together with Whitehead, of whom we shall speak shortly, he is the most organic and original mind in British neorealism. His main work *Space, Time, and Deity* (London, 1920) is one of the most significant works of our times. A disciple of Green and Bradley at Oxford, he soon departed from his masters' idealism. Besides the influence of Anglo-American neorealism, he experienced for many years that of French contingentism, of some Bergsonian theses and of Einstein's theory of relativity; yet, his thought draws inspiration also from Aristotle and Spinoza. For Alexander, philosophy is metaphysics and, as such, a system taking into account not only particular problems but the totality of the real which he endeavors to reduce to unity through a principle working in all the sectors of experience. If nothing else, Alexander has the concept of philosophy, which is wanting in almost all other neorealists. His naturalistic-evolutionistic pantheism has some obscure sides and deficiencies in its structure and method (which is the empiricist one used by the sciences); yet, it still is a philosophy elaborated with care and seriousness.

The fundamental problem in his metaphysics is that of the spatio-time relation—no contraposition or scission between the two, but a mutual bond. It is on this bond that Alexander, using the empiricist method, constructs his conception of the world.

As a result of science, nineteenth-century positivism accepted the geometrical-mechanical conception of reality; Alexander's neopositivism, on the other hand, is founded on a scientific conception principally resting on the theory of relativity and it strongly claims to be far removed from the static doctrine of materialism, which is unable to explain the qualitative formations emerging from the same reality in motion. The *space-time* quadri-dimensional *continuum* is the fundamental element (*stuff*) constituting the world; it is the sum-total of "pure events" or space-time points. This is the *primum* in reality and it is ordained by the *categories* constituting all things.

The introduction of time as an integral part of the cosmic system changes, almost radically, the vision of life as held by the old Galilean Newtonian scientific philosophies. Into a purely extended world a temporal becoming is now introduced: the causal order becomes irreversible and the creation of the new is justified. In this way Spencer's evolutionism is changed into an "emergent evolution." The primary element no longer is the atom, a point of space, suspending reality in a timeless void, but the *event*, that is, the spatial point taken in the instant of time. The world is not a whole of atomic aggregates but an emerging series of events being fulfilled in time; it is development and *advance in nature*. The world of mechanical and materialistic evolutionism is suspended in space, without either a yesterday or a tomorrow; the world of the quadri-dimensional *continuum* is lowered into time, and it has a past that is a propulsive energy pushing the present toward the future. As Alexander says with an effective expression, "time is the mind or soul of space and space is the body of time." It is on this concept of evolution, understood as an emergent evolution (a theory also enunciated by Lloyd Morgan independently of Alexander's), that the influence of the Bergsonian *élan vital* is felt particularly; and this corresponds to the principle of the *nisus* as a creative force that, continuously and inexhaustibly, is re-emerging in the diverse forms of experience (knowledge, morality, art, religion), of which it is the unique matrix.

Thus, "space-time" is a metaphysical principle, and the mould of becoming. All the various forms of existence emerge from it, beginning with the lowest ones and going to the highest as far as the superior forms of human consciousness; a unique principle of life passes through them all, as all are constituted by it, in the wonderful richness of their ever new and diverse differentiations. Every degree is a new one and the successive is unforeseeable; consequently, it cannot be known. The evolutional course, however, has some invariable, absolute characteristics, some immovable dikes, as it were, through which the grand river of the real is channeled. They are the *categories* or ideal levels of cosmic organization, which do not constitute the mind but the reality itself in the objects. Thus, more than in a Kantian sense, they are categories in the Platonizing sense of ideas. Arranged in the categories, the spatio-temporal becoming is specified, through degrees of reality hierarchically ordained from the least to the most complex; every finite being is made up of a determinate group of movements that are variously complex. Quality is excluded from the categories (existence, universality, relation, order, substance, causality, reciprocity, extensive and intensive quantity, and number), since for Alexander it is not constitutive of things but something emerging from the cosmic evolution. Thus empirical qualities constitute the different levels of empirical existence. "The emergence of a new quality from a level of existence signifies that at that level a certain constellation or placement of movements belonging to that same level is coming into being; and also that those movements possess a quality appropriate to that level, and that this placement has a new quality that is characteristic of a higher complex." Qualities emerge always new from a lower level in which they have their roots. Every new order of existence has its own law. Involution is impossible in that the temporal series is irreversible— emergence always is ascending.

The following are the different levels of empirical existence (or groups of empirical qualities) indicated by Alexander: *primary qualities*, forming "matter" with its various specifications (physical, chemical, biological, and so forth); *secondary qualities*, constituting what is material; *tertiary qualities* or "values" (aesthetical, moral, and so forth). Each order has its own "mind" or distinctive quality; the highest one is "consciousness," that which is mind true and proper (the mind belonging to every lower grade is not a consciousness inferior to the human one, for the latter alone is really consciousness). Mechanics has as its object the primary qualities (shape, magnitude, and so forth); physics has the secondary qualities (colors, sounds, and so forth); biology, the phenomena related to life; morality, aesthetics and science have the world of values; religion, the Deity. The *degrees* of being emerged so far are four: pure movement, of which time is the principle; matter; life; consciousness.

The group of empirical qualities preceding the formation of consciousness is the one pertinent to biological processes (life): consciousness (mind) is, then, an empirical quality emerging from the biological group. The subject-object relation is not its prerogative, in that it also belongs to the many relations in the scale of beings; it has its determinate place and is of the same quality as the other empirical realities. "Subjects are the most highly endowed members within a democracy of objects; and as in a democracy wherein talent is freely developed, the most gifted members exert more influence and authority."

What is knowledge, then? It is not the fundamental problem of philosophy but only a chapter or a part of a broader science, metaphysics. According to the tenets of realism Alexander admits that things are in themselves; their being, then, is not given by their being perceived. Knowledge is a rapport or a relation of simultaneous presence (*compresence*) or of coexistence (*togetherness*) of two finite beings, of which one is the mind (being conscious of this *compresence*), and the other, a finite being belonging to an inferior level of existence. In the relation of compresence there is the "contemplation" of the object and the "fruition" (*enjoyment*) of the subject or of the mind that cannot contemplate itself (only a being belonging to a superior level of existence, an angel, would be able to contemplate it); the object being contemplated in it by the mind is a synthesis of *sensa* or sensorial contents (images, recollections, and so forth); this synthesis is to be understood in the sense that it represents not the being of the object, but rather its being as perceived by a mind.

Reality in itself is neither true nor false, neither beautiful nor ugly, and so forth. The world of *values* emerges from consciousness; in order that the value may arise, the subject must react with respect to reality, which has no value. Each reaction is determined by the fundamental exigencies of the human spirit, namely, the exigency of learning (knowledge or value of truth), the exigency of doing (morality or value of the good), and by the exigency of expressing ourselves (art or value of the beautiful). Value is the elaboration of reality according to these exigencies. For this reason Alexander classifies values as "tertiary qualities": they have no objective foundation and they exist as relations between an evaluating consciousness and an object being evaluated. With respect to the sphere of learning or the theoretical sphere it is the object which determines the evaluation; with respect to the practical one, the evaluation pertains to the subject as an agent acting on the external world; with respect to the aesthetical, subject and object are reciprocally determined and beauty results from their relationship. The values are not constituted by a single subject but by the community of subjects.

The *nisus* of the emerging evaluation does not stop at consciousness, but it pushes itself toward a higher empirical quality, the Deity. The relation between God and the world is analogous to that between body and spirit; the world is the body, and Deity the mind. *God is the totality of the world qualified as Deity*. Just as the space-time tension (and time, the principle of motion, is infinite) leads beings from life to consciousness, so it leads them further from consciousness to the Deity, that is an unknown quality (superior to our level of existence), with which the universe is filled. The Deity, then, is effort, not a reality in act; if it existed actually, no longer would there be God as one and infinite, but God Himself—which is the universe tending toward the Deity's superior and unknown quality—would break into a plurality of finite gods. God (the universe) is unceasingly becoming toward the Deity; the whole world shares in this longing, in this begetting a superior perfection which as such (and like all empirical qualities) is not a value. Values are at the mind's level and imply the nonvalues; the Deity excludes them, in that it is only truth, beauty, and good without their correlative nonvalues. The world is the body; the Deity, toward which it tends, is its mind (different from consciousness); and since the universe is God, it can be said that God is the body of Deity, which will emerge from its continuous effort. The longing toward the superior degree of perfection is religious sentiment; religion is, then, a cosmic *nisus* toward Deity.

Alexander's evolutional pantheism has some accents that make one think of the very ancient cosmogonies, which were both naturalistic and mythical. His metaphysical realism is apparent; his is not a metaphysics of being, but one of empirical qualities resting on the presupposed principle of the spatio-temporal unity, which is insufficient for the foundation of a metaphysics in a philosophical sense; values have no reality, in that they are not qualities, but evaluations of the mind depending on the mind itself; consciousness is a pure event in the dynamic evolution; its emergence is incomprehensible. Diverse from life and representing an inferior degree, consciousness emerges from life; it is a product of biological activity; and this is a gratuitous affirmation. In the last analysis, for Alexander, as for Hesiod, in the beginning there was a Chaos and not the Logos; how the Logos emerges from the Chaos is inexplicable. Perhaps by fancying the advent of the Deity with accents of Jewish prophecy, Alexander realized that the God spoken of by him is not God, but simply a world in becoming, which, for this very reason, can only contradictorily be identified with God. It seems to us, however, that he is conscious of this contradiction pertinent to modern idealism in which he had been educated. In fact, here is why we think he is aware of it: idealism identified God with Thought in becoming; that is, being totally resolved in the world, God is made immanent in becoming itself and, with this, idealism thought it had satisfied the religious feeling. Alexander, however, thinks differently: as object of the religious feeling he does not posit God, which for him is the universe in becoming, but rather the Deity, toward which the entire cosmic effort belonging to becoming itself tends, as to something superior and unknown. This critical point is valid, but there is nothing more attached to it—Alexander's Deity is still an emergence from the cosmic evolution, a product of consciousness. And with this we go back to where we were before, to a naturalistic pantheism which, in agreement on this point with idealistic pantheism, makes God or the Deity come from things as well as from consciousness and not vice versa; that is, it makes God the offspring or product of the world rather than its Maker and Creator. In the case of Alexander there is only one alternative: either the Deity will emerge, then the world (God) will break into so many "gods," and a fifth degree of being will rise denoting the end of consciousness and of men (once the Deity is born, men die); or the Deity will not emerge and then it will always remain a purely messianic fancy, and religion a useless longing for a nonexistent reality. "This essentially mobile and progressive universe is leading toward a higher, divine quality lying ahead of it, like an ideal always likely to be attained but never attainable, because to reach it would mean to die." [3]

Neorealism, with Alexander, tries to build a metaphysics of which knowledge is only a chapter; and this is done against the prejudice consonant with modern gnosiology, whose conclusion is either agnosticism or a reduction of metaphysics to the critical problem of knowledge. Along the lines of a realism also colored with Platonism we find the Cambridge professor JOHN LAIRD (1887-1946), whose intellectual formation rests on Locke and Hume, and also on Reid.

For Laird (*Problems of the Self*, London, 1917; *A Study in Realism*, Cambridge [Eng.], 1920), realism is a description of the facts of knowledge which, divested of prejudices and overstructures, concerns the reality of the subject, of the object, and their relations. To know is to "analyze," that is, a pure description of the real relations of things and of their distinctions. Knowledge is a relation between two entities, subject and object, which remain subject and object. Things are known as they are, without aiming at a complete knowledge, because the mind is unable to discover all relations.

The foundation and beginning of our knowledge of the world is our sensorial perception, to which judgment and memory are to be added. The sense-data are as we learn them from all the points of view of which we are capable in that given moment; there is a mutual relation between single data. I perceive no single data but "facts," which also are "signs" (sign-facts). This does not mean that subjective activity creates the facts and that these are mental; things exist; the distinction between the world signifying and the object signified must be maintained. The world is an ensemble of sounds, that are different in the different languages; the object, on the other hand, is immutable in its reality. Knowledge requires, indeed, the elaboration of the datum (comparisons, logical properties, and so forth); however, even conceding that mental processes are a product of the spirit, knowledge must be considered as something not

[3] G. De Ruggiero, *Filosofi del Novecento* (Bari, 1934).

produced by the spirit itself. Knowing is not constructing; it is only knowing. The world is as we perceive it and the judgments founded on the sense-data are the same as those immediately formulated on the objects. It is true that the perceptions are subject to illusions and errors, but experiment and a greater attention can avoid them. Neither memory nor any other form of activity by the subject can modify the object, in that the recollection always is something both belonging and referring to the object. Even in judgment subject and predicate are objective, although the predicate is not the whole thing but only a characteristic that, together with others, belongs to it.

Laird distinguishes the knowledge-process regarding the object from that regarding the knowledge of the self. By knowing itself the subject simply becomes object to itself: the act by which it perceives itself is not the same as that by which it perceives a thing other than itself. Even if for a moment the personality stays suspended and half-asleep, upon waking up it always finds itself identical with itself. Personality, then, has a true and real existence. It is irreducible to that belonging to other individuals, although the ideas pertinent to various individuals are communicable. The reality of the world is not one absolutely; it is instead a pluralistic one.

Obviously Laird does *not* move far from the fundamental theses of neorealism, of which he was always a sturdy defender. More recently he has probed the problems of classical metaphysics in his two volumes *Theism and Cosmology* (London, 1940) and *Mind and Deity* (London, 1941). For Laird every idealistic position is "theistic" even if it rests on immanentism; *ergo* the confutation of idealism (in any of its forms) is a confutation of theism. He rejects Catholic theology on principle and, with it, the theistic thesis as contradictory; hence, his criticism of all the traditional proofs of the existence of God. His argumentation is compact and technical, but preconceived. The idealism-realism antithesis within the theological problem is presented as a God-Divinity antithesis, that is, a personal God and an impersonal Divinity. Thus, by rejecting idealism, even the theistic thesis, founded on an idealistic gnosiology and on an idealistic metaphysics, is excluded. Morever, once realism is accepted (Laird's, that is), it follows that the hypothesis suitable to it is that of the existence of a Divinity or, rather of an indefinite "divine," a conception which does not go beyond a generic pantheism. Both the confutation of theism and the affirmation of pantheism are, in Laird, true *idola theatri*, as his countryman Bacon would say.

C. D. BROAD (1887) is also a professor at Cambridge; in his writings, *Perception, Physics, and Reality* (Cambridge, 1913), *Scientific Thought* (London, 1923), *The Mind and its Place in Nature* (London, 1925), he develops and clarifies the theses of neorealism while remaining absolutely indifferent toward the problems of metaphysics, of religion and, in general, of the "human." He personifies the *ésprit de geometrie*.

According to Broad the task of philosophy is to clarify critically general concepts (number, quality, cause, substance, and so on), which the special sciences use, accepting them without further thought. The need for philosophy "is justified by the fact that these concepts are really obscure and that their obscurity may really lead to error; the possibility for philosophy, moreover, results from the fact that while all special sciences *use* these concepts, no one has them *as such* for its object. Critical philosophy, as far as I am concerned, in fact, has the task of defining them." Moreover, in our practical life and in our research, we accept a great many fundamental propositions; another task for philosophy, then, is to place these propositions under criticism. For this reason mathematics, physics, chemistry, and so forth are distinguished from the "philosophy" of these sciences. In the more concrete but less involved sciences the distinction becomes less and less precise. "For example, every discussion on mechanism and vitalism should be the province of critical philosophy and, instead, biology books are filled with such discussions. Erroneously considered a branch of philosophy, psychology is, in reality, a natural science based on observation and on induction; yet, every work on psychology in its own way takes up again the discussions that, by right, should be left up to critical philosophy. . . . But the confusion between particular sciences and the philosophy of them generally is an evil, in that it is difficult for one man alone to possess both the attitude and the learning required by two such diverse disciplines. The absurdities uttered by great philosophers when discussing scientific problems are largely counterbalanced by the absurdities being repeated every day by great scientists when discussing philosophical problems."

Philosophy, however, is not only "critical"; it is also "speculative"; that is, it is not only a clarification of the principles of which special sciences avail themselves but also a complex vision of reality, a study of man's place and destiny in that reality, as well as a comprehension of all the aspects of human existence. Yet, all experiences (scientific, social, ethical, aesthetical, and religious experiences) must be subjected to critical analysis. It follows, then, that no system of speculative philosophy can represent the ultimate truths: all speculative systems are only "conjectures on the real," so that they are subject to modifications. "The vitality of speculative philosophy, in my opinion, must be sought not so much in its conclusions as in the collateral effects it exerts—or may exert—on those dedicated to it. The speculative philosopher is, of necessity, led to look at the world from a universally comprehensive point of view; and he who does not endeavor to achieve such a point of view at some time or another during his life is bound to remain within a narrow and arid spiritual world. This is the danger threatening the scientist." Taken separately, idealism and realism for Broad are unilateral and they impoverish the infinite complexity of the real. That scientist is arid who ignores the spirit, as that idealist is poor who disregards physics and chemistry, which interest an infinity of objects of reality. "The error of idealism, then, is seeing the forest but not its trees, and that of realism is seeing the trees but not the forest. The great merit of idealism is the effort it makes in accounting for social, ethical, aesthetical, and religious facts; the great merit of realism is its facing in a precise and meticulous way the problem of matter and of the latter's perception. Yet, neither of the two great systems is a substitute for the other; and a truly speculative philosophy should unite the detailed study of the inferior categories to the acknowledgment of the higher categories, while making an effort to reconcile the general character of the former with the increasing importance of the latter."

As for the problem of knowledge, Broad (like Moore) admits, besides the other physical objects, the sensorial contents or *sensa*, which are a kind of intermediary entity between physical objects (whose vibrations stimulate our organs and produce sensations) and sentient subjects. *Sensa* or sensorial contents are not mental acts but objects in the presence of subjects, and they are sensed but not created through the act of sensing —images, indeed, but images in themselves, not depending on the subject representing them. A *sensum* of the color of an object exists in the physical object, even if not seen. The nervous system interposes itself between sensorial contents and subject, and explains the passage of the *sensa* into the subject. Indeed for Broad and also for another neorealist N. K. SMITH (1872)—a student of Descartes and Kant—the nervous system contributes to the formation of the *sensa*, that is, the content of knowledge, which also needs the space-time formal element (on the level of intuition) as it needs the categories on the logical level. However, to what extent do *sensa* exist in objects? And why does he admit that the physiological subject can act on sensorial data while excluding the action of the subject as a spiritual entity?

Broad saw this difficulty, so he wound up excluding—or at least attenuating to a great extent—the objectivity of the sensorial contents, in agreement with the "emergent evolution theory" of CONWAY LLOYD MORGAN (1852-1936). For Morgan (*Emergent Evolution*, London, 1923), the compound derived from those contents cannot be foreseen, with certitude, in all its qualities while taking into account the composing elements. Something new, that is, an *emergence*, always comes up in the compound. In other words, one cannot analytically deduce the compound in its entirety from the consideration of its various, composing elements; a new element emerges in the composition. On the basis of this principle, Morgan constructs his theory of the emergent evolution or of the grades of existence that are entangled with one another, though each of them cannot be deduced from the inferior grade, since something emerges in it which is not contained by it. Mind emerges from life, but this is not only life; life implies a chemical synthesis, but life is not chemism alone. Mind or consciousnes is the ultimate product of the emergent evolution.

If we now from this standpoint consider the objectivity of the *sensa*— both in Morgan and Broad—it appears to us to be highly modified along idealistic lines with respect to intransigent realism. The intellect is a new emergence with respect to the sense, and thus it partakes of the constitution of things. When consciousness arises, certainly there is already a constituted world whence it is emerging, but through the contact between reality and consciousness new qualities emerge. Sensorial qualities emerge from the relationship between physical objects and sentient subjects, as the beauty in a panorama emerges from the relationship between contemplator and thing being contemplated.

As one can see, the theory of emergent evolution makes an effort to replace the opposition existing between idealism and realism with their mutual agreement. The exigency on the part of neorealism to guarantee the reality and objectivity of the external world against idealistic subjectivism (the neorealists bear in mind particularly Berkeley's empiricist idealism)—so as not to reduce the world to a private property of the subject but rather to give it a "public domain" existence—is thus blended with the opposite idealistic exigency not to deny the rights of the subject, and not to annul the activity of the spirit in the presence of the object. However, if it is the merit of neorealism to have rejected the "mythical" foundation of idealism, that is, the concept of a subject creating the object and making all reality its illusory product, it is also its grave fault to have been unable to grasp what is truly idealistic within idealism and to have opposed to the latter a scientist pseudo-realism which is a gnosiological skepticism and a metaphysical materialism denying the spirit and with it, philosophy.

3. A. N. Whitehead's Philosophy of the Organism

ALFRED NORTH WHITEHEAD (1861-1947), the internationally famous English mathematician and scientist, came late to philosophy (when he was more than sixty years of age); he taught this subject at Harvard University until 1937, after teaching applied geometry and mathematics for many years in London. Philosophically, he perhaps represents the most educated mind amongst Anglo-American neorealists and scientists-philosophers; yet, people have greatly exaggerated in evaluating the speculative importance of his philosophy of nature. Even when making philosophy, Whitehead remains a scientist and, precisely, one of the greatest theoreticians on modern mathematical logic (particularly on account of the *Principia Mathematica,* written in collaboration with Russell). He is also a scientist and a student of the natural sciences. As a philosopher he constructs his philosophy on these foundations and with the methods of science: he is not a metaphysician but a cosmologist who, lacking a philosophical mentality, believes that metaphysics is only cosmology in the sense of a philosophy of nature. In his favor it must be said that, unlike other neorealists, he possesses a vast culture even outside of the strictly scientific field and shows even a certain humanistic sensibility; however, spiritual problems (aesthetical or religious ones) do not take a step forward in his case just as they do not attain a more mature speculative position in relation to others which are truly critical and philosophical. The main sources of Whitehead's thought are, first of all, the findings of science; on this basis he rethinks or utilizes theories of Leibniz and Spinoza, Kant and Bergson, as well as the relativity theory of Einstein, some fundamental aspects of which Whitehead criticizes. His influence on philosophy, above all North American philosophy, has been vast and in depth, notwithstanding the occasionally almost insurmountable obscurities in his writings. Indeed, his critical position regarding the formalism of mathematical logic (and, in this sense, it is a self-criticism) and materialism makes him the neorealist most conscious of the limitations confronting neorealism itself and, for this reason, he is the most serious one as well. Yet, he always remains steadfast in his conviction that a very tight bond exists between the sciences and philosophy, the latter ultimately being reduced to a cosmology. Thus, according to him, it is possible, on the basis of the new physics, to solve questions heretofore insoluble for philosophy which allowed itself to be seduced by the apparent simplicity of Euclidian geometry and of Aristotelian ontology and logic.

Whitehead has expounded his philosophical perspective in his works *Concept of Nature* (Cambridge [Eng.], 1920), *Science and the Modern World* (New York, 1928), *Process and Reality* (Cambridge [Eng.], 1929) and, in a more popular form in two lectures brought together under the title of *Nature and Life* (Chicago, 1934). A good number of articles is collected in the volume *Essays in Science and Philosophy* (London, 1948).

Whitehead's philosophical exigency arises from within science or, more precisely, from the way he conceives it, that is, from the formalistic conception of scientific knowledge as given by the *Principia.* He realized that purely analytical and formal knowledge leaves out reality as such; applied to scientific knowledge, mathematical formalism thus posits the problem of its integration. Now, since scientific knowledge, as such, is indifferent toward the real concrete from which it prescinds, the latter can be recovered only through the help of philosophy; philosophy is thus conceived as a cosmology, that cannot prescind from science, whose findings are to be integrated by it. In short, science is a formal knowledge; philosophy comes to its rescue by giving an account of the concrete, and by explaining some experiences (aesthetical, ethical, and religious ones) left out by science. Let us immediately notice how the philosophical problem of science is, at the outset, being entirely skipped, while autonomy (of method and of object) is being denied to philosophy. Whitehead does not question the affirmation that scientific knowledge is formalistic. Having posited this dogma and since scientific knowledge misses the concrete, Whitehead, always on the presupposition of a scientific formalism, requests philosophy to integrate the findings of science and to confine itself to that task alone. It is evident that philosophy is not called upon to question the results of science and hence to posit the problem of science itself at the philosophical level; on the contrary, philosophy is invited to accept those results outright and to confine itself only to their cosmological integration. Thus, both the problem of science and that of philosophy are not even posited. One of them is presupposed as logical formalism, and the other as cosmologism, that is, as an integration of the cosmological exigency which science (understood after the manner of Whitehead) finds arising within itself without being able to satisfy it. Everything is presupposed in a noncritical way, with a mentality I would call prephilosophical or, if you wish, philosophically ingenuous.

However, even with all these serious limitations one must acknowledge the following merits in Whitehead's thought: (1) it has denounced the abstractions which, originating from the generalization of a viewpoint valid only for a sector of reality, take the place of the concrete, while imposing themselves as indisputable dogmas; (2) it has defended the value of reason, independently of its practical use, against numerous anti-intellectualisms, including Bergson's, even if, ultimately, for Whitehead the rationality of the world is only a well-founded belief; (3) it has criticized the "materialism of simple location," which is precisely the outcome of an abstraction, that is, of an influence by science on philosophy to the point of having some (pseudo-philosophical) cosmological conceptions pass for scientific results, while they really are extravagances (like Russell's) which deserve no serious discussion. In this respect Whitehead notices that, conceived as "simple location" (a simple delimitation of place in space and time), matter is a double abstraction which makes time an accident of immutable matter, and the universe a paving-block of it—an impenetrable, instantaneous, and independent paving-block in which the instant is without duration. Modern and new physics no longer gives, according to Whitehead, any support to materialism because the latter has been defeated by the undulatory theory of light, as well as by the theories on the atom, conservation of energy, and evolutionism; and now it has been made impossible by the *quanta* theory which permits the replacement of matter, as a fundamentally metaphysical category, with the concept of "event," that is, with an organic conception of matter itself. "For the Aristotelian notion of the process of forms" the new physics had substituted that of the "form of process," which allows neither the isolation nor the instantaneousness of classical science, for it studies the forms of coexistence and of succession of events.

Even Whitehead remains within empiricism although his is an experienced and rigorous form of it. The starting point for every scientific (and philosophical) research is the "sensorial perception-data" considered with respect to the knowing subject or in themselves, in their reciprocal relations independently of the knowing act. Knowledge is not a fact to be possibly explained; one must confine oneself to describing it as well as to analyzing its content. Whitehead distinguishes between "apprehension" or knowledge of an object and "prehension" indicating the unity realized in the object of knowledge. In borrowing the term from Einstein, he calls it an *event*, by which the old term of "phenomenon" is replaced. The event or unity of a prehension is a "here" and a "now," *this* single event that cannot be repeated. The world is not made up of things, but of events, of what happens. It is a characteristic of the event to extend itself into space and time, so that as a result of events nature is becoming and development. Whereas the atom for materialism is static and indifferent toward change, the event has a present, a past and a future while being in an "organic" relationship with other events. Every event is a moment in the process of nature, which is the total event including all others. Unlike phenomenon, the event implies the entire universe; it is the universe itself as it posits itself *here* and *now*; it is a perspective that is different from other perspectives or events, which are, in turn, the universe as it posits itself there and then. *This* event has intrinsic reference to *other* events in *other* places as well as in *other* times. The event is, in short, prehension and organism; it apprehends in itself the entire universe and its parts make up a whole. Like Leibniz' monad every event is a "mirror of the universe," a perspective unification of reality, a synthetical unity of the universe as one; it is pure actuality: nature's development signifies that one event becomes part of another into which it enters and extends itself into the future.

For Whitehead there is neither an absolute space nor an absolute time, but there are spatial relations and temporal relations; space and time express certain relations between events. Space is not the common "receptacle" of all events but their very organization; time is the passage of nature from one state to another. Time exists for becoming; time is in nature and nature in time. Space is not static and not even instantaneous as materialism claims. Time is united to space, and nature not only extends itself spatially but it also is a "duration," that is, a past and a future —the space of concrete nature is made in time. Events, then, are extended and they last in their becoming through the spatio-temporal relations. Science arrives at space-time concepts through what Whitehead calls "extensive abstraction." Events have no substance. This is precisely the error of materialism, which considers space and time as attributes of a material substance. Instead, only *attributes* exist; in space we find "the red of a rose and the smell of a jasmine . . . so that space is not a relation between substances, but one between attributes."

The space-time complex allows Whitehead to delineate his organic conception of reality, which is an ensemble of events becoming and lasting: concrete entities are organisms. Each one of them is concrete within the process of cosmic realization and according to the organism in which it actuates itself. Every event, as we said, becomes and *is* what it becomes in relation to other events and in accord with the portion of reality in which it operates. In other words, the same physical atom becomes and behaves differently, according as it is a part, for example, of so-called brute matter or of organic matter. The reactions of matter, then, are always new and original. Reality is an organic and dynamic flowing of events.

What is science's task? We know that for Whitehead a sensorial object is an ensemble of events. When we notice that a certain group of events habitually concurs in a situation, we express this permanence by using the term "physical object." "And the origin of scientific knowledge in turn lies in its effort to express in terms of physical objects the *role* of events, as active conditions upon the coming of sensible objects into nature. Scientific objects emerge within the progress of this investigation." [4]

For Whitehead as well as for Alexander, even the perceiving subject is a "perceiving event" though it is higher than others. As he himself writes, "The primary situation revealed by the knowing experience is the ego-object amongst objects." The world does not emerge from the subject as it does in Kant: "For the philosophy of organism the subject emerges from the world." The emergence of a conscious subjectivity from the objective world of events is facilitated in Whitehead, in contrast with other neorealists, by his dynamic conception of the event as a becoming and a process. Consciousness does not arise inexplicably from a material atom, but from the objective data which are what they become. Moreover, for Whitehead the event taking place in nature is not extrane-

[4] G. De Ruggiero, *ibid.*

423

ous to us; it is a relation also shared by us. Being a complex and unique relation, the event comprises things and ourselves within a living unity. When Whitehead states that every event is in relation to another, he considers the event already as physical and mental at the same time, in that the fact of relation always is a mental thing more or less.

For Whitehead, as earlier for James, consciousness is a function: spirit, like matter, is not a substance. Whitehead rejects materialism, but he perplexes us about the relationship between spirit and matter. The immortality of the soul can only be admitted through religious faith.

Whitehead has also constructed his own theological theory: there is neither an intuition nor a demonstration of God (he does not accept either St. Anselm's argument or Aristotle's cosmological proof); he holds, nonetheless, that it is necessary to admit God in order to explain phenomena. According to his theology, God would have two aspects, a "primeval nature" (an immutable and nontemporal God, a full actuality) and a "consequent nature" or a limited God in becoming, a conscious universal prehension enriching Himself throughout the development of nature. As a primeval nature God is immovable, eternal, and infinite, but He is dead; as a consequent nature He is limited and immanent in the cosmic becoming—all of which amounts to saying that when He is God He is dead, and when He is alive He is not God but the cosmic becoming itself. This is a Neoplatonizing pantheism speculatively inferior to other similar forms (Bruno's, Spinoza's, and so forth). A kind of mysticism is engrafted on this Neoplatonic background; God, the principle of good, is in strife with evil, which is a positive principle; in order to free Himself He suffers together with those many who live and suffer the vicissitudes of life.

Founded on a conception of science and developed on presuppositions through the use of scientific methods, these so-called philosophies of nature betray their insufficiency, as well as their speculative poverty, when they face the problems of the subject or of man, of consciousness, of morality, of God, and so on. Like fragile or dead things they fall apart when compared with the problems of the spirit. Their failure is due to a very simple reason: their theories and hypotheses make sense as regards science, but they become meaningless when applied to the construction of a philosophical or metaphysical vision of the world. Science makes only one mistake when it builds itself up as a philosophy—that of trying to be what it cannot be. A critic opposed to abstractions, Whitehead winds up being a victim of abstraction, that is, a victim of the pretension to extend the narrow basis of science to a metaphysical comprehension of reality. Moreover, from a philosophical point of view, his complicated researches tell us nothing about the value and meaning of sensible experience nor about scientific concepts, so that everything remains in need of being justified. As has been pointedly remarked, the widest "point of view that the science of nature should represent with respect to science is constituted in Whitehead by nothing more than an extension (and in some way, an absoluteness) of the validity of the concepts pertinent to science." [5]

4. NORTH AMERICAN NEOREALISM

The neorealism which has flourished in the United States began in the form of a cooperative effort by several philosophers (E. B. HOLT, 1873; W. T. MARVIN, 1872-1944; W. P. MONTAGUE, 1876-1957; R. B. PERRY, 1876-1957; W. B. PITKIN, 1878-1949; E. G. SPAULDING, 1873), who in 1910 published the program of their philosophy; later this program was implemented with a volume in collaboration, *The New Realism* (1912), thus inaugurating the so-called *cooperative book* which, as already mentioned, has met with great success ever since. American neorealists proclaim their bonds with nineteenth-century materialism. Montague, in fact, defines his thought as a "materialistic-animistic" philosophy and, according to him, it should mean the same thing as "cosmological spiritualism" (poor spiritualism!); and according to all these neorealists the concept of matter comes out "purified" and almost transfigured; moreover, they profess an unconditional admiration for science so they extend the scientific-objective method to philosophy, in order to make it as "scientific" and "impersonal" as possible and thereby give philosophy a new "dignity." Such dignity is conferred upon philosophy not only by its being *ancilla scientiae*, but also by its freeing itself from the Absolute. In fact, R. B. Perry (*The Present Conflict of Ideals*, New York, 1922) attributes to James and Dewey the great merit of presenting us "the priceless gift of a world without the absolute" and also the merit of giving up the "humanizing of nature," once perpetrated by idealistic subjectivism, in favor of the "naturalizing of man," now consummated, we might add, by the new philosophy of scientificalism.

The world is representation, but not "a representation of mind" as idealism claims. In itself and by itself representation is *neutral* and indifferent, and it belongs both to the ego and to the nonego. There is no difference between appearance and reality; things are as they appear, and what appears is the thing or things. There is no need for a subject to which things appear; whether there is a spectator or not, it makes no difference for the spectacle of the world: neutral entities have no interest in appearing to someone. The subject is not necessary; reality can do without it very well. Does a man of common sense distinguish the sun

[5] L. Actis Perinetti, "Filosofia e scienza nella 'filosofia della natura' di W.," *Filosofia*, II (1952), 259.

in itself from the perception he has of it? No. For him the sun is as he sees it and he sees it as it is. Moreover, he believes that the sun continues to be what it is even when he is not seeing it, when it does not appear to him. Things are in themselves, and there is no difference between the thing as it is when being perceived, and as it is when not perceived— things remain in themselves what they are.

Neorealists deny a substantial difference between the psychical and the physical; there is no distinction between psychical, physical, and logical entities: spirit and matter are made up of the same "neutral entities" in diverse groupings (absolute monism). Contrary to popular belief, psychical entities are not distinguished on account of their incommunicability and intimacy from the physical ones, which are generally considered to be learned by many people. Even psychical phenomena being revealed in the intimacy of my consciousness may pertain to other subjects. They too are neutral and indifferent as to whether they belong to one individual rather than to another. Even pleasure and pain are not exclusively individual; they are, among others, the relations constituting my consciousness, but they exist also in the external world though they may not be known. The color and smell of a flower preserve their objective reality even when they are not producing a pleasant or unpleasant sensation in a sentient subject. Consciousness is not defined through the nature of its particular elements, but through the particular form wherein the elements are being grouped. It is a group of neutral entities chosen among many by the nervous system. Sensorial data are spatial projections of the objects, each of which is a group or class of simple or neutral entities capable of becoming a part of other infinite groups, among which there are even those particular classes called "consciousnesses" or "spirits"; and these are distinguished from known objects not because of a substantial difference but only on account of a difference of relation. The same entities can be variously grouped; the established relations are purely extrinsic, that is—according to the model of mathematical logic—they do not modify the terms constituting them.

Just as a searchlight, says E. B. Holt, illuminates now this and now that section of a landscape and causes one group of objects to become part of the illuminated section and another group to become part of the dark area (though the landscape remains integral in its complex), so the nervous system leads consciousness now toward one and now toward another group of neutral entities. Just as the landscape stays always the same, whether illuminated or not, so the entities remain always external to the subject, as they are in themselves. The brain (as North American neorealists repeat along with Bergson whom, otherwise, they reject) does not create images but impelling answers proportioned to them. The mind is not a darkroom in which "images" or copies of objects (according to

426

empiricist idealism) are formed: there are no images in the mind, only objects before it. In other words, out of the numberless, simple entities in the universe, the nervous system chooses or clips off those needed for the conservation and development of the self and of the organism. The system does not generate representations, but acts according to the vital interests, says R. B. Perry. Out of the infinite relations that can be established with objective representations, the nervous system carries out only one and this one is connected only with a limited number of those representations. Consciousness lies in this relation. "Consciousness is a transversal section of the world chosen by the nervous system." The science of this relation (one among many) is epistemology (theory of knowledge); likewise, that relation which is knowledge is one among the many being established between objective representations. For the neorealists everything is a simple entity; consequently, mental data, objects and logical entities represent the same thing—truth and reality coincide perfectly. The world is only an ensemble of neutral entities joined by extrinsic relations, which do not alter them; gradually, as the searchlight (the mind) moves about, they come out from the beam and enter into a zone of darkness without ceasing their existence; and they are ready to enter into another pencil of rays of light and establish new relations. Even illusion and error are real and true; they actually exist as simple entities. They are due to a cut in the nervous system not in correspondence with the vital ends; but, precisely in this way, illusion and error are real.

By suppressing the dualism between subject and object, neorealism had aimed at giving an immediate certitude of the knowledge of the world; and, instead, it winds up in the chaos of relativism and opens both doors to the nominalism of logical positivism. Reduced to a "private space" in each individual perceiver, without anything in common with the private space in another perceiver, perception stands out as an individual perspective and as an entity in a space being distinct from all other spaces. Once again, mathematical logicalism, which should serve us to know ourselves and the objects, prevents us from even being able to say that we have two eyes and one nose. It leaves us with: (1) a world "without an absolute"; (2) a myriad of perspectives and of "private spaces" opened on one panorama alone; (3) a consciousness reduced to a transversal section of the world, a section being chosen by the nervous system; (4) an error being as true as truth, and an illusion, as real as reality —all of this provides for and, indeed, assures a "new dignity" to philosophy!

American neorealism did not stop at the book published in 1912; some of its authors (especially Montague and Perry) have been very active both in defending their theories and in adapting them to new interests.

It can be said that the problem of perception and of knowledge in general has become secondary with respect to the more important one regarding the method and, especially, the methods of the natural sciences (see Montague's work, *The Ways of Knowing*, London, 1928), which tentatively are applied to the study of values. Perry, for his part, has more or less become a kind of philosopher of American democracy (*On All Fronts*, New York, 1941; *Our Side is Right*, Cambridge [Mass.], 1942; *One World in the Making*, New York, 1945). Previously he had written a *General Theory of Value* (New York, 1926), founded on scientific psychology. Thus (after destroying the objective value of knowledge and every other value, man and God, and after reducing everything to an ensemble of "private spaces" interwoven with extrinsic relations) these fine people think that with a bit of democracy and of optimism in technical progress man is heading toward perfect happiness; and so they think that in his personality and freedom man is safe against any possible attack, since he is launched after an ideal which naturally is also identified with a neutral entity.

5. CRITICAL REALISM AND G. SANTAYANA

Another group of North American philosophers reacted against neorealism through the publication of *Essays on Critical Realism* (New York, 1920) written by DURAN DRAKE (1878), ARTHUR O. LOVEJOY (1873), J. BISSETT PRATT (1875-1944), ARTHUR K. ROGERS (1868-1936), GEORGE SANTAYANA (1863-1952), R. WOOD SELLARS (1880), and C. AUGUST STRONG (1862-1940). This is a "critical" realism in comparison with that of the neorealists, which is defined as "ingenuous"; considered in itself, however, it too has its conspicuous dose of naïveté, even including the twenty pages written by Santayana who, in his stature as an essayist of taste with a European culture, stands apart from the others. As the authors themselves state, their agreement is confined to the "epistemological problem"; each one, then, professes his particular, ontological conception. Critical realism has never become a well-defined current or school; it has always remained vague. Even the denomination of "naturalism" (generically applied also to other positions comprising neorealism) is a vague one and, more than a body of doctrines or a system, it indicates an "attitude," a philosophical method, and a program. Neorealism feels the influence of empirio-criticism (above all Mach's), while the critical realists are under the influence of Meinong's doctrines; both are in agreement in their reaction against idealism, and the merit of this reaction is passed on to the "ingenuous" [neorealists] by the "critical" [realists]. Thus, it is a realism in the sense, as Drake writes, that all those are properly realists "who believe existence to be wider than experience, and the objects to exist in themselves and by themselves independently of our probing them."

According to critical realism neither mental states nor things are immediately present in thought; the presence in it is given by qualities (essence), which in the act of knowing are considered as qualities of an external object independently of a perceiving subject. We do not experience directly the existence of an object, but we affirm it (so Reid had said against Hume) through an intuitive and irresistible act of our spirit. Used by common sense and by science, experience and reasoning prove the legitimacy of this act from time to time. In other words, critical realism distinguishes the universal essences, which are the objects of an immediate intuition, from things and existing facts in which *essences* may or may not be realized (or have existence). Knowing an object means giving it a determinate essence, that is, conceiving it according to a given content of thought. Knowledge then is always *mediate;* the object is not known through an immediate experience but through our perception and ideas. Now, since we must ascertain indirectly (that is, through experience and reasoning) whether in the world of existence there is an object corresponding to the ideal essence, it then becomes evident that error is possible in such an ascertainment; it is also evident, however, that neorealism is unable to account for the error, because it sustains that the real object is immediately present in the mind, so that truth and reality are identified. Knowledge is true when the essence corresponds to the existence of the object to which it is referred; knowledge is erroneous when the essence is referred to an object held as real while it is not so.

Critical realism uses the *logical* dualism of essence and existence in place of the *ontological* dualism of dogmatic or traditional realism. According to the latter, essence (idea) and existence (things) are two independent realities. Hence arises the problem of their mutual correspondence. If, instead, as critical realism claims, the essence is of a logical nature, it can be identical with the essence in the object, as is so when knowledge is true. Essence in itself has no existence; it exists in that we attribute it to an existing object; and, furthermore, inasmuch as existence is thought of by the mind, it is but an essence. As a result we have the following important argumentation of critical realism against neorealism: real and living (existing) consciousness cannot be deduced from logical entities, because these are not existing things but only essences. Essence is not known but only *intuited*, while existence is known but not intuited.

The most renowned critical realist and the one who is most widely read on account of his qualities as an effective writer and a keen essayist, is George Santayana. A Spaniard by birth, he taught at Harvard until 1912 when he returned to Europe definitively. A pupil of Royce and of James, he felt the influence of Plato and Aristotle, besides that of Schopenhauer and Indian philosophy through the courses of study he pursued in Berlin from 1886 to 1888 under Paulsen and Deusser.

Because his temperament is more artistic than philosophical, Santayana is more successful in his polemics and his moral essays than in his doctrinal works. There is no doubt that the five volumes of his *The Life of Reason* (New York, 1905-1906) are more interesting than his *Skepticism and Animal Faith* (New York, 1923) or his four volumes on *The Realms of Being* (New York, 1927-1940). Santayana takes sides with the critics opposed to idealism: the spirit of idealists is "omnivorous"; idealists are "voracious thinkers" and metaphysical ostriches, making the thinking subject swallow up everything without realizing that, if everything is spirit, every spiritualization-process becomes useless. However, even his confidence in realism is scanty; in the last analysis, his is a skeptical position such as only a moralist can hold.

He proclaims himself a Platonist, but his is a curious Platonism laying stress on the dualism between "essences" (ideas) and existence, to the point that the former vanish in a kind of limbo while the latter is reduced to *animal faith*. He exasperates so much the qualities between the super-Urania of essences and the chaos of existence as to make both of them incomprehensible. It is needless to rebuke him for his obscurities and contradictions; his is a nonsystematic temperament like that of an annotator, a compiler of the keen and brilliant remarks that make up the coacervation (in which a great deal of good can be found) of his works in four or five volumes. Santayana remained a great "Spanish" essayist in the English language.

A dualism exists, we were saying, between the world of existence and the world of essence. Existence is matter: the spirit is determined by physiological and social conditions of which, as we have said, spirit itself is a kind of epiphenomenon. Whatever is taking place in cosmic life is a flux of events in space and time; even in the highest forms of consciousness there is nothing spiritual though they express something spiritual (the essences incorporated in matter). The "soul" is the life of an organism in which the "spirit," a mediator between matter and essences, is incarnated.

Besides essences there is nothing to justify logically the existence of anything. The primary and original affirmation positing an object independent of us is a spontaneous and irresistible act of the spirit without any logical justification. The *existence* of a thing cannot be logically inferred from the fact that the thing is *appearing* to us. Santayana arrives at this conclusion when, in studying the life of reason, he posits the problem of knowledge and its objective validity: How can our mental states, which are necessarily subjective, be descriptions of external things? How can we be certain about the existence of external things and even about our own ego? Santayana rejects the Lockian (and Cartesian) theory wherein our ideas or images are copies of the objects; he also rejects the neorealist doctrine of "neutral entities" and turns toward critical realism. He maintains the Cartesian dualism, not as a dualism between images or ideas and external objects but as one between "essence" and "existence"; the latter is spatio-temporal and a continuous becoming comprehending the physical as well as the psychical reality (that is, existence is "nature" or "reign of matter"), while the former is beyond time and space, a purely logical, eternal, and immutable entity identical with itself. For Santayana the essence is represented by any quality or concept man is able to think of, imagine, or feel; essences are intuited directly and they alone are the immediate datum of experience. How are we certain about the existence of external things? Not through an immediate intuition but because of an "animal faith," that is, because our organic life places us in contact with them continuously. The passage from the "appearance" of a thing to its "existence" takes place, then, through an extralogical or "alogical" act, or to be more precise, through a vital exigency. We notice the existence of a real world because we are active beings and come into contact with things, which may be either obstacles to be overcome or instruments of defense or dominion. If we were pure intelligences we would never notice the world. Instead, we are acting beings in a continuous exchange of actions and relations with the external world. We believe in the existence of the world because our will always feels the need to expand itself; in this irresistible exigency of life lies the root of the irreducible instinct of affirming the existence of things. In other words, for Santayana, our belief in the world is determined by the contact we "feel" with something else differing from us and which we cannot do without. It is an assured "animal faith" inducing us to affirm that "as long as life lasts, this faith must last in one form or another. This faith is the expression of animal vitality—the first sign that something is happening. It is implied in every feeling of hunger, fear, and love"; and "being an expression of hunger, tendency, impact, and fear this faith is directed to things; it does not assume the existence of extraneous beings developing by themselves independently of consciousness, but that of beings capable of being modified through action."

If we move from the world of material existence, which is the object of animal faith, to the world of essences or mental entities, thought can easily and quietly have intuitions and contemplations within this Platonic reign of ideas. Essences have a permanent character like the laws and symbols used by science. Essences as such are more real than things themselves, but inasmuch as they do not exist materially so as to be a reality

of fact, they are unreal. Things exist, essences do not: they are the totality of projections that can be expressed in the existing things. Thus, they
are not substances like Platonic ideas. Essence is the reign of pure being
in opposition to that of material existence; every essence is what is.
Universal gravitation, space, matter, time, and laws are only symbols
used by animal faith, that is, relation-schemes without a reality of fact.
Science and knowledge are a complex of significant symbols, not translatable into existing things to which they may by chance correspond.
Thus, Santayana has the reality of things lie in animal faith which, in
turn, lies in our vital need. Furthermore, he has another faith and another
activity, and these lie in the free contemplation of pure essences attained
by art through the free play of imagination, while science grasps those
essences in their abstract relations. The two worlds of existence and
essence constitute an irreducible dualism; life is divided and broken between these two reigns and human activity is only an absurd and tragic
effort at reconciling the idea with existence and existence with the idea.
Whatever men do or think (social institutions, religious cults, philosophical
systems, and the like) represents an immense, vain attempt at adjusting
animal life to spiritual contemplation, as if all this were a curse imposed
on humanity. However, as Christ, the highest figure in spiritual life, has
taught (*The Idea of Christ in the Gospels*, New York, 1946), the liberation, for Santayana, is achieved through suffering and death. We find it
difficult to understand what kind of "divine, immortal sufferer" is suffering with us. In spite of all, Santayana never forgot he was a Spaniard.
One of the topics often treated by him is the Christian religion, even
though he had long ago lost his original, Catholic faith. Of course, he
deals with religion in his own way, aiming at building a doctrine of the
Trinity in conformity with his materialism: God the Father is matter;
essences are the Son; spirit is the Holy Ghost.

"Pessimism" causes Santayana to run away from the world and to
identify the moment of "liberation" from existence, with that of poetical
and mystical contemplation, as did Schopenhauer. In this ascent, knowledge whose aim is the realm of truth and totality of essences stays one
degree lower than contemplation whose goal is the realm of spirit, that
is, the total detachment from existence, the annulment of every bond with
the world, in which the knowledge of values still has an outside end
instead of enjoying those values solely for the sake of enjoying them.
Even in this Santayana has remained a Spaniard at odds with America;
his contemplation is absolutely "inactive," "impotent," and most certain
(the only certitude overcoming every skepticism), and it delivers us from
the active and always problematical knowledge. This explains why he
criticizes not only every political form oppressing personal freedom, but

also the capitalistic-type society and contemporary American civilization as one in which conformism, technologism, and activism prevail over spiritual experience—the only authentically human type of experience. Santayana's criticism can be extended to almost the entire West.

In Santayana's position there is still another point we wish to draw attention to: his dualism between essence and existence denotes his thorough awareness about the insufficiency of critical realism and Anglo-American naturalism in general. Although indirectly, Santayana shows how the abstract formalism in mathematical logic does not help us to know the concrete world of existence, whose character (once that empty formalism of a thought-receptacle is granted) is nonlogical; and at the same time he shows the speculative deficiency (even as regards the problem of science) of so-called philosophies of nature, which do not account for the validity of knowledge, nor of moral, aesthetical, and religious values, nor for a spirit, by them almost identified with matter.

6. J. DEWEY'S INSTRUMENTAL PRAGMATISM

Even today JOHN DEWEY'S (1859-1952) form of pragmatism exerts a great deal of influence and provokes much discussion. A man of many interests and under various influences, he first came into contact with evolutionism, and with Comte's positivism, and later with Hegelian idealism; yet, as he himself states, his contact with James's *Principles of Psychology* was decisive. First an instructor and then a professor at the University of Michigan (1884-1894), he later moved to Chicago (1894-1908), where he conducted the noted experiment based on a school organized as an experimental laboratory of the University of Chicago. Finally he went to Columbia University where he taught until 1929. Of his many works we shall mention: *Studies in Logical Theory* (Chicago, 1903); *The Influence of Darwin on Philosophy and other Essays in Contemporary Thought* (New York, 1910); *Democracy and Education* (New York, 1916); *Reconstruction in Philosophy* (New York, 1920); *Experience and Nature* (Chicago, 1925); *Art as Experience* (New York, 1934); *A Common Faith* (New Haven, 1934); *Logic; the Theory of Inquiry* (New York, 1938).

Dewey's philosophy was also defined as an "experimental humanistic naturalism" with one important qualification: *nature* is the totality of the real of which *man* is a part; man "is living" *in* it and he "acts" *on* it. In nature everything is natural; every existence is an "event," a temporal "happening" not to be repeated and yet extrinsically bound up with the other events in a complexity of interaction. This is the whole reality; there is nothing outside of or beyond nature. Between nature and man there is, then, a tight and indissoluble connection. A part of nature, man is enrooted in it; yet he represents that part which is destined to modify nature itself and to realize its meaning.

Many levels of existence are distinguished in nature: physical, psychological, and spiritual levels, none of which is deducible from the other. Within the many forms of interaction there is a relationship of evolutional continuity or of change. The more complex forms of organization emerge from the simpler ones, and are irreducible, undeducible and unforeseeable among themselves. The evolutional continuity is not an absolute and univocal law but only a relation-scheme between events. Thus the coexistence and succession of more or less complex forms is thinkable. The essential characteristic of existence, then, is "temporality" (Dewey opposes not only the forms of naturalism which place becoming under a mechanical succession, or identify nature with matter, but also antinaturalistic conceptions), which means precariousness of existence and also openness—free from an order of necessity, it can go through changes and modifications. Moreover, the task for intelligence in its conscious proceeding is: to order reality which is always orderable and never entirely and definitively in order but as mobile as our intelligent proceeding, which is not mechanically determined by biological or social conditions, nor is it absolutely passive but dynamic and interactive.

Ideas and thought in general are instruments of future experience, and reason has necessarily a constructive function. It is the task of philosophy to place itself at the center and confluence of antitheses. In this sense, the validity of an idea is given by its *instrumental* efficacy to pass from a less harmonious or disharmonious experience to a more harmonious one. Facts are not imposed on us from the outside; there is in them what is due to our activity. This is not to say that we create facts (by now Dewey is far away from idealism), but we organize pre-existing experiences. Thought, in short, re-creates the world, and transforms it into man's tool; indeed, thought begins precisely from the conflicts presented by integral experience. We must be convinced that error, evil, disorder, irrationality and death are a reality (instead of deluding ourselves by calling them appearances); and the task for man and human society is to reduce their effects and limit their importance; this is to be done gradually (but never completely) through the active operation of human intelligence, which is "valid within the limits of its success." Every theory, doctrine, or mental construction is man's effective means (when it is really so) of transforming reality in order to guarantee the use and enjoyment of goods necessary to him. Men think when they are stimulated by need and inquietude, when they have to soothe perturbations, overcome difficulties, face a risk, surmount ignorance. "A life of rest,"—as we read in his *Philosophical Reconstruction*—"of success without effort, would be a life without thought. Men are not inclined to think when their action is dictated by authority. Soldiers have many difficulties and an abundance of restrictions, but as soldiers they are not famous for being thinkers. Thought is set for them from the top. Wherever an external authority reigns, there thought is suspect and harmful." Conflicts in experience produce systems, theories, reorganization-instruments for a given situation. Their validity, then, lies in their "success," that is, in their effective ability to carry out an intelligent reorganization of reality. Otherwise, theories and systems are false. On the other hand, once the instrumental value of ideas is granted, there are no theories or rigidly closed systems; through the use we make of it, every conception is instead susceptible of development and modification. Thought, in short, is only a norm for behavior; the concrete notion of the "good" surpasses the logical conception of the "true" as well as the metaphysical conception of the "real." Even the sciences of the spirit must be tested by contact with reality. However, while the physical world is to be subdued, the moral world is to be freed—it must be left free to realize itself through forms and structures that are always new and continuously in development.

Thus, the main aspects of Dewey's "logical instrumentalism" and "ethical betterment" are becoming clear. The first one tends to dissolve any rigid conception of logic and culminates in the *inquiry*, which is understood as "the controlled and guided transformation of an indeterminate situation into a situation that is determined in its distinctions and constitutive relations, to the point of changing the elements of an original situation into a unified whole." Intelligence always acts within an immediate situation, which is experience as a totality; and the latter, whether immediately known or not, always refers to a new immediateness. Thus, the inquiry is an ever open process taking place through a series of solutions; this process, however, is never concluded definitively since, determined under one aspect, a situation may become indeterminate under others; it may present disharmonies of relations and require new solutions within a multiplicity of possible results. Thought always is an endeavor toward solving a social and cultural crisis and toward re-establishing a "better" order which can always become still better as regards a given historical situation; history of philosophy is only the history of these attempts or plans of solution proposed by individual philosophers in relation to the social and cultural situation in their epoch. The crisis of our epoch, according to Dewey, is called upon to avail itself of that *instrument* which gave good results in other fields, namely, the scientific method representing the conquest of the modern age; and Dewey applies it to social and pedagogical, moral and aesthetical problems, as if methods or techniques that are valid for physics or biology could be good for pedagogy and morality. Indeed, if spirit is an emergence of nature and man's ultimate end is the betterment of this world, the only thing left is to confine the problems of philosophy and of religion to a better development and employment of man's intelligent behavior; thus, as a new earthly Eden man can be assigned the democratic behavior which, unlike abstract liberalism and dictatorial materialism, allows both the development of the individual in a society regulated by intelligence and the developments of society itself always being reorganized by man's perennially intelligent inventiveness.

Dewey's is a "concrete" and "democratic" materialism, but always a materialism; thus, although we acknowledge his merit for making his notable contribution to some particular problems and for a certain finesse of his toward moral and pedagogical values, we must conclude that: (1) he eliminates every trace of spiritualism even when he speaks about the spirit, which is no longer such since it emerges from nature; (2) he confines the function of intelligence to its actual ability to transform reality (any reality whatever), thus denying the existence of essences, substances, or immutable principles; (3) he makes of man a solely "historical" and "mundane" being since his needs and his stimulating inquietude can be satisfied only within the natural and historical order. Dewey's pragmatism does not differ much from the fundamental theses of Marxism, even if as a political and social conception his is poles apart. The philosopher is not only the "engineer of society" and, if he is only this, his function is indeed superfluous because it is inferior to the scientist's and the politician's functions. This explains the sympathies that Dewey's thought finds among some European theoreticians or followers of Marxism.

Until the beginning of the Second World War, Dewey's influence on contemporary American thought was vast and deep, and yet today it is notable even if other currents (to be treated later on) are predominant at the present. Among the pragmatists we should also mention ADDISON W. MOORE (1866-1930), first a student and then a professor at Chicago while Dewey was teaching there. His interests are essentially ethical and social (*Pragmatism and its Critics*, Chicago, 1910; "Reformation of Logic," in *Creative Intelligence*, edited by J. Dewey, New York, 1917) and even his pragmatism, which he defended brilliantly, can be defined as "humanistic": those ideas are true which, by acting upon situations, allow man to solve his problems.

CLARENCE I. LEWIS' (1883) "conceptualistic pragmatism" is an attempt at a compromise between idealism and naturalism, rationalism and empiricism. A professor at Harvard, his thought reflects the influences of Peirce and Dewey. The author of some valuable treatises on symbolic logic (*Survey of Symbolic Logic*, Berkeley, Los Angeles, 1918; *Symbolic Logic*, in collaboration with C. H. Landford, New York, 1932), Lewis reconciles the empiricist foundation of knowledge with the conception of the "variable *a priori*" ("The Pragmatic Conception of the A Priori," in *The Journal of Philosophy*, 1923; *The Pragmatic Element in Knowledge*, Berkeley, Los Angeles, 1926; *An Analysis of Knowledge and Valuation*, La Salle, 1946); that is, the principles *a priori* are the mind's initiative but they do not impose any limitations on experience because—as Dewey says—they are subject to change when they are revealed as inadequate intellectual instruments.

THOMAS V. SMITH (1890), a disciple of Dewey and a professor at Chicago, applied pragmatism to political philosophy (*The Promise of American Politics*, Chicago, 1938; *The Democratic Way of Life*, Chicago, 1939; *Discipline for Democracy*, Chapel Hill, 1942; *Constructive Ethics with Contemporary Readings*, New York, 1948). Democracy is not only a particular form of government, but a type of society in which all its members can freely develop their own economic, social, and intellectual possibilities; the philosophy implied in this society is pragmatism, since it upholds the idea that human personality and freedom are also social products. If this is so, if man and his freedom are purely social products, person and freedom are denied *ipso facto*, and the road is open, with all its consequences, for a man who is *only* "a social man."

SIDNEY HOOK (1902) is also linked with Dewey's pragmatism; a professor at New York University, he has dedicated his attention to political problems (*Reason, Social Myths, and Democracy*, New York, 1940) besides writing *The Metaphysics of Pragmatism* (Chicago, London, 1927).

7. SOME CONCLUDING REMARKS ON NORTH AMERICAN PHILOSOPHY

The currents in contemporary North American philosophy "are pragmatism, idealism, and naturalism . . . while the fields of endeavor are the philosophy of science and the theory of values." [6] We have already treated the three movements; of them, idealism and pragmatism no longer exist as specific currents; naturalism, remaining also as a generic characteristic, has turned its interest toward scientific methodology and its application, not only to social and political problems but also to problems of values, and so on. Regarding pragmatism we must say that it never was (like critical realism) a unitary current, both because of its eclecticism and because it is a method more than a doctrine. Obviously,

[6] G. H. Mead (1863-1931) sustains a functional point of view, and he endeavors (*The Philosophy of the Present*, Chicago, 1932) to transform the idea of the social into a natural category. Close to Dewey is also the "conceptualistic pragmatism" of C. I. Lewis, 1883 (*An Analysis of Knowledge and Evaluation*, La Salle, 1946), who expounds a naturalistic theory of the values which he studies from an empirical point of view.

many of its theses have been absorbed by other currents, so that we can say that even today there is no American philosophical movement without some elements inherited from pragmatism. Furthermore, it is not always easy to distinguish between pragmatism and naturalism (and even between naturalism and idealism); Dewey's philosophy, for example, is given both labels. Moreover, if pragmatism means, as has been written, "considering everything from a functional point of view and describing objectively the laws according to which things are relative," it can be said that, in this sense, American philosophy is pragmatist even today. Let us remember that C. S. Peirce's complete works, published from 1931 to 1935, called attention to the father of pragmatism, and that, in one way or another, Dewey's influence is effective on jurists, psychologists, sociologists, and so forth, as well as, though to a minor extent, on the philosophers properly so-called. Dewey is the philosopher of action, of the dominion over nature, and not of contemplation. His philosophy of experience draws from economics and science, in which he sees the forces that will transform the shape of the earth and the social systems; his instrumentalism has first of all that meaning, which draws it close to Marxist theories. Ultimately, even the naturalists do not entirely reject the concept of functionality although they disagree with Dewey precisely on the concept of instrumentality.

After all, even naturalism shows itself to be more a method and a program of studies than a doctrinal system. With pragmatism it shares the logical positivism, and with other currents of American philosophy it shares a more or less open materialism that makes the spirit emerge from nature or "matter." Naturalism so closely unites the spirit with the physiological functions that psychology becomes a chapter of animal biology; it affirms the existence of a world without an absolute (so that God is identified with the universe), and it is also marked by the negation of every form of "supernaturalism" in homage to a pure "humanism" founding nature on nature itself and man on man, so that humanity is assigned, as paradise, a universe fully dominated by technology and scientific progress. American philosophy substantially is almost entirely atheistic, even if the society making up the United States is Christian. Moreover, it is characterized by an idolatry of science, the instrument that, through production and technological development, will radically change mankind giving it all the happiness man with his "nature" is able to aspire to. Even on this point the "official" American thought is similar to the Marxist. The difference between Marxism-Leninism and pragmatism-naturalism-logical positivism lies in the lesser fanaticism on the part of Americans, who do not dogmatize an ideological system as orthodox Marxists do; likewise, the clash between them is determined by the difference in political method, that is, by the different manner of conceiving "democracy" and man's political and social freedoms. A naturalist or a neopositivist, no longer sure of his way of understanding democracy, would not have any difficulty in accepting the Marxist conception of life; nor would there be a religious difficulty, because he is an atheist; nor would there be any philosophical problem, because even for him the spirit, ultimately, is an epiphenomenon of matter, values are purely conventional or empirical, knowledge is a "technique," and science is the "grand Whole" transforming men and their lives which, after all, are engaged in the satisfaction of vital needs through economic goods. Besides the difference in political method, on the part of the American there is an almost sacred respect for the opinions of others; yet, this does not alter the fact that the two are nearly identical in their conceptions of life (prescinding from some ideological presuppositions that are typical of Marxism); and, when the significance of man, or the man of value, is conceived in a certain way, the danger of reducing that respect to a purely empirical fact, devoid of meaning, is not diminished. Such is the case if man is conceived solely as just another part of nature and subject to the same laws as all other things, and if value too becomes a conceptual fiction or a subjective feeling, more or less the same as any other animal feeling. We are not denying that many American thinkers believe in good faith that they are defending and founding a humanistic axiology as well as the rationality of values (for example, Sellars, who is inclined toward a more or less materialistic ontology); yet, it is just this good faith that worries us, in that the consequences flowing from certain premises are not fully realized. Many present-day currents in European philosophy, as we know, also affirm and develop a pure and absolute humanism (an atheistic one, and also "materialistic" in another sense). Yet, as we said, they are aware that their humanism is leading to the nullification of man and of all value, that is, to the position that "there is nothing serious"; they know that, carried to its ultimate consequences, pure humanism arrives at the negation of itself, to a "nullism" of humanism itself, simply signifying the "nothingness of meaning" in every purely humanistic conception (humanistic only in the order of immanentism and naturalism). American philosophy, instead, is still in the stage of exaltation and enthusiasm, idolatry of science and of scientific methods, believing that philosophical scientificalism or scientist philosophism is the infallible way toward progress and human salvation. It, therefore, is advancing boldly like an army that is certain of victory and does not know that all its weapons are unloaded or unfit to win the battle; and today (as always) the battle is not that of science, or of the philosophy of nature, not that of symbolism in mathematical logic or of techniques in the numerous logistics, but that of the spirit and spiritual values, of the humanity in man and his freedom in a metaphysical sense, and of truth, which is objective in an ontological meaning—and man, spirit, and truth are neither mathematical signs, events, neutral entities, essences without substances, nor things without being. Indeed, American naturalism was a reaction of optimism against European existentialist pessimism, as happens to young and powerful nations, or as Ortega would say, "ascending" ones: as happened to Elizabethan England or to eighteenth-century Europe—technology and science are exalted as instruments of man's power. We do not intend either to smother this optimism or to be backward. We only say that optimism is like a holiday: people are merry while it lasts; however, man's problems—the perennial ones—are not solved either with science, technology, optimism, or pessimism. An American scholar makes the following comparison between his country's philosophy and that of France: "American philosophers are inclined to seek the existential within objective relation rather than within their self-consciousness; they analyze experience in terms of problems and solutions rather than in terms of immanence and transcendence; their attention is focused on events rather than on mental actions and intentions; the study of the organic-whole shifts from the situation to the universe or to a solution instead of switching from the Ego to the Absolute or to Nothingness. However, once these approximate equivalences are established . . . we are able to understand that the similar study of the organic, existential, and circumstantial has given realism and naturalism the same central position in American contemporary philosophy that the diverse forms of existentialism occupy in France." No, we say, the difference is still there (and more so with respect to Italian and German philosophy), in that the problems of the "existential" in France are posited philosophically as problems of the spirit and in America, instead, as problems of "nature"; in France this is done with the awareness that, enclosed in its finitude, the "existential" is "nothing" and that its salvation lies in Being or in transcendence (whether this is denied or affirmed); but in America it is sought for within the world, in the pure, social life, which will undoubtedly be improved through the various "techniques."

The proof of this may be seen first in the arbitrariness with which the North Americans give the rank of general principles to methods and results that are valid only within a specific, narrow field; secondly, in the manner in which they extol a particular, scientific affirmation, so as to insert it within a general conception of man and of the whole universe (let us consider, for example, the arbitrarily extensive applications made of behaviorism and psychoanalysis); and thirdly, in the way in which they believe they can build everything, from aesthetics to morality, "scientifically" (actually, "empirically").

Lastly, one should consider how even Husserl's phenomenology, particularly in the writings of MARVIN FARBER (*Phenomenology as a Method and as a Philosophical Discipline*, Buffalo, 1928), has been stripped of every idealistic and spiritualistic element (for Farber the concepts of "spirit," "absolute spirit," and so on, are not different from the notion of ether in physics, and they are bound to undergo the same fate) and confined within the same limits of a "naturalistic" picture.

Husserl's phenomenology, according to Farber, must be divested of its idealism (*The Foundation of Phenomenology*, Cambridge [Mass.], 1943); its many "pretentious and deceptive" terms, such as "transcendental," "*a priori*," "constitutive," "pure," and "eidetic intuition," must be replaced; and we should accept from it only what may profit the formulation of a program "on the basis of a naturalistic or materialistic theory of reality," which is constructed with naturalistic methods, so that we may not go beyond the limits of a "descriptive philosophy"; and, on the basis of the results of the particular sciences, the latter is the whole philosophy, which can account perfectly for all the phases of experience."

Farber finds (and in this we agree with him) that phenomenology can agree and even identify itself with historical materialism, if the former is reduced to those suggested proportions and inserted in a naturalistic or materialistic conception making philosophy such a descriptive discipline as to comprehend all the logical, epistemological, and biological studies of the scientists. This confirms our thesis that in its fundamental principles the "official" American philosophy does not differ from the Marxist one. In fact, Farber (a critic of idealism and of existentialism) affirms: (1) value-judgments "are conditioned by predominant social interests and by biological interests"; (2) in so far as "theological criticism" is concerned, Kierkegaard is "far from having the importance of a Feuerbach"; (3) some theses of Lenin are "of an extreme importance for the struggle against idealism as a general philosophy," and so on. Finally, the following is Farber's historiographic scheme concerning the main directions of thought after Hegel's: "(1) the post-Hegelian current, with Marx and Engels, *via* Feuerbach; (2) the current of Darwinian evolutionism; (3) the renewal of a descriptive philosophy of experience, in which Brentano and Husserl (naturally reduced to the above-mentioned proportions) play the most important role; (4) the development of logic and of logical analysis in the different branches of philosophy." Thus, almost all of post-Hegelian world-philosophy does not represent any principal direction. Yet, I am convinced that those four directions suffice not only for Farber but also for many British and North American philosophers, for Russell, for Dewey and for logical positivists because, after all, even for them the problems of the spirit, of theology, of death, of man's destiny, and so forth, are "meaningless." Instead, as Farber writes, the truly "fundamental problems of an existence, properly interpreted, are problems of nutrition, shelter, clothing, sociability, hygiene, cultural realizations, and—conditioning all others—are the problems of economic relations." Perhaps Farber is a loyal friend of his country's democracy and one of the large number energetically affirming that they are defending "Western civilization" against communism.

441

VIII

THE PROBLEM
OF SCIENCE

---

1. Preliminary Considerations and General "Layout"

It would be beyond the scope of our work and also of our competence to give a technical treatment of this argument. In the present chapter, therefore, we shall confine ourselves to pointing out—in order to complete what has already been said in preceding chapters—some orientations in contemporary science always related to the problems of philosophy. This writer is absolutely convinced about the reciprocal autonomy of science and philosophy on account of both their methods and their formal objects; and I say this without implying that their respective independence invalidates the legitimacy of the problem regarding their mutual relationship or that it carries within itself an aprioristic underestimation of science; nor are we denying the existence of a problem of science itself, that must be posited and solved philosophically and with a philosophical method.

Our century has enriched science with quite a few theoretical discoveries, which have so transformed the classical conceptions that one can talk about a *crisis* of science, especially of its "principles." It even seems that the new scientific positions are denominated in opposition to the traditional ones: non-Euclidean geometry, non-Newtonian mechanics, non-Pythagorean arithmetic, and so on.

Already in the course of this work, as the occasion arose, we hinted at the problem of science in the individual thinkers and in the different currents of thought. Except in the case of Anglo-American realism we noticed the predominance of what has been called the "idealistic reaction against science" and so-called scientific intellectualism. The last quarter of the nineteenth century and the first decade of the twentieth were dominated, in fact, by the criticism against scientificalism generally coinciding with a criticism against positivism. Along this line we find Boutroux's contingentism, Bergson's intuitionism, Blondel's integral realism, the pragmatism and empirio-criticism of Mach and Avenarius, the neo-Hegelian idealism of Croce and Gentile, besides the critics of science such as Poincaré, Milhaud, Dehem, Le Roy, and others. Almost all these currents defend and sustain the autonomy of philosophy and of the rights of the spirit; they vindicate the "concrete" against scientific schematism, freedom against determinism, the "idealistic" and subjectivistic exigency against scientific "realism" and objectivism, and so forth.

During the last thirty years or so things have changed; the image of nature, as it had been constructed by modern science, has undergone radical changes; science itself has become subjectivistic. At present the scientist is not experimenting in order to discover the immutable objectivity in the data of nature, as if the infallible research would inalterably reflect a world in itself, but he is questioning all ancient and modern laws, which he considers as "hypotheses," "conventionalities," and "possibilities"; he is affirming the subjectivity and historicity of the scientific constructions. Hence arises the reaction against the objectivistic-positivistic conception of science, as well as against the last century's materialism and naturalism. Nineteenth-century science presents itself as an experimental inquiry into facts regulated by laws: observation and logical-mathematical deduction of consequences, with a view to establishing necessary and universal relations between phenomena of experience according to a causal concatenation. Twentieth-century science questions this conception, and formulates new hypotheses: "probability" and "possibility," non-"necessity"; nominalism of laws; not a material atom but a dematerialized matter. Eddington affirms that the substrate of all things, even the one that seems most material, is of a mental nature. Physics and chemistry no longer speak of material atoms but of atoms, photons and electrons having a mathematical characterization. It is not a question, says De Broglie, of real substances but of "realizations."

We are especially interested in the repercussions of, and influences exerted by, the "new science" on the problems of philosophy and on the mode of understanding philosophy itself and its tasks. In this respect we find it necessary to set forth some fundamental points, for the purpose of making necessary distinctions wherever we think that a great deal of confusion has occurred; thus, some order should be brought into the chaos caused by the mingling of science with philosophy, of the practical with the theoretical, of the empirical point of view with the speculative perspective; in this way, it will be possible to distinguish between empiricist praxism and philosophical reflection between science and scientificalism, the latter being a pseudo-science as well as an insensibility to the problems of the spirit.

(1) As already mentioned, nineteenth-century science was restricted to laboratory research and to the well-delimited contents of experience with the goal "of discovering the causal laws governing the world of material substance." From this point of view, its absoluteness (and the consequent conviction of the scientists that they were about to reach the bottom of the universe), was only an artificial one: the self-glorification as perfect and absolute knowledge was possible only because science "acritically" identified experience with laboratory-experiments. Hence arose the dogmatic conviction about the universality and necessity of physical laws and about a possible total description of the world within a complete and immutable table of categories or of "intellectual functions," through which the destiny of man and of mankind in the world would be defined and guaranteed infallibly. Science was then assigned even the normative task of directing individual morality and social ethics; it was given, in other words, an intrinsically "humanistic" content ("scientific humanism"), in which the religious question itself, now de-mythologized, was resolved. In short, science presented itself as absolute knowledge, objectively valid, and as a metaphysics of "material substance" of which the "spirit," "consciousness," and so on are manifestations or degrees of evolution. As an autonomous science with its own method and formal object, philosophy had no justification for existing, since it had revealed itself to be a collection of reveries (a sort of "pathology" of the mind) outside of experimentation and a collection of pseudo-propositions unfit to be the content of a scientific experiment. Philosophy was left with a secondary and servile task: summing up the results of the individual sciences. Thus positivism solved and dissolved philosophy into science, as transcendental idealism had solved and dissolved science into philosophy, in that science is a transitory moment dialectically overcome by it. Two total and absolute systems of truth are not possible; consequently, if such a system is given by philosophy (idealism), science can only be solved into it; if it is given by science (positivism), philosophy can only be dissolved into it.

The new science has widened its horizon so as to comprehend all experience, beyond that of the laboratory; and, above all, it has modified the very concept of experience on the basis of an exacting and absolute, rigorous empiricism which furthers, as it develops, the positions of the English empiricism of Locke and especially of Hume; nor does this new science neglect the consequences brought about by the Kantian conception of the categories as "intellectual functions," and by the Hegelian principle of dialectical *antinomism*, which as a law of thought and reality constitutes the essence of both. Thus, through the absoluteness and extrapolation of the empiricist principle, the new science solves spiritual and material "substance" into "pure experience" and, consequently, it denies that there is any substance whatever beyond the phenomenon: on the one hand, all experience is reduced to "sensations" and, on the other, sensation itself constitutes the whole reality and its substantiality. It is like saying: there is neither substance, nor being, nor essence, such words being "meaningless," mythical and "unverifiable." The remaining part— a criticism of the categories of causal or teleological necessity and of an absolute criterion of truth, nominalism, and so on—is only a consequence as we shall see later on.

It seems to us that the so-called revolution in contemporary science, which consists in a profound revision of the conception of the world as given by Galileian-Cartesian-Newtonian science, is connected with the gradual process of dissolution of being and disintegration of thought on which modern immanentist-historicist philosophy had embarked. Influenced by science, which in turn is conditioned by rationalism, modern thought, from Descartes to Kant, constructs a physics that is "metaphysical" in a certain way, and a metaphysics that we may call a "physics": Cartesian-Leibnizian rationalism is all centered on the cosmological idea; consequently, its conception of man and of God is cosmological. Like rationalism (but with more broadmindedness and indifference toward metaphysical problems), empiricism, from Bacon to Hume, in its turn considers nature as the proper object of philosophy and of science; sensorial experience is for empiricism the limit of human knowledge so that, on the one hand, metaphysics is solved into physics and is thus denied and, on the other, physics is divested of its metaphysical character at the moment that reality is identified with the sensorial contents, with "what appears" to (empirical) consciousness, in such a way that reality is what it appears to be. This explains the "scientificalism" and "philosophism" consonant with Enlightenment. Kant modifies deeply the *a priori* pertinent to rationalism (not an apriorism of "ideas" but one of "forms" or of universal and objective conditions in knowing) as well as the concept of experience, which is not the mere sensorial, but the synthetical act of form and content; in this way Kant moves a step forward toward the dissolution of the concepts of being, substance, and of categories in general, which are reduced to intellectual functions. Moreover, with his principle of transcendentality, whose valid "function" is limited to the systematizing of the contents in sensorial experience, Kant makes metaphysical "knowledge" impossible (metaphysics is left only with the task of positing itself either as a "natural exigency" or as a "postulate") and, thereby, he identifies knowledge as such with scientific knowledge or knowledge of nature. From this point of view the *Critique of Pure Reason* is a philosophical solution of the problem of science, the "critical" justification of the validity of scientific knowledge and, consequently, the disowning of metaphysical knowledge on the ground that metaphysics is not a "science" because its object is not a sensible one (that is, a content of sensible experience); and all this falls within the vision of the world, as it springs from Cartesian-Newtonian science. Post-Kantian idealism gives transcendentality a metaphysical value, as it identifies being with thought and thought with antinomic dialecticity; the adequacy between being and thought is perfect and immanence acquires a geometrical roundness. From this point of view, as an absolute immanentism idealism can be indifferently defined as a "philosophy of Spirit" or "philosophy of Nature." Nature is a moment of the Spirit (and thus science is a moment of philosophy, in which the spirit is wholly displayed), but the Spirit, which is all immanent in its natural and historical process, is Nature itself (and thus, as positivism claims, philosophy ultimately is resolved into scientific knowledge or becomes the systematization of the latter). Granting the adequacy between spirit and nature and the reduction of being to thought, whose latitude is that of the world, idealism and positivism are only two points of view—one moving *from* the subject, the other *from* the object—which tend to be assimilated; both represent the complete and, perhaps, conclusive development of cosmologism in modern thought and what we have called *metaphysical physics*.

However, if we consider the matter carefully, we find that with empiricism first and then with Kant and transcendental idealism, philosophy laid down the conditions for the deep evolution undergone by the *metaphysical physics* of modern science; philosophy did this through so-called criticism of the concepts of substance, being, and so forth, which were dissolved either empirically into the phenomenon, or critically into transcendentality, or dialectically into the antinomic movement of thought. Also it must be noted that such criticism is directed against the "substantialism" and "essentialism" pertinent to rationalism (therefore, against "this" metaphysics); consequently, this criticism is to be understood as an evolutional moment intrinsic in modern, immanentist and historicist thought; an evolution gradually revealing itself as a self-dissolution, and as an evolving and a dissolving of cosmologism, which characterizes this stream of philosophical-scientific thought from Galileo-Descartes to Kant-Hegel-and positivism. Yet, this stream must be carefully distinguished from the other proceeding from Campanella-Pascal to Vico-Rosmini; through a compact and critical debate with the former, the latter continues the traditional metaphysics (highly different from the metaphysics of modern rationalism) as well as the speculative tradition which assigns man (the problems of the spirit) to philosophy as its object; for this current, nature and science are looked upon subordinately, as problems interesting the concrete and integral man, that is, his existence as a spiritual animal living in the world.

After Hegel the Kantian-idealistic mode of understanding objectivity and necessity in knowledge begins to wear away until all objectivity and necessity are denied of human knowledge as such (negation of "theo- reticity"); and then, as a consequence, the supremacy of the practical over the theoretical, of action over thought, of facts over principles is affirmed (*praxis* is assumed as a criterion of judgment). Thus, after the idealistic reaction against positivism, the new science fully accepted the historicist principle and questioned the validity of the categories of causal necessity and of substance and, on the basis of a rigorous empiricism, it formulated new, epistemological doctrines revolutionizing the vision of the world held by Cartesian-Newtonian science, which nineteenth-cen- tury positivism had preserved even through the criticism of Kant. The doubt concerning the absoluteness of scientific laws led as a consequence to a strong emphasis on the "practical" value of science, which was in- dissolubly linked with *praxis* and was reduced to pure conventionalism, and so on. *Metaphysical physics was dissolved just as was physical meta- physics.*

Obviously such an evolution in scientific concepts confronted the sci- entists themselves (particularly mathematicians and physicists) with new philosophical and epistemological problems, which (as we noticed even in the preceding chapter) they tried to solve or to lead toward a solu- tion. Mathematicians and physicists, however, did not confine them- selves to the problems inherent in their disciplines (and, if the problem of science is posited as a philosophical problem, it must be solved philosophically, not scientifically), but they attempted to construct "philosophies" or deny philosophy with the methods of science by ex- trapolating their scientific conclusions. Hence arose the confusion of tongues, the arbitrary and hasty conclusions, the superficial hybridisms (harmful to philosophy as well as to science), the presumptuous affirma- tions, the many inconclusive "treatises" of a "philosophical science" and of a "scientific philosophy," which is like speaking of zoological morality and of moral zoology. On the other hand, some so-called philosophers with "scientific" heads, while engaged in extracting all truths and every criterion of truth from "facts" and from "praxis" for an ever greater "progress" of mankind, accepted the findings of science, its empiricism and its method, its technique, its object, and concluded that besides these findings there is no philosophy and that philosophy is this phenomenism, empiricism, naturalism, materialism, conventionalism, and so forth. A new- positivism thus came into being and, according to it, whatever is not "verifiable" (and the life of the spirit and its values, including the religious values, are not verifiable) is nonsense. We are not stating that science and scientists must abstain from positing the philosophical problems arising from science itself; nor are we saying that philosophers are to ignore the findings of scientific research especially when these affect problems directly connected with philosophy (such as those of time and space, of causality, of substance, and so forth). We are saying (and repeating) that scientists must posit those problems philosophically and that the philosophers must "reflect" upon the scientific results as philosophers and in relation to the object proper to philosophy; this object is spirit not nature, or it may be nature considered from the metaphysical point of view, and this point of view is not reducible to that of science; or philosophers may think about scientific results in relation to spiritual life, which is in no way an aspect or a part of natural life according to the scientific meaning of this term. It is one thing to eliminate from science any trace of metaphysics, and quite another to try to replace metaphysics with science and to draw up the death-certificate for the former in a language lacking philosophical sense. Likewise, it is right to emphasize the points of contact (where they do exist) between science and metaphysics or to reflect philosophically upon the problems and findings of science, but it is wrong to draw hasty, metaphysical consequences from them, and still worse to assume them as truths metaphysically valid or as principles on which to build a metaphysics. On the contrary: only on the basis of a metaphysics built through its own method, through the examination of its own object and for the purpose of solving its own problems, is it possible to draw conclusions suitable not for new, scientific discoveries but for the solution of the problem of science as such, posited as a philosophical problem; otherwise, the intellectual chaos will be ever greater and nobody will know any longer (neither the philosopher nor the scientist) what philosophy is or what science is. The "cause," "freedom," "unity," and so on, of which the philosopher speaks, are not the cause, freedom, and unity spoken of by the physicist and mathematician; the discrimination is given by the metaphysical or scientific use of the terms, without implying thereby a necessary contrast or contradiction; indeed, the distinction makes it possible to converge and integrate the meanings, which, if confused or extrapolated, cause many so-called philosophical views by the scientists to be simply inconclusive. Science was right whenever it claimed its autonomy against the fanciful and equivocal "philosophies of nature"; likewise, philosophy was and is right every time it has claimed (and today this problem is of an urgent reality once again) its autonomy against the no less fanciful and equivocal "philosophies of science" or "scientific philosophies." Nor is it a question of speaking, as some did, of a "divorce," for the simple reason that there never was nor is there ever going to be a marriage; the so-called collaboration-periods were either periods of tyranny of one over the other or of concubinage, whence came into the world precisely the miscarriages of the philosophies of nature or those of the scientific philosophies. Nor is it sufficient to say that the "exceedingly profound revolution . . . in the very foundations and fundamental concepts" of science makes urgent philosophy's rapprochement with science,[1] thereby legitimating a new philosophy of science on the basis that, on the one hand, the problem of the concept of method and that of the value of knowing must be posited as philosophical problems (that is, they are theoretical problems of philosophy and not a philosophy of science); and that, on the other hand, the transformation of the concept of nature operated by scientific theories is valid as a scientific viewpoint to be distinguished from the philosophical one on nature itself; if, in fact, the former point is not distinguished or is assumed as also having a philosophical validity, we will still be making a scientific philosophy which is neither science nor philosophy. "Philosophy of science is an expression as ambiguous as "philosophy of nature" is. There exists no "rapprochement"-problem and, even less, a problem of "accord" between philosophy and science, but only one of "relation," in that it is a question of two diverse (not contradictory) and irreducible levels, whose diversity is a *qualitative* one.

(2) The spiritual, moral, and social value of science represents another ambiguous problem, made extremely urgent and disquieting because of the progress attained in these last decades with all its prodigious technical applications. To recriminate against physics for discovering atomic energy and applying it to items of war, or against genetics for the possibility that it may generate monsters, or against the inhumanity of science in the name of morality and of spiritual rights, means persisting in the confusion of problems which must be distinguished. In fact, he who recriminates against these inconveniences caused by science implicitly recognizes that science as such possesses a moral value; that is to say, something is being attributed to science which does not intrinsically belong to it; and, in making this attribution, he causes science to take the place of philosophy and of other forms of spiritual activity. In other words, the one recriminating against science paradoxically is already a "scientificalist." Now science is not a moral "science" though it is a human activity; in itself it is not "humanistic," and it does not possess a morality. To the researcher, a worm and a man from the science point of view are "scientific material"; in creating a monster, genetics is experimenting on one of its possibilities, and so forth. Only art, morality, and

[1] P. Filiasi Carcano, "Concetto e problemi della filosofia della scienza," *Giorn. crit. della filos. ital.*, III (1952), 290.

religion can give science that humanistic "soul" which science by itself does not have, nor is it expected to have: science is only an ensemble of results obtained through experiments conducted on a given scientific material. Therefore, science is neither evil nor good nor more evil than good according to a calculation of the disadvantages or advantages it brings about. It is not the research which is moral or immoral but the scientist, the *man* of science—it is he who gives science that sense of humanity science itself is lacking, according as he abides or not by his deep humanity. The fact that science today does not draw back in the presence of anything, even in the presence of a radical negation of the human person, or in the presence of brutality, is not its fault; this is simply one of the consequences (perhaps the most disastrous one) of the "crisis of principles" provoked by historicist immanentism, and one of the consequences due to the rejection of being and the disintegration of thought, which can be defined as a crisis within "theoreticity" and its objective validity. All the intellectual and spiritual values, even including the moral and religious ones, are involved in the crisis of principles. The scientist, who within himself has disowned and destroyed them, is not going to respect anything any more; being devoid of them, he cannot give science that humanistic soul which it is lacking, and consequently everything becomes perfectly normal and licit for him. Ironically, the most implacable recriminators against the inhumanity of science and against the man who has placed himself "in opposition to the human," are precisely the existentialists (whether atheistic or theistic), the "relativists" and others, that is, those who have doubted all evidence and made vain all spiritual values which, at best, they reduced to an existential experience or mental states by proclaiming that their objectivity and theoretical validity are no more than an illusion—and then they expect that science should have a spiritual, moral, and social value!

Ultimately, in spite of all apparent contradiction, there is here an extreme coherence though, perhaps, an unconscious one. In fact, once the theoretical value and the "illusion" of the metaphysical point of view have been destroyed and practice accepted as the evaluative criterion, those persons cannot ask of a "liquidated" philosophy what only philosophy can give and so they appeal to science—among other reasons, for these two: first, once the philosophical-metaphysical point of view is denied, one can only adopt the scientific-empiricist view by extrapolating it; second, if "truth" is practical only, then of all human activities science is the best qualified, with its technical applications, to convalidate the pragmatic point of view. Thus, once all value has been denied together with the objective validity of thought, we have the solution of the value of the problem of science from the "scientificalist" standpoint and, with it, the confirmation of scientificalism itself. If philosophy is no longer called upon to understand but rather "to transform the world" (and within a conception in which the principles spring from *praxis* itself), then there is no room for it any longer; in fact, science is much more fit for carrying out this task and for assuring for itself an undisputable supremacy, although as theoretical validity it fails because, like every coherent historicism, it leads to absolute relativism; this is, in fact, the scientificalism with which "naturalism" and neopositivism, instrumentalism and Marxism coincide—whether "Western" scientificalism or "Eastern" scientificalism they are substantially identical. There is also another reason: granted that every individual man and all mankind have only historical and natural ends (absolute immanentism), it follows that the end of history (of each individual and of mankind) is the total conquest of the world, its dominion and its exploitation for the purpose of civil and social progress. Hence arises a new confirmation of science's absolute supremacy as well as the uselessness of positing the problem of respect for the human person as a limit for science itself. Man as such does not count any longer; what counts is the realization of progress, whose efficient and sovereign forces are scientific and technical research. Francis Bacon, who lived when modern science was being formed, understood this very well: *scientia est potentia,* in that the more we know nature the more we dominate it. Hence arises the other consequence: as a dominion over nature, science is an instrument of political power, which is *praxis par excellence,* "realism," and thus "possibilism." In fact, philosophy is being identified with politics, today; or rather, it is politics which has taken its place while action has taken the place of thought, which no longer fathers the action but is determined by it, so that thought is "instrumental," "practical," "possible," and as contingent as "contingency" itself. In this total dissolution of philosophy or of "theoreticity," no longer is there any sense in positing the problem of the morality or nonmorality of science and of the scientist, and not even that of man; what is left is only the power of science *as a matter of fact,* outside of every moral evaluation and every consideration of the "humane"; and science is an instrument of political power which, whether democratic or dictatorial, nullifies the person within a monstrous, materialistic mankind devoid of any gleam of spirituality. This is not a cry for "less science, less technology!" but an insistence that there be "more art, more philosophy, and more religion," so that there may be (at least) an equal affirmation of the beautiful, of the true, and of the good and sacred, while science is allowed to advance and technology to progress.

(3) So-called *methodology* has gained an ever increasing importance through the evolution of science. It is understood both as a determination of procedures for the sake of their increasingly effective and rigorous use in the individual sciences (methodology is today identified with so-called

analysis of sciences), and also (with respect to problems no longer held to be scientific) as a clarification of the procedures themselves for the purpose of applying them to other fields of inquiry. Methodological research has led to an increasingly rigorous distinction of methods, so as to delimit more precisely the field of each science and to determine the most rigorous concept of each: this is a process of clarification and dissociation that had many important consequences in the determination of the concepts of geometry, physics, logic, psychology, and so forth. Besides the analysis that each science has made and still can make of itself, and precisely from the necessity for this same analysis, has arisen the need to elaborate independently of each single science,[2] a general technique applicable to the analysis of the individual sciences. From this same need arose the *analysis of language* (to which the so-called Vienna-Circle and other similar currents have devoted themselves), whose main task is to examine the logical structure of scientific theories, their meaning and verifiable nature—all this for the purpose of distinguishing between problems and pseudo-problems, between words "making sense" and others "saying nothing," and for the purpose of discriminating among the various languages in order to avoid unfruitful polemics.

We shall have occasion to consider again the meaning of methodology; now we are interested in remarking that, as a technique, it has such a limited scope that it can even be ignored by philosophy, because the analysis of philosophical assertions belongs to philosophy itself (indeed, it is philosophy itself being constructed); it is not a technique, and it is not formalistic at all. For philosophy it is completely irrelevant that its assertions are "insignificant" from the viewpoint of a neopositivistic methodologist. Philosophy has no use for a logic without *logos* and for a thought without being, precisely because it is metaphysical intelligibility. If one objects that its affirmations are "unverifiable" and its language "without a meaning," philosophy replies that, if the verifiable is limited to scientific assertions, its affirmations can only be unverifiable although they are equally "true" concerning philosophical truth; also, that its language has a philosophical sense, which is not the scientific one, and that it is not without a sense by any means, unless one claims that the only true meaning conveyed by words is the scientific meaning. However, this is a gratuitous and arbitrary affirmation and a dogmatic scientificalism which, once philosophically analyzed, shows itself to be devoid of any meaning. It is not philosophy that must undergo a trial by the methodology of the sciences and by the analysis of language as understood by neopositivism; philosophy invites both to analyze themselves, and not assume dogmatically the concepts of logic, of language, and so on, which constitute the foundation of their analyses. The analysis

[2] Cf. Carcano, "Concetto e problemi . . . ," *op. cit.,* pp. 295 ff.

of science without saying what science is and why it is, or of language without saying what language is and why it is, is merely formalistic and a nonphilosophical moment, because it analyzes while prescinding from the concept and the intelligibility of what is being analyzed. It is mere simplicism to pretend that from such a methodology or technique one can draw philosophical inferences (as often happens), or that on its basis one can even ostracize the concept of "spirit," of "being," and so on. Trying to understand the sense of philosophy and its problems from this point of view amounts to trying to understand music with one's feet and painting with one's touch, a thing that may happen, indeed, but to those who, in the first case, are born deaf-blind and, in the second, to those born blind, provided that they are re-educated.

(4) The results arrived at by science may appear to be revolutionary not only to science itself but also to philosophy; in reality the more serious scientists present their results as "hypotheses" (though recognizing their fundamental importance), and the philosophers, those who are really such, know that the revolution in philosopy can be carried out by a philosopher, that is, by philosophy itself from within, with its methods and from its speculative point of view, which is not the scientific one.

According to some epistemological currents, the following is the most conspicuous result of the new science: mathematics is not founded on evident truths having a logical, absolute validity, but on "conventional propositions" chosen amongst the most idoneous for its logical organization; consequently, it is possible to have the coexistence of diverse, logical-linguistic systems, each with its conventional propositions and with its own logical and coherent discourse, and with its own criterion of formal coherence; and therefore, there are no universal and necessary truths founded on a sole and absolute criterion of logic. However, the matter does not stop here; logic is identified with mathematical logic. Hence comes the reduction of logic to a technique and a conventional, mere formalism. Moreover, according to the methodologists themselves, physics is identified with its own methods, its very methodology. Consequently, the latter's task no longer is that of discovering and formulating the immutable and necessary laws of nature, but that of determining with a greater precision its methods so as to make them always more effective. Unlike Cartesian-Newtonian science, physics has given up the description of the world in its totality immutably governed by necessary laws—for scientific methodology such a world is meaningless. Methodological inquiries, furthermore, have pointed out that science is historically conditioned and thus relative. Nor is it a question of progress but only of a different mode of perceiving truth, of a new choice. As some wrote, the new science is not the "result of a superior capacity of ours, but of a changed attitude on our part." There is no "science in itself"; scientific theories are not outside of history, but within its dynamism; their logic has nothing absolute and immutable about it, without their being for this reason arbitrary constructions.

We are here interested in putting things each in its place and in pointing out the arbitrary extrapolations in order to achieve a minimum of clearness in the confusion of tongues, which was increased, as a matter of fact, by the analysis of language often made by those who either do not understand or are unable to grasp the depth of the philosophical language—which they do not distinguish from the scientific one. Let us notice, first of all, the following: it is affirmed that science has discovered its historic and relative character (there are no absolute and immutable, scientific truths), or, as they also express it, science has discovered the conventionality of its laws, "arbitrarily . . . posited" by the scientist "in order to establish experimental protocols or axioms and postulates (that is, grammars and vocabularies) which are also arbitrary"; then, from these affirmations the conclusion is drawn that, today, "the traditional concept of reason is in crisis." Obviously, we have here an unacceptable confusion between the "reason" of the philosopher and that of the scientist, between "rationalism" in the philosophical sense and scientific "rationalism," without saying that no distinction is made between modern rationalism and classical rationalism and, consequently, between their two diverse metaphysical conceptions. Therefore, to identify logic with mathematical logic is only a whim and an intrusion of mathematics into the field of philosophy, as well as a confusion between the language of philosophical logic and that of mathematical logic. Evidently, the terms "knowledge," "principle," "judgment," "concept," "abstraction," and others have in philosophy a meaning that is irreducible to the mathematical one, just as the terms "causality," "necessity," and "finality" have in metaphysics a sense that is not *tout court* the physical one. To deduce metaphysical illations from so-called new physics is to blunder both as a scientist and as a philosopher. There is no doubt that Plato's and Aristotle's concept of geometry or of physics is no longer the same as today's after Einstein, Planck and others; just as there is no doubt that, like every form of human knowledge, science has a historical development. However, it is one thing to say that the human knowledge of truth is historical, and it is another to say that truth itself is a historical product and thus contingent and valid only with respect to a given historical situation. Moreover, we do not hold that philosophy and science are two contrasting truths perhaps in opposition to each other, but simply that the scientific perspective is diverse from the philosophical one (and "diverse" does not mean "contradictory"); and also we sustain that knowledge has some levels or moments that must not be confused. Indeed, in the infinity of truth the diverse modes of knowing can meet and converge. Therefore, only those scientists who are dilettante and superficial philosophers can hastily conclude, from the conventionality of the logical-syntactical schemes of their scientific theories or from so-called in-determinism and relativism of physics, that all logic is conventional, and that the causality-principle is to be put aside, as if the concept of "cause" in the metaphysical sense were identical with the one in the physical sense. This kind of scientificalism is nonscientific and pseudo-philosophical.

We are not arguing against scientificalism alone but also against phi-losophism, that is, against the extending of philosophical methods to the sciences, whereby those "metaphysical physics" are produced; the latter are worth as much as the "physical metaphysics," that is, they have no worth either scientifically or philosophically. The fact that, from the end of the sixteenth century, modern science has established itself in its own concept and with its own method by differentiating itself from the con-cept of Aristotelian-mediaeval science, is certainly a great progress; in-deed, it represents the conquest of the very concept of science and of the end of aprioristic science founded on metaphysical concepts. However, all this signifies only the surpassing of Greek-Scholastic science and not of classical metaphysics in its twofold orientations, the Platonic-Augustin-ian and Aristotelian-Thomist. The rise and formation of modern science implies only the criticism of "metaphysical physics," that is, of science constructed with the methods of philosophy and having, as its object, the "essence of things," but in no way does it imply an extending of this criticism to metaphysical knowledge; modern science marks the end of "metaphysical physics" not of "metaphysics." From this point of view all classical metaphysics remains intact, even granting that not a single iota in the whole of Greek-mediaeval science can stand up any more. This metaphysics can have (as it did have in fact) its own deepening-process, not because there came into being a new science, diverse from the one which metaphysics itself had built, but because of an internal reflection upon itself within the horizon of philosophical truth and of metaphysical perspective. This argument can be shifted to another historical level. Diverse from Greek-Christian rationalism, modern rationalism makes the world an absolute image of the Cartesian-Newtonian science and then it has its own physical metaphysics coincide with that image; by furthering empiricism's critical thesis in an original way, Kant modifies the concepts of objectivity and experience, and through the principle of transcen-dentality he believes he is guaranteeing the validity of science. However, it is at this point that the two equivocal positions—opposed and yet substantially identical—take place: the reduction of science to philoso-phy (idealism) and of philosophy to science (positivism); and all this either in the name of the absoluteness of the Idea and of dialectical necessity, which is as unavoidable as destiny, or in the name of the necessity of modern law, which is invincible in its determinism. Thus, on the one hand, philosophies of nature which build a pseudo-science on philosophical presuppositions are appearing again and, on the other, there is a rebirth of the scientific philosophies, which arbitrarily and naively consider the conclusions of science to be valid for philosophy. As already mentioned, an idealistic reaction (science is criticized for its abstract intellectualism and for its being reduced to the categories of the useful and of the economic) developed between the final decades of the last century and the first decades of this one; this reaction vindicated the "contingency" of natural laws, nature's initiative and freedom, the autonomy of philosophy, the rights of the spirit, and so forth. The new science began just when the idealistic reaction against nineteenth-century science was in swing; and with its new theories it has come to confirm what the critics of the same science had sustained against the scientists in their times; that is, the new science convalidates the criticism against nineteenth-century materialism and determinism, thus paving the way for new conceptions, from which the scientists of the last century were dogmatically shut off.

At this point we have to distinguish between serious scientists, who proceed with much caution, and a flock of dilettanti; with an enthusiasm matching their naiveté and swearing by the truth of the new science while drawing gratuitous inferences therefrom, the latter arrive at some metaphysical conclusions; indeed, their view is so vast and deep as to engulf and exhaust metaphysics. Furthermore, with respect to serious scientists we have to distinguish the activity directed toward the elaboration of their scientific theories from the other activity devoted to extrapolations or philosophical reveries, to which some of them have abandoned themselves through an irresistible temptation. Just as it was naive to draw a materialistic philosophy from Cartesian-Newtonian and positivistic science, so today it is equally naive to draw, from Einsteinian-Planckian science, a spiritualistic philosophy, and a confirmation for the existence of God, of freedom, and so on. No science can lay down the foundations of a philosophy; nor can it posit and solve a single philosophical problem. Therefore, some scientists show no respect for the limits of science when they say they are favorable to religion and believe in God on the basis of their scientific "hypotheses"; likewise, some philosophers do not respect those limits either when they rejoice about the "contributions" of the new science toward the demonstration of the existence of God, of freedom, and so forth; in both cases there is a deplorable confusion of science, metaphysics, and religion. Most intemperate of all are the so-called methodologists of science, who go beyond the results of the same new science when they affirm the conventionality of all scientific theories and of principles; they also go beyond a minimum of scientific and philosophical seriousness when, on the basis of the conventionality of sciences, they talk about the crisis of reason, the end of the absoluteness of logical discourse, thus dismissing all principles even in their metaphysical use; and this they do as if the "logicity" of sciences were identical with that of philosophy, the meaning of terms, the same, and as if physical determinism and causality in a metaphysical sense signified the same thing, and so on. Apparently on the basis of an exigent criticism, these exponents of scientificalism are extremely dogmatic. Their position is as follows: science is the truth and there is no truth which is not scientific; yet, the truth of science is as conventional as its logical coherence; therefore, truth as a whole and "logicity" are conventional; and if philosophy claims to possess its truth and "logicity" and metaphysics claims its absoluteness, this means that they are clinging to mythical, archaeological, and obsolete positions which, in any case, make "no sense." Senseless, instead, is all this discourse. In fact: (1) the latter postulates the scientific truth as the only existing truth, thus echoing positivistic scientificalism; (2) it considers the conventionality of scientific truths as an established and indisputable truth, without such a definitiveness being authorized by science itself (since science presents its theories as "hypotheses") and by philosophy; (3) it entangles itself in the most naive contradiction when, having accepted the principle of conventionality as absolute and definitive, it denies that all truth is conventional, precisely because it takes as definitive and absolute the principle of the conventionality of truth; (4) it arbitrarily applies the conventionalism of scientific theories (supposing that it is valid in this field) to philosophical and metaphysical doctrines, as if "scientific reason" and "philosophical reason" were the same thing. Supposing that there is a crisis in the "principles" of science, what is there to authorize the conclusion that all "logicity" is conventional, so that even metaphysics and its principles are to be involved in that crisis without any possibility of appeal? Obviously this conclusion originates from an "acritical" attitude toward science (in contrast with the very affirmation that scientific theories are relative and of a historical character) as well as from an incomprehension of the philosophical moment.

With its conventionalism and abstract formalism of a "logic without *logos*" and of a "physics without nature," methodology, ultimately, coincides with that crisis of theoreticity characterizing contemporary thought.

(5) Inasmuch as the "logicity" intrinsic in scientific theories is essentially conventional it must be concluded that the theoreticity consonant with the sciences is pure "conventionality." This is very close to a denial of the theoretical value of the sciences in favor of a practical

and utilitarian one (as in the case of pragmatism and idealistic philosophies). If logicity is, ultimately, formalism and a technique ("without logos"), something must be found to fill it up; the content given to it is empirical; logicity is understood as an instrumentality serving practical ends. Conventional methodology joins with other forms of *praxis* and above all with the Marxist-type *praxis*. This explains why quite a few methodologists are Marxists, and those who are not so because of political reasons or convenience equally coincide with it in their conception of man and history. In fact, if that conventionalism is extended, for example, to morality, politics, and so on, it follows that the principles regulating man's spiritual life are conventional and without an absolute meaning: one can give them any meaning whatever or no meaning at all; such principles can be accepted on faith, voluntarily; but their objective and universal validity cannot be demonstrated. Even at this point the theoretical criterion is substituted by the pragmatic one which is based on convenience, on fitness and on relativity to a circumstance, situation or contingency, and so forth. These are the consequences of a logic "without a logos," a "physics without a nature," and a "psychology without a soul": man is emptied of his being and, like an empty bag, he can be filled out with anything whatever, according as this or that principle, which in itself has no truth, is conventionally assumed. Man is an amorphous material to be "manipulated" at pleasure by using techniques suitably valid according to circumstances and possibilities. These consequences result from a logical and conventional formalism arbitrarily extended to all logicity (even to that logicity being intrinsic in the same objective intelligence and thus in the structure of metaphysics and not of science). Someone has said that this formalism represents "the price we had to pay for the progress" made by science and philosophy toward the solution of their problems. In my incorrigible backwardness I insist on saying that this is a well-deserved punishment for having perpetrated the ruin of being and the disintegration of thought.

2. The Theory of Relativity

Classical science is founded on certain fundamental principles: absoluteness of the spatio-temporal localization and universal determinism. The image of classical physics is that of an objective world which can be described in its completeness and defined independently of the observer. Difficulties and problems left in suspense by this science did not shake the trust in its principles, which were considered capable of overcoming all difficulties and solving all problems.

It is believed that the revision of classical science began in 1830 when Lobacevski questioned the validity of the Euclidean postulate; the series of non-Euclidean geometries ensued thereon. However, the most important innovations are due to the theory of relativity, which is linked with the name of ALBERT EINSTEIN (1879-1955). With the introduction of the *time*-factor, the classical three-dimensity of space is superseded by the new conception of the four-dimensity of space-time and of spatio-temporal relativity. The elaboration of the spatio-temporal continuum and the formulation of the new, four-dimensional geometry are due to Minkowski. The introduction of time has modified the classical concept of space as a "place" having its objective properties. The geometry of space has become, says Eddington, a geometry of time or, at least, space has been closely bound up with time. According to the theory of relativity, space-time are not absolute but relative to the reference-system and they change with the changing of the velocity in the world where the observer is. In other words, the measurements and laws judged by us as absolute are valid for our world because of its motion, but they are not so for other worlds whose motion differs from ours in velocity and direction; thus they have no absoluteness whatever. The phenomena being observed cannot be regarded independently from the observer; consequently, what a phenomenon is independently of our observation cannot be determined in an absolute sense but only by way of *hypothesis*. The classical principle of relativity held the spatio-temporal intervals to be constant; Einstein, instead, holds simultaneousness, distance, velocity, and time to be relative: when the reference-systems are different, the measurement of spatial distances, and of temporal intervals within a reference-system, does not coincide with the measurement in other systems. The space measured by an observer at rest differs from that measured by an observer in motion. Similarly, two events being simultaneous for one observer are successive for another. Hence arises the impossibility of an absolute spatio-temporal determination of a reference-point that is unique and absolute. Time and space are not independent of each other but are conditioned reciprocally: time is the fourth coordinate to be added to the three spatial ones in order to determine a phenomenon (*four-dimensional continuum, or spatio-temporal continuum*).

The doctrine of relativity as well as the quantum theory (which, moreover, are two discordant syntheses of science) are not definitive and certain, even in the opinion of authoritative scientists; this fact should suggest caution to scientists and philosophers when they draw metaphysical consequences or make arbitrary extrapolations. As was prudently remarked by an expert, one should not think "that the systematization of the quantum-relativity theories through Dirac's equations—no matter how satisfactory and stable it may be—has attained an absolute value (this was not achieved by the two theories nor by that of relativity alone). Both are and still remain physical theories; indeed, they are better than any previous theories in that—through the use of a smaller number of postulates—they allow for the interpretation of a great many phenomena, some of which were first foreseen theoretically before being discovered experimentally; yet, they still are *purely physical theories* and, according to the Galilean experimental criterion, their collapse could be determined by even a single experience clearly showing some effective contrast with experimental reality." [3]

3. THE QUANTA-PHYSICS AND THE POLEMIC ON DETERMINISM

In 1900 MAX PLANCK (1858-1947) enunciated the principle of the new *quanta*-physics or of the *discontinuity* of the phenomena of emission and absorption. Through his studies on the radiations affecting a dark body, he arrived at the "conviction that energy is emitted and absorbed in a discontinuous manner; thus, atoms of energy occur in the same way as atoms of matter occur. These atoms of energy are the *quanta* and they are proportional to frequency and multiples of a certain elementary constant magnitude called h, Planck's constant, that is." [4] After development by today's most important physicists, the great German physicist's intuition brought about the new physics called quanta-physics. Bohr places the discontinuity within the atom itself; Einstein introduces the quantum of light or photon; Rutherford finds out that the atom has an electrical structure and that the electrical charges that are negative are distanced among themselves. If the void existing between charges within the same atom is nullified, matter is reduced to the smallest dimensions. The unique, indivisible, solid, and continuous atom of classic physics is found to be made up of parts separated by an emptiness, to be *porous*. On the other hand, the principle of continuity (Huygens' ondulatory theory confirmed by Hertz and by Foucault) was still held valid for the explanation of irradiation-phenomena. "The synthesis of the two conceptions—the corpuscular and the ondulatory—was brought about through the ondulatory mechanics of De Broglie and the quantum-mechanics of Heisenberg, while the equivalence of the two was later demonstrated by Schrödinger. De Broglie's theory rests on the affirmation of an indissoluble union between the ondulatory aspect and the corpuscular aspect in every energetic phenomenon, in that the corpuscle would be a singularity within an ondulatory phenomenon. Heisenberg, instead, deprives the wave of any real meaning and refuses to single out the corpuscle

---

[3] P. Straneo, "La relatività della fisica," *Humanitas*, VI (1951), 557.
[4] F. Amerio, *Epistemologia* (Brescia, Morcelliana, 1948), p. 315. As regards this chapter, I have also considered the volume of F. Albergamo, *La critica della scienza nel '900* (Florence, 1951).

and, upon rejecting the possibility of remaining within the conceptions of classical mechanics, he founds, leaving out corpuscles, waves, and so forth, a new micromechanics to be developed along mathematical constructions (Hermite, Dirac, Fermi)." [5]

Although remaining a hypothesis, quanta-physics has revolutionized the classical atomism. With respect to philosophy it seems to us that these are the two most significant consequences: (1) material elements (corpuscles) are no longer conceived as definite, physical individuals but as an ondulatory phenomenon, as a something no longer being matter but a symbolical entity; (2) the so-called principle of indetermination which we are about to consider.

Classical physics is deterministic: phenomena are governed by a constant connection, which is always reproduced independently of space and time. In other words, as Heisenberg[6] writes, classical physics had rested on a fundamental premise that seemed to be obvious and indisputable—that is, the study of the behavior of things in space and their modifications in time with the tacit admission that there exists an objective course of events in the same space and time independently of every observation, and with the tacit admission that space and time are schemes independent of each other, in which everything happening must be ordained and by which an objective reality shared by all men is therefore represented. Classical physics rested, then, on two presuppositions of a rational order, seemingly confirmed through experimentation: the objectivity of the physical order—of facts and laws—and the most rigid causal determinism. Hence we had that "scientific image" of the world, which, from Galileo to Newton and as far as the nineteenth century, seemed to be the ultimate result of science. The new physics came with Einstein's theory of special and general relativity; with Planck's discovery of the "quantum of action" and *quanta*-theory; with the other discoveries concerning the structure of the atom; with the new experiments on light (which is an ondulatory phenomenon showing, at times, corpuscular properties), and with the dualism between ondulatory and corpuscular conceptions discovered by De Broglie even in the behavior of matter. With these discoveries and theories, the new physics has compelled classical physics to revise its concept of time and of the geometrical properties of space, as well as its rigid determinism, and to modify its realistic certitude, wherein events are developed in space and time objectively and independently of every experience.

Thus, the deterministic interpretation of nature has been questioned by the new physics: the criterion of rigorous necessity is superseded by

[5] F. Amerio, *ibid.*, p. 316.
[6] W. Heisenberg, *Physics and Philosophy; the revolution in modern science* (New York, 1958).

the calculation of probabilities. Scientific precision is confronted with insurmountable limits; the world of the infinitely small (microphysics) is anarchical and it does not seem to obey a criterion of necessity. The quanta-physics has pointed out that mutation always is discontinuous and that the passage from one state to another, within the same system, occurs by leaps, not according to a constant law. The only thing left is a statistical criterion, or one of probability—laws express the immense number of cases in which phenomena have occurred but not the necessity of their occurrence in any other point of space and time. It is not necessity but chance that is predominant within the microscopic domain. It is well-known that for the British physicist Ernest Rutherford, a radioactive atom can expel an electron or a nucleus and become another electron; it is *able* to expel, that is, a phenomenon occurs when it occurs, not through necessity. Rutherford's hypothesis on the constitution of the atom and of radioactive bodies has been extended to the atom of any body by the Danish physicist Bohr.

The principle of the new physics formulated by Heisenberg is known under the name of *principle of indetermination;* it is not possible to determine both the position and the velocity of a corpuscle, so that it remains indeterminate in so far as the observer is concerned. It is also impossible to foresee necessarily its successive development—one cannot go beyond the limit of probability. Thus, it seems that the principle of determinism is problematical at least within the field of microphysics. It is not a question, however, of an upsetting of physics: "Modern physics has by no means changed the great classical disciplines of physics, such as mechanics, optics, and the heat-theory. However, with the knowledge we had of a limited part of the world, we prematurely delineated a picture extending to the still unexplored parts of it—such a picture has undergone a radical change." [7] That which is the object of our immediate, sensorial experience remains the domain of classical physics, while that which falls beyond our daily experience is investigated by the new physical theories which in this field may have a structure differing from that of classical physics.

However, things are not so settled as it might appear. Determinism is still advocated by those who consider the indeterminateness of phenomena only as a temporary fact caused by a lack of instruments suitable for investigating the microphysical world. In short, this would not be a question of *indeterminateness* but one of *indeterminableness,* a thesis sustained by both Bachelard and Metallmann. Moreover, there are those who, like Winter and Morand, try to reconcile the two hypotheses. Still others deny objective value to both determinism and indeterminism, like Enriques and Eddington for whom determinism is, in fact, a hy-

[7] W. Heisenberg, *ibid.*

pothesis that experience cannot confirm and indeterminism, likewise, is a purely negative hypothesis. Determinism and indeterminism are two metaphysical hypotheses and neither can be verified by science.

Although De Broglie—the founder of ondulatory mechanics—accepts the indeterminism theory, he remarks that everything is still *sub judice* and that it is "perfectly permissible to think that physics may go back sooner or later to the path of determinism. Nor is the judgment of Einstein, Planck, Rutherford, and others less prudent. Be that as it may, it is certain (that is, recognized by the very theorists of the new physics) that determinism has nothing to do with the principle of causality; the confusion is so banal that it is unworthy of confutation. The determinism in question, as De Broglie further remarks, regards the prevision of phenomena in so far as the physicist is concerned; every inference regarding the principle of causality is purely arbitrary, as arbitrary as the subjectivistic consequences drawn by the British astronomer A. S. EDDINGTON (1882-1944); the "world of physics," according to the latter, "is a world contemplated by the spirit, measured by instruments that are part of the same spirit and are subject to its laws." The new science (and this will be true as long as the research is kept within the limits of science itself) does not authorize any well-founded conclusion for the solution of the problems (pertinent to philosophy) of knowledge and of its validity, of the meaning and essence of reality, of freedom, of God, and so forth. An ignoring of distinctions and a failure to respect limits have not only caused much confusion but have also barbarized philosophy and indirectly discredited science. Today's metaphysical inferences drawn from the new physics are nothing but extrapolations, just like the conclusions drawn from scientific materialism and from scientific determinism by scientists and philosophers during the age of positivism. It is not a question of inviting philosophy to posit again the problem of the category of natural necessity and, still worse, to justify the principle of causality (which, we repeat, is another thing), or even to re-examine the question of freedom after the new physics of relativism and indeterminism; it is a question of taking into account scientific hypotheses in so far as this may be of use to philosophical research and always from the speculative point of view, without building up any metaphysics based on science's results, which moreover are hypothetical. The polemic is not between science and philosophy; it is between the picture of the universe held by classical (deterministic, and so forth) science and what seems to be the one delineated by the new science today, also between the scientific philosophies imprudently founded on the said picture in the last century and the philosophies being not less imprudently elaborated on another scientific description today. Therefore, philosophy does not have to justify its principles before the new science; its principles and its problems are to be justified philosophically, though not ignoring the progress in scientific research. In any event, philosophy has the authority to weigh the cognitive value of science and its scope.

Now that we have determined these points and have emphasized (with a polemical liveliness that is appropriate and perhaps necessary today) the arbitrary extrapolations and facile illations, we are going to point out the importance that, in our opinion, the new science has for philosophy. We note, first of all, that confining the validity of scientific knowledge to more modest proportions has been advantageous to philosophy. The myth of the absoluteness of science and of the indisputability of its results weighed heavy on the development of philosophical thought from Descartes to positivism: philosophy felt the impact of science to the point of conforming its metaphysical views to the interpretation of the world given by classical science; for this reason philosophy respected the Newtonian determinism or the scientific materialism of the last century. As was noted [8] apropos of the religious problem: "In contrast with the difficulties and doubts of the past, the believer is able today to understand better the action of his God on creation, and he need not take seriously any longer certain old objections, that formerly had represented grave obstacles, because the new physics has once and for all destroyed certain overhasty objections against faith." Only half a century ago it was a scientific heresy to speak of free will, as opposed to determinism; and it was also a philosophical heresy in so far as positivists were concerned; speaking of Providence was a sacrilegious act against the inviolability of natural determinism; questioning the theory of evolution and expressing a timid doubt concerning man's common ancestry with the ape meant being pitiable victims of religious superstition. Being more cautious and more critical, modern science redressed not its previous conquests but the superstition of science and the idolatry of dogmatic rationalism. In fact, supposing that the results of science are infallible, for the scientist it becomes easy to reject and very difficult to accept those metaphysical affirmations which conflict with the said results; likewise, it is possible that the philosopher will make these his own and, then, it will be difficult for him to construct a philosophy that is not confirmed by these results or one that is not their consequence. Once science, by itself, renounces the monopoly on truth and the privilege of the absoluteness of its conclusions, the obstacle has been removed, and even the reciprocal spheres of activity can be better defined. Yet, precisely on account of this we must not repeat the mistake of the past; that is, we must not be "relativists" and "subjectivists" in philosophy solely because science is "relativistic" or "subjectivistic" (or, rather, because it is interpreted in this exaggerated way), as in the recent past they were "determinists" and

[8] B. Bavink, *Science and God* (New York, 1934).

"objectivists"; we must not reduce reality to a symbol, only because some theorists of science are leaning in this direction and so on and so forth. Otherwise, we continue to give science an absolute value, contrary to one of the results of the new science which has destroyed this myth. Just as in the recent past nothing authorized us—except for an almost fanatic dogmatism—to consider determinism and materialism as established truths with a metaphysical scope, so today nothing authorizes us to consider the new science as the ultimate and absolutely valid world to which philosophy must conform. In any event, we think it necessary to repeat that the scientific interpretations of reality (natural and human reality) cannot be assumed as a solution of the problem of reality itself (that is, natural and human reality) in a philosophical sense, and as a solution of all the speculative problems included therewith; otherwise, we fail to see how the criticism of one scientific position made by another—which is also a deepening of the former—can, even indirectly, be of any use to philosophical research, at least in the sense of not having science as an obstacle. The critical problem of the philosophy-science relationship makes no sense unless the two levels of inquiry are kept distinct from each other. On the positive side, science (although its results cannot be held as arguments demonstrating a metaphysical affirmation) can coincide with philosophical theses; as it is also possible that the scientific interpretation of reality (valid only with respect to that reality which, experimentally, is the object of science itself) may agree with the philosophical intelligibility of reality itself, as understood in a metaphysical sense.

This critical caution of ours is shared by the founders of quanta-physics. Planck, as is known, rejects (*Wege zur Physikalischen Erkenntnis*, Leipzig, 1933) the pragmatist thesis as well as the idealistic one: "It is not we who create the external world just because it suits us, but it is the external world that imposes itself on us with an elementary violence"; it is the world that posits as a "foundation" and a "preliminary condition for any science," the "metaphysical hypothesis" of its existence "completely independent of us," of "our sensations." Hence a decisive realism which is an act of faith for the scientist who is not building a metaphysics; it is the task of philosophy, not of science, to justify rationally its own existence. Science has some definite tasks and thus some limits, both with respect to the object and task of philosophy, as well as with respect to religion: having arrived at a point "beyond which it is not possible to see," man is left only with the alternative of "looking for another guide . . . , religious faith." Planck is here arguing as a philosopher, for he is positing the philosophical problem of science within the framework of speculative problems.

In describing the relations between classical science and the new one, and in his evaluation of the latter, Heisenberg (*Philosophical Problems of Nuclear Science,* trans. F. C. Hayes, New York, 1952) is no less cautious. As a starting point classical science had confidence in the possibility of performing a rational analysis of every reality; today, on the other hand, scientific systems "must be always self-contained in order to be right," and thus "the extending of the scientific inquiry to new fields of experience does not take place by simply applying the old principles to the new objects." This does not mean that the change taking place in the exact sciences has revealed new limits for the application of rational thought; it has only assigned a narrower field to some forms of thought. "The edifice of exact science cannot then become a coherent unity in the naive sense previously hoped for, so that one is able to reach any part of the same edifice only by moving from a given point and simply following the prescribed itinerary. This edifice, instead, consists of single parts, each of which makes up a self-contained unity, regardless of the many relations each part has with the others and even if the single part contains in itself other parts and, in turn, is contained by others." It seems to us that in this way even the boundaries of science compared to philosophy (and of philosophy in relation to science) are better defined. This fact becomes more evident through the remarks made by Heisenberg apropos of the history of physical doctrines: the old science claimed to be the "explanation" of nature; more modestly the modern one claims to be its "description." Furthermore, the "modern description is distinguished from the old one on three important accounts: its propositions are quantitative not qualitative; different phenomena are brought back to the same origin; and no 'whys' are asked." Consequently, "the pretensions of our science to a knowledge of nature, according to the original meaning of the word, have become increasingly smaller." Naturally, we add, precisely because defined in the sense given by Heisenberg, science has no right (the opposite of what science did in the eighteenth and nineteenth centuries) to extend its very agnosticism, about the intelligibility of nature, also to philosophy; and it has no right to deny the possibility of a conclusive research in metaphysics just because its descriptive scope is limited and its relativism is fundamental. Modern physics does not invalidate the laws of classical physics; it only limits their applicability. This necessity for "surpassing the boundaries of classical concepts has arisen principally from the technical amplification of our field of experience. Classical concepts were no longer fit for the situation nature confronts us with." Modern physics discovers only new possibilities of thought, which can be revised without falling into skepticism. On the contrary, this "is only another expression of the conviction that the amplification of our field of experience will bring to light ever new harmonies."

Heisenberg, on the other hand, remarks that we are still far from having

realized the unity of science in spite of the progress already attained. ·
The unity of method that is making some headway is not yet sufficient
to carry out the unity of the scientific image of the world. We have
abandoned the Utopia, adds the author, of explaining all facts according
to the model of Newton's mechanics; likewise, we are able to understand
that side by side with vital phenomena, there is the sphere of consciousness and that of psychic processes. "More than science ever was in the
past, we are now aware of the fact that there is no one sure starting-point
for all the ways leading to the many fields of knowledge, since every
branch of it is somehow hanging over a bottomless abyss; we also know
that we must speak about reality in terms that only gradually gain a more
precise meaning through their daily use, as we are also aware that, in
spite of their logical and mathematical exactness, even the most precise
conceptual systems represent only groping attempts to guide us into
limited fields of reality."

The above words may be said to express the position of the new science, which has abandoned the dogmatic certainty of classical science
in favor of a more critical position; and precisely on account of these
self-imposed limitations, modern science succeeded in questioning the
dogmas on which classical science had built its image of the world—
the dogmas of determinism, mechanism, and materialism which the nineteenth century held as an ultimate and indisputable result. Except for the
beginning, science was then so imprudent as to draw some bold and
arbitrary conclusions regarding morality, religion, and the life of the
spirit in general. In view of the changes undergone by science we must,
at present, exert all our caution in order not to draw hasty conclusions of
a metaphysical and religious character from today's scientific findings;
and we do this while acknowledging that with respect to philosophy and
the problems of the spirit, the results of the new science—if understood
properly—are less prejudicial than those which took place during the
eighteenth and nineteenth centuries. We must not, therefore, dramatize:
the new theories concerning the pluridimensional spaces and the non-
Euclidean geometries, as well as the relativity and indeterminism, modify
indeed the notions of space, time, matter, and so on, as regards Cartesian-
Newtonian science, but they in no way modify the notions of classical
metaphysics concerning the same concepts; nor is the new science (whose
value is merely mathematical or physical) in contradiction with the old
science which, though diverse, continues to have its validity.

4. Mathematics and the Mathematical Character of Modern Science

As we know, for Galileo, the language of the great book of nature is
"mathematical"; today Eddington writes that "when we determine the

properties of a body in the form of physical qualities, we produce this knowledge as an answer coming from the reading of the numerous quadrants, and nothing more." The tendency to make physics a mathematical science is so stressed that physics almost disappears within mathematics: physics is interested in measurements (quantities) or, rather, in numbers. Its character is not explanatory: physics does not care to know, for example, what inertia is but only to measure it exactly. "Measuring" is the methodological principle which, according to Heisenberg, conditions physical research. This tendency involves the risk of causing the intuitive content in the initial experiment to disappear within the mathematical symbols through which the physical world is made "intelligible." As Heisenberg again writes, "The atom of modern physics can for the present be symbolized only through a partial differential equation in a limited pluridimensional space." On the other hand, even at this point one must be cautious about making unjustified illations, identifying the whole reality with the one that is measurable, and the latter with the measure and number as symbols. Opposed to this "mathematical" tendency prevailing in the field of microphysics, there is an "intuitive" tendency: a physical explanation of physical phenomena and a distinction between mathematics and physics. The intuitionist current reacts against this overemphasized mathematical character which, in giving up the immediate understanding of the qualities in favor of "a kind of analytical comprehension," produces a scientific image of the world far apart from that offered by concrete life, in such a way that one cannot say which one is true and which one is false. To the objection that intuitionism is always tempted by the pretense to offer a metaphysical explanation of the world, its advocates reply that such a temptation does not spare even its adversaries, who tend to conceive reality as a mathematical structure, that is, they make a metaphysics out of mathematics.

Between "formalistic" and "intuitionist" tendencies, the polemic is extended also to the problem of the cognitive validity of the mathematical disciplines, in which no character of absoluteness has been recognized by mathematicians since the appearance of non-Euclidean geometries. The logical-formalistic currents (initially of a Platonic tendency) try "to construct the mathematical world as coherence and formal rigorism"; mathematical systems are hypothetical-deductive systems constructed through a logical deduction from a certain number of fundamental concepts whose relations "are regulated by a certain number of propositions called axioms and postulates." The difficulty of defining the primary concepts has increased the formalistic tendency, thus making mathematics a purely logical science, or a system of pure relations, capable of assuming different meanings according to the different interpretations of the elementary notions. This tendency, identified with that of *logistic* or *mathematical logic*[9] (associated with Whitehead and Russell—for whom the numerical signs have a meaning with respect to the sensible world—and also with Hilbert, for whom the numbers are symbols or pure and indefinite signs devoid of any meaning) already contains within itself the developments actually given to it by the Vienna School and other currents: every mathematical system (and they are many) arbitrarily develops the consequences from some hypotheses, according to rules that are also arbitrary, and whose coherence constitutes the so-called mathematical truth. This is a pure and simple conventionalism.

Lively reactions against this formalism and its conventional conclusions are not lacking; an example is the "neointuitionist" school of E. J. Brouwer, who admits an original intuition of primary notions; likewise, Gonseth's empiricist realism is not to be overlooked. Apropos of the question of mathematical method, the same divergence of opinions exists between advocates of the deductive (analytical, and tautological) method and those sustaining the empirical or creative method. As has been remarked, "neither the conventional thesis, which at present enjoys so much credit, nor the idealistic thesis responds to all the data and all the exigencies of the problem. Their share of truth can and must be recognized in so far as the two theses are both possible on the basis of the acknowledged essence of mathematics, which is fundamentally theoretical and realistic: the conventional part and the part played by the subject, or that related to creativeness and 'atheoreticity' do not exhaust the explanation of the mathematical world, neither when the latter is considered in its process nor when it is considered in its content." [10]

5. BIOLOGY AND PSYCHOLOGY

As can be deduced from our exposition (which indeed is an imperfect one since we lack a specific competence), the prevailing character of the new science is shown both by its abandoning the claim to an absoluteness in its conclusions and by its renouncing the explanation of reality. The new epistemological currents insist on the hypothetical and probabilist character of science, whose task is confined to the formulation of quantitative relations, of laws and previsions. Leaving aside the exaggerations on the part of symbolism which makes the concrete vain, and on the part

[9] I. M. Bochenski, *Contemporary European Philosophy* (Berkeley, 1956). Semeiotics (W. Morris), a theory of symbols, is closely connected with mathematical logic, and it is divided into *logical syntax* or theory on the relations among symbols; *logical semantics* or theory on the relations between the symbol and what it signifies; and *logical pragmatics* or theory on the relations among symbols, their meaning, and men utilizing them. The first two were elaborated particularly by A. Tarski and R. Carnap. (Cf. Bochenski, *op. cit.*)
[10] F. Amerio, *op. cit.*, p. 344.

of conventionalism which reduces scientific propositions to a *flatus vocis*, we recognize that the new science has the merit of getting away from the presumption shown by nineteenth-century science, which fancied itself to be able to explain the whole physical and human universe in its essence, through determinism and mechanism. Indeed, it is necessary to avoid making scientific relativism so absolute as to extend it to all forms of human knowledge unless we wish to fall back on the presumption of a new scientificalism which once again identifies all valid knowledge with scientific knowledge. The difference between this scientificalism and the last century's lies only in the fact that the latter believed in the absoluteness of scientific knowledge while the new one believes in its relativity; yet, as regards the arbitrary and dogmatic extension of science to all the fields of reality and of knowledge, there is no difference between saying that all human knowledge is identified with the relativism of science rather than with the absoluteness of science. The problem is not that of substituting one form of scientificalism for another, but that of not falling into the error of scientificalism as such. In this respect it is unimportant to object that nineteenth-century science was dogmatic whereas today's is critical. This may be so, yet present-day science which calls itself "critical," and not naive, is still a dogmatic and ingenuous scientificalism if it claims to be the whole of knowledge so as to extend its methods to the problems of the spirit. In such a case it may be critical as a science, but it is certainly dogmatic in its extrapolations and unwarranted illations. It is this scientificalism that we oppose, not science.

The same remarks are also valid as regards biology and the still live polemic between "mechanism" and "vitalism" (which correspond to the two theses of "materialism" and "spiritualism" in the last century). Laid down in these terms, obviously the discussion has a metaphysical scope surpassing the potentialities of biological research. "Explaining life" is a problem to be laid down and solved only philosophically, while the contributions made in one way or another by biology are secondary. It seems to us that the finalistic principle cannot be abandoned, as it is the only one making the biological world intelligible. However, even at this point one must not go beyond the limits of science by conceiving finalism in an animistic and anthropomorphic way, which would amount to making a naive metaphysics; on the other hand, the said principle cannot be reduced to a purely methodological canon or even to a mechanical or physico-chemical determinism. There are those who would like to apply to biology the so-called physicalist method of neopositivism.

Concerning psychology some hold that its progress would be more conspicuous if the "physicalist" method had been decidedly applied. We have already amply treated psychoanalysis and have mentioned Jung and the so-called psychology of form; our discussion, then, will be very brief, for another reason also: so-called experimental psychology is now very far from psychology understood as a philosophical discipline. We do not deny the contributions afforded by the psychology called scientific; we only say that the latter has not yet defined itself as a science: as for its new object and its new method one does not know what they really are. Those who sustain that the psyche is its object and introspection, its method, may be, perhaps, less "scientific" but theirs is the merit of recognizing that psychology has an object and a method of its own. On the other hand, the advocates of a "soul-less psychology," whose object is only "behaviorism" and whose method is the "reaction" or response, may be more scientific, but their psychology is not human; it pertains to man inasmuch as he is an "animal" and not inasmuch as he is a "spirit," that is, a spiritual animal. If one prescinds from the soul (even without denying it or reducing it to physiological phenomena), then it is not man that is being studied but an abstraction, in that there is really no human act that is not the act of the whole man as body and soul. What are the human acts in which the spirit is absent? The inferior ones? If so, this is a psychology of the "sub-man" not of man. If the "psychic" is distinguished from the "spiritual," as a "psychicalism" belonging to man and other animals alike, then the study is confined to the animal not to man, who is not only an animal, and, in this case, one falls back on an abstraction. Yet, perhaps, one prescinds from the soul only in appearance; and in reality, the expression "psychology without a soul" literally signifies that man has no spiritual nature but only an animal one, also corporeal but endowed with a particular characteristic (the so-called consciousness) marking him off from other living beings. In such a case, one is a materialist, that is, one has proceeded from an arbitrarily metaphysical presupposition. Materialism, in fact, is the behaviorism which neopositivists have also accepted. What is there to authorize this preconceived materialism scientifically and philosophically? And why should one complain that the psychology "with a soul" makes up a metaphysics when an inferior type of metaphysics is produced by the so-called psychology without a soul? What sense is there in the "reaction" or response of a "behaviorism" which does not belong to man but only to a biped called man? Moreover, such a psychology no longer is distinguished from physiology, biology, and physics. The "psychology with a soul" is unable to define its limits with respect to philosophy; the one "without a soul" is a "physics" neither more nor less. Scientificalism is thus extended to another field. Gemelli correctly writes that modern psychology "is seeking a way to free itself from all its bonds with philosophy." This is not enough; it must not be identified with physiology and physics— otherwise it has only succeeded in becoming a psychology that is merely animal and not human at all.

6. A. Pastore's "Logic of Strength"

ANNIBALE PASTORE (1868-1956) holds a notable place among the students of scientific logic; he was a professor of theoretical philosophy at the University of Turin until 1939. Already in his paper at the Fourth International Congress of Mathematicians (1908) there is a first sketch of his "logic of strength" which he later developed in the two volumes, *Il problema della causalità* (Turin, 1921); the said sketch had been preceded and was followed by a series of notes and articles later gathered in the work *La logica del potenziamento* (Naples, 1936). Pastore does not wish "to have anything to do with an exclusively analytical or an exclusively dialectical logic detached from the fervid work of the sciences operating through calculus and experiment." The new logic is that of power and of relations, an expression of the relativity in the *entia* in that every logical *ens* varies according to the concrete *entia* with which it is in relationship. The starting point in Pastore's theory is the analysis of the principle of identity. In classical logic "identity appears as a proposition without a logical justification." In it "the logical principle is lost in the unchecked darkness of the extralogical, and the abstract basis of the sciences becomes really incomprehensible when such a basis is transferred to logic. In order to eliminate the inexplicable (a thin veil hardly concealing a real contradiction) we must give the principle of identity a logical meaning, or else we must exclude identity from logic." Pastore remarks that it is necessary to remove "the tautological principle from any logical calculus whatever that refuses to sacrifice the principle of identity $(a = a)$. In fact, by positing $a\ a = a$, one affirms, as relatively identical, two logical quantities between which there is an undeniable diversity of content or of extension."

In order to safeguard the pureness of logical calculus one has to admit that "the only truly and properly logical object is the concept; the latter, in fact, does not have to exist in order to be since it only needs to be thought in the mind. Hence it follows that in positing the $a\ a$ the logical concepts involved herewith are unquestionably two in spite of the fact that the concept in the first a is identical with the concept in the other a; thus, the concept of their simultaneous affirmation is irreducible to the simple concept pertinent to a, unless we wish to lose the two concepts of unity and of multiplicity that are fundamental in any calculus. . . . Every concept is a mental *ens* and every mental *ens* is conceptual as often as it is conceived, independently of the fact that there may or may not be any corresponding object really existing outside of the mind."

The variation in the logical *entia* (they vary in function of one another) can only come from the relationship that an *ens* has with the other

472

entia. The *entia*, then, are strengthened reciprocally so that none of them remains inert. This fact makes it necessary to have a new logical means of research and of testing. Three are its fundamental principles: "(1) the solution of the *ens* in its 'wherefrom' relation; (2) the relative variation in the *ens,* that is, the variation taking place in the *ens* itself by virtue of the sole variation taking place in the *entia* with which the former is a 'wherefrom' relation; (3) the reciprocal strengthening of the *entia,* which require that every logical *ens* be individuated for its distinctive identity as well as strengthened for its relation—a new logical means of research and of testing is thus constituted, and this is not only irreducible to the models of classical logic but is also enriched with new results either in the sciences, in gnosiology, or in metaphysics. The relativist thesis in a 'logicity' understood as a universal, productive activity is founded on these principles, which are able to bring about a new concept of relation." In this way, the logic of strength replaces the uniformity of the *ens* with the variation arising from the relation with other *entia* and, the principle of identity being safe, it introduces the concept of "strength" not as a product but as a power of production. We have here a radical relativism "which upon evicting the irrelative knows that nothing is left behind."

7. E. MEYERSON'S THEORY OF SCIENCE

EMIL MEYERSON (1859-1933), a naturalized French citizen of Polish descent, had only one philosophical end in view: to define the nature of science. This end he pursued in all his writings—which are powerful more for their amazing abundance of erudition than for originality of thought—from his *Identity and Reality,* trans. K. Loewenberg (New York, 1962) to *Du Cheminement de la pensée* (Paris, 1931). He holds a place of distinction among contemporary epistemologists.

In opposition to the pragmatist theories giving science only an economic value, Meyerson vindicates for it its theoretical essence; in opposition to the empiricist currents reducing science to a description, he assigns it an explanatory character. Indeed, for Meyerson science not only aims at knowing the laws of nature but also the causes of phenomena; that is, science is directed toward a deep understanding of reality as well as a progressive rationalization of phenomena. The scientist believes that in nature there is an order, and he endeavors to discover it through science; the latter is a form of intelligibility of the real.

What are the methods used by science for the attainment of this goal? The inductive method does not go beyond the reduction of phenomena to natural laws, but science is not simple "legalism." The deductive method, instead, is explicative and not descriptive, and it endeavors to

473

explain phenomena by reducing them to an underlying permanency. Now, for Meyerson, the main task of science is the reduction of the diverse to the identical. The *principle of identity* is the supreme and unique principle of intelligibility; indeed, it is the very law of the thinking process and the ideal of thought as such. Reducing multiplicity to unity and the diverse to the identical (in quoting Plato, Meyerson writes that "reason's only tendency is to adapt with force the nature of the Other—a rebellious nature—to the nature of the Identical") is the work of common, scientific, and philosophical reason, of reason *sic et sempliciter*. However, the identity spoken of by Meyerson is dynamic and synthetical and not static and analytical—identity as a continuous "process of identification." Even the principles of sufficient reason, of inertia, and of conservation of energy and matter are for him ultimately reduced to the principle of identity, in that they too try to lead back the apparent change and variety in phenomena to identity and to deep permanency.

The object of science is not represented by our sensations, that is, by the immediate data of consciousness: science always tries to resolve qualities into quantities, because only through renouncing the qualities and concreteness of the phenomenon can it work out the reduction of the heterogeneous to the homogeneous, of the diverse to the identical. To rationalize reality means to sacrifice its qualitative variety for a permanent uniformity. Thus science proceeds from laws to hypotheses, theories, and principles—the unification, through mathematics, of all that is knowable is science's supreme ideal.

Is science able to reduce the infinite, qualitative variety of phenomena to a permanent identity, to a uniform homogeneity? For Meyerson it is not; science is always an actual and infinite identification process never really achieved absolutely. At a certain point the process of identification stops; it finds something unexplainable and irreducible to the identical, a something resisting rationalization and as such irrational. "Reason on the march" is always moving: it always finds *irrational* oppositions that must be overcome so that reason itself may not be denied. This is not a serious evil after all; if at a certain point the order of nature were identical with the order of thought, nature might cease to exist. The resistance offered to thought by nature is almost dictated by the latter's instinct for self-preservation: it is like a defeat imposed on reason by a multiplicity that refuses to disappear within uniformity, a revenge taken by the concrete against the presumptions of reason. On the other hand, the movement of reason would cease without this resistance; the irrational is an obstacle for reason but also its life; reason finds a rest only in identity, but if everything could be reduced to the identical this permanent rest would be its death. Ultimately, it is the irreducible irrationality that makes the movement of reason possible and with it science and philosophy. Thus there persists in reality an obscure and irreducible depth of a still unknown structure, and this always arouses science to engage itself in a further process of unification. A depth that is unknown (not unknowable) so that it differs from the "unknowable" of Spencer and of the positivists: it is something rather closer to Ardigò's "indistinct." Science does not stop before the "wall" opposed to it by reality; it knows that the wall will be demolished one day, as it also knows that beyond that one another wall will be met. There are infinite trenches behind which the concrete defends itself in order to avoid a total assimilation in the identity.

However, this is not the only irrational aspect of reality. Science presupposes the existence of objects distinct from consciousness and producing our sensations—for Meyerson this is unexplainable. Also unexplainable is the transitive action exercised on each other by bodies, either through contact or by action at a distance. To these irrationalities one must add the other concerning irreversibility: what in the real is modified is irreversible. "Four and three undoubtedly make seven; but if the former number represents a beam four meters long and the second a beam of three, the architect cannot use them when he needs a beam seven meters long. In every real mutation there is always something that is irreversible, and this makes the mutation be irreducible to reason's identification process."

Between thought and reality there is, then, no collaboration but clash and struggle: thought affirms the principle of uniformity and permanency, while reality confronts it with that of an irreducible diversity, and of an irreversible moment; thought aims at identity while reality confronts it with multiplicity and mutation.

What then? The only thing left, then, is to take notice of this continuous disproval inflicted on thought by reality. It is true that Meyerson states that the disproval is wholly detrimental to reality, which does not impair the truth of reason but, rather, reveals its irrational depth through its opposition to the identification-process; yet, it is also true that reason is powerless in the presence of the inexplicable in reality—reason can only acknowledge its failure. After all, Meyerson is not assigning reason the task of explaining the world, but that of abolishing it at the very moment that reason should by any chance succeed in explaining it. For its part, a world not allowing itself to be entirely explained winds up abolishing science. Science and reality are antinomial terms: science tends to deny reality in the uniformity of the identical; reality tends to deny science by preventing reason from understanding its obscure and irrational depth. Moreover, since, for Meyerson, no one phenomenon in its variability is completely reducible to another, all phenomena maintain a residuum of irrationality, which means that all reality is irrational. Thus the philosopher of identity winds up destroying the very validity of this principle. In fact, common reason, whether scientific or philosophical, can never carry out the identity; the irrational persists as a limitation within science itself, that is, within reason. The fact is that Meyerson's conception of identity is inadequate. After all, he conceives it dialectically, after the Hegelian manner; there is identity because there is multiplicity; the *no* of the irrational is the life of reason and of the principle by which reason itself is governed. Hence the following paradox arises: identity is the conclusion of every movement made by reason and, at the same time, it is the premise for any new rational effort in that the irrational is immanent in science itself and not only its limit. Explaining the world would be the same as destroying it (the ideal on the part of identity is the absence of a world: the conceived identity is the destruction of the perceived diversity); yet, not to explain it is the "failure of reason." At the bottom of Meyerson's philosophy there is an irreducible dualism between reason and reality; on the one hand, there is a science constructing reality in its own way, according to the process of identification; on the other, there is a reality that in its own way remains irrational before the rationality aimed at by science. Science and reality come to deny each other.

8. "Physicalism" and the New "Scientistic" Barbarity

We noticed how the revision of classical physics involves the Cartesian epistemology, which is founded on the intuition of simple and distinct natures. These are precisely the concepts being questioned by the new, scientific criticism: "Whereas Cartesian-inspired science used to construct the complex by moving from the simple in a very logical way, contemporary scientific thought endeavors, instead, to read the real complex under the simple appearance supplied by the phenomena counteracting one another." [11] The so-called simple is, as Bachelard adds, the result of a compilation; and it is a simple "example, a mutilated truth, and an image that is only sketched." The simple can be understood "after an intensive study of the complex." Naturally, the historical importance of the Cartesian method or of Euclidean geometry is not minimized, but it is clearly affirmed that the new science has surpassed the stage of Cartesian-Newtonian science. Scientific thought aims at a "realization of the rational"; it proposes to reduce the latter to experience in order to find verification therein; that is, it aims at overcoming the dualism of reason and experience, of rationalism and realism. "The scientific world is our verification.

[11] G. Bachelard, *Le nouvel ésprit scientifique* (Paris, 1934), p. 180.

476

Modern science is founded on the project, both beyond the subject and beyond the object." [12]

The epistemological question and the problems connected with it have been given a vigorous impulse not only by the so-called Vienna-Circle but also through the developments attained in Europe and in America by Viennese neopositivism.

There were in Vienna historical precedents favoring the development of the radically empiricist tendency professed by the "Circle." In fact, in Vienna the logical trend within Brentano's school had been followed by Alois Höfler, a professor at that city's university. Furthermore, under Mach's influence, Stöhr taught there a philosophy of language founded on the "algebra of grammar." Mach himself promulgated there his empiricist and antimetaphysical tendency. At the same university there was also the active influence of Avenarius, Poincaré, James, Russell and, through Neurath, that coming from the *History of the Inductive Sciences* (London, 1837) by Whewell, a nineteenth-century English thinker. Moreover, it is necessary to add the influence of Einstein and of other theorists on the theory of relativity, as well as the empiricist and antimetaphysical attitude of the physicist Frank and the mathematician Hans Hann. In 1929 the school left Schlick's seminar and appeared under the name of *Wiener Kreis* and with a program (*A scientific conception of the world*); in 1930 the periodical *Erkenntnis* began its publications (it can be considered as the continuation of the *Annalen der Philosophie*, edited by J. Petzoldt, a pupil of Avenarius) under the editorship of Reichenbach and Carnap. Until 1938 it was the official organ of the E. Mach Association of Vienna and of the Society of Experimental Philosophy of Berlin; in 1939 it was replaced by the *Journal of Unified Sciences*. After the Congress of Prague (1929) and that of Königsberg (1930), the Prague International Congress for the Unity of the Sciences (1934) laid the foundations for a permanent contact aimed at an international exchange of views; and the Paris International Congress of Scientific Philosophy (1935) saw the followers of the new school at the forefront. Other conventions followed in Denmark, France, England, and in the United States where the most important exponents of the school later took refuge from Nazi persecution. During the last twenty years the school has continued to exert some influence in Europe; however, it was in America that the school affirmed itself and spread, giving rise to several associations, periodicals, and minor schools. The influence of neopositivism is, on the other hand, secondary in the Latin countries. The Vienna-Circle, nonetheless, still remains the irradiation-center for scientific empiricism, which opposes systematic philosophy and any metaphysical tendency.

[12] G. Bachelard, *ibid.*, p. 11.

The Vienna-Circle theorists propose to arrive at a scientific knowledge, the only one really deserving this name, without a need for a "metaphysics," a "philosophy," a "theory of knowledge," a "phenomenology." It is a question of "presenting a scientific language that, while avoiding all pseudo-problems, makes it possible to express predictions and formulate the conditions for their control through the observation-data." In other words, this means extending empiricism to the entire domain of thought so as to get rid of any metaphysical appearance that may be hidden behind our words. Nominalism is considered an excellent reagent against the theologic-mathematical tendency. Language-criticism has an important role in achieving this goal. The new scientificalism presents four main traits: "an opposition to metaphysics, an empiricist general attitude, a bent for using logic methodically, and a 'mathematicizing' of all the sciences." [13] Hence a neopositivism presented as a *logical empiricism*. Science is understood as a scientific "comprehension" (and not as an "intuition") of the world and therefore as a science without metaphysics. Science is only "a collection of propositions which are printed in a book and which have a meaning, and are directly allusive to experience. The experience-data come to science duly 'recorded,' that is, under the form of propositions. Science has the task of arranging these 'records' in a coherent system by submitting them to all the transformations of formal logic, thus attaining new propositions, which in turn become subject to an experimental test." [14] Experience and language complete each other: experience must be transcribed in the form of propositions which, in turn, are truly such in that they are expressible.

Let us try to determine the position of neopositivism with respect to philosophy. It seems to us that such a position is clear and dogmatically negative even if lately there has been some attenuation. In the 1929 program, already mentioned, it stated that "the Vienna-Circle is composed of men having a scientific orientation in common"—an orientation that F. Frank confirmed with a polemic tone in 1934 in the *Erkenntnis*: the Circle is "the storm troop of the anti-metaphysical current, and thus the supporter of a scientific thought." Thus we are in the presence of thinkers deeply engaged in the solution of the problem of scientific knowledge, its value, and its meaning. If they had kept within these bounds, we would not have spoken of a new philosophical barbarity, though we would have maintained the right to discuss their epistemological doctrine. Instead, at the very outset neopositivism presents itself as a kind of crusade against philosophy and metaphysics and, from this point of view, as a noisy and dogmatic form of scientificalism. It starts with a presumption: the carrying out of a systematization and unification of all valid knowledge. The

---

[13] O. Neurath, *Le developpement du Cercle de Vienne* (Paris, Herman, 1935), p. 41.
[14] P. Filiasi Carcano, *Antimetafisica e sperimentalismo* (Rome, 1941), p. 41.

science taken as a model is physics, whose methodological principles have been adopted; and out of these principles, the one (fundamental for the physical order, according to Einstein and Heisenberg) which sustains that only the measurable "makes sense" whereas the nonmeasurable "makes no sense." This methodological principle is extrapolated and arbitrarily applied *not only* to the physical but also to any form of knowledge, so that whatever is not measurable makes no sense; a proposition that is not susceptible of "verification" is devoid of meaning. Hence *"physicalism"* follows: that which is and makes sense is what is physically verifiable; since all metaphysical propositions (indeed the whole world of the spirit) are not "verifiable" they are meaningless, because the spirit and its acts are not measurable quantities. Let us notice that the neopositivists do not confine themselves to saying that scientific (physical) knowledge has to free itself from the metaphysical residua and that, from the scientific-physical point of view, metaphysical affirmations cannot be evaluated in their scope and meaning. We agree with them up to this point; indeed, their having purified science of the spurious, metaphysical residua due to a metaphysical physics is undoubtedly a genuine contribution, as is a contribution to purify metaphysics of the cosmologism that is due to a physical metaphysics, and to rescue it, we say, as a "meta-anthropeia." However, the fact is that they hold metaphysical affirmations to be meaningless from the scientific point of view (a meaningless claim on their part, because physics has no right to pass judgment on and reject metaphysical problems for the simple reason that this science is an "incompetent" judge). For the neopositivists, the only meaningful knowledge is the scientific one, which is restricted to the model of a physical knowledge, that is, only to the measurable or the verifiable. There is nothing to authorize such a radical position on their part; neither science nor philosophy gives them such a right, which they take upon themselves either because of a naive preconception or because of a dogmatic scientificalism that, while being coherent to itself, pushes itself too far, namely, since only the scientific, physical knowledge is logical and makes sense, the metaphysical propositions and any others that are unverifiable (moral principles, for example) are illogical and nonsense. In short, philosophical problems are a game of words. Carnap writes that "neither God nor the devil can any longer give us a metaphysics." God and the devil certainly not, because they never gave us one; but the philosophers yes, because this is their task. Moreover, metaphysics is due not only to the philosopher but to man as such whenever he is reflecting upon himself, gaining consciousness of himself, of his being within being, and is not degrading himself by reducing the spiritual level to the verifiable quantity; whenever he is a "philosopher" and not a scientist, who is always a *parvenu* with respect to philosophy.

For these people there are indeed no insoluble questions, for the simple reason that those that are said to be such are ill-posited questions. It suffices to define their precise meaning through "language analysis." Through the analysis of the scientific language one is able to distinguish the idle and ill-posited questions from the others, fix the definition-rules, and give science the maximum of rigor coincident with the adoption of a univocal language, so that unification of the language and unity of science can both be achieved. Moreover, what can be gained from the analysis of philosophical language? The answer is simple: it is ascertained that the nonverifiable philosophical propositions are meaningless; and since all of them are unverifiable, the triumphant conclusion is that, once philosophy is well determined in its language, it makes no sense, is all illogical, and is sent down the drain! Conclusion: in order to be rigorous the scientific language-rules must be purely formal, tautological, and so forth; the rules of philosophical language (which is irreducible to the scientific one) acquire an absolute rigor when they all show themselves to be without meaning. . . . In order to arrive at this conclusion the neopositivists organized themselves in so many cooperatives of scholars (school of Vienna, school of Chicago, and others): a work based on collaboration is indeed antithetical to philosophy which, just like artistic creation, is based on personal work. For the past thirty years or thereabout, with their language analyses these people have tried hard to express philosophical propositions that are meaningless, without thinking that precisely their work is devoid of any meaning whatsoever. These people are like an *équipe* of children trying to draw water from an empty well; and they do not even suspect that the well from which they wish to draw a philosophy is filled only with measurable things; like small children they go on and on lifting up an empty pail from an empty well, not even seeing that the real well from which philosophy can be drawn is their own spirit. Failing to realize the real problem, their research is fundamentally mistaken even if stubbornly pursued. However, there is no point to continuing these considerations since in this work we are dealing with philosophy, that is, with a discourse on man as a spiritual subject, on values, on the metaphysical sense of the world (to be discovered through the sense of man) and on the ultimate intelligibility of existence, rather than on combinations of symbols or on measurable quantities. Thus we proceed to only a brief mention of the most important neopositivists both for the sake of the completeness of our exposition and for the minimum of interest that their analyses may have. The term neopositivism "may be ambiguous and generic in that it designates a variety of doctrines, which at times are different from each other though they may have a common platform; even the expression "logical empiricism" cannot be identified with the expression "neopositivism." According to

Hempel, neopositivistic empiricism went through three phases: (1) "narrow" empiricism pertinent to the Vienna-circle (Schlick, Carnap at the beginning, and Neurath); (2) "liberalized" empiricism as represented by Carnap's "physicalism" and more precisely by *The Logical Syntax of Language*, trans. A. Smeaton (Paterson, 1959) and by *Testability and Meaning* (New Haven, 1954); (3) "broad" empiricism as seen in the developments it has had in America after the last war. On account of the nature of this work and because of the way we understand philosophy, as already stated, we shall limit ourselves to only a few allusions without pretending to give a complete and detailed account of this school.

MORITZ SCHLICK (1882-1936) established the program and the canons of the Circle: the sole criterion of significance in language is its reducibility to the immediate data of experience; thus, only propositions that are reducible to these data are significant; on the one hand, then, there is a logical analysis of scientific language which is the only one having a meaning and, on the other, there is the exclusion of all philosophical (metaphysical) problems as these are pseudo-problems devoid of meaning. We have, then, not a theory of knowledge but a logical analysis of language, whose significance is confined to its reducibility to facts. Neopositivism is thus formulated as a *logical empiricism:* an empiricist thesis or one regarding the synthesis of the content (the immediate data of experience, the facts, and the verifiable) and a logical thesis or one regarding the analysis of the form. In this formulation (which only superficially reminds one of the Kantian way of positing the problem of knowledge as a synthesis between a content *a posteriori* and a form *a priori* whereby Kant surpassed the two opposed theses of empiricism and rationalism) there is, already implied, the main difficulty faced by neopositivistic epistemology: What is the degree of objectivity or of truth in science, that is, in the only knowledge having a meaning according to this preconceived scientificalism?

After discussing this problem at length the neopositivists have parted company. Neurath and Carnap develop the logical motif (coherence in the logical construction and a nominalistic and conventional epistemology), and Schlick the empiricist one (adequacy with the experimental datum). At first, both Carnap and Neurath accept the theory regarding the *correspondence* between proposition and content in experience, to which the former is related while being able to express the latter in a verbal form. Later, however, due to the difficulties, both abandon this theory of correspondence in favor of that of *coherence*, which is formulated by Neurath as follows: "When an enunciation is given, it must be compared with the totality of existing enunciations; if the former agrees with this totality, then it can be added to the others; if it does not agree, then it must be classified as 'non-true' and dropped out, or else all the existing enunciations in science are to be modified in order that the new one may be inserted; yet, the latter is a difficult decision to take and so it is generally avoided. There cannot be any other concept of truth in science." Instead, according to Schlick (see "Über das Fundament der Erkenntnis," in *Gesammelte Aufsätze*, Vienna, 1926-1936, as well as the collection of articles published in 1938) there are enunciations he calls *ascertainments*, which describe only facts (for example, "this is yellow"); that is, they are experience-data in conformity with the rules of observation, so that their truth or falsity is established exclusively by their correspondence with experience itself. The language-question is, nonetheless, fundamental even for Schlick ("Philosophie und Naturwissenschaft," in *op. cit.*), for whom "every knowledge is an expression and a description of the state of things about which knowledge is attained . . . all that which can be expressed is knowable as is all that which lends itself to sensible questions." Logic is the method of philosophy, whose essential role is "to find out and clearly formulate the meaning of enunciations and of problems." Only in this way is it possible to avoid the danger of altering the pureness of the scientific method, and it is also possible to "profess empiricism with a full awareness about it. Only the rigorous separation of the logical form from the material content in the enunciation allows us to grasp permanently the empirical character in every knowledge of reality."

However, in Schlick himself there is a dualism between the empirical and the logical even if, as it seems, he gives so much importance to the empirical datum; and this dualism is attested by his concept of science as structure (which is expressible and defined, and thus knowable) and content (which is real, but personal and beyond cognoscibility). The distinction between philosophical knowledge and the scientific knowledge of the structure is only apparent; the former explains the meaning of propositions on the basis of grammatical and logical rules; the other, instead, decides about their truth, that is, it studies whether they are verifiable according to the scientific processes. Thus, philosophy is all gone; the propositions whose meaning it tries to explain are only those that are scientifically verifiable, that is, not its own, but those of science, of which philosophy is a humble handmaiden. It is clear that only science can decide about the truth of verifiable propositions. From here to Carnap's position there is a short step—philosophy is the analysis of language or a logical syntax; that is, it is not, in that it is a moment within science and, precisely, that one that explains and makes "clear the concepts and scientific propositions through a logical analysis." Schlick protested against this reduction of philosophy to a logic within science but without any good ground, because the coherence of his scientificalism exacts this conclusion. Perhaps remembering Pascal he writes that "the clarification of moral concepts is to man infinitely more important than all theoretical problems." True. But moral problems also are theoretical ("speculative") and their clarification is metaphysical. However, for Schlick, unfortunately, the content of metaphysics is personal and beyond cognoscibility, and thus inexplicable and outside of "theoreticity."

OTTO NEURATH (1882-1945), a sociologist and economist, is animated by "nonheroic" furors against metaphysics; constitutionally inept as regards philosophy, he dusted off some attitudes belonging to nineteenth-century positivism. His natural need to understand everything is pursued by man through the historical development in thought (Neurath follows Comte's theory of stages); this need is, according to Neurath, expressed through and satisfied by science alone (*Empirische Soziologie*, Vienna, 1931), as this is the only significant human activity. No theologic-metaphysical residuum is compatible with the "unitary science," whose unique elaboration-form is *physicalism*. "Whatever is not done through enunciations either is devoid of sense or is a mere instrument of lyrical emotion" ("Physikalismus," in [*Scientia*, 50], 1931). Neurath's physicalism is radical: unitary science is constructed through scientific language, "which is itself a physical construction"; language is a physical fact and not a symbol. Thus, the problem of adequacy between language and reality or data exists no longer, and so the significance-criterion is not to be looked for in this comparison. The doctrine of language is "totally united to the doctrine of physical processes, which are characterized by the spatio-temporal structure; therefore, all propositions have a spatio-temporal character"—language is a physiological process. With all this Neurath thinks he has eliminated the metaphysical residua, which, according to him, are still found in Wittgenstein and in Schlick, who followed in the latter's foot-steps. All propositions with a meaning are scientific propositions and there is no room for philosophical data having a content of their own, such as the propositions relative to reality, or pertinent to a conception of the universe or to any given theory of knowledge. On the contrary, unitary physicalist science absorbs in itself the theory of knowledge. An enunciation is true when it can be reduced to a proposition affirming the happening of something in a given place and at a given time. It is not a question of comparing one enunciation with "reality" in order to prove its truth, but a question of comparing one enunciation with a system of other enunciations. The theory of truth as *coherence* replaces for Neurath that of truth as *correspondence* between a proposition and a datum. Moreover, since only the scientific truth has significance and value, it follows that there is no absolute criterion of truth because for Neurath there are no "linguistically privileged" propositions;

any proposition can be rejected and the whole scientific system changed. That this may or may not easily happen is only a point of fact, a principle.

All sciences must use the universal language of physics, which includes all the contents found in the other scientific languages. Thus, unitary science results from "the diverse, scientific disciplines being unified within the same language and connected together in order to arrive at global predictions." Thus, an antimetaphysical "scientific monism" is permanently established, so that there is no longer any need for philosophy or metaphysics; the distinction between natural sciences and sciences of the spirit is abolished. Psychology is the study of human behavior, which can be "intersubjectively" described through physical language (*behaviorism*); sociology is the study of the behavior of human groups (social behaviorism). The latter does not study "norms *in se*," "values," and "essences," all of which are words "without any sense" (Neurath even puts them on the "index of forbidden words"); but it studies human groups in their mutual relations. Ethics and philosophy of law are also metaphysical residua. Neurath (and he is really serious!) replaces ethics with a behaviorist "felicitology." Even if, for the time being, no logically perfect study has been arrived at in unitary science, it still is an appreciable result to have been able to define the concepts in the particular sciences, so as to combine all their enunciations and establish transverse bonds from science to science. An ample systematizing and "axiomatizing" are possible thanks to the progress in modern logic, but not even the process of this marvelous instrument is, for Neurath, an absolute guaranty against metaphysics. "Nothing will prevent the metaphysicians from making use of it and soon we shall be concerned about a metaphysics *modo logico demonstrata*." Indeed, the metaphysics of the past, from Thales to physicalism, is all illogical and nonsense. Until he died Neurath took great pains with his unified science. Edited by him and sponsored by the University of Chicago, the *International Encyclopedia of United Science* began its publications in 1938; it was to be, according to Neurath, the heir of the French Encyclopedia. In fact, it repeats the scientific optimism of the latter, as well as the dogmatic and naive conviction that mankind's infallible progress lies in science and not in philosophy. It would be superfluous to ask of Neurath a critical justification and a valid foundation for his convictions: the tone of his writing is that of a propagandist and not that of a serious scholar.

Neurath's physicalism was elaborated again by RUDOLF CARNAP (1891), who taught philosophy at Vienna, Prague, and Chicago. Carnap is the "logician" of the school, the pure scientist who identifies philosophy with the analysis of scientific language: philosophy is the study of the logical syntax in scientific enunciations (*The Logical Syntax of Language*, *op cit.*). He accepts Neurath's thesis of the universality of physicalist language (*The Unity of Science*, trans. M. Black, London, 1934), from which metaphysical propositions are excluded. The logical grammar of language determines the limits of significant scientific propositions, and it clarifies the single concepts in the various branches of science showing their logical-formal and gnosiological connection. Thus, language-illusions and the controversies arising from purely verbal problems are avoided, and words lacking a determinate, corresponding meaning are not introduced. Pseudo-propositions spring from the equivocal and vague use of words; they can result either from words lacking a meaning or from others that, considered separately, have a meaning but put together, against the rules of syntax, produce phrases making no sense. The first elimination must affect words that, like those used in metaphysics, cannot be substituted empirically. What corresponds precisely in experience to the terms absolute-relative, subject-object, and so on? Nothing. They are spurious products of language, and the cause of interminable as well as useless controversies from which science must free itself as from a harmful burden.

According to Carnap's "logical syntax," the language-forms, on the one hand, are considered prescinding from the content to which they are applied and, on the other, the formation-rules are established; according to the latter, the propositions and transformation-rules are constructed (those which in logic are called rules of reasoning), wherein the conditions allowing the deduction of a third proposition from one or more given propositions are established. Words are divided into types; in each type there is a grouping of those words behaving in the same manner with respect to the formal rules wherein propositions are constructed. A distinction must be made between synthetical and analytical propositions; the former constitute the science of the real, the latter formal science. Reducing our observations to propositions or determinate language-symbols would amount to constructing a science with only synthetical propositions. However, in this way there would be no possibility for making previsions. Thus it is necessary to transform some synthetical propositions into other equivalent ones, which are to be deducted and tested experimentally. Analytical propositions are used only as an auxiliary calculation. Formal science is only a convenient transformation of scientific language symbols (*Die Aufgabe der Wissenschaftslogik*, Vienna, 1934). Being independent of science, the rules of logic are "tautological," and are merely grammatical rules through which the data of sensorial experience are elaborated. Once the principles and rules of deduction are laid down, some consequences follow, but the foundation of logic is purely conventional. The formal treatment of the speech-structure warrants the scientific character of the logical analysis. The scientist determines the nature of facts and the property of objects; the philosopher treats the formal structure in the scientific discourse through logical methods. The remainder is "metaphysics" and devoid of meaning. The verification (and, as we know, only verifiable propositions make sense) must be "intersubjective," that is, it must be performed by at least two observers; since the senses are the only source of knowledge (only sensation is the object of experience—the existence of things cannot be verified), only enunciations regarding what is measurable, that is, body and motion, can be verified. Even psychology ("Die Physikalische Sprache, etc.," in *Erkenntnis*, 1932), which coincides with J. B. Watson's form of behaviorism, is reduced to physicalism. Also at this point verification is intersubjective and thus limited to behavior only; introspective psychology, soul, and spirit are meaningless words. Carnap himself calls the language of physics the basis for the entire language of science, or "thing-language." His whole "philosophy" is a mere "thing-philosophy."

In the latest period of his activity Carnap has extended language analysis toward semantics or analysis of the rapport between the linguistic sign and its designatum (*Introduction to Semantics*, Cambridge [Mass.], 1942).

HANS REICHENBACH (1891-1953), a professor at Berlin, Istanbul, and Los Angeles, is to an extent the heretic of the school; after taking part in the foundation of the Vienna-Circle and contributing to "Erkenntnis," he left the predominant current and disputed with it. When compared with Carnap's dogmatic position, he, with his probabilism, is the Carneades of the School (*Ziele und Wege der heutigen Naturphilosophie*, Leipzig, 1931; *The Theory of Probability*, trans. E. H. Hutten *et al.*, Berkeley, 1949; *Experience and Prediction*, Chicago, 1938). It seems to us that Reichenbach is of particular interest for his bringing to light the difficulties and internal contradictions of neopositivism. One of them is (as we have noticed) implied in the expression "logical empiricism": empiricism is synthesis, but it is also uncertitude and probability; logic is analysis and certitude, but analysis is tautological. The scientific enunciation does not go beyond the limits of probability—absolute certitude is impossible. Previsions are only probable; they are only "stakes"; we "bet on them as a player on his previsions" (*Prediction and Terminology in Physics*, Chicago, 1938). Reichenbach's dilemma is peremptory: either the certitude of analysis and resigning ourselves to "saying nothing," or "saying something and allowing room for doubt." If all philosophical-metaphysical propositions are meaningless, we are left only with mathematical and physical knowledge; the first of the two is tautological and says nothing about reality; the other is empirical and does not go beyond induction. Thus it is not possible to go beyond probability.

Reichenbach's position modifies Neurath's and Carnap's principle of verification. In fact, he makes a distinction between forms of verification (*technical, physical, logical,* and *super-empirical* verification). The choice of one form instead of another is purely conventional. The true-false dilemma aimed at determining the meaning of an enunciation cannot be maintained; it can be determined only by its degree of verifiable probability. Thus, the neopositivistic thesis (derived from empirio-criticism), according to which sensation is the object of experience while the problem of reality is a pseudo-problem, is placed in doubt and a meaning is given to the realistic thesis.

Some theses adopted by neopositivism are contained already in the *Tractatus logico-philosophicus* (New York, 1922) by the Austrian LUD-WIG WITTGENSTEIN (1889-1951), from 1929 to 1947 a Cambridge University professor, who together with Moore, Russell, and others, gave life to so-called Cambridge School. The study of logic and of philosophy of mathematics led him (under Russell's influence) to anticipate the Vienna-Circle's scientificalism; he had contacts with the latter although his position always remained autonomous. Made up of aphorisms, the *Tractatus* is a sibylline and in many points an unintelligible book for people not equipped with a specific preparation. Yet, the influence of this volume and of its author's personal teaching, together with Russell's and Whitehead's, has been considerable both at Cambridge and on English thought in general. Of his numerous manuscripts only the *Philosophical Investigations,* trans. G. E. M. Anscombe (Oxford, 1953) and the *Remarks on the Foundations of Mathematics,* trans. G. E. M. Anscombe (Oxford, 1956) have been published posthumously up to date. Wittgenstein's thought, according to these writings, may be divided into two phases: one pertinent to the *Tractatus,* and the other pertinent to his teaching at Cambridge and represented by his posthumous writings.

Going back to Moore's linguistic analysis and Russell's logical conceptions, he makes, in the first phase, a synthesis of empiricism and rationalism; in the other phase, he elaborates a conception of philosophy as a linguistic analysis free from the schemes of Vienna's positivism, and he also contributes to the formation of the two "analytical" schools at Cambridge and Oxford.

Besides dealing with logical and mathematical language, in the *Tractatus* Wittgenstein deals with the analysis of the nature of language and its capacity of symbolic representation. The "sense" (*Sinn*) of a proposition is the descriptive capacity of possible facts; that is, language is significant in that it is an image of the world. For Wittgenstein there are simple facts ("atom-facts"), that is, the immediate data or sense-data, to which there are, in correspondence, simple or "atomic" propositions and nonelementary ("molecular") propositions, the latter ones resulting from the connection of the former through logical constants. The totality of atomic and molecular propositions having an empirical meaning constitutes science, and outside of it there are no propositions with any meaning. Thus, the affirmations of formal logic and mathematics are pseudo-propositions without an empirical meaning (*sinnlos*); they are transformations of linguistic signs being valid not because empirically verifiable, but because of the essential and intrinsic form of the signs themselves. Logical laws and inferences are tautologies. The propositions of traditional philosophy also are pseudo-propositions; they are not *sinnlos* but "senseless" (*unsinnig*). The task for philosophy is to bring to light the logic of scientific enunciations. Thus, rather than a doctrine, philosophy is an action whereby the logical structure of science-affirmations is analyzed. Philosophy is being denied, *sic et simpliciter;* deprived of an object of its own, it becomes simply sterile. If philosophy goes beyond the task assigned to it by Wittgenstein, it is bound to say meaningless things. This means that all philosophy in the past not confined to the exploration of the logical structure of scientific enunciations stated meaningless things. In short, all philosophical problems are pseudo-problems, so that they do not call for a "solution" but rather for a "dissolution." Wittgenstein (who winds up saying that even what he has been arguing is meaningless) writes that "one must remain silent about what one is unable to say," that is, one must not talk about philosophy. With this he grants that he has been talking about everything except philosophy, unless he too has been speaking about it saying things which, according to his theory, are *unsinnig*.

On account of the difficulties presented by the *Tractatus*, Wittgenstein worked out a new perspective which, far removed from Russell's while closer to Moore's, gave rise to the "analytical" school as we already mentioned. According to this linguistic-therapeutic new positivism, philosophy is a "struggle against the bewitchment of our intelligence by our tongue." Granted! But man remains just the same, even when we have cured ourselves of all "linguistic maladies," have discovered all the errors that, according to Wittgenstein, are hidden in every philosophical problem, and have clarified all man's linguistic games through "linguistic analysis"; that is, we still are confronted with a "man" who is a problem to himself. It is precisely at this point that philosophy begins as solely a philosophy of man as a problem to himself and as an investigation of being and value. Only in this way will the real "equivocation" be clarified; in short, it is not a question of clarifying the errors that, according to Wittgenstein, are hidden in all philosophical problems, but rather a question of clarifying Wittgenstein's own error, namely his belief that only scientific language makes sense while philosophy is meaningless.

In recent English positivistic empiricism, along with the influence of classical empiricism (especially Hume's and Stuart Mill's) we also find the influence of Moore, Russell, Wittgenstein, of Viennese neopositivism, and others. Yet, English neopositivism does not consider itself (and in fact it is not) a derivation of Viennese or North American neopositivism. In fact, the so-called Oxford School is connected with the "common sense" philosophy of Moore and with Wittgenstein's analytical techniques, and it develops its own form of analytical philosophy also called "analysis of common language" or simply *Oxford Philosophy;* its characteristics are: (1) analysis of common language or description of the modes (carefully exemplified) wherein a given expression is commonly used, so as to eliminate the linguistic confusions which give rise to problems or philosophical *puzzles* ("therapeutical method"); (2) a systematic study of the numerous linguistic expressions; (3) a criticism of attempts at the formalization of the natural language and hence a polemic position toward the forms of semantics and logistic characterizing the neopositivism of the American schools of Carnap, Quine, and so forth.

The initiator of the Oxford School is GILBERT RYLE (1900), who succeeded Moore in the editorship of "Mind." According to him the task for philosophy is to perform the analysis and clarification of concepts, that is, it must correct the philosophers' . . . "mistakes." "There is no doubt that some of the cardinal problems in philosophy are caused by the existence of 'logical tangles' that are present not in this or that special discipline, but rather in the thought and discourse of each philosopher, whether he is a specialist or a nonspecialist." And what then? Then, nothing, or rather, since fortunately the philosophers will always make "categorical" and noncategorical errors, philosophy—as a pure analysis of language—will correct them endlessly; yet, on its own, philosophy can never say anything; it will always remain correctly silent and this will be an excellent position for avoiding all mistakes. A "logical geography" for concepts must be set forth; that is, the logic of propositions in which concepts are used must be studied; propositions are to be shown in their compatibility or incompatibility with others, showing also which propositions can be deduced from them and from which propositions they themselves can be deduced (*The Concept of Mind*, London, 1949; *Dilemmas*, Cambridge, 1954).

Besides Ryle other thinkers have made contributions to the Oxford School, namely, JOHN WISDOM (1904), one of Wittgenstein's pupils, who more properly represents the "therapeutical" current. According to him, metaphysics is a "neurotic fancy," one which could nonetheless (a real concession!) give meaning even to ethical, aesthetical, and metaphysical propositions, whose language differs from scientific and from common language (*Problems of Mind and Matter*, Cambridge, 1934; *Other Minds*, Oxford, 1953; *Philosophy and Psychoanalysis*, Oxford, 1953). Other contributors are: J. L. AUSTIN, F. WAISMANN, H. L.

HART, J. BERLIN, and among the younger ones, S. N. HAMPSHIRE, R. M. HARE, P. H. NOWELL-SMITH, P. F. STRAWSON, and G. J. WARNOCK.

ALFRED J. AYER (1910), wishes to make logical neopositivism part of the English empiricist tradition; at first a professor at Oxford and since 1946 at London, he has been influenced by the Vienna-Circle, particularly in the work that made him renowned, *Language, Truth, and Logic* (London, 1936; reprinted in 1946 with an introduction to the second edition), which represents one of the most complete and clear expositions of all neopositivistic theses. Moving from a number of presuppositions Ayer argues with clearness and coherence. Significant enunciations are either analytical or empirical: consonant with mathematics and logic, the analytical ones do not express any knowledge; the others are "verifiable within sensible knowledge." Metaphysical enunciations are neither simply analytical nor verifiable within sensible experience: thus they are neither false nor true; they are only meaningless ("Demonstration of the Impossibility of Metaphysics," in *Mind* [43] 1934).

Ayer has again elaborated his point of view (so-called phenomenalism) in *The Foundation of Empirical Knowledge* (London, 1940) and in *Thinking and Meaning* (London, 1947). The question whether we perceive things as they really are (realism) or as modified by the physical and physiological conditions of knowledge ("idealism"), is ill-posited; perceiving a material object does not necessarily imply either its existence or any affirmation about its reality whether or not we perceive it as it is. Immediate objects of knowledge are the *sense-data*, that is, those objects whose existence cannot be doubted in that the latter depends on their being perceived—their being is their being perceived. Thus, the distinction between true and false perceptions and the dualism of reality and appearance are abolished. Ayer discards the metaphysical hypothesis of a reality in the objects beyond perception, as a problem having no foundation in experience. Yet, the phenomenon ("what appears") has no cause of its own; and since its cause cannot be identified with another phenomenon, does it not have to be identified with the real object transcending perception itself? Instead, like Hume, Ayer reduces causality (without noticing that causality is one thing in an empirical sense and another thing in a metaphysical sense) to a relationship between phenomena, that is, between groups of *sense-data*, in such a way that nothing can be inferred about the existence of objects; and necessity (to be thus replaced by "probability") is reduced to a psychological habit. Material objects are only a permanent possibility for perceptions, and only this is to be understood when it is said that they are "real." Semantics is important so as to avoid the false problems arising from metaphysical hypotheses.

"Physicalism" and "Scientistic" Barbarity

On account of racial persecutions the greatest exponents of the European neopositivistic currents in Berlin, Prague, and Vienna emigrated to the United States where they came into contact with the pragmatist schools of Mead and Dewey. European neopositivism, as a result, felt their influence which, at times, was really profound, particularly as regards the broadening of language analysis, which is enriched with more themes, with a more complex methodology, and includes even nonscientific language. As a consequence mathematical-physics has lost its supremacy, physicalism has gone down, and the analysis has been extended to the value-discourse, to the rhetorical one, and so on, that is, to those language-patterns called "emotive." The change of location on the part of some of the *Wiener Kreis'* representatives has produced a symbiosis-process between neopositivistic currents and local philosophical traditions making the mutual contacts already existing prior to 1938 closer and stronger. After all, some of the themes of the European neopositivists—antimetaphysical attitude, empiricism, and language-analysis—were already alive and active within American pragmatism and experimentalism even before the spreading of neopositivism; likewise, the signification-empirical criterion affirmed by ALEXANDER B. JOHNSON (1786-1867) in his *Treatise on Language* (New York, 1836), is already a point of fact in Peirce. Moreover, studies on the methodology of experimental science had been cultivated by PERCY W. BRIDGMAN (1882), author of *The Logic of Modern Physics* (New York, 1927), which is considered a fundamental work. His other works are: *The Nature of Physical Theory* (Princeton, 1936), *Reflections of a Physicist* (New York, 1950), and *The Nature of Some of Our Physical Concepts* (New York, 1952), in which he sustains an operational theory (operationalism) in the expression of physical concepts. Other scholars to be mentioned are C. I. LEWIS (already treated in this work) and the physicist VICTOR F. LENZEN (1890), a professor at the University of California and the author of *The Nature of Physical Theory* (New York-London, 1931). In the span of time between the two great wars, studies on formal logic and on mathematics were also developed in America by Lewis and by W. O. QUINE (1908), a professor at Harvard, who in 1934 published *A System of Logistic* (Cambridge [Mass.]) followed by *From a Logical Point of View* (Cambridge [Mass.], 1953), *Mathematical Logic* (New York, 1962), *Methods of Logic* (New York, 1959), and other writings in which, independently of philosophical doctrines, he sets up a modern symbolic logic like the one developed through the research on the foundations of mathematics. Even in 1934 there is *An Introduction to Logic and Scientific Method* (New York) by MORRIS R. COHEN (1880-1947) and ERNEST NAGEL (1901); concerning the latter, a professor at Columbia University, we also recall his *Principles of the Theory of*

Probability (Chicago, 1939). Thus, European neopositivism came to place itself within an environment already set to receive and transform it.

A pupil of Mead, CHARLES W. MORRIS (1901) has been a professor at Chicago since 1931 and he is the author of works (*Six Theories of Mind*, Chicago, 1932; *Foundations of the Theory of Signs*, Chicago, 1938; *Sign, Language, and Behavior*, New York, 1955, and others) giving him an outstanding place in contemporary American philosophy. Morris engrafted the themes of the language-analysis of European neopositivism on the trunk of pragmatism around the empirical criterion of signification and the syntactical determination of formal structures. For Morris even "semiotic" moves along the lines of scientific empiricism; yet, being free from the neopositivistic schemes "semiotic" coordinates the "pragmatic" course in the research with the semantic and syntactic courses. Morris made an inquiry of his own not only with a view to founding a behavioristic-biological theory for the sign but also with a view to offering a phenomenology of that type of behavior represented by the choice and by the evaluation-attitude of man before life.

MAX BLACK (1909) has devoted his studies to the philosophy of language; a professor at Cornell University he moves along the methodic lines of the English analytical school of which we have already spoken (*The Nature of Mathematics*, New York, London, 1933; *Critical Thinking*, New York, 1946; *Language and Philosophy: Studies in Method*, Ithaca, 1949). In his work, *Ethics and Language* (New Haven, 1944), CHARLES L. STEVENSON (1908), a professor at the University of Michigan, worked out a theory on evaluation along the lines of the semantic-pragmatic analysis of language. According to this theory the ethical discourse is contradistinguished by an exhortative function and its judgments, by an emotive meaning and a dispositional property, that is, one that is apt to arouse emotive reactions.

HERBERT FEIGL (1902), a professor at the University of Minnesota, was a pupil of Schlick and a member of the *Wiener Kreis;* he was among the first to make the theories of European neopositivism well known in the United States with his articles published in the *Journal of Philosophy* (1931), in *Philosophy of Science* (1934), and in *Twentieth-Century Philosophy* (1943). In the latest phase of his thought ("Existential Hypotheses," in *Philosophy of Science*, [17], 1950; "Logical Reconstruction, Realism and Pure Semiotic," *ibid.*) he sets forth his own "semantic realism" consisting both in separating the signification-criterion from its relation with the immediate datum and in claiming for the theoretical constructions of science a semantic validity equal to that of directly testable entities; he proposes a "pure pragmatics" as a new semantic dimension. Together with WILFRED SELLARS (1912)—who teaches at the same university—he published an anthology of scientific philosophy entitled *Readings in Philosophical Analysis* (New York, 1949). On the other hand, Sellars published a *Readings in Ethical Theory* (New York, 1952) in collaboration with J. Hospers.

A professor at Yale, FILMER S. C. NORTHROP (1893) sustains the necessity of not conforming to one single method arbitrarily imposed on all the sciences; the nature of each different method, instead, must be analyzed according to its own evaluation and structure. Such a test enhances the understanding of each method and causes a verification of the mutual relations in the natural and social sciences together with the different phases of development in each of them; each development leads to a unity, which is a normative unity and, as such, represents the central problem in the methodological and epistemological inquiry (*Science and First Principles*, New York, 1931; *The Logic of the Sciences and the Humanities*, New York, 1947). On this basis Northrop made an interpretation of cultures with a view to clarifying reciprocal misunderstandings (*The Meeting of East and West*, New York, 1946; *The Taming of the Nations*, New York, 1952).

As in Northrop also in SUSANNE K. LANGER (1895), who is a professor at Connecticut College for Women, there is a critical position with respect to dogmatic scientificalism together with a sensibility to humanistic values. Under Cassirer's influence in particular, Langer finds that the key of philosophy lies in the investigation of symbols in all the forms of human activity (science, art, religion, and so on). According to her, such investigation prescinds from an established metaphysics: the starting point is the study of symbols rather than arriving at them by proceeding from a metaphysics of man (and in this she moves away from Cassirer). In this way philosophy is kept within its proper task, which is that of positing problems rather than moving from solutions already given. Langer opposes empiricism and holds that symbols are not to be confused with signs (*An Introduction to Symbolic Logic*, New York, 1953; *Feeling and Form: A Theory of Art Developed from Philosophy in a New Key*, New York, 1953).

Apart from the differences not only between the numerous currents discussed above but also those existing within each single one, there are some established points that can be set forth from what we have been expounding: (1) sensation is the only source of knowledge and existence pertains only to that which is measurable or verifiable within sensorial experience, that is, to the physical fact; on the other hand, we are unable to leave our skins and thus the problem of the existence or nonexistence of objects and whether these are as we perceive them goes beyond the immediate datum and cannot even be posited; therefore, this is a *physics without nature*; (2) that which is not verifiable (which is not a physical fact) is devoid of meaning; all metaphysical propositions (even the

493

ethical ones) are unverifiable (they are not measurable physical facts); all metaphysical questions, and so on are meaningless and illogical; therefore, this is a *philosophy without philosophy;* (3) philosophy has the sole task of clarifying scientific concepts and propositions by means of a logical analysis; no truth is discovered by philosophy, which is not even a doctrine but a simple "activity"; the only "knowable" language that is philosophically interesting is scientific language; being an "emotive" one instead, that of metaphysics and of ethics represents a "nonrational" language; (4) logic is analytical and thus it is tautological; its laws are grammatical rules being fit for an elaboration of the data of sensible experience; syntactic rules are drawn from arbitrarily posited principles which, once they are set forth, are followed by consequences; yet, the foundation of logic is purely conventional; besides, whether it be deductive or inductive, logic needs no absolute truths, "in that it expresses rules according to which one proposition implies another without any concern for their truth"; a proposition is accepted and inserted within a complex in conformity with a system of conventional rules; therefore, this is a *logic without either a logos or a truth;* (5) physicalism and naturalism must be extended even to psychology, sociology, philosophy of law, ethics, and so forth; thus, even at this point, only that is knowable which is measurable (that is, behavior and reaction), prescinding from the "myth" of the soul, from that of natural law, and from every norm; therefore, this is a *psychology without a soul,* an *ethics without law or values,* and a *law without norm,* and so on.

At this point it is no longer a question of the problem of science and its relationship with philosophy; of epistemology and methodology in science; of freeing physics from all metaphysical residua; of assigning a limit to the invasions of metaphysics into the field of physics. Here the real question is the total and radical destruction of the human and natural universe: a destruction pursued mercilessly by employing the most refined weapons of logic and the most subtle analyses of words. Of man and nature the only thing left is a complex of sensible data without reality and a complex of symbols and grammatical rules without truth. And only this which we have just said would make "sense"; it is as if we were to say that that makes sense which is senseless. If the simplicity of illations whence neopositivism moves is confronted with the complexity and gravity of the results arrived at, one can fully detect the simplemindedness of its inferences and procedures, the superficiality of its scientificalism, as well as the erroneousness of its antiphilosophical and antimetaphysical claims. Perhaps, Western thought has never gone through such a period of absolute and radical disintegration; never before have man and things been emptied with such a subtle fury by using the gimlet of a mad logic which delights in its aimless twisting and capricious manipulation of formulas and signs—a logic being avid for nothingness and repugnant to being; never before was empty "logicity" so illogical; nor have people before now ever seen a rationalism so irrational and unreasonable.

This is not the place for a detailed critical evaluation of neopositivism and similar currents. Nor do we think that it is worthwhile to confute its philosophical simple-mindedness, because its inconsistency is so obvious; philosophically it is a mere verbalism manifesting the presumptuousness of every sophistry and eristic; and this is not only our opinion but the opinion of all the scholars who have undertaken an objective and intensive examination of it. Yet, we do not intend to disregard whatever positive contribution it has made in the epistemological field, though this same positiveness, to be effective, must be recovered in opposition to neopositivism itself. The distinction between the scientific and metaphysical domains is not only an advantage for science but also for metaphysics; and, as has been said, it is the merit of neopositivism to have "deontologized" scientific language and eliminated nonscientific ("poetical" and "metaphysical") meanings from the words used by science, so that the terms were clarified and defined. However, the presupposed and prejudicial scientificalism in neopositivism places the latter both in contradiction with its own method and in a position of "physicalizing" metaphysical language at the very moment that the scientific one is being "deontologized." Thus, while rightly fighting against the error of an "ontologized" physics, neopositivism perpetrates the same wrong against a philosophy it has "physicalized." On this point its dogmatism is affected by a fundamental acrisy: led by physicalism, neopositivism assumes as a categorical-universal principle what is only a methodic-physical principle; the latter cannot unify science at all, but can simply make it uniform on the basis of presuppositions that are metaphysical, materialistic, unjustified and thus arbitrary. And what are the results of such a subtle "clarification"? Nihilism of thought and nothingness of truth; besides, by subtilizing and sophisticating so much on empty words, the linguistic confusion becomes such that even the neopositivists themselves understand very little. The scientist Utopia of a unique, universal language and of a unity in the sciences has ended in the chaos of conventionalism. The neopositivists object that, in spite of everything, it cannot be denied that neopositivism moves from deeply critical exigencies; the latter compel it not to accept any dogmatic presupposition, but to conform both to the use of a most exacting rationalistic method and to a discussion clarifying ambiguous words such as "intuition," "evidence," and so forth. Properly speaking, authentic philosophy always has been a critique of dogmatic presuppositions, rationalistic in its method and exacting in the clarification of terms. Philosophy always has taught what scientist neopositivism claims to be teaching: indeed, rationality and criticalness are its component parts. On account of this, philosophy rejects neopositivism in that the latter moves from dogmatic presuppositions and an acritical, elementary, and naive metaphysics (such as its physicalism, physiologism, and materialism); on the basis of the latter there is no longer a clarification of such terms as "evidence," "intuition," "being," and "spirit" but only their misunderstanding and final denial as entities devoid of meaning. Now, if one ought to oppose the presumption (first rebutted by empirio-criticism and then by neopositivism) of some philosophers whereby philosophy and metaphysics were to be made the science "governing" all scientific doctrines, one must oppose even more strongly the neopositivists' absurd pretense of making physics the mother-science and its language, the only one having a significance. Philosophism may be harmful to scientific progress; yet, scientificalism destroys man as it arbitrarily denies spirit and spiritual values, debases logic within the twaddle of conventionalism, and finally repeats its initially presupposed materialism. Nor is it sufficient to remark that some neopositivists are sensitive toward moral problems (Schlick, for example): a personal and "emotive" exigency is not enough when the system as a whole denies every rational and metaphysical foundation for it and pushes itself to the most radical moral nihilism.

We shall not insist on the internal difficulties and contradictions characterizing neopositivism (that is (1) impossibility of reconciling the logico-tautological moment in knowledge with the empirical one; (2) lack of critical value in the sense-datum presupposition, wherein reality is built on pure contents of consciousness, and the same lack in the verification-principle which dogmatically fails to account for the non-sensorial moment in knowledge; (3) arbitrary limitation of the concept of experience understood as purely sensorial, and a naive reduction of the intellectual and internal experience to an insignificant and nonknowable one; (4) reduction of language to a physical or biophysiological fact—and this is found even in Carnap's theory of "protocols"—and a reduction of science to a merely verbal game; and so on), but we cannot refrain from still insisting on its nihilism.

It has been said that the proposal of a unitary language for all sciences has a methodological character; thus it cannot be either rejected or accepted *a priori* but rather evaluated according to its results, that is, whether through its application the proposal meets with the expectation. Such applications were performed in sociology, ethics, psychology, and so forth. As a result of these experiments it is evident that only on the surface has the proposal a methodological character; in reality it presupposes a materialistic metaphysics of its own, as well as a reduction of morality, psychology, and so forth to physical or biophysiological facts.

Physicalism does not confine itself to saying that there are inferior manifestations both in society and in the individual man, but it maintains that whatever is knowable and significant in social and individual life, in ethics and morality, is reducible to biophysiological facts. Therefore, the value of the results of this methodological principle is absolute rather than confined to the range of applicable facts. And this amounts to changing a methodological principle into a universally valid category; this, in turn, is made possible only because of the implicit denial of anything else but measurable facts. The sophism of physicalism lies precisely in this: it says that it has no concern for the metaphysical problems regarding the soul, morality, and the like (and this could imply that there are other forms of knowledge that are more idoneous and more valid than the discussion and solution of those problems), but at the same time, by affirming that they are insignificant and illogical, it denies any other knowledge but the physical knowledge, and it denies the existence of a soul and of moral values not identifiable with the same biophysiological facts. Now these materialistic negations are dogmatically presupposed in the research and are at the foundation of the methodological principle used by physicalism which only on the basis of these negations can accept behaviorism and reduce sociology, morality, and metaphysics to so many chapters of biophysiology or, perhaps, to chapters of neuropathology since, as it seems, everything is explained through nervous processes and neurotic involutions. It has been properly remarked that behaviorism can describe Socrates' behavior in prison but is unable to explain the reason for it. The physicalist, however, does not give up: it is a question of an "emotive" experience, he may say. And yet, in criticizing the "highly physicalist" Anaxagoras it is precisely Socrates who in the *Phaedo* remarks (and the remark applies to behaviorism) that through his procedure Anaxagoras can explain the fact of Socrates being seated in prison but not *why* the latter is there. However, it is precisely on account of this *why* that Socrates died—a *why* that for physicalism is meaningless and illogical.

Now, as it has been properly remarked, "The rejection of God, freedom, and immortality as arguments consonant with a mature consideration and discussion, and the abandonment of metaphysics in favor of word-analysis are not things of little account."[15] Exactly—they are simply the annihilation of man and of the human. Man, like a bag, is emptied: God, freedom, immortality, soul, justice, and so on are pulled out of his mind as meaningless words, devoid of an objective value; man is left with Carnap's "grammatical rules," Neurath's physical language, and Watson's behaviorism. This "void," like Sartre's can be filled up with anything, although nothing—freedom and necessity, spirit and immortality, just

[15] C. E. M. Joad, *A Critique of Logical Positivism* (1950), p. 19.

and unjust—has any value whatsoever. Why respect the human person if what counts in it is only that which is measurable and is a physical fact? Why a moral and social justice rather than the most merciless injustice? On account of a conventionality? Or because it so pleases? Alas, no! With conventionalisms people may write books, play with words, or have a chess game, but they cannot think or live, and exist as men especially. In spite of all physicalist idiocies and of the idle talk of logical syntaxes and logic-mathematical treatises, man has a spiritual life, an "inwardness," the only one that makes sense and gives a sense to everything; yet, in the circumstances, being unable to think and live in the void, man deviates from his fundamental vocation (which is metaphysical and theological) and tries to fill up that void with the first dogmatic and irrational creed presented to him as an ideal and as a possibility of living for something. The need to believe leads him to believe as true even what he knows is not, and to profess as a religion that which is fanaticism.

Like Marxist materialism and atheistic existentialism, physicalism is the death of humanism. From different directions they all converge in the same destruction—man and every spiritual value. Here is the only difference: Marxist scientificalism is instrumental because it works for the economic-social *praxis;* thus its materialism is positive, "practically effective," and has an ideal (it is closer to Dewey's instrumentalism). What is essential they have in common: they admit only the level of "quantity" while denying that of "quality"; consequently, they deny philosophy which is qualitative, and identify man's essence (and also the essence of culture) with the physico-economic, that is, the *qualitative essence* of the individual and of mankind with the *quantitative degree* (scientific and technical progress). All this simply means lack of "humanity," that is, inability to grasp the level of the spirit due to a constitutional crudeness. No wonder, then, that on the basis of their common materialistic platform denying all spiritual values, the void in the neopositivists (and in those who permit the absorption of their souls by accepting these doctrines) can be filled up with the Marxist "ideal." What is there to prevent it? Not religious, moral, and metaphysical principles (indeed, the latter are identical); neopositivism itself is unable to do so since for it these principles are neither true nor false, but simply meaningless. Perhaps, the difference in political method? But what sense does it make in a conventionalist position? And, then, is a difference in political method sufficient to distinguish the "West" from the "East"? Only this and no more? Yes, it seems to be so; such is the baseness arrived at by so-called West. And the West today would seem to be as follows: existentialist nihilism, neopositivistic nihilism, and Marxist nihilism, all united by a materialistic metaphysics. Yet, it seems that the Westerners are wearing blinkers; they see one danger facing them but not the other; they see the "materialism of the Left" and fight it; they accept (or they do not see) the "materialism of the Right," which tomorrow, having emptied them completely, will leave them to be filled up by the former, which will then give thanks to the "democrats" for their generosity in preparing a most suitable ground for its ideological "*promenade.*" After what we have been saying no one will be surprised if we now touch on contemporary Marxist currents in this same chapter.

9. Leninist-Stalinist Marxism

We have already devoted some pages (besides the numerous hints and allusions) to Marx and other pages to the relationship between Marxism and existentialism. The nature of this work and our manner of understanding philosophy prevent us from dealing exhaustively with Marxist ideology, which for the most part is outside of the problems of philosophy; yet, we consider it proper to mention some of its positions.

As we remarked in Chapter I, Marx reproaches Hegel for having severed thought (dialectic-logical motion) from reality (historical motion); the former is unable to act upon the latter and remains isolated from concrete action. According to Marx the synthesis between logico-dialectical moment and historical moment is given by *labor,* which in overcoming the individualistic ("lordly") moment of the ego unites men in the contribution-bond that each man, for himself and others, brings to the common well-being. Labor is the ethics of a complete man; through labor the subject man masters the real by changing it; thus the logical moment is transferred into history "effectively." Through revolution or a struggle against alienation, wherein the "serf" is redeemed and "equality" attained, the future of mankind is fulfilled. This logico-historical synthesis is lacking in Hegel, whose dialecticism is still a conquest of self-consciousness, or an affirmation of the "unique" against the principle of equality. Here the question is not to "understand" but to "create" truth; and man is the creator in that he is activity and *action.* Yet, action is the nonlogos; and if philosophy is theoreticity and categoricalness, Marx's philosophy is the "nonphilosophy" or the dissolution of the theoretical moment into the practical one. Labor is everything for Marx; through revolution the workman puts an end to the labor-alienation (whence capital arises), and he brings about the workers' society in which he produces for himself and for others. Individual or egoistic consciousness must yield to the collective one or to the infinite Ego through which Marx solves the religious question: socialistic society is God, the Whole by which the supreme synthesis of logic and history is realized. Hegel makes religion fade away into philosophy, which is the conclusive moment of the absolute Spirit. Marx transfers it into the workers' society: two diverse ways of secularizing the sacred and of making absolute the mundane—Hegel on the "qualitative" level of philosophy and Marx on the "quantitative" level of economics—but two substantially identical ways; in fact, both arrive at the same conclusion, according to which the Whole or Infinite can be fulfilled by man within the historical process. Flattened along a horizontal and extensive process, even Hegel's "qualitative" level becomes a "quantitative" one by implication: immanently *equalized* by Nature and History, the level of the Spirit still is that of Nature and a purely historical one in which the essence of man is identified with the historical situation (the same as in Marx), even if it be the global and total situation (the whole of indefinite time) of universal history.

Marx is not Hegel indeed, but Hegel contains Feuerbach and Marx. Ultimately, for Hegel Spirit is the history of man, as an individuality (subjective spirit) and as a partaker of society (objective spirit): the reduction of morality to ethicity is the anteroom of Marx's collective consciousness through which the logico-historical synthesis or synthesis of the Whole representing "humanity" is carried out; thus humanity is able to construct itself through the historic process. From this point of view Marx still is moving within a humanistic-idealistic conception in the Hegelian sense; a radical humanism (which is antihumanism) rejecting the existence (be it God or nature) of an objective world outside of the logico-practical or dialectical-historical action (that is, labor) of man. The "materialistic" moment in the economic structure, which is the moving cause within the historic process, expresses the essence of this humanism; through the latter, nature is reduced to man's practical-productive possibility, to the "real" moment that can be converted into the "logical" moment by means of labor or action; action implies the redemption of labor itself (a human-social problem), and the conquest of that collective consciousness which achieves its fullness through the realization of a homogeneous society. No theoretical moment is autonomous but is completely immanent in actual history and is identified with it; likewise, no morality, no metaphysics, no religion is autonomous. "By developing their production and their material trade" men "transform their own thought and the latter's products at the same time." It is not consciousness that determines life but life, consciousness, which is conditioned and determined by the material and historic situation. And thus Hegel's immanent idealism is pushed to its consequences, that is, to reveal itself as a negation of idealism itself and hence as a negation of the spirit as such. In fact, Marx makes "thought and its products" (that is, the "essence" of man) be the effect of "production" and of "material trade," that is, the effect of the "economic" degree of a society.

On the other hand, Marxist "materialism" retains the Hegelian dialectic that is to be understood as a conflict between two social classes; that is, this is an "effective" or "historic" dialectic (not one belonging to a thought being independent from *praxis*) to which the "alienation" moment is essential. Without this split there would be no history, and mankind would stand even now in the presence of its immediate animality. The process runs from immediate unity to a society split into two opposite classes and from here to a concrete or mediate unity to be realized through the cessation of alienation; alienation then is the moving element producing the historic process whose end is the supreme unity or synthesis in a classless society, that is, in a society without history any more. In any case, the Hegelian dialectical triad is retained by Marx who understands it in economic-social terms, as a law within the economic structure and a dynamic principle in the historic process (Marxist-Engelsian dialectical materialism).

We have emphasized (compare Chapters I and V) the consequences implied in Marxism and how its absolute humanism is a radical negation of man and of the human; we also have acknowledged the truth of its theme concerning the rescue of labor from servitude and exploitation as well as the truth of the concept that labor itself is not "the means" of the server (in which case labor is servile) but of every man as a man (in which case labor is "human"). Yet, labor can be human—we add—only within a spiritualistic (and thus anti-Marxist) conception in which, being transposed in terms of spirituality, even the economic value is a means of spiritual elevation. Also the anti-individualistic quest has a truth of its own if individualism signifies egotism and antisociality, but it becomes negative as regards the individuality if the social importance in man is not recovered within the person in which the individuality of value lies. The Marxist collective consciousness is still on the same egoistic and materialistic level of individualism: it denies the individuality (as Hegel does, after all) without recovering the authentic sociality, which no longer makes any sense if man is denied as a person and if it is not an expression of spiritual values. "Collectivism" is not a society of persons; men's society is not human if it is not realized as a communion of spirits. Marxism does not solve the problem of the relationship between person and society (or rather the problem of the "reciprocity of consciousnesses," as promotion and affirmation of the autonomous personality of each individual within the absolute society) but suppresses the inner consciousness—the person's autonomous being—in the collective consciousness. And this occurs when Marxism makes man an essentially and exclusively social being and consciousness, a phenomenon of evolution whose content is determined by the situation and modified by economic progress; in this way, whatever is conceived and desired by man is a consequence of his material needs resulting from methods of production and from social relations which, in turn, are determined by production itself. All this, however, does not mean overcoming individualism but creating the idolatry and fanaticism of sociality in which both the individual and the person are denied; and, on account of its essential materialism this sociality identifies the content and progress of consciousness with the dialectic of the economic. Certainly, the debate on the problem of person-society relations can no longer be posited in terms of nineteenth-century individualism; yet, unless one falls into the opposite abstraction, it cannot be sustained that society has a structure while the person, whose consciousness-content is determined by society itself, has none. The person as such has its social structure constituted by its own profound interiorness, which must be respected, not denied.[16]

It must be recognized that today not only Marxism denies the person and the values constituting it: the organization principle is by now the tyrant of man whose activity is controlled; every individual is a cog in the gearing-wheel. The victory over misery and the securing of a degree of material well-being, the right to work and to a place in the sun seem to exact as a price the renunciation of freedom, as only a minimum of personal life is allowed. Being violent and imposed by the social order, extroversion causes the life of every individual to be identified with his public life. It seems that today there are no longer problems requiring a personal initiative and decision: it is the "machine" or the social "plan" which solves all of them, almost as if an anonymous, blind, and uncheckable force had taken the place of the individual's will. The choice of our behavior is imposed upon us; "progress" chooses for us, the organization assigns us a place, technology rules our work. Evidently, there is no longer room for moral problems; social ethics, whose goal is the well-being of each and everyone, assigns each his "place"; and the individual's "worth" rests on the function he performs as an instrument for the common interest. Perhaps never before has the common interest so emptied the individual's life of every interest: "subjectivity" has been emptied and man prevented from finding himself before himself; he has lost his inward life and instead of being "someone" he is only a public and impersonal "something." The so-called educative techniques take it upon themselves to manipulate consciousnesses, to make one for man at will according to the whim of the one maneuvering the technique. This radical negation of the person, of morality and religion, and so forth, is perpetrated not only by Marxism but also by neopositivism and behaviorist psychology or by whatever other "inhuman" doctrine and irrational fanaticism (even skepticism is a form of fanaticism) that are persistently

[16] Cf. M. F. Sciacca, *Interiorità oggettiva*, 2nd ed. (Milan, Marzorati, 1958), chap. V; *idem., L'ora di Cristo* (1953).

opposed to man and spiritual values. The ultimate result is unmistakably the despotism of an idol: the State, Race, Political Party, Communist Society and even so-called Democracy. It is important to insist on this point and to demonstrate how—from dictatorships to democracies—all political forms compete with each other in the destruction of the person and its values with a view to procuring the utmost of well-being for man.

Soviet or Russian Marxism (in reality that of Lenin and Stalin) certainly is Marxist but not reducible to Marx's Marxism. I do not believe it can be called humanistic or that the term "humanism" can have for it any meaning whatsoever. Its materialism is obvious: "Nothing exists in the world but matter in motion"; consequently, everything is a product of matter in motion. This is the dogma on which Russian Marxism builds its political and social theories, its conception of history and of man. It is the philosophy of a political party strictly controlled and imposed without any possibility for discussion; its evolution and criticism are the task of the party itself, which is called upon to make it fit for all changeable situations. Russian Marxist philosophy is, in short, identified with the communist State, that is, first with VLADIMIR J. LENIN (1870-1924) and then with JOSEPH STALIN (1879-1953). Such was the birth of Leninist-Stalinist Marxism which sovietism has spread by means of encyclopedias, volumes, and small catechisms as the new religion of mankind. We are not going to follow the numerous phases of this philosophy, whose interpretations have all been condemned one by one from that of G. A. Deborin to those of G. F. Alexandrov, V. F. Asmuss, M. A. Markov, and others.

Lenin thought he had accepted the most orthodox Marxism, which he defended from all mechanistic, empirio-critical interpretations, and so on. In reality, however, he adapted Marxism to the cultural and social situation in Russia and made it retreat toward less critical positions than that attained by original Marxism or those attained in its developments in Europe. Marxism is unable to overcome one of its internal contradictions: on the one hand, it states that man changes with the changing of economic conditions (the only true forms making up existence), whereby he is acted upon rather than be the agent and whereby he is the resulting effect rather than an initial cause (a deterministic conclusion); on the other hand, it holds that man creates himself through labor and is capable of acting upon and modifying his environment. Thus, on the one hand, there have been some deterministic interpretations and, on the other, some idealistic ones (for example, in Italy, by Labriola, Gramsci, and others). As is known, Marxism believes it solves the problem with the illusory concept of upsetting the "praxis," whereby man becomes the agent and the determining factor rather than being acted upon and determined.

The idealistic motif was abandoned by Lenin; nature is a datum, a reality before the subject. Nature is matter in motion and is precisely defined as the "philosophical category indicating the objective reality." Everything is produced by matter in motion; the so-called spirit is produced by a material organ, the brain. Ontologically there is only matter; the consciousness-matter opposition is only gnosiological. Lenin defines consciousness as "a copy, a reflection, a photograph" of matter without which consciousness cannot exist: first there is matter and then consciousness which is determined by the former. Man's freedom consists in making the laws of nature productive. However, how is this possible if man himself is determined by these laws and if even as consciousness he is their product? The answer is that matter does not determine consciousness directly but through society. With this, however, the problem is not solved but simply shifted. Freedom, as human freedom, makes no sense in a materialistic-deterministic system.

Unless thought itself is dialectical, it cannot be adequate to and reproduce the external movable world; yet, always approximate and never perfect, adequacy is relative only; the changeable external reality exists independently of our consciousness, a copy or reflection of matter, which is objective only within the limits of its imperfect and partial correspondence with it. The continuous evolution of matter excludes, on the one hand, the existence of immutable substances and, on the other, the eternal principles or absolute truths; matter alone and the laws of its changes are eternal within universal motion. Evolution moves toward the better (the last degree is more complex and higher than the previous one) and is "dialectical"; by accumulating, the small quantitative changes produce a tension through which a new quality comes into being once the balance has been broken. The gradual conquest of nature is possible to man through productive work or the utilizing of the means of labor; thus, on the one hand, thought is an effective means of action and, on the other, being a mediator between nature and man (it sets forth the "interaction" uniting the world to man), it becomes identified with technical-scientific progress. And it could not be otherwise since—as Marx teaches—this is not a question of "understanding" but one of "transforming" the world. This being granted, it follows that the only valuable actions are those that are fit for the purpose of the conquest and transformation of nature. Likewise, the only valuable "knowledge" is that which allows an always more productive work and an increasingly effective action by man, namely, technology and science whose truth is not theoretical but practical, that is, it is measured in terms of its efficacy in transforming and producing. Marxist-Leninist materialism is (and it cannot not be) "scientistic" and pragmatic. To "think" of a nature in motion simply means to look for forms of effective mastery that are more and more adequate, that is, forms making work more effective and achieving an always less approximate correspondence, so that interaction between the natural world or matter in becoming and man may always be less inadequate. In short, the only true knowledge is science united to technology; nor is there anything "unknowable" that could authorize any form of agnosticism whatsoever; nor is there any contemplative knowledge or a knowledge resting on pure "comprehension." A purely "comprehensive" knowledge not transforming the world for our needs, makes no sense, is devoid of truth, and is the betrayal of labor; knowledge can only be class-knowledge and its criterion of truth is practice alone, that is, success in productivity.

Science as the instrument of man's power over the world and man's highest happiness on earth is a myth coeval with its inception in modern times (a myth already explicit in Francis Bacon); in this respect, science was met with great enthusiasm by the Enlightenment, positivism, and original Marxism; today, a new and childish enthusiasm is shown for it by the North American and soviet pragmatist scientificalism while some currents in European thought give evidence of mistrust and concomitant pessimism. The difference (and, if you wish, the opposition) is not in the premises, which are identical, but in the conclusions. If man's end is to be fulfilled in this world and his supreme aspiration is the conquest of and dominion over nature, man as a whole is equalized by the natural and historical order; human goals, in fact, do not transcend nature and history (according to idealism and Hegel, these goals are attained within the knowing-process centered on thought; for Marxist materialism and other forms of pragmatist scientificalism, they are instead attained within the pragmatic-process centered on labor which uses science and technology as its instruments). In this way, however, the conqueror of nature winds up being conquered; if nature is everything he is longing for, the conquest he achieves is nature's victory over man. Immanent idealism's "philosophy of spirit" changes into what it implicitly is, into a "philosophy of matter"; that is, the spirit-nature adequation implies in itself the burying of the spirit in the world. Being far from the critical maturity achieved by European immanentism, Leninist-Stalinist Marxism (and North American naturalism, as well) is still in its phase of enthusiasm and faith in progress; it is still dogmatically convinced that the communist society (that is, that Whole, that Absolute longed for by humanity) will be arrived at through social revolution and a dictatorship by the proletariat (Lenin), and through a "scientific" plan for the socialist industrialization and collectivization of rural economy. On the contrary, other European currents of immanentism lack this faith and any faith whatsoever; completely disenchanted, they envisage the death-destiny and nothingness of man in his radical historicity and in his being in time. For them, the dominion over nature through science, which is an instrument of nature's conquest by means of labor, is a "useless endeavor," a fall, and the loss of man's authenticity.

Leninist-Stalinist Marxism is not satisfied only with enslaving man to nature of which at first glance he is to be the master, but it also makes him a slave of society; the "assimilation" of man and his ends to nature is accompanied by the assimilation of the individual to society because the latter represents man as a whole and is the whole of man. As has been written, Lenin (who was an engineer, a technician, and a "scientist") "considers the world, mankind, and individual men as raw materials to be technically worked out by him, in the same way as he would in a ship-building yard." Hence his "realism" and "rationalism." Lenin "is a realist because as a man of action he cannot admit that the world on which he is working and which he seeks to transform can be other than a reality; and he is a realist because this is the natural and necessary inclination in a man of action. Likewise, his rationalism bears this character: busied with the reformation of the world through technology, Lenin is unwilling and unable to admit the existence of a world of factors that cannot be seized by knowledge; in fact, such factors would be inaccessible to the conscious activity of a man of action." [17] The so-called Leninist-Stalinist philosophy is thus reduced to the realization of a political and social program; consequently, not philosophy as such (which is denied at the outset as idle-talk or bourgeois rhetoric), but science, morality, every human activity, the whole man, "the complete man" of Marx are identified with this program. On the one hand, the Leninist-Stalinist dialectic deprives the synthesis of almost all its importance so that the importance can be given in its entirety to the thesis-antithesis conflict, which is carried to the point of suppressing the thesis, that is, the bourgeois class (no longer a "passage" as in Hegel, no longer a dialectical and theological "surpassing," but only a negation); on the other hand—having identified man with his social nature, the moment of knowledge with the transforming action by a technically organized labor, and the task of all mankind with the realization of a political and social program—the Party shall be the whole "truth" of the "new man"; and, at the same time, it shall be a violent imposition, a dictatorship, and an unquestionable control by its leaders over philosophy and science (and also over the individual's thoughts, feelings, and sighs), which are reduced to instruments serving the activity of the Party itself.

Even morality and art must be "engaged" in this class-struggle and contribute to the destruction of the middle or capitalist class; art, for instance, must exalt the heroic efforts of the proletariat in its struggle

[17] Cf. G. Semerari, "Sul materialismo dialettico sovietico," *Riv. Intern. di Filosofia del Diritto,* IV (1952).

toward the said destruction and the concomitant construction of the new, socialist world. "Socialist realism" requires that everything be at the service of this class-struggle, and that a Marxist philosophy be built along with a morality and an aesthetic also being Marxist and, with it, even a Leninist-Stalinist physiology, mathematics, and cosmology. In the Soviet Encyclopedia one reads that until now mathematics has had an "unquestionable class-character" and that "it is necessary to fight mercilessly against the middle-class cosmology" of Galileo and Newton or of Einstein. The only thing not serving this class-struggle is religion, which instead must be suppressed as a collection of superstitions, errors, and lies condemned by science through which alone we know everything. Born of man's fear before the forces of nature (a fear ending once the technical-scientific progress totally and irresistibly dominates these forces), religion has been a means to keep the proletarian classes enslaved and asleep in the hope for a better life after death. But by now religion is no longer needed by humanity which has progressed; the latter can transform bourgeois philosophy, science, morality and art, can also make religious superstitions disappear, and can cause their place to be taken by scientific truths and by unfailing happiness in this new society of labor.

Such a gross simplicity and such an acritical naïveté are beyond any possibility of being discussed critically. Yet, it must not be forgotten that sovietism posits some problems that must be taken into serious consideration and that, in any case, today it is a conception of life which must be dealt with even outside of the political and military domain. However, the Soviet conception of life can be properly dealt with only by a conception of life that is authentically spiritualistic and by a philosophy not resting on immanentism. Immanentist positions (historicism or naturalism, existentialism or neopositivism) have nothing to say against sovietism since they are bound to be either assimilated ("converted") or destroyed on account of the many essential points they have in common with it. Leninist-Stalinist Marxism denies religion, but it posits itself as the true and sole religion. Thus it has become a monstrous idolatry (the "deification of the party-leaders") and a fanaticism perhaps without precedent. However, it is exactly in this absolute lack of criticism that its strength lies; and being an offspring of the same immanentist philosophy, the anticommunist, skeptical, disheartened, and academic West —be it existentialist or neopositivistic—has nothing to oppose to it except its egoism, its decadence, Byzantinism, materialism, and scientificalism lacking the merit of being efficacious even on practical grounds.

Imposed by force, the Leninist-Stalinist ideology, rather than being critically elaborated, is repeated and divulged by the rigidly controlled Marxist philosophers so-called, and their task is confined to the acceptance and apology of it. Hence the lack of critical value even in the German, French, and Italian philosophical literature of Marxist stamp. We shall indeed overlook it outside of some allusions.

"Western" Marxists have been formed in a cultural climate quite different from the Russian one—the "Western" environment being one in which the word culture has had a humanistic and critical meaning for centuries. Hence their uneasiness (often leading them to heresy) and their effort to acclimatize Russian Marxism. In reality, they go back to other traditions, for instance to Cartesian mechanism, to La Mettrie and Holbach, or to Enlightenment, and so forth. Their efforts at adaptation to historicism or their attempts to give a critical evaluation of contemporary philosophical currents, such as idealism and existentialism, would have greater interest if the preconceived Marxist scheme and the doctrinal presuppositions did not deform the historical perspective making quite questionable their critical evaluations. We have already mentioned Lukács, and now we cite the names of the Frenchmen L. Lefebvre and A. Cornu, who use the Marxist theses as rigid canons through which they interpret every cultural movement and philosophical thought as such, arbitrarily generalizing principles which are valid only in the area of economic and social phenomena and even here only within certain limits. The so-called new rationalism in French Marxism is still that of Lenin (even if more learned and more acute); in fact, as Cornu writes, this is an effort toward achieving "an always greater rationalization of concrete reality and of human life through action." Even for the French, the Marxist scheme is absolutely valid: art, philosophy, morality—every cultural movement—are only the transference of an economic phenomenon onto an ideological level. Thus, for instance (still according to Cornu), existentialism transfers to the ideological level "the bankruptcy of the bourgeoisie, by now incapable of leading in a rational way the forces of production due to the increasing worsening of the internal contradictions which disconnect the capitalistic system and prevent it from functioning within the framework of free production and free exchange that once were characteristic of it." The preceding evaluation is identical with that of Lukács, which we have already discussed.

Although influenced by Lefebvre, Cornu, and Lukács, the most recent Italian Marxism draws its inspiration from Croce's interpretation (which, as is known, reduces historical materialism to a historiographical canon and particularly to a methodology of politics) and from Gentile's (who sees an implied idealism in Marx's *Glossae*). There is also the influence of Labriola whose interpretation is taken up again by Mondolfo, who brings into evidence the humanistic aspect in Marx's philosophy. This explains why this most recent Italian Marxism emphasizes—better than its French counterpart does—more man's action on environment than environment's

action on man, and why it attributes less importance to economic determinism so as to present itself as social humanism and historicism with a
stress on its being more an open problem and a method than a closed
system and an absolute knowledge. In short, Marx is interpreted along
the lines of idealism and historicism, and he is being elaborated again
through themes pertinent to existentialist philosophy and currents of
scientific methodology, such as neopositivism. This is not a dogmatic
Marx but a critical, antimetaphysical, and detheologized Marx, one who
makes man, the subject of philosophy, a problematical and historical
entity. The importance of Marx's anthropology is emphasized (and this
is detrimental to his theory of economic development) together with his
criticism against Hegelian theologism. Obviously, this Italian Marxism
does not fully account for the fact that Marx makes philosophy an absolute; that is, he converts it into politics or "nonphilosophy" in which true
philosophy is nullified.[18] For Hegel metaphysical reason is supreme as
scientific reason is for Marx; yet, precisely on this account Marx represents, on the other hand, a remarkable moment in that process of self-
dissolution which modern, rationalistic, and immanent thought has experienced—a thought that converts itself into a materialistic humanism
denying and exhausting man within historical situations. Of the Italian
Marxists we shall briefly mention only Gramsci and Banfi.[19]

ANTONIO GRAMSCI'S thought became known with the publication of his *Quaderni del Carcere* (Turin, 1948) and his *Lettere dal
Carcere* (Turin, 1947) and thus his influence is very recent. Undoubtedly,
he holds a conspicuous place among the interpreters of Marxism. Although he calls Lenin "the great theorist on the philosophy of *praxis*,"
his Western mentality trained by historicism possesses a critical sensibility
lacking in the Russian revolutionist and more so in orthodox Leninists,
to say nothing of the Party's propagandists. For Gramsci, Marxism is
concrete, historical consciousness, absolute historicism and philosophy of
praxis quite different from metaphysical, traditional materialism. Historical materialism furthers the philosophy of immanence, "freeing it
from all its metaphysical apparatus and bringing it onto the level of
history" (*Il materialismo storico e la filosofia di B. Croce*, Turin, 1948).
In fact, as total historicism, Marxism is critical awareness of the present,
historical consciousness and not a system or a scientific truth. Hence, with
an antiscientific attitude Gramsci states: "To install science at the basis of
life, to make science the conception of the world *par excellence*—one
that clears the eyes of every illusion and places man before reality as

---

[18] Cf. A. Del Noce, "La 'non filosofia' di Marx e il comunismo come realtà
politica," *Atti del Congresso internazionale di Roma*, Vol. I (Milan, 1948).
[19] For complete, critical information cf. N. Matteucci, "La cultura italiana e il
marxismo dal 1945 al 1951," *Riv. di filos.*, I (1953).

reality is—all this means to fall back on the concept that the philosophy of *praxis* needs philosophical supports from the outside. But in reality even science is a superstructure and an ideology." He is far from the naive optimism of a science "which will create a Utopia on this earth," as if "through increasingly more perfect mechanisms and without the intervention of human labor, the forces of nature" could "plentifully" give "all that society needs in order to satisfy its wants and in order to live comfortably." This criticism against science reveals the fact that, basically, the Marxism of Gramsci rests on historicism and idealism. Leninist realism advocating an objective reality that is reflected and photographed by thought is thus rejected. To know is not to reflect the rational structure of nature in motion and to adapt thought to it; it is, instead, a historical "creation." Therefore, neither science nor common sense (on which Lenin builds his naive realism) can be asked to give proof of the objectivity of the external world. It is "an error," says Gramsci explicitly, "to ask science as such to prove the objectivity of the real since this objectivity is a conception of the world, a philosophy, and it cannot be a scientific datum." Scientific "objectivity is that reality ascertained by all men; it is independent of every standpoint that is particular or belonging to a group. Ultimately, however, even this is a particular conception of the world, and thus an ideology." Precisely on account of its absolute historicism, Marxism cannot be subordinated either "to a materialistic (popular) theory, or to the idealistic one."

Consequently, Gramsci assumes a critical position with respect to Croce's historicism, which is still "metaphysical" and the "restorer" of bourgeois culture. Thus even Croce must be "purged" of his transcendental and theological residua through Marxism, which is true historicism and true humanism. "Regarding Croce's philosophical conception, it is necessary to perform the same reduction made with respect to the Hegelian conception by the first theorists of the philosophy of *praxis*. This is the only historically productive way to bring about an adequate revival in the philosophy of *praxis;* because of the necessities of practical, immediate life, this conception has been "popularized" and it must now be elevated to the height needed for the fulfillment of the more complex tasks proposed by the struggle at this stage; that is, it must be so elevated as to represent the creation of a new and total culture. . . ." Thus Gramsci arrives "at the equality or equation between philosophy and politics, thought and action"; in this way the only "real" philosopher is (and it could not be otherwise) the "political" philosopher. Consequently, "the theorization and realization of the hegemony carried out by Ilyich (Lenin) has been a great metaphysical event." In this way, philosophy is denied, in a Marxist way, in the "nonphilosophy," in the political action or action by the Party, which fatally leads to fanaticism, "superstition," and "infatuation" of politics. Gramsci replaces scientificalism with politics and everything becomes the latter's tool. This proves how it is impossible to salvage and justify man within a Marxist conception, even in Gramsci's conception otherwise so characterized by idealistic motifs.

ANTONIO BANFI (1887-1957)—a professor at the University of Milan—developed his "critical rationalism" (*La Filosofia e la vita spirituale*, Milan, 1922; *I principi della teoria della ragione*, Milan, 1926) in a sense even more decisively dependent on historicism and to the point of making it agree (so he states) with his recent Marxism.

For Banfi the philosophical exigency as a universal value is autonomous. Such autonomy is noticed when the world of experience appears to us not as a dogmatic certainty but as a "problematicity," into which philosophy endeavors to probe deeply. "Problematicity" is for Banfi the discovery of an ideal relationship between data, wherein their reciprocal indifference is resolved. Philosophical problematicity is both "the full and free certitude of thought in itself and the absolute and unavoidable incertitude of the world posited as objective reality." To know is precisely to be conscious of incertitude as ideal and the ideal position of this incertitude is the very act of philosophical thought, "an ideal position of thought before or, better still, on the inside of every datum." In its ideal form, knowledge appears to us as the positing of thought as absolute and universal incertitude of the "datum," whatever the sphere in which the datum is given and whatever the activity in which it finds its dogmatic foundation. "If reality is to be totally assumed by thought in an ideal form, no dogmatic foundation, no definitive sense, no absolute must or can have any *value* for this reason; every absolute, as well as every "immediate," is, at its being affirmed, simultaneously rejected by the thought itself, which is irreducibly problematical in the form of knowledge." At the very outset Banfi was confronted by two essential problems: the problem of systematic knowledge and that of the organism of culture. Systematic knowledge appeared to him as an "open problematicity": "Knowing is, in this way, problematicity itself which is absolutely unsolvable, since here the separation of data is not outside the resolving activity but lies in the resolving activity itself; in short, this is problematicity in its typical and universal form." The very particularity in the points of view pushes thought toward a universal systematization. "In the presence of the infinite richness of knowledge, of its forms and its directions, and of the intricacy and development of these forms we are to grasp the basic, theoretical lines characterizing such organism and its life, without pretending to prescribe for it any essential form or to assign to its many directions either a relationship or a fixed method" ("Per un razionalismo critico," in *Filosofi italiani contemporanei*, Corno, 1944). With respect to "critical rationalism," ontology, theory of being, and so forth, are "mythologies destined to exemplify reality in an edifying way rather than to explain and illuminate it." For this reason, Banfi was never interested in the problem of the "why" but only in that of the "how." Speculative concepts were used by him "in a *meta*-logical sense—as instruments of rational research rather than in an ontological sense as objective forms of reality itself" (*La mia prospettiva filosofica*, Milan, 1950). Thus philosophy is not "absolute knowedge in the sense of a knowledge of rationally absolute contents. This is the metaphysical illusion for which reason pays with the contamination of its exigencies through particular contents or exigencies, with the succession of dogmatic systems superseding one another paradoxically and, finally, in our times with the denial of its own self in a metaphysics of the irrational. Philosophy is absolute knowledge in so far as it is a critical consciousness of the rational foundation of knowing, principle of its freedom and of its dialectical organicism. For this same reason philosophy is consciousness, not of an absolute reality hiding itself beyond or beneath experience but of the gathering of experience according to structural laws and lines of organic and dynamic unity—laws revealing a manifold and living reality, which is never given but always gives itself with an admirable richness of harmonies and contrasts. Thus critical rationalism, which we already identified with dialectical realism, reveals itself as leading toward a philosophy of life." For a philosophy of culture, then, it is not so important to indicate the absolute forms of validity pertinent to each of its fields as a judgment-criterion, as it is to indicate the conception of these laws regarded as a system of relations in the numerous fields and as a structural, dynamic, and living unity of culture.

For Banfi, in conclusion, philosophy is systematization of the data of experience in the widest sense of the word; it is also dissolution of the dogmaticalness of the datum within critical thinking; in other words, philosophy is a "togetherness of problems" which eliminate every dogmatic foundation lying in the immediate datum, as well as every definitive or metaphysical affirmation. A perennial and always open systematization of the particular moments characterizing historical experience, thought is concretely open to numerous points of view and to manifold perspectives and directions. Philosophy, in the last analysis, is a critique of historical knowledge and it coincides with the history of culture.

According to Banfi, during the Resistance-period "Marxist-Leninist doctrine filled with its historical humanism and its realistic-dialectical consciousness the space which critical rationalism had cleared of every mythical-metaphysical structure and of every edifying dogmatism, and which it had predisposed, with its problematicalness, toward the active universality of this solution."

From this moment on, Banfi is filled with "enthusiasm for the victory of the October-Revolution and for the development of the Soviet Union."

Such new enthusiasm obviously places Banfi in a tight spot; on the one hand, he endeavors to present his acceptance of Marxism as a logical consequence of his critical rationalism—and to a certain extent it is possible to derive from Banfi's problematicalness a Marxism understood as a "truth drawn from historical knowledge" which "always exists in and knows itself through history, but as one which frees itself from the domain of the past in a sphere of self-consciousness which is freedom from the present and an omen of the future" (*L'uomo copernicano*, Milan, 1950); on the other hand, wishing to remain loyal to Leninist-Stalinist Marxism, he must attenuate his interpretation of Marxism itself as having a sense that is absolutely historical and problematical. And so the "coinciding of a critical rationalism with a dialectical realism," as "the truest and most universal result of contemporary thought," is very problematical. Banfi knows very well that the "historicist" and critical interpretation of Marxism, such as it took place in Italy, was and is possible only through the influence of Croce's and Gentile's idealism; he also knows that the Leninist-Stalinist interpretation is another thing. Yet, "orthodoxy" obliges him to employ the same style used in the political propaganda of the party; in fact, he writes that idealism is an archaic form of philosophy serving the ruling class (perhaps even in the service of Vatican obscurantism), which "the flood of history" will sweep away "as useless rubbish."

Between pragmatism (of the Dewey type), naturalism, and neopositivism on the one hand and Marxism on the other, there is an undeniable relationship (that between Marxism and existentialism has already been considered); after all, this affinity has been pointed out even by some students of idealism and historicism, who are in sympathy with the Marxist philosophy of *praxis*. All these currents proclaim themselves to be antimetaphysical and opposed to philosophy understood as "theoreticity" or a moment of "comprehension"; and for this reason they turn to science which is a means for transforming nature and also a practical criterion of truth, and which is such only if engaged with and historically resolved into *praxis*. Implicitly or explicitly, all said currents ultimately are materialistic, even if their materialism differs from the classical one and presents itself as dialectical and critical. Even if not unified, they are all characterized by their antimetaphysical spirit, their scientificalism (which may be in accordance with the new conceptions of science), pragmatism and materialism.

For the so-called logical instrumentalism or instrumental logic of Dewey, ideas and doctrines are tools of action which transforms experience and the human condition. "Reflective knowledge is instrumental in mastering an abnormal situation," as it also is "a means to enrich the immediate significance of previous experiences." Hence the social character of Dewey's "humanistic naturalism," which is a neoempiricism according to which, as we saw, thought is the product of biological evolution and has a social finality consisting in achieving a collaboration and communication among men. Thought arises from vital needs and its function is to quench them; its end is essentially "instrumental," that is, to change and resolve real "situations," not individual situations but *social* ones. Being reduced to an "instrument of labor" and to its practical function of changing and resolving situations, logic and its truths obviously become as changeable as the situations, and their validity is limited to this or that situation (no matter whether the latter is individual or social). "Logic is an evolutional discipline. Reason is nothing but logic resting on the analysis of the best methods of research (considered such in relation to their results in the continuative investigation) existing at a given moment. As the methods of the sciences are perfected, corresponding mutations take place in logic. A change of great importance has taken place in logical theory since classical logic formulated the methods of science existing at the time. This happened as a consequence of the development in mathematics or in physics. . . . When, in the future, research methods are changed once more, logical theory will change also. . . . The idea that logic can be formulated once and for all is only an *idolum theatri*" (*Logic, op. cit.*). Dewey's distinction between "instrumental" and "operative" is also to be pointed out: "As a general term 'instrumental' signifies the relation in the *means-results*, as a fundamental category for the interpretation of logical forms; 'operative,' instead, expresses the conditions thanks to which matter (1) is rendered appropriate to serve as a means, and (2) effectively functions as a means in the act of carrying out the objective transformation, which represents the end of the inquiry."

In spite of the opposition between "democracy" and "dictatorship," the coincidence of Dewey's instrumentalism with Marxism is evident (a Marxism, indeed, which does not dogmatize science as absolute truth, but which accepts historicity and does not dogmatize itself in a materialistic metaphysics, though remaining materialistic). However, the communists have violently reacted against this *approchement;* they denounced Dewey's "bourgeois" subjectivism, which denies the reality of matter in becoming, and Dewey's "reactionary" enlightenment, which prevents him from totally transmuting human nature into social nature.

The same considerations can be repeated apropos of neopositivism, whose relationship with Marxism is even more evident in certain aspects. In fact, even neopositivism presents itself as critical and concrete materialism rejecting "in principle, every metaphysical interpretation of nature"; even for neopositivism, vital philosophy (not the one which is an archeological relic) is identified with the logic of the sciences, and the only truth is the scientific truth. Yet, the communists have energetically reacted even against this *approchement*.

All this has an explanation which seems to us evident. Within Western culture there are two forms of Marxism: one represented by sympathizers or even by Marxists, who are unable to give up the critical habit which is characteristic of the West; they try to free Marxism from its dogmatism and insert it within a historicism which does not permit matter in motion to be given a reality independent of man; they also try both to consider man as a pure product of material becoming and to accept science as objective truth and absolute knowledge. The other form is represented by Leninist-Stalinist Marxists; in their loyalty to Soviet Marxism, the latter consider all these attempts as concessions to Western philosophy and as regurgitations coming from the bourgeois world, which is skeptical, decayed, and bound to disappear. All this proves how ineffective and naive are the attempts at "Westernizing" Marxism, which (rightly from its own point of view) defends its dogmatism, lest it be involved in the same dissolution-process characterizing immanentism. Certainly, the skeptical and nihilistic conclusions held by Western thought are more critical than those held by dogmatic Marxism; they also represent the coherence of immanentism; but, precisely on this account, Russian-type Marxism fights them vigorously, because it knows very well that without a faith there is no effective action and the world cannot be dominated. A doctrine identifying philosophy with politics (of which science and technology, both transforming the world, are the most effective instrument) and making the latter the sole truth cannot afford to be "problematical"; and it cannot accept the "conventionalism" of scientific laws, nor can it be only a "historiographical" method. It is superfluous to object that this is "dogmatism" or even "reactionism"; their answer would be that outside of this dogmatism there is only the skepticism of the moribund bourgeoisie and the true reaction, which is the enemy of proletarian progress.

Outside of this polemic between squabbling relatives, there remains their substantial affinity and even their very identity. Apropos of Alexandrov's "excommunication," Zolanov condemned every concession, even a veiled one, to Western philosophy, and he proclaimed the total elimination of philosophy by now absorbed by science. "Physicalists" and "language-logicians" do not speak differently, whether they are Marxists according to Russian orthodoxy or not. Philosophy has nothing to rejoice about; the same barbarism bringing the same dogmatic presuppositions —though with the pretense of a most radical antidogmatism—is advancing from the West and from the East on Europe; the latter, in the meantime, engages in subtle discussions and "Byzantinizes" around a decadent immanentism, which by now is incapable of any speculative vigor as it is occupied in its sophistications on nothingness and in its flirtation with death. By now metaphysical immanentism is truly a philosophy of the past. Otherwise, it is a philosophy of the present, either as academic and decadent Scholasticism or, else, as heavy scientificalism and materialism with a discouraging simplicity, such as that shown by neopositivism, or with an acritical naiveté, such as that shown by Soviet Marxism; the latter, with Lenin, "consciously sets at the basis of knowledge the naive conviction of humanity." All the great human (philosophical) problems are left aside as being meaningless and unimportant to a physicalist or Marxist man; the latter's destiny is to be decided by science which, as an instrument of politics, will produce a monstrous society without spirit, morality, art, or religion. At present, nothing is philosophically so poor and so worthless as neopositivistic and Marxist scientificalism.

IX

NEO-SCHOLASTIC THOUGHT

1. NEO-THOMISTIC CURRENTS

A. General Considerations and Principal Orientations

It suffices only to compare the thought produced by Catholics in the
half century between 1860 and the beginning of the First World War
with that produced in the last forty years in order to become aware of
its powerful reawakening. There is, today, a living and operating Catholic "culture" occupying the forefront, though remaining within the
furrow of tradition—a culture that is actual and experienced, critically
exacting, and keenly sensitive to the problems of the modern and contemporary world. Certainly, the half century preceding this generation
had its Catholic thinkers, writers, and scholars, even some of great re-
nown. However, that period was dominated by so-called secular culture
according to which a Catholic must, by definition, be a repeater of old
doctrines surpassed by science. A Catholic was considered constitutionally
"dogmatic" and thus unfit for "free research" and critical thought; his
superstitious, religious beliefs prevented him from understanding things
according to reason. Indeed, in order to pay homage to freedom of
criticism, "secularism" has always made this intransigent and contemptu-
ous dogmatism stand out; and this was done not in the name of intelligence (which, in this case, "secularism" does not possess) but in the
name of the superstition of philosophy or of science, or, undoubtedly,
in that of reason which, in this way, renounces the very freedom of
criticism it tries to affirm.

From this point of view, in the presence of the new crude and un-cultivated dogmatisms (like the scientificalism and naturalism of neo-positivists, naturalists, and Marxists), it can be stated, without fear of being justifiably confuted, that at the present time the only thought that is rational and a free and critical seeking of truth is the thinking of Catholics. It can be objected that today's tendency is characterized by its antidogmatism going beyond agnosticism and as far as relativism and the most negative skepticism. We hold that even such an attitude is extremely dogmatic, though this dogmatism is the opposite of that of the rationalism of the eighteenth and nineteenth centuries; in one case we have a "reason explaining everything" and in the other a "reason explaining nothing" and standing—like a man hanging from a rope—suspended before a problem, an insurmountable doubt or some conventional proposi-tions; in both cases we have acritical, nonrational, and equally dogmatic modes of conceiving reason. In the past, Catholic philosophers were accused of being dogmatic only because they were not pure rationalists and because they did not worship philosophical or scientific reason; today, once more they are charged with dogmatism, only because they are not skeptical or because they sustain—not on the basis of faith but with the most exacting, rational weapons—that man is capable of truth and that the philosophical point of view is not the scientific or economic one, but the metaphysical, that is, not a particular or partial point of view, but a universal and comprehensive one, capable of giving an organic and integral conception of reality. According to contemporary secular-ism Catholic philosophers are dogmatic and "reactionary" for the follow-ing reasons, which are all without philosophical foundation: (1) they still admit a rational order of truths universally valid, that is, because they are not skeptical and refuse to accept as categorical principles some methodological hypotheses of science; (2) they still insist on building a metaphysics, that is, because they are not dogmatically antimetaphysical, and this amounts to saying that they are at fault because they do not accept an arbitrary and primitive, materialistic metaphysics; (3) they still distinguish philosophical from scientific knowledge and uphold the auton-omy of the theoretical or comprehensive moment, that is, because they are not grossly "scientistic" and integrally pragmatists; they are at fault because they critically defend the very existence of philosophy and refuse to take part in the pseudo-funerals celebrated for the good or bad soul of philosophy by different currents; yet, the officiants do not perceive that the corpse in the casket is not philosophy but the dogma of absolute immanentism together with its absolute historicisms and humanisms; in short, officiants and casket-bearers are not aware of the fact that they are celebrating their own funeral; (4) they still insist on demonstrating the existence of a God-creator and on saying that there are moral and natural laws; they also insist that man is a person and that he is such in that he is a spirit and expresses spiritual values, that is, because they attribute a nonempirical meaning to the words justice, freedom, and virtue and because they refuse to reduce thought to a brain-function, and spiritual values to words devoid of meaning or to superstructures within the economic structure—namely, they are accused because for them the words *man* and *human* have a meaning that is not biological, and man himself, in the wholeness of his being and fullness of his problems, is the primary object of philosophy; the latter, therefore, must give an integral and global answer and not one that, being partial and particular, is arbitrarily generalized afterwards.

However, although certain intransigencies of secular culture still make it difficult to have a fruitful dialogue, Catholics are presently conducting their own concerning the most lively exigencies of modern and contemporary thought. The following, in our opinion, is the most significant event of the last thirty years: the fact that the culture expressed by Catholics has come out of its isolationism, that is to say, from seminaries and pontifical institutions where secular thought had succeeded in confining and exiling it away from the world of militant thought; its condition of inferiority was felt deeply even by those talented Catholics who were playing an important role in the world of living culture. The passage from this isolationist attitude—the two worlds ignored each other and were mutually indifferent except for excommunicating each other—to a position of constructive criticism and understanding marks the beginning of the awakening and formation of a true culture on the part of Catholics. Certainly, this is a traditional philosophy but in the sense of a renewed tradition being lived through with a new sensibility; in this way, though not dressed according to fashion, this philosophy becomes pertinent to the present time and is "actual" in terms of that perennial actuality characterizing truth; the latter, precisely because of its perenniality, is capable of renovating things while renovating itself; it can open up new perspectives confirming and enriching it at the same time so that while being an "ancient" philosophy, it is always "original" and true in the "present," which is also its "past" and will be its "future." In this sense, one can speak of a true rebirth of the culture and philosophy of Catholics, which can no longer be ignored because it is not the *quantité négligéable* of the end of the last century and because, as we said, it is one of the dimensions to be dealt with in today's cultural and philosophical world. And this treatment must be given according to the rules of fair play, that is, not by dogmatically proclaiming that this philosophy is dogmatical but by discussing it in the light of most objective and exacting criticism. At present, we are confronted with a confusion of languages, a destruction of the nineteenth-century idols created by immanent historicism, and with "scientistic" and materialistic determinism; in short, modern thought is undergoing its own dissolution and, in its incapacity to renew its own immanentism, it sometimes accepts as truth its own dissolution and the disintegration of being as well as that of all values; other times, with a lack of criticism, it proposes again scientistic and materialistic conceptions already surpassed by the same dissolutive process affecting the presuppositions on which those conceptions are founded. In the presence of all that and undoubtedly favored by this crisis (favored, that is, only in a psychological sense due to the fact that the ground has been cleared of the many prejudices—*idola theatri*—produced by dogmatism in science or in philosophy), the thought of Catholics undertakes philosophical problems with a philosophical method, that is, the problem of the whole man and that of philosophy as a whole are regarded as the ultimate intelligibility of reality and as metaphysics; being understood in this sense, the latter is the solely concrete and universally valid truth, not a closed system but one that is always open to the new inquiry into the infinity of truth; thus, as a constantly and rigorously critical system, metaphysics rejects the double abstraction and the twofold dogmatism of a (scientific or philosophical) reason explaining "everything" and of a scientificalism "enclosing itself" in a total uncertitude that makes no sense.

Naturally, this open attitude toward the exigencies and sensibility of the modern world implies some risk unless the problem is adequately and critically examined. Moreover, having an open mind does not mean counting the "concessions" that can be made (a method to be avoided because it is political and pragmatical rather than philosophical and critical); nor does it mean accepting, as "philosophers," the opponents' positions that lead to the same conclusions as our own to which we, as Christians, can then add faith from the outside; and, least of all, does it mean trying to meet the opponents' antithetical positions "half-way," so as to allow our own positions to be assimilated for the sake of a "Christian collectivism," a "Christian Marxism," or a "philosophy without metaphysics" (as if metaphysics were a question of "choice" or a personal "exigency" or even a question of "mysticism" rather than an intellective and philosophical truth). These and other similarly equivocal solutions proposed by superficial (and thus intemperate) thinkers reveal a lack of awareness concerning the true problem, as well as a confusion between reason and faith, philosophy and religion. Such thinkers also give credit to the opponents' charge that Catholics either produce a dogmatic philosophy founded on the truths of faith or they arrive at the same conclusions as the others if they really produce philosophy—the only difference being that of religious faith which, in this case however, is their own personal characteristic; the latter is of no interest either to philosophy or to science. Evidently, the problem is quite a different one; the breach ("crisis") effected by modern thought (beginning with Luther) between man and God (and this is the true problem) is a fact, so that either there is God denying man (antihumanistic theologism) or man denying God (absolute humanism)—that is, either God without man or man without God. Now, because of this, the problem is to recover the unity of man by regaining that metaphysical point of view wherein man is given the profound intelligibility of his integrality: a goal to be attained through reason, not through faith. Furthermore, while utilizing the most exacting and exhaustive criticism, it must be proven that in its dialectical, concrete, and real movement, the very "nature" of man contains all the elements which prove the existence of a theoretical order of truths; this order regulates both thought and action since it constitutes the very humanity and value in man; that is, it constitutes the person and gives foundation to the reasons for the existence of God. The truth of faith is the completion of this objective order critically discovered and founded; faith is so because once more it shows the convenience, concordance, and convergence (not external, but "vital" and "living" convergence) of the two distinct and immeasurable, though not separate or superposed, orders.

The culture of Catholics today is not only a voice that is present and alive in all European countries (except those countries where it is being violently suffocated) and in the Americas, but it is also a culture engaged in the discussion and solution of problems of philosophy and science, namely, moral, social, political, and aesthetical problems; moreover, it is a voice aimed at renewing tradition itself within orthodoxy (there being but a few exceptions and intemperances). We shall deal only with the activity of the philosophers, while regretfully passing over in silence (except for some brief mention) that of eminent writers, theologians, sociologists, psychologists, and others.

Within the lines of scholastic tradition, this rebirth of philosophy developed, earlier than anywhere else, in France and Belgium with first-rate representatives and repercussions in all countries. The most important centers are the *Institut Supérieur de Philosophie* at the University of Louvain founded by CARDINAL D. MERCIER (1851-1926) and the *Institut Catholique* of Paris. Particularly in France the currents of Christian-Catholic thought present, even within one single movement, some diversities that are irreducible to a common denominator; the same thing can be said of Italy where, however, the different currents have since 1945 found a point of fruitful contact and of intense activity in the annual Convention of Christian Philosophers held at Gallarate, as is attested by the twelve volumes of the *Proceedings* published so far. However, the oldest and most active center in Italy is still the *Università Cattolica del Sacro Cuore* of Milan, which was founded by Father Agostino Gemelli, not to mention the centuries-old Roman institutions like the Gregorian University run by the Jesuit Fathers and the *Angelicum* run by the Dominicans, and so forth. The most important center in Switzerland is still the *Albertinum* at Fribourg. During the last fifteen years or thereabout, Spain has its irradiation-center in the *Instituto Luis Vives de Filosofía* of the "Consejo Superior de Investigaciones Científicas" in Madrid, which has been added to the already existing centers run by Jesuits and Dominicans. The first affirmations of Catholic thought have also been noted in Portugal, a country until recently dominated by secular thought particularly of French and German importation. Even in traditionally Protestant countries, either there are recently formed philosophical centers (in Holland for instance) or there is some interest in scholastic thought (England). Very active Catholic centers for philosophical studies have risen in the United States and in Canada; the centers in the South American countries are well informed about the European movement. The revival-movement is vigorous in Germany, where it had begun after the First World War not only as an intellectual movement but also as one of renovation in religious life. Besides the names of Przywara and Wust, whom we have already discussed, we may add those of Adam, Guardini, Martin Grabmann (1875-1949), a renowned historian of mediaeval philosophy, of Lippert, Dessauer, Hildebrand, and others. Nor is the activity by the Jesuits of Pullach to be forgotten.

For ROMANO GUARDINI (1885) there is no Christianity without Christ, who is the incarnate God (*The Humanity of Christ*, trans. R. Walls, New York, 1964; *The Lord*, trans. E. C. Briefs, Chicago, 1954; *Das Wesen des Christentums*, Würzburg, 1949). Although independent of each other, these three works form a *corpus*, and they transcribe a continuous and unitary meditation on the life of Jesus, as this is presented in the New Testament; consequently, from the whole of hints and fragments, the unity of Christ stands out irresistibly, as "a whole of an ultrapowerful being, irreducible into history and the purely human." It is, in short, the divinity of Jesus which imposes itself, of Christ the God-Man, as He was experienced by the first witnesses, by the apostles and, above all, by St. Paul for whom Jesus is "more a power in act, a creative energy, an enlightening light, an irradiating and proving life than a physical figure at which one can stare, or a visage to be contemplated."

And Christ Himself is, for Guardini, the "essence" of Christianity; this essence is not an abstract determination, but it is the concrete Person, the incarnate God. This is a thesis that is opposite of the one held by Harnack which reduces Christ to human dimension and builds a Christianity without the divinity of Christ, and this amounts to saying without Christ. Guardini instead makes out of it the essential element: to be Christians means not to follow a moral system or an ideology, or to obey an abstract principle, but it means to place ourselves "under the

Lordship of a concrete person." The choice of Christ "is not of an ethical nature alone, but it aims at the person of Jesus and signifies the personal gift one makes of himself, and love. . . . There is no abstract determination of such essence. There is no doctrine, no structure of moral values, no religious attitude or order of life which can be separated from the person of Jesus, and of which one can say that they represent the essence of Christianity. Jesus Himself is Christianity—that by means of which men receive, and the relationship which through His means man is able to establish with God. A doctrinal concept is Christian in that it comes from His mouth. Existence is Christian in that its motion is determined by Him. He must be compresent in everything that is to be Christian.

In His historical unicity and in His eternal glory, the person of Jesus Christ is, *per se*, the category which determines the being, action, and theory of what is Christian. This is a paradox. Every sphere of being contains certain fundamental determinations which characterize it in its particularity and distinguish it from the remaining ones. As soon as thought tries to embrace theoretically such a sphere, it abstracts from there these fundamental determinations, and so it obtains the presuppositions for all possible assertions related to the objects of that sphere. These presuppositions or categories must be general; in our case, instead, the matter is different. Whereas there we are confronted with a general concept, here we have the appearance of a historical person. . . . The same thing is also valid for the moral behavior. Even here there are ultimate norms of rectitude and dutifulness. These norms, *qua* norms, have always a general character. For this reason, they can assume in themselves any situation, and they receive from action their concrete application. On the other hand, Christian action is confronted with the historical person of Christ in lieu of a general norm."

At this point, the sense of the incarnate, of the existential and, I would say, of the personalistic achieves the maximum of interiority together with the "dialectical" sense which belongs to Christianity in that Christ is the insertion of the divine into the human. This dialectical character is always present, after all, in Guardini's writings with a twofold meaning: as immanent in the spiritual life of the Christian, who is conditioned by his finitude and, at the same time, attracted by God transcending him though innerly present in him as an operating and stimulating force; and as a twofold attraction which almost divides the heart of man into two opposite directions, one toward God so far as to despise the world, and the other toward the world so far as to disdain God—so to use one famous expression of St. Augustine's. The first dialectical moment is a moment of *tension*, the other of *contrast*: the living and experienced drama of the Christian is to compose the contrast in order to regain the integrality of life by maintaining the tension. Obviously, the contrast between the kingdom of man and the kingdom of God has become more acute in the modern world than it has in the Middle Ages and, consequently, the Christian man's drama is more lively and complex in the Christian of today.

For KARL ADAM (1876), an apologist and a theologian (*The Christ of Faith*, trans. J. Crick, New York, 1957; *The Spirit of Catholicism*, trans. J. McCann, New York, 1952), the whole of man is engaged in religion.

There are three ways of faith: sentiment, reason, and grace. The function of sentiment in religious knowledge is not directive but contemplative, "hence in a constant and close dependence on the preceding judgment of the intellect." The sentiment must rest on a rational basis in order to draw near the spirits in a durable way. However, sentiment is indispensable: "it enters into the fact presented by reason in its deepest strata, releases from it the intimate life, the blazing warmth, and thus it establishes an intimate meeting in which the profoundest fibers of our being become open—a personal union between object and subject, known and knower." But, besides sentiment and reason, we need grace, that is, that God gratuitously reveal Himself.

Before Him, when His word reaches us, this is the sole attitude that becomes us: to believe in Him, to abandon ourselves with confidence in Him. "The revelation of God on the one hand, our faith on the other—this is the only road on which Christ can meet us." There is collaboration between nature and grace: "It is certain that the sound reason of man, which endeavors with its natural resources following a rigorously scientific method, is able to deduct by itself certain and sure conclusions on Jesus and His work and to elevate to evidence the credibility of His person and affirmations regarding it, provided that reason itself is excited and inflamed with a religious feeling. And it is also certain that his conscience, due to this evident vision, is immediately called upon to decide in favor of Christ . . . to a complete conversion and renovation of the inner man. On the other hand, however, it is also certain that man, oppressed by the consequences of original sin—man subject to bad concupiscence—is in need of the vivifying force of grace in order to be able to free himself from his earthly bonds . . . and in order to be able to achieve that independence of vision allowing him to decide freely in favor of Christ and His kingdom. . . ." (G. Ceriani, *Orientamenti teologici del Novecento*, Milan, 1938, pp. 56-57). The experience of Christ has found a passionate expression in two contemporary French writers, among many others: FRANÇOIS MAURIAC (1885) and PAUL CLAUDEL (1862-1955). Mauriac (*Life of Jesus*, trans. J. Kernan, New York, 1937) draws Christ through the path of love; Christ satisfies the inquietude of our heart and senses. "If I did not believe in the word of a certain man born under Augustus and crucified under Tiberius, if the whole Church rested on a dream or on a lie (the same thing to my eyes), its dogmas, hierarchy, discipline, and liturgy would lose for me every value and also every beauty: its beauty is the splendor of truth. If Jesus were not the Christ, I would feel nothing but an immense emptiness in the cathedrals." Christ is the heart of human hearts, the source of every love satisfying every love, and the concrete love which lives in us. "The Christ living in the Church, living in the saints, and in each of us is the authentication of the Christ of history. . . . He is the knowledge of the river which distracted me from every inquietude related to its source; He is the great tree spread and crowded with birds, which made me consider the little grain of mustard with simple eyes." To the visage of Christ the King, of the triumphant Messiah, Mauriac prefers "the humble tortured figure which the pilgrims of Rembrandt recognized upon breaking the bread in the inn of Emmaus: our brother covered with wounds, our God." What persuaded him to write the life of Jesus is "the need to find, to touch somehow the living and suffering Man whose place remains empty in the midst of people—the incarnate *Verbum*, namely, a being of flesh, of a flesh similar to our own." Christ is Christianity. And yet, "how many efforts to obscure the divinity of Christ, to conceal this unsustainable visage, to cast down the Christian fact, to wipe out its contours under the crisscross little rulers of erudition and of doubt! Broken to pieces, the Gospel became a pile of incoherent and suspicious materials, where the amateur went to look for the elements of a construction so pretentious as ephemeral."

Paul Claudel is the poet of Christ, of the Mystical Body. He finds in Christianity the Christ eternal through the centuries, the mystical unity of all souls, the "new and holy reality"—to live in the Church where all are present and living, where everyone lives the life of Christ. God who made Himself man died and returned to life: "It is not the signal of the Angelus, but that of Communion, that is, of the participation of the soul in the incarnation, passion, and death of Christ." The universe is a poetical art, says Claudel in his book bearing the same title, that is, a process of continuous creation. The pretense of science to reduce the universe to clearness and to force it into the laws of mechanics is then unfounded. Claudel, who wrote this at the time of the philosophical polemic against science, criticizes the concepts of causality and time as they are conceived by the physical sciences.

Due to the theme of our work, these few hints at theologians and writers who confine themselves to the figure of Christ should suffice to give the reader at least some information on the theological and religious orientations. (For a more detailed treatment of this topic see M. F. Sciacca, *Il problema di Dio e della religione nella filosofia attuale*, Brescia, Morcelliana, 3rd ed., 1953.)

Because of the limited size of this work we cannot take into account all the currents, which are articulated in such a diversified manner as to bear notable differences, though all of them move within the classical distinctions of Augustinianism, Scotism, Suarezianism, and Molinism. We note that Augustinianism (in its widest sense and without special reference to its mediaeval form, particularly Scotism), at present, stands in the forefront among Catholic philosophers, both ecclesiastical and nonecclesiastical, and nourishes the most lively currents. In this respect, it suffices to point out that the German movement we have just mentioned is almost entirely inspired by Augustinianism; the same thing can be said of the "philosophy of spirit" in France and of "Christian spiritualism" in Italy, and so on. This does not mean that these currents are anti-Thomistic because many Thomists (particularly in France and even in Italy) no longer profess a closed and rigidly Aristotelian Thomism. Besides other thinkers whom we shall have occasion to mention later on, we may at this point list J. MARÉCHAL, J. GEYSER, A. SERTILLANGES (1863-1948), and others. Of the most rigid Thomists, we may recall first R. GARRIGOU LAGRANGE (1877)—a pupil of A. GARDEIL (1859-1931)—G. M. MANSER (1866-1949), and the Spanish Dominican J. M. RAMÍREZ (1891). Suarezianism is still very influential in Germany and Spain; besides P. DESCOQS and L. FUETSCHER, we may cite the Spaniards J. HELLÍN, R. CEÑAL, and J. ROIG GIRONELLA (the last two are also very active writers), and others.

B. *Louvain's Neo-Thomism*

The Neo-Scholasticism of Louvain (and, in general, the revival of Thomism) was effectively prompted by Leo XIII's encyclicals (*Aeterni Patris*, 1879; and *Rerum Novarum*, 1891) and eventually realized by Cardinal Mercier, who was joined in his effort by other scholars, among whom we should mention De Wulf—the historian of mediaeval philosophy. The *Cours de Philosophie* by the Louvain professors can be considered the *summa* of their Neo-Thomism. At that time the opponent to be fought against was positivism. As a philosophical position, scientific naturalism was confuted at the same time that the contributions of modern science were given their proper value and utilized within the limits of Thomistic thought; it was not, therefore, an attitude of condemnation but one of constructive criticism. The very position that Mercier with his "criteriology" held with respect to the gnosiological problem is a rethinking of the Thomistic doctrine of knowledge in the light of the solutions which this same problem has had in modern thought from Descartes on.

The new generation of Louvain represents a strong evolution with respect to the previous one: Mercier's Neo-Thomism is modified, thought anew, and criticized in some fundamental points; the new generation's attitude is decisively critical even as regards St. Thomas. Present-day Neo-Thomism—the one interesting us here—is different from the former: its principal exponents are Balthasar, De Raeymaeker,[1] and Van Steenberghen.

The thinkers at Louvain are metaphysicians in the classical meaning of the term and thus their starting point is the *notion of being,* whose knowledge cannot be reduced to a simple abstraction. They speak of an "implicit intuition" of the idea of being, of a "contact," and an "intellectual experience"; however it may be, they admit a fundamental intellectual intuition that is present in all human cognitive activity and on which the abstractive function is engrafted. Outside of being there is nothing as nothing can prescind from it; the idea of being cannot be obtained through abstraction, nor is it possible to abstract from it. It can be said to be "abstract" in the sense that amongst all ideas, the idea of being is the poorest in content; this is the one and most general idea (*explicit* meaning). It, however, has an *implicit* content extensible to all reality, in that nothing (except the unthinkable nothingness) escapes it as it grasps and expresses everything. Inasmuch as it is all-inclusive of reality, it possesses the maximum of richness and concreteness. Every knowledge presupposes the implicit intuition of the idea of being, which transcends and includes all knowledges; Rosmini would say that it is the mother-idea, and John of St. Thomas that "everything is drenched with being." All human knowledge is one; that is, it is knowledge of being, whether it is sensible or intellectual (even the sensible is knowledge of being), or whether it is scientific and philosophical (the former is subordinated to the latter in that every knowledge draws its value and meaning from metaphysics).

The implicit intuition of being lays the foundations for both gnosiology and metaphysics. The analysis of consciousness enables us to discover the unconditioned which conditions everything, that is, the absolute value

---

[1] "In order to have St. Thomas' system revived in the twentieth century, it is necessary to treat it as the Angelic Doctor would if he returned among us. . . . He would omit or he would posit in a different way some questions examined in the thirteenth century; he would study new problems and would take into account all the developments of science, making an appeal to principles not formulated explicitly in his epoch and applying methods of work not as yet practiced in the Middle Ages. In short, he would belong to his time." There is no other way "to bring about a synthesis representing a new and fecund stage of *philosophia perennis.*" De Raeymaeker, *Introduction à la philosophie* 3rd. ed. (1947), pp. 177, 180.

of the affirmation of being. Sensible experience is the necessary condition for every actual knowledge, as it is the one "awakening" knowledge itself; man grasps being in the sensible, *immediately*. Once being as one and many is posited, the very indeterminate idea of being implies the whole concrete reality in its individuality; "formal" object and the "material" object coincide with each other in metaphysics. These are some of the fundamental concepts of recent Neo-Thomism at Louvain; we shall now proceed to examine them briefly as they are expressed by some of that institution's scholars.

NICOLAS BALTHASAR (1882-1959), for about forty years a professor of metaphysics at Louvain, seems to us the most vigorous thinker of the whole group. His metaphysical temper was blended with what I might call an "artistic" disposition, so that more than a systematic philosopher he was one with original intuitions; yet, he was neither fragmentary nor freakish. *La méthode en métaphysique* (Louvain, 1943) and *Mon moi dans l'être* (Louvain, 1946) are two documents of a high speculative level. The "method of metaphysics" gravitates toward what Balthasar calls the "interiority of the transcendental." The human spiritual ego or consciousness holds the first place in metaphysical knowledge; the ego has an immediate and intuitive knowledge of itself; though imperfect, this knowledge is "metaphysical" and through it the ego grasps itself in its value of being. Although independent of the senses, such knowledge is conditioned by sensible experience which effects the passage from "habitual" to "actual" knowledge. In short, in self-consciousness the ego grasps the absolute value of being and its structure. Hence, we have: (1) an *interiority* or metaphysical value of self-consciousness; (2) an *actualism* or awareness of being within the act lived through by consciousness; (3) an *intrinsicness* or proof of being within its intrinsic structure; (4) an *analogism* or grasp of being in its analogical value. "The metaphysician analyzes the ego in its intellectual and spiritual life, that is, his own being in the world and his unlimited capacity for being, knowing, and willing in the world and beyond death, *sub specie aeternitatis*. He perceives the self as being identical with himself and, nonetheless, manifold in its operations; he unceasingly renews himself in this fundamental, personal unity lying at the source of his acts which, undoubtedly, externalize him without, however, suppressing his interiority and the intrinsicness of transcendental values. Through these values and within his own general individuality, he communicates with men in the world, that is, with spirits being, like himself, inserted in matter and having analogy in the value of being, which is essentially common to them and makes them exist. It is not a question of *looking at a spectacle from the outside* but of *living it through from the inside*, because it stands *per se* and not only for others."

His other work is "the application of interiority, intrinsicness, and creational analogism to the value of being." This work was dedicated to Blondel and it is significant that Balthasar notes how there is a "manifest concordance between the method used by us and Blondel's ontological method. It is an interiority-process fully valued within the intrinsicness of analogous being created for the pure Being. *Omnia tendunt assimilari Deo.*" Even the Platonic-Augustinian influence is evident (the fundamental texts always are those of St. Thomas). Just as we grasp our spiritual being as a being emerging from the world, so we grasp God as a creative, pure Being; our intelligence grasps truth not only in consciousness but as it truly is in itself (the mind is capable of truth, says Augustine, and therefore Truth is in itself); what we intuit is not God but the exigency of God. God is not the cause of Himself but His very reason for being; nor is the world an "effect" of God, but His "creature." The *participation-*concept serves as a base in this metaphysics (it has a supremacy over the potency-act theory): "Partaking is taking one's own part of what constitutes a superior unity. Determinable matter partakes of determinate forms; substance partakes of accidents; from another point of view, accidents partake of substance which they multiply secondarily—made accidental, the essence partakes of existence, which is the last act; finally finite beings, *ens commune qua ens,* partake of God." Indeed, we are far away not only from what Balthasar calls "the still too empiristic atmosphere of Mercier's general metaphysics" but also from that closed Thomism which still is bound to the letter and to unilateral interpretations.

Being is the formal object of metaphysics; thus it is from the point of view of being that one has to construct a solid and coherent metaphysics, through which an integral solution to the problem of being will be given. Such an endeavor is pursued by LOUIS DE RAEYMAEKER (1895) in his essay on metaphysical synthesis, *The Philosophy of Being,* trans. E. H. Ziegelmeyer (St. Louis, 1954). A richness of historical references, a systematic rigor, and a clear and linear exposition characterize the writings of this thinker, who has been the director of Louvain's Institute in recent years. The separation between "ontology" and "theodicy" (natural theology) is abolished on the basis of the centrality of the principle of participation: ontology and theodicy constitute ontology undoubtedly (that is, Aristotle's "first philosophy"). De Raeymaeker aims at demonstrating: (1) that true metaphysics is not an abstract science for its great theses spring from the concrete experience of reality; (2) that as man's natural and insuppressible tendency toward "positing himself from the point of view of the *ensemble of things* in order to seek their explanation," metaphysics comes to be ultimately identified with philosophical research true and proper; and thus to eliminate metaphysics amounts to eliminating philosophy; (3) that, once understood and penetrated in its spirit, the Thomistic synthesis has present-day value especially because the concepts of being, essence, existence and so on have been the subject of a most lively discussion by the many existentialist currents.

The object of metaphysics is the fundamental explanation of things in their wholeness; thus metaphysics must rest on a *transcendental idea*, that is, on a knowledge whose content is both "universal and concrete": universal, because being necessarily limited, human experience cannot be extended to the whole of reality, and concrete, in order that the individuality and existence of things may not be neglected and reality may be grasped in the fullness of its richness. The *idea of being* responds to these conditions; that is, it is concrete as regards its content and transcendental as regards its extension. Consequently, general metaphysics cannot consist in a study of abstract essences, that is, in an "essentialism," because "the abstract will never give an account of the concrete." Present-day existentialism is right in reacting against the philosophy of abstract essences, but it is wrong in limiting itself to the concrete alone and to phenomenological descriptions of experienced reality or of human existence. Essentialism neglects concrete existence and encloses itself in the universal essences, while existentialism misses the universal and remains imprisoned in the concrete. The two opposite and erroneous metaphysics can be surpassed by considering the essences not only in themselves (essentialism), but as real, individual, and concrete essences—that is, as *modes of being*, or incomplete and open realities that are relative with respect to what is *beyond* themselves, namely, being. They are not identical with being in that they are concrete modes of being, but precisely on this account they are understood only through being from which they cannot be separated. Thus there is a distinction (imposed by the real data) between value of *being* and *modes* of being. The former is unique and absolute; the latter are manifold and relative. A distinction, not a separation: the modes are meaningless outside of the value, and the value is only manifested through the modes. Moreover, the modes of being are so opposed as to be incommunicable; they subsist in their own being and are autonomous and independent of each other in their action. Thus, as absolute and unique value, *being* comprehends an order of beings which have no consistency outside of the value of absolute being in which all are reunited. The reality of the modes of being is thus *relative* and the modes make up the unique order of beings not as parts within a whole (as in Hegel); every being is subsistent and autonomous (a "whole"); yet, every being *partakes* of the value of being, which is absolute and unique. Every being *is* and it truly is and realizes the value of being in a particular and distinct manner. "The whole of things is not made up of a congealment of 'parts,' but is an aggregate uniting autonomous 'participations.' The ontological order is an *order of participation*." The problem of participation is fundamental in De Raeymaeker's metaphysics, to the point that the metaphysical problem is identified with it; every mode of being is a complete and subsistent being, but one that is opposed to other beings on the same level of being; thus every mode of being is not the whole being, nor is it a part thereof; therefore, it is necessary to conclude that it *partakes* of being. The ontological order is identified with the concept of participation.

If the idea of being signifies the absolute value and every being possesses it in a particular manner by partaking of being, the idea of being can only be *analogical*. Formally signifying the perfection of being, this idea of being involves everything in its content; thus this idea must be attributed to particular beings in a proportional manner, that is, in proportion to their degree of participation in being. "The analogy of the idea of being is an *analogy of proportionality* because the order of being is integrally founded on the participation of subsistent beings in the value of absolute being." Even the analogicalness of the idea of being is thus brought back to the problem of participation and so is the solution to the problem of the one and the many, and the problem of the intelligibility of finite being; inserted in an order of being, finite being can only be understood in relation to other beings. This consideration leads to the conclusion that finite being is not simple but is intrinsically compound and has a *structure*. In fact, the particular being results from the close connection of two real principles, the one pertinent to the mode of being representing the root of individuality and the principle of being representing the root of subsistence. If the two principles could be united in a simple reality, there would be no participation. From the participation in being there is, as a necessary consequence, the becoming of the activity characterizing the finite and participating being which, however, preserves its "substantial identity" through becoming.

On the other hand, no matter how autonomous it may be, since it is so relative the particular being cannot be explained by itself nor can it be the explicative "reason" concerning the order of beings. In other words, the absolute foundation of beings cannot be identified with particular beings from which it is distinct without ceasing to be perfectly real. Thus there is an absolute Being representing the absolute reason for all beings, which are created by Him and depend on Him—the absolute Being is their absolute Cause. Thus "causality is closely tied up again with participation and supplies its ultimate explanation." It is *creation* which solves the problem of participation on the level of being. "This divine cause is thus the beginning of every real order: the *supreme analogué* in the *analogie of being*."

The evolution in the School of Louvain led its representatives to substitute the old *Cours* with a new *Cours de Philosophie*. The *Epistemology*, trans. M. J. Flynn (New York, 1949) and *Ontology*, trans. M. J. Flynn (New York, 1952) by FERDINAND VAN STEENBERGHEN (1905) are a part of this new *Cours* and, although they bear a note of originality, they conform to the character and principles already expounded. Van Steenberghen, too, moves from the scrutiny of consciousness and divides gnosiology into descriptive and critical epistemology; the former is equivalent to descriptive psychology and represents its starting point. "The formal object of epistemology (or gnosiology) is the study of the nature of knowledge," which has to precede the construction of a metaphysics. "On the other hand, to have the critique of knowledge depend upon an ontology previously elaborated amounts to remaining still and hopeless in a vicious circle, since the value of knowledge rests on the results of a science whose premises have not been justified."

In the description of knowledge this author adopts the point of view of phenomenology (knowledge is a relationship between a knowing subject and a known object). "The critical problem is only a problem regarding the value of knowledge, posited in function of the finality manifested in it." The affirmation of being "realizes the ideal of perfect knowledge, the absolute value or ultimate end of my knowledge; it posits a truth that is absolutely evident and absolutely certain. However, this ideal is realized in my consciousness in a very imperfect manner. Hence it follows that the affirmation of being leaves my desire of knowledge partially unsatisfied, even if it offers me a norm through which I am able to appreciate the other elements of my knowledge." The intuitive experience of reality is superficial and limited; the transcendental conception of reality wherein the absolute is grasped gives an abstract and confused representation of the universe; "through it the subject is capable of an affirmation adequately true, perfectly evident, and absolutely certain; yet, this same affirmation is still a confused expression of reality."

Being has a supremacy over knowledge, and, within knowledge, the real order has it over the ideal order. Thus knowledge has a radically idealistic character.[2]

The new Louvain philosophy is not an extrinsic bringing-up-to-date but a true endeavor to satisfy the deepest exigencies in modern and contemporary thought on the basis of a renewed Thomism, or rather on the basis of a Thomism which does not only account for its Aristotelian direction but also for its essentially Platonic component. This is what

---

[2] In his *Ontologie*, of which the principal lines are those already expounded, van Steenberghen reduces the proofs for the existence of God to one: the finite, as such, is essentially and totally dependent on a transcendent Cause. St. Thomas' five ways are simple "approximations" to the proof. Cf. the (highly questionable) criticism which van Steenberghen makes of them in "Le problème philosophique de l'existence de Dieu," *Revue philos. de Louvain*, 1947. For a full treatment of the most recent activity on the part of the thinkers of Louvain, cf. Noël, *Le réalisme immédiat* (1938); A. Michotte, *La perception de la causalité* (1946); F. Renoire, *Eléments de critique des Sciences et de Cosmologie* (1945); J. Leclercq, *Les grandes lignes de la philosophie morale* (1947).

some exponents of "Christian spiritualism" have been maintaining for over a decade in Italy independently of Louvain. This also explains why some theses of the Louvain thinkers recall the thought of Rosmini (who, it seems, is not very well known by them). Indeed, we agree with this new orientation of Thomism but cannot share some viewpoints of the Louvain philosophy, for it seems to us that they are not sufficiently examined and clarified as yet. What they say on being and on the intuition which being itself implies remains obscure and unprecise for us. Also it seems to us that, though profound, the idealistic exigency is not truly substantiated and satisfied by their metaphysics of interiority. Even for this writer, authentic metaphysics (understood as substantiation of Platonic and Aristotelian, Augustinian and Thomistic problems and theses) is only the metaphysics of interiority; yet, precisely this principle, as it appears after Rosmini's ontology and subsequent idealistic probing, must be examined in a different way and grasped in all its metaphysical depth. It seems to us that even the existentialist thesis (which, like the phenomenological one, is present in Louvain philosophy) should be better founded and clarified. There is, however, a fundamental agreement, namely, self-consciousness (man) is the starting point for philosophy and pre-eminence belongs to being; metaphysicalness and criticalness are the essentiality of philosophy.

C. Italian Neo-Thomism and the School of Milan

The Thomistic tradition was defended and preserved by the Jesuits even in the last century. The Aloisianum Philosophical Institute at Gallarate kept, then, the torch of Thomism alive through Fathers Sordi, Cornoldi, and Anselmi. Contemporary Neo-Thomism drew its origin from the said Institute as well as from the Gregorian University in Rome and from *Civiltà Cattolica*, the latter being a magazine of general culture, whose history (from 1850) is identified with the vast portion of Italian Catholic thought and its practical influence on the political and social field. This magazine fought a valid battle against modernism; later it undertook a critical analysis of the main points in Hegelian idealism and in other contemporary philosophical currents, always remaining alert and attentive to all new voices in every field of culture.

FATHER GUIDO MATTIUSSI (1852-1925) belongs to the *Aloisianum* group; his teaching exerted a vast influence even outside of the Society of Jesus. He, in fact, contributed effectively to the establishment of Thomism both in Rome (he also taught at the Gregorian) and in Milan through his private discussions with those who later founded the *Università Cattolica del Sacro Cuore*. FATHER CARLO GIACON (1900) has also made his contribution to Thomism; a very active scholar, he brought St. Thomas' philosophy into contact especially with the experimental sciences and with contemporary speculation. According to him, Neo-Thomism has a "fundamental and essential" task, which is: "To present the central nucleus of Thomism—the best, if nothing more, of the philosophical systems of Scholasticism—in its genuine significance; presenting it to contemporary minds in its best form and in relation to present exigencies, for the purpose of a solution, consistent with Christianity, of the problems of culture and life."

However, the center of contemporary Italian Neo-Thomism has been the Catholic University of Milan, which differs fundamentally from Louvain University. Essentially, it defends an intransigent Thomism that is averse to any concession in the field of metaphysics. This is explicitly stated by FATHER AGOSTINO GEMELLI (1878-1960), who was the organizer and promoter of this school. He wrote: "With the name of Neo-Scholastic philosophy we properly understand the restoration of mediaeval thought within the scope of modern civilization; thus mediaeval thought is not considered as a transitory expression of a civilization but, in substance, as a definitive conquest by human reason in the field of metaphysics, a conquest brought to maturity through Greek speculation and Christianity, and having realism and theism as its fundamental characteristics."

As regards philosophy, the most important men (of those belonging to a later generation we shall speak separately) are FRANCESCO OLGIATI (1886), EMILIO CHIOCCHETTI (1880-1951), and AMATO MASNOVO (1880-1955). We shall mention only Olgiati for he represents the most complete figure in Italian Neo-Scholasticism. He reduces to two the fundamental characteristics differentiating Italian neoschoolmen from Thomists in other countries: a more lively, more comprehensive, and wider sense of historicity, and the most absolute intransigence regarding everything pertinent to St. Thomas' metaphysics. The program of historical inquiry and of philosophical speculation developed by Olgiati in many of his works is synthesized in the words just stated. His first task was to lay down and insert in Italian Neo-Scholasticism (and in this perhaps lies his principal merit) the problem of the relationship between mediaeval philosophy and modern philosophy—namely, What kind of attitude must present-day Scholasticism assume in the face of the development attained by philosophy from Humanism to Descartes, Kant and post-Kantian speculation?

Ancient philosophy is "philosophy of being"; modern philosophy, instead, is a continued and uninterrupted effort to conquer the "subjectivation of reality." Does there exist an irreducible contrast between the two philosophies? If by modern philosophy one understands the exigency of the subject to create reality or the opposite exigency affirming nature as the center of everything, there is no possibility for a reconciliation with ancient and mediaeval philosophy. Olgiati denies precisely this, namely, that ontological reality has been proven to be a false conception. The "truth-value" of modern speculation is not found here and its historical significance lies in something else; while ancient philosophy studies reality above all with the abstractive process, modern philosophy studies it according to the method of concreteness. In other words, ancient philosophy is an elaboration of abstract concepts such as ideas or the universal; modern philosophy, instead, has turned to the individual, to the concrete universal or, as Olgiati states, to *concreteness. Abstraction* and *concreteness* are two diverse but not opposite directions; they are two mutually necessary orientations.

His studies on the history of philosophy led Olgiati to recognize the pre-eminence of an *initial metaphysics* in every system, that is, the pre-eminence of a conception of reality in whose light alone the unification of every system is possible. While antiquity had affirmed the conception of reality "in function of being," modern philosophy has elaborated new concepts of reality. Thus for Olgiati the gnosiological problem is already, and always has been, inspired by an initial conception of the real. It is necessary "to rewrite the history of modern philosophy not from the point of view of gnosiology and that of the critical problem but from the point of view of metaphysics . . . I think that the philosophical battles of the future will be fought on this field: *the true concept of reality.* We must not heed the alluring voices which would have us abandon— *even for a single instant*—the metaphysical concept of *ens.* We cannot and must not *ever* prescind from our metaphysics because there is no other field that is neutral, indifferent, and that does not already imply another metaphysics." With this he does not mean to condemn gnosiology as such "but only that gnosiology which pretends to examine knowledge by prescinding from the value of the concept of *ens* and the principles derived therefrom, that is, a gnosiology aiming at gaining independence from initial metaphysics." With the "historical method" on the one hand, and with the "metaphysical position" on the other, Olgiati aims at realizing the synthesis of ancient and modern, of abstraction and concreteness, which alone can legitimate the Thomism of our times.

A different position from Olgiati's (and, in general, from the Neo-Thomism of the Catholic University of Milan) is represented by GIUSEPPE ZAMBONI'S (1875-1950) pure gnosiology. The most speculative mind in Italian Neo-Thomism, Zamboni is closer to the first Neo-Scholasticism of Louvain; yet, even throughout his studies on Kant and Rosmini, the point of view he elaborates is his own; and this is evidenced particularly in his *Sistemi di gnoseologia e di morale* (Rome, 1930) and *La persona umana* (Verona, 1940).

He distinguishes between *phenomenal reality* and *ontological reality*; in the former we have "l'esserci" but not "l'essere"; in the latter, instead, we have "l'è," "l'esiste," "c'è," "esiste," "even independently of my thinking of it; that is, *existing* contains the "esserci" but adds to it all its *ontological significance*. The pictures in the movies *are there* as pictures, but the screen, the light, and so on, on which the "esserci" of the pictures depends, not only *are there* but also exist really." Those philosophers who deny *being* confuse ontological with phenomenal being. In short, being is "that which is most fundamental and constitutive in the substance and individuality," that is, the *actus essendi* of St. Thomas or that energy (*energia, actus*) by which, as Rosmini says, "being and everything it has within itself, actually exist." The sensible content alone does not, however, present itself either as a substance or as an accident, so that the senses give us the "phenomenal actuality" of the external world and not the "ontological actuality." Thus there is a need for two metaphysics: the "metaphysics of existence" and the "metaphysics of being," which alone coincides with Scholastic metaphysics.

Zamboni does not admit that the concept of ontological being can be, through abstraction, extracted from sensation, from which the concepts of the metaphysics of existence but not those of the metaphysics of being can be drawn. "The real and experimental foundation for the concept of being is to be found" not within sensorial experience but in the "supra-sensitive" experience.

The analysis of popular metaphysics reveals that the center of philosophy is represented by the subject. In fact, the subject possesses the experience of its states, of its very being, and such experience is so intimate that the subject is able to penetrate its inner structure: "In the knowledge of the ego lies the origin of the idea of *ens,* which is the means *a priori* for the knowledge of external bodies." In fact, the ego is "the fundamental reality beyond which one cannot go"; it is "the sole basis of reality for all cognitive, sentimental, and practical functions." The concept of substance is given us "within the consciousness which each of us has of himself as an individual, substantial, intelligent being or person. Thus 'substantialist' metaphysics is founded." We know about the existence of other substances, besides our own ego, "through the consciousness of our modifications which do not come from within ourselves, and through the testimony of other men who inform us that they feel themselves to be substances like any one of us." At first "activity and substantiality are felt in myself; then they are deindividuated (and universalized), and finally invested with the individuality of the phantasm standing opposite me."

More open to non-Thomistic theses, another group of Neo-Thomists endeavors to examine and also to understand the exigencies of modern thought. Not all in this group belong to the School of Milan, either because they are younger or on account of their different intellectual formation (they all belong to the lay world and studied with idealist teachers or have more or less felt the influence of idealism). Almost all the neoschoolmen belonging, let us say, to the first generation are clergymen; thus their Thomistic formation, having taken place in seminaries, antedates their direct encounter with modern (and generally non-Thomistic) thought, which they always see from the outside as something extraneous to them, and which they judge according to the most rigid rule of Thomism. Almost all those belonging to the second generation were, instead, formed in lay universities and by lay teachers; their contact with modern philosophy was direct, while their Thomism is the result of an internal criticism of that philosophy; or else they availed themselves of certain Thomistic theses in order to construct their own point of view, which aims at inserting in the tradition new exigencies and new problems whose solution is sought for in accordance with a renewed Thomism that is not to be regarded only in its Aristotelian aspect. Obviously, in their very formulation such positions involve the risk of appearing equivocal or undecided, and even the risk of a juxtaposition of unreconcilable elements. Notable, nonetheless, is their effort to insert Thomism within the range of modern problems, to bring to light its fecundity, that is, its truth, and also to defend the inalienable rationality of philosophy, its metaphysical essence, and the validity of reason. We should mention the names of U. A. PADOVANI (1894), CARLO MAZZANTINI (1895), NICOLA PETRUZZELLIS (1910), VINCENZO LA VIA (1895), GUSTAVO BONTADINI (1903), MARINO GENTILE (1906), and CARMELO OTTAVIANO (1906). A learned historian of philosophy and a mind open to present-day problems, Mazzantini has elaborated (*Capisaldi filosofici*, Turin, 1945) his own theory on "virtuality" and a theory on "evidence," which is potentially endowed with original developments; Petruzzellis has been engaged in a profound criticism of historicism and of modern idealism from the point of view of classical metaphysics; La Via and Bontadini have developed an internal criticism of idealism and modern thought in general (as did Ottaviano also); Gentile has been able to grasp some aspects of "humanism" understood not as a historical moment but as a theoretical value. We are going to mention, in some detail, two of the most characteristic positions in this new generation of Neo-Thomists.

Considered in its metaphysical and integral sense as a problem of life, the moral problem prevails over any other in Padovani's thought; a pupil of Martinetti, he still feels his influence though it may come by way of Schopenhauer.

For Padovani, philosophy is the *"science of the primary causes necessary to solve the problem of life.* This means that if the solution to the problem of life is the ultimate and most complex end of philosophy, such a solution is highly human and practical and, at the same time, highly speculative and theoretical; the problem of life can only be solved through a system of reality of which life is a part and which life presupposes. And this is true in spite of every practicalism and every ancient or new pragmatism." A metaphysical conception is necessary to life precisely because man cannot not live. "And as regards man, living amounts to choosing, and to choose means to motivate an end, and the numerous ends in empirical actions are necessarily included within an absolute end—however it may be conceived. Inasmuch as this end is absolute, it can only be motivated by an absolute knowledge, that is, by philosophy as metaphysics." The latter "justifies itself integrally with respect to every other valid knowledge, namely, as an integral solution to the problematical character of experience, which is absolutely contradictory, while being (which is enucleated from the very same experience) manifests itself to knowledge as noncontradictory—and thus as rational." The metaphysics accepted by Padovani is the Aristotelian-Thomistic metaphysics: the starting point is pure experience in its mere presentness and immediateness. Now experience *is* and if it is, it is not nothing. Indeed, the existence given by experience is a being tainted with nonbeing; yet, every being, as being, is what is, identical with itself. The principle of identity and thus that of noncontradiction establish rationality, the non-contradictoriness of being and, hence, that of knowledge.

Instead, on the historical, concrete, and existential level, human nature is filled with fractures both in the spiritual order and in the material order; these fractures constitute moral and physical evil. Man cannot prescind from the problem of evil in that he lives it; yet, philosophically, he does not find for it an adequate and definitive solution. And still he must find one; otherwise he will be compelled to admit the irrationality of the human being and to accept pessimism. Thus philosophy alone is unable to solve the problem of life and, more than that, in its presence philosophy acquires consciousness of its own limitations. Hence the two consequences: (1) a necessity for the "ascetical *praxis*" or detachment from the world, in which Padovani sums up Christianity as morality of life, that is, as *praxis* realized by the Saints, "the supermen of the Christian conception of life" (*La filosofia della religione e il problema della vita*, Milan, 1937; reprinted with the title, *Il problema religioso nel pensiero occidentale*, Milan, 1951); and (2) the impossibility of a unitary and total vision of history from a rational and philosophical point of view (*philosophy of history*). "A unitary and universal (but not a scientific and philosophical) vision of history is possible from the theological point of view—which is revealed (*theology of history*)—because as a matter of fact the plan of history is supernatural, as Augustine proved in his *City of God*."

We fail to see how Padovani harmonizes these two points of view: on the one hand, a metaphysics which does not solve the problem of life and, on the other, the problem of life that is solved only by Christian Revelation. It seems to us that the authenticity of Padovani's thought lies in that Augustinian interiority which he made his own together with an essential Thomism; yet, the latter is not as yet sufficiently welded with the former. Padovani himself (*Filosofia e teologia della storia*, Brescia, 1953) remarks that while "keeping critically within the essence and historicity of classical metaphysics, he thinks he must appraise spiritually all of humanism as well as the Augustinian-Pascalian interiority, so inadequately felt by the Aristotelian-Thomistic current."

Bontadini until now has confined himself, on the one hand, to delineating a historical-critical methodology and, on the other, to indicating the "task" for contemporary philosophy, which is that of constructing a Neo-Scholastic (or "neoclassical") philosophy. He himself, however, has not as yet accomplished such a task in the sense of a critical recovery of the essential truth in classical metaphysics. According to Bontadini, the "critical" character so peculiar to modern philosophy has not been "constructive"; instead, through positivism and idealism it has produced—with existentialism, problematicism, neopositivism, and so forth—a state of crisis in the sense of the historicity of philosophy. In other words, like other thinkers (especially Catholics) Bontadini holds that contemporary philosophy is both the outcome and the critique of modern philosophy; moreover, in a certain sense its crisis is salutary in that it has laid bare the mistakes of immanentism and has proposed again the problem of the foundation of metaphysics, that is, the problem of whether it is possible to found the metaphysics of being or classical metaphysics; the latter, according to Bontadini, establishes the very meaning of the word metaphysics, so that it posits itself as a unique metaphysics or as *the* metaphysics and no more.

For Bontadini, then, the task for philosophy is to found the concept of experience on which a metaphysics of experience itself can be built. The unity of experience is the totality of a reality (unified in the form of consciousness) affirming itself on the basis of its simple presence

(*Saggio di una metafisica dell'esperienza*, Milan, 1938; *Dall'attualismo al problematicismo*, Brescia, 1946; *Dal problematicismo alla metafisica*, Milan, 1952).

D. French Neo-Thomism: J. Maritain and E. Gilson

Generally speaking, French Neo-Thomism is not bound to a school nor to those preoccupations and responsibilities from which a Catholic institute or university cannot prescind; thus, in a certain sense, it is more broad-minded (but also intemperate and bold, at times only for the pleasure of being so and because of a fondness for the new). Undoubtedly, the attempts (which we are gradually examining) to "modernize" Thomism have the merit of bringing to light some of its previously neglected or unnoticed aspects; yet, when they are not controlled, these attempts present the danger (which is a sign of their speculative weakness) of accentuating—according to fashion or circumstances—now the "existential" aspect of Thomism and then its "social" aspect or even others; and this is carried to the point that it is hardly possible to see how (and I say this only with respect to some thinkers) such a revision can harmonize with the essential theses of Thomism. In short, more than new syntheses that are original and faithful at the same time, they seem to be punctual revisions in which what is new is either an external addition or what is old is only a cloak serving an alien content. Moreover, the importance attained today by the problem of science and the new epistemological doctrines has caused in some Thomists (particularly French ones) a twofold temptation: (1) they envisage a kind of anteroom to religion in the new science which has departed from the dogmatic mechanism and determinism of the nineteenth century; at any rate, they see in it a vision of the world open to the theistic thesis, without noticing that present-day epistemologies warrant all hypotheses and reduce even principles to hypotheses; (2) they perceive a kind of rebirth of Thomism and of Thomistic logic through the so-called realistic conceptions and through the interest in the studies on logic (even in logistic itself), without sufficiently reflecting that the various "realisms" and diverse "logics" are today the negation of Thomistic realism and of classical logic. In addition, the relativism characterizing modern science and epistemological doctrines as well as the (existentialist and pragmatist) positions which reject any rational mediation or "objectivation" have been accepted in France with a certain ease, so that metaphysics is entirely transferred from the level of reason to that of faith. And thus, especially in France, we have Thomists or scholars belonging to traditionally Thomistic religious orders, who are anti-intellectualistic or against metaphysics, and even skeptical or pure "fideists." In this way neither Thomism nor anything else can be renewed; nor is one a Thomist with or without the "neo"; in this way one is not only anti-Thomistic but one also remains outside of the principles of classical metaphysics, whether Platonic or Aristotelian, Augustinian or Thomistic. We are unable to discuss here all these attempts, which after all do not make any serious contribution to philosophical research; let this critical sketch suffice while we turn our attention to two important personalities.

Among French Neo-Thomists JACQUES MARITAIN (1882) is the most complex and representative personality. His philosophy (especially his political and social thought) has aroused enthusiastic agreement as well as bitter criticisms; his influence is very strong in both the Americas, though less in Europe. Maritain moves within the limits of Thomism whose fundamental theses he accepts; he holds a realistic position (critical realism); his philosophy is a metaphysics of being which in an effort to comprehend all forms of human life elevates itself to the supernatural and to a mystical contemplation through *the degrees of knowledge (Distinguish to Unite*; or *The Degrees of Knowledge,* trans. G. B. Phelan, New York, 1959). "We do not need truths which serve us but only a truth which we may serve. Metaphysics is not a means; it is an end, a fruit, an *honnête et délectable* good, a free man's knowledge, the most free and indeed real knowledge, the entrance to the comforts of the great speculative activity in which intelligence alone can breathe, on the summit of causes." The possession of metaphysical truth is the reconciliation of the spirit with itself. This does not mean that metaphysics is everything or the only knowledge; the latter, instead, has certain hierarchically ordained and convergent degrees, according to Thomistic doctrine, in which the sciences occupy their place; it is necessary to avoid both a narrow scientificalism and a no less narrow philosophism. However, the archetype of philosophy still is metaphysics, which posits problems as they are related to our cognitive faculty and to the means at our disposal. Knowledge is right when it "respects the essences" and recognizes what is formal and true in every order of reality. The "degrees of knowledge" are the roads leading to wisdom. Beyond the possible and the abstract, intelligence tends toward the perfection of existence and also toward bringing back upon existence the affirmations we make on essence. Rational knowledge finds its completion in suprarational knowledge: within the natural order, metaphysics; within the supernatural order, "Christian wisdom," which is subdivided into "theological wisdom *à mode humain*" and "mystical wisdom" inspired by the spirit and proceeding "par voie d'amour fruitif." For Maritain the problem of our epoch consists in "restoring the preeminence of knowledge, the supereminent dignity of a knowledge purely ordained for the possession of truth" and in "reconciling the sciences—now conscious of their value and power—with knowledge and natural knowledge, with the wisdom of a superior order."

This last problem was treated by Maritain in many of his writings, among which his *True Humanism,* trans. M. R. Adamson (New York, 1950) is the most significant. "Humanism" does not signify the exclusion of every superhuman order or the abjuration of every transcendence. We can say, instead, that humanism "tends in its essence to make man more truly human, and to manifest his original greatness by having him participate in everything capable of enriching him within nature and history ('by concentrating the world in man,' as Scheler more or less used to say, and 'by expanding man in the world'); at each proper time humanism demands that man realize the potentialities contained in him, his creative forces, and the life of reason, and that he endeavor to make the forces of the physical world instruments of his freedom. Humanism, thus understood, is inseparable from civilization and culture, once these two words are taken as synonyms." Nor are humanistic epochs in opposition to "heroic" periods. The proof for a "heroic humanism" is given by Western humanism, which has religious and "transcendent" sources in its twofold origin and confluence of classical and mediaeval roots. Homer, Sophocles, Socrates, and Vergil are the "fathers of the West"; and, on the other hand, because of the fact that the regime of mediaeval Christianity "was a regime of unity of soul and flesh or one of integral spirituality, it contained in its consecrated form a virtual and implicit humanism." In the Middle Ages, "a communion in the same living faith of one individual with other real and concrete individuals and with the God they loved and the whole of creation made man amid a thousand misfortunes as fruitful in heroism as he was active in the pursuit of knowledge and in the creative arts; and in the purest hearts a mighty love, exalting nature above itself, extended even to things the same fraternal piety. Thus a St. Francis understood that, rather than being exploited by our industry, material nature also demands in some way to be acquainted with our love—I mean to say that in loving things and the being in them man should draw things up to the human level rather than reduce humanity to their measure."

If, however, we observe humanism in its contemporary forms, it appears to us to be removed from any metaphysics of transcendence and, at the same time, to be engaged in defending human dignity, freedom, spiritual values, in a word, the most genuinely Christian heritage. But, sundered from the trunk of transcendence and set in a no longer Christian climate, these values have lost their original character. It is necessary to bring things back to truth, "reintegrating in the plenitude of their original source these hopes for justice and this nostalgia for communion on which the sorrow of the world feeds itself and whose impetus is now misled, thus raising a cultural and temporal force of Christian inspiration capable of acting upon history and of coming to the aid of men." Only in this way can there be hope for a new civilization characterizing itself as "integral humanism" and representing before the eyes of contemporary men "a new Christianity no longer sacred but secular in its forms." This new humanism, which has nothing in common with bourgeois humanism, is all the more human since it does not worship man, but has a real and effective respect for human dignity and recognizes the integral exigencies of the individual. "We see it as directed toward a socio-temporal realization of that evangelical concern for humanity which ought not to exist only in the spiritual order, but which ought to become incarnate so that the ideal of a true brotherhood among men might be attained. It is not to the dynamism or imperialism of a race, of a class, or a nation, that it asks men to sacrifice themselves; it is rather for the sake of a better life for their fellows and for the concrete good of the community of human individuals, so that the humble truth of brotherly love may advance—at the price of a constant and difficult effort and of poverty—within the social order and the structures of common life. In this way such a humanism can make man grow in communion; and in this way only can there be a humanism which is heroic."

The dissolution of mediaeval Christian humanism is a consequence of the Renaissance and the Reformation, which lean toward an anthropocentric "rehabilitation" of the creature. Protestantism is characterized by a "darkly human" sense "of human misery and of sin. The creature speaks only of his nothingness." Calvinism portrays the dialectic and tragedy of Protestant consciousness: man is nothingness, but the predestined one is certain of his salvation, and herein is the antinomy. Moreover, through Molinism (a "mitigated humanistic theology") one arrives at the theology of rationalism or "absolute, humanistic theology" through which human freedom is to be released from its dependence on divine causality. It can be said that Protestant theology is a theology of grace without freedom, while humanistic theology or metaphysics is a theology of freedom without grace. However, both arrive at the affirmation of an anthropocentric humanism that is at variance with theocentric or truly Christian humanism. The latter recognizes "God as the focus of man and implies the Christian conception of grace and of freedom." Now for Maritain, anthropocentric humanism "deserves the name of inhuman humanism," and "its dialectic must be considered as the *tragedy of humanism.*" In the modern and contemporary world this tragedy has three aspects: tragedy of man, of culture, and of God. Nietzsche, in fact, feels the terrible mission of announcing the "death of God."

In today's tormented and bewildered society, Maritain finds that

Christian, integral humanism will have a decisive task, namely, to cure man's conscience of the atheistic humanism of Marxism and communism and to substitute itself for the already surpassed bourgeois humanism. "At this stage in the history of Christian culture, the creature cannot be disregarded and annihilated before God; it cannot be rehabilitated without or against God; its rehabilitation will be *in* God. There is only one way out for the history of the world—the Christian regime. The creature must be truly respected *in* its bond with God since it receives everything from Him; humanism, indeed, but a theocentric humanism implanted there where man has his roots, that is, an integral humanism or a humanism of Incarnation." This should be the new Christianity: "An era of civilization whose animating form is Christian and in correspondence with the historical climate of the age which we are about to enter."

This does not signify a pure return to the mediaeval ideal of society. "Considered in its essence, the mediaeval ideal of a Christian, consecrated society certainly is not bad since it *was proven* to be good. Yet, existentially it corresponds to something already finished. If, by way of paradox, we are allowed to apply the language of metaphysics to the philosophy of history, we may say that this ideal or this programmatic image was truly an *essence*, that is, an intelligible complex capable of existence and requiring existence; yet, in the present time and in relation to concrete existence and *because* of the historical era we are about to enter, such an ideal is only a *being in the mind* known *ad instar entis*, and thus incapable of existing. If St. Thomas had lived at the time of Galileo and Descartes, he would have stripped Christian philosophy of Aristotelian mechanics and astronomy in order to be more faithful to the metaphysical thought of Aristotle. Likewise, concerning the social and cultural order, were he alive today he would free himself of the phantasms and images of the *Sacrum Imperium*, as being a temporal regime no longer consonant with the Christian spirit.

ETIENNE GILSON is a great historian of mediaeval thought (though he occasionally deals with modern thought). His interest is more historical than theoretical. In fact, he is best known for his studies on St. Augustine, St. Thomas, St. Bonaventure, and others. Theoretically, Gilson presents himself as a Thomist and an advocate of realism. However, even his most theoretical work (*L'être et l'essence*, Paris, 1948) is to a great extent a historical research on "being," "essence," and "existence"; its last section, which should have given a new synthesis or solution, seems to us to be its weakest and least original part. Gilson advocates an absolute realism, and every attempt aimed at a critical analysis of the problem of knowledge (such as that made by Picard, Maréchal, or others) is considered by him as a dangerous concession to idealism, the source of many misunderstandings. "The opposition between realism and idealism is absolute; we must, therefore, think consistently and say what we really think and how we think" (*Réalisme thomiste et critique de la connaissance*, Paris, 1947). The knowledge of being is attained through sensorial knowledge and abstraction: accepting realism in its pureness means "remembering that the sensorial perception has the nature and value of a principle of knowledge within the order of existential judgment."

Gilson's fundamental problem is to surpass the abstractness of the two opposed positions: that of "essentialism" which dissolves the metaphysics of being into an aprioristic, logical formalism, and that of "existentialism" which, likewise, dissolves it into an existentiality without objectivity. Thus, the question is not to oppose a "metaphysics of existence" to a "logic of essence" but rather to recover the existential element lying at the source of the metaphysics of being. Unable to justify becoming or existence, idealism, according to Gilson, ends in essentialism or even in pantheism whether it be ancient (Parmenides and Plato), Christian (Augustine and Augustinianism) or modern (Hegel). According to him, only the Aristotelian *ousia* produces the concept of ontological unity between essence and existence (only the concrete individual is real); however, because of his Platonism, Aristotle once more loses it in the essence which is unique and identical with itself. Only St. Thomas makes existence the very act of essence by giving back to being (which intrinsically constitutes the essence) its existentiality. Thus existence is not, as Avicenna thought, *id quod accidit quidditati;* its relationship with existence is not accidental—existence is the act of essence. Here St. Thomas introduces the Christian principle (lacking in Aristotle) of the creative act of God. "For St. Thomas Aquinas, the Creator's *Esse* creates a finite *esse* which, as the act of the essence, constitutes an actually existing being."

Modern thought has lost this metaphysical concept; with Hegel it went back to an "essentialistic" metaphysics (existence is a "logico-categorical" determination of essence); with Kierkegaard's protest, which has been resumed and exasperated by contemporary existentialism, it has destroyed the universality of values as well as objectivity. Now the question is to find again and recover the unity of essence and existence in the *actus essendi* as a primarily metaphysical act, and this in spite of the antinomy between existence and philosophy.

There is no doubt that this is the real problem of metaphysics today (and since it is not only a historical "today" it is actual always), as Gilson posits it with such exactness and clearness. Yet, the solution he offers does not convince us: his theoretical conclusion is inferior to his historical research, which is also debatable. Gilson distinguishes between common or spontaneous consciousness and philosophical consciousness; the former gives us the immediate comprehension of the "judgments of existence," which are not reducible to the purely logical form of the "judgments of predication" and vice versa. "The very fact that there are judgments of existence proves that existence is accessible to thought. In order that such judgments be possible, the intellect must be able to grasp directly what is most deep in being and express it in a formula—the simplest formula that the intellect is capable of and one that in its internal duality reproduces the duality of the very structure of reality. It must be admitted that this fact is amazing and even mysterious, but its mystery is that of knowledge itself and of being expressed by it. To distinguish the judgment of existence thus understood from the judgment of predication is not the discovery of a new mystery; rather it is a deeper penetration into the heart of what philosophy has always probed and sometimes forgotten without being able to suppress it."

E. *Other Neo-Thomistic Positions*

This presentation of contemporary Neo-Thomism would be even more incomplete if we failed to mention other considerable efforts to go back to the sources of Thomism and grasp it in its profoundly Christian inspiration and also as an original synthesis of Platonic, Augustinian, and Aristotelian elements. The aim of these efforts has been to bring Thomism into the heart of contemporary philosophy, as a doctrine that is still able to offer clarifications and solutions. Such was the task undertaken by the Belgian Jesuit, JOSEPH MARÉCHAL (1878-1944); however, he encountered such adverse criticism and obstacles (due not only to his precarious health) that he was unable to complete his most profound work, *Le point de départ de la metaphysique* (Bruges, Paris, 1922-1926).

"Metaphysics is a human science of the absolute. It translates immediately the seizure of our intelligence on the part of the absolute—a seizure in no way constituting a yoke endured from the outside, but rather an internal principle of life." In these words belonging to the first draft (1917) of the work just mentioned, one can identify the whole Maréchal: the dynamism and finality of our intelligence which is led from within to allow itself to be "seized" by the absolute (rather than to seize the absolute as in idealism); that is to say, this is not an external imposition but a natural orientation toward such an end, and it is due to the very dynamism of our intelligence. The latter is an inborn "appetite" for the absolute; knowledge is not a passive reflection but an activity oriented toward the intelligibles, and a tendency to receive them, which means a tendency toward perfect intelligibility. Through its internal movement directed toward the absolute, intelligence (not as intuitive intelligence but as intelligence bent on the intuition of itself and on its fullness) gains its significance within this finality. Inwardness is a characteristic of modern thought and Maréchal seeks to satisfy this exigency.

However, he points out (his writings on modern and contemporary philosophy, particularly on Kant, are remarkable) that the manner in which such an exigency presents itself in modern thought creates not only an opposition to Thomism but also a dissatisfaction within itself; in fact, it is lost within the erroneous solution because it is unrealistic and not in conformity with the nature of the spirit. The solution, he points out, is to be found in the Thomistic gnosiology and metaphysics, whose principal merit and lasting value consist in having constantly rejected any "unjustified wedge" "between life and consciousness, act and thought or, more generally, between act and form." Maréchal felt strongly about the "integration" of all human acts, and this represents another characteristic of his thought: "The form of internal unification respondent to our normal psychological condition is a *strong integration* of all the elements of consciousness—representations, values, sentiments, and tendencies. It can be accomplished through a long and intimate endeavor that is both moral and rational."

In his interpretation of Thomism, the French Jesuit, JOSEPH DE FINANCE shows points of contact with Gilson, Forest and even with Blondel. He demonstrates the originality of Aquinas with respect to Aristotle through his analysis of *Etre et agir dans la philosophie de Saint Thomas* (Paris, 1943). St. Thomas' interpretation of the Stagirite "maintains intact the rigor of those concepts" while "allowing them to express new values," that is, Christian values. However, it is difficult to understand how the Aristotelian concepts can still preserve "all their rigor" in a St. Thomas who modified them profoundly with his introduction of the principle of creation and his overcoming of so many gaps (justification of becoming, of moral action, of the will, and so forth). St. Thomas' metaphysics based on creation is a metaphysics of *esse* and not of essence, of *esse* as *act* "charged with dynamism." The absolute being, which is pure being, undoubtedly is *activity* with which it is identified; the being, which is not pure being (one having limits, that is), is also activity *tending* to add something to being itself. This is the relationship between *être* and *agir*, which De Finance develops in his interpretation of Thomistic metaphysics and qualifies in fact as dynamism. Thus finite being is *tension* toward the infinite Being—to exist is *to be for Being*. Understood in this way, St. Thomas is on the same line not only with St. Augustine but also with the best contemporary thought. Rather than being the "lien" of the universe, action is a "retours" toward God. In the limited being there is a need of "depassement." On the basis of this Thomism of his, De Finance studied, in a compact volume, *Existence et liberté* (Paris, 1955).

De Finance's Neo-Thomism shows a strongly Augustinian influence as does that of REGIS JOLIVET (1891), a professor at Lyons and the author of widely known studies on Kierkegaard and existentialism as well as on St. Augustine. From the latter he borrows the principle according to which the inward experience of truth is antecedent to any other form of knowledge and is like an illuminating light guiding man from within toward God. This does not prevent Jolivet from accepting the fundamental theses of Thomism, of which he avails himself with dialectical ability in order to criticize some positions in contemporary philosophy and to clarify some aspects of Augustinianism. In his most personal and theoretical writing (*Essai sur le problème et les conditions de la sincérité,* Lion, Paris, 1951)—which is to be recommended also for its qualities of style—Jolivet has found the argument suitable for his power of psychological penetration and for his capacity in the analysis of moral life. In the last analysis, sincerity is acknowledgment of truth, adherence to it, and respect for man as a person both in himself and in relation to others, since all are beings sharing the same values. By considering others not as things but as individuals who meet one another within values, communication becomes a communion, and communion, a personal revelation. In this communion to which we are led by sincerity, there is the presence of God, who is the foundation of inwardness; He is in us, but transcends us for He is immeasurably greater than we are.

Whether Spanish Neo-Thomism is expressed by Dominicans (leaving Suarezians aside) or by lay scholars it is less inclined to concessions and more bound to tradition, though some encroachments have been made lately. LEOPOLDO PALACIOS (1916), a professor at Madrid, has focused his attention on the political and social thought of Maritain and on that of the movement which originated with it. He finds points and suggestions of some importance in this French thinker, but he strongly criticizes *El mito de la nueva Cristiandad* (Madrid, 1951). According to Palacios, the sociological and individualistic conception suffers "from a malady which destroys it from within and which was brought about through the modern concern of giving man his rights just because he is a man regardless of his finality in the universal common good, which is God." A Catholic humanism presents itself with a *media tinta crepuscolar.* This movement "shares its name with atheistic humanists and individualists, but then it pretends to share its principles only with Catholics. Led by the strategy of two opposed enemies, it seeks kinship and friendship with both of them, but winds up alienating everybody. If one accuses this movement of being secular, it appeals to its Christianity; if one accuses it of being Christian, it invokes its unholy and secular character. Cowardly by nature, obscure by vocation, and confused by procedure this movement will end up by being the fodder of its enemies."

JUAN ZARAGÜETA (1883), formerly a professor of metaphysics at the University of Madrid, has, since 1947, directed the *Instituto Luis Vives de Filosofía* with the active collaboration of MANUEL MINDÁN. He moves in the climate of Neo-Thomism as expressed by Mercier, of whom he was a pupil at Louvain. A student of sociological, psychological, and pedagogical problems, he has dedicated a good part of his manifold activity to the study of metaphysics, always remaining within the bounds of Thomism even if his attitude is critical and independent (*Introducción general a la filosofía*, Madrid, 1909; *Contribución del lenguaje a la filosofía de los valores*, Madrid, 1920; *El lenguaje y la filosofía*, Madrid, 1946; *Una introducción moderna a la filosofía escolástica*, Granada, 1946). His method can be called a method of convergence or of synthesis of the different points of view: "More than any other system, philosophy offers such a flexibility and variety that it is possible to enter it from different points, as happens with monumental structures furnished with numerous portals giving access to their interior; once on the inside, one finds the visitors proceeding from different entrances with perspectives initially diverse, but then all coinciding in the contemplation of the final whole." Scholasticism "is a living and not a mummified doctrinal organism"; being Neo-Thomists does not mean "reinstalling among us a literal and petrified Thomism" with all the intellectual baggage pertinent to the Middle Ages. The methodological progress of modern thought and the study of the "human compound" represent an asset that should not be neglected. Philosophy is a "constant becoming" and a perpetual dynamism; thus, the everlasting importance of a philosopher makes sense only if we consider his perennial quality "as a historical condition that in every epoch is attached to a nucleus of specific preoccupations constituting its center of gravity; and it is within the duration of this nucleus that the different schools, which have claimed to reflect and even to monopolize philosophical truth, are realized and have gained their peculiar character."

The starting point of philosophy is life or as Zaragüeta specified later, "human, mental life," which he undertook to analyze in a vast work in three volumes, *Filosofía y Vita*, Madrid, 1950-1954 (*La vita mental*, in *op. cit.*, 1950; *Perspectivas y problemas*, in *op. cit.*, 1953; *Soluciones*, in *op. cit.*, 1957). "Only one task, but one that is of capital importance, is incumbent on philosophy" in the presence of life—the *rationalization* of life." This is neither vitalism nor rationalism but a synthesis of life and reason. It is a question of first describing or delineating life in its components, then of explaining and evaluating it, and investigating its foundation and its reason for being—such is the task for the philosopher of life.

The German, FRITZ J. VON RINTELEN (1898) is a professor at the University of Mainz and also a student of mediaeval philosophy. He is a thinker for whom the solution to the crisis troubling contemporary consciousness lies in a new synthesis of "life" and "intellect." His most recent works (*Dämonie des Willens*, Mainz am Rhein, 1947; *Von Dionysos zu Apollon*, Wiesbaden, 1948) reflect, with their pessimism, an existentialist environment and the situation of postwar Germany. Rintelen rightly (even if at times he exaggerates with his negative judgment) identifies the cause of the chaos, of the "demoniac," and the spiritual desert of our times with the loss of Greek and Christian philosophy of being, and also with the prevalence, from the Renaissance on, of a most unrestrained activism. The latter has come to be a pure "demonicity of the will" characterizing the present-day existentialist and decadent climate wherein every objective order and rational limit is denied. An everlasting becoming has been substituted for the order of being; hence the insurmountable pessimism and nihilism, which are here to stay until a metaphysics of being has been restored. Rintelen's affirmation concerning the uselessness of political or economic remedies is true: the evils caused by a metaphysics require the remedy of another metaphysics. It is not a question of choosing between "Dionysus" and "Apollo," "Nature" and "Spirit," *eros* and *logos*, but a question of avoiding a scientific "intellectualism" confining itself (and confining the intellect) to the measurable. Moreover, that "vitalism" which relies on pure instinct and impulse is also to be avoided. Endowed with a remarkable literary culture, Rintelen is more successful in his phenomenological descriptions and criticism than he is in the construction of his new synthesis, which still remains rather generically sketched.

CORNELIO FABRO (1905) occupies a distinguished place in contemporary Neo-Thomism, and this is due to his compact and profound research on *La nozione metafisica di partecipazione secondo S. Tommaso d'Aquino* (Rome, 1952). In it the author (who is also a recognized student of Kierkegaard and existentialism), with his vast knowledge of Thomistic texts and literature, demonstrates the speculative value that participation has in Aquinas. In fact, it can give "a total understanding of life in every direction, according to a progressive harmony of intelligible values without scissions and discontinuity." Fabro has discovered and evaluated new aspects of Thomism, and the problems he has been able to formulate give him the right to be at the center of the most lively discussion today. Even the Louvain School, as we know, gives preeminence to the principle of participation over that of potency and act. Yet, it seems to us that Fabro is the scholar who, better than anybody, has emphasized the metaphysical importance of it; and this is certainly due to his knowledge of modern thought, particularly from Kant on (a knowledge not usually found in Thomists with an ecclesiastical formation), and also to the systematic method with which he examines this problem.

Let us review for a moment the efforts made by these Neo-Thomists: Gilson and De Finance emphasize the existentialist aspect of Thomism as well as its "essentialist" aspect, and they also stress the importance of the *actus essendi;* the School of Louvain, Forest, and Fabro bring to light the great metaphysical importance that the notion of participation has in Thomism. All this enables us to see how advanced the interpretation of St. Thomas is today: the "Aristotelian" St. Thomas of the old Thomism has been superseded by a "Platonic" one, but by a St. Thomas who, while making Aristotle and Plato more veracious, carried out a new synthesis in which, as Fabro writes, the two Greek thinkers "are enabled to live again and complement each other." This simply means "rediscovery" of that nontransitory Platonism, which is essential to authentic Thomism and by which the latter often assumes a position of criticism with respect to Aristotle. Until recently some people used to point to the concept of participation as one of the fundamental points of distinction between Augustinianism and Thomism. At present, however, this principle is emphasized as the one which points out the historical and theoretical originality of Thomism. Thus it follows that St. Thomas' originality really lies with his thorough study of St. Augustine's Platonism which he views through Aristotle, and with which he does not entirely agree. St. Thomas "fully accepts the *causal transcendentalism* as well as the *divine exemplarism* so that it can be generally stated that the metaphysical content of the notion of participation as held by the two Doctors is very much alike. Moreover, this mutual agreement is the topic of many articles in which St. Thomas posits the Augustinian question. For example, in the *De Potentia,* q.III,a.5, St. Augustine is skillfully introduced as a mediator between Plato and Aristotle with respect to the rational solution of the problem of creation; hence, it can be argued that from the outset the Augustinian speculation has exerted a positive influence on what we called the *synthetic assimilation,* which St. Thomas uses as a personal characteristic when he is confronted with other systems from which he draws the elements suitable to his own synthesis."

The participation-notion allows St. Thomas to harmonize abstract thought (universal element) with "real thought" (concrete element). In other words, intellect and sense are the faculties of a unique substance, and this allows the intellect to grasp reality in its mode of being concrete. Furthermore, as Fabro points out, St. Thomas distinguishes between "predicamental participation" (genus, species, and individual) and transcendental participation. The former represents "a true partaking" in a metaphysical sense, that is, in a sense understand as *partialiter habere* which is opposed to an *habere totaliter* and a *totaliter esse* rather than being opposed to a *substantialiter esse.* On the other hand, transcendental participation in Being on the part of beings represents "the ultimate, metaphysical reason concerning the Thomistic position on the real composition of essence and act of being." *Esse* expresses the transcendental and metaphysical totality of which real and finite beings are a participation.

2. NEO-AUGUSTINIAN CURRENTS

A. *Neo-Thomism and Neo-Augustinianism*

The currents we are about to discuss are not opposed to Neo-Thomism (or, at least, to some currents within Neo-Thomism). They only differ from it because they are linked to a tradition which is more markedly Platonic, and because they are represented by thinkers endowed with a different mental formation which leads them to criticize modern thought from "within" rather than from "without." For most of these thinkers, all of whom have a non-Scolastic formation, it is not a question (as is the case with Neo-Thomists with respect to St. Thomas and Thomism) of modernizing St. Augustine and Augustinianism, of showing some of its heretofore ignored aspects, or even of renovating some of its theses formerly understood differently or unilaterally, so as to demonstrate that modern exigencies and modern problems can find valid help for their solution in the Augustinian tradition. Moreover, they need not (as Neo-Thomists have to do when St. Thomas is placed in the midst of present-day problems) point out that in Augustinianism (1) the participation-principle is a fundamental one, and (2) that its metaphysics is based on creationism, or (3) that its starting point is consciousness or inwardness (and hence "intrinsicness") so that there is an "implicit" or "abstractive" intuition of being, and so on; they need not do so because these are the themes which characterize the philosophy of Augustine or that inspired by Augustinianism. In other words, with respect to what Neo-Thomism had been in the last two centuries (and this is one of its merits), it has had to be profoundly renewed in order to keep pace with the development of European thought, while Augustinianism has always moved along with it. The fact is that after the so-called second Scholasticism, for almost three centuries Thomism had shut itself up within rigid schemes, adverse to any productive development and only able to produce some ineffective manuals for the schools. In short, it had drifted away from the movement of ideas. On the other hand, precisely on account of that nucleus of thought which Neo-Thomists now try to discover also in St. Thomas, Augustinianism has always been one of the most effective elements in modern thought from the Renaissance onwards, even with respect to thinkers who are not affected by religious preoccupations. Moreover, Augustinianism represents a well defined current even within modern thought itself; in fact, it suffices to recall the names of Campanella,

Pascal, Malebranche, Vico, Rosmini, Biran, and the Italian and French spiritualism of the nineteenth century. In short, in order to become a living and productive element of present-day thought, Neo-Thomism had to recuperate and restore the elements of Thomism which are fundamentally Augustinian; that is, it had to "Augustinize" itself (I am not saying that it had to "Augustinize" St. Thomas by introducing extraneous or contrasting elements), while Augustinianism has continued its internal development and has moved from within modern thought in such a way that throughout the course of the history of philosophy its "value" has been uninterrupted. Today, Augustinianism has a greater sensibility and a greater spirit of penetration as regards modern thought, of which it is an essential element and a philosophical perspective; it has also a greater ability for a constructive and positive criticism as regards modern problems and their solution, and all this is due not only to the intellectual formation of its thinkers but also to its doctrinal content.

At this point we would like to ask: Could the more openminded Thomists arrive at the new interpretation of St. Thomas without the pressure coming from (Italian and French) new Christian spiritualism? The latter, in fact, has thoroughly analyzed the most metaphysical and more properly speculative aspects of Augustinianism; it has also criticized Aristotle and Aristotelianism pointing out its fundamental cosmologism as well as those elements which are irreconcilable with a spiritualistic and theistic metaphysics. On the other hand, we have to remark that these new studies on Thomism have helped some Christian idealists to define their speculative position better and to come in contact with a new Thomism from which they now have less reason to dissent since the unilateral and intransigent positions of the past have been abandoned. Thus we must recognize that if Neo-Augustinianism has led Neo-Thomism to renew itself and be "Augustinized," the latter has induced some Neo-Augustinians to recuperate some Thomistic theses and develop Augustinianism in its highly metaphysical and speculative aspects; and this was done without indulging either in a tradition which is more mystical than philosophical or in voluntaristic solutions, which may be inclined to satisfy even the exigency of an "edifying philosophy." In short, although each current maintains its own peculiarity and distinction of positions, both of them can meet and find a common ground beyond what is transitory or simply an abstract and artificial opposition. Today, in fact, Neo-Thomism makes room for metaphysical theses which are characteristic of Augustinianism, while Augustinianism is being restored to its theoretical character and its essentially concrete intellectualism. All of this seems to us a *very important achievement and one of the most positive, significant, and productive elements in contemporary thought.*

All this should induce us to render justice also to the Augustinian tradition which, as we said, is so great a part of modern thought, and I specifically refer to that metaphysic-speculative tradition (and not to the other which is based on exigency and voluntarism) from Campanella to Rosmini. Perhaps, many theses presently sustained by Neo-Thomists are already found in Rosmini, who is the first great thinker to have re-newed Thomism along the lines just mentioned, although he is basically inspired by Platonic and Augustinian thought; he is, therefore, a "Neo-Scholastic" in the strictest meaning of the word. It must be noted that the new interpretations of St. Thomas aim—within the scope of Thomism —(1) at satisfying the exigencies of modern thought in opposition to some of its solutions; (2) at surpassing both rationalistic "gnosiologism" from Descartes to Hegel which causes the concrete to die in the abstract, and existentialism which causes the universal and the objective to die in the concrete; (3) at restoring the metaphysical sense of philosophy and the principle of being which has been dissolved in becoming; and (4) at emphasizing and justifying the intellectual intuition of being (as idea) as well as the metaphysical intrinsicness. From what we have just said it appears more evident that Rosmini—through the criticism of rationalism, empiricism and the enlightenment, Kant and idealism—was the first to carry out a great synthesis within the framework of Greek and Christian philosophy. Yet, even at present people continue to ignore him as they dispose of this great thinker simply by classifying him as an "ontologist" and a "pantheist." Even now some people endeavor to identify the origins of Neo-Thomism and the revival of Thomism with the work of the two Jesuit Fathers, Sordi and Cornoldi, of happy and forgotten memory.

It must be borne in mind that since the publication of the *Nuovo Saggio* (Rome, 1830), the Rosminian current represents something con-stant and alive in all Italian thought from the nineteenth century to date. In spite of what is erroneous and non-Rosminian in the interpretations and developments which the philosophy of this Roveretan has ex-perienced, the fact remains that it influenced Italian thought not only up to 1860 but also afterwards, from Spaventa to Gentile and from Varisco to Carabellese; nor is it possible to understand the metaphysical develop-ments in present-day Christian spiritualism without the influence of Rosmini.[3] Rosmini and authentic Rosminian thought are still today the most significant and most speculative part of modern "Neo-Scholasticism"; and they are so because of their influence on thinkers belonging to other (even antithetic) currents and also because of their internal development

[3] Mention is made only of the two large volumes devoted to "metaphysics" in 1947 by the *Giornale di Metafisica* (IV, V) and the *Revue de métaphysique et de morale* (III, IV), as well as the ample discussions which ensued in these same periodicals and in the *Rivista di Filosofiia Neoscolastica*. Cf. also the issue of June 4, 1956, of the *Giorn. di Metafisica*, devoted to the topic "Che cos' è la metafisica."

which has kept pace with both modern thought and the metaphysical nucleus of classic-Christian thought in its twofold (but not divergent) Augustinian and Thomistic orientation. With its most recent developments, Neo-Thomism permits the possibility of bringing the positions of the two currents close together (not by virtue of compromise or by leaving aside the most burning problems); and if this goal is fully attained, Neo-Scholasticism may experience a new epoch in which the richness of its positions will develop to the full extent of its metaphysical vigor. Notwithstanding the philosophically irrelevant noise which scientists from so many schools have made, there is a revived interest in metaphysics today. This is not evidenced only by the Neo-Scholastic currents but also by German existentialism, certain syntheses made by neorealism (Alexander), and neonaturalism (Whitehead), and finally through the debates at philosophical conventions and in periodicals. Of course, all this is not gold since most of it is a purely descriptive phenomenology and a pseudo-metaphysics founded on scientific hypotheses. The fact is that metaphysics becomes nonmetaphysics whenever its problems are ill-posited or relegated to the limbo of what is metaproblematical, existential, and even "mystical."

We believe that after saying all this, the reader will better understand why we have gathered together Neo-Thomistic and Neo-Augustinian movements (to them one must also add some of the thinkers treated in other chapters, Blondel, for example) under the common heading of "Neo-Scholastic currents." In fact, Augustinianism is one of the main currents of mediaeval Scholasticism; together with Thomism, it continues in the late Scholastics and at a certain point it alone represents the Scholastic tradition, effectively and valiantly. Finally, Augustinianism and Thomism coincide in many essential points, and this is as it should be if St. Thomas is understood in his integrality and is not treated simply as a "pure Aristotelian." After all these clarifications let us hope that the reader is not going to be surprised when he finds under the "Neo-Scholastic" label the names of thinkers who seem to be far apart (one should not think only of the unilateral and narrow meaning given to this word "Neo-Scholastic"); let us also hope that the thinkers themselves will not complain for being so "labeled."

B. *Philosophie de l'esprit: General Program*

Philosophie de l'esprit[4] is the title of a well known collection (sixty

[4] R. Le Senne, "Philosophie de l'esprit," in Farber's *L'activité philosophique contemporaire en France et aux Etats-Unis, etudes*, 1st ed., II (Paris, 1950), 113-130. We also avail ourselves, besides the work of Le Senne, of Lavelle's "La filos. dello spirito," gathered in the volume *La filosofia francese tra due guerre*, It. trans. (Brescia, Morcelliana, 1949), pp. 142-149.

volumes have already been published) which was founded by L. Lavelle and R. Le Senne in 1934. It represents a general philosophical orientation more than a current or a school, and yet this does not mean eclecticism. On the contrary, without being rigidly formulated, its programmatic lines are clear and well defined. Its remote inspiration is Cartesian and thus it is enrooted in the French philosophical tradition. From this tradition (that is, from Descartes to Malebranche, Hamelin, and even Bergson), this movement draws two essential affirmations: (1) the *cogito* or "existential" (not "existentialistic") element, in the sense that even in its universality thought is the thought of a subject; and (2) the idea of an infinite and perfect Being. These two points signify, then, man and God in an Augustinian way. Thus, as Lavelle writes, "this philosophy has within itself two central points which unite human personality and universality, whose origin is God and whose realization is the world." [5] One must sacrifice neither the human "pole" to the divine "pole" (Spinoza), for "man without initiative amounts to a mode of substance in which God becomes naturalized"—thus losing God and man both—nor the divine "pole" to the human "pole" (Sartre), for the human initiative becomes irrational and foolish—thus sacrificing man himself.

At the time when this "bicentrical" philosophy began, it felt the threat coming from "the progress of science and technology." In other words, there was a revival of positivism at that time, and this "always ends up by sacrificing the subject to the object in man, whether it presents itself as logical positivism as is the case with the *Wiener Kreis,* or biological positivism as customarily occurs with medical science, or even when its form is sociological positivism. This is a partiality involving "theoretical," "practical," and "spiritual" consequences, which may be so grave as "to not only disregard the transcendence of the spirit with respect to all its manifestations" but also "suppress man's personality because this philosophy considers only the nature from which such personality springs." Scientific progress and discoveries should not make us forget, writes Lavelle, that there are "other works of the spirit such as art, morality, and religion itself, which cannot become science unless we wish to overlook and even destroy their original and irreducible essence. Moreover, a certain distrust is increasingly shown toward the spirit itself, which produces science, but which science misses; and, in spite of the contradiction, the spirit is either easily denied or even made the object of science, in which case things and spirit are the same, for making a science out of the spirit amounts to materializing it." Morality cannot be changed into sci-

[5] "Provided that man is nothing but an objective whole made of laws, it is possible to arrive at a technique of man which permits to determine him and later utilize him with certainty. Positivism had then to favor the establishment of all sorts of techniques, psychological or sociological, so that man may fall under the domain of the scientist" (*ibid.*).

ence without "being reduced to a fact or habit," which science can describe but not regulate. "Science cannot be a substitute for morality, for it in fact may serve crime as much as it does virtue; and the very condition of the world shows that civilization is not measured according to the level reached by science in a given epoch but rather according to the purity of intention in the conscience of individuals or nations." Science and morality "represent two degrees: one seeks to define the concatenation of phenomena and their conditions of possibility, while the other avails itself of that order discovered by science for the purpose of subordinating it to a superior order which allows us not only to know the world but also to will it. Such is the task of the spirit, which continuously rises from phenomenon to being, from cause to reason for being, from what is given to the act giving it, and from the fact that is endured to the value justifying the fact itself. In this way, *Philosophie de l'esprit* attempts a new rapprochement between morality and metaphysics, beyond phenomenalism and scientific relativism, which cannot satisfy our conscience."

In opposition to those pseudo-sciences denying philosophy and man, the philosophy of the spirit—adds Le Senne—"aimed first of all at putting spirit in its proper place; and, obviously, spirit holds the first place" both in the (psychological and empirical) sense of *mind* as well as in the (metaphysical and religious) sense of *spirit*. Thus, this philosophy is linked to absolute idealism but with an emphasis on personality (in opposition to Hegel), as well as with a form of intuitionism which is derived from the teachings of the Cartesian Malebranche." Man's spirit is viewed in relationship to the universal and absolute spirit "in which truth and beauty, good and love find the source of their worth." This *"theocentric relationship* is the axis of the philosophy of the spirit," of the spirit "inasmuch as it is human," *a parte hominis* or on the part of concrete man as he is in the world; and in this sense, it is a "phenomenology," but a phenomenology of a Cartesian and Biranian, rather than Husserlian, origin. However, "whereas phenomenology aims at expanding science, philosophy of the spirit is oriented toward metaphysics which is conceived as the highest mission for philosophy." Thus the unity of spirits is realized through the "converging of all efforts and values in a supreme unity namely, Being, Act, absolute Value, God. It is from Him that the inexhaustible diversity of individual spirits irradiates together with the norms according to which each spirit pursues its determinate value assigned to it by its character, situation, and choice." This is still a philosophy of the spirit "inasmuch as spirit is universal; that is, after considering the spirit as spirit in man" this philosophy considers it "as a superhuman, universal, and absolute Spirit." Metaphysics "pursues two essential ends: it must elevate the human tension toward value, as such, and it must also serve

557

the converging of our efforts toward this or that value while turning them toward the unity of all values. On account of these two ends metaphysics is the highest meditation resting on the courage and peace of the spirit." The philosophy of the spirit ultimately presents itself as a "doctrine of salvation." It is also a philosophy of experience which is not solely confined to objects or things. As Lavelle specifies, it is a spiritual experience, "which is mixed with material experience indeed, but we are never able to isolate the one from the other. This is an experience which shows us the spirit at work, at the moment in which it generates itself and also the sense about things (rather than things themselves) wherein it calls upon other spirits to witness; and all the spirits cooperate unceasingly and become united through those things which, nonetheless, separate them as they separate each spirit from the pure spirit. Such is the experience which this *philosophie de l'esprit* endeavors to examine and promote and by which it pursues, through the domains of Being, that living and omnipresent reality of which materialism acknowledges only the body, that is, the cadaver."

Such are the main themes of the most significant and speculatively most valid current of thought which France possesses. However, precisely because it is a serious philosophy rather than dilettantism, it has not met with great success in the cafés and clubs nor among *reporters*.

Philosophie de l'esprit: Lavelle's Eternal Present

LOUIS LAVELLE (1883-1951) was a professor of philosophy at the Collège de France from 1940 to the end of his life. In the second edition of his work *De l'Etre* (Paris, 1947; 1st ed., Paris, 1928) he defined his spiritualism as a "dialectic of the eternal present." In it, "dialectic" signifies "an experience of participation in which we grasp a living relationship between our own being and the being surpassing us; not as a void beyond which nothing can be done, but as a living presence from which we unceasingly draw and which enriches us." Thus as this is clarified in his *De l'Acte* (Paris, 1937) dialectic means (in a Platonic sense rather than in the Hegelian sense of an overcoming of oppositions) that constant experience which "compels us to posit both the whole and the ego always according to that relationship which unites them." Hence this is a participation of the finite being in the infinite Being or God. The problem of "participation" represents, in fact, the central problem of Lavelle's thought. It can be said that in all his writings, from the first to the last, Lavelle (the greatest French metaphysician of the last thirty years) was principally concerned with a thorough study of the problem of the relationship between finite being and infinite Being. The two concepts of "time" and "freedom" have been profoundly clarified through this study, and the pages devoted to them represent the most original part of this philosopher's thought.

The intimacy of the ego thinking within itself is an intimacy with being. Consciousness is not only oriented toward being but it also recognizes itself in the interiorness of being. The act of consciousness reveals in fact this intimacy: to gain an awareness about the self amounts to drawing this primary and absolute datum through existence or through our making and creating ourselves. This is not a relationship between subject and object but rather an original inserting ourselves into the being which surpasses us. In short, being is within us; between being and us there is an "ontological kinship" which is thoroughly explained by *participation.* This is a Platonic (not a transcendental) idealism and an ontologism in which the Augustinian theme concerning "inwardness" is treated once again, not according to the genuine form used by St. Augustine but rather according to the form used by John Scotus Erigena and Malebranche who, besides Plotinus, Descartes, and Maine de Biran, inspired Lavelle. This also explains his method of philosophizing which is systematic and architectonic. Lavelle proceeds from a central point (the primary fact—constant and common to all men and which philosophy brings into evidence—is our communication with the whole and this is the act through which the human subject as such is constituted), from which everything is obtained, without adding anything from the outside through a discovery of particular acts; that original point is developed from the inside, like a light which irradiates little by little. In this way, Lavelle reveals the whole of himself in each and every page of his works. Yet, he does not repeat himself by moving around and about this central point, because he constantly probes into it more thoroughly, so much so that this luminous center becomes more and more clear as it reveals its intrinsic significance. And, it could not be otherwise since all the determinations are within the Absolute as the Absolute is in them, as that which is most essential, intimate, and profound, though the Absolute in its infinity transcends all of them. Erigena's Neoplatonic theophany is present in Lavelle and it gives his thought a character which is essentially theological and mystical.

His thought has also a moral aspect (*La conscience de soi*, Paris, 1933; *L'erreur de Narcisse*, Paris, 1939; *Evil and Suffering*, trans. B. Murchland, New York, 1963; *La parole et l'écriture*, Paris, 1942; *Les puissances du moi*, Paris, 1948; *Four Saints* [formerly *The Meaning of Holiness*, trans. D. O'Sullivan] Notre Dame, 1963), which is perfectly consistent with the metaphysical nucleus and is characterized by stoic and Spinozian motives besides Christian motives ("an ideal of wisdom finding its culmination in holiness"), as well as by a marked attitude of criticism toward the ethics of dissatisfaction, solitude, and anguish pertinent to decadent and pessimistic individualism. "During an epoch of distress most men are moved only by a philosophy which justifies their longing for the future as well as their rebellion toward a destiny which they are compelled to endure without ever being able to master it." In the last analysis, every pessimism is an evasion from one's own concrete, personal, and moral reality. Shutting one's self "within the lucid unhappiness of a separate existence" as spectators of an illusory world, or being seized by a desperate will to power in order to forget the self in an individual and negative activity amounts to a self-denial and an oblivion of one's own vocation. Contrary to the radical immorality of these tendencies, Lavelle's philosophy is wholly inspired by an ideal of vindication and rescue of the person's value, which cannot be done away with. He wishes to restore to men the "joy" of remaining loyal to themselves and of recognizing their own vocation. It is not a question then of evading and escaping from ourselves but of accepting our own limitations, which can only be overcome within the divine, present in each of us as we all are present (the whole universe is) before each other in the presence of Being. It is useless to swing hopelessly between a "complacent and melancholy" nostalgia about the past and a "hope and fear" about the future. What counts is living in the present with all our strength and fighting against the phantasms of our self-respect. The motif entirely dominating Lavelle's thought is the *in te ipsum redi* and the *transcende et te ipsum*. Man must not escape from himself but rather go back to his own self because God is in him and he is in God. "The dialectic of the eternal present" explains all this as we shall show by delineating its fundamental points.

Within our pure and original experience which perfectly coincides with its object we attain the Being present in us. To the fundamental difficulty, which has always been attributed to ontologism, of never being able to come out of subjectivity and therefore of never being able to grasp anything but a state of consciousness, Lavelle replies that "consciousness is within being and not the other way around." Hence this is an ontological rather than a subjective idealism. "In no way can being be considered as a mode of thought because thought itself must first be defined as a mode of being. Too often thinkers imagine that thought, by positing itself, posits a subjective character to be found in everything that can exist. However, in order to posit itself thought must first posit its own existence, that is, the objectivity of its own subjectivity." Thus, this is not a deduction of being from the ego, as idealism claims, because the genesis of the ego is in being, in which there is also the law according to which the ego partakes of being itself. Moreover, according to Lavelle, the moment of subjectivity is not denied at all in this position. The first aspect in the "experience of the presence" of being is our "inwardness with respect to being," that is to say, "the being whose total presence we have discovered and the being we attribute to ourselves are one and the same being considered under two diverse aspects. We are "within" being and thus the being which envelops us and our own being are one and the same, even if the ego is able to realize being only gradually. "The fundamental experience on the part of a limited being is the experience of its own being and its limits. Yet, thinking of one's own limits means surpassing them infinitely, as this also means apprehending the identity of nature between our own being and the infinite being containing it." The presence of being in us is an original intuition. Consciousness reveals the intimate being of the whole and remains consubstantial with it.

This ontology has a strong moral accent. Ontologically, every part is never detached from the whole and never existent by itself, although our attention or our desire seem to detach it. "Consciousness is not a pure form which is filled by objects, but a full reality *dont la conscience les detaches en la divisant*." Moved by curiosity and a yearning for particular things, men forget (on account of their indifference or "divertissement") the metaphysical experience of being, which is primary and permanent and from which no one can *s'affranchir* since the ego discovers itself included in it. Being then takes its vengeance on man's forgetfulness and "takes away all the flavor possessed by particular things." The experience of presence is "always actual" but very often it is "so confused and involved that it escapes us almost unceasingly." Our duty is then to hold it so that it may become clear to us. Instead, men are usually concerned with filling this presence, so much so that they "are attracted more by the object being present than they are by the presence of this object." "Narcissus' error is consonant with individualism, which believes itself to be self-sustaining; instead, it breaks the communion with the Whole, a communion attained by a participation in it. The person's gravest danger today is "to leave his salvation at the mercy of separation and all the delights derived from self-respect." The person cannot detach himself "from the infinite reality . . . without falling into nothingness." To unite the self beyond one's own individuality, to pursue the same value, and to partake of the same being, all this represents the communication between consciousnesses; and this is therefore possible only "within a profound and secret interiorness, which is common to all and in which each consciousness penetrates through the mediation exerted by the other." This is a Platonism after the manner of Malebranche and it founds the communion of spirits on their participation in God. Lavelle's philosophy is entirely permeated by the principle of "univocity" of being. It seems then that it cannot avoid pantheism, but we shall see later how he defends himself from it.

Lavelle denies that being is "collectivity," that is, the sum-total of all particular beings. Being is, instead, a simple and absolute unity without divisions or determinations; it is the foundation and not the multiplicity of finite elements; it is a positive indeterminateness from which every finite being "clips off" its own world. "Being contains and abolishes all differences." We are dealing here with the most difficult problem of Platonism and ontologism, the problem of the relationship between the one and the many. Lavelle endeavors to solve this relationship in a way that is original, indeed, and also worthy of being examined very attentively. In his *De l'Etre, op. cit.*, he already explains the truly obscure affirmation that Being is both a simple and absolute unity and also the perfect totality of all particulars, thus establishing an analogy with the Kantian theory on space and time. Neither space nor time is the sum-total of all places or instants even if such places and such instants are inscribed in the totality of space and time; but rather "each of them represents a glance cast at the infinity of time and space."

When he considers this same problem once again in his *La Présence totale* (Paris, 1951) and even more thoroughly in his volume *De l'Acte, op. cit.*, Lavelle insists on defining being as *act*, an "operation by which being posits itself eternally" as a pure efficacy, as the supreme source of every determination and of every value, "an act without limitations or, in other words, as pure freedom." Being as an act is not an object nor is it an operation from which we deduce existence by moving from its effects, but we grasp it as we grasp our will, always together with its effects and not only by arguing it from its effects. The experience of Being is "a creative experience by which we assist at and produce the advent of our own self and the world as given to us." "Necessarily" identified with the whole and yet not a collectivity, being "resides in an act which always is about to be completed and to which we are summoned to give our collaboration" (*Traité des Valeurs*, I, Paris, 1951).

This concept of Being as Act and pure freedom enables Lavelle to defend himself from the accusation of pantheism. "It seems to us" he says in the introduction to *La Présence totale* (quoted above) "that we should feel safe from every suspicion of pantheism and that, on the contrary, our doctrine in a certain sense could be considered as the opposite of objective pantheism in which the very ideas of a Whole and of parts are abolished because the law emanating from the Whole necessarily rules over the parts." In fact, although the parts cannot exist either without the Whole or outside of it, they cooperate with the Whole and receive a certain independence, an existence and a power which really belong to them. This is the way things stand, according to Lavelle, since total being is defined as an act without limitations or, with other words, as pure freedom. "Every creation is a communication of the being of Being; that is to say, *He can only create freedoms. . . .*" In his volume *De l'Etre, op. cit.*, he already states that "within the unrestricted generosity of the creative act, it becomes impossible for God to make things benefit from an existence which would be diverse from that He Himself enjoys eternally. There is no existence which is diminished or debased, because the existence of every object is its pureness in the divine act without which it would be nothing."

How does this freedom take place in finite beings? Or, in other words, what is the relationship between finite freedoms and infinite freedom? Lavelle replies with his "dialectic of participation." To begin with, the identification of "Being" and "Act" makes the participation of being possible, even if it had appeared to be denied or unjustifiably posited since being allows no gradation. Instead, "when it is a question of the Act, it is obvious that it stays identical with itself always as it is also obvious that, without being divided, it supplies each individual being with the power needed for its becoming what it is; in fact, the opposite of activity is not nothingness but passivity . . ." Lavelle introduces the concept of *interval* in order to explain this passivity. There is no participation unless the latter creates "a discarding between total act and particular act," in order that the first may inspire and sustain the second and this one may separate itself from the other in such a way that it will be able to fulfill a personal *démarche* and assume a personal initiative. This interval corresponds to Le Senne's *fêlure*, "that kind of ontological defect which would be essential to the very existence of the universe." In other words, this interval is that by which "life for us stays an uninterrupted initiative, an indefinite starting-all-over, an ever new promise, but also an unforeseeable succession of trials which we accept and of gifts which we receive." Absolute interval is the one which separates nothingness from being, but it can be passed through only by God. Our inability to posit nothingness other than as a verbal expression compels us to think of the interval in being itself as an interval between possibility and reality, essence and existence differently passed through by God and us. For God, existence follows essence along a process of eternal circularity, if we may so speak, since God is an essence that through participation changes into existence, continuously. In us instead it is existence which posits our essence. We must, says Lavelle, reverse the classical relationship between essence and existence and consider existence as the means to conquer its essence. "Instead of saying that essence is the possibility of existence, we shall say that the latter is rather the possibility of the essence. Only through the choice of our essence are we able to establish our eternal place within being." And we must choose within an infinity of possible choices—even nonchoosing is a choice. However, the reality of each man, whatever it may be, is inserted in one of these two philosophies, "so that his choice must fall on one of them: either he chooses Protagoras' philosophy according to which man is the measure of everything . . . or he chooses that of Plato, which is also Descartes', according to which God and not man is the measure of all things though He is a God who allows man to participate in Him."

The interval between essence and existence explains the classical opposition between subject and object, which "appears as the simplest expression of the interval that separates the partaken act from pure act." This interval also constitutes our consciousness of time, which is the very reality of time as it expresses the relationship established in us between our passivity and our activity. When we arrive at the perfection of the Act, time ceases not only to be felt but also to exist. "He who carries out his destiny, says Lavelle, and feels equal to the task of being and of life is always filled by the present. Time sweeps away only imperfect and unfinished things such as desire, effort, and sadness, which are unable to subsist and suffice to themselves."

The concept of interval is analogous with the existentialist concept of "fracture"; yet, it must not be confused with the latter because while the existentialistic "fracture" is a radical poverty of existence, the interval is "a lack only in so far as we are concerned; in fact, it expresses precisely that fullness of concrete being always present, always offered to us, and to which we continually reply with an action of our own which alone gives us its immeasurable superabundance."

The notion of interval reveals how freedom can be attained for finite beings. In us, freedom is the power to say yes or no, while God is the power which says only yes. Our freedom is the "power to determine ourselves," a free will which Lavelle defines as a power of option between an activity that can only be spiritual and a passivity that is imposed on us from every side as soon as our activity yields.

From what precedes we can now understand the reasons used by Lavelle to defend himself against the accusation of pantheism. He points to the solution of the problem of the relationship between divine and human freedom as the touchstone for his doctrine. Between finite beings and Being there is not a relationship of static appurtenance but one of dynamic cooperation. The sublime mystery of participation is that by which men are *created creators*. Lavelle remarks that pantheism has failed to understand that the Whole must be conceived as freedom not as a substance.

The Whole or pure Act is a Person precisely because it is freedom. This Act is neither an infinite plurality of persons, nor a relationship between finite persons, and not even a superperson. For Lavelle "the act is a person and the source of every personal existence at the same time," for "it would be paradoxical to give an individual who is able to achieve the universal the character of a person, and then not grant it to the universal itself from which the individual has received that character."

Moreover, the parts are not destroyed within the Whole since "the miracle of participation lies in the fact that, through it, we understand the endless additions it makes to us while no addition whatever is made to the infinite in act from which participation itself attains all that it can make us gain." Participation "never destroys the distance which separates a part from the Whole since it maintains a duality and a communion of all instants between part and Whole."

Participation, freedom, time and eternity are unseparable in this "dialectic of eternal present." In fact, according to Lavelle, for the finite being, time is a means of participation in the Eternal; it is an ever renewed present, the only one to exist in *act*. All the importance and seriousness of every man's life lies in the present, since in it he realizes his vocation and his real participation in Being. It is in the present that past and future acquire their true meaning while at the same time they lose the fallacious sense of depressing nostalgia or of illusory expctation. Every action of ours is limited and imperfect, indeed, but even the most humble one partakes of the eternal act.

The manifold actions which fragmentize the act infinitely carry out the cooperation among men and the cooperation with the eternal Act or God through participation. The problem of freedom is inseparable from that of time, which Lavelle understands in a different way from the classical conception (*Du temps et de l'éternité*, Paris, 1945) in which the future follows the past by which it is continuously generated according to the relation of cause and effect. He reverses the order of time, that is, "if the future is not considered as already realized, that is to say, as past and if it is considered as future, that is to say, as possible, it is evident that it is antecedent to the past because it is always the future which becomes past. Now the future always is what must still be born. It is only a possibility that is going to be realized and its realization makes it fall into the past. An order proceeding from past toward future is the order of realizations already completed rather than an order of realizations still to be completed, that is to say, an order according to which things have been already done rather than an order according to which they are done. Such an order is retrospective rather than prospective. It is an order according to which knowledge develops, which is the opposite of the order according to which action is produced; in other words, this is the order of history by which the order of life is recorded backwards. Being comes out of the nothingness of the future unceasingly, and it goes into the past whereby it is realized. As such, the future is the place of freedom, that is, of an act which starts again always." Considered in itself, the future belongs to time only by realizing itself, that is, by *becoming* past. "Until that time the future is only a temporal possibility; freedom, which realizes it, makes it go into time, and yet freedom does not belong to time.

Freedom is, then, the creator of time, and when we say that it is *first*, we say this in order to show that freedom has no place in time (nothing is first in it) though it makes eternity descend into time. Freedom can do this thanks to the instant in which it acts because its function is twofold since it is the *unmovable point* in which *the conversion of future into past*, that is, *the very genesis of time* takes place, unceasingly." Time is a relationship "between becoming, duration, and eternity—here is the movement which enables freedom to exert itself and which constitutes the three degrees of its exercising itself. It can be said that, without becoming, the act of freedom could not be dissociated from the pure act and that participation itself could not take place. However, becoming spreads freedom, so to speak, and enchains it to circumstances which must supply the matter for freedom's action instead of ruining it. Freedom, in fact, establishes its own independence first through this struggle against becoming; and thus it is necessary that freedom, within the very act of becoming, distinguish between what it lets perish and what it wishes to salvage, for it has found to incarnate itself in it, as it were. Moreover, freedom is threatened even within duration because it tends to become nature. Only in eternity does freedom find a never failing source of activity and renewal. In fact, here freedom is placed beyond all particular circumstances though it must always manifest itself precisely within the latter. Freedom is beyond matter and yet it runs the risk of being converted into nature on account of its everlasting efficacy, although, in its participated form, it is engrafted upon a nature which it modifies and enriches unceasingly. From this it can be seen how the aspects of time are inseparable from each other and how they constitute something like a journey which goes from becoming to eternity."

The sense and value of existence are determined through this dialectic. "In its most intense meaning, existing signifies the performance of a free and pure act which engages us absolutely. To be free means to be detached from being only to consider the self obliged to participate in it, that is, to draw an essence from it through a self-manifestation." During life we experience the personal immortality of our soul (*Sur l'âme humaine*, Paris, 1952) about which no conceptual proof is possible. "If we are immortal, we are not so only after death but also during this life." Death gives our lives importance and seriousness; when there is no tomorrow, everything we have done is an achievement. Death—"and already the thought alone of death makes all the actions of our lives absolute by virtue of the conversion to which they are subjected—transforms them from material and temporal events to spiritual actions of which we avail ourselves always; death finishes and completes things; it elevates the relative to the absolute, takes the tomorrow away from our life while compelling it to flow back toward our past, not in order to give the past a time-privilege over the future but in order to uproot the past itself from time and phenomenon and convert it into a spiritual or eternal present." Immortality is the presence of all our lives as an eternal present. We shall be what we have made ourselves. "Death creates a corporeal absence which reveals a purer presence."

Lavelle's ontological spiritualism can be summed up in this formula: being is being *in* Being and *for* Being, in which everything makes sense and everything is redeemed, spiritualized, and eternalized. This ontologism (in which we see everything in being even if through time and interval) undoubtedly has some Neoplatonic accents (more after the manner of Erigena and Malebranche than Spinoza), but it is characterized by a conception of time and freedom giving it a dialectic which no longer is that of being-substance but rather that of being-freedom. It seems to us, nevertheless, that Lavelle has not succeeded in avoiding pantheism with all the consequences derived therefrom. That the Act transcends the act, that Being is a creator and not a principle of emanation, freedom and not necessity, and so on—all these are antipantheistic affirmations indeed, but they are no more than affirmations in our opinion since, instead of solving the difficulties, they assume them to be already solved. Once the concept of "univocity" of being has been established—being is one and the same both as a creating and a created being—it is possible to sustain the transcendence of being with respect to the world and all its creations, but this is not enough to avoid pantheism as this did not suffice to Erigena and, before Erigena, to Plotinus or, later, to Spinoza. In fact, we find that Lavelle (notwithstanding some undeniable clarifications and attenuations between the time of the first edition of his *De l'Etre* and that of his writings on the "dialectic of eternal present") always engaged in solving the insoluble difficulties of a system, which is pantheistic at the outset though unwilling to be so. Being is freedom, but in the last analysis it must create even if it be on account of its "generosity" and superabundance. It cannot not create, and what has been created is the same Being manifesting itself. Lavelle writes, in fact: "The discovery of the infinite Act on which we depend and without which our finite being could neither posit itself, nor subsist, nor increase itself, compels us to posit the existence of an infinity of finite beings, unless we are to limit its creative power and measure the gifts coming from a limited generosity. . . ." There would be nothing without the creating infinite Act, but the Act *must* create. This almost amounts to saying that the created reality is a continuous process of realization of the creating Act. Lavelle does not go that far but the coherence of the system demands it. In fact, everything is *for* and *in* Being, but Being would not be without this everything. Now, that this is so is also proven by his undeniable ontologism, that is (1) we are in being and this is our experience or original intuition; (2) the ontological proof is not a proof (namely, an argument), but an evidence (yes indeed [we say], if we are in being and being is univocal and also directly intuited); (3) there is no proof of the immortality of our soul, but only an experience, and so forth. One may ask: Is this immortality an immortality of the individual soul? Or is the soul annulled in the Whole once the bodily appearance is lost? There is in Lavelle a strong tendency toward the *cupio dissolvi* beyond every interval, as well as the desire to be drowned in the great sea of Being. For him the world "is only in the instant, always fading away" and it is "nothing if it is not with and for the spirit." "The world and our body occupying its center are only appearances of the true being." Created being is a pure theophany.

Prescinding from these difficulties (and certainly we disagree with him on these fundamental points), Lavelle (like Le Senne) was an authentic philosopher at a time when philosophy was being renounced. He defended it in its theoretical and metaphysical essence, and he made himself a stern advocate of the supremacy of the spirit and thought over matter, and of spiritual values over vitalistic values. He upheld the autonomy of philosophy with respect to science and the metaphysical meditation on being with respect to the description of phenomena. Moreover, Lavelle was a deeply religious soul, and without compromise or uncertitude he always posited and solved the greatest problems of human life in the light of Christian truths. In times of intellectual clumsiness and spiritual deafness, he always reasoned according to the classical line of thought, like an ancient sage, in a French that is classical, clear, and solemn.

Philosophie de l'esprit: Le Senne's Philosophy

RENÉ LE SENNE (1882-1955) is the philosopher of *value* and *character* within the "philosophy of the spirit." From the first edition of his *Introduction à la philosophie*, Paris, 1925 (although recognizing that his immediate source is Hamelin) Le Senne presents his "experimental and psychological" idealism in opposition to that of his master, which is "dialectical and objective." In his *Introduction* of 1925, he is still under the strong influence of positivism, and yet the main traits of his own philosophy can already be perceived. In fact, the concept of value is grasped in the very concreteness of the subject, whose activity existentializes the value itself, which in turn substantializes "existentiality." The formula which can synthesize Le Senne's position is as follows: *being-for-the-values* (which we do not create but witness only), *which are a gift from the supreme and absolute Value.*

In his 1939 *Introduction*, he summed up the "intellectual vicissitudes" gone through by the spirit from common experience to idealism, which, in all its forms based on immanentism, historicism, and abstract dialectic, calls from within to be superseded by a philosophy of values. The latter is still idealism, but an idealism concerned with the transcendence of values, and with the supreme Value, that is, a theistic spiritualism. Science, art, morality, and religion—each of which emphasizes one of the ego's powers and satisfies a particular value—are the fundamental *démarches* through which the subject bears witness to the values and elevates itself to the absolute Spirit, God, Value of values, and perfect Person. It suffices to sound out these values "in order to discover their unique source, that is, the supreme and infinite Value, which all determinate values compel us to call God by revealing His personality to us." Thus the man-God relationship appears to be the central line of human experience. Like any other, this man-God relationship compels us to distinguish and, at its peak, to separate its terms, which at some other time are to be united through a relationship of interiority. Transcendence and immanence find here, correlatively, their logical foundations. If within temporal experience everything is realized through the concurrence of human freedom, then it is up to us to make a good or bad use of it. Naturalizing the value within pantheism through the reduction of the man-God relationship to immanence is easy, but unfair; and the same can be said, when in the opposite direction, we use a radical agnosticism to produce a wedge between God and man as well as a duality between God-without-us and us-without-God. Certainly, on account of His infinity, God escapes us and suffices to Himself. However, "if our good will is responsive and our life is a prayer oriented toward the supreme Value in its unique origin, then, according to our experiences, we are allowed to be more or less closely united, so to speak, to God's grace, which makes our search worthwhile."

For Le Senne, God is then the first Value and the creator of all values. This is an axiological and a metaphysical affirmation at the same time, and it makes Le Senne's axiology not a pure and simple axiology (namely, values are only a guide for and a denomination of human activity) but a *metaphysical axiology* (namely, values are manifested through human activity and have their source and ultimate "why" in an absolute Value). In this way, the estimation of a value is given by a source which transcends all values as well as by an ultimate finality (that is, the absolute Value), which man seeks to attain by carrying out these same values. The presence or gift of values nourishes in man the dynamism of his spiritual impetus toward the absolute Value. Everyone expresses in his own way a value or values which he does not create and, in doing so, he creates his personality on the basis of the *character*, which is a condition for it without being its cause; otherwise the whole of man would be reduced to his character. Thus, Le Senne's metaphysical axiology can also be called a *personal idealism*, which, without giving up its objectivity, is no longer "objective" in a Hamelinian sense. On the other hand, Le Senne's "moralistic" exigency is satisfied through the importance he gives the concrete datum or individual man, in whom he finds not a character in general but "this" character, and so also "this" individuality, and "this" personality. In fact, in the *Traité de moral général* (1st ed., Paris, 1942; 2nd ed., Paris, 1947), before expounding his moral doctrine he delineates ten "moral portraits" (from Buddhism to Bergson), that is, the "Christian man," "stoic man," "utilitarian man," and so forth; and in *La destinée personelle* (Paris, 1951), he exemplifies his schematism on character through his highly successful description of "portraits." Le Senne's essential thought lies in his value-character dialectic and in his metaphysics of value.

Moving from Hamelin, as we said, Le Senne states that "against the former's dialectic one must emphasize the existential aspect of experience." Freedom and responsibility, which come last on Hamelin's table of categories, are instead a condition for the others in Le Senne. Thus, the *primum* from which philosophy has to proceed is not relation but existence; and its task is "to make synthetically an object better than the one actually given, rather than "to make it dialectically." Hamelin's relation, which is valid as a law for the construction of the ego's activity, does not suffice as an explanation of this same activity. In fact, the sufficiency of the aprioristic and deductive thought breaks against the obstacle of this problem. Concrete existence is not only a sense of ideal continuity but also a sense of rupture and limitation, of defect and obstacle. The life of the spirit, in fact, is not only an ascending and univocal dialectic but also an effort, a contradiction, and an adventure on the part of consciousness. Immersed in consciousness, relation becomes a *contradiction* which *must* be resolved. Instead, the dialectical alternative constitutes the essence of experience, which is always surpassed and never concluded because the "rupture" is renewed and the obstacle shifted, continuously. However, our personality is created precisely in this decision to heal the rupture and overcome the obstacle. Freedom is realized in "being-for-the-value."

Once Le Senne has posited the contradiction within experience itself, he cannot refrain from criticizing all "dogmatic" philosophies, from Spinoza's objective dogmatism to the idealistic dogmatism of Hegel and Hamelin as well as the intuitionist one of Bergson. He opposes to them his dialectic of open contradiction and value (*Le devoir*, Paris, 1930) and his "obstacle-value" relation (*Obstacle et Valeur*, Paris, 1934).

No dogmatic system, in fact, can explain morality, since it is unable to understand why the good is not performed by the will, and it cannot understand this because it claims to be able to explain how the will performs the good. Le Senne asks: "Is morality derived from nonbeing?

Then it is inexplicable. Does it have its principle in being, perhaps? But then nothing is achieved. In order that morality be possible, it is necessary that its reason for being be the impossibility of any reason for being. This means to point out the contradiction." In fact, "relation is not the first fact, since no sensible or ideal being can ever be a moving fact for the spirit; what moves it is a contradiction which has been proven and felt. Nor can it be a purified contradiction like that between being and non-being, but one that is most confused and most brutal, that is, one that takes place between two beings, a clash, or even the clash willed by a belligerent." Contradiction is precisely what places us before our personal destiny (*destinée*) and shows us that we are not given this destiny, but rather that we are to create it for ourselves since the responsibility of finding ourselves before ourselves falls upon us. As Kierkegaard would say, contradiction gives us the feeling of "seriousness." However, one is conscious of his insufficiency only because he has an aspiration which forces him to surmount it. Contradiction, which is a limit and obstacle to the ego, permits consciousness to come into being at the same time. In fact, consciousness does not understand itself in a state of perfect harmony since it brightens up only after an impact, and then goes on with the feeling that its own ruptures must be healed though only to see bravely that they reopen once more. Consciousness is a conflict between two theories, a clash provoked by an unforeseen event, a cruel denial inflicted by reality, and a contrast open to infinity, and not an appeasing synthesis or a "leveling" and harmonizing dialectic as it is in Hegel. Yet, it is this sense of crisis that arouses the feeling of duty and the obligation to settle the conflict even temporarily, since contradiction comes again on a higher level under the everlasting impact of a "genetic inconsistency" and a "germinal mutability" on the part of consciousness. Consciousness is spirit, that is, activity and freedom, for contradiction and duty, for the duty to promote unity and harmony in the person, without surrender and discouragement, or any fatalistic resignation in the presence of uncertainty and nothingness. On the contrary, the decision must be firm so as to be able to build and rebuild and make the effort adequate to the obstacle.

Le Senne remarks that the contradiction he is talking about is not logical but psychological. The latter, unlike the former which is suppressed before coming into being, "must have some existence within consciousness if we are able to discuss it. This existence is that of an illusion or, if you wish, of an equivocation, but still an existence which as such is distinguishable from any other." We must recognize the existence, within thought, of what is irrational and incomprehensible, since no enigma would take place in us (and, hence, not even consciousness), and no disorder would ever be harmonized if we had not felt and suffered its real existence. Thus, at the origin of every conquest as at the root of every psychological experience, there is always an experience of contradiction.

The contradiction which forces the spirit into motion is the very root of Descartes' methodic doubt. Or rather, according to Le Senne, the originality of Cartesianism does not lie so much in the supremacy of thought as it lies in doubt, which always inheres in thought and urges it to gain its self-consciousness and also create its own truth, perennially. The worth of the *cogito* lies in the fact that "it has been prompted by an exigency affecting and satisfying the whole soul." Thought is "doubt thinking itself." But doubt is only the intellectual form of contradiction, and it must be felt, experienced, and suffered since suffering is its sensible and dramatic form. Before we experience suffering we do not distinguish ourselves from things, because only the consciousness of suffering delivers us from the automatism of our instinct. Suffering places us before ourselves and breaks the bond which unites us to the universe. An unforeseen failure arouses a conflict between the obstacle and our ideal. "I suffer; therefore, I am." Thought, in fact, lives in suffering, and it is not an abstract and passive contemplation precisely because of the "absence" of thought within thought. How must we behave in the presence of suffering? The answer is that we must accept and make it our own, and also question it and draw from it the means to enrich our deepest being so that it may be converted into a principle of joy. Voluntary suffering is the origin of morality.[6]

Suffering, however, is only the psychological and sensible object of contradiction, which still presents itself as the very condition of knowledge understood as a subject-object relation. Contradiction is manifested in knowledge as a contrast between thinking thought and thought that has already been conceived and established. No established thought is ever adequate to thought. Thought which has already been conceived is *not* yet everything that thought is able to think of. Thus nonbeing is that which prevents experience from stopping before the massiveness of a system or from being exhausted in its determinations or in what "has already been done." The object is an obstacle running through the process of intelligence, but precisely because of this it is also what arouses the activity of the spirit as a spring of life and morality. A philosophy understood as a description of total experience makes one feel "emptiness and solitude, past and future, error and illusion, and what has been lost and destroyed, forgotten and paid for. In short, it makes us feel other things as other things." The error of objectivistic philosophies and the source of their inhuman abstractness lie in the fact that they have not recognized the rupture between subject and object. "Why should reality be defined

[6] L. Lavelle, *Le moi et son destin* (Paris, 1936), p. 123.

in a manner which leaves out precisely what makes us feel every day? One can find refuge in truth and being as well as in illusion and nothingness." In opposition to all philosophies which "detotalize" experience, Le Senne desires a philosophy which consciously and profoundly acknowledges the original bipolarity of experience as a dynamic and suffered synthesis between being and nonbeing, "presence" and "absence," sorrow and joy, contradiction and duty, obstacle and value, and victory and defeat. On the other hand, recognizing "total experience" also means recognizing that the nonbeing of experience does not suppress being and that the irrational does not nullify thought. Thus it is necessary to avoid these two opposing abstractions: the one pertinent to a "dialectic which levels off everything" and is a characteristic of all dogmatic philosophies, which deny obstacle, error, and limit so as to extinguish the life of the spirit and morality; and the other pertinent to a "dialectic of anguish" characteristic of pessimistic and irrationalistic philosophies, which deny the joy of surmounting obstacles, the effort of overcoming errors, and the power of ascending on the part of thought. Both of these dialectics represent an evasion from the concrete reality of experience and from the responsibility of moral life; they do not describe but falsify experience. A conquest would have no importance without obstacle and suffering, in the same way as absence would be meaningless without having a presence beyond itself, at least as a presentiment. Science is limited precisely because contradiction is a law of the spirit. Knowledge rests on the effort to master the object on the part of the subject. On the other hand, it is necessary that this mastery remain always incomplete in order that the subject be able to keep its independence. This does not mean that the object is a "thing in itself" so as to be inaccessible to the spirit. In fact, as regards that which escapes knowledge, the object represents what is known rather vaguely and incompletely so far.

In the presence of a limit, of what is beyond, the subject may react as follows: either it regards such a limit as a means of conquest and enrichment of its spiritual life, or it accepts and succumbs to it as a condition wherein its spirituality is renounced and the subject itself is to be extinguished within the already concluded world of things. There is no experience of a limit without perceiving what stands "before" this limit as well as what stands "beyond" it. On this side of the limit there is determination; on the other side of it there is value. He makes himself a person who longs after this value and achieves it through a struggle; if instead he succumbs to the other alternative, he repudiates himself and becomes a thing among things. As the value, which is beyond the limit, is a "nothingness of determinations" or a "nonbeing," so determination, which is on this side of the limit, is a "nothingness of value." Experience carries within itself a presence of nonbeing, suffering, and defeat, that is, a presence which is an "absence" of being and completeness, and, for this same reason, a condition for the very progress of life. "Absence" and "presence," "value" and "determination" are closely connected with each other. In fact, as determination without value would have no existence, so value without determination would be lacking that "variety" and "efficacy" which make it such. Absence and presence are the two poles of experience, and the latter is always realized in them as a dynamic and mobile relationship between structure and existence.

As we said, the incomplete knowledge of the object preserves the independence of the subject and also gives it the power to distinguish itself from and communicate with other subjects. Each subject has an imperfect vision of the universe and the vision is its own, and yet by enriching itself the subject multiplies the points of contact with the vision of other subjects. However, knowledge is not enough to create a true closeness between spirits. There is a conflict between separate consciousnesses and, with it, the duty to establish an active peace in which separation is to be found once more not as a separation but as a means of "voluntary union." When duty is changed into love, then the union of spirits is stronger and closer. Yet, in order that this union remain alive, it must not be a complete one. There is a secretness of intimacy which the deepest love prevents itself from penetrating. This secretness is the protection of the person's independence and the true object of love rests exactly upon it. It must stay unimpaired in order that love may always preserve its decency, hope, and anxiety.

Is there a principle which permits the complete union of consciousnesses? Where can we look for it? In the warmth which nurtures their very activity as well as their unquenchable longing for an ideal toward which they naturally tend. This principle is God, pure love and perfect Person. If the ego makes itself a person by overcoming the limits of determination, we must say that value reveals itself as a personality in opposition to determination, which is impersonality. Value is God, but not "God without us"; it is instead "God with us," who lives in us, sustains and warrants our lives and freedom, and gives a meaning to our aspirations.

Are all contradictions perhaps abolished in God? No. God is neither a haven nor a refuge. God makes contradictions arise in order to give us existence and allow us to be the makers of our own destiny through the trial of life. He is the custodian of our personal initiative, as He "attracts us only in order to reject us." He does not take courage away from us nor does He act in our stead. He hides Himself not in order to condemn but only to love us. This "God with us" always gives us a dissatisfaction concerning the present and a hope for eternity. As Lavelle writes, Le Senne "defines philosophy as being itself a promise; and he identifies reality with a "troubled or an impatient consciousness," which seemingly makes us dedicated to suffering so that we may convert it to joy, and to war so that we may convert it to peace, and to peace in order that we may change it to love: undoubtedly, it appeals to duty only for the sake of making us gain a grace which will make duty useless. But, neither joy, nor peace, nor love, nor grace is a state in which we can settle ourselves. To imagine that consciousness can be satisfied is to think that it can perish. Such satisfaction is never present in consciousness because contradiction is always there ready to trouble it and force it to move on and on like the wandering Jew."

A philosopher of total experience, Le Senne rejects the dialectic of idealism for being unable to explain antinomy, whose two terms idealism denies in their positiveness at the very moment it posits them in their dialectical relationship. Le Senne, instead, recuperates even the positiveness of the obstacle. Man, in fact, "would not create anything if the obstacles surrounding him did not serve to increase his impetus as industry does with a dam, or if they did not also contribute by supplying him with those solid and resistant means needed for his task." Again opposing immanent idealism, Le Senne considers the ego's motion as being "vertical" rather than "circular." For him, the spirit transcends the world and surmounts every obstacle since it shows an aspiration capable of placing itself beyond things and of leading it toward a something which is neither a determination nor a nothingness, but is a "superdetermination" from which the validity of each determination is drawn; this is a value enrooted in every person, a value through which all determinations are spiritualized and yet it is never exhausted in any one of them. *Truth, beauty, good,* and *love*—these are the cardinal values, each of which cannot be taken separately and made absolute. In order to avoid the conflict of values, which arises from making one of them absolute, spirit must elevate itself toward God, the absolute source of every value, "first Spirit" and *causa sui* in that He is "absolutely conscious." Without God there is no love among men. Science draws them close to one another but only in order to have them kill each other, unless at the base of individual and social life there is a love for God, which is "the light of souls." "Humanity must oscillate between a reciprocal hatred and love for God."

Axiological experience is the conquest and almost the revelation of our profound interiority, in that it also reveals our fundamental vocation, which is our longing for God. But this is possible because value is not a man's creation ("the ego is unable to create value") but a gift of God. Hence we have its objectivity, not in the sense of externality such as that belonging to a datum, but rather in the sense of interiority (namely, the value is present in the spirit). Value reveals the Absolute to us and unites us to Him. We think that this is the most productive and metaphysical point in Le Senne's axiological doctrine.

His theses on "value" and "character"—which he has treated in specific works (character, for example, is studied in his vast *Traité de Caractérologie*, Paris, 1946)—are taken up once again in his volume *La destinée personelle, op. cit.*, in which Le Senne defines more precisely the relationship between these two terms. Character is a condition as well as a fact initially given to the person, and the latter must proceed from there. Value is the person's goal and it characterizes the success or failure of our lives, according as we are able or unable to achieve it. Character, nevertheless, which is a hereditary datum (that is, "a constitutional structure that the individual draws from his ancestors"), is only the starting point and not a determining factor; otherwise, life in its entirety would be the development of a datum or pure fact. Inserted in this datum, freedom or initiative acts upon it and dominates it as far as possible, so much so that instead of an obstacle the datum becomes the condition or means through which the end is realized. The value is discovered through freedom, which also changes the datum into a means for the end, and the person's "destiny" (*destin*) into a "destination" (*destinée*) of the person. It can be said that each man is given a condition which is fit to become a proper means for a given value (not for any value). On this basis, initiative aims at the realization of the end, and according to his success or failure, the person may realize it or fall short of it. The datum itself, however, cannot be modified. In fact, Kant could not have been Beethoven and vice versa, so much so that if the former had tried to write music and the latter had attempted to build a philosophical system, both would have failed because each one would have endeavored to do something contrary to his own character, which though not a determinant still is a necessary condition.

What is *a* man, then? (1) In his nature he is a *character* according to the meaning we have just clarified. (2) At the "center of his character," he is "a conscious *moi*, that is, one who, though put in a particular place by his own character, is able to react against events through his knowledge and action used in place of character. Nothing can be said about this ego; it can only be pointed out since it is not an object but the very existence of man." (3) "In the third sense of the word, a man is an *individuality*. In fact, this man, placed in his character, has always had a history of his own, whenever we encounter him: he was affected by events and he reacted to them. This history changes him in his behavior but not in his character as we understand it now. In a man's constitution, individuality is that which results from his character and history, that is, a solid and permanent complex that is conditioned by the inborn character and also by the acquisitions which are due to the person's adventures and decisions." "We call *personality* all that which in the ego's individuality manifests *sa visée de valeur et l'accès à la valeur visée par lui*. Personality is that which makes up the individual's originality and nobility because it manifests the ego's choice as well as the grace of value. In its bond with individuality, the ego is only an individual; but, through its connection with personality and to the extent of its devotion to it, the ego becomes a person."

Inasmuch as man makes himself a person through his access to value and value is a "revelation of God," his *salvation* is identified with the *confiance métaphysique*, the "highest good that can be given to a man," his authentic *destinée* in perfect correspondence with his essential and absolute vocation. If values are related to a transcending Infinite, which is the Unity, they prevent man from falling into a form of fanaticism about a value expressed by him. In fact, "man cannot *deify* himself because the Infinity of the universal spirit maintains an inexhaustible distance between itself and finite spirits; but, if this distance is inexhaustible, it is so only in order to prevent life from coming to an end. It is appropriate for man to try to become *divine* by gradually increasing his union with the Infinity of Value." Value in this way has revealed to man, "in his most noble and deepest experiences, the quest for the infinite Value as the source of being and of what ought to be, and the *universal* presence of God in what is legitimate, anywhere. The transcendental *je* has thus become a divine *je*, and it is placed, by its spouting eternity, beyond history, which makes it evident only to the extent that the cooperation among men together with divine design permits the realization of the value. It is not up to man to complain that this union with God is always partial: since it is a union between a finite soul (no matter how expanded it may be) and the infinite Eternity, it must always be limited." It is here that the motif of "grace," which is present in all of Le Senne's philosophy, comes to light. In the midst of doubt and sadness, the trust in transcendence awakens our hope and strengthens our freedom. Through joy we verify our harmony with the real Principle of things and of spirits, as well as the fundamental spirituality of the Universe. Moreover, what we have to do is to pity and try to help those who have lost the first Value, that is, "the metaphysical trust, which is closer to us than we are to ourselves."

It seems to us that this discussion should not be confined only to "faith in transcendence" and "trust in metaphysics"; instead, it should place the probing validity of reason—in the light of truth objectively present in the mind—as a foundation of faith and trust. In this way, philosophical inquiry would have an autonomous and objective value and not one resting on faith or one that is simply psychological. But, in Le Senne, the descriptive and phenomenal aspect prevails over the metaphysical properly so-called. We are not saying absolutely that his axiology is not founded upon a metaphysics. What we mean to say is that the metaphysical principle and the problems connected with it are not rationally founded; they are rather posited as an exigency or as a choice, to which we are led by a need deeply felt by the spirit. In our opinion, Le Senne's mediative moment does not reach the first mediation through which metaphysics can be critically founded.

Philosophie de l'esprit: A. Forest, G. Berger, J. Moreau, J. Chaix-Ruy, M. Nédoncelle

Of all the thinkers associated with the *Philosophie de l'esprit*, AIMÉ FOREST (1898) is closest to the line of mediaeval metaphysics. A professor at the University of Montpellier, he has successfully blended together Augustinian and Thomistic theses. As a first task, metaphysics has to know its starting point, which for Forest seems to be a certain disposition toward "meditation" in that it is consonant with the spirit to go back to itself. This meditation, however, is not to be undersood in a negative way, for it is not a halt in the thought's movement toward being but, rather, an attitude of distance with respect to the immediate data, one that is needed to initiate the metaphysical inquiry, since it is provisional and destined to prepare a new, a surer and more profound adherence to being. The task of philosophy is to find the full meaning of the spiritual meditation when it expresses itself through the activity of the intellect and will.

"Meditation" allows us to exercise a peculiarity of the intellect, the "receptiveness," of which the metaphysical affirmation is an original form. It is a *receptiveness toward being* which induces thought to give its consent to being itself. Metaphysical experience, in fact, "is the awareness of our relationship with being" (*Du consentment à l'Etre*, Paris, 1936). Thus our experience becomes a "correspondence." To know reality is to be "in agreement" with it in a certain sense. As Aristotle says, one "appreciates the nature of objects according to the soul's internal disposition." It is up to metaphysics to find a clear and precise expression of the truths to which we may be led by following the movement of thought (and this is the task for the introduction to an ontology), and also to show how the foundation of thought itself lies in the affirmation of the idea of being; there is solidarity between spiritual experience and ontological experience. Truth transcends the research and is not constituted by our own act; but the spirit comes in its presence, suppresses an inferior representation to which it cannot confine itself, and seeks in it harmony and its peace. This is what Forest intimates with the word "consent" in which lies the main concept of his *spiritual realism*, which in its ultimate result is a *metaphysical realism*. Being has a true consistency of its own, and when it is so affirmed it leads us to acknowledge the truth of participation. In this way, our access to the Absolute is given through the very mediation of being. Being, in its own depth, is not extraneous to the order of what it transcends. Existence and value are thus united through a very solid, metaphysical bond.

Dialectic, he writes, "not only ascends to the Absolute" by surmounting all appearances; it rather makes us find again, within diversity itself, that ideal truth and that pureness given to us when we are able to think of all things according to the Being which is present in them, everywhere. Such is the pure presence which supports all particular presences, and such is the meeting with Being—the highest experience for each one of us. The attention of the spirit which posits "determination" as existence makes the limit of it disappear, and shows in "being" a tendency to surpass itself by relating itself to the Absolute of being. "It is in relation to God that multiplicity is organized within the same universe, and it is from the same origin that the reality of what is concrete comes." The two notions of singularity and existence are concurrent and cannot be considered as reconstructed through a dialectical movement. "It is existence that, really distinct from being for its being created, requires the entire determination and, with it, the singularity, as Kant had rightly remarked. Now, existence is the very work of God. *Illud autem quod est proprius effectus Dei creantis est illud quod praesupponitur omnibus aliis, scilicet esse absolutum.* Consequently, if we think of a science that goes back to the first principles and that, on the other hand, reaches its conclusions with no inclination toward a direct intuition, then we can say with Spinoza (though our inspiration differs from his) that *the more we know singular things, the more we know God.*"

At the base of this metaphysics there is a concept of creation (as Forest says in his *Consentment et Creation*, Paris, 1943), which makes us recognize the fact that being is in conformity with the spiritual impulse leading us to it. Being is the place of our "spiritual loyalty."

Metaphysics is not an "abstract" research as nonphilosophers or pseudo-philosophers think. It is an activity of the intellect, indeed, but also of the will: "honesty of thought inspires a most pure direction of love. Philosophical intelligence transforms the will by proposing to it its object under a different light, and by permitting us to discern in things an ideal value—the object of pure will. It enables us to reach a profound experience, which is not only sensible but also of a different order, the metaphysical one, in which being is the object of a new attachment." The metaphysical representation causes us to grasp the "value," to become disinterested, and "to learn how to consider things in their selfness. It also makes love possible, which is the relation in which we wish being to be, instead of relating it to ourselves according to the isolated aspects under which it becomes an object of our desire. In the gift that consciousness makes of itself by submitting to the other, it seeks nothing for itself but rather learns that pure love which brings about the representation of value. . . . The object of love is given to us in this vision, which is the highest one allowed by metaphysics. Friendship becomes the metaphysical experience itself inasmuch as it would not be possible without the intuition of being." That which permits us to reach the Absolute and "be united to Him in the metaphysical order is, perhaps, that which is most elevated in our consciousness, that is, the experience of a relationship which is a solicitation on the part of things as well as a response on the part of the spirit. Consciousness penetrates into a truth whose entire value it does not know as yet; but, its loyalty already present in its original consent—which is the starting point in the metaphysical order— gives it peace. Consciousness straightens the will, gives it its unity and appeases it without overwhelming it; it is a form of possession in expectation."

Metaphysical experience "does not depart from concrete reality which it implies and comprehends in itself, precisely because it regards the highest abstraction, the universal being. The sciences deal with a reality that in itself is concrete; yet, they never regard it on account of those ultimate characteristics which are the foundation of the individual perfections bound to the idea of being taken in its fullest universality." Metaphysical experience alone makes us discern, beyond every individual characteristic, the "unity" that constitutes the determinations and the "infinity manifested by them." "However, if it is true that the natural movement of thought leads from a scientific explanation to the metaphysical reflection, this entirely new attitude presupposes a change of level which is clearly evident. The universality considered by metaphysics is of an order completely different from that pertinent to the partial abstractions of the sciences; it is the universality of a notion variously present in the object of each positive science. Consequently, the study of universal being has a different nature from that of any particular aspect of reality." Thus, philosophy cannot be simply confined to "grouping together all the findings of the positive sciences. This limit must be surmounted somehow; the relation directly linking the particular to universal being must be grasped; and we shall realize that it is not possible for us to pass from the one to the other through the series of determinations, which are the proper object of our understanding. Our thought is led to this point when it *places itself in an attitude of loyalty*. We reach the metaphysical level when we do not refuse to consider explicitly that which is the condition whereby we think of all the rest." In his more recent work, *La vocation de l'esprit* (Paris, 1953), Forest makes a more profound study and a clarification of this metaphysics.

GASTON BERGER (1896) is a pupil of Le Senne and a professor at the University of Aix-en-Provence. He represents the keenest interpreter of Husserl in France (*Le Cogito dans la Philosophie de Husserl*, Paris, 1947). The latter's influence, in fact, together with that of Descartes, is apparent in Berger's compact volume *Recherches sur les conditions de la connaissance* (Paris 1941). Both realistic ontology and empirical natural-ism implicitly imply knowledge, and the latter must be our starting point if we wish to develop a "pure theoretics," which is not a theory of knowledge as understood traditionally. An important place is given to the problem of values. In fact, there is no judgment on reality which is not a value-judgment, but truth is not a value like any other. Without a truth of values, these are reduced to mere individual preferences. We must "engage" ourselves in the world since action is imposed on us ("aloofness" is a refined form of egoism). However, once we have ac-cepted our part, we must act for the well-being of all and not for our own. We must choose between God and us. Hence we have a need for metaphysics or for a "meditation on the Absolute." We need not "stop our criticism and be content to live in the shadow; we must, instead, pursue the search for meanings to the utmost and carry on our criticism against all pseudo-evidences presented by things which seem to be get-ting on by themselves "as a matter of course." Moreover, if philosophy performs its mission well, even daily life will benefit from it. In fact, life does not wait, and action changes those hypothetical truths afforded by knowledge into categorical affirmations. That is to say, action *con-siders* certain premises to be *sufficient*. By once more placing the Abso-lute beyond the world, metaphysics delivers us from all fanaticisms. The latter always arise from the impressions of self-sufficiency given to us by certain experiences or structures: the state, party, race, pleasure, history. . . . Even in this epoch of ours, we are not without some false absolutes. All this signifies that we greatly need a true metaphysics."

This line of Platonism is also followed by JOSEPH MOREAU (1900), a professor at the University of Bordeaux and a famous historian of Greek and modern philosophy. His works on Plato, Malebranche, Descartes, and Leibniz show his profound scholarship, certitude of methodology, and speculative acumen. In fact, it is precisely in his historical recon-structions that one can already foresee Moreau's personal thought, which he has recently systematized in his compact volume, *La Conscience* (Paris, 1957). For Moreau there is an "authentic" idealism, which can meet the ontological problem and can satisfy the deepest exigencies of our spirit while opposing the phenomenological and existentialist doctrines.

JULES CHAIX-RUY (1896) was at first a follower of Blondel but later he moved closer and closer to the *Philosophie de l'esprit*. A professor at the University of Algiers, he is also a meritorious student of Italian thought (his essays on Vico are notable), and an effective writer (his "monographs" on Renan and Cortes are to be recommended even from the point of view of his style). With his volume, *Les Dimensions de l'être et du temps* (Paris, 1953), the first of his planned trilogy, Chaix-Ruy has begun a systematic exposition of his thought, which he himself classifies as *essentialisme existentiel*. Thus the author himself sums up the content of his own work as follows: "First we tried to discern the levels of temporality in which our efforts are situated in order to escape dissociation and in order to reintegrate ourselves in the unity of being; then, the degrees of transcendence to which that thought accedes which is still subject to the uncertainties of those functions needed by thought itself. Thus we endeavored to examine the abatement of our freedom and determine its position between the automatism of an animal behavior and the gratuitousness of an activity having its rules and ends within itself." Some of Chaix-Ruy's analyses on Heidegger's existentialism and on Lavelle's "philosophy of total presence" are very fine and keen.

The *spiritual personalism* of MAURICE NÉDONCELLE (1905) is decisively inspired by Platonism and Augustinianism. A professor of Catholic theology at the University of Strasbourg, he is highly respected for his studies on Newman. Of so-called French personalism (with respect to which we may mention the name of E. Mounier, who died prematurely), Nédoncelle is the best prepared and keenest thinker from a philosophical point of view. His is a Christian personalism indeed, but with a metaphysical rather than a psycho-empirical character (*La personne humaine et la nature*, Paris, 1943). Moreover, this is a metaphysics of interiorness with some influence from Blondel, Marcel, and Le Senne. Nédoncelle replaces the "logic of identity" with a logic of loyalty (to which he devoted his fine work, *De la fidelité*, Paris, 1953), the only one suited to a philosophy of the person. At the person's level, being is a spiritual *act* with a dependency on the body, and yet it can posit the conditions for its realization. "We consider the ideal ego as a superior form and the source of psychological reality. Now, in this case, essence is not opposed to existence but only to the empirical situation or exteriority of existence. This is not a diminished existence; it is rather a perfect one viewed in its eternal principle, which enlightens and allows its temporal manifestations to be received."

The *ego* does not realize itself in opposition to the *nonego* but in harmony with the *you*. Helping another individual to advance and become a person amounts to helping ourselves to be persons (*La reciprocité des consciences*, Paris, 1942). The *other is not the limit but is the source of the ego* through which the ego itself realizes the ideal ego. This communion of consciousnesses increases and deepens our interiorness rather than suppresses it. The subject cannot become a person by itself (Nédoncelle's personalism has a gregarious character and so it is critical of individualism); rather it loses itself in the impersonal—consciousness awakens through its relations with the other; the fundamental subjectivity is not an individualistic ego but is the *we* whence *the ego* and the *you* derive. "The communion of consciousnesses is a primitive fact"; hence the ego makes itself with and in the communion. This communion is original (that is, "inborn"), and so rather than a datum, personality is a conquest attained through the overcoming of obstacles (that is, evil). The degrees of this process (which is also an ascent to the Source or God) are as follows: (1) *science*, which does not complete the person since it would merely give him dominion over the world; (2) *art*, which brings about a unity of consciousnesses, but not a definitive unity; (3) *morality*, which produces the good, but not a true reciprocity of consciousnesses; and (4) *love*, which alone makes consciousnesses coincide with each other in perfect unity, since it also respects the personality of each one by maintaining a state of unity and distinction at the same time. Thus, Nédoncelle proposes a *metaphysics of charity* (*Vers une philosophie de l'amour*, Paris, 1940), because only through the acknowledgment of a God-creator (that is, of an "Absolute of love") are we able to realize a perfect and authentic communion among persons and also overcome the nature-person dualism. Eternity alone, when it is inserted in our lives, can purify and save everything. Death is not a *retour* to God; it is rather a *retournement* of our situation *par rapport* to God: "Pendant la vie, nous regardons Dieu, après la mort, nous voyons que Dieu nous regarde."

Nédoncelle's philosophy (like Le Senne's, Lavelle's, and Forest's) is also a philosophy of salvation, since this theme is common to all French thought of what we may call a Pascalian inspiration. In it the *philosophie de l'esprit* continues a tradition (together with the Cartesian one) that runs from Pascal to Blondel. However, the point is to see whether this "philosophy of salvation" does not endanger the autonomy of philosophy with respect to religion, that is, the distinction between the critical moment and the moment of faith, so that the solution of metaphysical problems would not be only an act of faith on the part of the will (and, hence, not a solution), an act "imposed" by the exigencies of the spiritual subject.

C. Christian Spiritualism: Characteristics and Problems

To date, Christian spiritualism is the last word of significance in Italian philosophy; it is also a most lively current that is widespread and much discussed. In the last decade, its problems and methodology have been better defined and systematized. It chose the term "spiritualism," for the concept of "spirit," which is essential to man and philosophy as such, is essential to this current in the same way as it is to Gentile's actualism from which all its exponents have derived. Yet, it is this assuming the "spirit" in all its scope and man in all his integrality that carries within itself the criticism of idealism—a criticism that is extended to every form of immanent and historicist idealism (that is, to every form of absolute immanentism or absolute historicism), because in its dynamism the spirit's activity reveals some elements which lead it to a theistic transcendence. Thus this spiritualism still is idealism but not subjectivism. Its philosophy is a philosophy of "interiority," which is taken in its metaphysical meaning rather than in an immanent sense. In other words, this is an objective idealism that rests on transcendence and is deeply inspired by the Platonic and Augustinian tradition; it offers an integral conception of philosophy and of life (according to a dialectic of implication and convergence), which only a metaphysical (or absolute) point of view can make possible.

Moreover, Christian spiritualism is opposed to every form of positivism, though the latter's legitimate quest for concreteness is acknowledged. In fact, it considers the spirit with its ever present actuality to be first, and not the fact, which, as a fact of experience, presupposes the spirit. It is opposed to any contamination of philosophy and science and any attempt to impoverish *experience*, which is not simply external and sensorial but primarily internal and spiritual. Moreover, it opposes all forms of neopositivism or any form based on scientificalism and materialism, which Christian spiritualism regards as being negative to philosophy. Any such form is regarded as a nonphilosophical position, which shows naiveté and presumption in both its dogmatism and unilaterality. It also opposes so-called antimetaphysical philosophy, which it regards as responsible for the decadence of philosophy, loss of values, disintegration of the individual and of society. This antimetaphysical thought is also held responsible for all primitive fanaticisms as well as for the degradation of man to the level of things, and for the abandonment of speculative positions, which were critically more mature, in favor of others which are inferior, materialistic, pragmatic, and "scientistic."

Neospiritualism, however, does not disregard the importance of scientific discoveries together with their practical and transforming efficacy, as it does not deny that the sciences are a moment of knowledge. Yet, it opposes with all its energy the idolatry of science, which implies the subjugation of the spirit to nature as well as the transformation of man from a conqueror into a conquered one at the very moment when the end of man is identified, after the manner of immanentism, with the conquest and transformation of the world. All this is done as if everything had to satisfy the interests of the body or the category of "vitality" and not, to the contrary, the superior exigencies of the spirit, in respect to which those vital values are to be held as a means and a condition for its development, completion and end. Moreover, the world itself is to be held not as a "stage" where man performs his part, but as an instrument used for the success of man's "trial," that is, for the success of the life of each individual. Science can give us the means for action but not the "norm" of acting, which is internal and objective, that is, a value and not a fact. Even science is indeed a work of the spirit as morality is, but the latter cannot become science without ceasing to be value in order to become a fact—that is to say, a "science of customs," an empirical description of phenomena, and no longer a morality, which is an objective and absolute norm transcending phenomenological ethics. Nothing can ever be more inhuman or more fatal to mankind than a science which prescinds from morality and denies it within the fact, or a scientist who is not also a "man" and assumes the rules of science as rules of his human behavior (such is the "scientistic" conception of life). Science does not go beyond phenomenal order, that is, beyond the sensible; morality and metaphysics (namely, philosophy in general) hold the values to be their object, and without them not even science would be possible since every activity of the spirit exists only because it expresses a value transcending it. It is not a question of there being two degrees but, rather, of there being a qualitative difference. In fact, there is a shifting of levels going from science to philosophy, and this does not imply opposition and divergence in a dialectic of implication and integrality such as is this one which governs the spirit. Philosophy cannot prevent itself from remaining loyal to its object and its method, as it cannot reduce itself to being a coordinator of sciences or a sum-total of scientific results. For this reason, Christian spiritualism regards empiricism or neoempiricism, positivism or neopositivism, phenomenalism, and so on, not as philosophical doctrines (even if they may have importance for scientific methodology), but as so many modes which deny philosophy or which "say nothing" that is philosophically valuable—so many modes of denying the possibility and validity of any nonscientific knowledge which is not reducible to a verifiable "quantity."

Christian spiritualism is a constructive movement. Its roots rest on the traditional, Christian philosophy with a marked preference for the stream of thought which runs from Augustine to Rosmini. It presents itself as an integral and authentic humanism as well as an integral philosophy of experience and, precisely because of this integrality and totality, it critically discovers that the foundation and end of man and of total experience lies in God—the absolute Person. A theocentric humanism, then, the only one that guarantees, in a rational way, the objectivity and superhistoricity of values as well as man's dignity and freedom. In it lies the spirit's original priority over the external world—a priority that belongs to a transcendent and absolute Spirit such as God is, and also to a finite spirit such as every man is. This movement does not represent a "reaction," but a thoroughly critical (and, therefore, antidogmatic) study of the fundamental exigencies of thought in order that thought reveal itself in its authenticity and profoundness and man knows, through his reflective consciousness, his supreme destination. Thus, Christian spiritualism is a criticism of the fundamental presuppositions underlying modern thought, which must be grasped at the root if we really wish to correct the existing errors and regain the essential truth. The latter can be made productive if it is reinstated in the perennial fecundity of those truths which the Greco-Christian philosophical tradition acquired with an everlasting value since what has been discovered to be true once remains true forever. From this point of view, this philosophy (and all the other philosophies moving along the lines of a spiritualistic metaphysics) is critical and revolutionary and not "dogmatic" and "traditional" as it is imagined to be by some superficial thinkers who are themselves victims of a preconceived dogmatism, so much so that they are not qualified to pass any critical judgment. Critical and revolutionary indeed, because out of the dissolution of immanent metaphysics with all its consequent pragmatic and "scientistic" positions, this philosophy knows how to regain a tradition that is renewed and critically thought through once more: a positively constructive philosophy and, hence, a philosophy of the present—of a present which is going to be the future of philosophy itself.

Moreover, Christian spiritualism is pledged to reconquer the very structure of human thinking, validity of reason, supremacy of spirit, and concept of philosophy which at present is threatened or denied by the non-philosophies of matter, *praxis*, and nothingness. At least through some of its exponents, Christian spiritualism lays down the foundations for an ontology and does not satisfy itself with the "description" of existence. It does not confine itself to phenomenological descriptions or psychological analyses; instead, it wishes to build a metaphysics, that is, a philosophy through a thorough reflection on the depth of thought rather than on its surface. Clearly, the current of thought that is closest to Christian spiritualism and shares many points with it (though the two currents are not reducible to one another) is *La philosophie de l'Esprit*. Thus it is not without reason that, when Italian spiritualism decided to establish the periodical *Giornale di Metafisica* as its organ, it requested the collaboration of those thinkers and of others who represent a metaphysical, spiritualistic movement.

Christian Spiritualism: Carlini's Realistic Spiritualism

ARMANDO CARLINI (1878) can be considered the initiator of Christian spiritualism because he is the one who posited its problems and

its exigencies. However, precisely because he is the initiator of this movement, he represents a starting point still attached to modern idealism and
above all to Kant and the Kantian concept of transcendentality.

Thus Carlini actually cannot abandon the subjective moment of the
exigency and the metaphysical problems (existence of God and immortality of the soul) are solved through an act of faith or they even
become "dogmas of faith." The stages of his constant, speculative search
are expressed through the following works: *La vita dello spirito* (Florence,
1921), *La religiosità dell' arte e della filosofia* (Florence, 1934), *Il mito del
realismo* (Florence, 1936), *Lineamenti di una concezione realistica dello
spirito umano* (Rome, 1942), *Christianesimo e pensiero moderno* (Rome,
1953), *Che cos' è la metafisica* (Rome, 1957).

For Carlini, the analysis of Gentile's philosophy leads to the transcendence of the act, which, by positing the problem of the self, generates
and upholds the world of experience and also consumes it within itself.
The act, nevertheless, transcends such a world and, beyond it, faith and
thought manifest their boundary which extends so much as to coincide with the infinite. The philosophical problem, as a problem of experience, is one of human self-consciousness, a problem of the *a priori*
and *a posteriori* combined together, of the reduction of the latter to the
former, and a problem of the "transcendental" demonstration of the
physical world. The problem of experience implies the reality of the
psychological principle (self-consciousness), which differs from what
can be called the *theological principle,* a pure and absolute principle
totally independent of the world of experience. Self-consciousness has
experience of itself as the experience of something other than itself. Interiority lives and develops within exteriority. Yet, exteriority itself
develops within a problem of spiritual life, indeed, "by virtue of its
form which is not an abstract form or an empty reflection upon itself,
but a positing of a pure, psychological problem in which the human self-
consciousness posits the problem of itself in its pure interiority as it
realizes its own inadequacy. In other words, exteriority restricts interiority which looks upon itself as a principle of pure interiority, and in
this new attitude it postulates and discovers a superior interiority. Here
lies the shift from the psychological to a theological principle, from the
transcendental to Transcendence, and from idealism to spiritualism.

"Sensibility" is the decisive note which distinguishes the psychological
from the theological principle. Sensibility is not to be understood "as a
property of human self-consciousness, but as human self-consciousness
itself in its transcendentality": it is the "very act of feeling oneself," a
pure sensibility, or sensible "aestheticity." Theoreticity and practicalness
are identified with "aestheticity" and this agreement is "the revelation
of a superior and absolute principle to man; the exigency of transcendence

arises as pure aestheticity within self-consciousness." Pure sensibility is the transcendental principle of a work of art, and as such the poet makes an empirical use of it. Yet, the poet wishes to live, also for himself, the pure sensibility as such. When the poet posits the problem of his sensibility not as a transcendental form (since this relates to a superior interiority), "he feels in his soul the possibility of a faith which is clearly and sincerely religious, that is, a faith leading toward a true theology like that of the Transcendent." In other words, as a psychological principle sensibility posits itself as a transcendental form when the poet turns interiority into exteriority; however, it posits itself also as a problem, but when this occurs the psychological principle changes into a theological one. Now, since the work of art is sensibility in its process of becoming exteriority (which is also interiority), and since from the problem of pure aestheticity rises the transcendence in a religious sense, it follows that the religious exigency lies within the same sensibility understood as a pure aestheticity.

As we have said, for Carlini the act as such is a problem to itself. In order to solve this problem it is necessary to consider not only the *critical* but also the *dogmatic* attitude. In its positing itself, the problem of the ego or problem of human personality also posits the problem of the transcendence of God. Thought alone is insufficient. Faith is still needed, and so philosophy must be integrated with religion: God is immanent and at the same time He transcends the act of self-consciousness. All modern idealism moves from this thinking consciousness, but the Ego, which is thought, implies an exigency with which idealism has to reckon.

This initial problem arises from the problem of the "transcendental no longer considered in relation to the world of knowledgeable experience (which, as in science, is an attitude of thought turned to exteriority) but of the transcendental considered in itself and for itself, in its internal life, as pure interiority. Thus, the spiritualistic problem, which is both a moral and religious problem, arises in Kant." The problem of God and man must be posited precisely in the act of pure spirituality, in the act which is consciousness of itself, and in which man finds a reason not only for the world of experience and history "but also for that deeper and original reality which alone makes man's world worthwhile; yet, though immanent in the human act, this reality transcends it. However, this immanent transcendence can be arrived at only by a thought which is supported and integrated by faith; it can be arrived at by a faith which respects the value of man and his world and is guided and integrated by thought." The act of self-consciousness thus performs a double function: one, as a transcendental act wherein the world of historical experience is made possible, and the other, as itself a problem of pure interiority, which can find a solution in an act of faith, that is, in an appeal to a superior interiority—the Transcendent or God. "As such, it will be a theological principle which can be defined as the act of the human spiritual act, as that transcendence which is in the depth of human personality: the point on which not the world is directly suspended, as in ancient metaphysics, but one on which man is suspended and, through man, the world." This is so because after Christianity "we cannot and must not continue to speak of God in the same way as Aristotle did in a common metaphysics, which is both physical and theological; for a Christian, instead, God is a spiritual and pure Personality, and no longer simply a 'being,' not *the* Being, and not even the much abused, Scholastic *Ens Realissimum*." In other words, we must distinguish metaphysics as a science of physical reality from theology as a science of God, unless we wish to persist in a pre-Christian conception of God Himself.

The transcendence of personality as absolute interiority bears, as a consequence, the sacrifice of the worldly individuality without, however, arriving at a contempt toward life and the temporal on account of an excessive fondness for the eternal. Modern philosophy, which considers the person only in the sense of worldly existence, as individuality, replaces faith in the theological transcendence with the myth of the divinity of History. However, the "divinity" of the world of history is troubled by "mortality." What is death? And why? This problem, which is so urgent and decisive, does not exist for historicism. Yet, it imposes itself on our attention, and in order to solve it we must consider man as he is, spirit and body; on the one hand, he turns to the world, to the body, which is the center of the sensible world, and, on the other, to God.

Carlini has pursued a problem which offers no solution. He has attempted to draw a theistic transcendence from Kantian-idealistic transcendentality, that is, from an *a priori* whose validity is confined to experience. For this reason, he is compelled to give up metaphysics and "add" religious faith to his Kantian position, that is, reduce the existence of God to an act of faith which is devoid of any rational foundation whatsoever.

Christian Spiritualism: Guzzo's Theistic "Idealism"

AUGUSTO GUZZO (1894), a professor at the University of Turin, has developed his "idealism" independently of Carlini, though he has been in contact with all of contemporary philosophy and the great masters of thought from Plato to Bergson. For Guzzo, thought is impassable (and, hence, idealism), but this impassable thought is a qualified thought—the thought of a world, one which contains or bears witness to the existence of a world. Thus, an idealism which is the opposite of that one which has the world "posited" by thought (*Verità e realtà*, Turin, 1925;

Giudizio e azione, Venice, 1928). In this way, we are able to recognize the three fundamental problems of Guzzo's spiritualism: (1) nothing is outside of thought, yet to know does not mean to nullify the object but, rather, to realize it; (2) spirit is essentially ethicity, but is guided by a *universal and compulsory* ideal, which it is free to realize or not; (3) this ideal is truth *in interiore homine*, the voice of God, who gives us existence, and who calls us to Himself. Thus, the three problems of knowledge, morality, and religion are the three aspects of a unique problem, which is the spiritual reality in its determining itself, in its becoming, and in its being (*Idealismo e Cristianesimo*, Naples, 1936; *Sic vos non vobis*, Naples, 1939-1940).

According to Guzzo, each one of us brings into common life something unmistakable and indestructible, which can be imitated but not reproduced.

We need to realize this "fact" of individuation: "Through it life presents itself solely as an individuation of characters." Individuation is the one which is free, a recurring determination like life, which contains in itself "what at first appears like a rhythm of desire and gratification, need and satisfaction." Thus, affirmation and negation are present in the act of individuation. "Gratification is an establishment and a positiveness, and it is unthinkable without a need or a negativity which it saturates." The useful is also a form of good. Is evil as real as the useful? Good and evil, like the true or false, or the useful and useless are dialectical concepts. There is "a struggle between good and evil—a real struggle between a real goodness and a real wickedness." Fighting against evil, however, does not mean nullifying it. We can only will a definite action, and yet to be shut in a good is evil. The contradiction is apparent. The universal or a duty is always willed as an individual volition. Duty always sustains a personal activity. If I turn my back on duty and go after what is immediately useful, I do wrong. In conclusion: "When the useful is willed as merely useful, it makes the will, which adheres to it, bad; but when the useful is willed as licit and equitable (that is, it is willed as useful, only mediately), it makes the will, which proposes it, good."

At this point, a problem arises: Is the value of life *in* life itself or must it be distinguished from life? If one accepts immanentism whereby the absolute spirit *posits* everything, evil can no longer exist; nor is there room for our freedom and autonomy; nor is the guilt of our wrongdoings attributable to us. Responsibility implies a duality between my behavior, which recognizes itself to be vacillating, and my consciousness, which is never hesitant in any case and which judges my acts. Consciousness is universal, indeed, "yet, the particular that is presented to it for judgment, that is to say, our individual behavior, is not simply something posited by the universal so as to have our responsibility nullified once more; the particular, instead, is to be conceived as endowed with its own causality and autonomy with respect to the universal to which it responds." The universal is in the particular, but it is not identified with it.

The same problem confronts gnosiology: "Does truth guide the search or does search guide the truth, in a research process?" Is truth a historical product (*filia temporis*) or is it the maker of history (*mater temporis*)? For Guzzo, truth guides the search and does not arise from it; yet, truth is not extraneous to the search, but it is present and active in our consciousness, which endeavors to reason. But here lies the main point: to be immanent does not mean to be identical with the single ideas. The true bears upon the single ideas which are true, but none of them is *the* true, but only *a* true, in the same way as an action is moral when it is dutiful, yet no moral action is *the* duty. In short, even here there is a duality between true ideas and truth, as between dutiful action and duty. True ideas and dutiful actions stand for truth and duty but not vice versa. This is "what makes thought an aporia: thought is not such without *the* truth and it is such only if it itself is not *the* truth."

The moral disposition is, for Guzzo, an irrepressible assumption not only with respect to ethical life in its entirety but also with respect to any other attitude on the part of spiritual life. In fact, "we must posit a will which is really moral at the beginning of any activity whatever in order that the latter may develop and succeed." The artist, for example, must subordinate himself to art if he is to create a work of art; and this is an attitude of morality toward art. One has to produce art when and until one feels and knows that one will succeed. He has to produce as long as he is sure that his production is going "to work."

Do idealism and Christianity reject each other? The former *resolves* being into thought while realism vindicates the *reality* of being. What is the meaning of "resolving being into thought" or of "philosophy of being?" To those who maintain that a philosophy of being is what Christianity needs in order to be valid as thought, Guzzo replies that philosophy of being is helpful to Christianity but it does not suffice to present the latter as such. In order that thought may be Christian, it does not suffice to distinguish intelligible being from sensible existence in time; but it is necessary to consider the intelligibles as created by, but not necessary to, God, in order to save the concept of creation which is essential to Christianity.

The analysis of modern idealism leads Guzzo to concede that "every act of thinking is indisputably an egoity because the *actus cogitandi* is essentially a subject, an ego," to which rhythmicality, that is, its surpassing itself, is essential. "But precisely because thought is rhythmicality and a tormenting inquietude leading it upward, spirit is not the Absolute."

591

An Absolute in becoming is not the God of religion. The Christian God is within man, but there is a radical incommensurability between Him who is intimate and the one to whom He is intimate. The resolution of reality into the experienced instant of the act of thought does not mean, as it does for idealism, the nullification of the reality of thought; it means, instead, *attestation* of a reality as alterity. God cannot be posited on the same level as man and the physical world. He is Cause and Logos, and also a Redeemer. If idealism is understood as that philosophy which reduces all reality to an act of thought and which identifies the necessity of the Absolute with its total immanence in human experience, this idealism, which is anti-idealism and positivism, does not agree with Christianity. "If man needs the Absolute and he expresses his need through an experience that can be renewed, man is not the Absolute; he belongs to the Absolute instead, and if some idealists identify him with the Absolute they are wrong, while those idealists are right who maintain the incomparable and unique dignity of man in the universe."

Human morality is a struggle and a conquest, and thus "morality is a discriminating consciousness which chooses a moral value and rejects its opposite; it is a consciousness of evil in contradiction with good." He is "good" who does not shut himself in his own selfishness, or he who does not work for himself and is aware that *his* existence was given to him. He is "good" who understands that what is "his" indicates only a usufruct which he must account for; he also "aligns himself, as a person, with every other being, and he does not take anything for himself as he makes use only of that which is given to him. Such a man is responsible for what he succeeds in doing and he is also willing to defend the fruition of that which is due to him. Yet, he must be constantly aware that as he has not given himself what he has, so he is not working for himself. *Sic vos non vobis*."

For Guzzo there are no "generic" values. Values are deeds and "human answers"; and thus every value is singular and is realized through the person's work. There is no epic genre, but there is Homer; there is no virtue of humility, but there is St. Francis. There exist no poetry and philosophy, but the *Divine Comedy* and the *Metaphysics*. These are the historical values, without implying thereby that "ideality" and "eternity" are illusions. As values, the historical values are posited as ideals and they jut into eternity. God created man and He stimulates him. Man *replies* with his works. Thus, "the Platonism of man's stimulation on the part of the divine remains eternal; it is a voice coming to man from God the person. Vulgar Platonism falls apart for it made the sublime poetry of essences-Ideas (sung in a few dialogues) change into a heavy starred curtain, which was interposed between what is divine and stimulates the soul to be a soul and what is human and is realized by the soul through its deeds, which cannot be repeated, and to which man's endeavor to respond (each man with his responsibility) to this divine exigency gives life."

As a stimulation, transcendence operates in the depth of the human spirit which responds with a need for justice; this need animates and regulates social living through moral incentives (charity, internal quietude, fairness to all), which are innovative and inventive efforts beyond, and often against, existing formulas. "Moral stimuli come from a profound intimacy and they express an innerly experienced need often borne in depth. Their way of manifesting themselves comes about neither through a resounding exclamation (which is generous only verbally), nor through a lyrical effusion (often Pharisaical and amateurish or, in any case, lazy and too convenient), nor even through a sentimental effusion (which is icily warm); their way is, instead, a tenacious, detailed and persistent work in digging, improving, learning how to wait, daring and hoping without abandoning the pertinacious endeavor."

Transcendence, a close solicitor of the soul, leads man to assume the responsibility of evaluating all choices rationally, the ones already made and those still to be made. Nor is evaluation less sincerely rational simply because it is animated by a moral bond which, far from disturbing it, makes it (*as much as it is able to*) all the more serious and equitable (namely, rational). On the other hand, if the rational evaluation must censure and struggle against a choice made by sensible spontaneity (when this choice is proven to be contrary), it also must approve the same (without scorching it) when it is proven to be concordant. Moreover, "if at the beginning reason itself appears to be very distinct and dissimilar from the impulse, it then will move in such direction as to find the signs of an impulse or gain a ready and instantaneous action, an immediate resoluteness, and a ready taking of position which is characteristic of instinct."

During the decade between 1940 and 1950, Guzzo decided to conceive and write about his "system." To date, he has published three large volumes, *L'io e la ragione* (Brescia, 1947), *La Moralità* (Turin, 1950), and *La Scienza* (Turin, 1955), which contain all his theoretical and practical philosophy in a systematic form. The analysis of human and particular activities, such as art, religion, and philosophy itself, will be developed later on in three other special volumes, whose plan is foreshadowed in the first sketches of his system, such as *La filosofia e l'esperienza* (Rome, 1942), *La filosofia domani* (Milan, 1943), and his work-program, *L'uomo* (Milan, 1944), besides some other essays published in recent years.

His "system" is conceived not as a "positive" or dogmatic treatise, but as a universal criticism of human experience. "Experience" is here understood as experience of values, which the human spirit seeks for or produces; and "criticism" is a form of analysis of human experience, which "regains its meaning when it questions, evaluates or discovers its possibility."

Although Guzzo's search is oriented toward human spirit (in fact, his entire system is entitled, *L'uomo*), it does not mean that he regards God and nature as realities unrelated to philosophy. The fact is that Guzzo sticks to a truly critical method which consists first in placing oneself within the consciousness that man has of nature and God, then in studying nature according to the experience and the science which man has of it; and finally, in studying God first according to the exigency and idea possessed by man and then according to the positive revelation man receives about Him. This should not lead one to believe, as we said, that for Guzzo the spirit "posits" or creates nature and God, as if they did not subsist by themselves. In fact, for him "idealism" has nothing to do with "ideism," as "ideal" has nothing in common with the current and accepted meaning of the word "idea." Moreover, if an "ideism" can sustain that nature and God are "reduced" to the "idea" man has of them, an "idealism," which is not "ideism," knows very well that human "experience" is "experience" precisely because it attests some active presences given to it to be known—that is, on the one hand, this existence of fact we call "nature" (including our body therein), and, on the other, the omnipresent and omnipotent Act, which is God.

In his *Io e la ragione, op. cit.*, Guzzo founds the whole system and presents, to this effect, an anthropology which establishes the notion of man, critically. "Far from separating me, as a pure thought, from my living, consciousness links me to it: I who think, live." My life (or, if you wish, my body, which is to be understood as a living body or life in act) is present to my consciousness in the feeling which I have about myself and which later becomes the object of a reflection; the latter must interpret this object if it wishes to understand it. "The work of interpretation of that which I feel is the task of the intellect and sense at the same time, because that which prompts me to sense is in sight and is ready to direct me toward understanding, and vice versa. The fundamental acts of consciousness are the distinctions which the intellect sees emerging from sensing itself; the latter is to be examined as it offers and makes itself known."

No knowledge comes to me, however, unless I take the initiative to look for and acquire it, for human knowledge is really a research. As a research, knowledge always turns to something particular, whatever its magnitude may be; but it wishes to establish what is true with respect to this particular. Therefore, knowledge is always relative as regards the object to which it is related, and yet it is aroused by an essential need to attain an unchangeably true concept concerning that object. "If, however, I grasp the true direction of a movement, though this ceases afterwards, it remains *unchangeably* true that it had this direction while it existed." The *validity* of a true judgment lies in its universal and necessary form. On the other hand, true judgments are such on account of the truth-value they grasp. " 'True' is a qualifying adjective which expresses the value of some judgments of ours; and 'truth' points out such value." It would be erroneous to confuse *true* with *real*. "Sensation is in myself an indubitable and unquestionable 'reality'; but, the clearer are the terms of the question it puts before me, the more I am urged to give a reply, and this alone can be true. Moreover, if the interpretation-process—when it succeeds—arrives at joining a true experience with a true interpretation, the true cannot even then be exchanged with the real and vice versa. They could be exchanged only if the true interpretation exhausted the real experience in such a way as to be able to exclude *a priori* not only the possibility of a correction but also the possibility of an improvement, a deepening, or development of the interpretation. As long as such a possibility cannot be excluded, the fact that true and real are so close together will not signify their coinciding with each other without any residua, not even at the end of the interpretation-process."

Now, whether or not I succeed in finding a true answer to the *real* question posited to me by the physical or mental situation in which I am, the fact is that my disposition to look for such an answer already "contains in itself the naive but ineradicable inborn inclination to believe that everything must have a meaning. This is the postulate of knowing the condition by which I engage myself, and, at the same time, the lesson I get from my own attitude toward anything whatsoever; this is the result I attain from every knowledgeable experience of mine, whether it is a lucky or an unlucky one, because even when I realize with regret that I do not understand fully or at all, I still acknowledge that certainly there is something to be understood, even if I fail to do so. The fact that everything has its own character, its own intelligibility, and its own reason for being, is both the *form* of knowing (since I can know nothing unless I look for an intelligibility) and the fundamental and general knowing *content* (since whatever I know, I know in it a particular determination of that universal intelligibility which I tacitly attribute to everything in the very act whereby I direct myself to know)." This manner of understanding how form and content are inseparable from each other is characteristic of Guzzo's thought.

Human knowledge, essentially a research, is discursive and "ratiocinating" above all. This discursive character is, according to Guzzo, indicated by three inseparable phases: (1) the phase of appearance of a possible, which manifests itself through all that is offered to consciousness as a physical or mental datum to be interpreted; (2) the phase in which we note what the object—about which the first interpretation proposed a notion—has become; and (3) the phase in which we reason on the hypothesis supplied by the interpretation, in order to see if its adoption logically implies the fact which we have ascertained through experience. In a Spinozian way, Guzzo calls the act of conceiving (or judgment in act) a *conceptus,* and "the notion by which the object is conceived through a conception (or judgment brought about through the mind's initiative) a *conceptum.*" He remarks that when thought arrives at demonstrating the truth of the interpretation given to the physical or mental situation that we wish to know, "the *conceptum* is still posited by a definite *conceptus* in the tested certitude of a demonstration which concludes as follows: the *conceptum* must be thought according to the *conceptus,* at the end of a procedure which has resolved the assumption of an *interpretation* and the *experiences* of fact into the ratiocinating *reflection* whereby the demonstration of the necessity of that precise manner of thinking has been arrived at."

After positing the tendency toward truth as that which expresses exactly the essence of man, and after establishing the fact that truth is always present in man—even while he is searching for it—Guzzo remarks that precisely because it is an object of research, truth does not impose itself by force; instead, it "proposes itself to him [to man] by asking him the loyalty of a sincere adhesion." Thus, man is always tempted to rebel against truth or to falsify it, but when he agrees to follow it, he "chooses" it. Morality rests on this choice or option. Properly speaking, "I have no choice, either with respect to what I must judge or with respect to the nature of my judgment, which the circumstances compel me to elicit without delay. However, it is I who must choose either to accept what I said in my judgment or revolt against it by violating or falsifying it."

Violence and falsity are the two forms of evil; "one is rebellious, the other fraudulent." Dissociation of the good, hypocrisy, and rebellion are an unintentional evidence of its unity. "The good or good will is an indivisible unity of objective truth and subjective sincerity. Rebellion pays homage to sincerity by sacrificing the truth against which it rises. Hypocrisy pays homage to truth, which it honors still, by sacrificing sincerity, which it renounces."

Good is useful always. First of all, if good is adherence to truth, the more I adhere to it "the greater is the lesson which I draw from it in order to know how to regulate my life. In other words, my subordination to truth and the use I make of it in order to learn how to behave are two reciprocal and indivisible movements. For this reason, morality and utility can and must be distinguished but not separated from each other."

Thus, as I am unable to act without giving myself to the activity to which I am devoted (so as to make it "assume the dignity and consistency of an end," which "makes a Universal out of it") so I cannot "thoroughly implement an activity without living it while I am serving it; and I live it if I participate in it and interpret its meaning for myself, so as to make it my own and my good, in the very act whereby I dedicate myself to it and become part of it as well as its realizer." In this way, the good will becomes universal because of its submission to an end; but the orientation which the will draws from it for its sake is personal.

The activity to which I devote myself as to an end, unites in a unique *civitas* all those who pursue it. Thus, morality lays the foundations for society, but society does not found morality. Society keeps itself alive with two movements: one (proceeding upwardly) is the affirmation made through the consciousness of the rights which it believes itself to have and which it vindicates; the other (proceeding downwardly) is the application of laws through the ideal person consciousness itself creates when the spirit of justice, which it makes valid through the affirmation of its own rights, personifies itself in the presence of consciousness as an organized justice or a State that is about to sanction the prevarication.

Consciousness gives existence to the State and keeps it alive by respecting it, that is, by endeavoring to give others the same justice it claims for itself. However, this externally organized justice which regulates the common life of men is inevitably summary and approximate. Consciousness, which nevertheless expresses itself through this justice, cannot be satisfied with it, and so its tendency is to overcome it in some way or another, that is, through forgiveness, sacrifice, love, enthusiasm, and faith. These impulses are sometimes excessive, in-co-ordinate, and often incoherent. However, they can be regulated through different ascetic ways, though once in a while they may bring consciousness below the level of that eternal justice which it had tried to surpass in its effort to arrive at charity.

The third section of Guzzo's *Moralità*, which treats charity in the same way as the second had treated justice, analyzes in fact those "moral impulses." It studies the relationship between morality and religion and distinguishes between natural religion and positive religion. According to a Kantian expression, moral-natural faith "is postulated" by reason in its practical use, that is, by morality in act. In this way, one can go from morality to natural religion and not vice versa, while positive revelation becomes itself a source of moral precepts, and the impulse that morality receives from revealed faith assumes the meaning of a positive inspiration and a positive promise and guaranty of absolute value.

Religion-inspired morality presents two inseparable traits: an exaltation of action and an acceptance of suffering and resignation. There are not only great sufferers and great doers; but, on the one hand, the suffering of some great saints is already active and even heroic and, on the other, their overflowing activity draws its meaning and value from their self-renunciation, their acceptance of destiny, and the offering of their activity to God.

The fact that positive religion gives morality a guaranty of absolute value implies the perpetuity of this value. This explains the religious foundation of the spontaneous faith in immortality. As for its rational foundation, this consists primarily in demonstrating that in order to suppress the ever renewed faith in immortality, it would be necessary to consider man's natural aspiration to morality as a baseless prejudice; and, secondarily, in demonstrating that this aspiration to morality draws its meaning from the categorical aspect inherent in duty and implying the absoluteness and hence the perpetuity of value.

Now morality, which is a devotion to all activities to which it applies itself, is the condition for all these same activities invented by man and carried within himself. Science, art, and so on are activities created by man and not "forms" which are "natural" to the human spirit. They all are indefinitely perfectible; they are eternal or, rather, permanent though they are due to free, human inventiveness, which does not compel anything to stay in its "purity" (a purity that, nevertheless, these activities have acquired through history), nor does it compel us to try to invent other differently devised activities.

Such is the result of a "discussion" which in his book, *La Moralità, op. cit.*, clears the way for the analyses contained in his subsequent volumes dedicated to man's scientific, artistic, religious, and philosophical experience. The plan for these books is found, as we said, in Guzzo's programmatic work, *L'uomo, op. cit.* The "discussion," which we have just mentioned, contains some general lines concerning Guzzo's system, while his essays, in which his outline was more or less foreshadowed, contain particular developments.

In his book, *La scienza, op. cit.*, Guzzo sustains a fundamental and precise thesis, that is, *mathematics is a construction while physics is an experimentation.* And again—"freedom of mathematical construction and freedom of formulation of physical experiments on the basis and pattern of freedom in the mathematical construction." There is neither a fixed program nor a fixed concept of science. "Science has always revised its program in accordance with the renewal of object and method in its research. The concept of science has thus become gradually adequate to the becoming of science itself." This does not imply any relativism but only an adherence of epistemology to science in act. Scientific concepts come to maturity through history and none of them is definitive and unchangeable. Therefore, the philosophy of science should not be subject to any one of them, not even to the most recent ones. "Not because they are not justified, but because they too are justified by the *historical* realizations of the science of our times. Hence, it would not be legitimate to transcribe what is a historically determined scientific program into a theory of science which aims at achieving a validity not to be confined to a particular time even if it is our own age." There is not *one* mathematics but there are several. "The use of geometry by the ancients, the use of algebra by the moderns, and the use of arithmetic by our contemporaries are three modes of constructing mathematics." It is not mathematics in the abstract but the several mathematics which make a given experimental science possible "after achieving a definite order historically; such a science could not have been even conceivable in another historical phase of mathematics." What we call the "truth" of all the mathematics is in effect their logical constructiveness with which their thinkableness and "utility" coincide.

When mathematical theories are utilized by experimental sciences, the intrinsic thinkableness of mathematics becomes the thinkableness of experiments. The type of "truth" which is characteristic of experimental sciences "is similar to the type of truth belonging to mathematics because those sciences are constructed *ad instar* of the mathematical ones. As mathematical research has a moment of pure position of concepts and a moment of verification of the consequences drawn from them, so experimental science has, in that model, a moment of planning related to the experiment and a moment of realization related to the theoretical results delineated in the experiment itself. This resemblance also implies a profound difference, nevertheless. Experimental science, in fact, verifies *whether* the experiment gives a result that is in conformity with the project, while mathematics can only gather *whatever* consequences may develop from posited concepts. In any case, even if observation modifies —though in a negligible way—the phenomenon that is being observed, the experiment can make the phenomenon take place according to predisposed conditions. Hence it is possible to predict that the phenomenon each time will be the same as long as the conditions set for the experiment continue to be the same. However, science can never dream of attaining the phenomenon in its absolute being, independently of these or other conditions which were or were not set by man at its beginning." The experiment establishes the legality of phenomena, a legality that is interpreted as "reality" but not as a "necessity" under any pretense.

In fact, neither mathematics nor physics obeys a "necessity" of human thought. "Euclid *chose* to consider only straight lines and planes while also treating the circle and sphere with the *sole* criterion of straight lines *within* a circle and planes *within* a sphere. Thus, Euclidian geometry was constructed according to a chosen program, and not as a description of 'necessity' on the part of human thought. Real numbers and imaginary numbers are equally possible. The function of postulates in the construction and the free choice that is made of them show that mathematics is mental freedom like poetry, which, however, is another thing altogether."

The historical character of the natural sciences is also evident as is that of inventions. Such historical character in the sciences impresses a similar historicity on the very world of nature as this is known, utilized, and mastered by man. "In fact, historicity implies becoming, not immutability," although becoming itself requires some "constants" of becoming, such as are, in effect, the "laws" of phenomena. "Man is unable to pass over his historicity, but from within it he is able to combine again the logical continuity of his present thought" with the past and future, which he himself moulds in continuity with the same past and present. This is the way with which the compactness of the "world" around man is recomposed.

Thus, the nonnecessity or historicity of the mathematical-scientific knowledge does not authorize any relativism, which is not even permitted by the fact that every science has given itself its own logic and its own particular method that is one and the same thing with its structure. But, against the pretensions of scientificalism, Guzzo rightly remarks that it is untrue to state that thought which is not science is devoid of every logic. There is a logic in juridical and economic wisdom, but "this one is not to be put together with each logic pertinent to the various sciences because wisdom is the opposite of every science, and yet wisdom is a logic in that it would be arbitrary to deny a theoretical value to it by pretending to restrict it to practice." There is no human activity that can be assigned to practice exclusively, because authority alone is practicable. If that were possible, the sciences, more than wisdom, would be exclusively assigned to practice rather than being the only privileged ones to have a theoretical value. "Even wisdom determines its content as this is done by any thought, no matter how nonscientific it may be. Thus, the determination-law concerns every thought and, in this sense, it is identified with every thought." In short, Guzzo endeavors to guarantee the "logicity" (which does not signify necessity of a unique logic) of every form of spiritual activity and, at the same time, the autonomy of each one with respect to the others and of all with respect to science. Even the autonomy of religion, which, by "giving man the awareness of the uncertainty of whatever is human, is the opposite of that 'science' which in its presumption to know everything considered itself to be man's ultimate 'creed.' "

Furthermore, *the certitude of religious faith is not the certitude of science*, since the latter "believes" what it knows, while the other believes what it "shall know." Scientific certitude requires continuous verifications; instead, "religious certitude postulates its own final and absolute verification, which is deferred, by definition, to an experience and a knowledge quite different from what man knows on earth." Even philosophy cannot be confined to being only a philosophy of science, but it can and must concern itself with other human activities, such as practical life, art, and so forth.

In the concluding part, Guzzo draws the consequences flowing from the thesis that mathematics is a construction and physics an experiment. Through a more thorough inquiry about the concepts of thinking and experimenting, the concept of nature in science, that of the science of nature, and the concept of nature in man and of man, he sets forth the new problem posed by the new science as follows: If both mathematical construction and physical experimentation are free, how is it that nature, which certainly is not created by man who studies it, fits the human mind's theoretical, experimental, and technical initiative? If natural spontaneity and human freedom were not in agreement with each other, it would be impossible for man to construct the human world of industry understood in its highest meaning. "When mathematics and physics were thought to be an expression of the mind's immutable necessity and nature was believed to be entirely regulated by a necessity in its phenomena, there was no problem concerning the convening of both mental and natural necessity with a unique necessity which was to govern every real or mental existence." However, if thought is initiative even in rational and spiritual constructions, and if physical phenomena are considered by science to be real but not necessary, that is, such as to determine themselves rather than being determined, then the meeting of two freedoms (human freedom and natural freedom) is a problem that we must solve. To which Guzzo replies: the fact that these "two freedoms (which are often in contrast as this is proven by the difficulties encountered by science in its process) *may* harmonize proves their common origin and determination to correspond to each other, which is the more important as it is the more difficult and always contested and in danger of not succeeding." The harmonizing between natural freedom and human freedom is only a possibility.

In the last analysis, for Guzzo, philosophy is an aware and critical reflection upon human activity; yet, it seems to us that such reflection does not go beyond description or beyond the phenomenological moment, and that it stops at the threshold of the theological problem and of the other metaphysical problems. In fact, Guzzo's philosophy (or critical reflection on human activity) makes man realize that his "answers" are not exhaustive and, hence, his exigency or aspiration toward the infinite, which can be satisfied only by faith. Science and philosophy (though irreducible to each other) share the same inclination toward faith because neither is able to give an answer to the "why" of my existence, thinking, and so on. In other words, they have in common the same inability to solve the problems of metaphysics and so they both send us back to religious faith on the basis of an exigency genuinely felt by man. [Let us say in reply that] if philosophy, understood as a critical reflection on human activity, stops at this point, it is not itself (or the whole of itself) as yet, but only an "introduction" to philosophizing. The latter will really be an integral, critical, and exhaustive reflection when, in a rational and critical way, it has solved those same metaphysical problems which are now entrusted, as problems, to an exigency and, as a solution, to faith.

Guzzo is the animation of a highly promising school which gathers a certain number of young scholars around the periodical *Filosofia* founded by him in 1950. It suffices to recall, among them, the name of LUIGI PAREYSON (1918), who has already a scientific personality.

Pareyson can be considered in Italy as both the "historian" and the critic of existentialism without being an existentialist. He has explored the existentialist themes in favor of Christian spiritualism (*Esistenza e Persona*, Turin, 1950). For Pareyson, the solution to be given to the crisis of philosophy presents itself as a dilemma between Christianity and anti-Christianity. "If anti-Christianity succeeds in demonstrating the impossibility of a renewed Christianity, the solution will be anti-Christian. If a Christianity is really found which is capable of overcoming the theses of anti-Christianity, it will be Christian." For Pareyson, philosophy is philosophy of man, that is, of the individual, which means "awareness of the very life of the person." Christian philosophy is thus constructed on the metaphysical concept of the totality of the person which in it finds at the same time the problem and the solution to the problem of God's transcendence that is simultaneously reflected on the universal and personal form of thought. God alone can guarantee the person's freedom and independence. "All this amounts to saying that, although not displayed in explicitly rational and theoretical terms, a Christian philosophy still is present, living, and active wherever there is a will to freedom and a respect for the person." In a systematic way, Pareyson wrote an *Estetica* (Turin, 1955) in which he develops Guzzo's concept of a character serving "to form" all human activity and art as a "specification" of this universal formativeness. In fact, the book's subtitle is "theory of formativeness" and this means "aesthetics of form"—a form which is understood in a particular way: not simply as the opposite of "matter" or "content," but as an "organism endowed with its own life and internal legality." Consequently, on the one hand, form means a "totality which cannot be repeated in its singularity; also it is independent in its autonomy, exemplary in its value, complete and yet open in its definiteness which contains an infinite, perfect in the harmony and unity of its coherence-law, and integral in the reciprocal adequation between parts and whole." On the other hand, the word "formativeness" expresses better the dynamic character of the form; and, as Pareyson understands it, its essential aspect is to be a result or, more exactly, the positive outcome of a formation "process" because "form as such cannot be seen unless it is perceived in its act of concluding and also including the production movement at which it arrives and in which it finds its success." Unless we are mistaken, it seems to us that "the aesthetics of form as formativeness" aims at emphasizing, on the one hand, the autonomy of art which lives on its own rules though within the unity of spiritual life and, on the other, the totality of the artistic work even within its singularity. Moreover, it shows the dynamic character resulting from conceiving form not as a mould or a motionless model, but as that which makes itself, so that it is the finished form of a formation process which includes the very movement of production. Thus, this is an aesthetics of "production" and "formativeness" rather than one of "contemplation" and "expression." Consequently, this aesthetics is not like that of Croce in a sense, even though it includes some Crocian points; nor is it like that of Gentile, even though it agrees with the latter on the manner of conceiving aesthetics as a speculative moment which is not separable from the unity of the spiritual process; and, finally, I would also say that it is "non-Platonic" because of the dynamism attributed to form, that is, to a form that is such not because of its "being" a form but rather because of its "becoming" a form; in short, form is regarded as an outcome or success of a production process and not as something that is preconstituted and presupposed to it. However, it seems to me that form can be conceived in such a way as to avoid the static character of the Platonic form while preserving the profound meaning attached to it by Plato; that is to say, form should be understood as that which is intrinsically capable of stirring the production process in which it is implicitly present. In this way, form is not a datum, for it is actual in the process itself, as it is finally in the act of its own conclusion not, however, as that which is made through the process but as that which makes this process possible; through it, form makes itself explicit and specified. In short, it is at the end because it is at the beginning and also because, as actual form, it accompanies the whole productive and formative process.

From his manner of conceiving form Pareyson is led to consider art more as a "doing" than as an "expressing" or a "contemplating," in conformity with the classical conception of art as *poieîn;* and he is led to study the life of forms in Goethe, for this author has made a keen analysis of its birth, growth, maturity, and productivity in the artistic activity and in nature. On the other hand, Poe, Flaubert, Valéry and others have prompted him to study the character of the artistic activity which is composite and constitutive, calculating and adventurous, while Bergson and Dewey have called his attention to the organic aspect of art.

In this way, as Pareyson himself writes, "the formative activity, as it presents itself in art, appeared to me as that which in itself harmonizes both endeavor and organization; hence came the task of explaining how terms which are so diverse and antithetical may come close together (and not only 'awareness' and 'spontaneity' as in the aesthetics of romanticism, which misses the 'trying' character of the artistic operation as well as the organization as intrinsic in the outcome; and it seems to me that the method I used to overcome this difficulty can also point out the main point of my research and the newest aspect of the theory proposed by me."

A philosophical problem, whatever it may be, cannot be posed and solved separately. Thus, posing the aesthetical problem means facing other problems, and also verifying the results on the philosophical level, and this proves that the problem itself is a speculative one. Consequently, Pareyson analyzes formativeness in the entire spiritual life by pointing out, in every human operation, that formative character which makes it both a production and an invention, that is, a realization which advances, through attempts, toward success. What are the content, matter, and law pertinent to that particular specification of formativeness in which art lies? Pareyson replies that "*content* is the artist's whole spiritual life in that his personality becomes not only a forming energy, but even a mode of forming, namely, a style, and only as a style is it present therein. All this invites to surpass the old *querelle* between content and form because, in art, spirit is style and style is spirit, and this permits to avoid any debate on the concept of expression since in art there is nothing to say except doing and the very doing is a saying. *Matter* is necessarily physical matter. If we realize this necessity we eliminate any dispute on the technique and evincement because, in art, forming means forming a matter, nor is the work anything except a formed matter. The artistic process is invention and execution *at the same time* since the determination of the formative intention and the adoption, interpretation, and formation of matter are the same thing. Moreover, spirit and body are identified with each other in a work of art, and spirituality and physicalness are the same thing. The *law* governing art, then, is success itself. The artist has no other law then the individual rule concerning the work he is doing, nor does he have any other guidance except his presentiment of success, so that, in art, the work is both law and outcome of a formation-process. Only in this way can we understand how endeavor and organization in art not only harmonize but even appeal to each other and form an alliance because the work acts as something that forms before existing as something that has already been formed."

If spiritual life is wholly formative, it follows that every successful work is beautiful whether it is a speculative, practical, or a utilitarian one. This fact should not be conducive to aestheticism, but it should simply enable us to realize that the knowing process is also a formative one, in the sense that it is an "interpretation in which one endeavors to produce the image which conveys the thing; and the 'success' of knowing is 'contemplation' in which image and thing are identified in a unique form. Hence the possibility for the naturally beautiful, for things are beautiful provided they are seen as forms, and to attain this much one must know how to interpret them and represent a relative image of them." It seems to us that at this point Pareyson agrees with some of Baratono's acute remarks on the "sensible form" through which being is revealed; and this is, after all, the Platonic concept of sensible "appearance" which is being thought anew and in which form is transparent so as to be truly an "appearance" rather than a "fiction." Moreover, this is still a form of "realism" filtered through a proper idealistic thesis whereby the formed image reveals (though never entirely) the *being* of the thing, which can transpire through infinite images, inexhaustibly. The identification of image and thing within a unique form is what I call (in my language which is idealistic indeed) an elevation of the thing to truth. Plotinus keenly remarks that thinking is feeling while thinking; and feeling is thinking while feeling.

In concluding this exposition, we wish to emphasize once more the fact that aesthetics is a decisively speculative concept. Pareyson rightly remarks: "It is true that aesthetics is credited with being able to supply the critic with valid criteria of judgment; also that idea is widespread which states that the verification of an aesthetical thought lies in such ability and, with it, the criterion by which to accept or reject such a thought. However, if aesthetics really supplied such criteria, it would indirectly prescribe definite norms to the artist, and this obviously exceeds its limits because the task of philosophy is to speculate rather than to legislate. Indeed, aesthetics is useful to a critic in the sense that it offers him a philosophical awareness about the experience in which he moves; it also prevents him from relying entirely on his taste both by defining for him the relationship existing between personal taste and value-judgment, and by pointing to him the very structure of the artistic operation on which he has to reflect to the extent required by his conscious reading. Yet, this does not mean either telling the critic what art *must* be or offering him a precise criterion for the separation of poetry from nonpoetry." Croce is not mentioned here and yet the polemic is against his mode of conceiving aesthetics; nor is Gentile mentioned though this was his view on the "theoreticity" of art held in opposition to Croce. Indeed, to affirm the speculative character of aesthetics does not mean to disregard the experience of artistic facts; "aesthetics must reflect upon such experience in order to determine its structure, explain its possibility, define its meaning, and study its metaphysical scope." Nor does it have to make us disregard or even deny the historical character of aesthetics, since in the last analysis this is identical with the historical character of philosophy itself, which does not signify, as is commonly believed, a succession, alternation, struggle, and destruction of systems and theories according to fashion and kind of men; it means, instead, process and growth, development and advancement of research through more penetrating studies and amendments within the unity of philosophy, which aims at a universal and absolute validity, even if it remains always open to further integrations made possible by the infinity of truth and hence by the infinity of a thought which tests and probes it and expresses it endlessly.

*Christian Spiritualism: Sciacca's Metaphysics of Interiority**

The Christian spiritualism of MICHELE FEDERICO SCIACCA (1908) is decisively linked to the Augustinian-Platonic current and is deeply influenced by Rosmini. A professor of theoretical philosophy at the University of Genoa, he is presently engaged in giving a completely systematic form to his thought.

One can clearly sense, in the confluence of diverse aspects throughout Sciacca's vast production, the recurrence of a question which though continuously satisfied comes up again; yet, it is only in his recent theoretical works that it has certainly found a substantial gratification though not a total fulfillment. Being present in his *Linee di uno Spiritualismo critico* (Naples, 1936) which centers on the problem of God, this same question is proposed once more in his *Problemi di Folosofia* (Rome, 1941; 2nd ed., Rome, 1944) and in the *Problema di Dio e della Religione nella Filosofia attuale* (Brescia, 1946; 3rd ed., Brescia, 1953), and again in the *Lettere dalla Campagna* (Brescia, 1945), while it inspires and directs Sciacca's entire historical production. In fact, his historical research constantly develops along with his theoretical inquiry, so that the quest for God is conducted in the two fields simultaneously, and it reveals itself as a need to overcome not only a personal crisis but the crisis of modern thought. The historical inquiry obeys theoretical interests or, more precisely, internal ones as it always leads the reader's attention to thinkers who can be defined *lato sensu* as "Platonic," from Plato himself to Ros-

* These pages concerning the author of this work were written by Professors R. Crippa and G. Roggerone.

mini. Sciacca develops his argumentations along a line of lively participation in what has always troubled man and in what man has said so profoundly about himself (an instance of this is given by the letter "Zaccheo o di Dostoiewsky," in the *Lettere dalla Campagna*, quoted above). However, in his most recent works there is an emphasis on the quest for a theoretical, valid, and lucid truth as compared with his previous "compassion" which had a stronger tone. Without becoming abstract, the inquiry has gained a greater fullness. Progressively and polemically, the problem which arose from a need to reject the "whole being" of Gentile's actualism has become a problem that can find its solution principally and primarily by appealing to reason. The internal quest for the salvation of the whole man within truth has become a quest and realization of the *rational* foundation of truth, and this has reopened the debate on the same idealistic doctrine which, though rejected, has always been operating in him effectively. In his *Filosofia e metafisica* (Brescia, 1950), Sciacca is very close to Gentile in a certain respect, and he is so precisely because of his contending with the idealistic doctrine on its more truly theoretical level. The long process of detachment finds here its conclusion and, at the same time, its way toward a systematization that was lacking until now.

Sciacca's thought has been nurtured by a long acquaintance with Rosmini. The primary function of moral activity—as that which in the "acknowledgment of being" carries out the complete "circum-in-session" of spiritual life—is affirmed in *La filosofia morale di Antonio Rosmini* (Rome, 1939; 3rd ed., 1958), and is essential to a correct interpretation of Rosmini's thought (cf. also his *Interpretazioni Rosminiane*, "Opere Complete," Milan, 1958), while it leads Sciacca himself to a more complete metaphysical systematization of his own thought. His philosophy demands a substantial respect for human concreteness through which we essentially perceive and affirm our relationship with God, which must not be an abstract and internally useless one. The quest to safeguard the validity of our human doing within the concreteness and responsibility of the moral act is always present and effective without any heterodoxy.

It is in this light that I can understand Sciacca's dialogue with Blondel. The philosopher of *Action* and, above all, the philosopher of the trilogy appears to Sciacca as a thinker who can supply him with a productive and valid perspective. The richness of Blondel's interiority does not fail to operate effectively. In fact, moving along with Blondel, Sciacca makes a more thorough study of the problem of moral logic as well as a study of the more difficult problem of the consistency of beings. However, just as he cannot fundamentally agree with Blondel's integral realism, so he is not satisfied with the scarce substantial clearness of his logic and the lack of a precise definition of the relationship between intellect and will

("Attualità filosofiche," in *Atti del terzo convegno di studi filosofici cristiani*, Padua, 1948, page 264). Nevertheless, Sciacca accepts Blondel's lively demand for a philosophizing that listens to and locates the whole being, so as to pave the way for its complete satisfaction. He also agrees with the theme of the internal proceeding from man to God.

However, this contact with Blondel—while Sciacca goes on with his probing on St. Augustine whose influence he feels ever more—accentuates in him the more properly metaphysical demand with respect to the moral one. Pascal himself, with his forcibleness and "scientific" lucidity in probing into the "human fact," but, at the same time, with his clear perception of the philosophical limit characterizing this probing, induces Sciacca to pursue (even distressingly) this more theoretical search, though not to forget the torment and richness of our concrete existing for the faith or in the faith (see the preface to the anthological collection, *Pascal*, Brescia, 1946).

In *Filosofia e metafisica, op. cit.*, the problems of the foundation of the existent and of thought—which together with the proofs for the existence of God were incomplete in the *Linee di uno Spiritualismo Critico* (*op. cit.*)—are met with a clear and concise method. It is not possible to speak of the nothingness of the existent, as many existentialists do, because this would amount to placing one's self outside of any possible answer. "When anguish reveals the nothingness of the existent, which reason disguises, it does not posit a problem or a limit to reason, but it justifies reason for becoming disinterested in the existent. If it is posited as a nothingness of the existent, existential *nothingness* is the most rigorous suppression of the individual, which was ever even attempted by a speculative philosophy" (*Filosofia e metafisica*, Brescia, 1950). He who says existent—and not existence because the latter is an abstraction —says concreteness and he speaks of and affirms a becoming whereby *this-being* becomes *not-this-being;* he affirms an opposition under which there is an order because, if there were no unity and permanence of being, that is, if being did not remain identical with itself, there could be no movement going from *this-being* to *not-this-being*. It is *this* being that is contradictory to *not-this-being*, yet the being of either *this-being* or of *not-this-being*, is always the same identical being. "Existing is not the insignificant existence of nothingness, but it is the significant existing of something, that is, the 'existentializing' of an essence; and thus the problem of existing is not to be posited as a problem of pure existence, but rather as a problem of the existence of a *quid*." Thus, "that which is," is and it exists as something that enjoys existence; there is no existent which is not an existing and the "existentializing" of an essence. "In an ontological sense, being is *being which is existent* and this is the object of metaphysics. In its fullest meaning, *esse* is a synthesis of essence and existence, that is, an essence that has been actuated by *esse,* which makes *a* being out of it."

As a condition of revelation and subsistence of being, the primality of the existent is affirmed in an explicit way. The act of existing is the condition whereby a being is; but to deprive an existent of being means falling into absurdity. For this reason, if the metaphysical inquiry on the existent cannot neglect the analysis of essence, neither can it fail to consider the existent itself inasmuch as it is an existent. To confine oneself to a pure "eidetics" means falling into the abstract, as happened to so many philosophies, including the Aristotelian one; to reduce ontology to a doctrine on the pure existent means to build a phenomenology, at the most. The existent, *qua* existent, is never a pure possibility or a nothingness, but it is the concreteness of a being, a concreteness which does not have in itself its sufficient reason, that is, the cause for positing itself. "If I were the principle of my existing, I would be the creator of my being, and the act of existing of my being would be identified with the absolute Act of existing which makes every being which is exist—my essence would be identical with my very existence. Whatever project man is able to devise so as to establish himself as a being *in se* is always a project aimed at founding his being by himself; and this is bound to fail, unmistakably, because it is a project against man's consistency and a plot that man makes against himself and against his natural, essential, and universal vocation. Our tendency toward the Other is invincible and it is a tendency toward God. *Existing is not an end but rather the means of subjectivity: God is the end of every subject. The person's consistency lies in the person's relationship with the absolute Being.*"

Thus, because of its structure, the existent is an existence of being, and so it is a continuous and intrinsic transcendence of the existent itself; moreover, ontologically and teleologically it is a continuous inclination toward, and foundation in, Being whereby the existent is. Existence necessarily implies a *consistency* and the latter can be had only in God, with respect to whom our conclusive reasoning—aimed at clarifying the reason of being for the existent—can be started at the level of faith.

At this point, the ground is clear for us to consider Sciacca's capital problem, that is, the problem of the existence of God, which generally recurs in all his works but is particularly evident here. In fact, this theme is faced by the author in his most recent and significant work, *L'intériorité objective,* Milan, 1952; 2nd ed., Milan, 1958. In it, Sciacca shows himself to be, once more, the old pupil of Gentile so that, at least initially, his reasoning leaves aside all the requirements of concreteness, in order to focus, with a scrupulous and critical process, on the problem of the structure of our thinking. This point can be detected when, at the very beginning, he is not speaking of God as such but rather of the hypothesis of God, as if to maintain a most controlled check on the detachment from every internal urgency. Yet, in the concluding section of the work just mentioned, the author states that the whole human being must converge toward God; and the God which Sciacca seeks to attain is not the God of philosophers but the God of Abraham and Isaac. However, such a conclusion, together with the moral points treated therein, is made possible by and hinges upon what is held to be truly decisive—the demonstration "of truth."

The starting point always is man, not so much because for us modern man constitutes our most immediate and valid reality, but because through him we attain the revelation of that external world which has represented the beginning of philosophical inquiry for so long a time and for so many thinkers even today. In fact, if out of the real data from which I have to proceed I choose the things of the external world as a basis, it is evident that I must "reflect" upon them and posit for myself the problem of their reason of being and of their meaning in order to give rise to the problem of their contingency and origin and hence establish the hypothesis of "God." In other words, it is necessary that I transcribe the external world into mental terms or terms of thought (and to posit it as a problem amounts to transcribing it into other terms). Therefore, it is not the natural world as such that posits the problem of its origin and of its explanation and, with it, the hypothesis of "God," but the external world which is made object of our reflection. "The problem of the existence of God presents itself essentially as an anthropological problem and only subordinately as a cosmological one—no matter how we may consider this question."

Only in this way can we overcome, without neglecting it, the critical demand which represents the thorn of modern thought. "The problem of the existence of God (as well as that of metaphysics in general) must proceed from a critical presupposition: not from one which aims at probing—before facing the problem—the capacity of reason (in which case reason is made the judge of itself, that is, the accuser and the accused, at the same time) in order to ascertain whether or not it has the right to go beyond experience (as Kant did), but from the other according to which experience itself and reality as given in our experience remain devoid of their consistency and metaphysically unintelligible if—once they have been critically and thoroughly studied—that problem is not posited and solved. *Consequently, the problem of the existence of God is inserted at the very root of the critical problem.*"

However, Sciacca does not move from man in his immediacy but from the Cartesian *cogito* in which lies the starting point of critical thought. The *cogito* gives me a real datum, it tells me about my condition as a thinking being, but it does not supply me with an explanation; it does not tell me who has thought me through. Sciacca, nevertheless, leaves aside any discussion of the Cartesian formula and, rather, accepts it in its primary meaning with a view to ascertaining whether it paves the way to a transcendental solution only or whether through it one must arrive, in a different way, at the theistic conclusion arrived at by Descartes himself. The *cogito* is a datum and a certainty, but not truth as yet; and, for Sciacca, truth is not indeed to be found in the idealistic deduction. Where is it then? And how does it transcend our own thinking? All this can be grasped in the unfolding of the very process which led Descartes to the clearness of his *cogito* as well as in the same methodic and hyperbolic doubt which, as Sciacca remarks in the light of St. Augustine, has no real consistency since it continuously shows the presence of a thought without which doubt itself could not be legitimized and sustained. "If it were really possible to block up our minds within an absolute doubt, thought would cease in that very moment, and a *cogito* would never rise from doubt. It is contradictory to think and at the same time annul thought through an act of thought (namely, through an absolute doubt). He who doubts, thinks, but if he is thinking he cannot doubt about the reality of thinking, even in the most negative stage of his doubt. Instead, it is sufficient to have a thought—even as thought of a doubt—in order to imply the existence of God."

However, what is the reason for this affirmation? And how can it be justified? Let us examine, says Sciacca, the process of our thought and, more precisely, that capital function in it which is called judgment. The elements that are essential to judgment are a thinking and judging subject, a datum to be judged, and some norms or principles by virtue of which reason judges. Such principles are the terms to which reason refers in order to judge not only objects but also itself as well as other thinking beings. For this very reason, we eliminate the possibility of affirming the derivation of the said principles from sensation, since sensation itself is judged by and illuminated through those same principles; likewise [we eliminate] the possibility of implanting in the always limited and finite judging subject—analogously as regards reason in itself—the very source of those principles. If reason does not judge the norms of judgment and is instead judged by them, it follows that these norms are not produced by, but "are given to, reason and, as such, they are superior to reason itself because, as St. Augustine remarked, there is no doubt that *eum qui iudicat de quo iudicat esse meliorem*" (it is clear, in fact, that if reason judges on the basis of the said norms, it cannot place them under judgment, because if the same norm could be judged it would cease to be a norm of judgment in the presence of those norms judging it, for the latter alone would be the true and nonjudicable norms of judgment).

The origin of truth, according to Sciacca, is not then to be found in reason itself but in principles which transcend reason though they are present in it. The Augustinian doctrine of illumination enables Sciacca to eliminate, together with every form of innatism, the contradictoriness confronting that idealistic position which, in its reduction of all thinking to our thinking, never succeeds in grasping the very certainty of thought it would like to establish; and so it oscillates between the relativism of historicism and the contradictory mysticism of pure Act, which is able to arrive at perfect immanence, but not at mediation, only if it completely balances thinking thought and thought already thought; when this is not done, it falls into a position of transcendence.

The ultimate conclusion for idealistic immanentism is, in effect, a total positivism according to Sciacca. In fact, "if reason is immanent (wholly immanent) in the world and the process of the world is the process of reason itself, and if there still is a perfect adequacy between real and ideal cosmos, it follows that absolute philosophizing is the same as making science absolute so that philosophy is reduced to and identified with science; and this means that science is the Absolute while philosophy becomes its methodology."

This is nothing but a complete cosmologism and this is the charge and criticism continuously made by Sciacca against recent thought; he also uses it as a canon for his historiography. By emptying the idea of any form of transcendence, Hegelian and post-Hegelian idealism resolves all its content into the "world." Once the Kantian "noumenality" has been eliminated, our thinking is no longer "perceptive" of truth but "constitutive" of it; and in a most consequential way, it develops, through the Kantian mediation, not so much the principles involved in the rationalistic position but, rather, the new concept of idea as posited by empiricism. In fact, first with Locke and then with Hume, the term idea assumes a new meaning. It no longer is an intelligible object (or an image *a priori* of Intelligibility itself), but rather an image of the sensible, a pure content of subjective consciousness. Kant endeavors to overcome this position by restoring apriority. According to Sciacca, however, not even his effort was successful and this is true because Kant was bound by a substantially empiricist and "scientistic" motivation. Although it is not the same idea as that of the empiricist, Kant's *a priori* is conditioned by experience through which it receives all its content. Moreover, one tries in vain to find, through experience, a passage beyond the subject which posits the *a priori* itself. At this point, Sciacca introduces the distinction between intellect and reason. What is consonant with "reason" is discourse, and though the latter is transcribed into conceptual terms, it moves and subsists through the principles, which, however, can be noticed only by "intelligence" since the latter is prior to and even without reason. There

612

cannot be a "reason" of God without an "intelligence" of God. On the contrary, even when there is no reason of God (or it becomes lacking) the intelligence of Him is equally preserved, even if it is inexpressible because reason does not possess the means to begin the discourse. And this is true because nothing can snatch away truth from the mind or the mind from the truth, which is divine and superior and given to man.

God's existence presents itself as a reasonable postulate now, and Sciacca can give a precise formulation of this proof: *"The intelligent being intuits necessary, immutable, and absolute truths; from things and by means of sensation, the intelligent, contingent, and finite being can neither create nor receive the absolute truths he intuits; therefore, that Truth exists which is God, and it in itself is necessary, immutable and absolute.* Otherwise, it can be stated by using a more properly Augustinian formula: *Nothing is in man and in the world which can be superior to our mind; but mind intuits some immutable and absolute truths which are superior to it; therefore, that immutable, absolute, and transcendent truth exists which is God."*

The proof "from truth," in itself includes the proof based on causality, and the latter is rescued from the risk of an application which may be too scientific. In fact, if we stop at the scientific application of the causality principle, we are going to face what was first a Kantian and then a Schopenhauerian objection according to which Cause is extraneous to the very effects which (always finite) it is supposed to explain. In such a case, the causality principle would be exactly like the coach which, as Schopenhauer said, will take us to the threshold of our house but not into the house. This can be avoided when we realize that the procedure from the world to God is in fact made possible by the presence in us of that causality principle which, as an intuited and illuminating truth, permits the passage from things to God; and this is so because even previously to such passage, it permits us to grasp the most direct bond between the principle in us and God. In order to be fully valid, even the cosmological proof has to be related to an internal reason. They are the *primary principles or primal truths which made every true judgment possible (that is, they give the knowledge of sensible things) and, with it, they validate every argumentation from finite and contingent things to the infinite and necessary being or God.* Every rule of judgment is *first of all* a rule of our mind. Therefore, all possible, cosmological proofs depend upon the proof "from truth."

From what we have been saying, one can understand how Sciacca is led to re-examine and re-evaluate the much-discussed ontological proof. It would have been impossible to move from thought and leave this proof aside. For Sciacca, the idea of God no longer presents itself as a logical fact against which every usual criticism can be advanced. Since I think, and I cannot not think if I exist, I think of principles which do not come from me but come from some other Source. My thinking implies the existence of that truth which is the object of my mind and on account of which the mind judges and is a mind. It is clear that there can be no thought without the presence of truth. Now, inasmuch as it is an idea, the idea of God implies the existence of a thinking being which, as such, is endowed with truth. The atheist denies God because he denies the possibility of a true idea of God. "If we convince him that the idea of God is present in the mind and that, hence, to deny His existence is contradictory, the atheist surrenders or at least he is ready to reason according to truth. Thus, once we have overcome the difficulty of how man attains the idea of God, the proof is irrefutable in that it suffices to think of God in order to think of Him as existent." The alternative presented by the ontological argument is as follows: either one thinks of God or one does not think of Him; if one thinks of God, God exists. The atheist denies Him because he does not think of God at the moment when he denies Him. His mind is outside of itself. Thus, to repeat, if God is thought of, God exists; but, in order that the mind think of Him (and because it thinks of Him), it must partake of truth since the idea of God is present in the mind only because the mind is capable of truth. If God is a being in reference to which nothing can be thought of as superior, in the act whereby it thinks of Him the mind acknowledges the presence of something which is superior both to itself and to anything existent or even thinkable; and, consequently, the mind concludes (this argumentation is identical with that of the proof "from truth") that the absolute Being exists. "The ontological argument presupposes the proof "from truth." The mind adheres to a truth that is present in it and makes it subsist. There is neither a mind without truth nor a truth which is not the object of a mind. "The idea of God," continues Sciacca, "is to be understood in the same way in St. Anselm; that is, as a matter of fact we see there is a man who thinks of God and this idea belongs to him as something which is part of his nature, of his essential being. Here the point is not a mind *and* the idea of God but a mind thinking of God. Thus understood, the proof loses its purely conceptual and abstract character, which it presents at first and gains all its concreteness. St. Anselm does not move from the idea of God, but from the real being who thinks God, that is, from truth which adheres to the mind because it is connatural with the human creature through the act of creation."

The examination of the many proofs thus confirms the primality of the proof "from truth," that is, of that proof which in the very act of thinking grasps the reason for the transcending of our thinking. The hypothesis of God ceases being hypothesis and becomes a truth, so much so that the contrary hypothesis according to which God would not exist becomes a *forbidden hypothesis*. The natural and at the same time critical procedure on the part of reason leads to the point to which man's age-old wisdom arrives, that is, at a God which cannot be a purely cosmological principle, precisely because of the manner of proceeding of our interiorness and the manner of converging of all our real and diverse motivations. Man's deepest quest is to arrive at the God of religious consciousness and, likewise, the Christian philosopher's aim is to prove the existence of God in whom he believes by faith. But, just as it is not proper to make the exigencies theoretically conclusive in order to satisfy the first quest, so in the case of a Christian philosopher it is not permitted to make arbitrary mixtures between rational research and faith. Thus Sciacca affirms once more his aversion to all diverse forms of fideism.

His opinion is that one cannot ever arrive at God without, or in opposition to, reason. No apologetics and, least of all, a truly internal apologetics can afford to neglect that which makes man be a man. Instead of overemphasizing one aspect or another, we should restore the convergence of all components of spiritual life.

However, such a convergence, as Sciacca reaffirms in his work, *L'intériorité objective, op. cit.*, can subsist only on account of a first act, which represents in fact the essence of the subject as well as the bond of its complex articulation. That on account of which the subject is, that which makes the subject subsist as an ego (because it does not exhaust itself in the immediacy of its appearing but rather permits the subject to grasp itself as an ego), is exactly the constitutive presence of an exclusively internal act, an original determination of that *objective interiority* which is the presence of the primary truth in our mind and which, in fact, constitutes the subject and gives it its infinite capacity of thought. "On the one hand, the presence of being in all its infinite extension makes our thought be an infinite possibility and, on the other, since our thought is the thought of a finite being, it follows that in the very act in which such a presence grasps and reveals itself as a primary truth, it also grasps itself as a subject's self-consciousness, that is, as an *I am* and hence as something being determined by the subject's being in which it inheres. 'Thinking' is limited and circumscribed by the ego (namely, by the subject or real being) whose 'thinking' it is." Not an infinity of the thinking subject but an infinity in the thinking and concrete subject; and this is required in order that the subject be possible, otherwise everything is drowned in the surreptitious total-comprehensiveness of the transcendental.

Sciacca, however, warns us not to think of the real being, through which objective interiority is specified, as a content coming from the outside. If such were the case, we would then deny the very possibility for a determination of interiority itself. In fact, the real being, which in self-consciousness specifies objective interiority, is "a fundamental and internal perceiving (a perceiving without sensible image, unlike the act of sensing any other thing or even my own body, when I consider the latter the same as any other sensation of a something outside of myself); in this way, self-consciousness is an entirely internal act and the synthesis of a real being and ideal being, or of a subsistent subject and a thinking subject; *ontologically*, this is an objective interiority specified by the feeling of existing, which itself is an internal one like a fundamental feeling because in the moment in which the subject grasps itself as thought it grasps itself as a thinking 'ego,' that is, as a subject and hence as a real being. *To the act of thinking one's self is internally joined the act of feeling the self as existent and, likewise, to the act of feeling the self is internally joined the act of thinking one's self."*

In this line of reasoning, the convergence-theme is determined in all its ontological "syntheticity" as an essential concurrence in the subject of fundamental intuition, and consciousness of the self through this intuition and in this intuition, which reveals the subject to itself as the latter, in its constitutive feeling, is engaged by its natural capacity to want to be and to love to be.

The total engagement of the subject with itself signifies—as this is clear by now—a total engagement of the subject in a colloquy which makes every sufficiency impossible; in fact, the infinity of the idea, of the truth which makes up the subject, imposes on it, right in its interiority, the necessity of transcending itself in order to fulfill itself. "The light of being—though the latter is the possibility always actuated by self-consciousness (and in this sense the possibility is always actual but never in act), that is, it is essentially present in every act of the spirit, which itself is its specification—has a *logical priority* for every further act presupposes it; and it has also an ontological *pre-eminence* since it constitutes the absolute and supreme possibility and makes man not shut *in his own limit and in the limits of the world and of history* (namely, in the limits of created things or of the finite), *but constitutively open to the absolute or supreme actuality, to the fulfillment of the infinite potentiality of the spirit or of objective interiority in the total and ultimate act. . . .*

In this sense, what we call death is a passage beyond the line of time and a fulfillment of the objective interiority in the full interiority of itself in God and of God in itself, that is to say, its total actuation, the entirety and fullness of self-consciousness, which by now coincides with the objective interiority itself rather than being its determinant and circumscribing limit. Objective interiority only then will be wholly in act and entirely self-consciousness, not in the absurd sense that man is identified with God or annihilates himself in Him, but in the sense that, while remaining a creature, he will be gratuitously elevated to the fulfillment of himself in the fullness of the divine vision [perhaps it can be said that the *lumen gloriae* or the supernatural beatifying vision is the supernatural limit of the *lumen veritatis,* which is natural]; only then self-consciousness will be no longer limitative, in that it is not limited as in the world of finite reality, and this is so because God will fill it with Himself and will make it coincide with the fullness of absolute and infinite truth."

From the presence of Truth in human thought to the final permanence of the subject in the Truth which constitutes it, Sciacca's discourse always remains decisively "intellectualistic" as it constantly seeks to grasp the total sense of life within truth, which is valid to man only if he conquers it rationally.

L'uomo questo "squilibrato" (Milan, 1956; 2nd ed., Milan, 1958) bears the subtitle, "an essay on the human condition," and supplies an example of this *engagée* philosophy which is characteristic of Sciacca, and which arises from a radically persistent need of surpassing what is "temporary" and "seeming" in order to grasp "the essentiality of spiritual life." This is an extremely important problem because "to be at fault in our life-behavior means failing our own life and irreparably living a wrong life." However, this is a highly complex problem at the same time, since in order to solve it "one must arrive at the bottom and search man in his most hidden roots so as to drive out truth and goodness as well as falsity and evil, even from the underground recesses of his life. . . . The content is to be pulled out and tested and even turned upside down, so as to avail ourselves of all those elements which are apt to reinstate the fullness of man once they have been raised to the level of order and of man's 'normalcy.' "

In the first section of the work just mentioned, Sciacca analyzes the structure of the *normal man* by emphasizing his being an "individual" and a "person." "All the active principles constitute the subject man, but the vital, sensitive and human principles represent his nature as an *individual,* while the spiritual ones constitute his *person.*" Hence there is a need for the perfecting of man in his twofold aspect as individual and as person. But the person is not an immanent value; it, instead, incarnates values which are not completely and absolutely realized within historical existence; their full and complete realization is instead to be attained only in the absolute and transcendent Value whence they draw their origin and to which they are inclined as to their end, which attracts them while hastening their development. Thus the person "realizes itself by responding to the fundamental and primal vocation coming from Being, which is its beginning and end." The person's authentic, radical, and existential "inquietude" lies in this vocation "which is man's true 'infirmity,' his most noble illness that puts him above all other living creatures." In

617

this way, human structure presents itself as characterized by a "total synthesism" between the person and its individuality and between the spirit and its body. This condition results from the *fundamental feeling* which reveals man in his "simple state" in which he lives in an original and direct way, and also from the reflex life which tends to confirm the primordial synthesism of body and spirit. Hence the perennial state of tension in which man finds himself in order to realize himself as harmony and equilibrium. Hence again, the continual "unbalance" which befalls man and hastens him to engage himself in order to carry out his destination, his *absolute future*. This "lack of balance" arises from an inadequacy between finite and infinite, which is manifested in man both as an impossibility of making our limited achievements be up to the intuited being (so that "in every particular realization of ours persist in us the impetus to move ahead, the further ambition, and the intact force which activates an inexhaustible dynamism"), and as a perennial inadequacy between consciousness of the self and the totality of the objective being. At the root of ontological existence there is, then, according to Sciacca, a primary and original intuition of our being, so that what we intuit first is indeed a being-Idea, but this is also an intuition of the subject as a being. Consequently, this which we intuit first precedes every reflexive knowledge. "The Idea is the first object of the intellect (as Rosmini says), but in this fundamental intuition there is, simultaneously, an intellection of the existential being or subject." On the other hand, there is in human nature a natural and irrepressible tendency which is conducive to a mediation between immediate consciousness and reflective consciousness. Our reason unfolds side by side with primary intelligence, so that what is experienced in immediate consciousness becomes a problem. In this way, the infinite problematizing of our existence comes into being, for there is no series of rational problems that can be exhausted, and, with it, rises the dialectic of intelligence and reason.

In this spiritual dynamism, a twofold transcendence is manifested "toward the inside and toward the outside": on the one hand, a transcendence of the objective being with respect to finite being and the tendency of the latter to come out of its subjectivity and reach for the world in search of other contents, and this is the transcendence of *reason* or of knowing; and, on the other hand, a transcendence of the existing being thinking in the infinite light of truth, that is, a transcendence of the objective interiority with respect to every knowing. The latter is a tendency whereby *intelligence* moves within itself (or it penetrates within another spirit) in search of the spiritual and absolute Being. Thus the dialectic of intelligence and reason expresses the two fundamental conditions characterizing the immediate and the reflective; and since in intelligence there is always an infinite content that surpasses knowledge, the existing being always feels in itself its own inadequacy, and this acts upon the mind as a powerful lever. In this being insufficient to one's self lies the internal, perennial tension characterizing life in its concrete dynamism.

The moral act requires the employment of intelligence, an original and internal illumination, which in its "penetrativeness" goes beyond the "consequentiality" of reason. This, however, does not mean that reason is to be expunged from moral practice, but only that there are forms and modes of ethical reason, which though not immoral are in no way moral either. They are due to virtuousness "on account of habit, custom, tradition, and education, and also because of convenience or mediocrity." This is a kind of ethicity which "does not require efforts or sacrifices, nor does it call for a struggle against egoism and evil; instead, it tames egoism, accommodates it and reaches a compromise with it; it is an ethicity that behaves diplomatically and, under any circumstance, it goes no farther than reaching a certain equilibrium. In effect, it manifests a certain temperament that is convenient because the renunciation is confined to what is needed for a nonviolation of virtue and nothing more, so much so that our being virtuous cannot go so far as to call for a drastic intervention." Now, even this attitude is a virtuous one, but it cannot properly be said to be moral because it is devoid "of that 'intelligence' which alone makes virtue be moral and reason be a safe guide of knowledge and evaluation." "To possess virtue is a matter of 'ethical reason,' but to be good is a characteristic of moral intelligence." It is necessary that virtues be vivified by love and illuminated precisely by the *intelligence of love* in order that they may fully acquire their moral importance. But this is possible only if we use no hypocrisy and act with all sincerity. Then the *ethica minor* of reason is completely converted into the *ethica major* of intelligence, while the possessive, immanent, and antihumanistic tendency on the part of ethical reason is transformed into the givingness, transcendence, and humanism of moral intelligence. In other words, "moral intelligence is opposed to ethical reason when the latter represents the egoism of the virtuous person, or of a virtue resulting from calculation and dosage, or that of an ethicity consisting of rules and relations. Again, the same opposition occurs when ethicity results from a logic that arises and constitutes itself on its own, and then is applied to action as something extraneous to it, as something that instead of regulating the action functions as its shutter or extinguisher. Moral intelligence, on the contrary, is not opposed to reason and logic when these, jointly with the former, are kindled at the flash of intuition and are allowed to descend into the infinity of being and in the transport of the will at the moment of initiative in the acknowledgment act with which the will loves every being in its degree of being and makes every virtue be virtue." This is not a question then, as some used to say, of an abolishment of reason but a matter of a refusal to understand it in its purely notional and discursive form, isolated from the other forms of spiritual activity, so as to be abstract, abstracted, and abstracting"; this is a refusal which implies the pursuit of solidarity as well as that of deep convergence, which stands at the basis of the superficial opposition between moral intelligence and ethical reason.

Atto ed essere (Milan, 1956; 2nd ed., Milan, 1958) is closely connected with the problems discussed so far; and, more than that, it completes them substantially through the analysis it makes of the ontological basis characterizing the human structure, which in *L'uomo questo "squilibrato,"* *op. cit.*, is dimly seen in the background. Once the autonomy of the ontological inquiry is stated in the introduction, Sciacca then affirms the "humanistic" character of metaphysics as a metaphysics of man and not of the real as real. In fact, the "real" is not "being" but only one of the forms of being, namely, its natural form which, as such, is philosophically irrelevant, because "philosophy is a reflection on spiritual life in its existential concreteness, that is, a life which is incarnate and living in the world." Being is dialectical, but not according to the dialectic of "exclusion" of contraries or of "resolution" of opposites; it is so, instead, according to the dialectic of *implication.* The latter "implies, without denying the being of a thing, the being of its contrary or of its diverse in new syntheses," and represents a dialectic which is characteristic of the philosophy of integrality; for example, in the "whole" of a many-colored flower garden the diverse colors coexist "spatially," making up a "physical" ensemble which is just external but not a "unity." "But if we overcome the realistic, spatial, and material illusion on account of which the garden is a thing which results from the "ensemble" of so many things standing one beside the other, and we feel the garden as a unity of colors, it is no longer an external thing but rather an internal existence; it is as my feeling makes it exist, and to me who am feeling it, it reveals that being which I disclose in its appearance." In other words, "being is the contrary of nonbeing and each one is identical with itself; but these two identical-contrary ones are simultaneously present and they make up (in the finite being) a unity, though they remain being and nonbeing, respectively." Thus, through the analysis of the essence of being and of the dialectic of its forms, once more Sciacca takes up the concept of *objective interiority,* which is not a possibility of feeling, thinking and willing, nor is it feeling, thinking and willing in act, but rather is a "feeling-act," a "thinking-act," and a "willing-act" representing the condition for any further feeling, knowledge, and volition. Objective interiority is then a fundamental feeling, the very act of existing. The synthesis between fundamental feeling which represents the *principle of pure sub-*

jectivity, and what is intuited of being which represents *the principle of pure objectivity*, is a *primitive ontological synthesis*, and this is an "initial" one with respect to all further determinations through which it is specified and always partially realized. It also constitutes the primitive, actual power, while reason is an actual power resulting from the former so as to be a derivative one. Thus, being is the essential object of both intellect and reason. However, since being extends infinitely—inasmuch as it is an Idea—the intelligent subject which intuits it extends itself beyond the real and the knowledge of the real. "The exceeding of the spirit over nature is not an exigency but, rather, an ontological, original, and essential condition." Hence a double dialectic, one concerning the *implication* of the Idea in the first intuitive act, and one concerning the *tension* between the infinite of the Idea and the subjective act, which intuits the Idea and by which it is constituted. God alone is being in itself; every other being is not in itself but only *in relation* [to others] and in this sense it is *dialectical*. It, in fact, needs a mind, which is external to it and which thinks it. The Idea can only be in relation to the mind and the latter is a mind only in relation to the idea, which is its constitutive object.

Dialecticity characterizes both the being which Sciacca calls "existent," that is, the spiritual being which is a finite subject, and that one which he calls "real," that is, the material being which is an object or a thing. The distinction of forms implies the unity of being, and this is not to be understood as a multiplicity within unity or as a multiplicity consisting of parts of being but, rather, as an *ontological* synthesism or a synthesism of being according to what we have already said.

Thus we come to the consideration of another aspect of the ontological problem, that is, to the dialectic of existence and reality. The *existent*, which is characterized by its self-feeling, self-volition, and self-intellection, is not reducible to the *real* or thing which does not feel and does not know that it exists. Not only this, but existence precedes reality and every real, which is in fact a real in relation to existence and only in relation to it. Thus, being-act is opposed to the real-thing, "but such opposition excludes dissociation while synthesis is included"; and, furthermore, the dialectical nexus between existence and reality rests on implication and not on opposition. Neither can there be a real without an existent, nor can an existent without a real live and "exist." "Vitality" is accidental with respect to existence, but, in so far as man is concerned, it is necessary to his existence in the world. In its accidentality, life has then a positive function that cannot be eliminated because it allows the existent to have its try, develop its personality that cannot be repeated, and carry out the "project" which the existent is. In this sense, *economy* and *technique* acquire a very marked ontological character; the real in general is seen as a "sign" of values and as something which arouses values and nonvalues infinitely. "Stars are rocks . . . unless they are a firmament being contemplated as an aesthetical or a scientific value."

A threefold ontological relation is thus delineated, and it represents a triple alterity or a moral relationship between man and nature, man and another man, and man and God. This dialectical and harmonizing nexus brought into evidence by ontological inquiry establishes the harmony of the moral world that we have just considered. In this sense, the last pages of this small book *Atto ed essere, op. cit.*, are closely linked to *L'uomo, questo "squilibrato," op. cit.*, as they succeed in achieving a more complete and exhaustive ontological justification. Finally, with an effective synthesis this small book recalls the nexus between ontology and metaphysics, as well as between being in the unity-distinction of its forms, on the one hand, and, on the other, the principle of every being; in this way, it links explicitly the present construction to the themes and problems of *Filosofia e metafisica* (*op. cit.*) and of *L'intériorité objective* (*op. cit.*), so that the substantial unity of this "philosophy of integrality" gains an obviously organic consciousness.

Christian Spiritualism: F. Battaglia, L. Stefanini, R. Lazzarini

FELICE BATTAGLIA (1902) (like Carlini, Guzzo, and Sciacca) shows the influence of Gentile's idealism. A professor at the University of Bologna, only recently has he arrived, through a self-criticism of idealism, at a form of Christian spiritualism as is evidenced particularly by his works, *Il valore nella storia* (Bologna, 1948), *Il problema morale nell'esistenzialismo* (Bologna, 1949), and *Moralità e storia nella prospettiva spiritualistica* (Bologna, 1953).

Gentilian idealism means an assuming of the spirit in its dialectical logicity which can give a significance to the world. But once the idealistic itinerary has been concluded, Battaglia thoroughly examines the necessary logicalism of the spirit, which to him appears to be naturalism. "Spirit is nature if it is bound to its structures and functions, is completed and perfected by its intrinsic logicity and has only the task of being itself. . . . The fact is that a living spirituality cannot be enclosed in a cocoon as it were, wherein one digs without a way out." The logical cycle of idealism, like that of any philosophy of immanence, is human and only human since to it philosophy is solely worldliness and consciousness of worldliness. The other contemporary philosophies (logical neopositivism, existentialism, Marxism, and historicism) are also at the level of absolute worldliness, and this makes them close to idealism in whose criticism they are involved. Each of these philosophies criticizes the others "although they result from a common mould and have in common a fundamental aspect. Existentialism has sprung from the negation of idealism in a completely 'alogical' way; neopositivism has arisen, on the other hand, from its refusal of metaphysics while giving its assent to logic in so far as the latter is a producer of hypotheses. Likewise, Marxism and historicism are genetically bound to idealism, even if for obvious reasons they oppose existentialism and neopositivism. However, regardless of the relationships and connections characterizing these trends in contemporary speculation, all that really counts for them is the finite or concrete, and this alone is given to us for our understanding and for our trouble. Neopositivists and existentialists, Marxists and historicists are immersed in the finite and concrete, which amounts to saying in worldliness. This is the first time that philosophical speculation appears to be totally worldly in its general directions. Worldliness joins together the most opposing trends of thought."

Nevertheless, finiteness and worldliness, which these philosophies of immanence made absolute, cannot satisfy man. The circle of the microcosm, which epitomizes and summarizes the macrocosm, and the macrocosm which develops and unfolds the microcosm—so that, ultimately, the natural cosmos is made equal to the spirit and the spirit finds its adequacy within the world—present a gap and an unbalance which signify the inadequacy between spirit and nature. Just on account of this inadequacy we depart from naturalism and move instead toward the foundation of spiritualism. But not the whole of idealism, says Battaglia, is to be rejected; [some aspects of it are to be preserved], as for instance "the critical premise from which idealism moves and its critical plan of inquiry according to which there is neither a theoretical nor a practical process which consciousness is not able to attest and guarantee." However, the act that takes roots in consciousness is never perfect and complete because at any moment it meets with error and sin which idealism cannot account for. "In short, the spirit to which we go back is one that critically attests and guarantees all processes for us, one that is involved in all knowledgeable and practical vicissitudes, whatever they may be. And wherever this spirit is led to in order to unfold itself, it finds a limit and a residuum, and, right in its own depth, it encounters an irrationality which upsets its acts. Man cannot be defined within the rational, as an animal wholly rational, but rather within the simultaneous presence of the rational and irrational, as one who tries to master the irrational and never succeeds perfectly if error threatens his truth and sin disturbs his goodness." Here is how, then, the religious demand attains its legitimacy within the same concept of spirit. Ours is "a world marked by God, and though it is what it is—finite and imperfect, 'arational' and irrational, narrow in its limits and agitated by its errors—it has before itself something that certainly is Value, a Value which in fact makes it worthwhile. There is still a process of tension wherein man, who religiously turns to the hereafter, also turns back to the world once more, so as to transform it. The mere valorization process as assumed by the worldly and idolatrous philosophies is opposed by a process in which the highest value is gained in a worldly way, exactly because, religiously, it is posited as a distinct one." Consequently, "any conscious philosophy or any philosophical anthropology must seek a solution which can only be spiritualistically religious. Religion is a conclusive solution that philosophy offers to us in so far as the problem of life is concerned."

Evidently, the passage from immanent idealism to theistic spiritualism is made possible for Battaglia on account of the problem of *value* or, more precisely, on account of the spiritualistic justification of value, which this thinker is able to restore through his criticism of the Crocian and Gentilian concept of history. He poses the following question of historicism: "If history is logicity and if speculatively viewed, the problem of history leads us to consider reason as the sole root of historical thought and of historical becoming, is there not the danger of nullifying all values through the reduction of both series in terms of rationality wherein the more we exalt history as logicity the more we lose it as morality?" In order that value may escape death it must escape the "immanence of a whole that has been made logical and rational as well as impersonal and transcendental." Duality is within the act, which is inseparably consciousness of its own being and consciousness of what it ought to be. It is exactly the value which gives history a significance that transcends it. History is no longer *per-se*, but for *something else*, for personal and moral consciousness which, though realizable within history, is related to an irradiating center of values, which is God or the absolute Value.

LUIGI STEFANINI (1891-1956), who was a professor at the University of Padua, at first called his philosophy a "Christian Idealism" (*Idealismo cristiano*, Padua, 1931), then, a "Christian spiritualism" (*Spiritualismo cristiano*, Como, 1942), and finally, a "metaphysics of the person" (*La metafisica della persona*, Padua, 1948). His thought was influenced by idealism and existentialism, and also by Gioberti. "Being is personal and whatever is not personal in being is included in the person's productivity, as a means of manifesting the person and of communicating with other persons." Thus, the starting point of any demonstration is the experience I have of myself because the ego is the primary and central fact of experience. Moreover, the ego is a *person*. If the sense of the primacy of the spiritual in the internal experience of each individual is lost, it is no longer recoverable. "No metaphysics can be constructed unless its first chapter is psychological."

Evidently, this is not subjectivism. The person, which is not exhausted within sensible experience, becomes discourse, mediation, and reason. Yet, it is necessary to avoid the danger of making reason a spectacle to itself; it should be a "reasoned reason" (namely, a logical process that is impersonal and constant) instead of a "reasoning reason." "To be rational means acting and thinking always with all my soul, so that in every word and gesture of mine I may feel the vibration of my total life."

More than "unity," the person is *unicity*, an unmistakable reality that cannot be repeated. God created us as similar to Him as possible, that is, as free beings. But this unicity does not mean absoluteness. Regardless of my finitude, I continue to exist in being though I am not *the* being. "The primality of the spiritual, which first of all I have experienced in myself, rouses me in order to indicate to me the first absolute which makes me real not by resolving me into its substance—which is fulfilled in the personal infinity of self-possession—but by giving me that personal substantiality which distinguishes me from Him at the moment He holds me suspended at a gesture of giving liberality. *Transcendence becomes a constitutive form of my being and hence a category of my thought* in that I am not able to think anything absolutely or to will anything as an absolute value, unless I think the Absolute belonging to me not as a condition of my own but as a presence in me of its act supporting me. The derivativeness of my being from God is compared to the transparency of my act on God; or, better still, this relationship can be reversed and placed in a rigorously critical perspective—*inasmuch as my act is significative but not constitutive of the Absolute, I affirm the derivativeness from the Absolute of the being in which this act is expressed.* I am always confronted by my expressive act, always shut in the limits of my own insufficiency. But, since it is the hand of God which touches me and supports me, I cannot with my word bring to light the depths of my being without including in it some meaning related to that God to whom, in this way, I am united and which, as it were, is causally prolonged in me."

Stefanini amply applied his metaphysics of the person to aesthetics (*Problemi attuali d' arte*, Padua, 1939; *La metafisica dell'arte*, Padua, 1949; *Trattato di estetica*, I, Brescia, 1955; Vol. II consists of fragments only), to the social problem (*Personalismo sociale*, Bergamo, 1952), and others. For him, art is singularity and expressive absoluteness, "absolute expression and spiritual absoluteness; hence the moment of singularity indicates that art is not expressed by means of universal and abstract concepts but as something absolutely individuated and personal, which is also absolute in its expression. Although there is in art a certain unavoidable surrealism, there still is a bond between art and reality. Art is "nature and more than nature; it can make a leap only from the earth to the earth, but is, at the same time, metamorphosis, transfiguration, and translation." Art is "ahistorical" ("it fixes the instant" and "is solitary"), and yet it has a historicity of its own. In fact, "every literary document, every architectonic form, every shade of color are highly sensitive recording-instruments reflecting the soul of generations." Through art, one elevates oneself to the divinity. Art is "word" and the artist creates with the "word" as God does. "Modern aesthetics is a secularized theology." Through art nature surrenders to the spirit, but only in a "juggling" way, "in the reality of the dream." Therefore, instead of abolishing philosophy, art makes it necessary. The absolute in art is not the absolute of metaphysics. "By experiencing the unsolvable in life, man must surmount art and the paradise of omnipotence that it gives him, in order to define with an idea of his own the meaning of the *absolute* not belonging to him. From the immense dignity conferred upon us by art, we must proceed to an understanding of the sobbing of existence which, as Baudelaire writes, echoes throughout the centuries and breaks at the feet of God on the edge of eternity. Reason surmounts art from which it abstracts the most adequate image of the absolute."

RENATO LAZZARINI (1891), a professor at the University of Cagliari and a deeply mystical spirit, aims at constructing a moral metaphysics or, if you wish, a metaphysical morality, which he is unable and unwilling to separate from experience and from the religious idea. For him, a philosophy of life is essentially a philosophy of salvation (*Saggio di una filosofia della salvezza*, Rome, 1926). The problem of evil (*Il Male nel pensiero moderno. Le due vie della liberazione*, Naples, 1936), relates of necessity to a conception of life which is either eschatological or antieschatological. His study on intention (*L'Intenzione*, Rome, 1940) enables him to show how the form of personality can be only found in an essentially and fundamentally intentional, real relationship between man and the divine absolute; without it, the concept of perdition becomes plausible and understandable. Philosophy must have an essentially religious character in that it has to assume an attitude as regards our destiny. When it is not a purely gnosiological methodology, philosophy is for Lazzarini a commentary on life and, hence, a science of the last problems more than a science of the first ones. Moreover, the solution of these problems is not one of necessity; hence the great importance and ontological value of this philosophy, on which not only a vision of life and of the world depends but also a *determination* and a realization of it, in one sense or another.

In the volume *Intenzionalità e istanza metafisica* (Rome, 1954), this author once more treats his favorite themes, and his solution of the metaphysical question is given in terms of an "option" on the part of the will. Lazzarini's argumentation is here influenced by the concept of intentionality as expressed by phenomenology and by the concept of option as developed in Blondel. These two concepts, however, are thoroughly studied and their meaning surpasses both phenomenology and Blondelianism; in fact, they are united in a synthesis which extends to Augustinian and Bonaventurian themes and, through Kant, this synthesis meets with existentialist exigencies though not with existentialism proper. Thus Lazzarini hopes "to find an orientation and a light (however dim) in the concept of possibility and intention. Intention is understood as free and, as such, capable of presupposing freedom of option in the presence of those conclusions—perhaps the last ones—on the part of our destiny."

In its basic meaning, intentionality is "an act of reference to something else, and it indicates the constant mode of being of spiritual life." In an earlier work, Lazzarini studied the difficulties and antinomies which are present in moral metaphysics, while in the one mentioned above he studies more thoroughly two exciting themes, critical gnosiology and problematical metaphysics—"critical gnosiology" only in the sense that "a critically founded gnosiology makes a metaphysical theory, which is formulated as hypothesis, not only possible but also necessary." Moreover, such a metaphysics is necessary in that, for Lazzarini, a theoretical metaphysics "can only be problematical and hypothetical, that is, it stands far away from that univocal dogmaticalness which is claimed by some currents of thought commonly classified as intellectualistic or rationalistic. Only a hypothetical metaphysics is able to make room for a pure choice, that is, one which is free from any psychological or historical condition." Regardless of Lazzarini's efforts, it seems to us that a critical gnosiology does not imply a problematical metaphysics or one that is formulated as a hypothesis. On the contrary, the most exacting gnosiological criticism implies a metaphysics that is neither hypothetical nor dogmatic. Nor does this choice or option belong to this or that metaphysics; instead it stands *before* univocal metaphysics, whose logical strength is in no way compelling as regards the will. On the other hand, in the case of hypothetical metaphysics which, as Lazzarini claims, is the only one to allow a choice, we find that its truth undergoes exactly that psychological conditioning that he tries to avoid. The same intentionality, which Lazzarini amply analyzes and assumes as a suture-point between critical gnosiology and problematical metaphysics, is weakened exactly in the function that should be performed with regard to option.

From his point of view, instead, Lazzarini believes intentionality to be the principle that satisfies the metaphysical exigency. His manner of arguing is coherent: "The call to alterity is a motif that is inseparable from every spiritual act. . . . We arrive at the self when we (intentionally) relate our being to ourselves as if our starting point were something different from us." Thus, otherness has a pre-eminence over the ego in this intentional process; yet phenomenology is able to surmount the

boundary of pure phenomenality and consider itself at the level of existence. "However, where does this constant referring to something else
lead? Does this reference to something else, and then again to another
thing and so on and so forth, reveal a perennial instability, temporariness,
and conditionalness? Or does it tend to stop at an Alterity that is in some
way definitive and unconditioned?" Now, the pre-eminence of alterity
would be illusory without the admission of an unconditioned alterity. On
the other hand, "the unfolding of the subject's intentions is not necessitated but is free, so much so that it can relate to this or that alterity
according as the spirit directs it. Some of these references will be sterile
and in a potential state, while others will be completely unfolded and
brought to light. That capacity of choice, which is unfolded exactly in
its looking after or in its being intent upon this or that otherness, is
closely connected with the intentionality-process. We are free in that we
have freedom of choice. We are free, that is, not because we create but
because we concreate reality.

This freedom of choice is exercised even in the presence of an Alterity
that may have been posited as absolute. In fact, we may or may not accept
it. Moreover, we are able to choose between two models of Alterity in
such a way that we confer absoluteness upon one of them and deny it
to the Other. Upon doing this, we are prepared to accept the consequences
of this final choice unconditionally.

We realize then that we must look into optional intentionalism in order
to find the primary cause of such a choice. Being present in every intentional act, the choice element must be laid bare exactly when we have to
give our existence a general orientation. Choice is not determined *a
priori*, absolutely. The determination *a priori* pertains instead to the terms
of temporary or final alternative but not to choice, particularly when the
latter is considered at its own level, that of pure intentionality."

This is all very well, but the choice of a metaphysical hypothesis can
never make the hypothesis true. I can simply believe that it is so, even
with some foundation. The value of choice is not theoretical in itself, as
the will is not, even if it is true that there is a theory of the will. The
solution of the metaphysical problem and, in Lazzarini's case, of the existence of God, which is absolute Alterity, cannot be given through option,
which is always a subjective act, an act of faith.

Anti-intellectualistic positions, based as they are merely on exigency and
faith, do not represent the essentiality of Christian spiritualism. The
latter is intent upon building a critical metaphysics of man, rather than
one of nature—a metaphysics that can rest on a rational foundation, that
is, on a reason that is grasped in the concreteness of existence as well as
in the totality and integrality of spiritual life.

Christian Spiritualism: Its Influence

Of present-day Italian philosophical currents, Christian spiritualism is the only one (besides Croce and Gentile) to have aroused some interest outside of Italy; its influence extends to several areas of philosophical thought in the postwar period. In fact, this current is the only one to be considered and discussed in works dedicated to contemporary speculation; and its exponents are among the few Italian writers of philosophy to be translated into the principal European languages.[7] To mention a few, we cite ROBERT CAPONIGRI (1914), who is a professor at the University of Notre Dame, and A. DE MIRANDA BARBOSA (1917), a professor at the University of Coimbra, who in the book *A essência do conhecimento* (Coimbra, 1947), delineates a "critical realism" that is elaborated through an analysis of modern thought and shows some Augustinian influences.

A closer position to Sciacca's form of spiritualism is that represented in Spain by ADOLFO MUÑOZ ALONSO (1915), a professor at the University of Valencia, who is decisively oriented toward a Neo-Augustinianism with some influence from Rosmini. In Argentina, Christian spiritualism is represented at the University of Córdoba by A. CATURELLI, and at the University of Tucumán by M. GONZALO CASAS; in Brazil, it is taught by E. FIORI at the University of Porto Alegre. Muñoz is also a brilliant, effective, and polemical writer, whose power of style expresses that of his faith (*Andamios para las ideas*, Madrid, 1952). A raiser of problems, he has spread new ideas in Spain. The unity of his essays is given by an ideal nucleus of thought, which is expounded and sustained with a sincerity that is free from rhetoric. His research is dominated by a central concept: criticism against immanentism in all its forms; yet he does this with the sensibility of a modern man as well as with the awareness that the truth of traditional philosophy must be reconquered and not simply repeated. "El afán penoso" of Science is not enough; what is necessary is "el gozo" of Wisdom: "Quien añade ciencia acrecienta dolor, quien logra sabiduria satisface metafísica y voluntad." The separation of science from wisdom is the great ruin caused by the "epoch of physics and mathematics," and the great scientists of this (modern) age are "genios desolados y desangelados."

[7] Among younger exponents, we note Maria Teresa Antonelli (1922), Alberto Caracciolo (1918), Romeo Crippa (1916), Pietro Prini (1915), Michele Schiavone (1929), and others.

D. Other Positions: Realism of J. Chevalier and G. Capone Braga

Though moving along the lines of classical philosophy, the thinkers we are going to mention in this section cannot be assigned to any of the currents already treated. There is in all of them a prevailing Platonic-Augustinian aspiration which, in some, takes the form of an accentuated anti-intellectualism and, in others, the form of a marked realism.

JACQUES CHEVALIER (1880), a pupil of Bergson and formerly a professor at Grenoble, propounds a "critical realism" of a Platonic type showing some influence from Pascal and Blondel. His most significant theoretical writings are four essays gathered in the book *L'Idée et le Réel* (Grenoble, 1932). In it the author confronts himself with the problem of "individual knowledge" or knowledge of the "real" of which, according to Aristotle and Scholasticism, there is no "science" since the latter belongs only to the universal. The solution of this "real-science" problem (individual-contingency-freedom and universal-absoluteness-necessity) is given, according to Chevalier, by the Christian doctrine of the free creation of a world of individuals on the part of God, who creates all of them out of love and knows and discerns *each* one as a *single* being. Divine intelligibility is then an intelligibility of the individual. Consequently, "the highest degree of human science" does not lie "in the science of the necessary, but in that of the contingent," which in this way "does not appear to us as a lack of intelligibility but rather as a principle of intelligibility."

Being present in man's mind, ideas are a "sign of the real," from which we can ascend to their cause or God through "the movement of our thought toward being." The individual's foundation or foundation of the real lies in those Ideas eternally existing in the divine intellect, each with an eternal reality independently of us, and all as pure, individual essences which we intuit as existent beyond and outside of us; they induce us to go unceasingly beyond ourselves in our search for them; they are the divine models of a possible creation, which are sent into being by God, through an act of his free and creative will; this gives rise to the world, which in fact is an idea of God being realized on the outside. True realism is true idealism. Idea is the real, not man's idea but God's idea as this is thought and realized by Him.

GAETANO CAPONE BRAGA (1889-1956) propounded, instead, another type of realism. A professor at the University of Florence, he conceived his Platonism in the light of Kantian criticism (*Il mondo delle idee*, Città di Castello, 1928-1933; "Lineamenti di un realismo teistico integrale," *Ann. della Facoltà di Filosofia e Lettere dell'Univ. di Cagliari*,

1932-1935). Every reality of which we are able to speak must be a reality that has been thought through, but the analysis of the act of thought leads us to affirm that there would be no knowledge without something to know, a real object. This is particularly so as regards sensorial knowledge. To sense is to sense something, and the sensorial qualities come to us as "data" and not as "modes" of being of the subject. They can mean something only if related to a consciousness, to a spiritual being; and since they cannot be produced by the spiritual subject (namely, man), they must be understood as produced by a spiritual Being, which creates and presents them to our perceptive activity as *data*. We have to admit then a Spirit which creates reality, of which sensorial qualities—even those called secondary—are products really existing outside of us. We do nothing except reproduce them and, while reproducing them, we may err on account of our subjective conditions.

Intelligible data and sensorial data are closely connected with each other within reality. The former in fact are as if they were enclosed in a network of intelligible relations having an ideal nature; we do not create them—we only have to acknowledge them. Two things are neither alike nor different just because we think them to be so; nor do they cease to be as they are when we no longer consider them. Now, these intelligible aspects once more connect us with norms and eternal principles, which regulate the facts of experience though they are not subject to the contingent vicissitudes of the world because of their character of necessity and eternity. The necessity and absoluteness of these principles are explained only by admitting an absolute Spirit, a creator of reality, who ordained the latter on the basis of the necessary laws of His intellect and who endowed the human intellect with the same laws.

Other Positions: The Philosophy of E. d'Ors

The philosophy of the Spanish thinker EUGENI D'ORS (1882-1954) stands at a different level from that just explained. He was an essayist, a brilliant writer, and a well-respected art critic whose mind was open to all suggestions and cultural experiences as is evidenced by his *Glosario* (*Glosario d'Eugeni d'Ors*, Madrid, 1947-1950)—a collection of essays on themes which are aesthetical, philosophical, religious, and so forth. D'Ors had a taste for culture. He was fond of anecdotes and paradoxes, and he had the acumen of a man who is "curious" about the human world, and of a moralist who is sometimes indulgent in a friendly way and, at other times, terribly ironical. Because of his "aesthetical" temperament, we could not expect him (or, likewise, a Unamuno) to produce a system or even a systematic development of ideas. The unity of his thought lies in certain inspiring themes that remain constant within the fragmentariness of his intuitions. He finds elements of inspiration in St. Augustine and St. John of the Cross, in Schiller and Goethe, as well as in pragmatism and Blondel. However, the Platonic concept of "form" (or that of "form" as expressed by aesthetical Platonism) seems to prevail in him over everything else. Of his many writings—remarkable are his original conception of the Baroque and his theory on style—we shall mention only those aspects which are more properly philosophical (*Los argumentos de Zenón de Elea y la noción moderna del Epacio y del Tempo*, Madrid, 1913; *Religio est libertas*, Madrid, 1925; *El Secreto de la filosofiá*, Barcelona, 1947).

Philosophy is "dialectic," that is, "dialogue," which is a synthesis always open to new positions and even to new contradictions. It is dialogue and "irony," which is a synthesis of the philosophical "dialogue" according to the principle of "participation of contraries." Philosophy is even thought, which is essential to philosophy, but a *figurative thought*, an "art of drawing." The "intuición aparencial o figurativa" is for d'Ors the overcoming of vitalism (of the "intuición emocional") and of abstract rationalism, of concrete and historical irrationalism and of mathematical abstractness. "Intelligence" or *nous* (*seny*, in Catalan), which is the "primary organ of knowledge," resolves the antagonism between reason and intuition. "The norms which must preside at the construction of philosophical science are not norms of reason but norms of intelligence." This is a "neointellectualism" or a philosophy of the universal concrete, a priority of *razón* over *vida*, that is, a priority of concrete reason which seeks the "figurative" (to philosophize "is to think with the eyes"), "the idea in the symbol whereby it can express itself in a concrete world." This is not a motionless and conceptual transcription of reality, which in its constant mutation can never be given perfectly through a concept; this is instead a ductile figuration of it; not a *monofocal* or "Copernican revolution" like that of Kant, but a *bifocal* or "Keplerian revolution" which explains the movements of the stars through elliptical orbits; the *seny* is synthesis of both theoretical and practical. This neointellectualism, to tell the truth, hardly seems intellectualistic and rationalistic. In fact, it leaves out the rational principles of "sufficient reason" and "contradiction," which are replaced by those of "función exigada" and of "partecipatión de los contrarios." In it lies the difference between philosophical demonstration and scientific proof: the latter is given through "elements of logical determination," while the former is produced through "suscitación de fuerzas interiores dicisivas" or by means of "persuasión y adesión vital."

The two great characters of life and of the philosophical dialogue are nature and man, that is, man and that which opposes or resists him. *Poética* or creation is that part of human activity which is engaged in the domination of nature. It has three principal modes: "reason" (*homo sapiens*), "work" (*homo faber*), and "play" (*homo ludens*). Work and play are two aspects of the same act. In this sense, *poetica* embraces the whole field of the "science of culture," which d'Ors understands as the "colonization" or "spiritualization" of nature. "Nature" is that which is original, primitive, and unconscious; in a word, it is a datum; culture is that which is traditional, conscious, produced, and artistic. Culture subjugates nature and time, on which it imposes the "historical constants" (used by d'Ors in place of the so-called historical laws), through which the temporal rhythm is given a cyclical process. These constants (or *eoni*) are always manifested through certain *forms* or *styles* as supratemporal elements. There is then a morphology of culture as there is a morphology of nature, and it has an immanent reason whose principle is "rhythm" rather than "natural law." These rhythms or cultural styles correspond to natural rhythms. Science is a "pathetic knowing" and *Patética* (that which is only passion or passiveness) studies all that comes prior to reason (that is, the physical and psychical) without conforming to it. D'Ors utilizes the Einsteinian theory of relativity for his cosmology and as a confirmation of his criticism of the contradiction principle (reality does not conform to this principle in that it is contradictory). Evidently, even *homo ludens* or the creative act is not subject to the principle of contradiction. The "gaya ciencia" alone can free itself from this principle of contradiction.

The essence or "substantivo primario" of the person is freedom, of which the sentimental, intellectual, and voluntary facts are symbolical objectivations. Moreover, d'Ors identifies religion (at least at the time of his *Religio est Libertas*) with irreducible freedom. Yet, body and soul which define man as an individual are not sufficient to define the person. "Man as a person is composed of soul, body, and angel." The "angel" in man is "supraconsciousness" (opposed to Freud's "subconscious"). The union of soul and angel during man's earthly life is realized in a way analogous to the union of soul and body. This is, it seems, a question of an "authentically ontological union" "though only a functional one since the duality of the respective substances is safeguarded." [8] Living, as d'Ors writes, "es gestar un angel para alumbrarlo en la eternidad."

With respect to d'Ors, we have to make the same considerations we already made for other Spanish thinkers. He is a provoker of ideas and a writer endowed with a strong ability for genial intuitions; he can uncover new and hitherto unthought-of aspects even within things that appear to be old and fully exhausted; he is fond of paradoxes which at times are given only for the pleasure of telling beautiful ones. However, philosophy, whose foundation is the intellectual intuition, is discourse.

[8] J. L. Aranguren, *La filosofía de E. d'Ors* (Madrid, 1945), p. 105.

It is an art indeed, but an art of concrete reasoning and a "music," but a music made of discourses, as it is defined by the Platonic Socrates. Moreover, discourse is a logical mediation but there is no logic without principles or at least a principle of truth. D'Ors speaks of "intelligence" and we agree with him; but a *nous* which does not demonstrate through elements of logical determination is no longer a *nous*. Philosophical demonstration is not possible through "persuasion and vital adhesion," as it cannot be demonstrated in the abstract. Demonstration is accomplished through logical power with the whole man and, hence, demonstrating also implies our vital adhesion to a truth logically arrived at. To persuade is not to convince. Gorgias wishes to persuade but he is a skeptic and reduces everything to the persuasive ("alluring") power of words (and d'Ors writes that "ideas are the same as words" and that philosophy "is composed of words"). Plato, who is truly "dialectical" (and there is no ςιαλεγεἰν without λόγος), wishes instead to "convince"; there is no convincing without the absolute validity of rational principles, among which are those of sufficient reason and of noncontradiction. It can be added that if understood as a dialectic of implication (which in my opinion is a characteristic of Christianity), the "participation of contraries" implies and accepts the principle of contradiction in all its validity rather than excluding or substituting it. One must also distinguish between "diverse" and "contradictory"; what is diverse is not contradictory and two diverse things are not contradictory (a geometry that is "diverse" from the Euclidian one is not contradictory to it); and more than that, their diversity can be established precisely and solely on the basis of the principle of noncontradiction. After saying all this, we must recognize the fact that d'Ors has clarified, with an uncommon keenness, the concept of "culture" as he has also struggled against vitalism and, in spite of everything, against irrationalism by advocating the supremacy of the *nous* over life (of a concrete, and I would say effectual, *nous*) and of spiritual values over nature. We agree on all these points while we regret our inability to say the same thing as regards his angelology because of our incompetence in this area. With times as they are, we are more inclined to see in every man a horned devil rather than a little winged angel. In effect, it is better to regard man as he is—a substantial unity of soul and body.

Other Positions: Zubiri's "Unidad Radical"

Not more than a few, at least in Italy, know (and then only by name) XAVIER ZUBIRI (1900), a former professor at the University of Barcelona and, according to the canonical meaning of the word, perhaps the greatest philosopher in today's Spain. Unfortunately, he has until now confined himself to the publication of just some essays, which are rich with thought and have been gathered in the volume *Naturaleza, Historia, Dios* (Madrid, 1959). In it, the author delineates more the question of positing philosophical problems than a systematic and organic, speculative position. In any case, the reading of this book points out Zubiri's authentically philosophical vein, which is strengthened by a vigorous dialectic and a vast and assimilated knowledge of the great classics of thought.

It is entirely mistaken to consider Zubiri an existentialist. His thought follows the line of classical metaphysics, and the latter is viewed in conjunction with modern philosophy and more closely with Heidegger whose lectures were attended by Zubiri in Germany. Moreover, a comparison with Heidegger enables us to see the extent and the manner in which the problem of existence and the exigency of the existential (not existentialism) are present in Zubirian thought. Such a comparison also enables us to see how far he stands from existentialism and even from Heidegger himself.

Three are the essential traits which, according to Zubiri, define the present situation in philosophy: the leveling "positivización" of knowledge, bewilderment, and absence of the intellectual function. This constitutes the *"radical danger* affecting intelligence, the imminent *risk* of having life in truth cease to *exist."* This is a factual reality we must accept together with the problem it poses—"the restoration of intellectual life."

Truth is the intellectual possession "de la índole de las cosas" or, according to the traditional formula, an agreement between thought and things. Such agreement is possible under three conditions: (1) by conforming to things themselves, which stand before our intelligence in an obscure way; (2) by questioning them; (3) by keeping in mind that the system of questions arises not only from things but also "from the total structure of the situation in human intelligence." These three conditions must be expressed in a reverse order: "In his concrete situation man sketches a plan, a mode of getting close to things so as to be able to question them; only then do the latter give us the answer in which lies truth or our agreement with things."

Thought conquers things because it has already been moving in and about them. As an agreement with things, truth always presupposes a previous staying with them. "There is . . . a radical and primary truth on the part of intelligence—its structural immersion in them"; and only because intelligence stays previously *with* and *in* them, does it become possible to propose whether or not we stay in agreement with them. A primary unity between thought and things lies in and constitutes the three conditions of truth just mentioned. According to Zubiri, positivism, pragmatism, and historicism reduce thought more and more to a mere impression, and they push it "dizzily" toward the loss of things, which are its object. "But, if science is held as an ever deeper and wider penetration into a world of objects in which we are immersed by our constitution, everything changes immediately. . . . Then our efforts are imposed on us by things themselves. For this reason, science is a simple addition to the truths which man *possesses*, and not the unfolding of an intelligence *possessed* by truth. Consequently, sciences are not merely placed side by side, but they need one another, reciprocally, in order to get the diverse faces and levels of a varied depth belonging to the same real object. Intellectual life is a constant effort to keep oneself in this primary and integral unity." Thus, we must urgently reconquer the "object" *desde nuestra situación*. The present uprooting of intelligence from things is only one aspect of the uprooting of our entire existence. The first task for intelligence is to clarify the situation confronting it and then to convert this situation into a problem.

Mens or *nous* illuminates the object so as to make it "visible" while man is given the "capacity" to see; it makes the former a *nóema* while the latter is made a *nóesis*. The *nous*, as Aristotle says, is the "principle of principles." The principles of things are expressed through primary truths (for example, the principle of noncontradiction)—*axioms* or *dignities* innate in the mind—"which constitute the primary sense of that which is truly being." Science is engaged in verifying whence, when, and how phenomena present themselves; the *epistémè*, what things must be as they so manifest themselves in the world. *Things* are discovered only in a *universe* and their inclusion in it is that which fashions the meaning held by their *reality* in each case. "Science holds as real that which is, was, and will be in the eternal pureness of its temporal notation; in short, for science *being is happening (ser es acontecer)*," "holding a place" in the world of phenomena or sensorial impressions. For the Greeks, reality had another meaning as it signifies being a part of the cosmos or existing. It is the meaning of *ousía* that Zubiri translates with the term *entity* rather than with the term *substantia;* and existing is not simply happening. The problem of *philosophia prima* is that of *ousía*: what it consists of, where it is, and whence the thing receives its *ousía*. This term indicates the state of having (that on account of which a thing suffices to itself, is independent, and has its own reality in the world) and "the abstract form of the present participle of the verb to be," namely, "la cualidad de lo que está siendo." In the last meaning it represents the "happening," which has reality only when it is the unfolding of that state "of having which belongs to and is a peculiarity of the thing" (*ousía* as having). To be is "to exist substantially." Science tells us how things go about in the world, and, for it, reality "simply signifies happening before our eyes"; *epistémè* tells us "how real things are and real being signifies having an existence of its own."

Man finds himself "implantado en el ser . . . para realizarse." "This radical and incommunicable reality that the person is realizes itself through the complexity of living. In fact, to live is living with things, with others and ourselves as living beings. This 'with' is not a simple juxtaposition between person and life; the 'with' is one of those ontological and formal characters in the human person as such and, in its virtue, the life of the whole human being is constitutionally 'personal.'"

At this point Zubiri enumerates some fundamental propositions which help to clarify his critical dialogue with existentialism. Man *already exists* as a person, in the sense of being someone whose entity lies in his being compelled to realize himself as a person and to perfect his personality during his lifetime. Rather than his being "enviado a la existencia," existence "le está enviada" as it has a *missive* character. Life *has* no mission but *is* a mission. Nor is existence "una espléndida posibilidad"; it is something more than that. Man is "compelled" to exist because he was already *religado* to that which makes him exist. "On the part of the human being this bond is a *religación*," something that inclines us intrinsically, as a tendency making up what we *are*. "La 'religación' makes the *fundamentalidad* (namely, the root and support) of human existence evident and real. To exist, then, is existing 'with' (with things, with others, and with ourselves); this 'with' belongs to the very being of man and is not an addition he makes to himself." That which binds existence also binds the entire world with it. "Religación" acts both upon man and all other things, but *se actualiza formalmente* only in the case of man; "yet, in this formal actuality of human existing constituting the 'religación,' everything (material universe included) appears like a field illuminated by the light of this binding *fundamentalidad*." Thus, in its primary meaning, *religación-religión* "is a dimension which makes up existence formally."

It is not a question of whether or not man has "religion." Man is essentially "religación o religión" which belongs to his "personalized nature." "Religion" is not a property or a necessity but something diverse and superior; it is "a formal dimension of human being," and in it we do not feel an aid to action beforehand; we rather feel a basis for being. Being which is so bound makes man realize that "there is" someone binding him, that which constitutes the fundamental root of his existence, God, to whom we are bound in our entire being. *Deity*, rather than God, is evident to us: "La religación no nos coloca ante la realidad precisa de un Dios, pero abre ante nosotros el ámbito de la deidad, y nos instala constitutivamente en él." Deity shows itself to us as a simple correlate of "religación" upon which "we are founded," while deity is the "founder" as such. God's "fundamentalidad" "belongs" to man's being "not because God is fundamentally a part of our being but because He constitutes *the formal part of it—el estar fundamentado* or 'religado.'"

Externality and "religación" have contrary signs: man is open to things and lives *among* and *with* them and thus he moves *toward* them. But he does not meet *with* God—"God is not a thing in this sense." Man is not *with* God, he is *in* God; he does not *move toward* God because he draws his life from God. Thus, any additional *movement toward* God means *being led* by Him. "We move, live, and are in Him." This *in* means "estar religado" and "estarlo constitutivamente." As a problem, that of God is the problem of "religación." All this, insists Zubiri, is not a demonstration or anything resembling it; this is only an ontological analysis of one of our dimensions. The problem of God is not a scientific or vital problem which may or may not be posited, but it is a problem already *planteado* in man for the simple reason that man finds himself *implantado* in existence. Any discursive demonstration of the existence of God's entitative and operative attributes presupposes the "religación" of all things to God so as to be never a "primary" discovery of God. "The fact that human understanding possesses the bare faculty of demonstrating God's existence" does not mean by any means that this discursive way is the only and primary one intellectually possible." Demonstration is the explication of an implicit knowledge from which it proceeds.[9]

Many points are still obscure in this philosophy; and they are the ones which affect the metaphysical problems. It is not yet possible to see clearly what it is that Zubiri calls "primary truth"—whether it is a pure datum or an intellectual intuition. The same thing can be said as regards the distinction between God and deity and their relationship, besides the fact that the word deity rouses many suspicions. Furthermore, the relationship between man and God does not appear to be clear; nor is man's metaphysical structure clearly defined, precisely because the concept of *religación* has not been given all its ontological articulation.

[9] J. A. Marias (1916) is a pupil of Ortega and a follower of the philosophy of *razón vital*. He discusses the ultimate problems concerning the immortality of the soul and the existence of God, *Reason and Life: the Introduction to Philosophy*, trans. K. Reid and E. Sarmento (New Haven, 1956).

X

PHILOSOPHY
IN LATIN AMERICA

---

1. Some Preliminary Remarks

We have purposely devoted this short chapter to the philosophical activity of the main countries of Latin America, which, perhaps for the first
time, is taken into consideration within a panoramic synthesis of world
philosophy written by a European and published in Europe. Generally,
it is said that there is no philosophical tradition in the Latin-American
countries, and that the few and isolated lovers of this subject represent
only influences from European currents which are echoed without originality. This, in part, is true as it is recognized first of all by Latin-
American scholars themselves. But, besides the fact that the same thing
can be said for other countries including some European one (in Europe,
original, philosophical production and great movements of thought are
the characteristic of four or five countries), it must be pointed out that
the most important Latin-American countries have achieved—in the last
fifty years—what Romero calls a philosophical "normalidad." No longer
is it the case of a few isolated thinkers, who came up by themselves
without a favorable environment and with insufficient means (making
them all the more praiseworthy), for there are now organized university
"studies" animated by a vivid interest in philosophy, which is held in an
esteem never known before. It is not possible to speak of originality as
yet, but the highly significant fact is that, today, philosophy is considered
as the highest form of intellectual activity, without which there is no
true culture; and this is so because every particular discipline, whatever

it may be, posits the problem of its method, its object, and its meaning—all problems that are to be adequately illuminated by philosophical research. To be aware of the decisive and absolute importance of philosophy in intellectual life, is already an indication of philosophical maturity; and perhaps this is the true "originality" in most recent Latin-American thought.

From this point of view, if a comparison were to be made between Latin-American and North American philosophy, one could say that the former (although it lacks the outstanding philosophical personalities that are found in North America) is perhaps more original than the latter. In fact, North American philosophy finds it difficult to conceive philosophy in its theoretical moment, that is, philosophy as philosophy; it can see philosophy only in its practical moment, as an instrument of *praxis*, which cannot be distinguished from this or that positive science. For the North American philosopher there are "urgent" problems of daily life, which are vital problems (of organization, technology, social life, and so on) and they can be solved "scientifically." For this reason, he stops at the practical and social aspects regarding man and reality without assuming any radical or extreme position. He remains almost indifferent toward "philosophia prima" which considers the "ultimate" and highest problems. He lives a "penultimate" existence with a "philosophia secunda" —the one that is apt to produce success in individual and social life. Even at present, with all its vast organization of philosophical studies and the more consistent cultural and philosophical contribution from Europe, the United States has not progressed toward the acquisition of an authentically philosophical "mentality" or a critical sense for speculative problems. On the contrary, it has regressed in a sense, if we consider the popularity attained there by neopositivism and materialism, behavioristic psychology and psychoanalysis, although an interest in and a consideration for philosophy are greater than ever before.

As we have noted, now that Latin America has surpassed the preparatory stage and has come to philosophy with a respectable number of thinkers, it shows a truly philosophical sensibility especially in some of its exponents. From this point of view, Latin America then is closer than North America to European culture. Moreover, if we consider the following facts: (1) present decadence of "intellectual" life in Europe; (2) prevalence even there of the vital urgency and of "scientificalism" in such a way as to be detrimental to intellectual and spiritual values (in effect, Europe today is mostly unable to think in depth and it has become the land of "nihilism," "problematicism," and "practicalism" as if things made any sense without truth and as if man had only vital problems to solve through "technology"); (3) gradual loss of the sense of philosophy and culture (both discovered by Europe) as well as that of metaphysics in favor of a sort of "supertechnology," which is nothing but a "sub-science" and an "infraphilosophy"—then it is not unlikely that the young countries of Latin America (and this is a consolation since what counts are not the forms of a civilization but rather the "values" expressed by it) will be able to continue the best philosophical tradition of Europe and perhaps become the "colonizer" of our "continent," which seems to be determined to throw away its cultural "content." We do not exclude the possibility that even the United States of America may be able to perform this task (or contribute to it) and, in any event, attain such a maturity as to be able to "understand" philosophy, that is, the problems of the spirit and the meaning of the words "truth," "idea," "being," "intellect," and others. But, as things stand at the present, the latter possibility seems to us to be uncertain for two main reasons: one is that unless Europe finds itself once more, its metaphysical and cultural "soul" (I might say its intelligence) will end by being either "Americanized" or by becoming entirely "Marxist"; and the other reason is that, on account of its political and military power, the United States will inevitably believe itself to be a "superior" people and will mistake power for "wisdom" and its superiority in means for intellectual and cultural maturity. In such a case, its people will be inclined to consider themselves more as teachers than as pupils, so that they will wish to spread—with their characteristic, missionary ardor—their "philosophy" or conception of life as the most advanced one. Success and riches should be accompanied by a corresponding intellectual and spiritual advancement and by a tradition that has stood for centuries—a tradition that gives a fine sense of detachment and, with it, the ability to look at them in perspective, so as to see their limits and understand the true dominion of man over things; if this is not so, then they turn one's head and create the illusion of an unconditional superiority—the offspring of a naive conviction according to which everything can be bought or built with money, even a head philosophically well made and a spirit culturally well educated and mature.

These dangers are not so threatening in Latin America and if the latter should become a politically and militarily great power in the future, it would be safeguarded by the fact that such attainment would be accompanied by a philosophical and cultural maturity of its own (in the above clarified sense of conquest and awareness concerning the concept of philosophy and culture), even if at present its philosophical and cultural production is still lacking and secondary. In all these considerations, it must not be forgotten that the United States was colonized by England, and Latin America by Spain, that is, a nation whose culture represents one of the essential dimensions in the authentic spirit of Europe. Moreover, this signifies something highly important, that is to say, the United States of America, which until some decades ago was not really receptive to other cultures, was molded by an ideology that was made up of elements coming from the Puritan tradition, the 1688 English Revolution, and the culture of the Enlightenment—all movements which, prescinding from what there is positive in them, are partially responsible for the present "crisis" in the European consciousness. Protestant (Calvinistic) "lights" and Enlightenment "lights" are two faces of the same coin. In fact, from the very beginning great capital and great industry considered themselves Calvinistically "possessed" by grace and chosen by God (hence their satanic pride which arises "dialectically," from the annihilation of man through sin) as this is evidenced by their "success." Besides, the Enlightenment sees in scientific progress the means by which success— in the sense of conquest of the world—becomes total, the absolute guaranty of earthly human happiness. This helps to explain how the "useful," the "success," the "practical," and the "vital urgency"—which do not need intellectual truths, spiritual values, and ultramundane satisfaction but only such means as science and technology that are in conformity with their aspirations—have become, through English mentality, the essential categories of North American mentality.

Certainly Spain did not nourish a lively thought in its colonies, which were kept under the control of a rigid religious and political orthodoxy; but she spread Catholicism, and with it a conception of life which puts spirit and its values (namely, God and not the world) in the first place; in short, Spain nourished in its colonies an aristocratic and "noble" sense of life which is ready to sacrifice itself on behalf of an ideal of faith, glory, honor, and dignity. When the old colonies became independent nations, the secular-rationalistic reaction had more of a political than a doctrinal character. Even Latin America was subject not only to the influence of the utilitarian spirit of the Enlightenment, but also, from 1870 on, to the invasion of scientific positivism and naturalism which, after all, responded to a momentary need and practical urgency of organization and transformation in these new nations just born to freedom. However, we must emphasize that as soon as Latin America went beyond the years of infancy, it reacted against "scientistic" positivism and its dogmatism (like all forms of absolute rationalism, "scientistic" positivism was fanatical, devoid of any critical sense, and negative to freedom in the *name* of "free thought.") In this way, it began its youth with a new start which is, as we said, a sign of its maturity. Positivism was beneficial in a certain sense, but Latin America has built on the foundation of what Spain left deep inside it. On the other hand even after the state of infancy was surpassed and present-day power achieved, the United States of America is still confined to the ideology by which it was fashioned from the very beginning of its colonization. This is so true that instead of reacting against enlightened utilitarianism in a wide sense, it has more than ever opened its doors to scientificalism and materialism, as well as to the worse influence of decadent European culture, and thus today more than before, this country is not as yet philosophically "mature" in a full sense. This aspect is further complicated by the fact that the United States believes itself to be ultra-advanced and holds the truly great intellectual movements of Europe (those which refuse to erase the words "spirit," "idea," "God," and the like from their vocabulary) as something which is backward and surpassed in comparison with the new logical "techniques," genetics, biochemistry, psychology of behavior and subconscience, philosophy of hormones and glands. All this represents a hindrance to the progress of philosophy, which is philosophical maturity when it is philosophy of spirit—a concept that has gained ground in Latin America even if the latter has not as yet acquired it critically.

2. GENERAL CHARACTERISTICS AND PHASES OF DEVELOPMENT

Latin-American countries have always been receptive to European philosophical currents, which they endeavored to assimilate with a greater or lesser degree of originality. They have shown their own personality by accepting some currents and rejecting others. With a few exceptions, since the time of the antipositivistic reaction they have distinguished, more clearly, between the two fields of philosophy and politics which had previously been confused. They have defined their preferences and these bear the almost universal characteristic of a deeply humanistic sense—a humanism of the spirit rather than of matter. Without denying the value of science and technology, they believe that the latter cannot by themselves either exhaust the human field of knowledge and activity or carry out man's destination or accomplish the satisfaction of his deep exigencies through their progress. Their present-day philosophy, in fact, is immune from the easy optimism of a human happiness entrusted to scientific progress and an even "higher level" of material well-being. Even their undeniable pragmatism has an ideal purpose; they believe in man's creative energies, which are spiritual energies expressing the values of the spirit. Latin-Americans maintain the sense of the individual, of the "heroical," and of a qualified human personality in an age which extols only what has weight and extension, that is, the "collective," the "organized," the "democratic," and the "mass." Indeed, some of them still believe that man and his values can be established on and guaranteed by the principle of immanence and within the purely historical order because they fear that the principle of transcendence may deny man's autonomy and freedom. However, let us hope that the experience of what happened in Europe and a more critical sense concerning spiritual problems will lead them to that metaphysical thoroughness through which the transcendence of truth or value is revealed as the sole principle corresponding to the genuine and not superficial nature of man.

Another feature in this Latin-American thought is its strong need for independence. "We do not wish to assume a role of producers of raw materials and consumers of spiritual products." [1] Obviously, this is more of an aspiration than a reality—South Americans know very well (as was confirmed at the 1936 convocation of the *Instituto de Cooperación Intelectual de la Liga de las Naciones*) that their culture still moves within the orbit of the European one; they are still lacking a national philosophy (according to the best meaning of the term "national") as well as a "national philosopher" who gives a new sense and a new determination to philosophical values. It is interesting to notice in this respect that their need for independence led to the acceptance of some theories and to the interpretation of others in a singular way. Thus, for instance, Spengler's famous thesis according to which cultures are independent, impenetrable, and historical realities—the only realities to give a meaning to the life of a collectivity—produced in Bolivia what has been called the "mystique of the land" (its theorist was *Franz Tomayo* at the beginning of this century). According to this theory, "landscape and the telluric possess a sort of spirit and act upon man so as to create forms of individual and social life wherein cultural types are brought into being with their own characteristics just like the geographical environment producing them." In this way, Spengler has been used by some Bolivian writers in order to point out that in their exceptional land there is a source (principle of individuation) of national and independent culture which is able to give a content to that country. When Latin-American philosophy is evaluated, this nationalistic motif must be accounted for, even if it has not attained a sufficient degree of critical value as yet, for it still remains in the emotional phase that pertains to those who wish "to be someone."

Besides the Cuban positivist E. J. VARONA (1849-1933), who was more important as a writer than as a philosopher and whose activity falls beyond the chronological bounds of our exposition, the initiators or *fundadores* (as Romero calls them) of the development of Latin-American philosophy were ALEJANDRO O. DEÚSTUA (1869-1945) of Peru, CARLOS VAZ FERREIRA (1871-1958) of Uruguay, ALEJANDRO KORN (1860-1936) of Argentina, and ANTONIO CASO (1883-1946) of Mexico. Their influence lasted about twenty years (from 1910 to 1930) and it is not completely extinguished even today.[2] Intellectually, they grew up in the climate of positivism, but they reacted against it

---

[1] G. Francovich, *La filosofía en Bolivia* (Buenos Aires, 1945), p. 155.

[2] *Contemporary Latin-American Philosophy* (an anthology with an introduction), ed., A. Sanchez Reulet (Washington, 1949), pp. 13 ff.

from points of view which in themselves are different though all share in the criticism of this system for its "scientistic" conception, dogmatic narrowness, and deterministic mechanism affirmed in the name of the rights of culture and freedom.

Under the influence of Kant, German idealism, Krause (the latter, perhaps, through Spanish Krausism), and Bergson, Deústua elaborates an aesthetical metaphysics or, more precisely, he gives beauty an absolute value (*Las Ideas de Orden y Libertad en la Historia del Pensamiento Humano*, Lima, 1917-1922; *Estetica General*, Lima, 1923). According to this Peruvian thinker, "order" and "freedom" "represent the moments of rest and motion in all spiritual activity, although in the course of history the idea of order has been predominant while the idea of freedom has never attained a dominion of its own." Freedom expresses its creative power only through the artistic moment. The artist's activity is a free creation and "grace" is the expression of freedom in the work of art. However, in art, as well as in any other form of human activity, freedom presupposes an ideal "order" created by imagination and apprehended by feeling in which the infinite impulse of freedom itself is reconciled with the exigencies and impositions of nature. The beautiful realizes "*a reconciliation between freedom and nature through an ideal order created by imagination.* This is a conciliation that is *felt* and not simply *perceived;* it is real and not *formal* as Kant thought. Furthermore, this conciliation is an exigency on the part of sentiment, which considers as beautiful all objects in which freedom is expressed through *grace.* The latter springs from an inborn necessity of harmony with nature and as a means of achieving a greater freedom; it also results in harmony and freedom on the part of sentiment, as freedom and productivity of the work of art result in harmony." In this conciliation there are three elements: "Nature and Freedom as real elements, and Order as a formal or ideal element in which reconciliation takes place; the first element is connected with our sentimentality, the second, with our will, and the third with our intelligence. Intelligence permeates the *ideal* with the data of nature, and these data are chosen by sentiment in its intuitive function and at the service of a *free* force. This conciliation expressed by *grace*—which, in turn, is an ordained and free form—realizes the beautiful. The latter can thus be defined as the *ideal and experienced reconciliation between nature and free force expressed by grace.*" The forms of free activity are economics, science, and still higher, moral action and religious experience. However, the creative activity of the spirit achieves its highest expression only in art (this is true also for Schelling), in which freedom also realizes itself in its full pureness because there alone it can create its own order. Thus, the aesthetical value is superior to all others and it represents the fullness of the spirit.

The Uruguayan C. VAZ FERREIRA was a man of wide culture, an "essayist" and a writer (of a moralistic tone) more than a philosopher. He was fond of paradoxes and opposed any system which pretends to enclose physical reality within rigid formulas. As reality is fluid and mobile so must be ideas. Like Unamuno in Spain (with whom he has many things in common), he is, above all, a raiser of problems and inquietudes. In conformity with his temperament, his best work is his *Fragmentario* (Montevideo, 1938)—a collection of short essays and aphorisms.

The Argentinian ALEJANDRO KORN began as a psychiatrist inspired by Lombroso and ended as an influential and heeded professor of philosophy. The reading of Schopenhauer revealed to him his philosophical inclination and induced him to read the oriental and Spanish mystics, Plotinus and Eckhart. However, his philosophical inspiration is sustained by the criticism of Kant, who "cured" him of metaphysics. A passionate and vehement writer, he never forgot his positivistic origins, which he contaminated with Kantian "apriorism." According to Korn, the limits of experience on whose data our knowledge is founded coincide with those of consciousness. The world of objects is not an ensemble of purely mental phenomena, but we know it only according to the terms of consciousness. Its law is necessity and in it lies its opposition toward the world that belongs to the subject, which is freedom; the latter is a concrete datum of human existence and a creative impulse (*Ensayos filosoficos*, in *Obras*, La Plata, 1938-1940; herein are his best writings). The first freedom is "economic" freedom in which there is an "ethical" end. "Neither determinism of the objective world nor the sovereignty of utilitarian egoism can be denied. However, the consciousness of our freedom and responsibility cannot be suppressed either. Trying to suppress this duality is a useless endeavor and a nonrecognition of the psychical conflict in which human personality struggles in defense of its dignity and in order to attain an even greater liberation. Making use of objective determinism is only a pragmatic means to realize our material freedom. Yet, to be confined to this aim alone, means to enslave ourselves to the machine which we have invented." Science is the quantitative interpretation of reality; philosophy is a theory of knowledge and values. There are no absolute values existing by themselves; facts alone exist, and man has the privilege to deny them. Affirming freedom is denying reality. The unity of consciousness is consciousness of a conflict, and metaphysical anxiety is nourished by the exigency of making the opposites coincide. Man's duty in his daily life is to realize the unity of his moral person through oppositions, that is, his "relative freedom in each individual case, and his absolute freedom as an ideal goal. Culture began its action from this impulse, and so did the historical effort by the species as well as its affirmation of freedom when it was confronted by a dominating necessity. Since freedom is not given to us, we must win it in the short span of our individual lives as well as in the progressive evolution of collective life. This final aspiration is productive; for this reason we have called it *creative freedom*."

ANTONIO CASO, the renovator of Mexican philosophy, abandoned positivism under the influence of Boutroux and Bergson. He worked out a "pragmatism" of Christian inspiration while keeping away from excessive voluntarism. Endowed with a good philosophical culture, he was an effective writer attentive to all the principal movements in contemporary thought. Not too trustful of pure intelligence, he conceived philosophy more as a mode of being than as knowledge. This mode extends to action beyond the abstract and partial schemes of science, which never adequately correspond to concrete reality.

Man is not an egoistic (utilitarian and economic) activity alone, but is an unselfish impulse manifested in aesthetical and moral action (*La existencia como economia, como distinterés y como caridad*, México, 1919; 2nd ed. México, 1943). The highest unselfishness and the realization of our personality lie in moral action inspired by charity. "Disinterestedness, charity, and sacrifice are what is irreducible to the economy of Nature. . . . The world is the will of egoism and *good will*, which is irreducible, is contradictory to it. This proves, experimentally, that in connection with the order and life firmly ruled by what Darwin (in a primitive way) called *struggle for survival*, there is another order and another life." For Caso, good "is not a categorical imperative or a law of reason without enthusiasm, as Kant thought of it. It never commands, it inspires. It never imposes nor does it come from the outside; it springs from the inner consciousness of sentiment, whose roots reach the depths of spiritual existence. It is like music which conquers and enchants. Good is easy, spontaneous, and intrinsic—that which is innermost in our soul. It is not a compulsion on the part of pure reason, nor is it one coming from external life; it cannot be attained either through induction or deduction; nor is it to be respected—it *creates itself*. Good is freedom, personality, and divinity. In short, to use the expression of a famous Mexican thinker, it is "the supernatural that is felt like the most natural thing in the world." Christianity is not the apology of weakness, as Nietzsche thought of it, since "charity is strength and goodness, inseparably; strength because it is goodness, and goodness because it is strength."

Individualism and communism are for Caso rightly "identified as two forms of egoism." [3] They are two errors having "the same harmful root

---

[3] "The community is selfish, it demands its own continuity and priority over the individual. Community comes before individuals. They were born and are in it. It is the whole and they are the parts. Part of a whole, the individual must subordinate

—the super-evaluation of intrinsic and vital egoism." The only solution to this conflict is the axiological, ethical, and juridical solution. "Persons are not individuals, they are a spirit; States are not justified as individuals, but as politically organized persons which must treat each other with mutual respect and morality. Nobody is ever going to be free as long as he confuses his individuality—an essentially biological thing—with his personality, which is love and culture. In conformity with pure logic, individualism and communism are two contrary positions which in their exclusiveness are held as true by their respective followers. But, even in conformity with pure logic, where there are two contrary propositions one can be false and one true; or they can both be false—as in the present case—but never true together."

In itself not original but vigorous in thought, this idealistic reaction completely changed the philosophical situation in Spanish-speaking Latin America. Gradually, it not only freed the universities and other circles of learning from the predominance of positivism but also earned for philosophy a new prestige and a social respect unknown until then. Furthermore, with their regular activity the four *fundadores* gave dignity to teaching as well as to philosophical studies.

As is easy to ascertain, all these thinkers, with the exception of Korn, are under the predominant influence of French philosophy (particularly that of Boutroux, Bergson, and Meyerson), along side that of Italian philosophy represented by Croce and Gentile. The present generation, instead, is strongly influenced by German culture not only because many young men attended German universities but also on account of the influence exerted by Ortega y Gasset through the publications (which are mostly translations from German) in the *Revista de Occidente* which is now continued in Argentina. In fact, since 1930 South America has been principally under the influence of such European thinkers as Dilthey, Husserl, Scheler, Hartmann, and Heidegger, besides Maritain, Blondel, and Marcel, in a minor degree, to another area of Latin-American thought. Philosophical activity has been increasingly intense while the method is more rigorous, and production more effective. The decline of positivism has led to a renewal of Catholic philosophy, of which the most important current is represented by Neo-Thomism. At present,

---

himself to the community. Such is the selfish essence of communism. Here also lies the selfish essence of individualism; the individual in turn states that his being is the only real being. He says: I conceive the state as a means to my happiness; society was established in view of it. I am myself. The divine belongs to God; but I am not God; human is the Humanity. I am that which is real. My good is that which I wish to have, not that which others wish to give me; and, if they do not give it to me, I shall try to take it. The two rival positions are false because they place the value of life beyond culture and spirit." *La persona humana y el Estado totalitario* (México, 1941) by A. Caso.

however, the other Catholic current, more lively and original, is taking its place beside Neo-Thomism under the influence of the French thinkers just mentioned; to it we can add the first echoes coming from the French "Philosophie de l'Esprit" and those, which are even stronger, from Italian Christian spiritualism.

We shall now mention what seems to us to be most significant.

3. PRESENT-DAY CURRENTS

A. Argentina

JOSÉ INGENIEROS (1877-1925) may be considered the last positivist of some importance. As a writer, he enjoyed an international fame in his youth. He remained attached to the old generation and to the culture prevailing at the close of the century. On the other hand, ALBERTO ROUGÉS (1880-1945) was, in our opinion, the greatest Argentinian thinker of the last decades. His *Las jerarquías del ser y la eternidad* (Tucumán, 1962) is a work of importance containing vigorous and original pages. He reacted against positivism, scientificalism, and materialism in the name of autonomy in our spiritual life. Influenced by Bergson, and an authority on St. Augustine, he draws his most authentic inspiration from the Neoplatonic and Augustinian sources which keep him away from scholastic formalism.

For Rougés, the reduction of spiritual life to the physical world and vice versa makes no sense. The former is characterized by interiority and temporality; it proceeds from the past toward the future, and each stage preserves the past while anticipating the future so as to have a coexistence of past and future in the present. "The past in the creative act is not irrevocable as if it were dead like the past in the physical act; instead, *it creates itself together with its future which in a way is being anticipated. Past and future come into being and grow together mutually interpenetrated and inseparably united.*" Clearly, Rougés is bearing in mind the Bergsonian conception of "duration," but he modifies it fundamentally. The physical world is different, however: *"The being of the physical world at any given instant is that instant alone because it lacks past and future.* A movable thing in motion cannot be here and there at the same time. A monochromatic body changing coloration cannot be red and blue at the same instant. On the contrary, *the being of our creative act possesses, at any moment whatever, a past and a future and thus it is a period of time.* In other words, *the coexistence of the successive, which is impossible in the physical world, is essential to our creative act.* Physical becoming is opposed to Plotinus' eternity, which is not like a physical rest but is like a living of all its past and all its future in a present.

On the other hand, in order to be master of a past and of a future, our creative act participates in eternity, *es un jalón en el camino hacia la eternidad.*" A unitary conception of the physical reality is impossible. We must choose between a becoming without being and a being without becoming. In modern physics, mechanism sees reality from the point of view of permanence while phenomenalism grasps its changing nature.

Placed between past and future, the spiritual being is directed toward eternity of which it partakes. For Rougés, eternity contains time in its totality though the former transcends the latter. Eternity is a "temporality without time." The more a spiritual being dominates time the more it comes close to eternity. In the hierarchy of beings the lowest level is occupied by the physical being, the highest, by God. Between the two extremes there are the other forms of being—beings and spiritual lives. "Placed thus between physical being and highest spiritual Being, all hierarchies of being are . . . the dramatic moments of a divine enterprise."

Among living thinkers, the most renowned in Argentina and perhaps in all Latin America is FRANCISCO ROMERO (1891). Of Spanish descent, he was a friend as well as a pupil of Korn to whose chair of metaphysics he succeeded in 1931 (though he left it for political reasons only to return to his teaching afterwards). Strongly influenced by German philosophy and above all by Hartmann, he attaches to philosophy more of a problematical than a constructive significance ("the right to doubt" is one of the rights held by thinkers). The problem of man is at the center of Romero's meditations (*La filosofía de la persona*, Tucumán, 1944; *Papelos para una filosofía*, Tucumán, 1945), and all his anthropology revolves around the concept of "transcendence" (not in a theological sense). "The person functions as a bundle of transcendent movements; it is pure transcendence. Its being is to transcend. It transcends toward the objects in knowledge and in the aesthetical pleasure; it transcends toward the values. It also transcends especially toward other persons, because as it is consubstantial with the individual to deny other individuals so it pertains to the person's essence to affirm the other personal unities. Personal religiosity is, likewise, a pure transcending toward God, while the individual's religiosity is a mere effort to reconcile itself with the supernatural powers, as well as an attempt to bring them within the scope of the individual's interest and make them immanent." Each being is the realization of some latent possibilities that are in relation to other beings so as to make up a greater totality. Transcendence hardly manifests itself in the physical being, while in the spirit, which is absolute transcendence, it achieves its maximum. In his spiritual life as an "individual," man makes himself a "person" by transcending his psycho-physical individuality. Man acts on the basis of his egoistic impulse when he obeys the immanent tendency; but, if his action is based on universal values then he follows the expansive tendency coming from transcendence. The former tendency has become dominant in modern European thought because, as an outcome of the loss of mediaeval transcendentism, it rests on mechanism, materialism, and individualism. In this way, European thought has followed a process of involution in its attempt to make everything immanent (spirit is explained through the psyche, the psyche through life, and life through physical processes). Against all this, Romero, who inserts the notion of transcendence in the idea of "structure," opposes the transcending process in which as a spiritual structure the person transcends itself in the value. "What is essential and defining lies in the absolute transcendence of the act, and this transcendence would be denied if the act were diverted to the opposite direction of immanence. On account of its essence, the ethical act holds the agents of spiritual acts to be its ends, because transcendence would not be complete and effective in its acting if it were not directed toward centers of action that are transcendent in a similar way. Furthermore, absolute duty is only toward persons, toward nuclei of spiritual acts, of transcendent intentions. To sum up, action is ethical if it is deliberately regulated by transcendence itself, which each time appears with an ever-increasing evidence as the positive component of the whole, as the being of *ens*."

The transcendence of which Romero speaks is pure immanence; it moves along a horizontal line and concludes itself in the self-affirmation of the act which is pure immanentism. As European thought based on immanence has already demonstrated through its process of self-criticism, immanentism (be it idealistic or spiritualistic) does not justify either the values or the person; it is bound to lead only to that nihilism against which Romero complains (and we with him).

OCTAVIO DERISI establishes his philosophy of the person (*La Persona*, La Plata, 1950) on authentic transcendence (the latter is either theological or is not transcendence at all). He is the most active and best prepared representative of Neo-Thomism, which, in a homonymous volume (1941), he compared with modern philosophy in order to bring to light a new concept of Christian philosophy (*Concepto de la filosofía Cristiana*, Buenos Aires, 1943). Another important exponent of Neo-Thomism is NIMIO D'ANQUIN, a former professor at the University of Córdoba, a profound scholar on Aristotle and Hegel, and an illustrious teacher to a generation of promising youths. Worthy of mention are the names of I. S. QUILES (*Más allá del existencialismo*, Buenos Aires, 1958) and C. PICCO; also that of A. VASSALLO who has re-elaborated some theses derived from Blondel and Marcel.

Together with Neo-Thomism, which is in full development at the present, there is a current of German-inspired existentialism that is represented by C. ASTRADA (*El juego metafísico*, Buenos Aires, 1942) and

M. VIRASORO (*La Libertad, la existencia y el ser*, Buenos Aires, 1942). These authors have delineated a metaphysics of freedom as a foundation for existence and being.

B. *Mexico*

Along with Argentina, Mexico is the country that has made the greatest contributions to philosophical activity in Spanish-speaking America. JOSÉ VASCONCELOS (1884-1959) was Mexico's most renowned thinker following the death of A. Caso. He was a brilliant writer with an artistic rather than philosophical temperament, as is generally the case with Spanish or Spanish-speaking philosophers who are deeply sensitive artists and mystics more than dialecticians. Nourished with Platonic and Plotinian readings and influenced by Schopenhauer, Nietzsche, and Bergson, Vasconcelos considers philosophy as a vital necessity and, after the manner of the great German romanticists, he believes in its universal character as well as in its task of giving a unitary and total vision of existence. But, intelligence is unable to realize this vision since, instead of unifying, it divides and separates reality into irreconcilable dualisms, thus stifling the vital impetus. Unity is expressed through a "feeling of totality," through an "aesthetical intuition." His is an "aesthetical monism" (*El Monismo estetico*, Mexico, 1918) blended with Plotinian and Bergsonian elements which convert it into an "aesthetical pantheism" whose final state is mysticism (*Estetica*, 2nd ed., Mexico, 1936; *Tratado de Metafisica*, Madrid, 1929; *Etica*, Madrid, 1932).

For Vasconcelos the world is the product of a primary, creative energy gradually changing into an "atom," in which there is a mechanical repetition, and into a "cell," which already possesses a purpose, as well as into a "consciousness," which is freedom and creation. It is not a question of degrees of evolution or of passages, but of qualitative changes and of revolutions. "The semiconscious, semispiritual breath comes from the very depth; yet, it is necessary for us to determine the *instant of sudden mutation*, without which there is no definitive passage from one cycle to another, and *the specific leap which causes the mutation of orientation as well as the substantial passage*." Moral activity is neither utilitarian nor obedient to a categorical imperative—it is creative. Within spiritual dynamism, values are categories *a priori*, vital forms of action. Ethics transforms itself into aesthetics (for Vasconcelos, the "image" is a fundamental operation of the spirit and it draws its "essence, reality, and value" from "emotion"), which is converted into a religious impulse and a mystical fervor.

Converted to Catholicism, Vasconcelos subjected his aesthetical-mystical monism to a critical revision and then called it a "philosophy of co-ordination." In it, the transcendent and personal God has taken the place of primary creative energy. The theory of thought as co-ordination "leads us to acknowledge a highest being, an ultimate existence that is not like sensibility, nor intelligence, nor even the will; all this is expressed . . . as an absolute consciousness which guides and sustains the worlds." God is a dynamic Unity, the One-Whole, "the support of perennial harmony and co-ordination of all parts within the whole." This, nonetheless, is still pantheism inspired after the manner of Plotinus.

Both Caso and Vasconcelos belonged to the so-called Americanist and Nationalist movement of which they were the promoters. "The formula of our patriotism," writes Caso, "is that of our race; yet, Mexico is the axiom, and Spanish America the corollary. That is to say, first and foremost is the reality which sustains us and, second, the ideal which inspires us." This "Americanist" movement (which, as we mentioned, is common to all Latin-American countries) has been joined by thinkers like SAMUEL RAMOS (1897) and LEOPOLDO ZEA (1912) who come from other currents of thought. The latter explains the motives by which the movement is inspired and also the aims pursued by it: "In these present days of ours and in consequence of this cultural crisis, the various American countries have felt the need of seeking, within their history and traditions, elements apt to produce a culture that is their own." He also recognizes that Latin-American philosophy does not have the universal value possessed by European thought; yet he remarks: "However, this does not imply that *our* positivism, *our* Cartesianism, or *our* Scholasticism are without importance. Through this term *ours* we express, precisely, a personal as well as an original experience. This is a human experience, one that concerns some given men in a given circumstance."

Both Ramos and Zea belong to the current that stresses culture and history and their aim is to establish a philosophy of culture. As a matter of fact, this is a pragmatic and relativistic conception of history, one that shows the influence of Ortega. In fact, from the latter's formula, "yo soy yo y mi circunstancia," these thinkers draw their motivation with a view to establishing the historical "circunstancia" of Mexico on the basis of historical and social facts.

More recently, the Ortegan motif has been combined with the influence of existentialism. For Zea, every philosophical conception is the offspring of a "circunstancia." Thus, this is more the case of a "philosophy *in* history" than that of a "history *of* philosophy" (*Ensayos sobre la filosofía de la historia México*, 1949). In it lies the need for an American philosophy as a basis for a philosophical reflection on the concrete reality of Mexico in its structural relationships with European culture. Consequently, existentialism is being utilized in order to define the problem of what the Mexican man is. As E. Uranga (a member of the

Grupo filosófico Hiperión which was founded by Zea) states, it is necessary to establish an "ontology" of the Mexican.

A great contribution to the existentialist current in Mexico was made by certain exiled Spaniards, above all by JOSÉ GAOS (1900), who, among other things, is a translator of Heidegger, and by JUAN D. GARCÍA BACCA (1901), who is now a professor at the University of Caracas. Gaos, who "por los clavos de Jesús!" does not consider himself to be an existentialist, made his contribution to the definition of the Mexican man. Existentialist elements, however, are not lacking in him in spite of this declaration of his (and, indeed, Dilthey's and Ortega's influence is rather strong in this author). In fact, Gaos writes: "There are as many philosophies as there are philosophers, and philosophy is a confession, an autobiography." "To ask what philosophy is amounts to philosophizing" and this is "the philosophy of philosophy" (*Filosofía de la filosofía e historia de la filosofía*, Mexico, 1947): "The philosophy of philosophy is, above all, a reflection on a concrete experience, a questioning on the part of the philosopher-man." Philosophy is a research, but it is also "pride," because "philosophy is one's own existence, that is, a being in himself and for himself; and being in himself is simply a being who stands above the others," and this is what "pride" is called. However, he stays away from existentialism on a fundamental point: "Mere existence excludes every essence and reason; it cannot philosophize. Pure essences exclude every existence and philosophers alone allow room for existence. The existentialist can be a man but he can no longer be a philosopher. The existentialist can be a philosopher but he can no longer be a man." Thus, this is neither pure existentialism nor a pure essentialism. As a solution, Gaos points to Ortega's "razón vital."

García Bacca, like Gaos a scholar with a wide philosophical culture, holds a position resting more on historicism than on existentialism (*Invitación a filosofar*, Mexico, 1946; *Nueve filósofos contemporáneos y sus temas*, 2 vols., Mexico, 1947). In this author, remotely Scholastic (Suarezian and mystical) influences mix with others from Ortega and from existentialism. For García, the person is an anxiety toward transcending and making itself "supernatural." Thus, existence is neither finite nor infinite; it is *transfinite*, that is, an impulse toward transcending its limits. On account of this need to go beyond its nature, existence is consciousness of such a limit. Each philosophical epoch has its particular conception of the world as well as its repertory of ideas. Consequently, each epoch has its "type" of philosophy.

EDUARDO NICOL (1907) occupies a place apart. He too shows Ortega's influence as well as the influence of existentialism, but with a personal thought which he expounds systematically in his volume *Metafísica de la expresión* (México, 1957).

Scanty and confined to academic surroundings is the influence of Neo-Kantianism (of the type propounded by the Marburg School), at the present. FRANCISCO LARROYO and GUILLERMO E. RODRÍGUEZ, who are declared enemies of metaphysics, are the most conspicuous exponents of the current. Rodríguez, who must have a very personal idea of metaphysics, writes: "Aside from the laws of logic which make science possible, it is not possible to construct any science; consequently, it is not even possible to have the science of *Being in Itself* or metaphysics. There is no being beyond that which is in and by the laws of logic."

Even in Mexico, Neo-Scholasticism is fully active in its threefold directions of Neo-Thomism, Suarezianism (among the Jesuits), and Scotism (among the Franciscans). The Thomistic movement is even more widespread. We shall only mention the Neo-Thomist OSVALDO ROBLES (1904), a follower of Maritain, and one whose mind is most open to the exigencies of modern thought. However, writes Robles, "I give a shade of meaning of my own to my living Thomism. To the ideal synthesis of truths I add some conclusions from philosophical currents which are not taken into consideration by Maritain, for example, those of contemporary German phenomenology, in which I notice a great analogy with St. Thomas' theses. I dissent from Maritain in almost all that concerns his political philosophy because I consider it hardly reconcilable, in its extreme conclusions, with the morality and politics deriving from the Gospels."

C. Brazil

On account of its tradition and its tongue, Brazil is a world of its own when compared with the other Latin American countries, which, in turn, have their remarkable differences among themselves. Nevertheless, the development of philosophy in Brazil is very similar to that which is taking place in the Hispano-American countries.

Brazil, too, has known the predominance of positivism, which imposed its influence almost unchallenged (opposed to it were Tobias Barreto and the so-called School of Recife) even on politics and the public schools. The spiritualistic reaction began with RAIMUNDO DE FAZIO BRITO (1862-1917); his theory is a "pan-psychic" pantheism inspired by Spinoza and Schopenhauer and it transcends the limits of our exposition), and since 1920 it has been consolidated in a vast movement of Catholic thought. The latter received its first impulse from JACKSON DE FIGUEIREDO (1891-1928), an ardent mystic who died young, exhausted by his internal anxiety and a skepticism he never succeeded in overcoming. Figueiredo is a complete fideist who believes ardently and devotes himself wholeheartedly to the work of proselytism in order to counteract, through faith, his fundamental skepticism.

Having been a student of Pascal (*Pascal y la inquietud moderna*, Montevideo, 1922), he sees in the French thinker only that aspect which, after the manner of Montaigne so to speak, is apt to demolish reason. For Figueiredo, scientific knowledge is utilitarian and the intellect has a pragmatic function. True knowledge "does not come to us from any speculative effort; it comes to us *de ser, de ser lo que somos.*" Now, consciousness is only faith in our inner bonds which unite us to being; it is also a total possession of our being which is a longing for the totality of being. Everything is faith: life, existence, and consciousness are acts of faith. Religion is, after all, the true and only philosophy—it is the "knowledge of salvation." *Credo quia absurdum esse.*

Catholic thought in Brazil follows other lines today. Besides the Neo-Thomistic movement, we notice other independent currents such as that led by H. BARBUY, who endeavors to renovate Thomism through Bergson.

Side by side with some sustainers of Marxist humanism, existentialism is also making notable inroads; it has influenced the thought of VICENTE FERREIRA DA SILVA. RENATO CIRELL CZERNA moves along the path of idealism and is strongly influenced by the school of Baden and by Gentile.

The philosophy of culture finds its exponent in MIGUEL REALE —a Neo-Kantian, influenced by Hartmann on the logical level and by Scheler on the axiological plane. Reale's "critical realism" has given its best results in connection with the philosophy of law which is not considered in this work. Reale is perhaps the most noted personality in contemporary Brazilian philosophy, precisely because he gave it an animating impulse.

According to custom, I should close this work with a conclusion. However, the conclusion of a book on contemporary philosophy can only be a theoretical one. In other words, I should present my own thought, and this was done by others. If I, too, were to do the same thing, it would be nothing but presumption on my part since I would allow myself the privilege of saying the last word. On the other hand, because of the critical character given to our exposition, the reader has had the opportunity to get a clear idea concerning our point of view. Moreover, in its fourth edition (if there should be one), this work will be amplified and re-elaborated to the extent of including all the material that should have made up a volume *per se*, that is, *giudizio sulla filosofia contemporanea*. Such a future edition will contain, implicitly and explicitly, a real "judgment" on today's philosophy—a judgment that is not lacking throughout these pages after all.